DARTMOOR MINDSCAPES

Re-Visioning a Sacred Landscape

Peter Knight

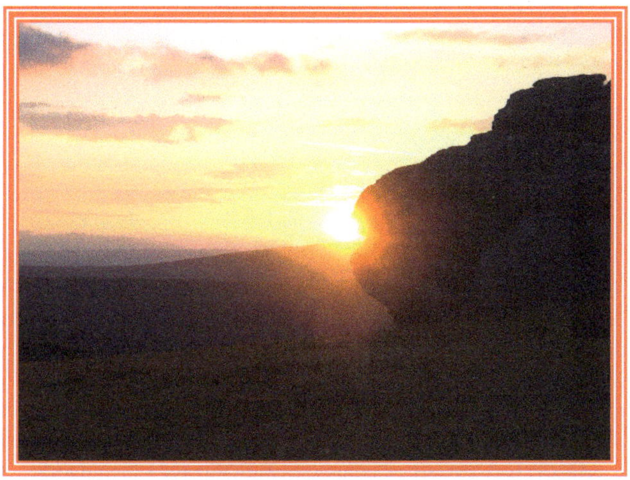

This book is lovingly dedicated to my ancestors.
In particular to my parents Joyce and Ernie Knight (RIP).

Stone Seeker Publishing
Wiltshire UK
Honouring ancient wisdom and the Earth

Published 2016
by Stone Seeker Publishing,
Wiltshire, England, UK
www.stoneseeker.net
email: stoneseeker@waitrose.com

ISBN: 978-0-9560342-5-0

Also by Peter Knight

Ancient Stones of Dorset - 1996
Sacred Dorset: On the Path of the Dragon - 1998
Dorset Pilgrimages: A Millennium Handbook (with Mike Power) - 2000
Earth Mysteries: An Illustrated Encyclopaedia of Britain (CD-ROM) - 2004
Thirteen Moons: Conversations with the Goddess - 2007 (& 2012 ed.)
The Wessex Astrum: Sacred Geometry in a Mystical Landscape (with Toni Perrott) – 2008
West Kennet Long Barrow: Landscape, Shamans and the Cosmos – 2011
The Cerne Giant – Landscape, Gods and the Stargate – 2013
Calne – Gateway to Ancient Wiltshire (with Sue Wallace) - 2014
Stolen Images – Pagan Symbolism and Christianity – 2015

website: www.stoneseeker.net
Follow Peter Knight on Facebook

Cover images:
Front cover: Top: Great Staple Tor. Left: Vixen Tor. Bottom: Sunset at Over Tor.
Back cover: Top left: Nine Stones, Belstone. Top right: Great Staple Tor. Centre: Rock basin at Kestor Rocks. Bottom: Sunset at Longstone, Merrivale.

Cover images and design: Peter Knight

FSC Printed and bound by CPI Antony Rowe, Melksham, on FSC paper.

Contents

1. Introduction 4
2. The Archaeological Background 10
3. Shamanism – Into the Dreamtime 19
4. Symbolic Landscapes 24
5. Phenomenology – Walk This Way 38
6. Stone Faced – The Case for Simulacra 50
7. The Sanctity of the Tors 64
8. Enculturing of the Tors 85
9. Balanced Rocks 102
10. Propped Stones 108
11. Rock Basins – Cauldrons of Life 118
12 Stone Rows and Their Landscape Setting 140
13. The Merrivale Shamanic Landscape 158
14. Circular Stone Settings and Their Landscapes 184
15. Settlements - Design and Landscape Settings 191
16. Sun, Moon and Stars - Prehistoric Astronomers 197
17. Earth Energies - the Pulse of the Land 205
18. Open Hearted Moor 210

Acknowledgements/About the Author 215
References 216
Also by the Author 219
Index 220

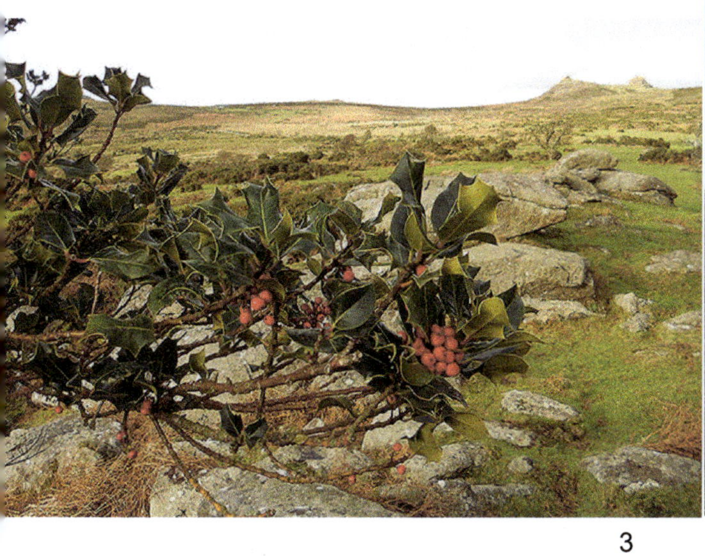

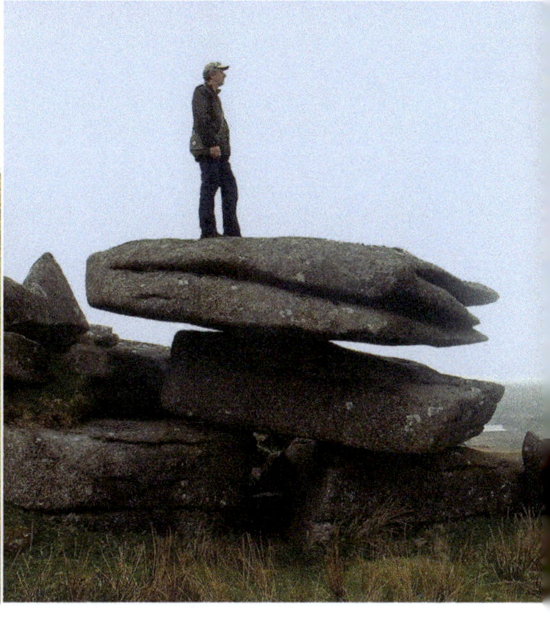

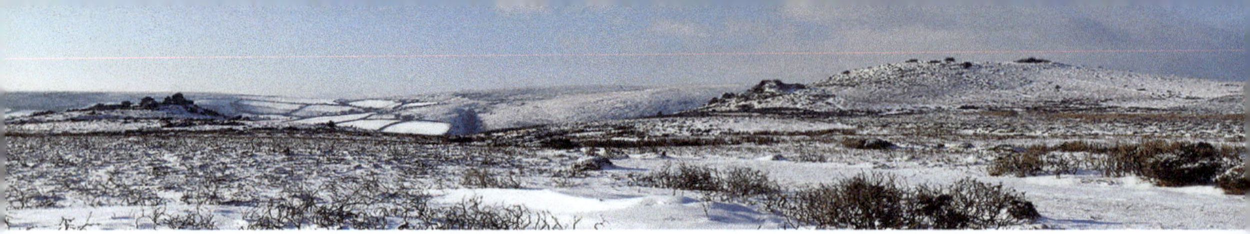

1. Introduction

'Tell me of the landscape in which you live, and I will tell you who you are.'
(Jose Ortega Gassett, 1883 -1955)

Will the real Dartmoor please stand up?

Dartmoor is one of Britain's natural treasures. It has inspired poets, naturalists and archaeologists for centuries and, in recent times, played host to ever-increasing numbers of tourists, cyclists, ramblers and other adventure seekers. Dartmoor is no longer, sadly, a true wilderness, and is, of necessity, a managed landscape; over four million people make day-visits every year (Newman 2011). And yet, in the moor's relative desolation, we may still encounter rugged beauty and enchantment.

Many come to experience the solitude of the open expanses of empty moorland, a mosaic of granite, ridge, valleys and marsh, and the raging torrents of rivers that cascade off the heights of this primal landscape. However, the lure of Dartmoor is nothing new. Thousands of years ago our prehistoric ancestors also ascended the heights of this granite upland. Sometimes this was for hunting game, or for agriculture, or often just for a place to live, be it in an often hostile environment. The landscape is heavy with memory, and the relics of Man's early forays and dogged occupation still litter the moor today. Compared to many other parts of England, Dartmoor's sacred sites are extremely well-preserved and apparent in the landscape, and although this book primarily focuses on ancient sites and landscapes, it is very much about how people *related* to them.

For there is another story to be told about the moor, one of the spiritual connections of its early inhabitants to the land, close reciprocal associations of which we have only begun to scratch the surface. In this volume I will evidence how our Mesolithic, Neolithic and Bronze Age forbears had an intimate, spiritual and, to them, crucial relationship with the valleys, rivers, rock basins, and the extraordinary rock formations of the tors. This symbiotic association led them to purposefully locate their monuments in relation to natural features; in those distant times, people revered the tors as sacred places, reference points in a landscape permeated with the spirits of their ancestors, and of the *'spirit of place'*.

For centuries, Dartmoor's granite and mineral deposits were plundered, the land sacked, regarded as a mere industrial resource. The scars of this abuse litter the moor today, as 'industrial archaeology'. Yet although the landscape has been battered and bruised by humankind, especially in recent centuries, it has somehow retained its dignity and character. The multi-layers of Dartmoor are much like an artist's old canvas, reused many times; the moor preserves traces of the older works in a stratified 'palimpsest' (Gerrard 1997). Although much of the skin of the land has gone, through farming and deforestation, its ancient, wizened bones remain, in the form of the tenacious, eternal tors, and the organic, ever-evolving rivers.

Part of Dartmoor's alluring character, undeniably, is its ancient sites, timeless vestiges of the Neolithic and Bronze Age. These people embodied the land in a more sensitive and cognitive manner than was later the case. And the moor's prehistoric sacred sites seem to somehow belong there, bestowing genuine value to the landscape; an engine house or quarry is certainly part of the heritage of Dartmoor, and yet, to me, represent its sorrowful rape and pillage. Likewise, vast china clay works are deep and unsightly lacerations, mercilessly cut into a sacred landscape.

Thousands of years ago, people had a different world view, one in which they took only what they needed, living a more conscious existence, in tune with natural cycles. They were driven by a respectful and reverential attitude to the landscapes in which they dwelt and moved through. The ancestors were all around them, in the form of the rocks of the tors and other landscape features; this is still the case with Australian Aborigines, American Indians, the Maori of New Zealand, and other indigenous cultures. With just a small change of perception, prehistoric shamans experienced a liminal landscape, a place bristling with magical potential, into which they embedded themselves with the full range of sensory experiences available. Their walking of the land was cognisant, for they saw no separation between themselves and the landscape. Movement was of prime importance to their knowing; walking mindfully can be mind-bending.

Unfortunately, we do not perceive landscape features in the way people once did, and I believe we are culturally impoverished as a result; nowadays a face in a rock is just a coincidental action of weathering, whereas it may once have been perceived as an ancestor or an element of tribal myth, or evidence of the 'spirit of place'. To the shaman there is never one landscape but rather many – all ubiquitous, overlapping, interconnected. It is somewhat appropriate that *'One Land, Many Landscapes'* is the title of a series of papers from a meeting of the European Association of Archaeologists, held in Bournemouth in 1999. The prehistoric shaman would have related to that.

Rethinking landscapes

'A mystery is concealed in the very bones of a landscape, once universally acknowledged.' (John Michell 1979)

I believe that we can again forge similar relationships with Dartmoor or, indeed, wherever we find ourselves. To this end, I have walked the moor in all seasons, all weathers, all temperatures, night and day, clear days and foggy white-outs, through horizontal rain and under hot sun, in an effort to truly connect with the deeper persona of Dartmoor. The moor taught me who was boss: 'The wilderness can be a ferocious teacher' (Snyder 1990). But the pain enabled the gain.

I have explored how my ancestors positioned their sacred sites within the land, and how they included natural features in their cosmology and spiritual practice. I have come to realise that there is not just one Dartmoor to be encountered, but many. For it is all about how we perceive the world around us, as it was thousands of years ago. So although, to a large extent, this is a journey back in time, it is also my sojourn through the present, and, ultimately into the future. Quantum physics tells us time is an illusion, that past and present are happening simultaneously. I get the feeling that, thousands of years ago, a solitary shaman surveying the moor from a windswept tor was well aware of this concept.

There was a time when academics saw little connection between astronomy, geology, geography and archaeology. Archaeologists, for instance, were chiefly focused on digging holes in the ground. During the last forty years, however, these disciplines have undergone a remarkable convergence. The mutual medium that has united these previously sporadic bedfellows is the landscape or, moreover, the new 'general systems' way of looking at it. New disciplines are examining the landscape holistically, looking at how space is a vessel, in which sensory experiences occur, affording ways of seeing the landscape as it may once have been perceived. For too long archaeologists have studied sacred sites as being unrelated, isolated and disconnected from others on the landscape. In recent decades, Paul Devereux, Prof Christopher Tilley, Richard Bradley and others have lead a charge to encourage academics to raise their heads out of the earth and see beyond the confines of their excavation trenches, to add deeper dimensions to their research. The *Landscape and Perception Project*, under the auspices of Britain's Royal College of Art, has been exploring how Stone Age eyes and ears once perceived the world (Devereux 2013). For many years I too have been advocating that sacred sites are not *on* the landscape, but rather are *held within it* (Knight 2007, 2011, 2013). To this end, I shall later outline the concepts behind *phenomenology*, and show how it has influenced my perceptions of Dartmoor, and how it led me to some remarkable discoveries, including those of self-discovery.

Every landscape offers a creative interaction with, and indeed receives a creative response from, people passing through or residing within it. The golden thread running unbroken through this book is the intimate and enduring tripartite relationship that once existed between Dartmoor's landscape features, its prehistoric indigenous inhabitants, and their ancestors. To these people this relationship was symbiotic, as they interacted with both a metaphorical, and a dynamic, 'spirit of place'. People created their landscape by embodying themselves within it – they were as much co-creators of the landscape as they were products of it (Tilley 2010). Creation myths and cosmologies were a key element of their knowing; the mighty, intimidating tors were central elements of how they made sense of their world. Knowledge was passed on from land to the shaman at defined places, within a mythologised landscape, which was the medium through which knowledge was disseminated.

Perhaps by simply perceiving an anthropomorphic feature on a tor outcrop (which may or may not have been previously venerated) we are briefly removing our psychological filters, momentarily dwelling in what Aborigines call *Dreamtime.* Our human brain/mind is designed to perceive a great variety of subtle signs and messages of which only we are capable. We were given the apparatus of a receptive manifold vision. Modern Western rationalism has closed the door on this way of thinking, dismissing simulacra as mere coincidence; this was not the case for most of Man's spiritual and cultural evolution. The very act of walking the *song lines* of the land was to enter the Dreamtime, the multisensory mindscapes of Dartmoor. Monuments were places to move to, around, and from, and as such mimicked the movements to, around and from the fantastically sculpted tors. That rocks are the abode of spirits is an ancient and universal concept, natural features which self-evidenced cosmologies. Throughout prehistory, shamans and their initiates underwent a myriad of unique and personal sensory experiences (Knight 2011), depending on the mindset and perception of the individual. Today we may dare to cross over to the liminal mind-scapes, sense-scapes and soul-scapes of Dartmoor.

To this end, I would suggest that we seek to approach the past by being fully in the present. By walking the same landscapes as our distant ancestors, but this time with 'new eyes', we may see more deeply than before, to see *as* deeply as before. This process can evoke a range of emotional states, including fear, awe, sensual yearnings, and a connection with the 'spirit of nature'. After repeated visits you may even find that a landscape (even one which you may have once feared) has now changed into *many* landscapes, all of which may be experienced to the full, with all our senses, even embracing fear as a teacher and guide. It is no less than a spiritual experience to explore and intimately learn every curve, nuance and distinction of a landscape, just as you might learn the landscape of a lover's body. The experience can be just as compelling and sensuous.

Granite - the bones of Dartmoor

Geology has played an important role in the evolution and social structure of Man, more than many have previously believed. Each geological element, be it chalk, granite or sandstone for example, produces different possibilities and affordances, in terms of resources, settlement and social identity. The gently rolling hills of a chalk downland would have produced different cosmologies and mythologies than the rugged uplands of Scotland or the tor-dominated landscapes of Dartmoor. The various building materials available for ancient sacred monuments also led to marked local variations in design. Each sacred site was very much of the place, which is equally true of the people who dwelt there.

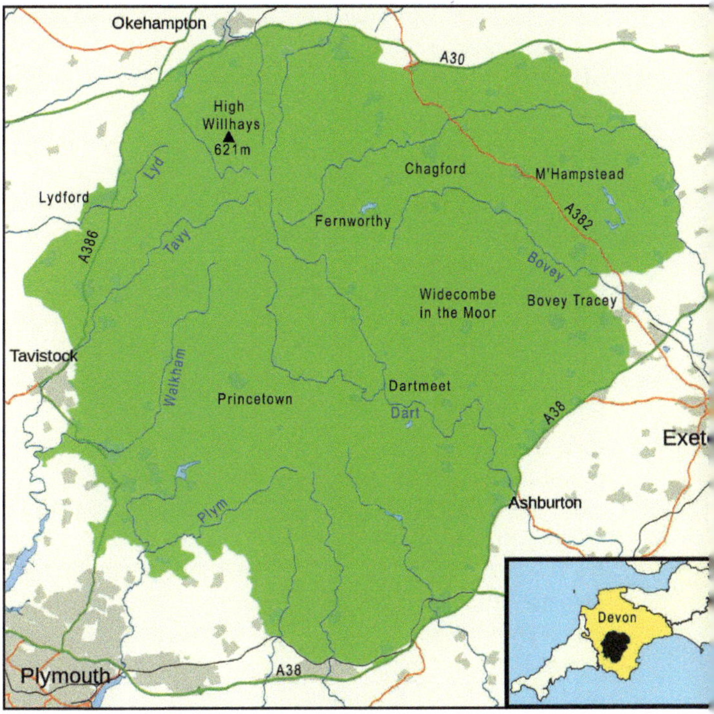

The word topography comes from a combination of *topos,* the Greek for *place*, and *grapheim,* meaning *to write* (Tilley 2010). This suggests that the importance of landscape to ancient people (in terms of their myths, heroic tales, their very identity) boils down to the landscape in which they live. Landscape is layered in myths, memories, cultural association and character, which are all rooted within it, just as an author layers the characters and sub-plots in a novel. Like some novels, the land does not have one story to tell, not one narrative, but rather countless narratives, each of which entwine and weave themselves into that which we call *landscape*. All myths are a product of a culture's immersion in their world. Landscape has never merely been a passive backdrop, but rather a dynamic element of culture, art and religion. And on Dartmoor we have an amazingly mystical landscape.

What we know today as geography, geology, astronomy, ecology and meteorology (disciplines we use to unravel what we call the 'natural world'), were once elements of the mythologies and cosmologies of ancient cultures. I have always been somewhat of a nerd when it comes to geology and geography. They have been my lifelong interests, along with astronomy – all natural sciences. Little did I know that later in life my nerdiness would hold me in good stead as I began to look at the archaeology and spiritual beliefs of my prehistoric ancestors. I have discovered how various aspects of the natural world, from the landscape to the stars above, were intertwined in the mind of Man since the earliest times.

Dartmoor is the largest tract of upland in Southern England (Newman 2011), an elevated and often trackless plateau covering about 46,000ha. In 1951, it became one of the first National Parks, covering an area of 954sq km, the extent of which is shown here **(image, previous page)**. The highest point is High Willhays, which stands at 621m (2039ft), the highest summit in the Southwest. Over 50% of the National Park's territory is over 300m, and around 50% is open moorland.

Dartmoor comprises mainly of a huge uplifted fist of granite, an igneous massif of Carboniferous to early Permian Age, which rose through the earlier Devonian and Carboniferous strata of the Palaeozoic Era. It is part of a huge mass that breaks the surface at various points in SW England and the Scilly Isles **(left)**. The largest exposed area of this granite is Dartmoor, which also forms the easternmost development of the batholith. The granite derived from the melting of sedimentary rocks and is composed of four main minerals – quartz, feldspar, biotite, and mica. Dartmoor granite is characterised by a relatively high proportion of tourmaline, which appears black. It consists of two main textural types, a coarse-grained rock with abundant large alkali feldspar megacrysts, and a finer-grained granite with few megacrysts. Interpretation of the gravity field over this batholith suggests that it is sheet-like, with a thickness of nearly 10km. It has a root at its southern end that extends to a depth of about 17km, and which may represent the original conduit that carried the molten magma up from deep within the Earth.

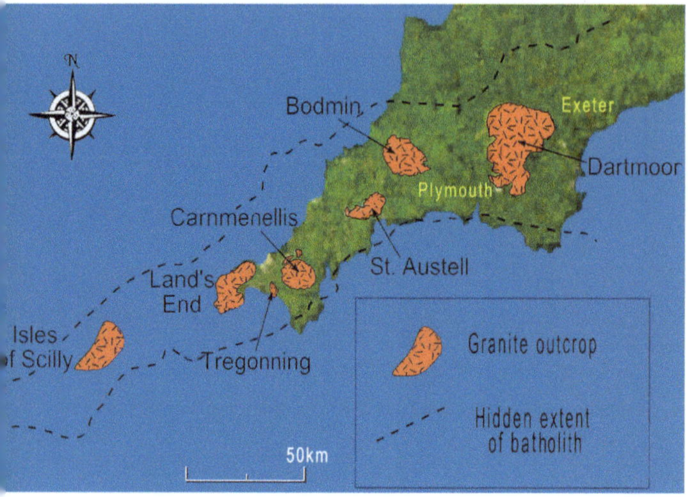

As erosion removed the sedimentary rocks which had later been deposited over the granite, the weight compressing it was reduced and the huge mass rose. Erosion of these exposed granitic outcrops has probably taken place since the top was unroofed in the Permian and Triassic periods; the topmost layers of granite were eroded away and deposited their minerals in rich alluvium sediments. The megacrystic granite, with huge crystals of feldspar, is thought to have been formed near the roof of the batholith, where it was cooler, enabling the growth of larger crystals.

The Dartmoor granites slope gently with a NW - SE tilt, due to Alpine earth movements during the Tertiary period. The Sticklepath Fault runs from Bideford to Torquay and slices through the east side of Dartmoor, evidenced by a series of NW-SE valleys. There are 35 regionally important geological sites (RIGS) within the National Park.

Recent research suggests that Dartmoor was an island in the Early Ice Age and may have been covered by a thin ice sheet: 'Dartmoor was the location of the southernmost independent ice cap in the British Isles' (David Evand, Durham University, 2012). Dating of 28 Dartmoor tors shows that most are surprisingly 'young', geologically that is, being less than 100,000 years old, with none over 200,000 years old; they probably emerged at the start of the Devensian, the last big Ice Age (Gunnell et al 2013). Both mechanical and chemical weathering, especially since the Ice Age, has created the form of the tors that are characteristic of Dartmoor. Rainwater mixing with carbon dioxide produces a weak carbonic acid that breaks down the granite and its weakly radioactive minerals (Klemen 2015). These erosive forces have sculpted the amazing and numinous landscapes of Dartmoor. As far as human interaction is concerned, the tors have not been majorly modified for 10,000 years (Bender et al 2007).

Dartmoor is also about water. Some of the main rivers of the southwest, such as the Plym, Tavy, Teign, Taw, Dart and the Erme, are birthed high up on the moor and drain radially out from the high moor from two isolated core foci. The landscape up here is often boggy, festooned with seasonal rivulets and in places impassable in winter. From certain viewpoints, the sea can be seen to the south and southwest, the place where the rivers reach maturity – their end game. Our ancestors were closely linked with the spiritual aspects and metaphorical nature of these life-giving waters, and many sacred sites, both natural and monumental, are close to watery places. I shall therefore look at the tor rock basins, which were seen to hold the purest of waters gifted from the skies; here rock and water co-exist in a kind of alchemy, the crystal-rich granite being the receptacle, the chalice, for the holy water.

Later I shall look in more detail at the wind-whipped granite tors, and their rock basins and simulacra, and how sacred sites are often exquisitely positioned to take account of them. I shall look at how subtle changes in topography, the proximity of marshes and rivers, and how the gentlest of slopes influenced the location of megalithic sites. These monuments became *permanent elements of the landscape*, not merely objects placed upon it.

Without granite, there would be no Dartmoor – it is the fire in the belly of the moor. It has been used, mercilessly, in historical times, giving birth to the characteristic and enduring granite crosses and dry stone walls of the Moor **(below)**. I shall look at the qualities of granite, and how around the world we have had a close cultural and spiritual connection with this magical rock for thousands of years. Granite is also rich in quartz, regarded in ancient times as having magical and conductive properties, as it is today with New Age healers and dowsers - granite was used in most Dartmoor monuments. People were transporting and re-embedding *'pieces of landscape'* or *'pieces of place'*, enhancing locations, to be conduits between Man and an omnipresent Spirit.

'I am drawn to stone itself. I want to explore the space within and around the stone through a touch that is a brief moment in its life. A long resting stone is not an object in the landscape but a deeply engrained witness to time.'
(Andy Goldsworthy)

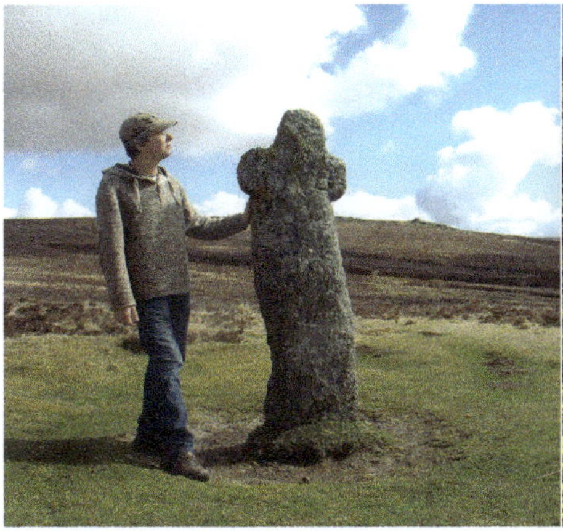
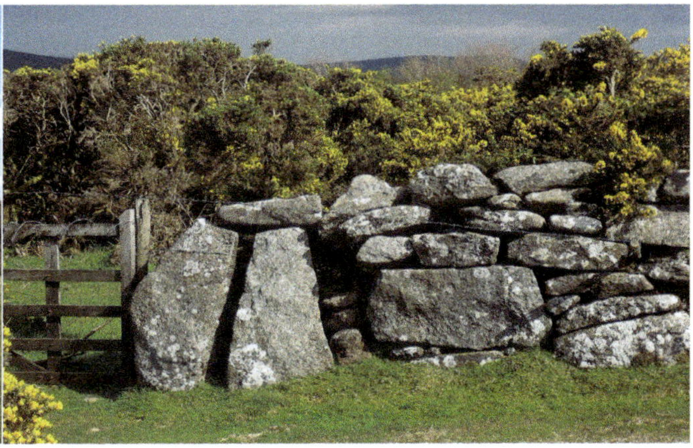

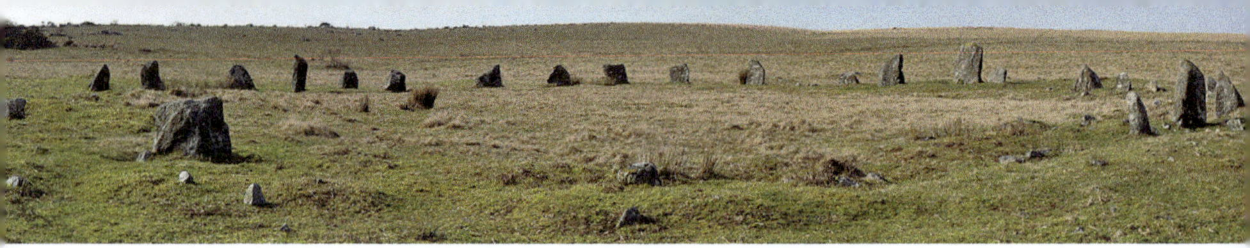

2. The Archaeological Background

'For in these stones is a mystery, and a healing virtue against many ailments.'
(Geoffrey of Monmouth, 12th C.)

Palaeolithic (prior to 10,000 BC)

Evidence for exploitation or habitation of the Dartmoor area during this long period is limited to a few flint strands and the cave deposits found at Kent's Cavern, Torquay, which marked a warmer interglacial period. Early human activity is evidenced by a 10cm long hand-axe found at Brent Moor in 1931, which was dated around 60,000–500,000 years BC. Finds like this are rare in upland areas, with only one from Exmoor and none, to date, from Bodmin Moor. Devon was probably unpopulated due to severe weather conditions during the Devensian Glaciation - c.16,000-13,000 BC (Gerrard 1997). Around 11,000 BC open grassland moved in to both Bodmin and Dartmoor, followed by areas of birch woodland. The caves at nearby Kent's cavern were reoccupied, and its inhabitants hunted and enjoyed deer, bear, wild horse and other small mammals. Other finds from the Palaeolithic have been found across Devon, but few on Dartmoor, and even then may mark summer forays. So, up until about 10,000 years ago, the high moor was almost certainly a true wilderness, which was, '... untrodden by Man' (Pettit 1974).

Mesolithic (c. 10,000 – c. 4,000 BC)

The Mesolithic can be seen as transitional, a time between the last Ice Age and the Neolithic, between nomadic and farmer lifestyles (Knight 2011). The climate was drier and a few degrees milder than today, with dry, warmer summers, which produced less extensive boggy areas than on Dartmoor today. The winter climate was still very cold, similar to the Siberian tundra and forests of today. Much of Dartmoor was covered with woodland (and by 6,500 BC the maximum extent of forestation was reached). The pollen record shows that all native tree species were present, dominated by hazel, birch, alder and woods of huge creaking oaks; remnants of the latter can be found at Wistman's Wood and Black-a-Tor Copse. Open grassland probably still held grip on the highest parts of the moor. Some clearance and burning was carried out as the Mesolithic progressed, although the population was still essentially leading a hunter-gatherer lifestyle. Nomads, **(left)** driven by seasonal movement, followed semi-wild herds of cattle.

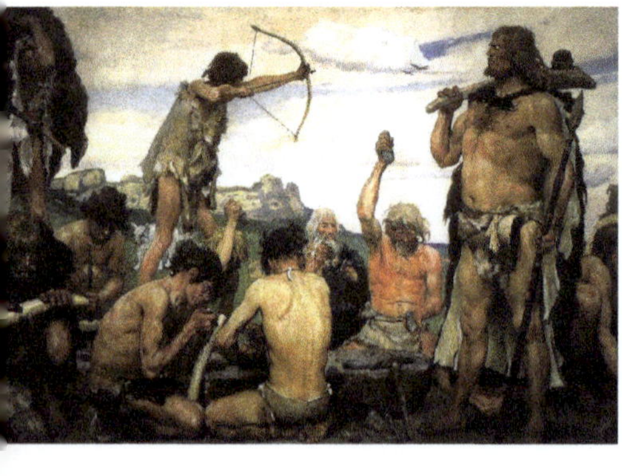

As the climate warmed around 10,000 BC, people

came to stay in the area permanently, in small family groups of up to 20, although their visits to the high moor were still transitory. These Mesolithic visitors were already driven by the spirit world, which would have been recognised and honoured in natural features – the terrain was already being mythologised, and they paused at special places to pay their respects. The spiritual foundations were being laid in the landscape for the monuments that would be erected by later generations.

From around 8,000 BC, people began to penetrate the moor (Pettit 1974). Several Mesolithic flint toolkits have been found on Dartmoor, such as at Gidleigh Common, Fernworthy and Taw Marsh, which have yielded flint flakes and blades, not naturally occurring locally. A Mesolithic site at Week, NE of the moor, suggests a winter encampment in a lower, sheltered landscape near springs. Lack of occupational evidence and scarcity of finds on the high moor suggests that it was visited only seasonally, probably via the main water sources (Newman 2011), following herds of deer as they moved to higher pastures. Studies on Bodmin have shown Mesolithic flint finds occur near water sources, or former ones (Tilley 2010); further Dartmoor finds may be interred under the peat (Gerrard 1997).

Woodland cover is estimated to have extended over much of Dartmoor by the end of the Mesolithic, except for the highest tors and extensive clitter spreads. Tors were good vantage points from which to watch for deer herds on the open moor, so already had 'value'. Prof Chris Tilley suggests that high eminent tors would have been named as far back as the Mesolithic, investing them with myth, endowing striking topographical features with metaphor, as Maori and Aborigine cultures do today. Tilley concludes, 'It is hard not to imagine that the fabulously weathered tors would have been great sources of symbolic potency and power, signifying a wide range of enduring relationships among people, the land, time, and space' (Tilley 2010).

The height of the tree line was about 415m, with a fringe zone of hazel and some oak. Below this, the world of the Mesolithic hunter-gatherer was a world of deep forests, sliced through by thin tracks, a world of small clearings, streams, marshy regions and occasional pools. Contours and scarps were less well-defined as the landscape was 'softened' by tree cover. The shapes of the hills were obscured: 'In the upland areas of southwest England, such as Dartmoor and Bodmin, only the tips of the granite tors would be exposed among the trees, invisible from below' (Tilley 2010).

In forests, touch, smell and hearing were more important than sight; seeing 200m away would have been unusual for the most part. There were strong contrasts between dense areas of canopy and the narrow tracks and small scale clearings. Some of these clearings were around the tors, which burst out of the canopy. The tors enabled the sensory input of long-distance sight. Where the woods ended and open moor started were magical liminal places, where one stepped from the dark of the woodland out into illuminated open spaces. This is was an equally powerful experience when reversed, entering woods from the open moor.

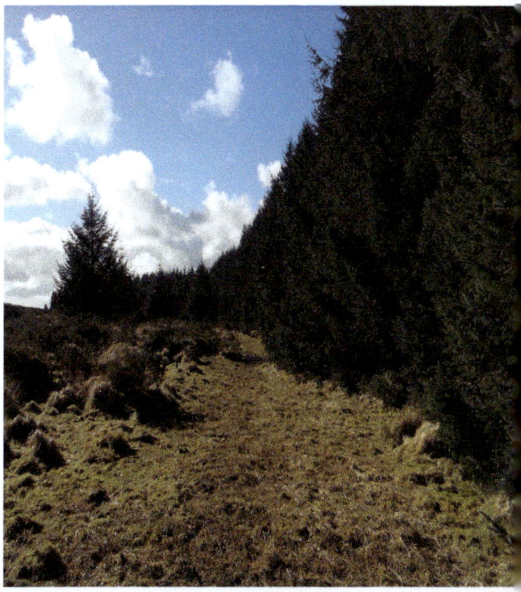

We can get glimpses today of how this Mesolithic landscape may have looked. On one of my visits to Bellever Tor I approached the tor through the forest, and I was struck, especially on an overcast day, how the plantation is a dark, even foreboding place, particularly noticeable on exiting the open moor **(right)**. I stood at a liminal boundary between these worlds of light and dark – open moor and distant views behind me, a confining world in front. Once in the wood, my vision was limited as my world closed in on me, my attention now drawn to close quarters as I followed an unusually narrow, barely managed path. The wind in the trees sang and made the sound of waves crashing on the seashore. I walked over granite pebbles and blocks of white quartz, and rivulets made the going boggy in places. This gave me glimpses of those times long ago when the open moor met the primal Mesolithic forest.

Another place I felt was congenial in feeling how Mesolithic Man may have encountered tors is at Gidleigh Tor (grid ref: 671878), where outcrops of rock occupy a small clearing, surrounded by trees. I visited the tor twice in the winter of 2015/6. As one reaches the edge of the woods, the rocks are suddenly there, majestic and mysterious **(left)**. Simulacra returned my gaze as I was drawn from the dark of the forest. From the top of the tor I could see long distances, to Kestor and Haytor. The land plunges away down to the Teign valley below, and I could hear its rush of water, unseen and yet part of my experience. Water is here too; as I surveyed my new world, I sat next to a water-filled rock basin, covered with a veneer of ice.

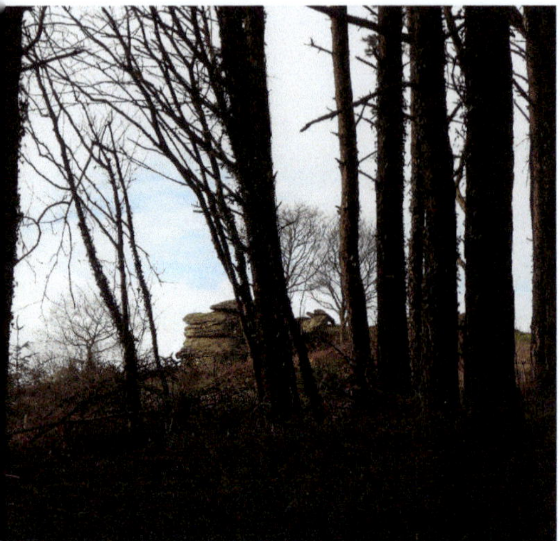

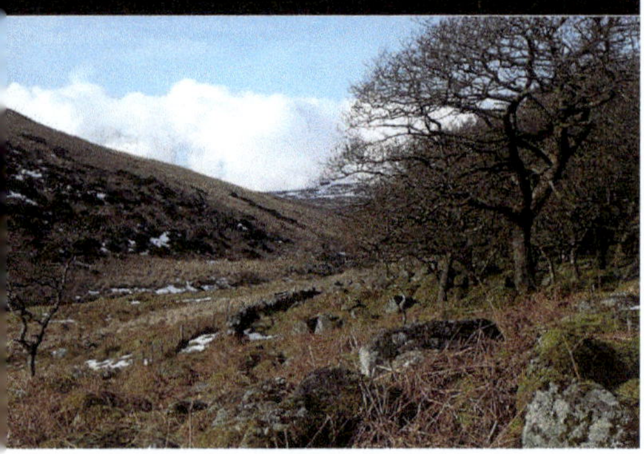

Wistman's Wood, north of Two Bridges, is another magical place from which we may get glimpses of the Mesolithic landscape. It is likely a remnant from the ancient forest that covered much of Dartmoor c.7000 BC, before Mesolithic hunter-gatherers cleared it sometime after 5000 BC. On arrival at the wood, I paused at the edge, where three large flat stones lie – the famous Dartmoor clitter! I could see **(left)** the open moor and the slopes of Beardown Tor on the left, contrasting with the clitter-strewn, claustrophobia of the oak wood on the right. This threshold is a liminal place in every sense; outside there is space, plenty of it. Once one enters the wood the going is tough, as rocks and oaks lock horns in an eternal tussle for the very limited space. Within a few feet my experiences were worlds apart. This phenomenological and experiential method of approaching the land can give us glimpses into the distant past. We have the opportunity to develop enriching and intimate relationships with landscapes, beyond scientific methodology, but with the potential to be just as valuable and insightful.

Neolithic (c.4,000 BC – 2,000 BC).

Things were to radically change on Neolithic Dartmoor, as the contrasting light/dark, open/closed experiences of the Mesolithic hunter-gather were to be greatly extended. The moor was being opened up through deforestation, and with it a new range of contrasting sensory experiences became available, such as wet/dry, steep slope/plateau, rocky tor/boggy valley, long distance/restricted views, high/low, hard and soft. It was on to these landscapes of ever-expanding sensory encounters that the first permanent monuments were built. Man had learnt how to grow food, not just hunt it.

Early Neolithic enclosed sites at White Tor (or Whittor) and Dewerstone were larger than their Bodmin equivalents, and can be classed as seasonal gathering places rather than settlements (Newman 2011). These would have protruded above the woodland cover, and it has been demonstrated that the tors deemed appropriate for enclosure were predominantly on routes up to the high moors. These routes were defined by rivers, or the main streams that fed them, sometimes marked by tomb monuments. Tors were the first major granite outcrops encountered when following rivers upstream, marking the boundary between the lowlands and highlands, the visible edge of the granite (Davies 2010). Both White Tor and Dewerstone have commanding views of the landscape and of Cornwall beyond.

The establishment of enclosures around tors in SW England, including Dartmoor, may represent early 'ownership' of land, and a formalizing and controlling of access to the tors, and their power. Some are clearly not designed with defence as the primary intent (Davies 2010). They were places of feasting and negotiation, of mitigation and gift exchange – all overseen by the spirits of the tor, giving legitimacy to proceedings. It was a period when people *appropriated* the land, staking claim to it as never before; 'The monuments that define the earliest Neolithic are clearly part of this desire to dominate and domesticate' (Russell 2002). Monuments served this purpose, even though it was the landscape features that were key. Features in the topography were referenced for the first time by means of the erection of sacred sites, as I have demonstrated in Dorset and Wiltshire (Knight 1996, 2011). The enclosure of specific tors would suggest they were as much a reference to mobility as for settlement, confirming Prof Tilley's views that *movement* across the landscape had meaning beyond the practical; people were spiritually bonding with the land (Tilley 2010).

The scarcity of palaeobotanical evidence for the Neolithic to the Early Bronze Age on Dartmoor has led to this period being seen as something of a 'black hole' (Klemen 2015). No cereal pollen was found at sites at Postbridge and Taw Head. Simmons (1969) suggests that either agriculture was practised on the periphery, and did not extend to the upland areas, or that small patches of cereal were grown some distance from higher areas where peat was forming, and so pollen did not become deposited into it.

People were now coordinating their efforts in monument building, a departure from the previous objectives of subsistence and survival. People were expressing a sense of a cultural past, of 'ancestor reverence'. Communities were upping their game in terms of sophistication and organisation, far surpassing what had gone before. There was a radical change from chasing food to growing it, a transition from a nomadic to agrarian lifestyles. Farming had a profound impact in our relationship with water, as rivers became vital factors in social organisation; the Egyptian civilisation would not have happened without the Nile. Even the peat of Dartmoor, which was used as fuel, was created on land saturated by water.

Farming was now the predominant lifestyle; 'The hunter-gatherers dropped their spears and picked up ploughs' (Russell 2002). With deforestation taking place on a large scale, for crops and livestock, people could now see for longer distances, unimpeded by trees. Vision became a more important sense in terms of orientation, visual perceptions of landscape being dominant. The subtle contours and profiles of landscape were now perceptible, and one could see for miles for the first time. This opening up of their world led to major monument building by early Neolithic people, often on high places, where the results of their labour could be seen from miles away and, indeed, from where one could see for miles. In the Neolithic, manmade monuments symbolically replaced the huge, ancient trees, which had, in effect, been the cultural markers of the Mesolithic. It is as if the features of the landscape are no

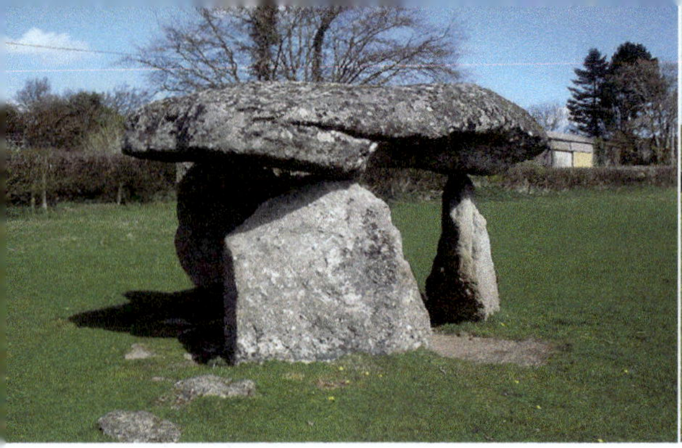

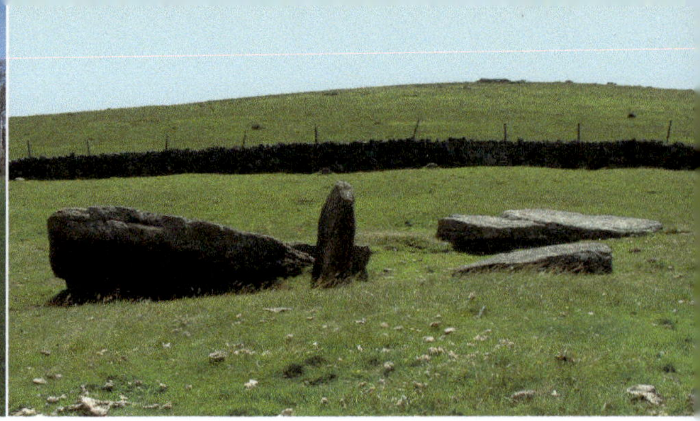

longer enough, perhaps due to the loss of forests - the land now needed to be permanently marked by monuments. With the ancient reference points (such as huge revered trees) now gone, new ones were needed as cultural anchors.

Across Europe and beyond, the Neolithic ushers in a period of monument building on a substantial scale. The people of the Neolithic provide the first legacy of permanent monuments of Dartmoor, in the form of long barrows and chambered tombs, notably at Spinster's Rock **(above left)**, the magnificent dolmen (grid ref: 701908), Corringdon Ball (669612), Gidleigh (657885) and Cuckoo Ball (659582); the English Channel can be seen from Cuckoo Ball Barrow on a clear day. Spinster's rock once had outliers and an avenue of stones **(map p. 198)**, which has been destroyed. Corrington Ball **(above right)** is the best preserved chambered long barrow on Dartmoor, originally 42m long with large boulders at one end representing the collapsed chamber. The mound is aligned with the midwinter sunrise. These sites must have been of great significance, as they were erected in a landscape otherwise devoid of manmade features. The radical new concepts of territorial ownership, a sense of belonging, and new perceptions of landscape, are developed at this time (Knight 2011): 'The Neolithic is all about the attempt to incorporate the 'wild' into a cultural frame' (Tilley 2010).

Formerly there would have been very few *inland* striking rock outcrops in Southern England. Now, with Neolithic deforestation, the tors of Dartmoor and Bodmin, as well as the sarsen fields of Wiltshire and Dorset, stood stark in the landscape. These provided new sensory experiences, both visual and tactile (Tilley 2010), exposed places woven into the myths of the people. One could now feel the surface of living rock, examine flints and chunks of granite, see what had been hidden under their feet. The Neolithic mind was driven and grounded by the new experiences of these open landscapes – people were changing not just the landscape, but themselves.

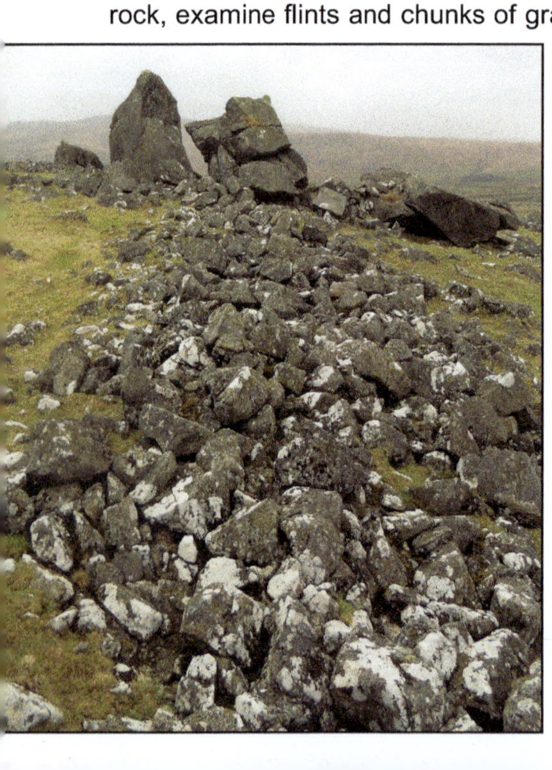

Clearance of woodland continued unabated during the Neolithic to facilitate grazing and hunting, which was improved on open ground (Newman 2011). Coppicing was also carried out, crafting woodlands with a thinner canopy, encouraging a greater variety of plants and animals. Occupation on the high open moorland itself was still infrequent, though it was present, if only seasonally for feastings and gorsedd-like gatherings. At White Tor (542787), the walls were incorporated into boulders and outcrops **(left)**, early signs that this and other tors were being encultured, a practice that was to continue into the Bronze Age.

One problem for archaeologists is that Neolithic buildings were of wood and thatch, and therefore 'biodegradable', leaving few traces. Flints and pottery are the most affordable evidence. Lack of finds may suggest that White Tor and Dewerstone were seasonal sites, used for feasting and the exchange of goods. Both sites have extended views towards Cornwall, suggesting they were carefully chosen (Newman 2011). At Gidleigh and Batworthy, Mesolithic and Neolithic flints have been found together, suggesting either continuity of use or that similar habitats had been sought (Gerrard 1997). A high-status dolerite axe was found at Haldon Ridge, just east of Dartmoor. Chris Tilley has suggested that natural flint simulacra found casually on the land by Neolithic farmers may have been collected and deposited as spiritual artefacts at sacred sites (Tilley 2007). They were regarded as gifts from the spirit of the land.
I shall return to the Neolithic later, in terms of shamanism and the positioning of monument in regards to natural features.

Bronze Age (c. 2,000 – 700 BC)

The Late Neolithic and Early Bronze Age ushered in the arrival of *permanent* domestic settlements on Dartmoor, bringing in changes through farming practices and subsistence strategies, such as enclosures and field systems. Metals, such as copper, bronze and gold, was used for prestige, high-status artefacts, which are particularly notable after 2000 BC. For the first time, Man was leaving a solid habitation imprint on the moors, and this coincides with a deterioration of soil quality, resulting in increased peat deposition. There was widespread deforestation to create space for the sowing of cereal crops, and to facilitate a change from grazing pigs to sheep and cattle farming - People were now in a contest with Nature. Dartmoor never recovered.
People become hoarders of food, but also acquirers of land. Over 5000 stone-built round houses have been identified, some of which had porches, forecourts and cooking pits inside. At many sites the door is on the south side, avoiding the colder winter winds as well as letting in the low winter sun. By the Middle/Late Bronze Age people had erected a complex network of boundary banks, known as reaves, which probably denote tribal territories. These boundary constructions also occur on Bodmin. They typically connect and make use of natural features on the landscape, such as clitter fields and tor outcrops.
On Bodmin Moor, Chris Tilley (2010) found that the higher outcrops and tors were where larger cairns and hill top enclosures were built. On sloping ground (often in clitter fields) was where settlements, enclosures and smaller cairns were sited. Saddles between higher ground were where stone circles and stone rows commonly occur. I think these criteria apply equally to Dartmoor. On Bodmin 79% of large cairns (over 10m diameter) are on prominent positions, and at least 16 cairns are built on or around the tor rock outcrops (Tilley 2010). Some actually encircle rock stacks, which were enhanced and became part of ritual activities. This relationship between monument and rock is hardly discreet. Rough Tor, on Bodmin, is the centre of a vast ritual landscape, a hub around which sacred sites are situated. Its summit is a key vantage point from which to view many of them. And so too with many of Dartmoor's 150 or so tors. Most Bodmin and Dartmoor tors display unusually weathered rocks, simulacra, caverns and overhangs, with cairns close by. These were all elements to be used in ritual and initiations. Tilley advocates that one purpose of reaves may have been not just for defining land ownership and domestic grazing restriction, but also for symbolic purposes; some reaves on Dartmoor are orientated to tors (Bender et al 2007). In other words, people not only claimed the natural resources, but also the *ritual* resources of the land (Tilley 2010). These defined places were where knowledge of

fertility was passed on from landscape to shaman, the very landscape itself being the medium through which knowledge was disseminated.

Bronze Age cairns and round barrows are the most numerous prehistoric monuments in Britain, numbering in excess of 30,000. There are around 700 on Dartmoor, which have been studied since 1752 (Grinsell 1978). More than 90% of cairns have been damaged through early unsympathetic 'treasure digs' (Gerrard 1997), and even when undisturbed, the acid soil of Dartmoor is usually merciless in terms of skeletal preservation. The Whitehorse Hill burial finds were a welcome exception; amber, bearskin, tin studs, and a woven bag show the sophistication of Bronze Age life.

Stone Circles on Dartmoor may number 12 (Newman 2011) or 18 (Gerrard 1997), as there is debate as to whether some circles are in fact cairn circles or 'ring settings', associated with burials. Most are generally dated sometime between 2,000 -1,300 BC.

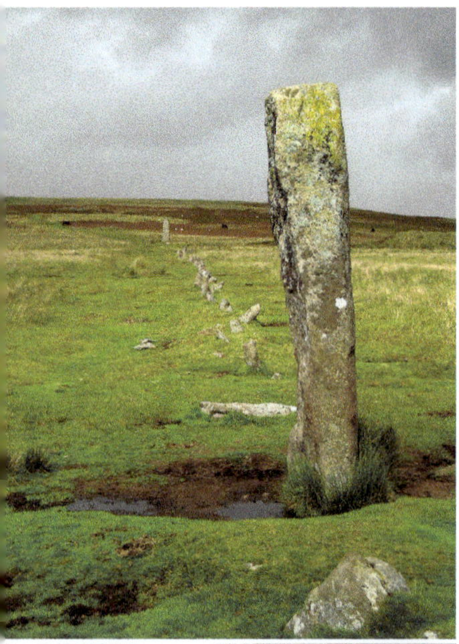

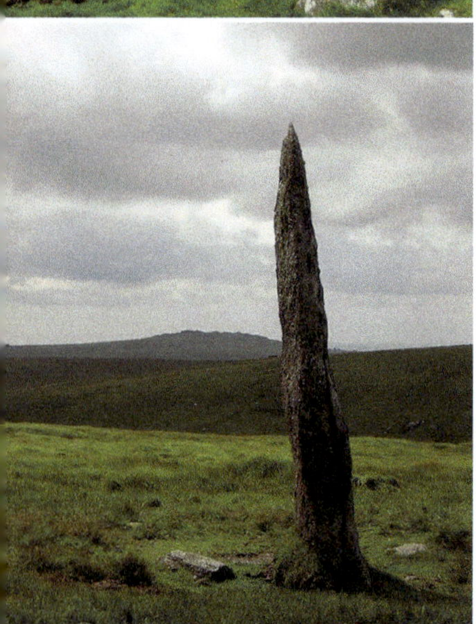

Some circles consist of multiple concentric arrangements of thin stone slabs, such as the fourfold circle at Yellowmead (which some think is a cairn circle). Several 'circle settings' contain no evidence of a central burial. Sometimes, however, there is evidence of an enclosed mound or cairn, such as at Shovel Down, which I think may have actually been a walk-in spiral. At some stone circles, a layer of charcoal was found, suggesting that fire played a role in ceremonies. The location of circles will be dealt with in detail later, as they are intricately positioned on the landscape, often where multiple tors are visible.

Standing stones and stone rows are perhaps the moor's most iconic and mysterious Bronze Age monuments (although some, at least, may be Neolithic). There are over 1000 stone rows in Britain, and Dartmoor has the largest assemblage in the UK, with around 80 known examples; here is Drizzlecombe stone row **(left)**. New rows have been discovered in recent years as they reach up to the sky from their entombment of peat. The majority of Dartmoor's standing stones are associated with stone rows, although some solitary examples occur. Standing alone on the moor at 3m tall is Beardown Man longstone **(left)** near Devil's Tor (596797).

Like stone circles, the *location* of stone rows appears to have been paramount, and their design seems to imply that *movement* along them is of prime importance (Tilley 2010). I shall discuss later my visits to several rows, by way of getting some principles across in terms of their relationship to the landscape across which they march. Some stone rows enter and exit granite clitter fields which show no signs of clearance to facilitate walking them. Neil Mortimer has recently made the case for a link between stone rows and water (Mortimer 2013), and my studies confirm this. Dowsers have found powerful earth energies flowing along stone rows, and I have also employed dowsing on occasions.

Other commonly found elements of Bronze Age archaeology are the hundreds of cairns, tumuli and burial cists (or kists) that festoon the moor. Many of these are in close proximity to stone rows, particularly the smaller cairns. Larger 'prestige' cairns were built on hill summits, often in groups or 'cemeteries', with some cairns entirely surrounding a natural rock outcrop or boulder. We shall look into this cairn/outcrop relationship in detail later, as it brings home the idea of adoption and enculturing of the tors and other high places. Dartmoor also has a vast number of stone burial cists, with over 180 recorded, compared to around 60 on Bodmin and just a handful on Exmoor. In them, several elitist 'beaker' pots have been found, dated c. 2500 BC.

Hut circles are the stone walls of round houses, formerly covered by timber and furze roofs. They may superficially resemble stone circles, and this may have been intentional. There are in excess of 4000 examples on Dartmoor, showing a variety of sizes, designs and construction techniques. They are usually defined by a single entrance, and often the upright door jams are still in situ. Hut circles may congregate inside boundary walls, forming enclosed settlements, as at Grimspound, Legis Tor and Dean Moor. The Grimspound enclosure wall encircles 24 huts, most of which have a diameter of around 4.5m, whilst at Watern Oke, 90 huts are evident. More than 100 settlements survive on Dartmoor (Pettit 1974).

The work of Bender, Hamilton and Tilley (Bender et al 1999 & 2007) has changed former perceptions that domestic and ritual were separate, and that 'never the twain shall meet'. I shall look later how the ancestors were omnipresent in people's everyday lives, even in the places where they dwelt.

The tors were also used as foci for boundary walls, called reaves, which can be traced from hut circles, through clitter fields, right up the slopes, such as at White Tor, Roos Tor and Sharpitor. These landscape-straddling features are often mistaken for modern walls by walkers. The one shown here **(right)** is the Great Western Reave, visible as a dark line in the low winter sun, climbing up the slopes of Roos Tor, as seen from Little Mis Tor. At 10km long, it is the longest known Bronze Age boundary on the moor (Gerrard 1997). These stone walls cross Dartmoor with little or no regard for the topography, although the majority respect and avoid stone rows (Newman 2011).

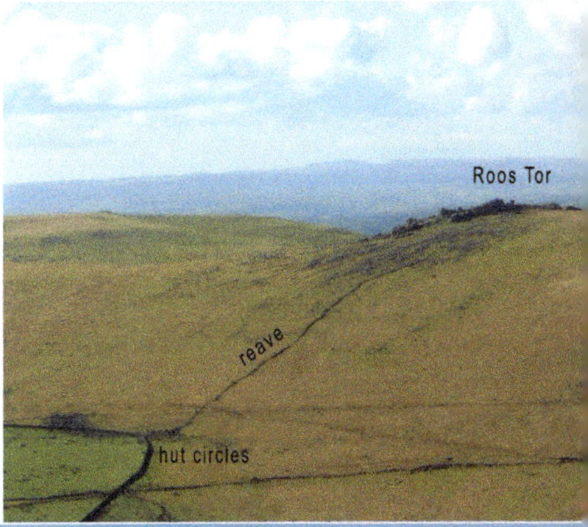

There are places where the ceremonial and the domestic seem to have been side-by-side, such as at Merrivale and at the Black Tor/Raddick Hill complexes. People were living in close proximity to their sacred sites, similar to how a church and its churchyard may occupy the heart of a village. This demonstrates that the worlds of the ceremonial and the mundane were never truly separated. Intervisibility between sacred sites, the tors, and domestic structures is also starkly demonstrated on Dartmoor. This image **(right)** shows the view east from the 'blocking stone' at the end of the triple stone row on Challacombe Down (690808) on a crisp winter's day. From here can be seen a cairn (far left),

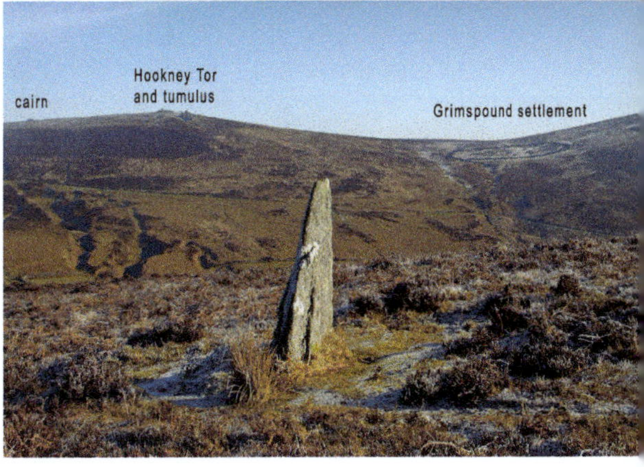

Hookney Tor with its tumulus, and the Grimspound settlement site, shown as an oval enclosure towards the right. If we were to pan further to the right, barrows and cairns on Hamel Down would be seen. The row is positioned on a gentle slope, a recurring theme I shall return to.

There seems to have been a rapid depopulation of the moor from around 1600 BC (Bender et al 2007). A cooler and wetter climate from the middle of the Bronze Age onwards (after 1395 BC) initiated farming and settlements to generally move down into the sheltered valleys, with their richer soils. The depopulation of the higher moors has ensured that hundreds of settlements, circular buildings and cairns have survived to this day, sprinkled across the vacated moor. By the end of the Bronze Age, the world was forever changed, and the symbiosis between Man and Nature was becoming fractured (Trwoga 2006). Hunter-gathering was in decline as farming arrived with a vengeance and with it a schism in people's relationship with Nature. There was a decline in the reverence in ancestral places and, as a consequence, a weakening in the influence of the shaman as a spiritual conduit.

Iron Age (700 BC – 43 AD)

I will not dwell on the Iron Age of Dartmoor in this volume, for I am primarily concerned with how earlier people related to the moor's natural features in a spiritual context. Compared to the richness of Bronze Age monuments, the Iron Age is certainly poorly represented, which seems to suggest a downturn in the fortunes of the moor's inhabitants. A movement down to the lowlands led to the abandonment of previously occupied areas. It has been suggested that increased rainfall, a colder climate, over-cropping and soil degradation all combined to make the uplands less attractive than before. However, this has had an upside: 'One positive aspect of this is that significant tracts of the earlier landscape have remained undisturbed for centuries...' (Gerrard 1997). The area was not completely abandoned, however, and there were settlements such as at Kestor. There are 12 hillforts on the periphery of the National Park (Newman 2011), some of which were heavily-defended, such as Hembury, Brentor, Hunter's Tor and Cranbrook; defence was now high on the agenda. The Dumnonii were Iron Age tribe of Dartmoor, whose name derives from the proto-Celtic root *dubno*, meaning *deep, earth*, or *lords*. Of course, the early antiquarians associated the prehistoric monuments with the Iron Age Druids. Although there is no evidence that this authoritative priesthood stepped onto Dartmoor, I find it inconceivable that they did not. As late as 1862, Dartmoor was termed '... a natural Druid Temple' by the President of the Archaeological Association. Every hillfort would have had a priest, its local variation of a 'Druid', and the moor still offered the same scope for initiation, ritual and solitary solace as it had ever done.

With the ascension of Iron, and perhaps even before, the symbiosis between the landscape and the people that lived on the moor had been ruptured, split apart, and the shaman, who had provided the spiritual connection between clan and land, was somewhat disempowered. The focus was no longer on the ancestors of the high moor, but on survival in increasingly violent times.

Lastly, mention also needs to be made of clapper bridges that span the waterways of the moor. Even though most are thought to be Medieval, some may be older. When one considers the capabilities our prehistoric forebears possessed in hauling huge blocks of granite for monument building, I find it inconceivable that they lacked the skills to span the rivers of the moor.

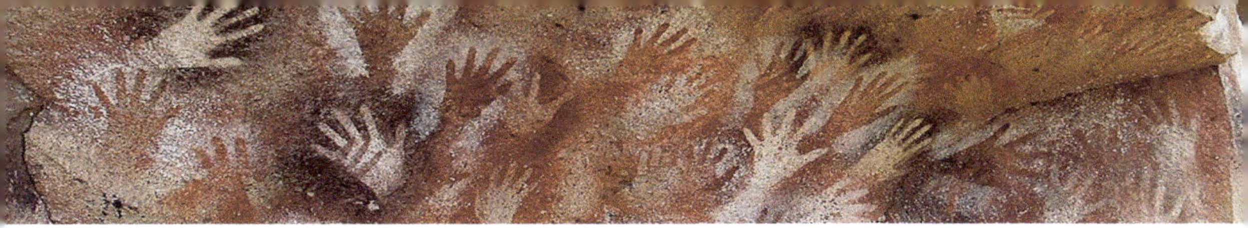

3. Shamanism – Into the Dreamtime

'What space is depends on who is experiencing it.'
(Prof. Chris Tilley)

Shamanism - meet the Ancestors

In tribal/aboriginal cultures, there have always been intermediaries between this three dimensional world, with its cycles of birth, life, and death, and some 'Otherworld', the realm of nature spirits, totem animals, and the ancestors. The generic term 'shaman' is used for someone (man or woman) who intercedes between this world and the 'spirit world', as it is defined by various cultures. These necromancers have been known by various names, such as Druid, wizard, witch, sorcerer, oracle, soothsayer, medicine man and witch doctor; to the Kogi of Colombia he is called a *mama*, to the Australian Aborigines a *karadji*. The image here **(right)** is of an Aboriginal elder standing on a rock, shielding his eyes from the sun as he surveys his landscape. This is how I envisage a shaman standing atop a Dartmoor tor back in prehistory. He is at one with his land.

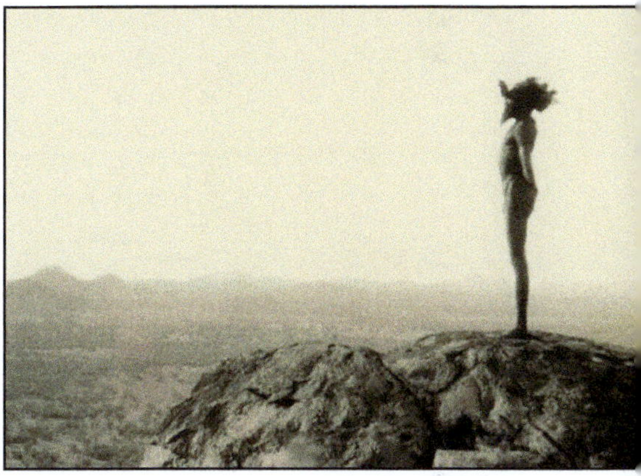

To the shaman, experience is everything, with interpretations and quests for meanings coming lower down on the list of priorities. The shaman really could have related to modern phenomenological thought; Science is often *re-discovering* that which has been lost.

For thousands of years shamans have entered trance states and 'journeyed' to these other dimensions to bring back information of use to their tribe, including knowledge of healing: 'To use shamanism to explore the possibilities for spiritual growth is to begin at the beginning. It is to explore human spirituality before cults and creeds and the Age of Priesthood' (Trwoga 2006). To ancient tribal peoples the shaman was of the same status as a tribal chief: 'The shaman was the guardian of esoteric knowledge and the technician of sacred power, whose secret wisdom was of natural laws and psychosomatic dynamics. The shaman knew, and could interpret, the cycles of nature, the workings of the heavens – the cycles of the Moon, the progress of the Sun...' (Moore & Gillette 1993). Shamans reached a profound connection with the heavens at Merrivale, with intricate alignments with the sun and the moon.

In recent years more archaeologists have acknowledged that shamanism was practiced in Neolithic Britain. In his authoritative *Prehistoric Avebury,* respected archaeologist Aubrey Burl cites evidence of shamanic practices. Regarding the 'Upton Lovell Shaman', he concludes that, '... the unusual burial position and the unique articles of clothing were the remains of a shaman or witch-doctor' (Burl 2002). Other archaeologists concur: '... the shamanistic element in prehistoric and early historic tradition in both Europe and Asia cannot be ignored' (Woodward 2001).

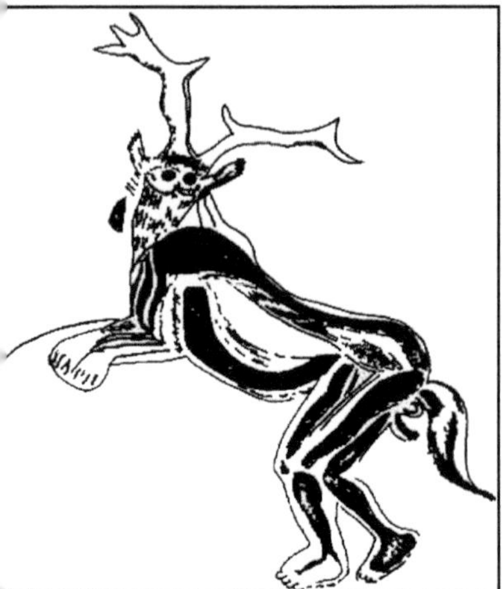

The Sorcerer is one name for an enigmatic Ice Age cave painting **(left)** found in the cavern known as *The Sanctuary* at Trois-Frères, Ariège, France. It was crafted around 13,000 BC, and the figure is often interpreted as depicting a shaman shape-shifting into a deer, or else one who has donned antlers. Shown here in a drawing by Henri Breuil, this and other cave art reflects the practice of 'sympathetic magic' ceremonies long ago.

At the Mesolithic site at Star Carr, North Yorkshire, were found a large number of objects, amongst which were red deer and elk antler, elk bone, aurochs bone, bird bone, and other artefacts thought to be the oldest known Mesolithic art in Britain. The most outstanding finds are the twenty one 'antler frontlets', from red deer stag skulls, some with attached antlers. These are sufficiently complete to see that they had been modified by the creation of two holes through the skull with a flint tool; the inside of the skull cap was smoothed off, and the antlers on each frontlet had been carefully trimmed to reduce weight. It seems very likely that these modifications enabled the frontlets to be used as headgear. This can be favourably compared with this old drawing of this drumming Siberian shaman **(left)**, and with the antlered shaman depicted on the Gundestrup Cauldron (Knight 2015).

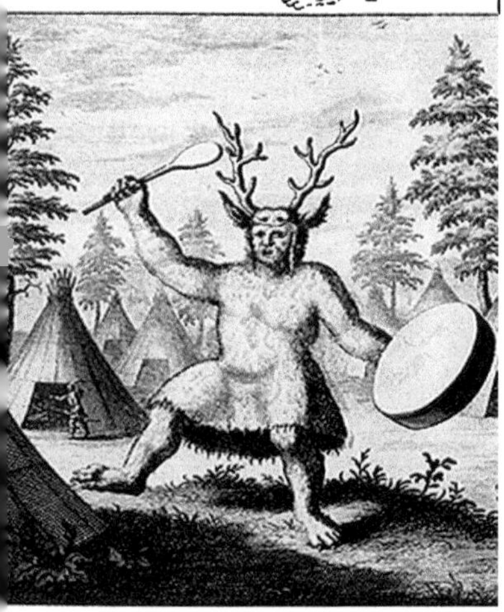

In my survey of West Kennet Long Barrow, I advocated that shamanism had underpinned the daily lives of our prehistoric ancestors (Knight 2011). To Neolithic people, the world was whole and complete, both wonderful and at the same time frightful, a world that both inspired and threatened. It was shaman who had the power to offer the clan protection from wolves, disease, adverse weather, famine, threats from other clans, and perhaps even from themselves. Their main role, however, was conversing with their predecessors: '... the ancestors may well have been considered 'supernatural' beings. The ancestors may ward off evil, ensure the fertility of the crops and herds and protect the community' (Parker Pearson 1993).

This stems from a primeval belief that part of us survives physical death: 'Their bodies may have returned to the land, but their souls are free, and can be contacted' (Knight 2007). By undertaking trance journeying, a shaman could contact the ancestors, which could be a powerful recourse. Perhaps only when corpses had defleshed would they have become a 'collective ancestor', losing any individual identity and having made their journey to the Otherworld.

It is possible that the interior of chambered tombs and caves, and even some of Dartmoor's tors, would have been taboo to ordinary folk; these were the domain of the shaman. The mystique of any sacred site gave the shaman power and high standing. The ritual knowledge embedded in the stone circles, stone rows and sacred tors could be selectively conveyed by a ceremonial specialist, the shaman. This knowledge was that of the spirits, a power rooted within the landscape. To Neolithic and Bronze Age shamans on Dartmoor, time was irrelevant when communing with the ancestors, as the

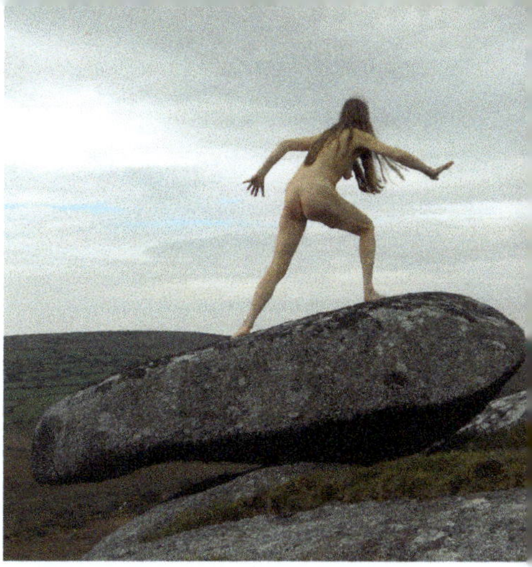

past touched the present. Dartmoor can be a wild place, where shamans/shamankas lived life on the edge, standing balanced in their power **(right)**.
Shamans would have also facilitated rites of passage and initiations, aiding adolescents during their transition to adulthood, or orchestrated elder ceremonies. Today we still have 'rites of passage', such as taking one's driving test or an exam, etc. These are often solitary challenges, involving separation, a test of some kind, and then a return. Tribal cultures often demonstrate these aspects, including incarceration and exclusion from the rest of community. A person must show their resolve, to pass through a physical or psychological barrier, to be 'reborn'. I have personally experienced this inside the chambers of West Kennet Long Barrow, when my shaman teacher, Heather, guided me through a ceremony and into meditation to meet my departed father, face to face.
I have already described the stories of people who had profound experiences, some of which changed their lives, at West Kennet Long Barrow (Knight 2011). They connected with 'something' or 'someone' who gave them knowledge from the ***past*** that could be of used in the ***present*** and in the ***future.*** This was the basis of prehistoric shamanic practice, which people carried out over thousands of years *because it worked!* The shamans were not obsessed with death, quite the contrary - they were embracing life! Kahlil Gibran put it excellently in *The Prophet*: 'You would know the secret of death? But how shall you find it unless you seek it in the heart of Life'. Life and death have always gone hand-in-hand.

Stone Age acoustics

'The world is not only watching, it is listening too.' (Snyder 1990)

Most tribal cultures today incorporate music, especially drumming, into their rituals and ceremonies. Whistles, flutes and drums have been found at many prehistoric sites around the world. Paul Devereux's *'Stone Age Soundtracks'* is the seminal work concerning ancient people's enduring and vital relationship with sound (Devereux 2001). It was noted over many years how drummers, and others present, were affected by certain fast beats, resulting in some participants experiencing changes to their speech, breathing, and pulse rates. Mike Williams comments that, 'It was drumming that enabled me to enter trance. The regular beat of the drum slowed my brainwave pattern and caused hyper-quiescence' (Williams 2010). I have confirmed this inside the chambers of West Kennet Long Barrow, where I have found that a beat of around two beats per second, influences me physically. At times I have felt very 'heady', and one has to ask what effects were experienced there in the Neolithic, when drumming was supplemented with periods of sleep and food deprivation, and the ingestion of hallucinogens. I have noted acoustic 'hotspots' inside the barrow (Knight 2011) and have also experienced the acoustic properties, through chanting, inside Neolithic rock-hewn caverns on Malta and Minorca; I was quite literally creating 'rock music!'
The *Landscape and Perception Project,* coordinated by Paul Devereux, has undertaken acoustic work at sacred sites. As a result of this, Devereux demonstrated the acoustic properties of the Bluestones at their outcrop in the Preseli Mountains. When struck by a small 'hammer stone', some rocks issued a 'clang', like a bell

(Devereux 2001, 2013). Some of the primary skeletons inside West Kennet Long Barrow were overlaid with flat slabs of stone, which were balanced on the bones. Were these simply to protect them, or were they also there for their acoustic properties? Were they struck to create sound - messages for the ancestors? All of this makes me wonder about the thin overhanging slabs of the tors.

Neil Mortimer and Mark Pilkington have recently experienced echoes at the Grey Wethers double stone circle, west of Fernworthy Reservoir. In October 2010, '... an unexpected echo' was clearly audible, particularly inside the southern circle. The echo was audible 50m or more away from the circles. A range of simple claps and calls all produced the pronounced echo effect, while echoes from one circle could also be clearly heard in another, creating more complex audible patterns that, '... would have offered a powerful experience for the prehistoric observer, to which these echo effects would have contributed a significant part' (Mortimer and Pilkington 2011).

Granite tends to reflect sound, rather than absorb it, creating amplification and echoes in the process. This may have been interpreted as the stones 'talking back'. Echoes played an important role at caves across the world: 'To a shaman, an echo is a communication between himself and the landscape' (Devereux 2010).

One powerful and evocative source of landscape sound is that of running water, which may range from the babbling whispers of brooks to the roars of plunging waterfalls, from the gentle patter of raindrops striking a rock basin, to the raging torrents of a swollen river in winter. I have drummed at night at the base of the White Lady waterfall at Lydford, which was a powerfully moving experience. Sue Wallace has found herself spontaneously singing to the land, evoking a powerful connection to it.

I shall later describe my own experiences in chanting, drumming and striking stones during my journeying the Dartmoor landscapes, particularly on the tors. A practice I often partake of is shouting, at the top of my voice, 'I AM HERE!' as I step on to the open moor. I am introducing myself to the landscape, so to speak, letting it know I have arrived. I also frequently howl, wolf-like, across the open moor, often from the top of an outcrop. This is to call in the spirit of wolf, my totem animal. This is wonderfully energising and connecting, as my howls are lifted by the wind and carried to the realms of the ancestors. On one winter walk, I found a sheep skull on the moor. I took this to the summit of Cosdon Beacon, holding it aloft on one of the cairns as I howled across the landscape **(left)**. I felt that I was not the first person to have done this here; I was connecting to the ancestors of the place.

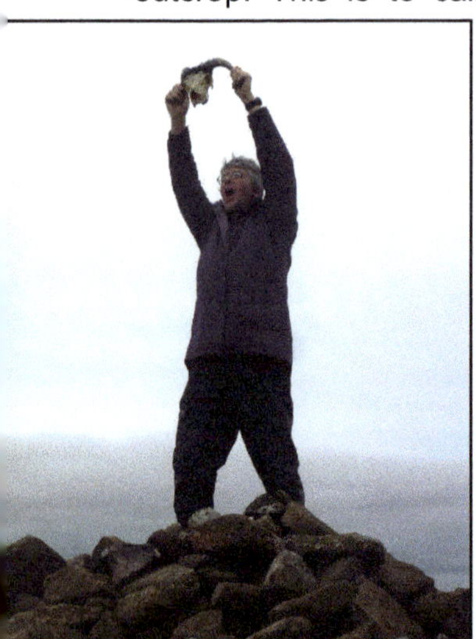

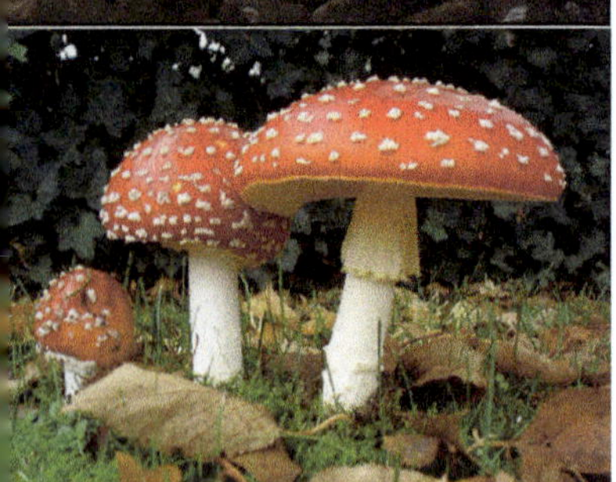

Ancestral tripping

The term "psychedelic" is derived from the Ancient Greek words *psychē* ("soul") and *dēloun* ("to make visible, to reveal"). Speaking of the Neolithic, archaeologist Mike Pitts states, 'It seems we are justified in hypothesising that altered states were indeed a component of some ceremonies...' (Pitts 2000). One aspect of 'out-of-body experience' is where one 'flies' across the landscape, like a bird, a practice spoken of in many cultures. Worldwide, one of the elements used by shamans to attain altered states is through the ingestion of mind-altering substances. There are around a dozen types of 'magic mushrooms' in the UK today, including the Fly Agaric **(left)**, Liberty Cap (popular with the 1960's hippies), Panther

Cap, Ergot, and Chicken of the Woods. I have recently seen Fly Agaric growing in Fernworthy Forest. Fungi expert Dave Shorten has informed me that all these were growing in Southern England in the Neolithic (pers. comm.). Dave also told me that the favourite growing medium for the Fly Agaric is on dead or dying birch trees. Archaeology has shown that in the early Neolithic, dense oak and hazel forests were being felled for agriculture and settlement. In these cleared areas, smaller woodland species thrived, such as ash, elder, and birch - Fly Agarics' favourite host.

It has been suggested that one use for the Neolithic 'grooved ware' pots was for ritual, such as receptacles for hallucinogens; some were large enough for fermentation purposes. Grooved ware pots excavated in Fife have been chemically analysed, and some of the vessels were used to contain black henbane (*Hyoscyamus niger*), a powerful hallucinogen. Grooved ware has been found in the SW of England. Pots thought to have been used as braziers for burning substances have been found at other British sites (Knight 2011). British Archaeologist Richard Bradley has speculated on a connection between entoptics (images seen by participants during trance) and the markings on grooved ware pots, which he thinks were used by 'ritual specialists'. This style of pottery spread from Scotland to southern England between 3000 BC and 2400 BC. Paul Devereux concludes that, '... we can envisage a hallucinogen-based shamanic cult... spreading through the British Isles' (Devereux 1997).

With this in mind, it seems highly probable that hallucinogens were being used by shamans on Dartmoor. One can imagine him or her perched on the edge of an outcrop looking at a huge simulacra etched out of the granite, its eyes staring back at the observer. How must this have been experienced if they were under the influence of a psychoactive substance? Did the face become animated, or its mouth speak? The effects of the substance were further enhanced by the flickering flames of torches illuminating the rocks, the chanting of nearby elders, and the smell of incense. These ancient necromancers were breaching the veil between worlds.

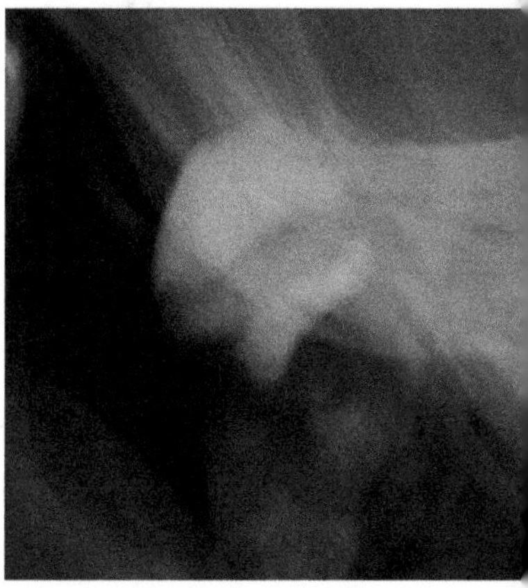

During my gatherings in West Kennet Long Barrow, people have observed how flickering lights make it appear as if features on the internal megaliths are moving (Knight 2011). Incense smoke further adds to the effect, as inanimate stones suddenly reveal faces, such as this 'beaked head' **(right)**. On my after-dark tours of Avebury, I ask attendees to replicate naked fires by waving their torches, which animates features on the stones, bringing the spirits of the stones to life no less.

I have produced similar effects on my night time visits to the tors, as wizened granite faces are roused from their slumber (see p. 176). Perhaps being exposed to radon gas in enclosed spaces, and the low radiation properties of granite, also assisted the process of 'journeying'.

We have looked briefly at the shamanic world view; to shamans, a landscape is a dynamic place, replete with spiritual essence. Now let us look at the way the ancient people viewed that landscape, which to them was mythologised and symbolic. Let us also see if we can stand on the weathered edge, and gaze with ancient eyes across newly-perceived landscapes.

'Come to the edge, he said. We are afraid, they said.
Come to the edge, he said. They came to the edge.
He pushed them off... and they flew.'
(Guillaume Apollinaire)

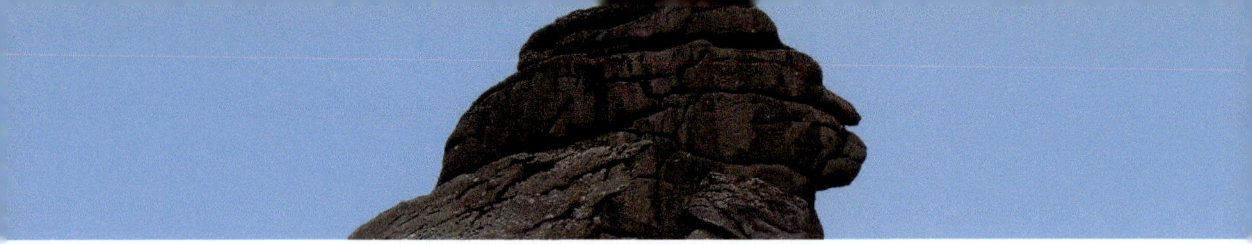

4. Symbolic Landscapes

'A landscape is captured in the very outlines of the landscape...
living books in which the myths are inscribed'.
(Lucien Lévy-Bruhl, *Primitive Mythology*)

Our amazing journey from cave man to astronaut has only been possible due to our ability to imagine and dream. To tribal cultures, the land holds memory, and imagination is a key element to pick the lock that releases arcane wisdom. But today we have devalued imagination, asking ourselves, 'did that really happen?' or 'did I imagine that?' To ancient cultures, imagination wasn't some valueless or poetic process of 'creating' from the non-existent, but rather an unveiling of a hidden reality, a revealing of something normally concealed. The retellings of myths, the perception of simulacra (both of which utilise our imagination) were once tools with which to unlock an 'Otherworld', a deep ocean of collective human and planetary consciousness; this is still the case with indigenous cultures today.

Prof Richard Bradley suggests that, 'Natural places have an archaeology because they acquired significance in the *minds* of people in the past... There are good reasons for suggesting that unaltered features of the landscape should be studied more systematically by archaeologists... we need to investigate the archaeology of monuments alongside that of 'natural' places' (Bradley 2000). Prof Chris Tilley concurs: 'A more holistic perspective is required, one that links bodies, movement and places together as a whole, and this is why the term 'landscape' has utility... as perceived and embodied sets of relationships between places, a structure of human feeling, emotion, dwelling, movement and practical activity within a geography' (Tilley 2004).

That natural features were held as sacred is also suggested by any physical changes that people may have made to natural places, such as rock art, and by evidence of human activity found at or near them. Only later may some embellishment take place by erecting monuments. Around the Stonehenge landscape it has been realised that monuments were raised with a direct relationship to the River Avon, and that natural glacial ridges also determined part of the route of the Avenue on its approach to Stonehenge. This process is evidenced on Dartmoor in the form of tor cairns and enclosures which incorporated the rocky outcrops.

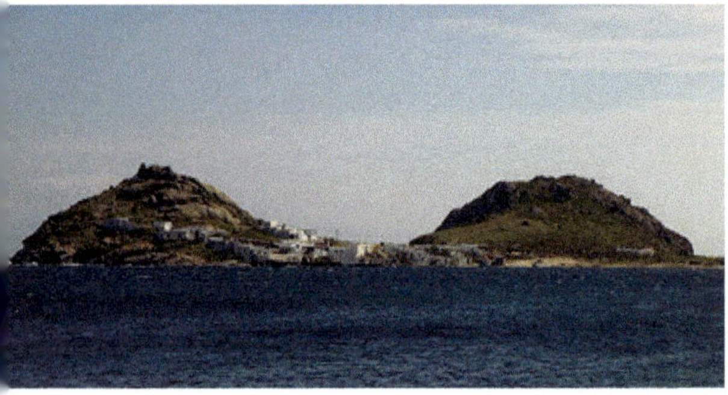

Across the Classical world natural features were imbued with layers of myth, such as in the naming of the *Breasts of Aphrodite* for twinned peaks at Mykonos, Greece **(left)**. The Paps of Anu or Danu are breast-shaped hills near Killarney, Ireland, said to be sacred to the Earth Goddess **(right)**. The features are accentuated by nipple-like cairns on their summits! The Paps of Jura (Scotland) are a similar configuration (Devereux 2010). I have demonstrated how a twin-peaked hill aligns with West Kennet Long Barrow (Knight 2011). Another landscape form resembling breasts can be seen from the Grey Mare and Colts, Dorset (Knight 1996). Clefted or double-peaked mountains are intervisible with many temples on Crete. They are sacred to the Goddess, as are those evident at Eleusis and the Acropolis, Greece; the rugged twin-peaked Mount Kerata (meaning *'horns'*) rises above the major temple complex of Eleusis. In Britain, the moon at lunar standstill sets into the Hills of Hoy as viewed from Ring of Brodgar, on Orkney. The sensuous curves of the landscape straddle the skyline, ready to receive the moon into its body.

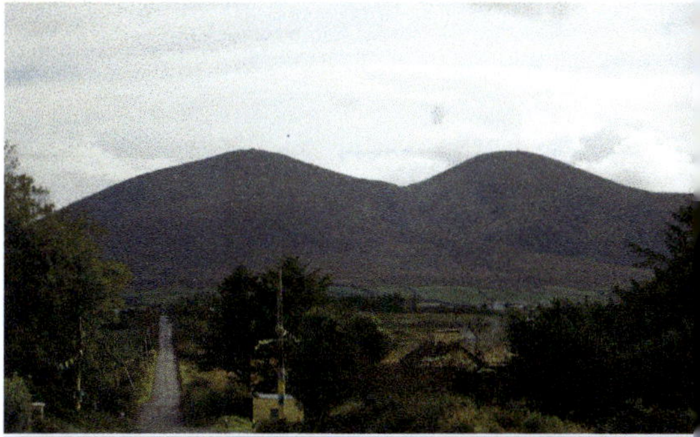

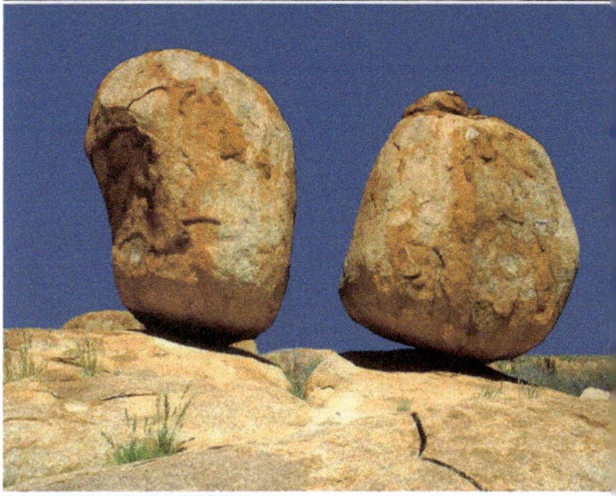

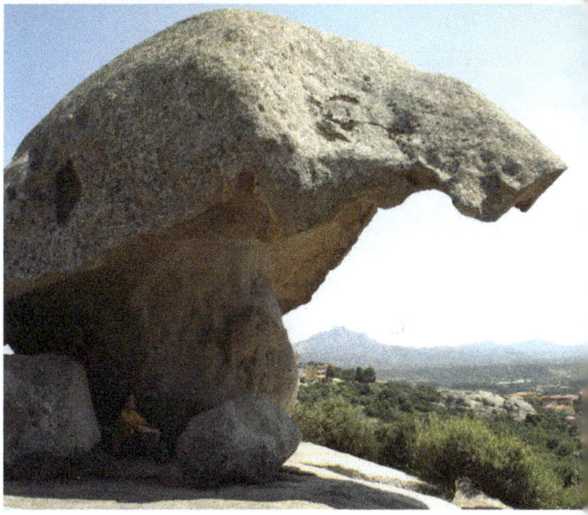

Most early myths concerning natural features, as well as stone monuments, have not survived into the modern era. This said, around the world there are surviving nuggets of folklore and superstition that *have* endured. There are enough to make us certain that thousands of years ago notable or unusual natural features were regarded as having special significance to people, as they do today to indigenous tribal cultures. The abandonment of these special places, plus the demonisation of many by the Church, led to the loss of oral traditions that had previously been handed down for hundreds of years. Relics of former worship, however, can be gleaned from place names, such as sun and dragon hills, and places now assigned as the work or abode of the Devil; Evil Coombe (605678) may be an example. Propaganda strove to stop people visiting these ancient Pagan places; there was a new God in town, which could only be accessed through Jesus, via a priest.

The Devil's Marbles at Warumungu, NT, Australia **(above, centre)** is a fine example of a natural sacred site. It is called Karlu Karlu to the Aborigines, who believe the granite boulders are the eggs of the mythical Rainbow Serpent. Other balanced boulders in the area are uncannily like the logan stones on Dartmoor, and are likewise made of granite. Two more massive boulders in the Ulamba region are sacred to the Aborigines of the area; one rock is perched on top of the other, thought to be the bodies of mythic ancestors, and where rituals are carried still carried out. I came across a huge rock outcrop shaped like a mushroom at Arzachena, Sardinia **(bottom image)**. It is called Roccia El Fungo (*Mushroom Rock*), and was a ritual centre in the Bronze Age. It is now the site of a Christian altar shrine on the slopes below. You can gauge its scale as I am dwarfed sitting under the mushroom.

Fine Dartmoor examples of revered natural places include the association of Belstone with the Devil and his *Wish Hounds*, the local variant on the Wild Hunt of many cultures, and in the naming of Devil's Tor. Vixen Tor and Bowerman's Nose were said to be the handiwork of the Druids, whilst various local places linked with troublesome pixies is the result of more negative Church press concerning supernatural places. From formerly being a hallowed place of the ancestors, the moor was distorted into the abode of all manner of evil forces. Folklore concerning the Devil, dragons, serpents and other mythical beasts, are vestiges of our Pagan past, garbled echoes of ancient mythologies.

Mythologised landscapes

'Nature always speaks of spirit... the world is a divine dream.'
(Ralph Waldo Emerson. *Nature,* 1836)

Myths are woven into culture through deep, embodied, consciousness connections with an animistic landscape. Any landscape is imagined, a construct of belief and spirituality, a crucible for imprinted mythology, a product of the eye of the beholder. Landscape is the bones of tribal myth-making, and exists by virtue of how it is perceived and contextualised by the people who really know it. As Paul Devereux observed: 'All sacred geography is an externalisation of inner states of being; a projection of the mind onto the land, forming mindscapes' (Devereux 2002). Since our earliest times, we have used our eyes to perceive shapes and symbols manifest by Nature, and used our imaginations to layer them with significance. In this age of modern rationalism, we have closed the door, save in some indigenous tribal cultures, to the notion that such 'coincidences' have any relevance. The way we see the world is how our culture has programmed us to see it. What is 'real' or what is 'imagined' was never an issue in times gone by.

That the land holds memory was an almost universal concept in prehistoric cultures, as it still is today in less Westernised societies. John Michell concluded, 'Socrates said that the ancients were uncomplicated, and if a certain rock was known for telling the truth, they would listen to it' (Michell 1979). It is an interesting question as to whether this repository of wisdom is something that is invented or recognised (Devereux 1996). A place that has been deemed 'sacred', whether natural or manmade, would have been, '... expected to support the imagination... it organises sight and sound, introduces light to present clarity and order, or makes things dark to suggest unseen presences and hidden power' (Walter 1988).

In 1936, visionary poet Antonin Artaud observed, 'There are places on the earth where Nature, moved by a kind of intelligent whim, has sculptured human forms, for it is over the whole geographic expanse of a race that Nature has chosen to speak. I shall not argue if anyone says that all these forms are natural; it is their repetition that is not natural'. He goes on to say that the simulacra seen in rocks and other natural features are usually similarly perceived as significant by indigenous tribes the world over. Further to this, these natural formations provide proof and validation of ancient myths and cosmologies.

Sean Kane has the following insightful views concerning myths, that they '... take their inspiration not from texts, temples or other monuments at the centre of human effort, but from the life of nature surrounding it, because people co-evolve with their habitat, who walk the paths their ancestors walked... myth-telling assumes that the stories already exist in nature, waiting to be overheard by humans who will listen for them' (Kane 1998). We still possess corners of the human mind that once streamed information from the land, from nature, with which to download data held dormant in the land.

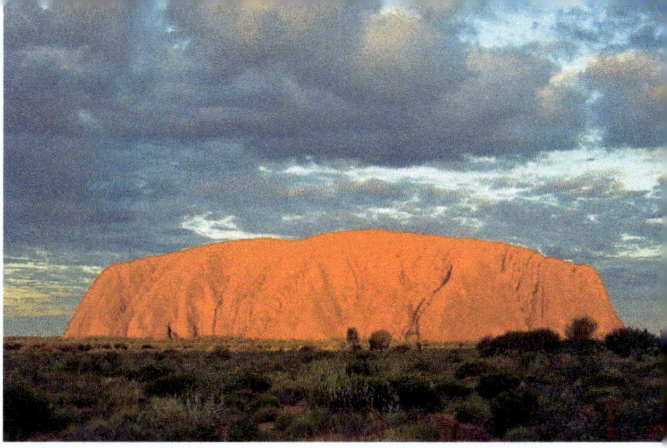

The Dreamtime of the Australian Aborigines is etched into the fabric of the landscape, as time is collapsed into place and into space. Their land is one that is freighted with myth, epitomised at Uluru, one of their most sacred sites **(above)**. For it is not the people that possess or create the legends, but the landscape itself that births the myths - the Earth holds memory. There seems little doubt that a landscape is 'a reservoir of mythic concepts' which seem to be triggered into life when humans inhabit it (Devereux 1996).

Ancient peoples of Dartmoor were sharing the landscape with their ancestors, as if they were standing next to them. Incoming Australian Aborigines would, '... encase the land in a mythological envelope, thus securing it in what became a timeless reality which would serve as spiritual sustenance to the countless generations that followed' (Cowen 1992). Aborigines approach their land not so much in words, but rather in symbolic form, as visionary geography. Their lands were created by mystical beings, so the present landscape is the Dreamtime landscape, and as such is an expression of their spiritual attachment to it (Cowen 1992). The Great Snake of their creation mythology is still present on the land today as geographical features, and in moving from site to site they walk the body of the serpent: 'They walked through a landscape that was a topographic myth - the land harboured the Dreamtime; it enriched the inner lives of the people' (Devereux 1996).

The Aborigines refer to 'old men' or ancestors, who can be seen in landscape features, such as trees and notable rock outcrops, and which have assumed totemic significance. A journey through topography becomes an inner journey, an *innerscape* – where landscape and mindscape are fused and entwined. The 'holy book' of tribal cultures is the fabric of the landscape: 'When aborigines enter into a 'dream journey' the land is transformed into a metaphysical landscape saturated with significance' (Cowen 1989). It is interesting that in the Aboriginal mythic past, known as the Dreaming or Dreamtime, giants emerged from the earth, leaving traces of themselves in the landscape, before returning into the earth. A boulder on a hillock at Ngama is believed by Aborigines to be where Malatji, the leader of the Dog People, made camp in the Dreamtime stories. Elders break off pieces from the rock, releasing the *kurunba,* or life force, to be released into the landscape for the fecundity of the clan's soul (Devereux 1991).

The spiritual and cultural bond between a tribal culture and its landscape is always seen as more than geographically fortuitous. But rather a gateway to ancestral interaction, where everywhere some mythic presence permeates the land and manifests itself in topographical features, such as remarkable rocks. In the Sydney region, because of the soft Sydney Sandstone, valleys often end in a canyon or cliff, and so travelling along the ridge lines was much easier than travelling in the valleys. Thus, the songlines tend to follow the ridge lines, and this is also where much of the sacred art is located, such as the Sydney Rock Engravings. In contrast, in many other parts of Australia, the songlines tend to follow valleys, where water is found more easily. The New Zealand Maori also wove outcrops into their mythology.

The Australian Aborigines have inherited a lineage and heritage that is 40,000 years old (Cowen 1992). The entire landscape is analogous to their family tree in an intimate state of kinship with the land. In fact it is impossible to discuss their cultural history without referencing the land, as it is their cultural map through which they travel. What to us is a just boulder may to them be a Dreamtime creature or ancestor. There exists an intense bond between each group and their homeland, where they inhabit, quite literally, the Dreamtime inherited from their ancestors. Likewise, the Kalahari Bushman and the Native Americans see themselves a part of the whole, and thus live in harmony with the land. This is confirmed by anthropomorphic imagery at rocky crags, seen as facets of Great Spirit: 'The land became a repository for the tribal myths. It became sacred text' (Paul Devereux, 2010b).

A common feature of the cosmologies of ancient and indigenous people is that the Creation gods journeyed through their land, shaping the terrain, the essence of which still imbues the geography. This gives rise to the concept of a *genius loci*, or spirit of place, which influences everything in its domain and in fact has a hand in shaping it. Scientists today acknowledge that human beings are influenced by the land in which they live – people epitomise where they come from, just as plant species are determined by soil type and climate.

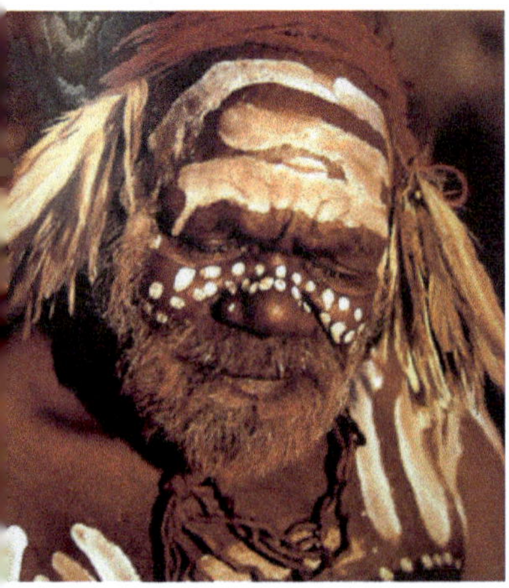

To the Australian Aborigines **(left)** their Dreamtime IS the landscape. In Britain, wilder places such as Dartmoor once provided an ancestral map, a mythologised environment, through which a shaman might travel, both physically and metaphorically; he or she knew that one was not possible without the other. Time is encapsulated into place, and landscape myths enable 'time travel', encounters with cultural mythical characters and ancestral memory. The ancestors still inhabit the land and share it with the living; '... the ancestors still sleep where they fell' (Trwoga 2006). To know a landscape is to know your identity, and where you belong in the world, and as such landscape is an active agency of cultural identity. When stripped of its mythology, a landscape is desanctified, becoming a barren wasteland, in which the stifling concepts of land ownership, real estate and property are born.

What really laid claim to any particular sacred landscape was the fact that people's ancestors had walked that land, and in their footsteps they walked across the same terrain, scaled the same tors, crossed the same rivers, and drank from the same sacred rock basins. People knew that the experiences of their forebears were embedded in that locality, and that their own experiences would leave a memory for those who would follow.

Speaking of his examination of the Neolithic sites of Orkney, Trevor Garnham (Kingston University) notes, 'Of the various disciplines we can bear upon to bridge the gap between archaeological remains and the prehistoric mind, mythology will be that most used here, as myth, amongst many things, is a form of explanation for primitive peoples' (Garnham 2004). And myth is never static: 'Myth in the landscape is both archaic and contemporary, and is always re-inventing itself in the context of the predominant cultural issues of the day' (Thorley 2012).

We shall talk in detail about simulacra later, but it is worth mentioning at this stage that rocks and other natural features that resemble something else are a key element of tribal cultures' world view: 'Dreamtime perception was particularly evident in the use of simulacra, in which the shapes of certain topographical features allowed them to be presented in anthropomorphic, zoomorphic, or iconic guise to both the individual and the culturally-reinforced gaze of society members' (Devereux 2013). Symbolic perception and thought allows the shaman to move between realities. Shamans navigated their mindscape, '... by constructing a mental map from a complex network of visual relationships, resemblance, differences, metaphors and other associations' (Garnham 2004). *Metaphor* is from the Greek *'to carry across'*.

Even though the whole landscape was once deemed as sacred, certain places were special; 'Perhaps sacred places were locations where *even more* information could be obtained.... The very fact that there are, and always have been, sacred places, demonstrates their psychological importance. They may be where we get a greater glimpse of reality' (Devereux 1996).

Mythologised landscapes have be perceived the world over. A outcrop of magnetic serpentine rock on Mount Tamalpais, near San Francisco, has Indian folklore about being a *'power place'*, that will mess up a compass needle. The rock has a 'seat' on which to perch and experience the vibe (Devereux 1998). In Chaco Canyon, New Mexico, steep ritual stairways, up to 7m wide, have been hewn out of the living rock in cliff faces displaying curious configurations. Some of the famous straight Chaco 'roads' focus on natural formations. Speaking of Greek temples situated in mountainous areas, Vincent Scully wrote (in *'The Earth, the Temple and the Gods'*), 'The landscape and the temples together form the architectural whole'.

So too on the Indian subcontinent. There are sacred rocks in the village of Phulgran, in Islamabad, where natural menhirs and rock shelters overlook agricultural fields. These were invoked by ancient people before sowing, and there are votive tables indicating that ancient people made offerings to their gods whenever the crop was good and in surplus. A number of such sacred rocks are located in the villages of Darwala, Bora Bangial, Peja, Gora Mast, and Bhimbar Tarar, where there are natural performance spaces still used for sacred rituals.

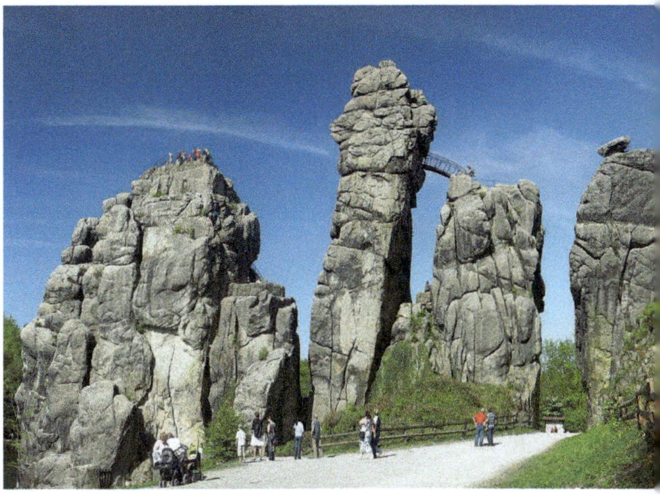

The indigenous peoples of the Arctic see distinctive landscape features as having magical properties, and although they sometimes build small cairns or wooden structures, they do not otherwise alter natural formations. The Saami of Finland make little use of monuments, using instead natural features that stand out on the landscape, to which they accord special powers **(lower image p. 66)**.

At Externstein, Germany, stand 30m high natural stacks **(right)**. Finds suggest that these spectacular columns interested reindeer hunters c.10,000 BC, and are said to have been a centre for Pagan worship until the 8th century AD. Huge steps are carved out of the rock which once led to shrines, and a bridge leads to a rock-hewn chapel. These stacks remind me of several that crown the Dartmoor tors.

In the southern part of the ruins of Machu Picchu, Peru, is the *Sacred Rock,* in the *Temple of the Sun*. It is an inclined natural rock outcrop that incorporates a small grotto; walls of cut stone fill in some of its irregular features of the rock. The shape of this rock mimics the form of distant mountains. Another huge natural stone at Machu Picchu is carved with steps and an altar, signifying its importance. Many other Inca sites use similar natural rocks as ceremonial foci.

That elements of geography were once regarded as sacred in their own right is proven, for instance, in the way the Preseli Hills Bluestones were transported to Stonehenge. These outcrops of dolerite were obviously regarded as significant prior to the selection of the stones, possibly because the stones possessed some special quality. The outcrops frequently form strange shapes which inspire the imagination. In Wiltshire, small pieces of non-descript oolithic limestone from several miles were built into the chambers of West Kennet Long Barrow, even though they added nothing to the strengthening of the structure. Some of the unworked boulders incorporated in the Newgrange and Knowth passage graves in Ireland came from the elevated landscape of the Wicklow Mountains, some 46 miles away. Again, few of these natural stones played any major 'engineering' role in the tomb's construction (Bradley 2000). In all these cases people were transferring geography, 'pieces of place', from one locality to another; elements of geography become artefacts on a grandiose scale.

Was this the case with the stone circles of Dartmoor? It is possible that the materials of the moor's stone circles may have been brought down from the higher ground of the sacred tors (just as Avebury's stones came down from the Marlborough Downs, and the Bluestones were transported from the Preseli Hills). These would have captured the magic of the forbidden tors, bringing their power down to lower and more accessible places. There may have been an acknowledgment that the clitter used in building the circles and rows originally came from this sacred high ground. Regarding the boulders brought from the Wicklow Mountains to Newgrange, the former is visible from the latter. On Easter Island the statues were obtained from higher 'sacred ground' of the remnants of a volcanic crater on the island. Concerning Dartmoor this is pure conjecture of course, but the precedents are there. I would suggest that every boulder of granite was sacred even as it lay on the earth; Dartmoor's granitic 'pieces of place' were valued by their very nature *before* they were even selected. By constructing a monument from local rocks a commitment and sacred connection was forged by the people to the tor from which components originated. And, as we shall see later, monument *location* was of prime importance; 'The location of ritual monuments may impart something about the way in which the landscape was organised to meet their spiritual requirements' (Gerrard 1997).

Landscapes were once perceived as being spiritually dynamic. Wise people with a deeper connection with the Earth have always lived within a landscape they perceived as animated and vibrant, one composed entirely of energy and spirit. Every atom on the planet is impregnated with life-force, and every landscape is sculpted through intent. This realisation is to look at the land through ancient eyes.

Seeing with ancient eyes

*'The concept that the visible world is an elaborated code,
which conceals, yet may be used to reveal, the metaphysical
causes behind it, is of great antiquity'* (John Michell 1979)

In 1932, George William Russell, the Irish mystic and seer, wrote that he preferred to interact with his native Irish countryside in isolation, shunning organised rituals, preferring instead a way which, '... gives wisdom rather than that which gives power'. He also looked at how memory can be transferred down to us through our minds and our bodies, and suggested that this is also true with nature and landscape. In *The Candle of Vision',* published in 1918, he wrote, 'In that acorn which lies at my feet is a tiny cell which has in it a memory of the oak from the beginning of the earth, and a power coiled in it which can beget from itself the full majesty of being an oak'. He also concluded that the memory of Spirit is the real origin of imagination. By extension, we come full circle to landscapes that remember, that pass myths onto new inhabitants – which Russell called the *'Memory of the Earth'.* As he walked across the land he had the realisation that, '... *all things were her dreams'*. Russell termed the phrase 'supernature' for the subtle levels of Nature. This telling conclusion by Russell directly relates back to ancient cultures and their relationship to the land: 'I believe that most of what was said about God was, in reality, said of that Spirit whose body is Earth'. He also came to believe there is spiritual aspect to any particular landscape and its sacred sites, which are, '... naturally charged with psychical forces'.

Perhaps we need to recapture that primeval eye, that mode of perception that finds sermons in rocks, and hears a song in a babbling brook. What is now the realm of the poet, dreamer and surrealist was once common knowledge, even science. A landscape is an entity that exists by virtue of its being perceived and experienced by beings that inhabit it, and is not inactive or a merely a static canvas across which to travel. Like people who cross it, landscapes also gather experiences. To ancient people the cosmos was made manifest from the interrelationship of everything that exists (not unlike modern quantum mechanics theorem!) and into this people wove their culture by metaphorical and reciprocal association. Our world really is a figment of the imagination, the result of the cumulative learning, experience and conditioning in whatever culture to which we belong. This can be equally applicable to our relationship with a landscape in which we inhabit, or travel through in a cognisant manner.

To have the assumption that only manmade monuments have any relevance in archaeological studies fails to recognise the input that landscapes influence perception. What we may see, hear and perceive at monuments may help us obtain some answers to questions, such as to why this stone row or that stone circle is where it is, rather than somewhere else. Peter Klemen suggests that, 'The very nature of prehistoric monuments means that they are often seen in isolation, as solemn, quiet entities and, with specific reference to Dartmoor, often in barren and lonely environments. However, not only is it important that the ceremonial monuments and settlements be viewed together as inter-related places... they are and would have been active and 'affective' places holding a presence and resonance' (Klemen 2015). This is the Aboriginal mindset.

'General Systems Theory' is a different way to view the world, which science is now embracing. It advocates that the world be viewed as an interconnected hierarchy of matter and energy, where, although it is not always possible to understand the parts, which in themselves interact with other parts, it all makes sense when the whole 'system' is studied. It is thus for a landscape, which is the product of all the composite parts. Take any element away and it is no longer the same landscape. 'The study of monuments has often seen them as separate from the landscape and has resulted in the monuments being viewed as separate entities divorced from the terrain around them. A useful way to bring the two together is by seeing place as containing a "certain influence" and "distinct potency", and thus is active' (Klemen 2015). In *'Monuments and Landscape in Atlantic Europe'*, C Scarre concurs, '... any attempt to understand a prehistoric monument which fails to consider the landscape setting is omitting one of the most salient characteristics' (Scarre 2002).

A person with an indigenous mindset and a shamanic worldview is not an individual in the way Western philosophy would have us believe. Rather, they are connected to everyone and everything in the world, in this context to the landscape around them, in such a way that even mundane everyday activities have magical significance. And this way of thinking is in no way inferior to the modern scientific worldview, but merely a different way of seeing things, and comes, in fact, with its own set of 'rules' and logic.

Science and modern life relates to things in terms of their usefulness, whereas a shamanic mindset sees things as possessing value because they are known. If something is perceived, it has worth.

Perhaps the act of experiencing a landscape as sacred is enough unto itself. Does the land recognise our recognition? Perhaps it does, perhaps it does not. The concept of James Lovelock's 'self-regulating Earth' asks us to enquire as to whether the Earth itself needs to be self-conscious to achieve this, or rather functions using the biological/physical processes of action and reaction, of check and rebalance? Whatever the answer, the very act of seeking is fulfilling for the soul, a genesis of sorts: 'Stories are still out there in the Earth, to be overheard by anyone who has patience to listen. This act of listening is not enough in itself to reach wisdom – but it's a start' (Kane 1998). Druid Penny Billington suggests we should: 'Internalise the landscape, for we are its mirror, as it is ours' (pers. comm.).

Our religious beliefs are firmly rooted in the concepts of animism and the sacredness of the natural world. Prehistoric peoples had great sensitivity to their environment and this is reflected in the huge amount of imagery inspired by Nature. Gods and Goddesses were seen to be omnipresent and eternal, and whilst contact with deities was sought after to harness their power for positive outcomes, what was equally acknowledged was that these divinities also had the capacity to unleash forces of destruction. In later religions, it was this *'fear factor'* that was centre stage, as Nature became something to be feared and ultimately subdued. Man has isolated himself from the magic of Nature, from the very energies with which he once lived in harmony: 'As scientific discovery has developed, so our world has become dehumanised, and with the rise in rationality has gone the profound emotional and spiritual connection that the symbolism that Nature once gifted us' (Knight 2015).

Symbolic landscapes of Dartmoor

'The landscape simultaneously passes on and encodes information about the ancestral past' (Chris Tilley 1994).

Archaeology has been slow to realise that the landscape setting of a monument is of equal importance as what was constructed. Nature and culture were never separated in ancient times, and in terms of research today we need to combine them again, seeing them as two sides of the same coin. Places that lack manmade monuments could still be highly significant to cultures (Bradley 2000), such as at Fen bog and Bath. Natural places form the backbone of the mythologies of the Aborigines and Native Americans, and the location of sacred sites is never chosen, but rather is revealed. The Shinto religion says that spirit/power, called *Kami,* is intensified in strength at certain outstanding natural places, two of which are curious boulders and waterfalls. Did Dartmoor's prehistoric inhabitants hold similar beliefs?

The prehistoric landscape was a product of people's comprehension of it. Landscapes were not somewhere 'out there', waiting to be exploited, but were conceptualised in terms of people's identities and understanding, as they observed, tasted, smelt, utilised it, regarded it as near or far away, or as dangerous or safe (Bender et al 1999). The physical landscape is also overlaid by a psychic/spiritual Mindscape – which could be traversed, and perhaps there existed a pre-requisite that it *had to be*.

A sacred place could be defined as where the physical world meets the spiritual world. Surely Dartmoor was once held as such a place. I believe it still is. Speaking of Bodmin Moor, Prof Chris Tilley surmises: 'Beneath the apparent surface of the landscape, but intimately bound up with it, there is a hidden topography best known to (and influenced by) ritual experts in these societies, but emotionally and cognitively pertinent to all' (Tilley 1994). This can equally apply to Dartmoor's prehistory.

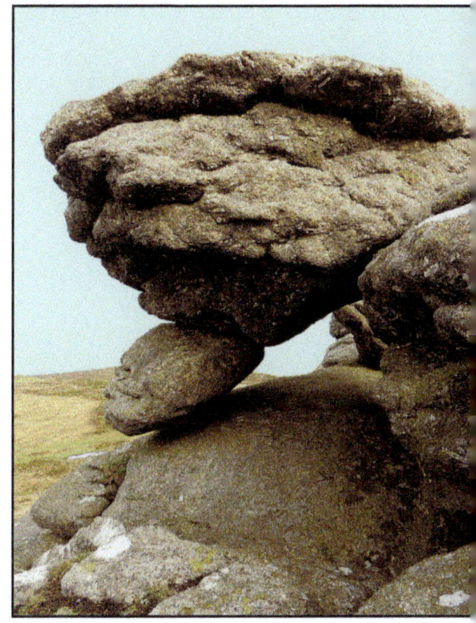

So, in the Bronze Age, the first farmers arrived on the stunning and unbridled landscape of Dartmoor: 'The presence of the landscape must have been of immense significance to these early farmers' (Garnham 2004). Ancient peoples embedded their myths and deities into the fabric of a land across which they moved and inhabited. These were often manifest as unusual or striking rock formations. This example **(right)** is from Saddle Tor, showing the amazing, gravity-defying balancing act that granitic tors produce. How did prehistoric people explain such things? As the handiwork of the ancestors or the gods?

The sound of waterfalls, how the wind whistles through the trees or crevices of tor exposures, the sound of water dripping from a rock basin into a pool below, all may have been taken as oracular portents. These are all expressions of nature, of the landscape – nature has a voice. The scarcity of local folklore to support this should not be taken as evidence that it did not once exist; if we did not have the tribal Aborigines to converse with today, we would be unaware of most of their culture and mythology. I believe that Dartmoor's tors, waterfalls and other landscape features possess their own spirit of place and would have been revered in their own right, and not because of anything humans projected on to them. Projection follows perception.

But projections surely followed, perhaps as far back as the Mesolithic, forging mythological and cultural connections between Man and his landscape. The idea of the sanctity of place was born, that locales did not need to be changed to make them sacred – they already *were*. The tors were eternal reference points, just as named places in the Outback anchor the Aborigine culture to their land; a red sandstone rock is seen as a red kangaroo of one myth. I find it hard to believe that the tors, the dominant features on both Dartmoor and Bodmin, were not likewise mythologised. It was the enduring quality of projecting myths onto natural outcrops, in this case the granite tors and clitter, that must have been reassuring, providing an eternal ancestral presence. These were places where you knew your ancestors had visited and retold clan myths to *their* generation. Lucid dreaming may have been practiced at such places, as it was by ancient cultures across the world (Devereux 1996). Shamans entered a dream state through which to receive profound messages from spirit. Perhaps this was undertaken beneath granite overhangs, or next to rock basins, inside cairn circles, or under the gaze of a huge zoomorphic simulacrum. Although monuments would later enhance and confirm interaction with those natural hallowed forces, it was granite that was the bedrock of their culture.

The ritually and symbolically effective placing of monuments became of vital importance in the creation and maintaining of authority. They also ensured the continuance of myths associated with particular places, and of the spiritual powers present; 'The landscape provided a primary medium through which power was reproduced' (Tilley 2010). It is possible that people believed that tor rock outcrops were endowed with spirits, even the ancestors turned to stone. The idea of Aborigine Dreamtime ancestor-creators settling down and becoming features in the natural terrain may be appropriate when considering Dartmoor's tors. Such striking and

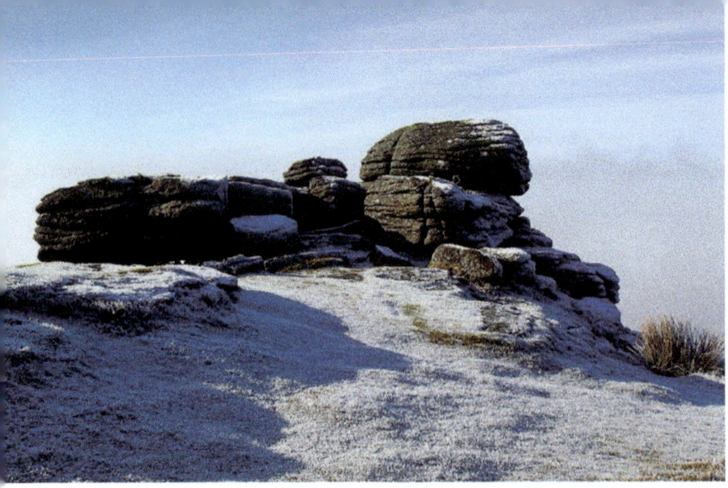

prominent features would seem prime candidates for spiritual and cultural association. The image here **(left)** is of a snow-dusted Birch Tor. The outcrop resembles a lion or a sphinx; it has looked similar to this for thousands of years.

Landscapes were once viewed through metaphorical eyes. Humanity speaks in metaphors. We do it every day: *'foot of a hill'*, *'blood red'*, *'soar like a bird'* and so on. We know that ancient cultures employed metaphors extensively in naming geographical features due to their physical form (Knight 2015), so why not the prehistoric people of Dartmoor? Prof Tilley concludes that, '... a metaphor does not tell us that one thing is like another (a simile) but that it *is* another... To be human is to think through metaphors and objectify them in material forms' (Tilley 2004). When we see a landscape in terms of metaphor, as it may once have been viewed, it becomes a product of both the past and the present, which is the mindset of aboriginal/tribal cultures. Seeing a landscape through metaphorical eyes is time-travel no less, minus the Tardis! The metaphorical ancestors, when included in ceremonies, brought the past into the present (Davies 2010). Perhaps high up on the tors, ancestor spirits (in the form of the granite simulacra) would 'oversee' meetings and rituals, ensuring everyone would follow the rules that had been laid down by the ancestors: everyone must act correctly, as people had done in previous meetings, reducing potential conflict. If gatherings took place around rocks that were regarded as spiritual embodiments of the ancestors/gods, conduct may have been ordered and constrained. Myths are often told from the land's perspective, ensuring that people retain the impulse to preserve the equilibrium between Man and landscapes.

In the Neolithic and Early Bronze Age, natural boundaries in the landscape, i.e. tors, rivers, lakes, and marshes, seem to have been important in marking the margins of sacred space. These were augmented by monuments in the Middle to Late Bronze Age, especially when there was a lack of obvious notable outcrops (Tilley 2010). Large cairns on bare hill tops were the new reference points, as the tors had once been, appropriating ancestral power, triumphant over the slumbering colossi of the granite tors. Intervisiblity seems to have been paramount. I noted this example on Cox Tor **(left),** which shows how the entrance of one of the cairns aligns with the remarkably pyramidal Brent Tor (or Brentor). At Loughcrew, Ireland, I observed how the entrance to Cairn H aligns with the sacred hill of Tara. Why were 'places of the dead' being aligned with hills many miles away?

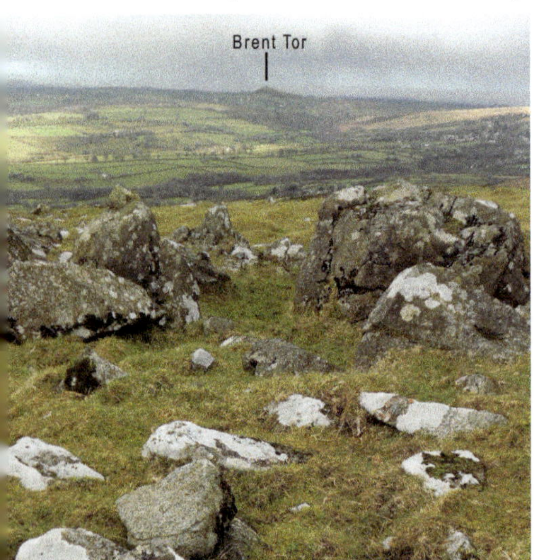

Natural features were almost certainly named back in prehistory. The naming of a place, such as a tor or river, imbues it with human and mythological meaning and significance. To name a place transforms it from a geographical element to something that is socially relevant, a fusing of time, space and people. In a way, names create landscapes, in terms of human relevance. Named features become part of the culture which has named them, and indeed may be a component that defines that culture, giving people a sense of belonging. It is like how actors draw upon a stage set, without which they could not perform. In this respect, landscape is never a neutral, passive backdrop, but always laden with meaning and potential, a dynamic agent, an interactive conduit. A landscape is embedded in cultural and individual memory, as the past influences the present and the future. It would have been impossible for these people to live on Dartmoor without creating myths and histories of the places that they inhabited. They were orientating themselves in their world, and their embedding of monuments in the landscape was a means of achieving this.

In my studies of West Kennet Long Barrow and several Dorset sites, I have been struck by the number of times that sacred sites are precisely positioned relative to natural features, and how intervisibility and alignment is sometimes determined by a matter of metres (Knight 1996, 2011). People did not see the landscape as 'background noise', but as much an integral component, just as they themselves. Several of the Bronze Age reaves, or boundaries, use tors as foci, passing close by or up the slopes of several, such as at Roos Tor, Sharpitor, and White Tor. This shows how 'permanent' features on the landscape were utilized to divide up the land, a practice that continued into historical times. It suggests that from very early on the tors were part of tribal cultural identity, as much as chambered tombs were to the Neolithic people of Wessex and elsewhere (Knight 2011).

A member of the Dartmoor mountain rescue team recently died whilst leading a training exercise, and his fellow team members scattered his ashes on an isolated part of the moor. As members of a team who regularly walk Dartmoor, the landscape has become woven into their individual lives, and thus their lives are inextricably woven into the landscape; such was the case with our ancestors back in prehistory.

By standing at an anciently venerated natural place, such as on a Dartmoor tor, we stand midst the vestiges of a lost way of seeing the physical world. And we can still enter aboriginal d*reamscapes* or *mindscapes,* embracing the ethereal, archetypal dimensions of topography. When I stand on a tor looking out over the moor below, I sense that a part of me is reflected in the landscape. I am it and it is I. And the landscape changes as I move around it; from one direction a tor outcrop may resemble a ruined tower, from another a gigantic beast. The landscape is always in a state of flux. As am I.

Speaking of the longevity of landscape features such as tors, Prof Richard Bradley considers that, 'Although these features may retain the same form over long periods of time, the ways in which they are perceived are very likely to have altered' (Bradley 2000). For instance, many wilderness regions of the world were previously avoided. Until, that is, the advent of tourism and extreme sports. Certainly tors inspire our imaginations today. This example **(right)**, shows Great Staple Tor just after sunset, as seen from Merrivale. Today, we see a pile of granite, whereas it may once have been perceived as the silhouetted ancestors, gazing down with authority on the proceedings at the stone row and the settlement below.

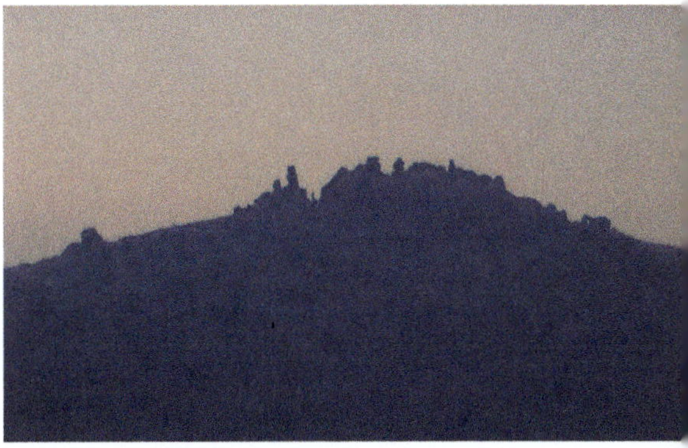

All human actions transform a landscape, no matter how little, such was the case on

Dartmoor even back in the Mesolithic. And I consider that there are also clues embedded in the landscape to help us glimpse what people believed. These subtle traces left behind by our ancestors may reveal arcane wisdom should we be open-minded and open-hearted. We can never more than partly deduce the thought processes and spiritual beliefs of our ancient forebears, but much of what we can may be achieved through walking the land. Peter Klemen concluded that, 'To be familiar with its qualities and character, walking the landscape day in day out, at different times of the day and year, would be extremely important for how I myself related to and felt about the landscape which I was studying' (Klemen 2015).

As I said before, I see sacred sites not as being ***on*** the landscape, but rather being held ***within*** it. A stone circle on a hilltop, a solitary megalith on a lonely moor, or indeed an overgrown cairn in a wood, are not separate from the landscape, but are part of it. The builders of such ancient places were reflecting their spirituality, which was a state of oneness with nature, at one with the land. The megalithic stone sites of Dartmoor were meant to last for an eternity, to be as immortal as the terrain. They were made from the rocks *of* the landscape, each component containing the crystals and minerals of the land; they were elements of the Dreamtime, *'pieces of place,'* repositioned to enhance a sacred landscape, a liminal landscape – *their* landscape.

I see Dartmoor as like a huge heart, which, from its sacred centre, pumps and squeezes out its rivers in every direction, coursing life into the land. The stone walls and ancient reaves are like the doodles of giants on the canvas of the land, and it has long been believed that isolated places are where Divinity can be contacted. I know there is a Wisdom here, which, although it cannot always be perceived, observes me from the darkness on a moonlit moor, or through the eyes of anthropomorphic granite simulacra. The landscape is a repository of cultural memory; strangely shaped rocks, the outlines of faces and breasts in hills, or a simple holed stone found in a riverbed, can reveal ancient timeless stories. I know that to connect with the spiritual essence of Dartmoor is to connect with my own Divinity. I know that when I go out onto the moor, I really go within. I have walked across a moor during midwinter, knowing that I am the only person for miles in any direction. Once, after walking miles across a sodden and cold moor in my wet gear, I made the acquaintance of a new friend, the standing stone on Langstone Moor. He seemed to have been waiting there for an eternity. For a few moments we shared both time and space **(left)**. I set up the tripod and set the camera timer for our photo call. My encounter with the stone will remain with me forever; I sometimes wonder if the stone remembers me? I certainly feel as if part of me is still out there, as if we are bonded, forever. For I have also found that the energy and presence of the Dartmoor landscape remains captured in the very cells of my body and my mind long after I have returned.

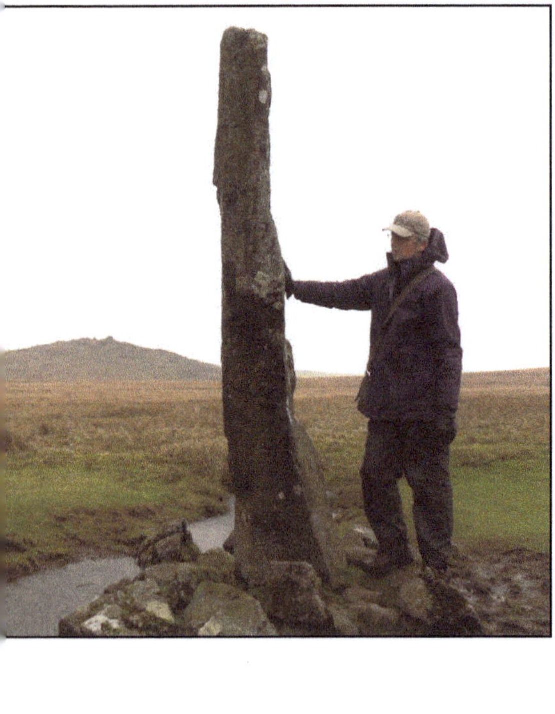

Sue Wallace and I came across an amazing granite simulacra nestling between Black Tor and Shelstone Tor, just east of the West Okement River. SW of Okehampton (563897). It measures an amazing 6m across and 3m high, and I was dwarfed by its bulk. It resembles a bison or auroch, or indeed a dragon, with arched back, its head resting on the earth, eye closed **(right)**. Many similar rocks are held as sacred by indigenous people today; there are 'Bison Rocks' in the Americas. This rock dominates the land between the tors, and would surely have been regarded as significant in prehistory. Today, it *is* still significant. On our visit to the rock, the mists shrouded the tors; it was as if we had stepped back in time. In a sense, we had.

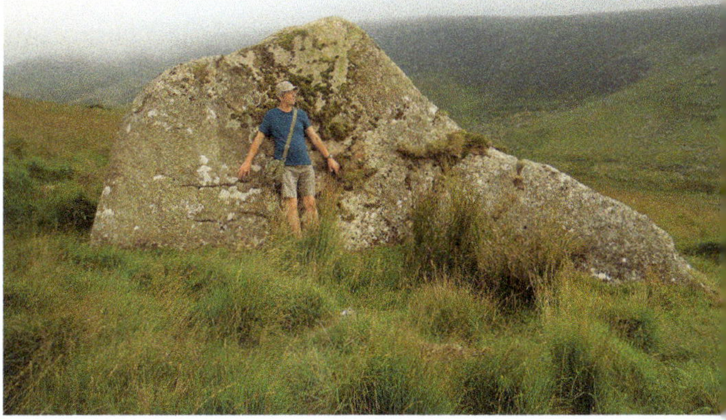

Religious and social dogma, Western philosophy, and science, have de-sanctified the land. Darwin stripped everything of its spirit and soul: 'Science delivered where religion and magic failed' (Trwogo 2006). Everywhere, nature has been forced to give up her secrets, and the Earth has been turned into a mere resource or commodity; land has become real estate, valued in units of acreage and money. Science is not the demon as such, but in its present dispassionate mindset, devoid of any acknowledgement of the sacred, it is doomed, destined to fail Mankind and the planet - a desperately sad state of affairs.

But there is hope. And it is the Aboriginal cultures of the world that hold the wisdom that gives hope for the rest of us. We too can change our perceptions, so that we can also be 'wisdom keepers'. For I now see the very landscape on which I walk as an open book into which the myths of my ancestors are emblazoned, and which I can tap into. And it is on to this canvas that I lay down my own story. Perhaps I am approaching the mindset of the ancient people of Dartmoor: their Universe was a dynamic place, alive with non-physical entities, and they possessed a rapport with a landscape bristling with myth and life-force, part of a living Earth. This is the cosmology of the shaman, whose campfire storytelling kept myths alive and vibrant.

This is the world we can glimpse through phenomenology, which we shall look at next.

Nature never breaks its own laws, and always knows its purpose. It is inspiring me to know mine. I endeavour now to see Dartmoor landscapes through ancient eyes, and to hear with ancient ears, through which archaic whispers may still be heard. A landscape may be beautiful to look at, but is even more beautiful to understand.

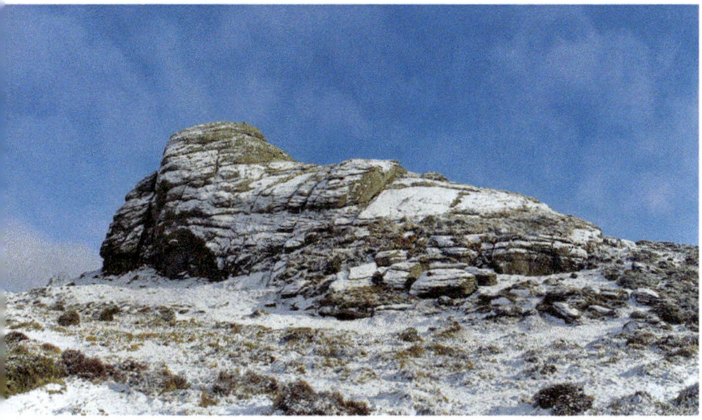

'Stories passed down over centuries, embellished by the fertile imagination of generations of tellers, expressed timeless truths' (Nanson 2011).

Left: the enchantment of Haytor after snowfall. Walking the moor in all seasons reveals diverse landscapes, resulting in disparate experiences.

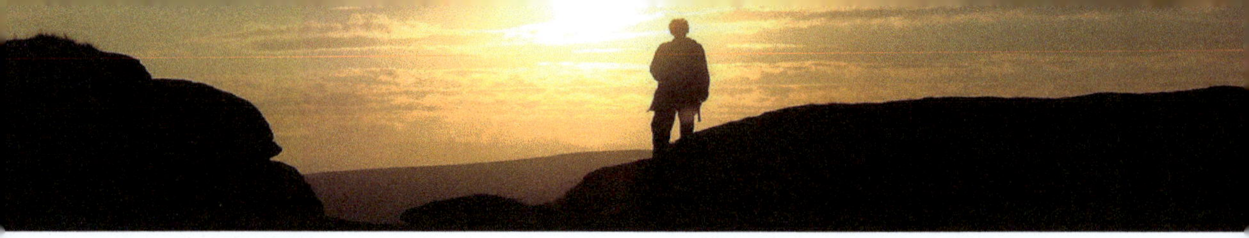

5. Phenomenology – Walk This Way

'What matters to native people is the path. What matters is to walk.'
(Chris Trwoga)

In 1994, Prof Chris Tilley published, *'A Phenomenology of Landscape'* (Tilley 1994), which sent ripples around the archaeological world, as it is still doing today. Phenomenology is a means of re-achieving a direct and somewhat 'primeval' contact with the world around us, using direct experience. It can reveal hidden meanings of landscapes and their monuments, as a means to study ancient cultures and *their* relationships to landscapes (Tilley 2004, 2008, 2010). It seeks to absorb the landscape through the full range of human experiences. It is more a way of thinking, a philosophical process, rather than a set of doctrines to be adhered to. It is perceptual, subjective and introspective, and sees our consciousness and our body as an entity of perception; the body, after all, is a product of our consciousness. In a similar way, sodium and chloride make up the emergent qualities of salt when they are combined, as opposed to when they are separate. All our bodily senses should be active and are essential in defining and experiencing what any space or landscape is. John Michell considered that, 'All that the world offers as clues to its own nature is the evidence available to our senses' (Michell 1979).

Until recently, rarely did archaeologists lift their eyes from the earth and consider how a site, field boundary or stone circle related to the wider landscape. Curiously, on the few occasions when archaeologists did look beyond a site, they by-passed the landscape to consider Man's relationship to the sun, moon, and stars. Academia often have a problem with the phenomenological/cognitive approach, like they have had with dowsing, because both disciplines rely on the experiences of the individual, and no two people can be expected to experience the same phenomena, or landscape, in exactly the same way. But to this argument we can add that there are countless Dartmoors; an inmate in Dartmoor Prison, a rambler, 'sunday driver', farmer, environmentalist, cyclist, historian, or horse rider all carry their own mental construct of *their* Dartmoor. And they are ***all correct from their personal perspectives.***

Perhaps we need to shift our enquiries from concentrating on the structure of monuments, to how they may have once structured people's perceptions. This phenomenological, cognitive way of thinking has the potential for us to experience new ways of sensing, to be fully present in the now as we walk across a landscape. We are invited to experience landscapes with all our bodily senses, grounded as they are in physicality, seeing ourselves intertwined with the world around us. We are coaxed to perceive *as individuals* as we move across the landscape, to emotionally reconnect through all of our senses, and through metaphor. We experience the landscape by embedding ourselves within it, ***not as an object separate from landscape, but rather an element of it***. How we perceive an object or landscape says as much about us as that which is being observed. It is the interaction between ourselves and the world around us that creates both it and us. Our bodies (through sensory experiences) are the medium through which we primarily know a place. It is the landscape around us that defines who we are through interaction. We must study the landscape from the inside, so to speak, embedding ourselves within it, for our bodies are the principal means of research. And the observer must immerse themselves in a landscape without prejudice or preconceptions. Peter Klemen states that, 'Applying a phenomenological landscape based approach, one that is concerned with archaeological and anthropological perceptions of Dartmoor's landscape, past and present, is to demonstrate that there are multiple ways to experience and embody those experiences' (Klemen 2015). The key elements here are *past and present*, which opens up the tantalising prospect of experiencing what our distant ancestors did, as an aid to finding out what was in their hearts and minds. We now have an extra tool by which to enquire as to how and why they walked the landscape, and why they erected monuments in particular places. Chris Tilley adds: 'Ancient stones in the landscape cannot be known or understood simply from publications, maps, diagrams, photographs and descriptions... there can be no substitute for the human experience of place – of being there...' (Tilley 2004). Without going out into the terrain, we will always lack the sensuous bodily experiences of place and space and, in particular, lack the implanted and constantly evolving individual memory. We should not regard a place as a fixed, definitive 'object', but rather something that is constantly evolving, like ourselves, fluid and non-permanent.

Cosmologies and creation myths explaining the identity of people are derived from their sensory explorations of the land. They are a product of their immersion in the land, as a fish is totally immersed in water. From the perspective of phenomenology, all our senses are engaged simultaneously, in a primal way, overlapping. We are invited to walk across a landscape by not focusing on a particular sense, but rather appreciate that it is a multi-sensory experience. I can simultaneously *taste* a rock's surface, *touch* its texture, *hear* the buzzard call overhead, *smell* nearby flowers, and *see* the colours of the minerals in the outcrop. To deprive myself of one of these senses, or to concentrate on less than the whole array, would be depriving myself of the full animalistic sensory experience of the place. Today's western cultures are dominant on visuals as the chief instrument of attaining knowledge, and as a consequence the other senses have been relegated to supporting roles. Not so with animals and birds, and the indigenous hunter–gatherer, whose worldview is a result of a total engagement in their environment using all their senses. Sound, for example, permeates all of the space immediately around you, whereas sight is very restricted to what is in front of you. Unfortunately we have become deaf to the archaic whispers of Nature. What was once common knowledge has been muted, now perceived and acknowledged only by poets, pilgrims and mystics, and thus dismissed by science as a whole.

Landscapes are constantly changing, always becoming something else, due to seasonal and weather variations. Every second we perceive a different landscape, depending on where we walk, or the direction we choose view from or to, or the variations in the light due to the weather, or the presence or lack of sunlight. A place can be a different experience every time depending from which direction it is approached, or exited. 'Temporality is thus at the heart of a phenomenological study' (Tilley 2010) and is the very basis of the way we experience and sense the environment around us. I walked to Roos Tor (543760) in December 2015. The day was rainy and a total whiteout as I literally walked in the clouds. Sometimes it was as if Dartmoor had woven a mist around itself. The tor outcrops were moody and only came into view just before I hesitantly reached them; it was as if I was being approached by a highwayman who had been waiting in the mist. On my second visit, just two weeks later, the day was clear and I could see for miles. The rocks were now clear-edged and sharp, as opposed to their somewhat menacing demeanour on my previous trip, when my trepidations had created different experiences. It was the same tor, the same rocks, the same simulacra – and yet it wasn't. Were my distant shamanic ancestors likewise coming up here under differing weather conditions to experience this multifaceted landscape? On a third visit to Roos Tor I was accompanied by Sue Wallace, and the interaction between us led to another set of experiences, which including a hailstorm! Same tor – or was it? Moreover, 20 different visitors to the tor would no doubt narrate 20 different experiences of their time there, of 'what the tor is' for each of them. Who is correct in their description of the tor? The answer, of course, is that they all are. This can easily be the outcome of 20 people seeing the same play or movie. How they perceived the performance was a unique experience to all of them; so too with landscape. There is never one landscape, but rather many. Even approaching the same tor for the 10th time, the experience will be different from all of the previous visits. The weather will be different; the angle of the sun and the bird song will have changed, as well as the seasonal plants. The tor will have even lost a few more grains of granite since previous visits; although imperceptible, the granite tors are never static, for geology is always on the move. Landscape can never have two days the same – ever! And landscapes are our mirrors.

I had a similar experience in two visits to Rippon Tor (747756) in the winter of 2015/6. My first ascent was during a total white out, with misty drizzle **(below left)**. This is an extract from my notes: *'Gloves on – I can feel temperature dropping. Haytor and Saddle Tor disappear from view halfway up the ascent, as I enter the Dragon's breath, weaving my way through the clitter. White out soon follows, visibility only 50yds on the summit. All is now calm and quiet. Hi Dragon – I walk amongst your teeth and scales'*. My second visit was on a crisp chilly morning under a blue sky **(below right)**, with wonderful uplifting vistas. I was led to my discovery of a rock basin and a simulacrum, which were completely hidden previously. Note how the images below show the tor differently, and this is because I ascended the hill from different directions. It really was as if I had visited two different tors, and, in a sense, I had. I believe that our distant ancestors likewise made a point of ascending the same tors under different conditions to obtain different experiences, and information.

During my studies of West Kennet Long Barrow I had visited the site during different seasons, varying times of the day and night, and in different weather conditions. The site underwent changes of 'mood' and atmosphere (Knight 2011). It was the same landscape to the lay person or academic – but not in terms of experience and memory. So it was thousands of years ago. As we walk across any landscape we undergo perpetually shifting experiences, and each one unique. Yet despite this distinction, we

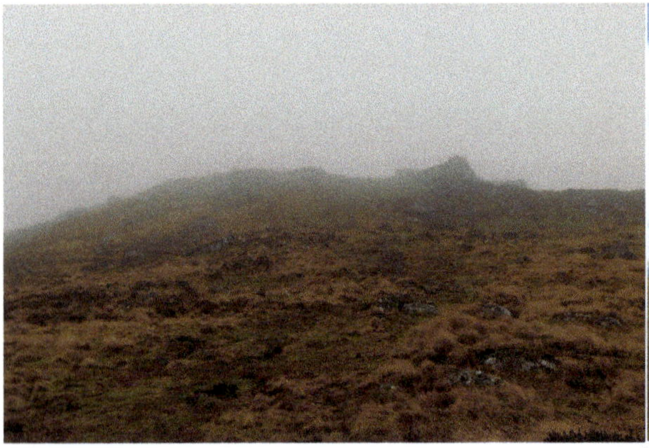

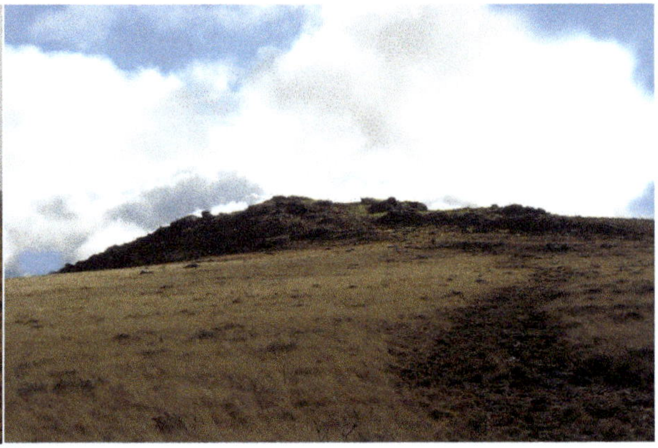

walk in the footsteps of our ancestors, whose own unique experiences added layer upon layer of meaning and memory on the landscape. Emma Kidd poetically sums up her view of experiencing Dartmoor:

'The moors have been weathered and beaten by the elements, shaken to their bare bones. This ferocity is worn by the haggered expressions of the twisted trees and bushes. Allowing my eyes to feel their way across this landscape I have a sense that depth perception is a capacity of the soul rather than of sight. My eyes provide the open doorway but it is my soul that stretches itself outward to meet this world, and revels in the opportunity to join with it in its wondrously creative expressions of earthly physical form." (http://sensinglife.net/)

Prof Chris Tilley gives an excellent list of eleven criteria (Tilley 2000), summarised below, which can be used as guidelines when working on any sacred site or monument encountered in the landscape. I myself regularly go down this checklist. Not all are applicable to every sacred site, but certainly many sites tick multiple boxes. We should take note of ...

1) The significance of the position of a site from a sensory point of view, such as whether it affords distant views, or that of a particular hill or outcrop, or is within earshot of the sounds of the sea, waterfall or river;

2) Whether or not a monument mimics local landscape features, such as the shape of megaliths mirroring the form of distant skyline or nearby outcrops, or long mounds or stone rows running parallel to ridges, reflecting landscape features;

3) Whether a monument references local landscape features, such as a door looking out to an outcrop or the long axis of a mound pointing to a landscape feature, or two megaliths aligning with an outcrop, or offering a restricted view of a simulacra. Tilley has noted how the long axis of Catshole Tor Long Cairn aligns with Catshole Tor, which sits on the skyline when viewed from the cairn (Tilley 2010);

4) Monuments that cluster around landscape features such as hill summits or rock outcrops, to *enculture* them, as has been identified with some of the cairns of Dartmoor and Bodmin. (I have found this to occur on Rippon Tor, Cox Tor, White Hill, Ugborough Beacon and elsewhere.);

5) The manner in which ones perspective of landscape changes as one walks around the site, including what comes into and out of view as one moves;

6) The sequencing as one walks from one site to another, in terms of the terrain crossed, such as hills, valleys, rivers and clitter, and whether one's experience alters markedly when one walks in the opposite direction;

7) The *directionality* between monuments and the different levels of sensory effects when one views hills and monuments from different places, e.g. where is the best place to experience maximum sensory effects?

8) Whether there is a temporality element to a site, as to whether any relationship to other sites and landscape features changes, such as limited or temporary access due to the seasons, river levels, boggy ground, etc;

9) The origins of the raw materials of the monument, and artefacts found within them, in terms of from where they were derived, whether from local sources or more distant locales;

10) Any *substitution* that may have taken place in the erection of a sacred site, such as a cairn built on a tor that otherwise has little or no natural rock outcrops. (I have found this phenomena on Cosdon Beacon, Eylesbarrow, Water Hill and elsewhere. Perhaps the abundance of round barrows on chalk hills and ridges, and on Exmoor, is to create more prominent features on landscapes where there are few. They were creating artificial 'tor outcrops' no less, 'false cresting' ridges and summits. Another good

Dartmoor example is King's Barrow, on King Tor (709814), which is a prominent feature on an otherwise featureless, rounded hill.);
11) Natural features which are incorporated into the monument itself, such as rocks that comprise cairns, or large round boulders inside cairns (such as at White Tor, and Easdon Tor), or fossils, rock basins, blocks of quartz etc.

I think that by applying these methods, we can glean even more from the landscape through which we walk. Peter Klemen concurs: 'By applying the concept of place and phenomenology, with an increased consideration of the senses and using the material remains of the past, a fuller 'holistic' understanding of how the landscape creates and conceptualises experience may be better understood' (Klemen 2015).

As I have worked more and more on this project, a realisation has welled up in me that I had become umbilically linked to the land, by a thread of energy pulling me ever to the moor. Often in my own home, lying in my bed, or doing day to day activities, it pulled at my being, at my heart, drawing me in as an angler reels in his catch. I soon reached a stage when it went to a whole new level. I realised that the connection I had previously had with the land was but a shadow of what I was now experiencing. I knew then that the landscape was replete with arcane knowledge, golden gems of wisdom woven into the geography, vestiges of times when people had a closer connection to the land. I have been gifted, and it is a hallowed gift, a connecting of my heart to the beating heart of the Earth. My eyes have been opened, and with it my heart. This epiphany, this awakening, changed my life path from straight, predictable and safe, to one of winding blind bends and rocky uneven tracks. Although I stumble, the rocks underfoot are now of the granite of the moor – and I know I walk the same hallowed ground as those who had gone before me thousands of years ago.

The impregnable granite, the road less travelled, the jagged tors, the harsh bliss of the moor – all these entwine to create that cord that links me to the ancestors. And I have come to realise that, after all, there never has been 'them and us' – there has only ever been the land. I feel I am coming home.

Space – the final frontier

'To enter sacred space is to enter sacred time' (Devereux 1989)

Dictionaries define 'space' as an area that is free, available and unoccupied, a boundless three-dimensional extent in which objects and events have relative position. However, disagreement continues between philosophers over what space is. Debates concerning the nature, essence and form of space date back to antiquity; Plato, Timaeus, Socrates and Aristotle all reflected on the nature of space. The Romans believed in a *genius loci, 'spirit of place',* which was a protective spirit of a locale. In Isaac Newton's view, space was absolute, in the sense that it existed permanently and independently of whether it contained matter or not. Other natural philosophers, notably Gottfried Leibniz, thought space to be a collection of relationships between objects. Later, the metaphysician Immanuel Kant said that neither space nor time can be empirically perceived, as they are elements of a systematic framework that humans use to structure all experiences. Kant referred to space as being a subjective 'pure form of intuition', hence it is an unavoidable element of our human faculties.

On planet Earth, space is never empty; around us we are surrounded by the invisible air we breathe; dowsers and psychics feel the vibrations of unseen auras and earth energies; gravity pervades everything on this planet (another unseen yet omnipresent force), and light fills the space in front of our eyes. So is space ever really 'unoccupied', as dictionaries would define it?

When archaeologist Prof Chris Tilley stated, *'What space is depends on who is experiencing it, and how'* (Tilley 1994), he opened up a can of worms. He suggested that space can now be viewed as a medium, rather than a container for action. Space only exists as a set of relationships between objects or places, and so is always the product of a relationship between these objects, or indeed places: as Tilley concludes: 'Without places there can be no spaces'. Space, in fact, only exists as a series of associations between objects, and has to be understood relative to those objects. As such, space cannot be divorced from events that take place within it – at places.

From a human perspective, space is really an individual experience, for it is egocentric. A person standing on a tor viewing a valley below (or rather the space we would call *a valley*) is seeing it differently from a person viewing the same valley (the same space) from an adjacent tor. And any point or object on the landscape can be viewed in terms of the space it occupies, rather than the place. If you pick up a small rock and move it to a few metres away, although the rock has gone the space it once occupied has remained. When I move from one piece of ground to another I am constantly occupying new space, which I may have looked at previously from somewhere else; over there is now here: 'Space is wrapped up in individual experience, and so is also relative, and far more abstract than place' (Tilley 1994). And as we move into a new space we are transporting the space we call 'ourselves' into it, our 'personal space' is now interacting with the new place, a new space. Our energies, psyche, physical presence and intent all interact and affect where we are. Quantum physics has confirmed that the beliefs of a scientist can affect the results of their experiments. We are entwined in any space in which we find ourselves. All is interconnected.

If I select a piece of ground in a field and put up a marquee on it, has the space changed because I have now enclosed it with canvas? Or is it merely my *perception* that has changed? What I previously viewed as outside is now inside, even though it is the same space. What makes a piece of music? Is it a construct of the notes on the page, or is it the spaces, the pauses and the silences between the notes? Does not the space within a circle exist before the circle is drawn? Karen French concludes that, 'The circle appears to be an empty void and is used as 'zero', to denote nothing, but actually it is a container of latent potential 'to be', making it both full and empty' (French 2012). So a circle is both a void and full at the same time.

I experienced a natural sacred space on a recent visit **(below)** to the collapsed 'Nutcracker' logan stone at Lustleigh Cleave (773815). The woods I walked through were like a throwback from a Mesolithic forest. Then I came to a huge collapsed rock, which was the fallen Nutcracker. It is over 3m thick, and now slants at about 45 degrees, creating a cavern beneath up to 3m high **(top image, next page)**. Inside there is a level 'altar stone' plus another ledge on which to lie. I paused inside this space and felt the presence of those who had been there before me. I sat alone and yet was not alone. I could sense the Mesolithic hunter-gatherers walking by me along the track nearby. Places such as this would have been highly valued back in those distant times, for shelter and ritual. I was also in a liminal space, where dark meets light, where without meets within. As I

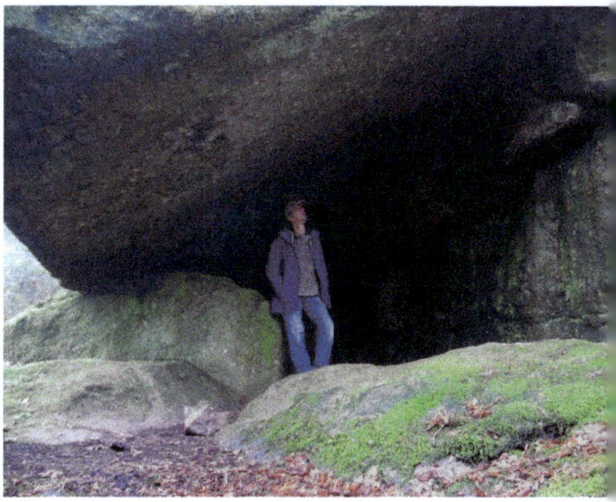

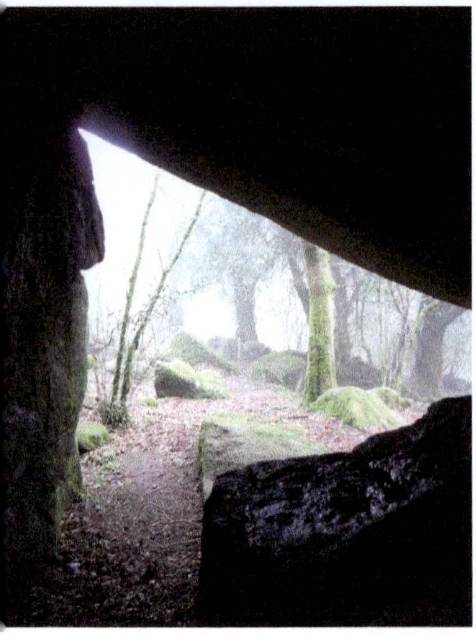

sat beneath this granite edifice, it was reflecting my own state of being.

Space can influence our experiences and perceptions. When I crawl beneath an overhanging granite slab into a space not much wider than my body, the feeling is somewhat claustrophobic. Yet a small terrier-like dog would think nothing of walking underneath it as it has more room to spare. As Gary Snyder observes, 'We learn a place and how to visualise spatial relationships, as children, on foot and with imagination. Place and scale must be measured against our bodies and their capacities' (Snyder 1990). When I sit inside the chambers of a Neolithic tomb at night, as the last nightlight goes out, that space suddenly 'closes in' on me. The concept of distance does not exist anymore, for an inky blackness is right in front of my eyes. My eyes are redundant, and yet my other senses are heightened. I am suddenly in a womb rather than a tomb. The space in which I am sitting is suddenly pregnant with imagination and potential, as the darkness consumes me. The pitch black tomb is the same 'space' I had occupied on other occasions to witness the sun stream down the passage to illuminate the ancient chambers. Just as Chris Trwogo experienced: '... the space beyond seemed to pour into me... that sense of that thin divide between the worlds of the living and the great well of ancestral souls...' (Trwoga 2006).

And so was the case on Dartmoor. Places and their space were deemed sacred because of what was experienced, which was always evolving: 'Like a mirror, a place can hold anything' (Snyder 1990). A place on any landscape can never be empty, like the circle. This is the world of quantum physics, and of the shaman. As we move in and out of places and their space, places that were 'out there' become 'in here'. Both time and space become fluid as we move across the land.

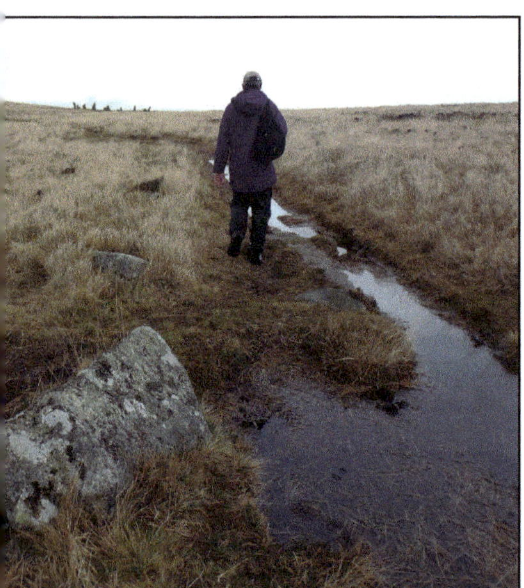

A walk on the wild side

'Moving was a process of revelation' (Tilley 2010).

The mere act of walking can induce a contemplative and meditative state of being which can be the soil for visionary experience. James Lovelock considered that, 'The simplest way to explore Gaia is on foot. How else can you reach out to her and be part of her ambience'. Chris Tilley concluded that, 'To walk is to fuse past, present with future... I am walking where others have walked, in the footsteps of previous generations and the ancestors' (Tilley 2008). I believe that we need to walk landscapes again in a mindful manner, to get to know them, to familiarise ourselves with landscape, in the same manner as those times when walking was the prime mode of getting about. When walking landscape we are in communion with it, we converse with it, but not with words. We sense the landscape through our bodies, through all of our senses, perceptions and experience, and through our inner sight, our intuition. The Australian Aborigines often pass on their stories whilst walking across the outback (Snyder 1990). 'Monuments express an attachment to the landscape and to specific locales within that landscape and one in which lifestyle was characterised by being mobile' (Klemen 2015). Walking can be, *'...an endless school of mysteries and magic'* (Endredy 2002).

The tempo of walking generates a rhythm of thought, and a passage through a landscape echoes the journey through a series of thoughts. This suggests that the mind is also a landscape and that walking is a means to traverse it. Today we must learn to walk once more, as infants learn to walk, barefoot wherever possible. We need to walk with all our senses, cognitively, in the here and now, perceiving ourselves as being an element of landscape. Peter Klemen: 'Walking is a central element in how both Bronze Age and present day individuals come to 'dwell' on and with Dartmoor. Through walking, the body becomes intertwined with the material properties of the Moor, the uneven terrain, steep slopes, areas of wet and boggy ground, the full sensual engagement experienced by all the senses' (Klemen 2015).

Many artists and poets already engage in such sensory attentiveness. I recently went to view an exhibition in Bristol by Turner Prize-winning land artist Richard Long. One of his works, 'Two Straight Twelve Mile Walks on Dartmoor, England 1980' struck a chord with me. He was clearly in the now, and with minimal text sums up his feelings and what he was sensing. His art expresses a fine-tuning of his sensory experiences of the landscape, as in this passage for example:

'Into a low sun. Glistening Frost.
Between the granite. Boggy and Slow.
Creaking Ice. Darkness.'

He cites his work as being a response to the environments through which he walks, and that the landscape is deliberately changed in some way by his interaction with it. In his video *'3 minute Wonder'*, Long speaks of being drawn to the, '... empty, stony deserts of the world', and that Dartmoor is his 'prototype landscape'. He adds that his art is best made in solitude, developing a 'one to one' with the place: 'My work is about the landscape... the walking is to make a piece of art... Dartmoor is my studio'. Long works directly on the earth, with the landscape as his canvas, his materials that of the land. He eliminates the need to represent the landscape through art. Like Long, contemporary land artist Andy Goldsworthy has cited his remit as being to work out in nature. Poet and bard Peter Owen-Jones said: 'When I walk the land, I walk into the sensuous' (pers. comm.). American poet Gary Snyder muses that, 'Wilderness is a place where the wild potential is fully expressed...to speak of wilderness is to speak of wholeness' (Snyder 1990).

As the 'bones' of the Dartmoor's 'wilderness/wildness' are essentially the same today as in the Bronze Age, we potentially have the same physical/sensory experiences as people in the past. And walking was once a vital element to connect with the landscape. Before footpaths and tracks had length and utilitarian purpose, they had worth unto themselves. People were 'Sauntering for the soul' no less, as the outer journey ignites an inner one (Knight 2000). It was all about movement: 'Through the act of landscape walking you are integrating both synaesthetic and kinaesthetic experiences, as you go along you give yourself to places and they give back (Klemen 2015). From a personal perspective, as I walk along I give of myself wholly to the landscape, which responds. Perhaps my intent is enough unto itself to trigger this reciprocity, to open the communication.

Movement is about constantly shifting perceptions. Take a skyline for instance. Unlike other geographical features, it is not a real thing. It is an eye-line, so as you move around the land the skyline moves up and down, or comes closer or goes further away. This is key to our understanding of the past, in that people did not just see things, they also experienced them mindfully and emotionally, from their own unique point of view as they walked around. When prehistoric people walked the moor, they became entwined with the landscape and its accumulated myths and memories, like pilgrims do today. To them landscape was a liminal interface. Travelling was not just an activity of moving from one place to another, but was also a way of being. As these prehistoric wayfarers walked, there was a constant active engagement with the world around them (Klemen 2015), just as Aborigines walk their *songlines* today.

When we walk a landscape mindfully, '... sensing, perceiving and understanding are conjoined in a fundamental way' (Tilley 2004). Our sensing and perceptions of landscape, and our subsequent understanding/knowledge (through writing, reflections, examining photos, map work etc) are all part of the whole – the process is incomplete and thus ineffectual if one of these elements is absent. In the past I have written books purely based on understanding/knowledge, through researching the work of others and adding my own. I have gradually come to realise that I have had to walk landscapes to really appreciate the intricate placement of sites, to experience those places from where they were meant to be viewed, or indeed what could be viewed from them. In my studies of West Kennet Long Barrow and the Cerne Giant, I walked these landscapes many times, to see where they were visible from and where they were not. In the process I developed a state of sharpened perception: I now walk cat-like across the landscape, using all my senses, from touch to smell, from hearing to taste, sometimes leaving maps in my pocket, leaving mental human constraints in the car. One becomes almost feral, becoming one with the terrain. In walking a landscape consciously, we are also walking inner journeys: 'These are journeys to an archaic region of our collective subconscious' (Krőnig 2001).

I have been amazed how quickly and radically a landscape can change over short distances, how perspectives change as one moves, sometimes in a matter of just a few metres. Even from different sides of a monument different landscape features present themselves, whilst others disappear. In areas such as Dartmoor, prominent landscape features are 'frozen in time' in terms of their imperceptibly small changes in appearance since prehistory, so we are able to see through prehistoric eyes, to see what people once saw. This is true 'experiential archaeology', and we can so easily put ourselves in the footprints of our ancestors, seeing as they did, smelling what they smelt, touching what they touched. Few other spheres of prehistoric research offer such 'action replays', for we share similar experiences to our distant forebears. Just like our ancestors, we smell the air, we walk on two legs, we touch with our fingers, we see with two eyes that are positioned well off the ground (unlike a rodent or a bird which will have different perspectives), all of which are the common elements of our humanity. To that I would add that we have a mind that is embedded in our body. The body and mind cannot be separated, including what they both encounter – the parts contribute to the whole sensory experience, and knowing. And there is such human delight in comprehension and revelation.

Satish Kumar once said, 'Walking in itself was an end, a form of meditation, a way of being… a trigger for an inner journey' (Kumar 1992). Personally, I found that to walk Dartmoor I had to release my busy mind from its chattering, from rambler mode, from map-reading mode, and let the land lead me. Whilst I am walking I am more than a participant, for I am an element of that landscape. The attributes of places initiate sensory overloads – the squelch underfoot in winter, the resonance of running water, moistness on the granite, the wind in my ears, my cold nose, the touch of naked rock - be it sharp, mossy or wet. This sensory bombardment became welcomed, even addictive, especially on my raw winter walks. Sometimes I have felt that it was enough for me simply to walk on the moor with an acknowledgement that the landscape has a spiritual dimension, to embrace this sanctity. The land knew of my recognition. Sometimes that was enough. No cathartic bolts of lightning, just a mutually reciprocated acknowledgement. This was probably the case long ago with the moor clans: '...primitive people construct a mental picture of the world from the sum total of their own direct experience' (Graham 2004).

I will give you an example of mindful walking, of 'cognitive archaeology'. In February 2016 I walked from Peter Tavy to White Tor (543786), and on to Langstone Moor to see the longstone (551787) and nearby stone circle (557782). The day was showery and windy and the moorland was saturated after heavy rain (both images below were taken whilst it was raining). It would have been very easy for me to keep my head down and just concentrate on getting from A to B. But I kept looking outward as I went, defying the horizontal rain that spat in my eyes. I noticed how tors to the south

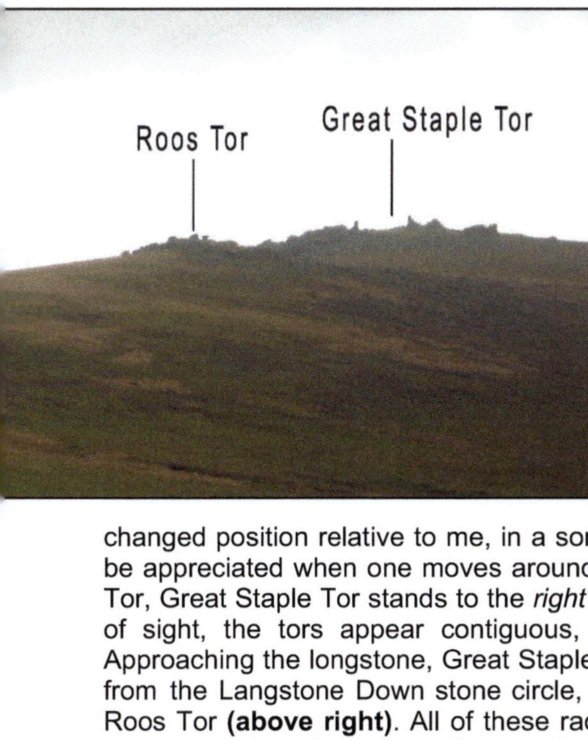

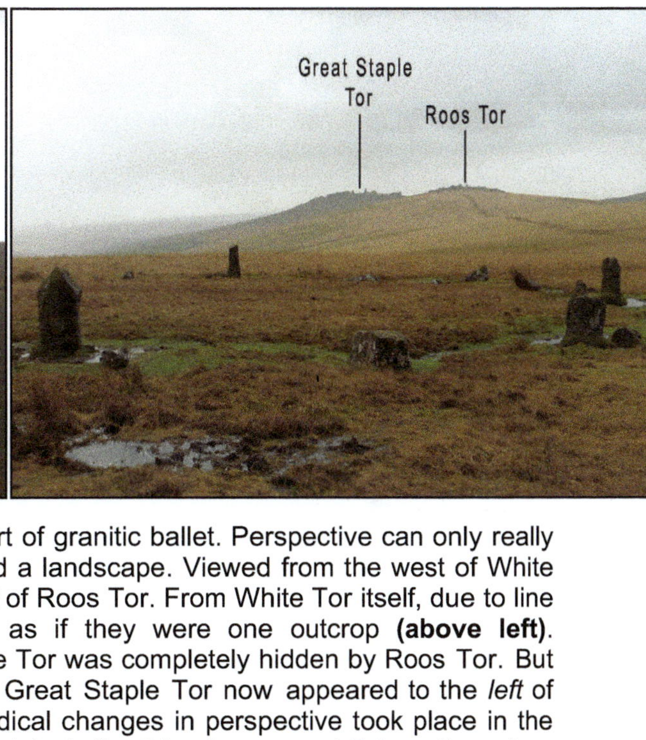

changed position relative to me, in a sort of granitic ballet. Perspective can only really be appreciated when one moves around a landscape. Viewed from the west of White Tor, Great Staple Tor stands to the *right* of Roos Tor. From White Tor itself, due to line of sight, the tors appear contiguous, as if they were one outcrop **(above left)**. Approaching the longstone, Great Staple Tor was completely hidden by Roos Tor. But from the Langstone Down stone circle, Great Staple Tor now appeared to the *left* of Roos Tor **(above right)**. All of these radical changes in perspective took place in the space of just a mile and a half of walking! A similar thing happens at Brisworthy; when at the stone circle, Legis Tor is to the *left* of Hen Tor **(image p. 187)**, and yet just a ¼ mile to the north is a stone row, from which Legis Tor appears to the *right* of Hen Tor **(image p. 188)**.

Life in general is all about how we perceive the world around us. It's the glass half full or half empty analogy. Here are three ways of looking at same walk:

1) I went out for a walk today, and it rained for two of the four hours. Shame.

2) I went out for a walk today and the sun shone for two of the four hours. Great!

3) I went out for a walk today and the weather contrasted greatly, enabling me to fully absorb a great variety of sensory experiences, to see the landscape in all its mood swings, which was inspirational. The British weather is what it is, and has of course moulded the beautiful landscape on which I walked today.

This is akin to how artists and poets of different genre will perceive the same landscape completely differently, projecting their own interpretations onto it, where each may even argue that their interpretation best captures the landscape. More than this, everything is relative – do I touch a stone or does the stone touch me? It is a mutual and reciprocal experience. Speaking of touch, the tactile nature of landscape is an important element of connecting with it. The surface of a granite rock is an interface, where radiant light is reflected, heat absorbed, where vibrations occur and, importantly, where the body meets it by touching and feeling. Rock surfaces all have distinctive shapes and texture, and are essential places of interaction, experience and perception through kinaesthesia.

I know that some of my biggest spiritual connections to landscape came when I have simply walked for walking sake; I was, quite literally, taking steps in the right direction. At other times I would sit in stillness, immersed in the 'sound of silence'. One can slip into an altered state of consciousness just looking out across the landscape, just as one can be hypnotised by a camp fire. In this state of near-bliss I have simply sent out my love across the landscape. I have so often felt that it was being reciprocated. I felt part of everything, a sense of oneness as my heart opened. Was this just a mental construct, 'wishful thinking' on my part? Love is energy, a vibration. So when we send it out it has to go somewhere. And who or what is returning my love? Is it an illusion? Is my own energy coming back to me, or is it coming from 'somewhere out there' on the landscape? Ultimately, if I am an element of the landscape, I am simultaneously both sending and receiving. Shamans and tribal cultures tell us there is no separation between themselves and the land. I am beginning to get fleeting glimpses of that which they speak.

As we walk and re-walk a landscape we are adding new experiences and new memories to it. We enrich not only ourselves but the landscape: 'The way to walk Dartmoor is to walk nowhere, without a watch or any regard for time, standing and staring and listening to the larks' (Smith 1966). Perhaps when we approach a landscape, we do it in a view to learn, be receptive. I think we should be obliged to pay attention and listen, rather than bombard the land with a long list of questions. Nature is giving us constant messages, and we can learn to be receptive. Pausing to feel is in itself an act of honouring. We may receive communication through osmosis, subtly, without the recipient even being aware. Mindscapes and landscapes become one: '... each state of mind provides us with a view of nature... changing how we see the world actually changes the world for us'. (Devereux 1996).

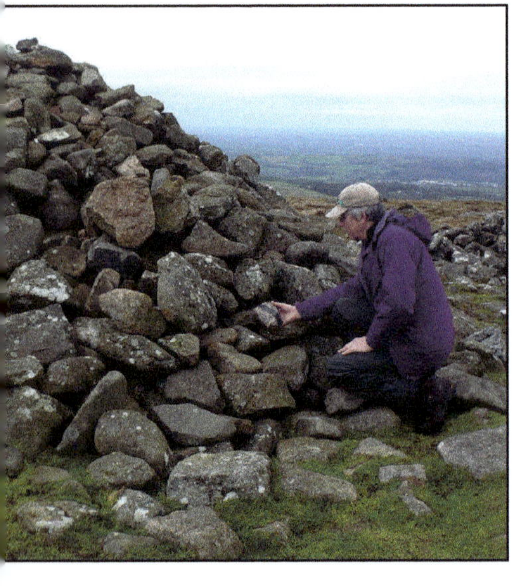

And it is also about giving something back, leaving part of ourselves behind. They say we should leave behind only footprints, but I think we leave behind more than that. Part of us stays out there too. I often replace a stone that has fallen from a cairn, placing it back on the pile, as here at Cosdon Beacon (636915) on a windswept and overcast day **(left)**. This feels an honouring act, and it seemed

reciprocated, as if a 'thank you' was returned to me, as if my efforts in walking through inclement weather to get there had been acknowledged. Perhaps our intent is enough, and the only thing we need to leave behind is our love.
I have captured hundreds of images over the years, many of which I have included in this book. Photographs, however, cannot capture the vastness of the Dartmoor landscape, that sensation of elevation, that sense of freedom. One has to be out on the landscape to get that - to really get it! And that, for me, is the bottom line.

'Walking is the great adventure, the first meditation, a practice of heartiness and soul primary to humankind. Walking is the exact balance between spirit and humility'
(Gary Snyder, 1990.)

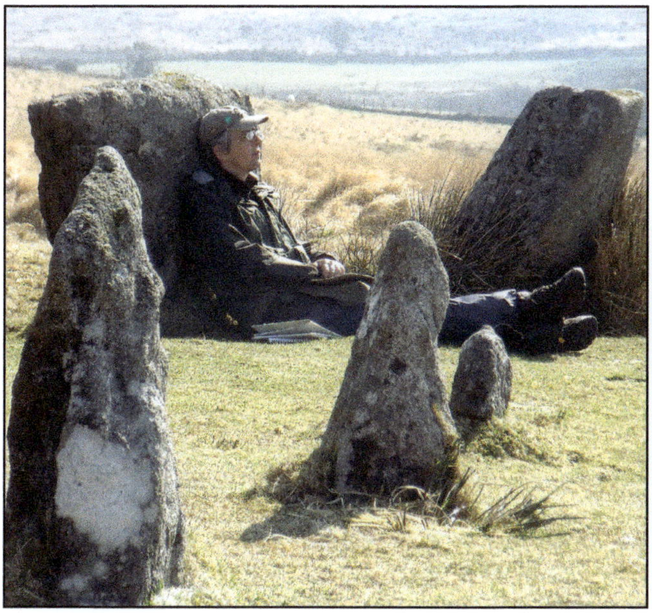

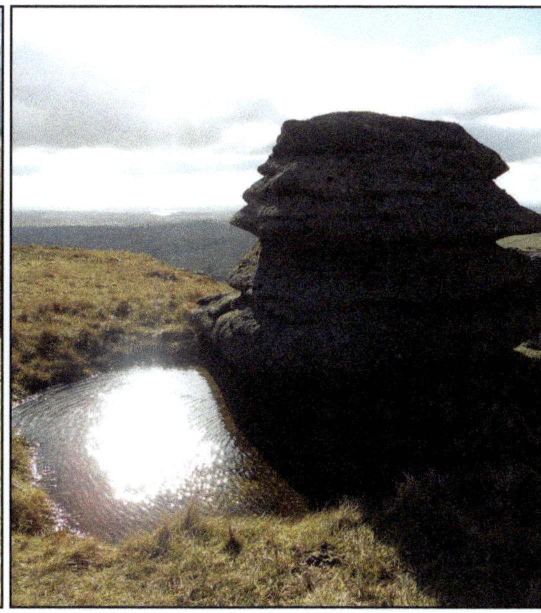

Above left: The author tuning in to the space and energies at Yellowmead stone settings. Experiencing *all* aspects of sacred sites is key to understanding them.
Above right: High on Great Mis Tor the sun is dazzlingly reflected in a rippling rock pool, as a granite zoomorphic stack gazes across the landscape to the sea. This mesmerising scene is imbued with mystique, and just as it captivates today, it would likewise have been appreciated in prehistory - the past and present fused by landscape.

'To walk is to fuse past, present with future...
I am walking where others have walked, in their footsteps'
(Chris Tilley 2008).

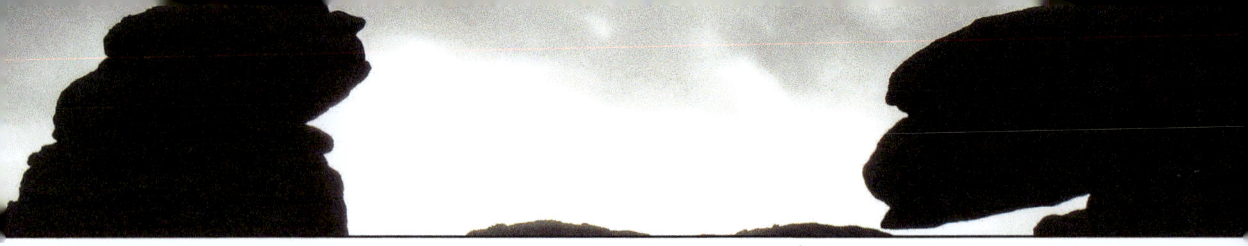

6. Stone Faced – The Case For Simulacra

'Our perception being a part of things, things participate in the nature of our perception.'
(French philosopher Henri Bergson)

The story of symbolism takes us on a journey way back to Man's early beliefs that natural objects possessed spiritual attributes, to the extent that they were endowed with supernatural qualities. These were things such as rocks that resembled animals, stalagmites that mimicked the human phallus, or faces that peered out of the bark of trees. Today, science interprets these as mere co-incidences, inevitable instances of pure chance. A non-scientific, more shamanic, mindset suggests that *everything that exists or is observed may hold a message.* Many see simulacra as products of blind chance. The mystics and shamans of old would not have regarded faces in rocks as coincidences, for the concept of '*chance*' cannot exist in a world that is the consequence of *divine* cause and effect. The pattern of bird flight, a flash of lightning, and all manner of other natural phenomena, become conduits for knowledge, often operating on many different levels (Knight 2015). From across the eons of time, folklore across the world speaks to us of the collective mythology of our ancestors and their creative involvement of the Earth.

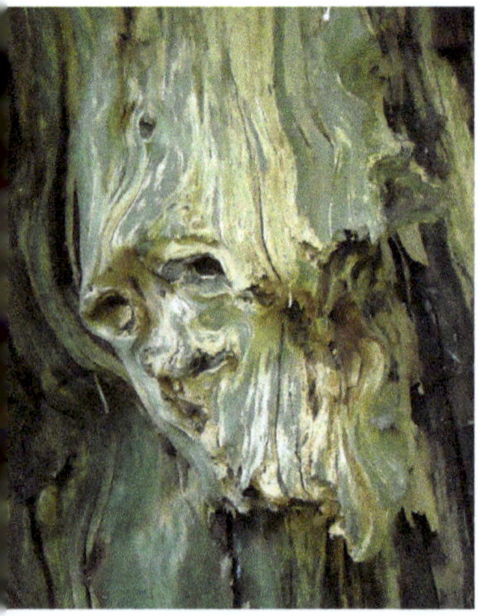

Human beings have a deeply intuitive tendency to project human features, to anthropomorphise, onto non-human features in our environment. I perceived this 'tree spirit' in an ancient Yew at Alton Priors, Wiltshire **(left)**. The suggestive forms of simulacra and other topographical features in the landscape were undoubtedly acknowledged by ancient cultures and incorporated into their Dreamtime scenarios, into their *mindscapes*. As early as 1928, Paul Wirz wrote: 'The outward shape and form of certain stones awakes in the native intelligence the reflection that it cannot be merely a stone that confronts him, but that he has now to deal with a superior being endowed with magical powers... Many of these stones have a markedly unusual look about them'. In 1965, Antonin Artaud (in *Concerning a Journey to the Land of the Tarahumaras*), considered, '... there is no lack of places on earth where Nature, impelled by a kind of intelligent caprice, has carved human shapes'. In 1836, Ralph W Emerson concurred when he said, 'Behind Nature, throughout Nature, Spirit is present'. In indigenous cultures today, simulacra are seen as the result of an influence

of the spirit of locality, the *genius loci,* which permeates everything, and influences folklore and even the spirituality of those who dwell in or visit its domain.
Prof Chris Tilley considered that, 'The relationship between peoples and their landscapes throughout prehistory was deeply anthropomorphic and animistic... the landscape was a kind of body, and this body was imbued with spiritual powers' (Tilley 2010). In other words, the land was animated and simulacra were an important element of this mythologised paradigm, objectified and tactile evidence that something unseen was manifesting. Creation and ancestral myths connected people to these forces, and these myths were not just perpetuated through word of mouth, but by natural forms, which 'held them' on the landscape. Mythic beings were transformed into landscape location, enabling people to access myths and the characters thereof, which were now visible before their eyes. How else could they explain the creation of these remarkable rock outcrops? The land then has the power to communicate information from deities or mythic characters through landscape features: 'A major topographical element that particularly attracted dreamtime attention was the presence of landscape *simulacra'* (Devereux 2013). Manmade sacred sites were an extension, a profound involvement, between *local* people and the creative forces of the landscape, a symbiotic relationship that was personal and enduring.
And how and why do simulacra even exist? Quantum physics suggests there is an inextricable connection between the observer and the observed. The landscape cannot be separated from the way we view it, we can't have one without the other, and this 'eye of the beholder' premise is very ancient. Prehistoric people were appreciating simulacra and locating sacred sites in relation to them. Once rocks are regarded as sentient beings, they are no longer mere objects, but rather subjects, possessing personality and spiritual essence, requiring respect and even reverence. They also represented permanence. To be associated with such rocks was to anchor a culture to that land, in the hope that they themselves would be permanent fixtures.
Boulders are sometimes, seen as ancestors or creatures turned to stone, such as in both Aborigine and Native American mythology. In 1992, British explorer Richard Schomburgk wrote how the Native Americans had a name, title or legend for remarkable shaped outcrops of rock. In Agua Canyon, in Utah, USA, is a large and well-known rock formation called 'hoodoo', 'the Hunter'. The Ashinanabe Indians of Manitoba, Canada, maintain the long tradition of making offerings at Buffalo Rock, at Tie Creek, a boulder presenting the likeness of a resting buffalo; although located in an isolated area, there is evidence of human occupation going back 10,000 years. The 'Garden of the Gods', Colorado Springs, are incredible red sandstone formations created during a geological upheaval along a natural fault line millions of years ago. Simulacra, stacks, balanced rocks/logan stones abound. One formation is known as the *White Buffalo* **(right)**. Archaeological evidence shows that prehistoric people visited Garden of the Gods about 1330 BC. At about 250 BC, Native Americans camped in the park, and used the natural overhangs in the rocks as shelters. The Apache, Cheyenne, Comanche, Kiowa, Lakota, Pawnee, Shoshone, and Ute people all have a spiritual connection to the area. In Nevada, USA, a huge natural and isolated outcrop of rock is known as Child Nest Rock, and is a simulacrum that displays mouth and eyes;

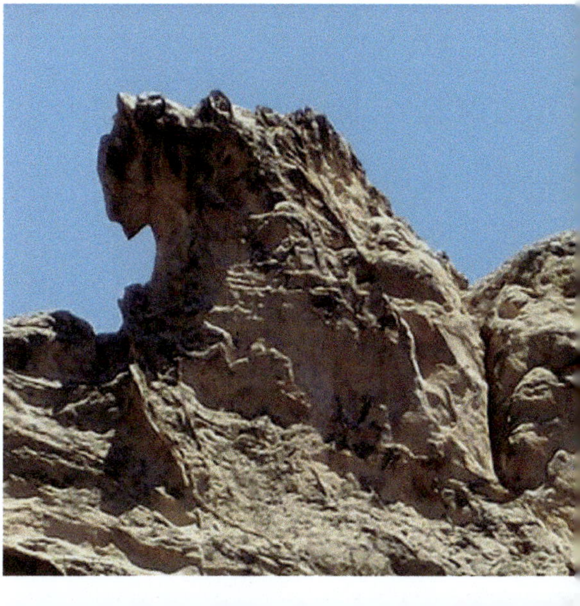

fifteen small graves are clustered around this rock, where ancient hunter-gathers left their kin. It is also the birth place of the 'Desert Culture Children' (Barlow 1996).

In the 17th century, Spanish Jesuit Bernabé Cobo found that the Inca, '... worshipped the works of nature that were unaltered by human contrivance', including features which possessed an, '... arresting visual characteristic or peculiar features'. The French postmodernist social theorist Jean Baudrillard argues that such simulacra are not copies of the real, but are a truth in their own right – they are the 'hyperreal'.

Anthony Donohue discovered an amazing anthropomorphic profile in a rock face behind the pre-dynastic Temple of Min, in Egypt (Devereux 2002), and eroded natural 'statues' can be perceived in the rocky outcrops behind the temple of Hatshepsut, also in Egypt; these include a pharaoh's head, complete with headdress and beard, with a cobra behind (Devereux 1996).

In NE China, a cave on Mount Haitang is sacred as it was used by a Tantric Buddhist monk, and this cave influenced the siting of the Temple of Pu'an. In the vicinity of this temple are boulders with carved and painted images of Buddhas, bodhisattvas, and other deities and holy warriors. They are interspersed with other boulders and outcrops displaying simulacra, which are unadorned, but which have names such as Mountain Eagle Rock, Toad Rock, Coiled Dragon Rock, Hat Rock, among others (Devereux 2013). Namsan (Southern Mountain), in the Gyeongju Province of South Korea, is sacred to Buddhists. The reason the mountain is such a spiritual focus is the many granite rocks which resemble animals and other objects, bearing such names as Old Man, Python, Fierce Tiger, Lion, Big Bear, Boar, Cat, and Dung Rock.

The Maori of New Zealand regard many remarkable rock outcrops as sacred places. These include the curious rock formations at Castle Hill Rocks, which are regarded as 'the highest ridge of learning'. This includes 'marotini', a rock stack said to represent an ancestral woman. Another huge simulacrum is named after Ra Kai Hau Tue, the 'great trail maker'. This hill is festooned with simulacra, many of which have significance to the Maori, and have been dowsed to be powerful energy nodes (Miller and Brailsford 2006). Many of them remind me of the Dartmoor tor simulacra we shall soon see.

Back in Europe, Sir Arthur Evans recorded that Mount Juktas, on Crete, resembled a man's head gazing skywards when viewed from certain directions, and he learned from locals that it was known as the *Head of Zeus*. The indigenous Saami/Lapp reindeer-herding culture of Finland has sacrificial sites known as *siejddes*, which are rock formations that usually resemble human heads, or else animals and birds. They may sometimes be encircled by low walls or circles of antlers. Some of the most distinctive are those rocks split open by weathering, forming natural caverns and fissures (Bradley 2000). Some of these features serve permanent communities, whilst others are on routes travelled at different times of the year, such as during reindeer herding. Wooden idols are left at these rocks, which are concerned with the fecundity of the local landscape. Decisions are reached using a shaman's drum, which acts as a compass to direct people to where game is.

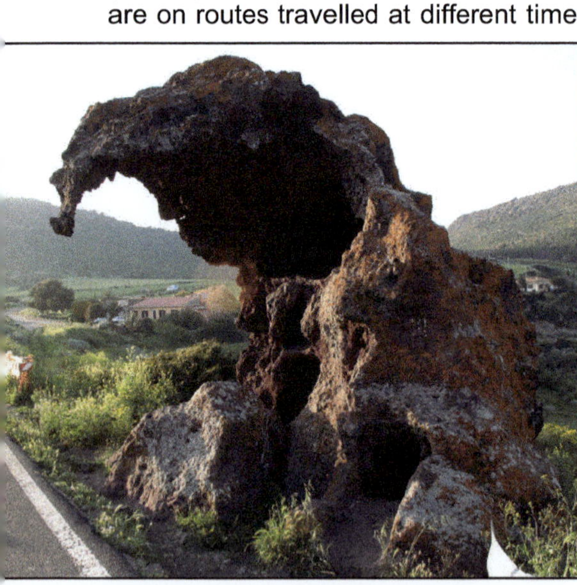

On Sardinia, I visited *'Elephant Dolmen'*, a remarkable natural outcrop **(left)** that had been modified to serve as a prehistoric rock-cut tomb, complete with carvings of horns. Also on Sardinia, I have already shown a huge rock shaped like a mushroom **(image p. 25)**. In Spain, the ancient city of Antequera, which includes a Neolithic mound, is overlooked by Enamorados, a hill that resembles a huge reclining head (Cope 2004). In Ireland, the Cat Stone is a skull-like rock at the sacred centre of the country (Biltcliffe and Hoare 2017).

In Britain, there are seemingly endless examples how natural simulacra have been named and embellished with myth and folklore. On the island of Islay, a former Neolithic stone row once aligned with the *Paps of Jura*, the breasts of Earth Mother. We have already seen two similar rounded peaks near Killarney on the west coast of Ireland **(top image p. 25)**, and many more are known. Another simulacrum of a reclined female figure in the landscape exists in the Preseli Hills of SW Wales, the source area of the Stonehenge bluestones. Here, a natural rock outcrop known as Carn Ingli (*Hill of Angels*) is said to be the body of a woman lying supine, her face turned skywards. She is either pregnant or has her arms folded across her stomach and her hair flows out behind her. How long this simulacrum has been noted cannot be determined, but if our eyes can see it now, one assumes it was perceived in ages past. Carn Ingli acquired its name because of the practice of a 6th-century anchorite, St. Brynach, who had his cell nearby. He climbed the hill to meditate and converse with angels (Devereux 2013).

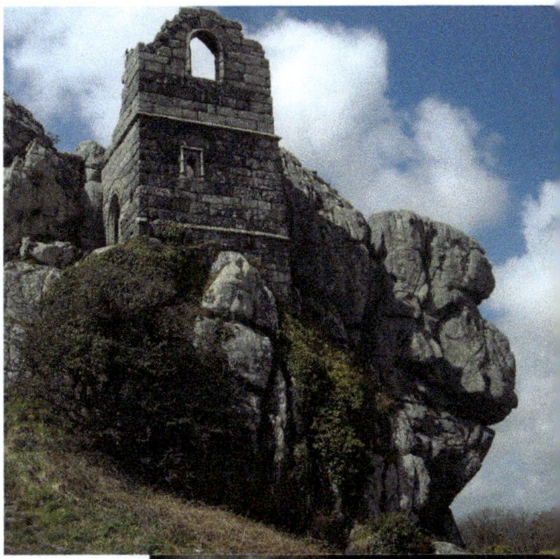

The Agglestone, at Studland in Dorset, is a former logan stone of gigantic proportions that also has Druidic folklore. On one rock face is etched anthropomorphic features (Knight 1998). According to dowsers, a remarkable simulacra, shaped like a dragon's head, at Trewavas Head on the Lizard peninsula, Cornwall, marks the flow of the Apollo current of the Apollo/St Michael axis (Broadhurst and Miller 2000). The chapel of St Roche, Cornwall **(right)**, sits atop a natural granite rock outcrop that displays a huge simulacrum; this rock giant looks east (right in this image) up the St Michael Line. In addition to this, a head, with check bones and lips, can be perceived in a granite outcrop in Carn Brae, Cornwall, next to a Neolithic camp. And from the Neolithic site of Callanish, the hills nearby have the semblance of a reclining woman, known as the 'Sleeping Beauty'.

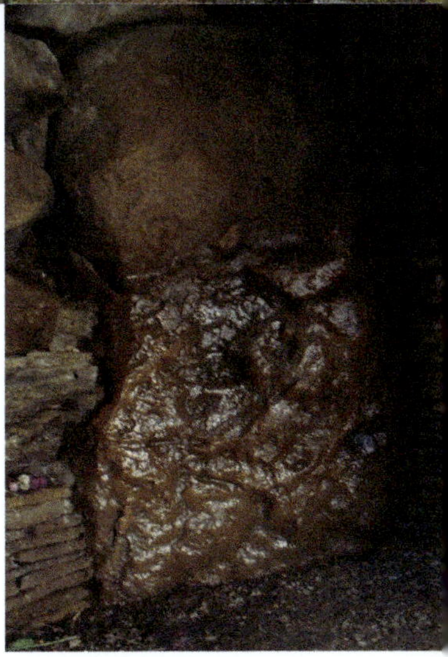

These are but a small sample of examples of the *enculturing* of natural places through features that sparked people's imagination, a theme I shall return to later. In terms of natural objects, John Michell concludes, 'Wherever it looks throughout the world, the innocent human eye sees anthropomorphic forms and a multitude of sightless faces. Human features are everywhere... anthropomorphism is built into us and inevitably conditions our view of nature' (Michell 1979).

In terms of *proving* a direct relationship between prehistoric Man and simulacra, the phallic-shaped nature of the huge megaliths of Brittany have long been noted, as well as others that were used in the Neolithic Breton chambered tombs. It has also been shown how many megaliths incorporated into the Neolithic monuments of Avebury (Meaden 1999) and West Kennet Long Barrow (Knight 2011) were *purposefully selected* because of the simulacra displayed on them. The example shown here **(lower image, previous page)** is the glistening '*Skull Stone*' from inside the long barrow. These examples are complemented by simulacra incorporated within the Neolithic temples at Malta, where no attempt was made to modify them; they were selected because of their suggestive and imaginative appearance.

Chris Tilley has suggested a methodology in which we can approach rock art by means of a more kinaesthetic approach, suggesting that how the observer is forced to approach and perceive rock art is vitally important (Tilley 2008). Likewise, simulacra can often only be perceived from a particular direction. Tilley tells of how Rough Tor, on Bodmin Moor, takes on different characteristics depending on from which direction one approaches (Tilley 2010). One is invited into the outcropping tor, to walk around, to view the same rock outcrop from a multitude of perspectives. Can one simulacrum be seen from another? Does a simulacrum change in appearance, or does its 'expression' change (such as smiling, grumpy or aggressive) when viewed from different places? Do the tor outcrops tell a different narrative depending on which direction I walk around it? What is the simulacrum communicating to me, if anything, and what mindset might I have to adopt to receive such communication? What does it feel like when one squeezes into a restricted space to view a simulacrum? **(top right image, p. 175)**. Is an anthropomorphic form being viewed as a silhouette in full sun, or under the full moon, both of which are generative of different experiences of the same object?

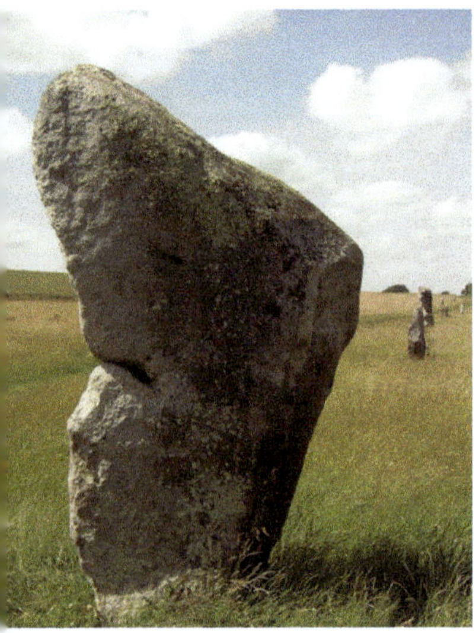

And what anyone perceives a simulacrum to mean is correct, even if others see the same outcrop entirely differently. I have suggested this is the case with the multi-interpretative nature of the megaliths at Avebury; this example is the *Shark Stone* **(left)**, but on my tours people invariably see it as different creatures. There is no right or wrong regarding interpretation. And this may have been the case thousands of years ago. Like any work of art, simulacra really are in the eye of the beholder.

'The eye is naturally inclined to anthropomorphize, and so too is nature'. (John Michell 1979)

Dartmoor *Dreamstones*

Many tribal cultures today embrace Dreamtime mindsets: *'The land is regarded as an ancestral creation and striking natural features are sacred places'* (Bender et al 2007). Perhaps when we see simulacra on Dartmoor (regardless of whether they have or have not been previously perceived or venerated) we momentarily dwell in the Dreamtime. By removing our psychological filters we may dip into that prehistoric mindset that there *actually are* spirits in the rocks. Across the world, natural features evidence the Dreamtime to indigenous cultures, and here too the ancient, seemingly dormant mindscapes of Dartmoor may be revealed. Perhaps in this shamanic context, we could see simulacra as *dreamstones.*

Some archaeologists are now seeing the cultural importance of the granite tors and boulders: 'We regard it as plausible to suggest that large impressive stones possessed individual names and had a specific significance. By contrast, the stones within the clitter masses had a more generalised cultural importance. Large stones might be embodiments of particular ancestors or spirits' (Bender et al 1999). After studying simulacra in relation to sacred sites around the world, Paul Devereux concluded that,

‘There is evidence that topographical simulacra represented not only a Dreamtime way of seeing, but that such features also directly influenced the religious lives and sensibilities of societies in terms of temple locations...’ (Devereux 2013). So is it unreasonable to suggest that such practices went on in Dartmoor during the Neolithic and Bronze Age? By mythologising simulacra and the tors, people were provided with continuity in an otherwise transient world; the tors had the quality of ‘over-sight’, over-seeing everything and everyone.

Simulacra were seen as evidence that these places held the omnipresent wisdom of the ancestors, of the land. The shamans were going directly to source – no middle man! When we look at a simulacrum on a Dartmoor outcrop, we not only look through a window into a bygone age of shamanism, but we may also be privy to a portal, through which spiritual forces and energy can flow through to this world, at this time. We may open up a conduit, a deeply rooted aspect of our psychology: ‘It might very well be that some of the rocks which look like gods, giants, dragons and demons, might in fact be the source of our mythologies... simulacra represent a link between human consciousness and the surrounding world’ (Krőnig 2001).

The image of the human face, and of the eye in particular, is a Jungian archetype. And, according to Carl Jung, this was the case throughout prehistory, ‘... conditioning our perceptions of the world around us’ (Jung1964). I have no doubt that thousands of years ago, people looked with awe into the wizened eyes that returned their gaze from a granite outcrop. With wonderment and knowing they knew that the spirits of place were always watching them (a precursor to Big Brother indeed), quite literally in their face! Remember, to the prehistoric shaman there were no coincidences, therefore these non-blinking eyes staring out of apparently ‘solid rock’ held deep meaning for them; remember that the amazing tor outcrops, with their incredibly balanced rocks and simulacra, were believed to have been created by the ancestors or the Gods. These granitic eyes looked through the doorways of time, which were always ajar. The following has been voiced about the simulacra seen at West Kennet Long Barrow, but equally applies to Dartmoor: ‘Did the shamans see these ethereal images as intermediaries between this world and the next? People considered the rock surfaces as permeable membranes through which spirits could pass’ (Williams 2010). In some ancient rock art, animals and people are depicted entering or exiting cracks in rock surfaces – these were liminal portals. This implies that the prehistoric shaman *interacted* with rock and stone, which may have ‘come to life’ when invoked to do so (Knight 2011). Perhaps the Dartmoor simulacra, when viewed at night under influence of hallucinogens and flickering torches, were coaxed into life; the gods or the spirits of the ancestors were manifest before their very eyes. I have ‘animated’ the shadow of a simulacrum at Over Tor (see p. 176).

It must be stated that the anthropomorphic megaliths used in chambered tombs across the world were once *natural*, in other words they had lain on the ground, embedded in the landscape. The act of setting them into a monument implies that they may have already been revered - relocated *‘pieces of place’*. I shall return to this concept later when I look at stone rows and circles.

Some Dartmoor simulacra

‘There were giants in the earth in those days’. (Genesis 6:4)

I shall now illustrate a small selection of Dartmoor’s countless simulacra, ones I have encountered on my journeying across the moor. As well as faces and heads, I will also look at phallic and triangular stones, which some archaeologists now see as having spiritual and cultural relevance. And I shall deal with the relationship between simulacra and the amazing balanced rocks, or logan stones, when I look at Dartmoor's tors in some detail in Chapter 7, and will show more wondrous simulacra in Chapter 13, when I look at the Merrivale Shamanic Landscape.

It seems fitting to *begin* with arguably Dartmoor's best known simulacra, the very anthropomorphic Bowerman's Nose **(below left)**. This 6m high granite stack stands on the north side of a small outcrop on Hayne Down (742804), north of Hound Tor. Legend says it was carved by the Druids, and early antiquarians described it as a 'granite god' and 'rock idol'. It is a small stack surrounded by clitter, and the Bowerman looks westward, with a projecting chin; is he sporting a cap? The name derives from the Celtic *'vawr maen',* (meaning *'great stone',),* which may have mutated into Bowerman. One legend says that the name came from a hunter called Bowerman whose dogs inadvertently ran into a coven of witches, upsetting their cauldron. As punishment he was turned to stone, and his pack into the simulacra seen on Hound Tor – hence the name. This is one of hundreds of examples of negative 'witchy' folklore assigned to places that had formerly been revered.

Just over a mile north of Bowerman's Nose, and *intervisible* from it, is Figgie Daniel **(below centre, and image p. 211)**. This fine simulacrum is visited by considerably less people than its better known cousin, but I think this feature is well worth the 30 minute walk. It rises above the eastern end of Easdon Tor, near North Bovey. It is a prominent granite stack (unnamed on OS maps, at 735823) as one ascends the hill and is visible from a mile or more away. A huge east-facing bird-like head with open beak sits at the top of the 6m high stack, which shows up as a feature on Google Earth. I climbed the stack with ease, and found two small rock basins on the top of its head! The simulacrum reminded me of an eagle, and only afterwards did I find out that Easdon means *'Hill of the Eagle';* references to this name go back to Anglo-Saxon times. Did the ancient tribe have the eagle as its totem; was it a bird clan? Some Bronze Age reaves converge on the hill and cairns adorn the summit, testament to its former importance. From this simulacrum one can see prominent outcrops to the south, such as Haytor, Hound Tor and Rippon Tor. He faces towards a thin sliver of sea to the east. It is almost as if Bowerman's Nose and Figgie are in a face off, and that Figgie is turning his face away. I came across another huge simulacrum **(below right),** on the

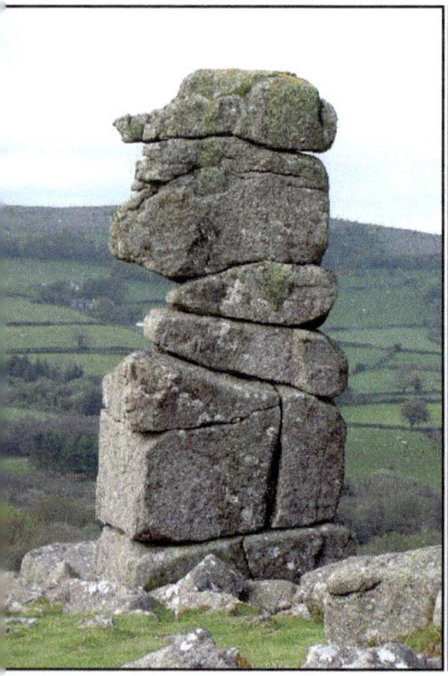
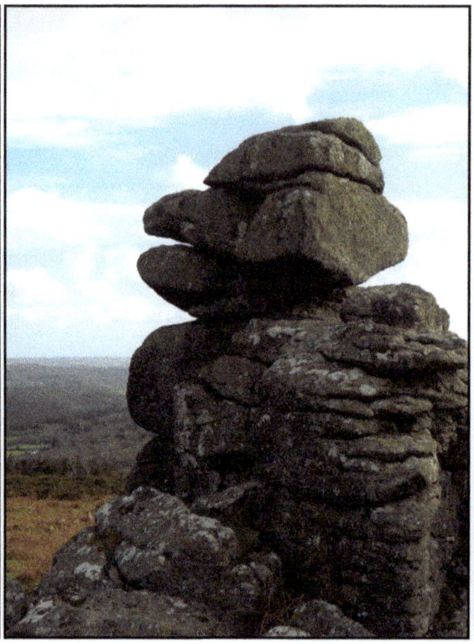
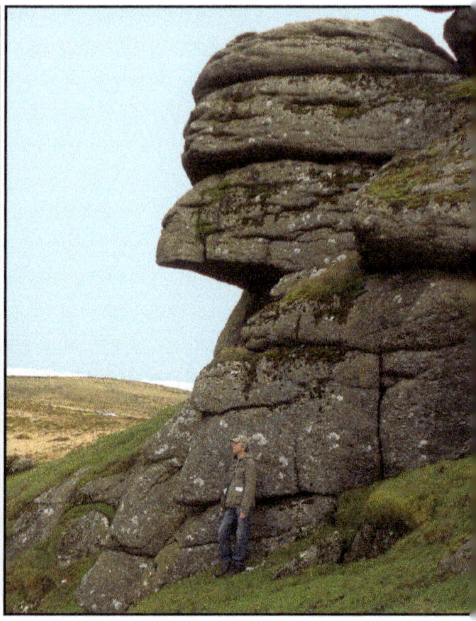

NW side of Saddle Tor (751763), which takes the form of another bird's head, with prominent raptor-like beak. The size of this feature is evident from me standing at the foot of the rock face. I estimate that the head is 5m high, forming the top half of a 10m high sheer drop. The creature stares eternally across the moor, and its 'bird of prey' features are virtually the same as in prehistory.
Hound Tor (743790) is a well-known destination for walkers, comprising a large rocky outcrop to the NE of Widecombe-in-the-Moor. Neolithic and Bronze Age remains have been found it its vicinity. I have visited the tor in rain and shine and have always found simulacra that I had not previously perceived. Such is the nature of our experiences and perceptions when we approach tors from different directions and walk around them following different routes. I present just three of many to you here, in the hope that this will inspire you to find more. All three anthropomorphic faces are on the western side of the tor and all look westwards. The first I call *The Crone,* for she appears as a toothless elder with archetypal witches' hooked nose **(right)**. Did people seek her wisdom in ancient times? She directly overlooks the next simulacrum; a small outcrop at the foot of the west side of the tor is capped by this feature, which I call *Pixie Rock* **(lower left)**. It has a turned up nose, and below it is a small cavern, large enough to lie within. See image on page 63 for the poem I received here. The last Hound Tor example I call *Long Nose,* for reasons which should be self-evident **(below right)**. Below the nose is a protruding upper lip or tongue. These features have only weathered a few centimetres in the last few thousand years, which in itself shows the resilience of granite. But it also reminds us that people were probably looking up in awe at these 'rock spirits' way back in prehistory, just as aboriginal cultures look to similar ones today.

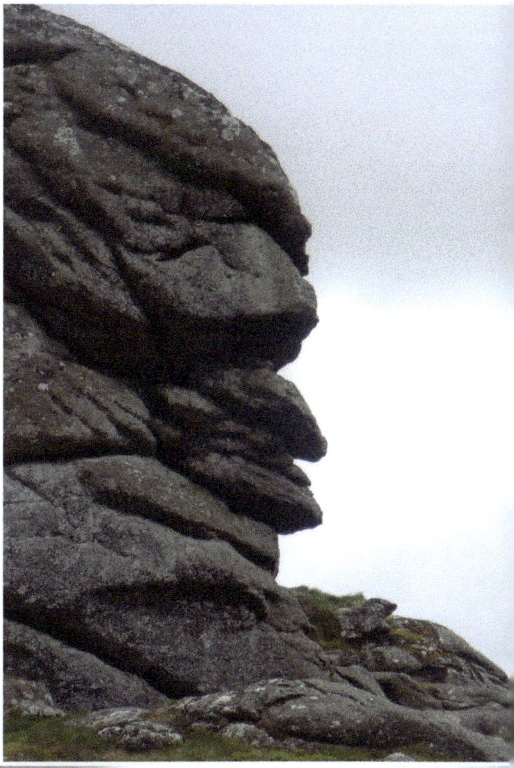

This next simulacrum **(top, next page)** is a striking one, which is on one side of the logan stone that

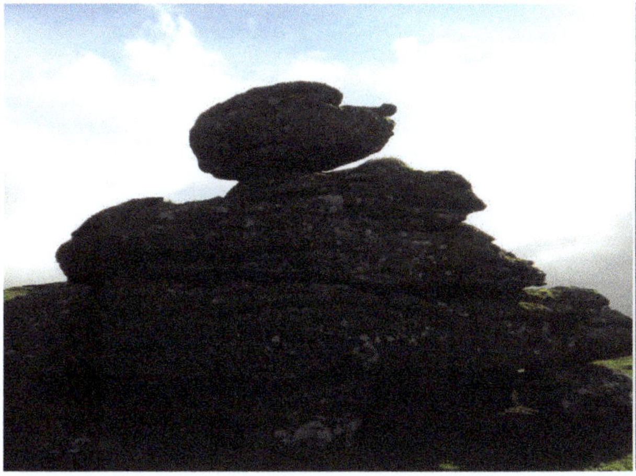

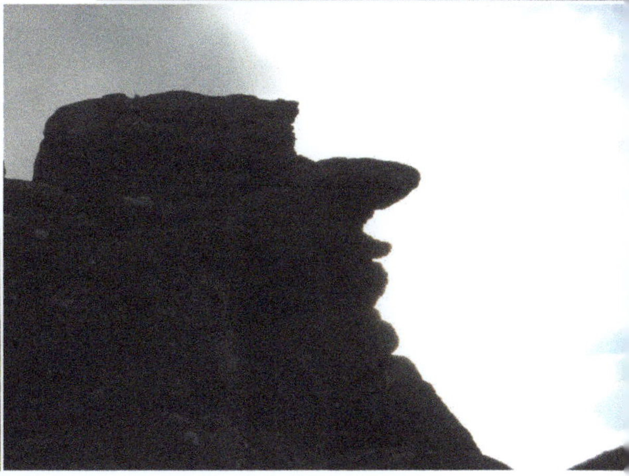

tops the north stack at Black Tor (573718), near Princetown. Complete with eye and lips, it creates a 1.5m overhang. The first time I saw this feature was on a very misty, overcast day and the head loomed over me, menacingly. On a return visit, the sunny day shown here, the face was friendly. This rock spirit looks east to stone rows.

Next is an amazing anthropomorphic head on the west side of Combestone Tor (670718), just south of Dartmeet. I call this lady **(centre)**, the *Combestone Hag*. In white outs and sunshine her 'moods' change with the weather. She is a totally detached 3D head, with long slanting eyes and hooked nose. I think she may have been a logan, or rocking, stone in the past, for she sits on a rock ledge and yet is barely attached to it. I would need some convincing that such an obvious feature would not have drawn the attention of our prehistoric forebears. She looks east, towards the main granite outcrop, upon which sits a rock basin.

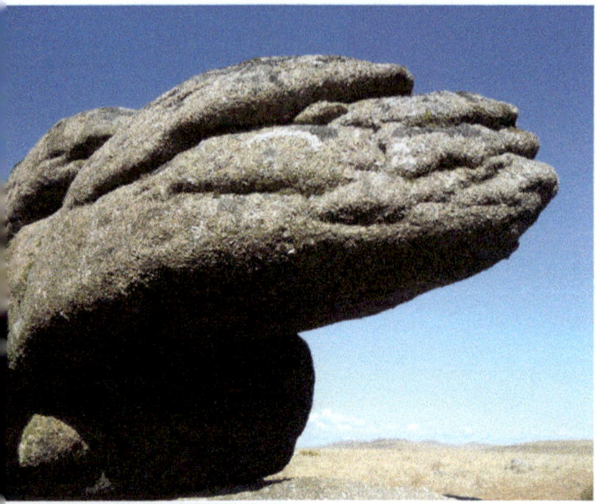

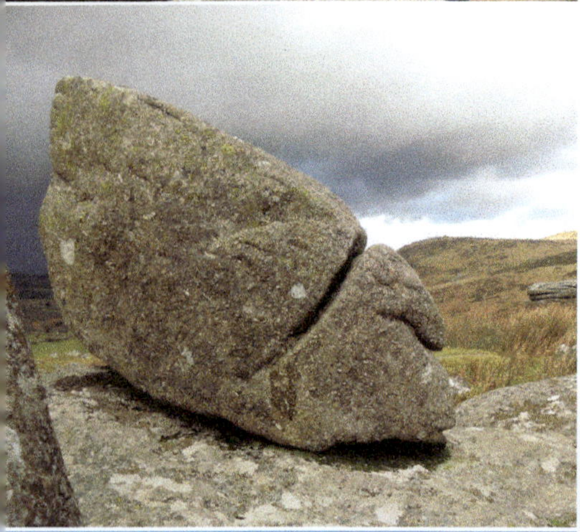

The next example is somewhat different. This time the simulacrum comprises the whole outcrop of Middle Tor (669858), SW of Chagford **(bottom left)**. Even from a distance the outcrop resembles a surfacing whale or dragon, erupting through the earth. It has eyes, a mouth and teeth, and thrusts forwards to create an overhang, under which several people may lie or sit. The view when doing so is to nearby Kestor. I have drummed beneath the overhang, and chanted with a group, and I knew we were in the company of those who had done similar long ago. Incredibly, on top of the beast's head I found a rock basin containing water **(top image, p. 132)**.

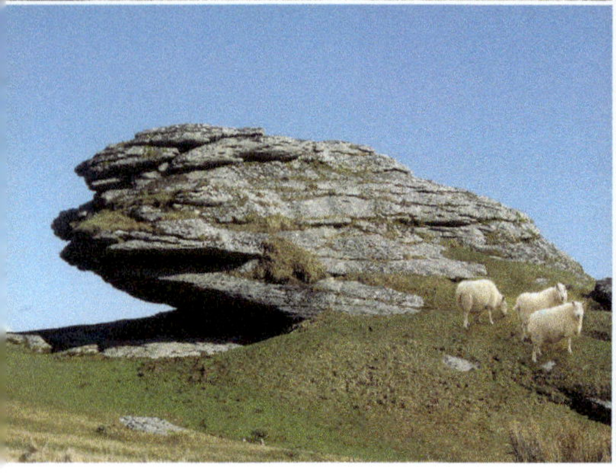

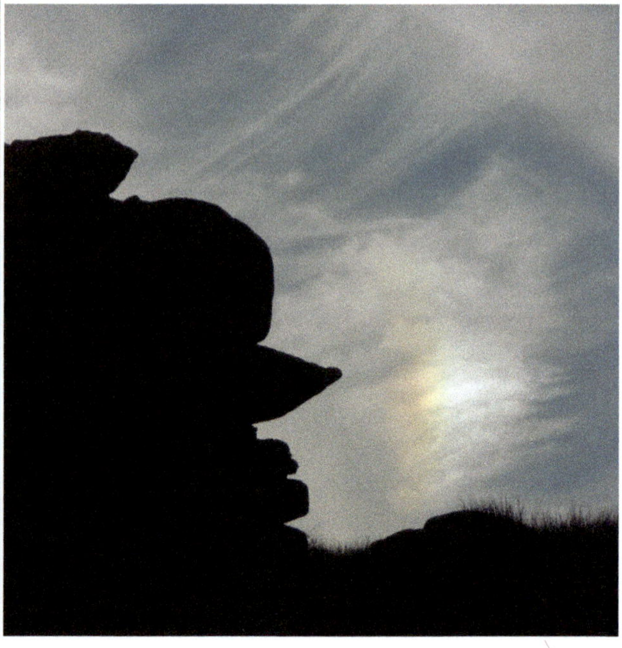

The last example **(opposite, below right)** is on the south stack of Black Tor, SW of Princetown. I captured its profile during a magical summer solstice sunset. It too stares across the moor, as if overseeing the rituals that took place at the nearby stone row.
These are but a few examples of the wondrous granitic simulacra to be found across the moor. Later I shall return to more, when I deal with the Merrivale Shamanic Landscape (Chapter 13).

The staff of life - phallicism

'The study of phallicism is the study of religion.'
(George R Scott, 1966)

Worship of the male member is very ancient and universal, and this reverence and the belief that the phallus possessed magical potency began way back in the Palaeolithic; our distant ancestors frequented caves that were filled with stalagmites and stalactites, emergent rigid phalli within the dark interior of the Earth Mother. Ithyphallic cave art from these distant times has been found in many such subterranean settings. Later, the Greeks, Romans, Hebrews, Babylonians, Egyptians, Chinese, and many other cultures (including the ancient British), all held the phallus to be representative of the fertility of Nature. The name of the Sumerian god Iskur means *'erect'*. The gods and goddesses of ancient cultures were all-powerful beings that ruled over Mankind, and were often sexually active, even promiscuous. Their myths echoed the forces people saw at play in Nature, so to honour their sexual merging was to honour both deity and the natural world.
In terms of ancient sites, many of the Neolithic megaliths of Brittany are decidedly phallic, some of them over 5m tall, such as the 9.5m Dol Menhir. Many of these were later Christianised with inscribed crosses (Knight 2015). Even in modern times, French women seeking to have children would visit such stones, as is recorded at the Stone Mare of Locronon. I have also found phalli at some of the Neolithic temples on Malta (Knight 2011 and 2013), where towering ithyphallic stones at Hagar Qim and Mnajdra were set into temple walls (Knight 2015).
The British Isles was not excluded from the ritualistic celebration of fertility, in which phallicism was often a central component. This is hardly surprising really: *'It was natural that the ancient Britons should worship stones and pillars, as emblems of the male principle, just as did the ancient Hebrews, Greeks, Romans, Egyptians, Japanese, et al'* (Scott 1966). In Ireland, a hand-held phallic artefact was found at Knowth, a Neolithic tomb complex in the Boyne Valley. At the same site, a 2.1m pillar stone stands outside one of the entrances, marking an equinox alignment. Another ithyphallic stone, called the *Stone of Destiny,* stands at Tara, the sacred centre of Ireland. The tallest stone in England, the 7.8m tall Rudstone Monolith, is ithyphallic, mirroring its huge Breton brothers.
Prof Chris Tilley considers the phallic-shaped menhirs of Brittany, and the bluestones at Stonehenge, were intended to be symbolic of huge axes thrust into the earth (Tilley 2004). These had enormous symbolic power, one of transformation, just as axes are created from the original rough rock from which they are fashioned. As farming took hold these stones may have represented a, 'dominance over Nature... as the land had become transformed from something which was a subject of human endeavour to an object of human authority and control'. Some also resemble bulbous rhizomes planted into the ground, a metaphor for fertility of the land and growth, the more phallic stones representing upward growth (Tilley 2004).

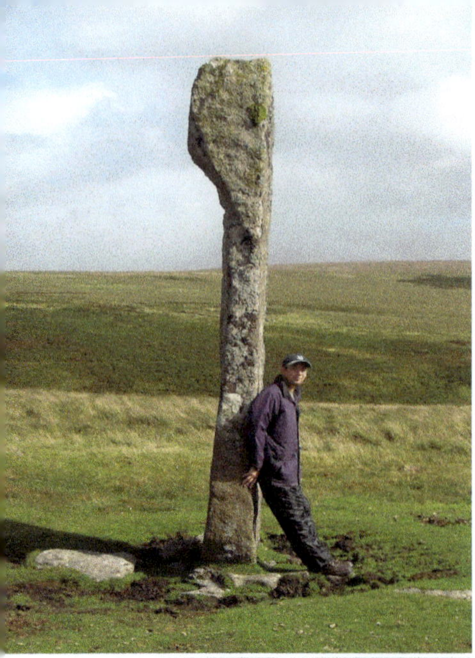

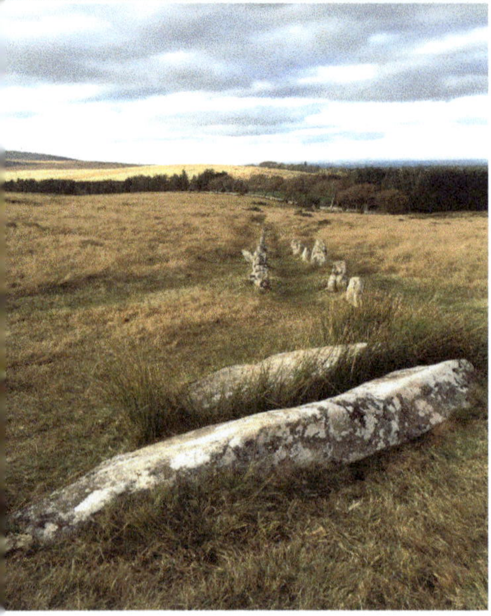

Dartmoor Phalli

'Long Men marching across the moor, keeping step, in a line, marking time.' (P Knight)

The above was my impression, in May 2016, of the row of phallic boundary stones and longstones linking Butterdon Hill and Western Beacon. The 'longstones' of Dartmoor are very often pillar/phallic-shaped megaliths, which punctuate the open, undulating moor with a stark and contrasting vertical presence. As the land was progressively cleared for farming in the Bronze Age these menhirs gained importance as territorial indicators, markers of social identity, which may not have been the original intention. These stones are often endowed with male attributes or names, confirming their ancient associations with the male member. Beardown Man, on Devil's Tor (596796) is phallic **(image p. 16)**. Aaron's Knock is an ithyphallic stone, with slit for the glans, on Hameldown Ridge. The tallest stone at Scorhill lends itself to phallic symbolism, and at the Yellowmead circles there is a fusion of phallic and triangular stones **(image p. 189)**. The tallest stone at the Hingston stone row is also phallic. I have also had the pleasure in visiting the isolated pillar-shaped longstone on Langstone Moor (551787), which is a slender phallus **(image p. 36)**. The tallest megalith at Merrivale is 3m tall and ithyphallic **(p. 182 & 203)**.

At the Hurston Ridge stone rows, one stone is decidedly taller and ithyphallic **(images p. 154).** The tallest stones at Drizzlecombe stone row (c. 592670), are ithyphallic **(image p. 16)** and one is the tallest on Dartmoor, standing 4.2m out of the ground. Its peculiar bulb or head has been noted by myself for some time **(top left)**; I am not the only one to have suggested the shape of the stone is significant: this 'head', '.... brings a very distinct dimension to the stone and gives it an almost anthropomorphic look.' (Klemen 2015). This head-like feature is in profile when viewed from three cairns either side of it. They are situated off the rows to afford the best view of the 'head', which is not otherwise profiled.

At the stone row south of Cobblestone Tor, the largest stones are prone at the east end, comprising a triangular stone and a fallen 3m phallic longstone. This same arrangement occurs on Shovel Down, where a slender prone stone lies straddled across the rows, next to a cairn **(lower image, above)**, and which may have been a focus of the stone row (Turner 1990). I have found phallic and triangular stones incorporated in Bronze Age hut circles at Merrivale and Grimspound; work on Bodmin Moor suggests that pairings of pointed and triangular stones in hut circles may have been for symbolic purposes (Bender et al 1999). It seems appropriate, therefore, that the Touchstone, a new millennium megalith erected near Rundlestone (578752), is pillar-shaped, continuing Dartmoor's ancient tradition of phallicism.

We have to ask the question as to whether the intention of the megalith builders was to present a phallus *rising* from the earth, or a phallus *penetrating it*. Perhaps both were appropriate. As I have said, Prof Chris Tilley also sees the tall slender megaliths as perhaps representing slender axe blades (Tilley 2004). They may have been regarded as the axes of the gods or ancestors, symbolic of their power of fecundity, thrust into the earth as an act of fertility. Many more examples of stone phalli can be found across Dartmoor. Most of the phallic longstones of the moor were probably that shape as they lay on the earth, 'ready to go' so to speak. They were a gift, and a sign, from the ancestors and the spirits of place. Bringing them into monuments gave the latter more 'clout'. As has been suggested, people were relocating 'pieces of place'.

I am also wondering if the tall stacks of many of the moor's tors were seen in a phallic context. On Hawaii, for instance, the phallic-shaped tall natural pillars in the Lao Valley (*Valley of the Flesh*) are the burial sites of ancient kings. I also draw your attention back to the 30m high phallic-shaped stacks at Externstein, Germany **(image p. 29)**. On the Dartmoor tors there is an interplay between the phallic stacks and the feminine symbolism of the gullies, the vulva-like rock basins, and the water they contain. This is an alchemical fusion of yin and yang, of the female and male principle.

Triangular stones

It has long been proposed that triangular megaliths, and even natural clitter, may have possessed symbolic significance in prehistory. Work on the symbolism of the Avebury megaliths (Meaden 1991, 1999), and at West Kennet Long Barrow (Knight 2011), has shown that people found triangulate stones to be spiritually important. The triangle has been variously been linked with the Triple Goddess, and even the shape of the pubic mound – another Divine feminine connection. Links have been made to the three aspects of the lunar cycle (waxing, full and waning), as well as the three aspects of womanhood (maiden, mother and crone). Sacred triplication is represented by the famous Neolithic triple spirals, such as at Newgrange, Ireland (Knight 2015).

Prof Chris Tilley has worked on the phenomenology of Bodmin Moor; Leskernick is a Bronze Age settlement where he found large, triangular stones incorporated into the walls of the houses, now preserved as hut circles (Bender et al 1999, 2007, Hamilton et al 2000, Tilley 2010). Several large triangular boulders collected from the natural clitter spread and purposefully embedded and erected in the ground, and were not the result of random settling. Structure 23 is a circular stone-wall structure, 4m in diameter, in the western settlement. Its excavation revealed it was not a roofed building, but rather a circular, open-air enclosure that incorporated a prominent triangular field boulder, 'of ritual significance'. The Bronze Age residents of Leskernick selected triangular stones, which may have represented less-pointed axe blades (Tilley 2004), setting them into the back walls. Also at Leskernick, a large boulder accompanied by an uprighted triangular stone was named the 'Shrine Stone' by archaeologists (Bender et al 2007), which reminds me of the roughly triangular 'auroch' stone near Black Tor **(image p. 37)**.

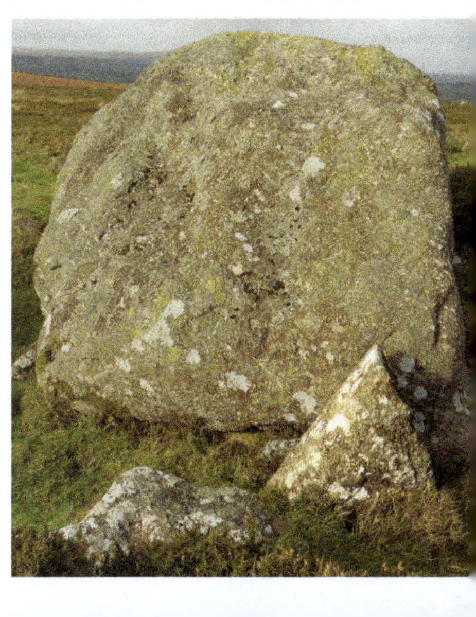

In the winter of 2015/6 I visited the eastern summit of Easdon Hill (734823), where I found a cairn that had been constructed so as to enclose a natural outcrop **(image p. 92)**. A huge boulder was used as a capstone, and butting up against it is a triangular stone **(right),** a juxtaposition that is repeated on White Tor. Below the west face of the main outcrop at Over Tor, is an alignment of stones, two of which are triangular, and one of which is pyramidal. At North Hessary Tor, under the shadow of the huge communication mast (578742), a triangular stone stands just north of the outcrop.

Triangular stones, many of which appear to have been propped up into the vertical, are common across Dartmoor, frequently occurring in a ceremonial setting. Several 'blocking stones' associated with stone rows have a pronounced triangulate profile, which I shall look at in more detail when I look at stone rows later, especially those at Merrivale and Drizzlecombe. A gnomon casts a shadow on to one of the triangular 'blocking stones' at Merrivale **(centre image, p. 203)**. At the triple stone row south of Combestone Tor, near Dartmeet, the main surviving features at the east end are a 3m prone longstone and an upright triangular stone (674711).

In February 2016, I visited White Tor (c. 543787), north of Merrivale, a site rich in Neolithic and Bronze Age remains. Bronze Age reave systems converge on the tor from the north and south. The one approaching from the south crosses an east-west track, to the south of which I found some large triangular standing stones incorporated in the reave (541282). They are obvious features to anyone following the reave to the tor. From here I could clearly see both the Langstone Moor Longstone and stone circle, which may be significant.

On Lakehead Hill, south of Postbridge, there are two excellent cairn circles adjacent to each other, one of which contains a cist (or kist) (643774). Bellever Tor was once prominent on the skyline from this locality. Both circles include triangular stones, such

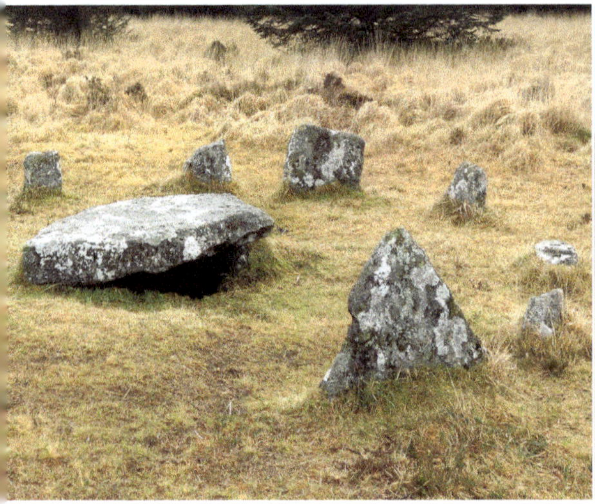

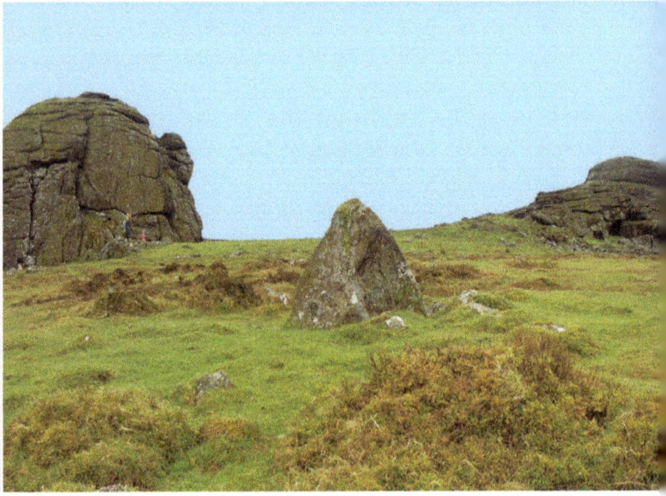

as the one in the foreground shown here at Lakehead Hill 6 **(above left)**.

On January 17, 2016, I visited Haytor to explore its magnificent crags and simulacra. Afterwards I was looking for somewhere to tune in for some earth-healing and to connect with the landscape. I noticed a 1.2m tall triangular stone, a true megalith, to the north of a clear area between the two summits **(above right)**. It is of red granite and is pock-marked on the south side. It is exactly north from centre of the natural amphitheatre between the summits, and its long axis is in alignment with Top Tor, to the west. The stone mirrors those found by Tilley at Carn Brae, Cornwall, which he thought may have represented axe blades. This stone at Haytor is not marked on any map and is not recorded, as far as I can ascertain, as being significant. And yet it is. It drew me to it: I tuned in to this stone and was compelled to walk around it anti-clockwise. With one hand remaining upon it, I had to say out loud the following words, repeatedly: *'I send love and healing out across the land in every direction with an open heart'.* I looked outward as the landscape revolved around me. I ended by asking the stone to hold the energy and the love until my return. I said my farewell with these words, *'Please receive the love of all those seeking to heal the land – and themselves. We are one. Good bye stone brother.'*

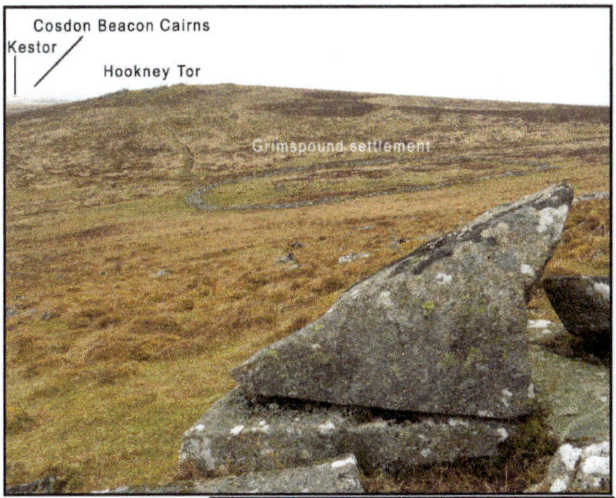

At Butterdon Hill, NW of Ivybridge, a large triangular stone was erected within metres of the summit cairn **(lowest image p. 98)**. At Yar Tor, I found a 1m triangular stone standing between cairns and the southern end of the stone row (682737), and near Lower Hartor Tor a triangular stone was uprighted (600673) between a settlement and a ridge top cairn. At Vixen Tor, a curvi-triangular stone **(right)** has been erected between the tor and a nearby cist. I think it relevant that the huge granite simulacrum **(image p. 163)** looks in this direction. At Yellowmead, there is a selection of pointed/phallic stones and triangular stones. This association is mirrored at the Hurston stone row, where the tallest stone **(images p. 154)** appears phallic from one direction, and triangular from another, a theme repeated at Merrivale. On the north slopes of Hameldown, there is a non-earthfast triangular stone, with pointed apex **(top)**, set upon a flat natural outcrop (702807). The view north from here is down to Grimspound and across to Hookney Tor. I observed that this stone marks where Kestor and the Cosdon Beacon cairns become visible as one ascends the hill. Inside Grimspound itself, some of the hut circles contain triangular stones. One 1.5m tall stone does resemble a huge flint arrowhead, a comparison Prof Tilley makes on Bodmin. At the Merrivale settlement (and elsewhere), I have found that triangular stones seem to be vital elements of hut circle design. Here there was a convergence of our world with that of the ethereal world of the ancestors.

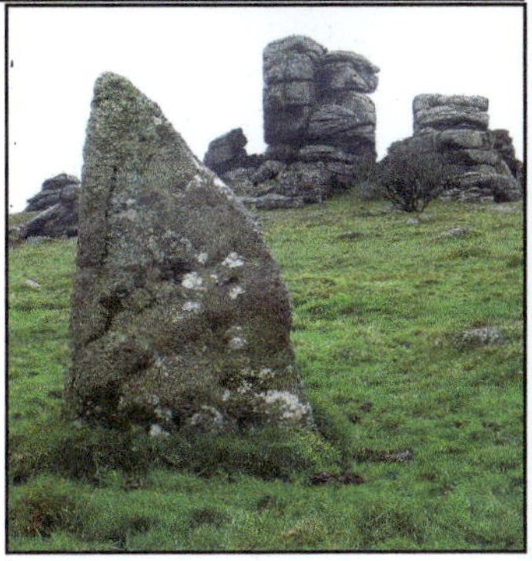

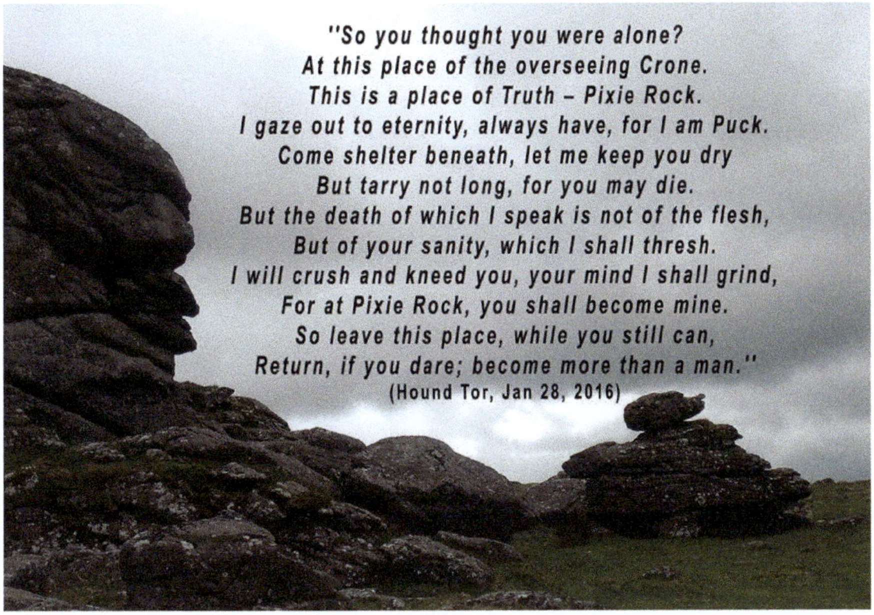

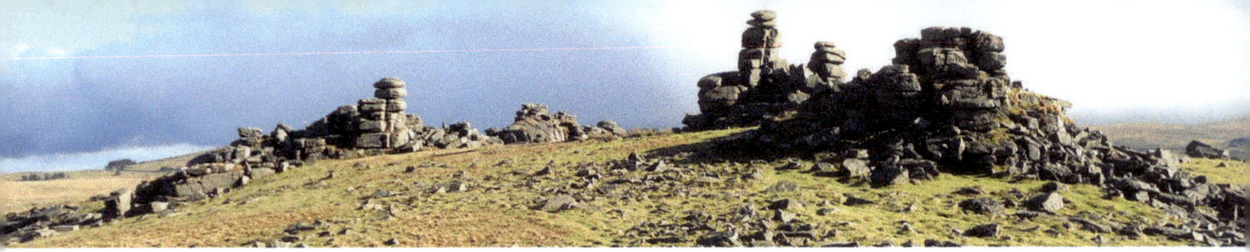

7. The Sanctity of the Tors

'The Mother has told us to look after the mountains, for they are alive'
(The Kogi, Columbia).

Elevated sacred places

For thousands of years, high places have been regarded as sacred components of cultural cosmologies and creation myths. As well as places of inspiration and aspiration, elevated regions are symbolic of transcendence and spiritual ascension, and are the abode of the immortals and the gods (Knight 2015). They are places where we may face physical danger, but also experience solitude. From them, we can look out not only to the land below, but also into our heart and soul.

Perhaps their significance is that they are close to the heavens – closest to deity. Mount Fuji is Japan's highest mountain and is sacred to both Shintoism and Buddhism, whose followers believe it to be a physical manifestation of God. Australian Aborigines revere Uluru as the site of the Dreamtime. Perched on Mount Kailash, one of the highest points of the Himalayas, the Potala Palace at Lhasa is a pilgrimage destination for Tibetan Buddhists and Hindus. The mountain has four pronounced sides which have been compared to a diamond by Buddhists.

As well as being a volcano, Mount Olympus **(below, left)** is the home of the Greek gods. The Greek oracle centre at Delphi also nestles within a mountainous setting. Devil's Tower is sacred to the Great Plains Indian tribes, and, as I have already mentioned, the 'Garden of the Gods', Colorado Springs, consists of enormous red sandstone formations held as sacred by many native peoples. The sacred Inca site of Machu Picchu is perched nearly 2400m up in the Peruvian Andes.

There are many instances of high places being associated with wisdom and shamanism in the Bible. For instance, Moses ascended Mount Sinai on a vision quest in order for him to perceive the Ten Commandments; Jesus gave his greatest homily, *'The Sermon on the Mount',* on an elevated high point in Galilee **(left)**.

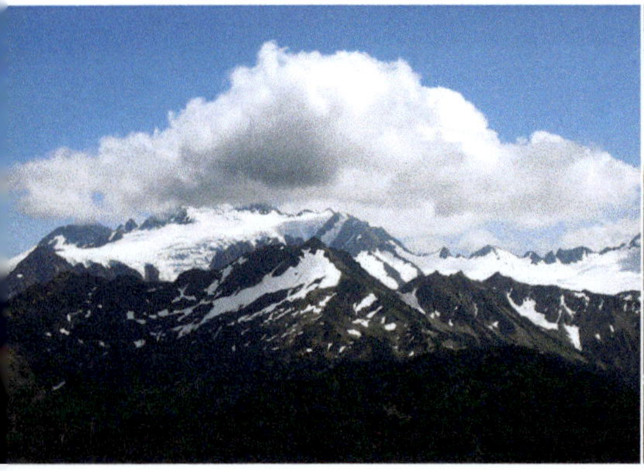

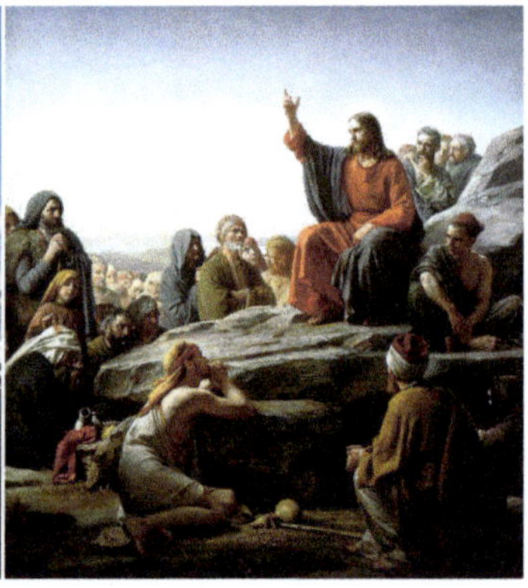

Around Europe, hills and mountains were the abode of dragons, trolls, goblins, and dwarves, where magical weapons and rings were forged (Knight 1998); *Hall of the Mountain King* by Greig, for instance, tells the story of a Troll King. King Arthur rests inside Glastonbury Tor, which is where the King of the Otherworld, Gwyn ap Nudd, holds court. Carn Ingli *(Hill of Angels)* is a sacred Welsh mountain, and the site of visions. One old Welsh tale says that if one spends a night up on Arthur's Seat, on the summit of Cader Idris, one will come down either a poet or a madman! Tower Hill, London, is where the oracular head of Bran was buried, as well as the site of the grave of Brutus, the founder of London. The Hill of Tara, Ireland, was the seat of the ancient Irish kings, and has monuments dating back to the Neolithic, demonstrating that it has been a holy hill for millennia.

'Hills will always be the haunts of him who seeks
to cultivate his original nature'
(Kuo His)

Natural outcrops as sacred places

Around the world, notable and striking topographical features are incorporated into tribal mythology. It is often the rocky outcrops that house the spirits of the gods and the ancestors. Within any landscape there is knowledge and wisdom, lying latent, activated by a shift of perception, which allows the nature of things to be revealed. High places are invariably those where the 'living rock' is exposed, often in sheer walls and incorporating features of a seemingly otherworldy appearance. Here the skeletal bones of the earth are laid bare, dominant and unyielding, and seemingly eternal. Academia has been slow to lay down the trowel, stand up, and look around at the natural features of a landscape. Prof Richard Bradley concurs: '... there are good reasons for suggesting that unaltered features in the landscape should be studied more systematically by archaeologists' (Bradley 2000). It is now becoming apparent that the prehistoric mind saw the world as a series of resemblance images and metaphors embedded on the landscape, accumulated over generations through intended action and reasoning.

In the Aborigine Dreamtime, the Rainbow Serpent swallowed up the ancestors and was forced to vomit out their bones, forming the rocky outcrops of the landscape. These outcrops were quarried to make axes, which were objects of great power due to them being fashioned from ancestral bones. The animistic Aborigines of Western Australia believe that the local quartzite rock holds the spirits of the ancestors. These are usually natural places which are impregnated with a magical power, the result of cumulative experiences of many generations. The Devil's Marbles, called Karlu Karlu by the local Aborigines **(image p. 25)**, stand at the Tennant Creek area of the Northern Territory. These huge, red, rounded granite boulders are strewn across a large area. Many of them seem impossibly balanced on top of each other. These amazing formations are traditional Aboriginal sacred sites of the Dreamtime. The Kaytetye people believe that the boulders are the eggs of the Rainbow Serpent and they remain very important to the tribe, and may be considered to be among the oldest religious sites in the world.

The Anasazi ruins of Boynton Canyon, USA, were built amidst huge natural formations, which have been likened to fairy castles (Barlow 1996). The canyon is said to be the home of a grandmother spirit called Kamalopukwia, whose form is seen in the 'Old White Lady' stone. The Anasazi would often build dwellings and shrines beneath over-

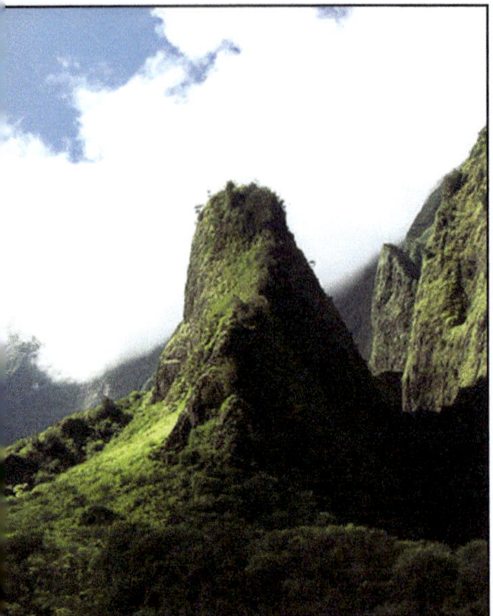

hanging outcrops, such as in the San Juan Basin, at Montezuma's Well, and in Indian Creek Canyon (Barlow 1996). In Tibet, three natural rocks in the holy region of La Phyi are thought to represent body parts of the deity Vajravarahi (Devereux 2002).

On Hawaii, tall phallic-shaped natural pillars in the *Valley of the Flesh* are the burial sites of ancient kings. Their bones were hidden to keep their mana (energies) from being used against the people (Barlow 1996). Kanaloa, the Hawaiian god of the underworld, is represented by a towering rock outcrop known as the Iao Needle **(left)**.

The Saami, the Lapland reindeer herders of Scandinavia, make little use of monuments, using instead elevated natural features that stand out from the background landscape, and which are accorded special powers. Some of these rocks serve permanent communities, whilst others are only visited at certain times of the year, such as during reindeer herding.

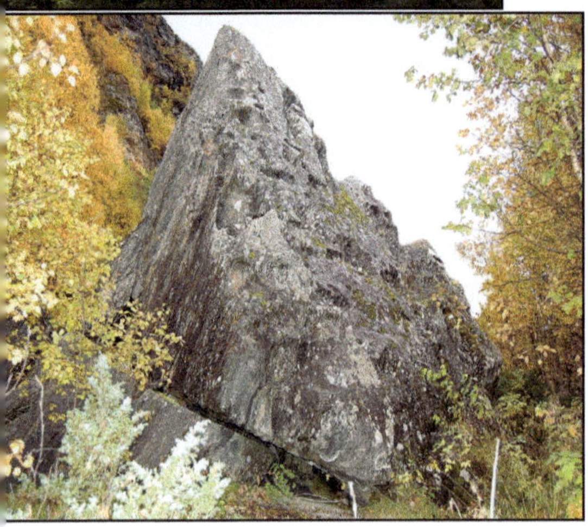

Many of these are huge striking rock formations (several of which display simulacra) which are collectively known as *siejdde* **(left)**. These features are rarely modified, and are the focus of animal sacrifice and the offering of anthropomorphic wooden idols (Bradley 2000). In some cases, reindeer bones are left at the sites in small cairns, with their antlers left protruding. Shamans reach decisions, such as where food is to be found, by consulting their drum, the sound of which gives them the answers. One of the reasons Saami carry out sacrifices at these notable rock outcrops is to ensure there is there is ample rainfall to nourish the moss and grass, so vital for their herds (Bradley 2000).

Sacred sites become especially potent if reinforced by the natural forms in the landscape. Icelanders held their annual midsummer gathering of twelve tribes, called the Althing, below a towering natural outcrop called Law Rock, where a major geological fault has caused a dramatic rift; a rock outcrop beside the deepest fissure was used as the rostrum. This gathering can be compared to Crockern Tor on Dartmoor (616757), meeting place of the local Stannary Parliament.

Schielallion Mountain is the central point of Scotland; in its shadow is an outcrop called the 'Rock of Initiation' (Biltcliffe and Hoare 2017). At Ffestiniog, in Wales, a large column of 'grotesquely shaped rock' rises from the waters of the Cynfal, and resembles a pulpit. Called 'Huw Lloyd's Pulpit Stone', the Huw in question is a colourful character from local folklore, said to be a poet and a bad-tempered wizard, who would curse all who crossed his path (Walker 1987). Is this the corruption of the memory of a former ancient, natural gathering place?

Many curious rock formations are scattered over fifty acres on Brimham Moor, Yorkshire. One of them is Idol or Hanging Rock **(image p. 104)**, which is some 6m high, weighs 200 tons, and precariously balanced on a small pivot. It is said to have oracular properties (Walker 1987). Other local formations include Elephant Rock, Porpoise Head, and the Dancing Bear. In the Shap area of Cumbria, two natural rocks called the Giant's Foot and the Cope Stone, were key elements of the local sacred landscape and its monuments. The Old Man of Mow is a 20m rock stack in Cheshire, said to have been the object of worship (Biltcliffe and Hoare 2012). Julian Cope regards such natural sacred places 'Proto-Neolithic Temples' (Cope 1998).

The sanctity of Dartmoor tors

In 1862, the President of the Archaeological Association called Dartmoor, "... a natural Druid Temple – one great mass of logan stones and rock idols". This is an early indication of how antiquarians thought that the natural rock formations of Dartmoor were once imbued with spiritual reverence. However, I believe that such veneration pre-dated Druidic gorsedds by thousands of years.

The landforms on Dartmoor are an eternal interplay between water incising into valleys and the erosion-resistant granite of the tors. There is an alchemical ballet playing out here, of hard and soft, whose tempo is very slow, with thousands of years between beats. There are around 150 tors on Dartmoor, although numbers vary due to eternal debates as to what constitutes a 'tor' and a 'hill'. The Dartmoor tors are visually dominant landforms, out of proportion to the relatively small part of the landscape they occupy. Each tor is unique and easily recognisable to anyone who knows the moor – as was the case in prehistory. The timeless sense of awe and wonderment of such places continues to this day. People are still fascinated with the dramatic and bizarrely sculpted forms of the tors, which are endlessly reproduced in tourism brochures; they are part of the cultural construct of Devon. Since the earliest human encounters with the granite uplands of the Southwest, we can reasonably assume that the tors had enormous cultural significance as landmarks and orientation points, and inevitably became places, '... invested with myth and meaning' (Tilley 1995; 1996).

The tribal boundaries of today's Aborigines of Australia are often marked by water courses, or else prominent topographical features such as hills. These natural features often play key parts in Aborigine Dreamtime mythos, and are referent in passing on encoded cultural knowledge. They literally anchor each culture or tribe to their land. Sometimes it was the creatures of myth that forged the shapes of rock formations, such as at Uluru, where ten totemic beings created its features; over fifty locations on Uluru are mythologically named (Tilley 1994). The landscape thus represents the myths, and these legends are apparent in the landscape – it is as if time has collapsed into space and landscape. Was this also the case with the tors of Dartmoor, and in particular with relevance to the simulacra?

However they were interpreted, the environments of tors would certainly mark them out as special places in prehistory. Exposed rock, a treeless area rising above the surrounding forest, water pouring down from them, water held within rock basins, areas of openness at the mercy of the whipping elements, and huge orthostatic crystals shaped like axe heads; 'Tors can be seen as metaphor for all of the elements of the world, both social and physical, brought together in microcosm' (Davies 2010). Tors literally burst out from the earth, like antediluvian giants surfacing for air. Surely their qualities of solidity and timelessness would have impressed people thousands of years ago, as they do now.

Tors are places separate from the heart of dwellings, and which required an effort of body and mind to reach. Once there, their uses and symbolic interpretation were multifaceted: 'Wild and sacred places have many uses. There are places where women go for seclusion, where the bodies of the dead are taken, and where young men and women are called for special instruction. Such places are numinous, loaded with meaning and power' (Snyder 1990). Different features of a tor may have determined where different activities and rites were acted out. Natural ledges, overhangs, rock shelters, vertical cliff faces, gullies and rock basins all present a variety of spaces for sacred theatre and practice; indeed, the tors were as versatile as the monuments built within sight of them, and, like monuments, formed a network in a mythologised landscape. The experiences, and subsequent storytelling, of the shaman was a medium through which the landscape spoke.

The tors of Dartmoor never fail to fill me with wonder and awe. As I clamber over them my senses are filled with unfamiliar experiences. Tors are often prone to sudden gusts of wind; they are touchy-feely, invitingly tactile, and often rough to the touch with weathering crystals. They present weird rock formations, and can be capped with mysterious pools of water, the rock basins. Perhaps the sudden changes in weather on tors, compared to lowlands and the forests, were another factor that made the tors special places. Sometimes their summits are covered in snow, whereas lower lands are not. Rocks rise from white surrounds, as if surfacing for air. Shown here **(left)** is Leeden Tor (563718) after snowfall. Tors may be blanketed with mist when lower down the sun is shining. I have had the pleasure of the moor's changeable conditions on many occasions; a mist may roll in 'from out of nowhere', to cover a tor within minutes of there being views of miles around.

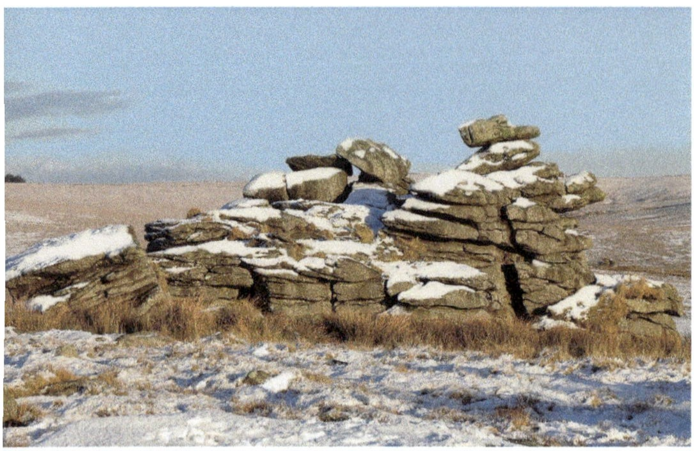

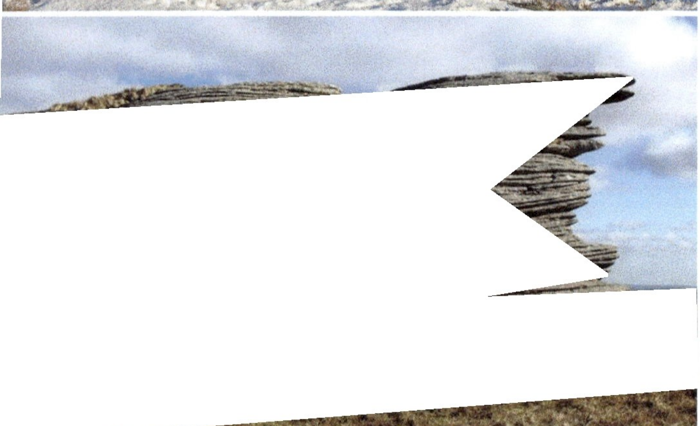

The Q'eqchi of Guatemala believe that atmospheric changes represent hill spirits talking to each other (Davies 2010).The major hills of the Q'eqchi are assumed to be male, whilst the valleys are feminine. Many Native American peoples also consider rock to be male and earth to be female. The way that granite outcrops burst up out of the ground could have been interpreted as a male symbol, while the receptive fissures and gullies between the stacks could have been seen as feminine.

So what did prehistoric people of Dartmoor really make of these towering and often isolated protrusions? The tors are all distinctive, each being a unique reference point on the land, which, with familiarity, can be recognised from miles away. Watern Tor **(above, lower image)** is notable for two outcrops which appear to be in conversation, having a head-to-head. The gully between them may have been regarded as an entrance to the Otherworld, or as a space through which one had to pass during a rite of passage; the voids may have been as important as the rocks.

To Neolithic and Bronze Age farmers, tors may have been related to how crops similarly rose out of the earth, and yet were rooted in it, as well as symbolic of the endless cycles of nature. The tors are like natural fortresses of the gods, rock-strewn and ancient. These sculpted edifices of granite, eternally whipped by the winds, imbue wonder and possess a dramatic aura which draws people in. They may have been tribal omphali, ritual centres on which individual clans were focused; by associating with a tor they embedded themselves into the land. In tribal cultures around the world today, repeatable offerings and rituals of a symbolic nature are made, directed at the transcendental Otherworldly forces, omnipresent in the land. Tors would have been potent resources for symbolism and mythology, particularly those with striking topographical features like simulacra. Tors are liminal places, and the presence of attention-focusing simulacra would have been seen as highly significant. They continue to inspire poets and painters today - a continuance of their ancient role as inspirational mindscapes.

The tors are the original sacred sites of Dartmoor, long before a single standing stone was erected. Culturally and physically, they carried a charge: 'Before they improved on nature by building temples and monuments, people venerated specific topographical features because they were considered to be the homes of mythic beings' (Devereux 2013). Perhaps it was felt that Spirit dwelt permanently in these tors, available if approached with care by those seeking communion. Generations of people would have been led up to them in prehistory, to be shown around by elders, perhaps for initiations and rites of passage, or clan gatherings. The following has been said of one Bodmin Moor tor: 'We suggest that Brown Willy was a communal place where people from different settlements came together, and that the ridge formed a ceremonial processional way' (Bender et al 2007).

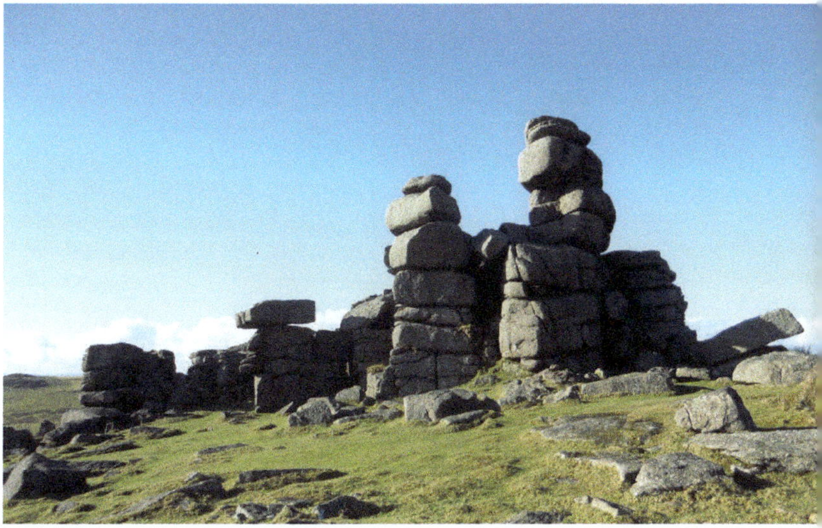

And in all that time, the granite and its simulacra would not change. On a recent trip to Great Staple Tor **(right)**, I stood on the tor rocks, surveying the timeless outcrops, which seemed like a time capsule - frozen in time, frozen in granite. The rocks had character and presence, as if they were watching my every move; I felt as if I was actually standing in the Dreamtime. The perceived ancientness of the rocks might have meant that only people of a certain age were permitted access to certain tors or certain rocks thereon, younger people being excluded. Others could only gain entry when guided by an elder or shaman. Indeed, rites of passage ceremonies may have taken place on the tors themselves. Getting up to a tor can be arduous, symbolic of the rite of passage. These liminal qualities may have been used to mark important life changes (Davies 2010), such as from child to adult, single to conjugal, adult to elder, or from life to death.

In crossing the psychological boundaries as one approaches a tor outcrop, the individual is changed in some way, and so tors might be understood as places of controlled transformation. This is due to both the physical nature of the rocks there, and by the overlaid cultural myths. These referenced such timeless places, linking the past to the present through association with ancestral and creator spirits.

Climbing up to the tors on the edge of the moor would have represented a notable contrast to life in the forests below. The rock outcrops are massive and tower above the viewer's head, exuding a powerful presence (Davies 2010). It is notable that many of the tors that were later enclosed have significant fissures and cracks within the rock outcrops. Tilley and Bennett (2001) suggest that these were seen as the routes by which the creator ancestors entered and left the world, thus further supporting the idea that the tors were liminal areas, offering access to other worlds. This is paralleled by the Vantu of the South Pacific, who view rocks as markers for people's arrival in the landscape, and as the concrete form of the ancestors (Davies 2010). In the Early Neolithic it seems likely that the only places from which good views over the landscape were possible were from the higher tor summits. This suggests that the views *from* the moorland edge tors were one of the factors that gave these outcrops value, attracting people up from the forested lowlands.

A parallel to this can be drawn from the ethnographic record of Madagascar. The Zafimaniry make their settlements on hilltops amid dense forest. The concept of clarity of vision is important to them, and they regard the expansive views, and the places from which these views are afforded, as very special (Bloch 1995). Bloch gives several examples of this. For instance, on returning to their village they would emerge from the forest and often stop at a clearing that gave a good view of the village. Here they would sit for an hour or more, sing songs and sometimes even cry. Yet for the Zafimaniry, and for people once viewing the landscape from the tors, there was an ability to view many places at once and to see how they were spatially related. Thus, any location from which such a view was encountered might be considered, by those doing the viewing, to be a very special place indeed. It was a place where they could look down onto the world as the spirits and ancestors do. An old metaphor for understanding something is 'I see that'. This quest for clarity led to tors being regarded as places at which to contemplate the wider world. If this method of relating to time via space was also prevalent in the Early Neolithic, then the ability to view the landscape from an elevated tor might have been related metaphorically to the ability to view time, and the past: 'The tors could have been used to orientate people both in the landscape and in the *pastscape*, and show them how to act or *get on* in the world" (Davies 2010). The tors were near to the sky, possibly nearer to the spirits, and more likely to represent a time of light, warmth and summer, when life was abundant and large game plentiful. Perhaps at the highland-edge tors, hunters were required to ask permission of Spirit before hunting these higher areas.

It is equally possible that the rock outcrops were themselves believed to be endowed with spirits or were the ancestors turned to stone. If gatherings took place around rocks that were metaphorically viewed as spiritual embodiments, conduct may have been closely circumscribed. The idea of Aborigine Dreamtime ancestor-creators settling down and becoming features in the natural landscape may be apt when considering the tors. Being such striking and prominent features, the tors would seem prime candidates for spiritual association (Davies 2010) Taking an example from northern Europe, each family of the Scandinavian Saami had their own sacred hill, associated with ancestors, of which the sacred rock formations, siejddes **(image p. 66)** were the most significant (Bradley 2000).

On Dartmoor, the tor outcrops emerge from the ground almost organically, similar to trees, giving the impression that they are alive and growing out of the earth. From this perspective, given that they out-last even the greatest trees of the forest, tors must

have been seen to have had a great depth of time, perhaps going back to the creator gods and ancestors, back to the Dreamtime (Davies 2010).
Locations become significant due to meanings attached to particular features and also through events that have taken place there (Tilley 1994). Don't forget that to prehistoric people the land was not 'natural' as we see it, but was created by the ancestors or gods. In this context, aboriginal cultures believe that they merely pick up on myths that are already inherent in the land. Successive generations perpetuate these myths, embellishing and adding their own layers. In this animistic mindset, all things are alive and have soul, and not just plants and animals, but also rocks and water, even flint and metal tools. The outer appearance of anything, be it outcrop or artefact, was the result of unseen forces, of which people were also a manifestation. The world had many layers of reality: 'To the shaman there is never just one landscape, but always many landscapes. Worlds and dimensions mingle, as mythical and physical landscapes intertwine and interact' (Knight 2007).

Folklore – What's in a name?

In many cultures, such as the Australian Aborigines, the Saami, and Native Americans, folklore and myth has survived more or less intact because of continuous, unbroken oral traditions, as has their constant association with landscape features and its sacred places. In Christianised Europe, we have lost the majority of our 'living' traditions. What surviving folklore we do have often represents vestiges of ancient beliefs and practices, such as the maypole, the Green Man, and some calendrical celebrations that are Pagan in origin (Knight 2015).
The Church unfortunately assimilated, and all but obliterated, most local ancient customs and mindsets, and Dartmoor was no exception; the 'old ways' were forgotten - there was a new God in town. Local myths and legends can be forgotten within a few lifetimes if there is no continuance through oral tradition. And, of course, many localities were demonized and renamed, now associated with the Devil, demons and evil forces. Hundreds, if not thousands more topographical features across Britain may have once possessed names which have now been forgotten, including notable boulders, standing stones, logan stones, and tors. However, all is not lost. Some relics do survive, giving us tantalising glimpses of times when tors and other landscape features were revered.

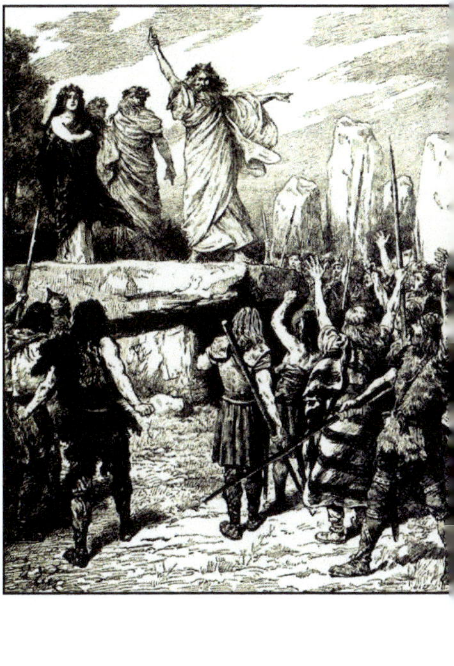

There is Druid's Chair, or Seat of Judgement, on Pew Tor, and the Tolmen Stone **(image p. 135)** has Druidic folklore. Drewsteignton is named after the Druids (this is also said to have been the site of the shooting of the last wolf in England around 1780), and there is Druid Cross (743707) near Ashburton. I find it inconceivable that these Iron Age priests did not visit Dartmoor's tors and other remarkable places, for ceremony, ritual and solace **(right)**. Woden's companion, Tiw, may have given his name to Dewerstone Rock (538638), in the SW corner of the moor. Folklore, however, says that the rocks were named after 'Dewer', the demon huntsman, who steals the souls of unbaptised babies. In a 19th century account, it is also where the Devil's footprints were seen in snow. The 'wish-hounds' are said to be heard in the valley, accompanied by the Devil, who is a deformation of Hurn of Hunter (Knight 2015).

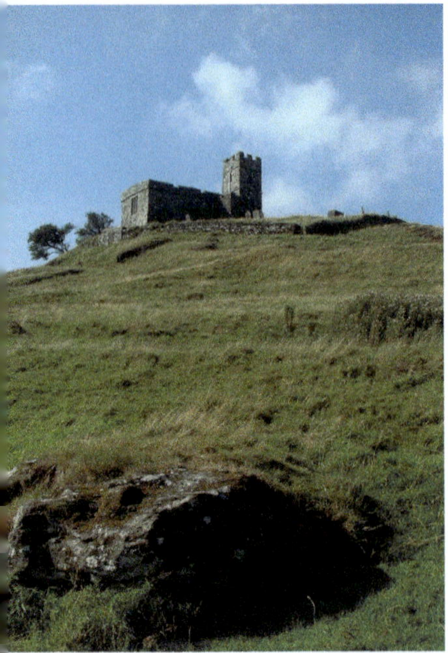

The spectral wild hunt is also associated with Hamel Down, and Devil's Tor overlooks the Beardown Man standing stone. The Devil's Frying Pan is the local name for a large rock basin on Great Mis Tor. On Brent Tor/Brentor **(left)**, the Devil was supposed to have kept moving the stones intended for the construction of the church until the intervention of St Michael. It is generally accepted by folklorists that places associated with the Devil are merely the result of the Church imbuing sacred sites with negative connotations. Brent Tor stands on the famous St Michael Line (see Chapter 17).

Most ancient clans had totem animals, as do indigenous tribes today. Memories of these are suggested in the naming of some of the Dartmoor tors, such as Fox Tor, Kestor (*Kestral Tor*), Vixen Tor, Lynx Tor, Doe Tor, Hart Tor, Hound Tor **(lower left)**, Rook Tor, Hawks Tor, Beardown Tors, Raven's Tor, Crow Tor, Feather Tor, and Easdon Hill *(Hill of Eagle)*. There is Giant's Hill, Giant's Grave, and White Tor (*whit* = holy*)*, and Grim's Grave; Grim was a pseudonym of Odin, the Norse god.

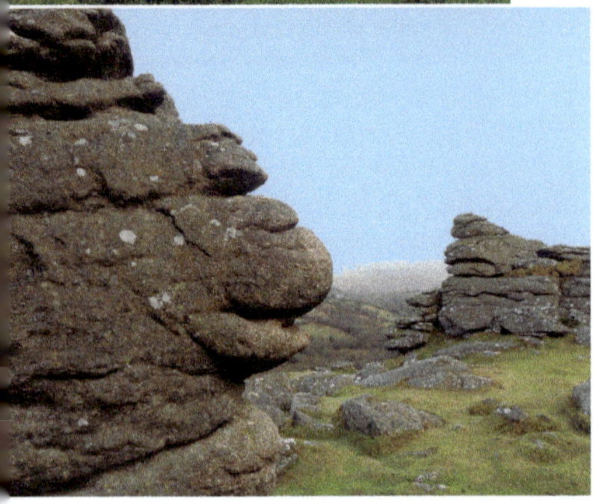

There are several Dartmoor places associated with pixies or piskies, such as Fur Tor and Dead Lake Well; there is a *Pixies House* on Sheeps Tor. King Arthur is said to have stood on Hel Tor (named after the Celtic sun god Hel or Helith) and been involved in a hurling match with the Devil. The wondrously slender waterfall at Lydford is called the White Lady, which may be a remembrance of a water sprit, or an association with Diana, the moon Goddess (St Leger-Gordon 2001). Near the waterfall, the waters of the Lyd cascade through the Devil's Cauldron. Dartmoor is sprinkled with more remnants of old lore, as Ordnance maps reveal. More suggestive examples can be found on Bodmin Moor, such as Temple Tor, Hawk's Tor, King Arthur's Bed, and Twelve Men's Moor.

Although some of these places may have been named from a local abundance of a particular wildlife, it is equally possible that some were named from rocks resembling animals or birds when seen from a particular direction. It is common practise for aboriginal/indigenous tribes to name themselves after topographical features, which are usually sacred to them, woven into their Creation myths.

'The roots of culture may be regarded as residing in nature…'
(Bender et al 2007)

A walk on the wild side - the phenomenology of tors

To view and admire these towering tors from afar is one thing, and that in itself must have moved our ancestors. But it is the intimacy that one gets when moving among these lofty places that gets us closer to the mindset of our distant forebears, as our imaginations are let out to play. Standing on a high Dartmoor tor, with its sense of immemorial antiquity and inspiring views, we are invited to change the perspectives of our own lives, our internal landscape, our mindscape, to recognise that there is always a 'bigger picture' unfolding. Landscapes are all mindscapes, constructs of our individual experiences, mirroring how our beliefs shape our lives. The striking natural features of tor outcrops evoke emotional responses. This is an often overlooked, yet important, element in experiencing and then understanding a landscape, and therefore the monuments sited within it.

The body is shaped by the places it comes to know, especially those who take up residence (Klemen 2015). All terrain offers personal interaction, whether you are resident or simply passing through. With several tors, it is now as if I am visiting old friends; I say 'hi' and 'farewell', as I forge my own personal relationship with them. Tors can be teachers, *men-tors* no less. They possess a numinous quality, offering us gullies, overhangs, balanced stones, simulacra, rock basins, confined places into which to squeeze, and frequent antisocial weather. I am invited out to play, to explore with my inner child perhaps. And every tor is totally unique, making it easier for me to relate to them as acquaintances - and mentors. I feel 'moored' – as if I am being tethered by the land, as a boat would be attached to the dock; it seems apt that I call this process *'mooring'*.

Many of the gullies between the rocky outcrops create natural portals that draw one in, not dissimilar to the way the entrances direct one into causewayed enclosures, or chambered tombs. They are liminal places, thresholds. As I approach the rocks of a tor I feel I am stepping into an alternate world, not unlike landing in the New World must have been like to Columbus, or to astronauts landing on the moon. The gentle, rock-free moorland is replaced by clitter, sheer slopes and 'in your face' simulacra; this world requires one to focus on the here and now. And it is the unpredictable nature of the weather on these tors that also adds to their mystique. On more than one occasion I have started an ascent of a tor under clear skies, only to walk into moisture-laden 'white-outs'. I was literally *'cloud walking',* surrounded by the breath of the dragon. Same landscape, and yet not. Poetry and snippets of wisdom have been revealed to me on such occasions, when I sit with a quietened, receptive mind. I once sat down and tuned into the simulacra at Hound Tor, and words entered my head, as if the rocks were speaking. The words were not kind or melodic, but harsh, as if a challenge was being laid down **(image and poem p. 63)**.

Even how we approach an outcrop, and from which direction, is relevant. Does it require physical exertion from certain approaches and not others? I often get the impression that I am being led into a tor outcrop along some well established and ancient route. Sometimes the 'doorways' can be narrow, as if I am gate-crashing on hallowed ground, being forced to walk in the very footsteps of my ancestors; Prof Bradley again: 'Particular parts of these sites had to be approached in a prescribed order, and one effect of reconstructing these places was to restrict the numbers of people having access to any one point at the same time' (Bradley 2000). Prof Chris Tilley tells of

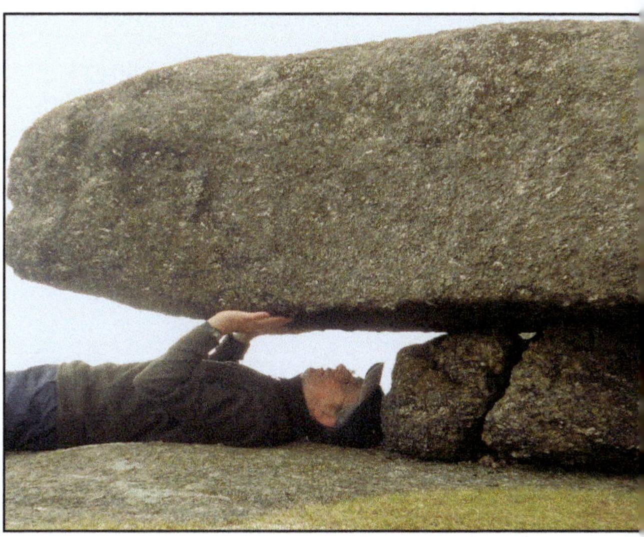

how Rough Tor, on Bodmin Moor, takes on different characteristics depending on from which direction he approached (Tilley 2010).

We are invited to immerse ourselves fully into a tor, to walk around the rock piles, to view any rock outcrop from a multitude of different angles. What does this rock surface feel like compared to that over there? How does my view of the terrain change as I walk around the summit? When I sit on this tor cairn, can I see why it was placed here and not over there? May I ask the 'spirit of place', 'what do I need to know? Why am I here? Am I being subtly persuaded or coaxed to follow a particular route around the rocks, such as through gullies? How is my experience of this place different under the full moon and the stars, and what responses does this generate? Does this place feel 'welcoming' or do I feel 'threatened' in any way, and why? Do I feel I need to be clothed or naked? Is the rock surface smooth or rough, warm or cold, dry or moist, and what does it smell like? What do I feel when I squeeze into, and lie supine in, a restricted space **(image p.73)**, such as a narrow overhang or gully?

Some spaces are indeed claustrophobic, and can present challenges, both physically and mentally. I have squeezed into spaces little wider than my body, knowing that hundreds of tons of rock were above my head; this can be emotional and can start the flow of adrenaline. And do these narrow passageways and crevices align with the sun or moon at certain times of the day or night or time of year? Perhaps the light of the solar god and the lunar goddess was also invited into these confines.

Interacting with rock outcrops, as with other 'sacred sites' on the moor, is multisensorial. The primary implement in studying rock outcrops in this manner is the experience of the participant. I would suggest that this was the case thousands of years ago. And whatever anyone perceives a place to be about is correct, and is so for everyone. At Avebury, I suggest this is the case with the multi-interpretive anthropomorphic megaliths. No matter what you think a rock feature resembles, you are correct - everyone is! Whatever you are given is the message for you. And this

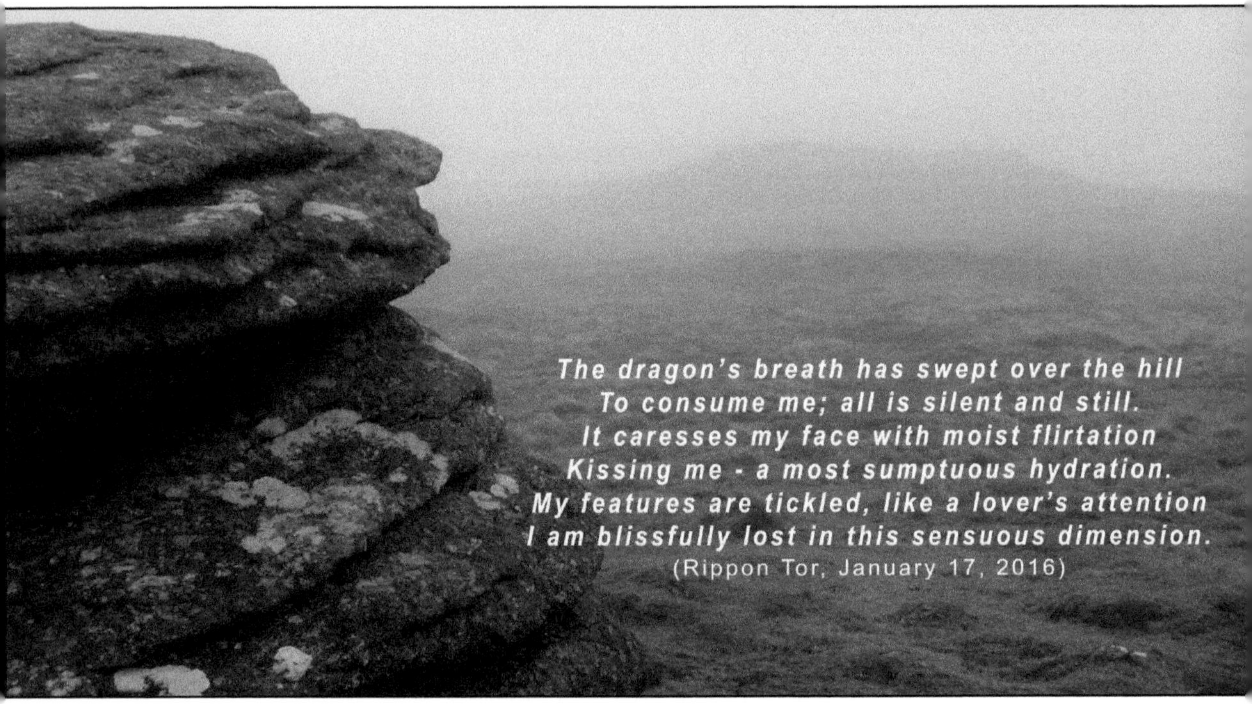

may have been the case thousands of years ago. Like a work of art, simulacra really are in the eye of the visual magpie within us all. This example **(top image)** revealed itself to me on Pew Tor (532735). The mouth is open as if to speak, and an eye seemed to watch me attentively. Did shamans use such simulacra like this one as oracle stones, under the influence of psychoactive plants and/or trance drumming, listening to their every word as animated mouths spoke ancient wisdom?

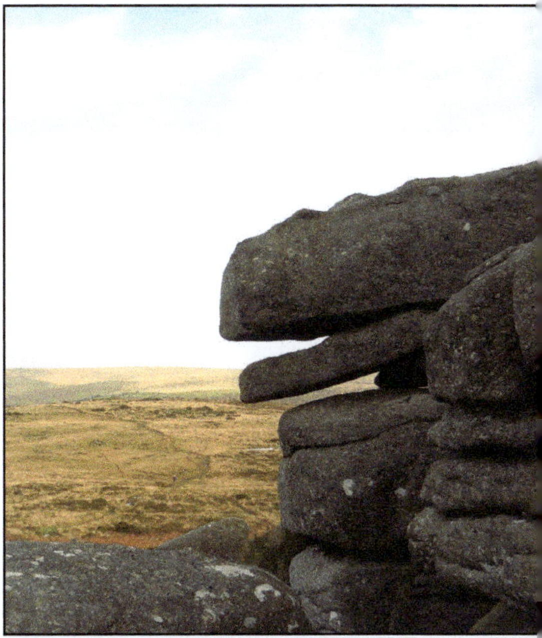

Great mystics and shamans have all shared the experiences of self-deprivation, and physical and mental challenges. When deprived of company and food and over-burdening sensual stimuli, the shaman's senses become more highly attuned; his psychic and animalistic nature comes to the fore. We are mammals, animals with culture, and it does not take much to bring out the beast within. Tales of human survival on desert islands and on mountains is proof of this. After spending time in caves, Kogi shamans emerge in a state of ecstasy and can see 'aluna', the spirit in the landscape. Solitude and silence are two key tools of the mystic; Mohammed, Jesus, Moses, Abraham, and Buddha (as did Merlin and Gandalf!) all spent time away from their people, a practice that is a prerequisite for self-transformation.

In similar spirit, I have been on the moor out of season, in total whiteouts, when I have lost my sense of direction. I found it uplifting walking around a tor in the rain, knowing that I was alone. These moments were essential for my spiritual bonding with the moor. It was as if my hardship and apparent foolhardiness had been acknowledged by some presence other than my own; I had not been alone after all. The veil of mist and drizzle had descended so that the veil concealing otherworldy realms could be lifted. My outer world had suddenly become the inner world of both my imagining and my perceptions. And, moreover, the outer landscape on which I stood possessed an inner dimension that I had not previously been able to perceive. The penny dropped, my heart was opened - the sword was drawn from the granite. I realised that 'imagined' journeys are just as authentic as physical ones; this is the way of the shaman – all experiences are valid. And that there is power in belief and that belief helps create experience. What is 'imagined' can then become a resource, as the world of spirit and physicality, of mind and subconscious (two sides of the same coin) merge and emerge. The landscape is the conduit.

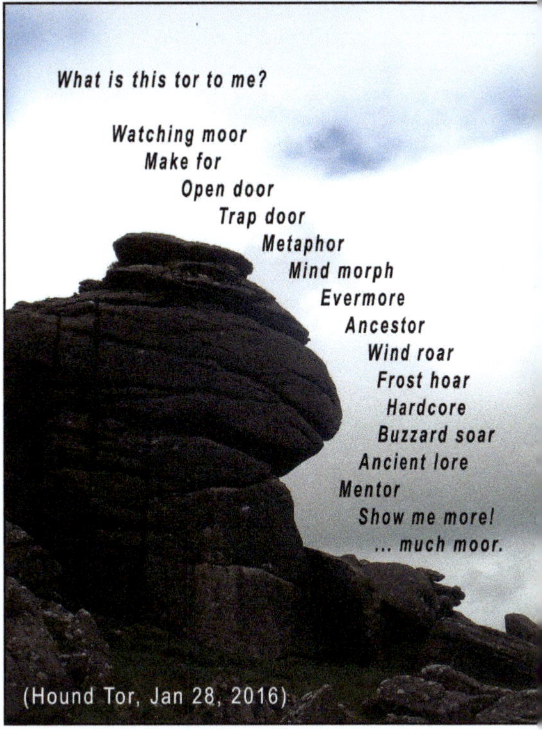

(Hound Tor, Jan 28, 2016)

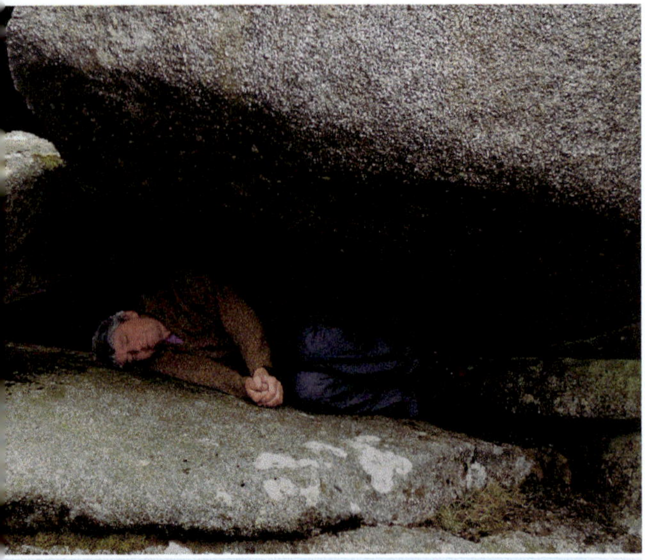

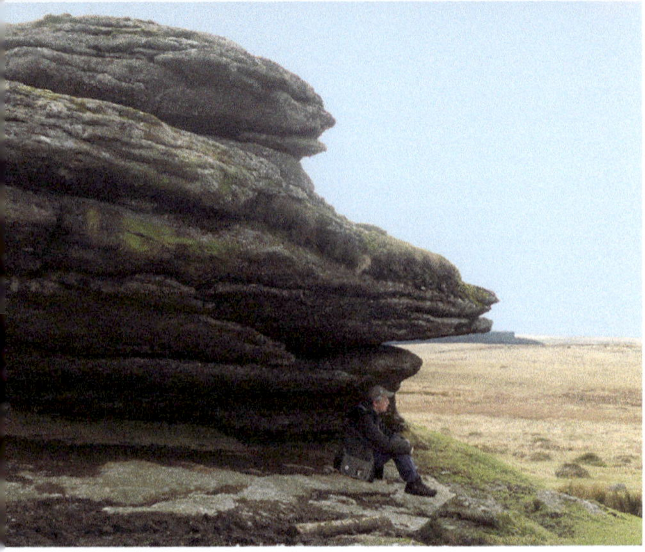

Another aspect of shamanism is 'dream sleep'. This involves a shaman or initiate sleeping at a sacred site, such as a chambered tomb, often through the night and with the aid of hallucinogens. Their dreams are then interpreted, seen as messages from spirit or the ancestors. I think there are good reasons for supposing that this ancient and universal practice was also carried out on Dartmoor. The tors offer plenty of places, such as rock shelters and cavities, where this could have taken place. Even today we are invited to close our eyes, to connect, to meditate, in isolation, on the moor's high places **(left)**.
At Middle Tor (669858), on Chagford Common, a huge simulacra rises from the earth, with a huge overhang beneath, which can receive several people at once **(left, and lower image p 58)**. I sat beneath, looking across at the stone row and longstone on Shovel Down. I closed my eyes and received these words: *'Connect with this ancient granite on which you sit. It will fire your passion and purify your soul. This is as hallowed a place as the longstone and stone row yonder.'* I dwelt on these words, wondering if I had just imagined them, if they were just in my head. I asked myself, 'Is imagination in fact the tuning in to another reality, which is just as 'real' and valid as this world I live in. Is it perhaps *more* real?'

The sanctity of granite

Around the world, granite has been connected with spiritual practice. The Inca temple of Machu Picchu is built on granite. One block of carved granite at the site, known as the Intihuataba, is said to open one's vision into the spirit world when one's forehead is placed against it. Also at Machu Picchu is a tower built of granite masonry, which seems to grow organically from the rock. The granite outcrops at Barker Dam California, USA, are sacred to local Indians. They include remarkable vertical and horizontal fractures, like those we see on Dartmoor.
In the Dragon Project, Paul Devereux and his team found that the inherent radioactivity of granite led to anomalies in stone circles and dolmens made from granite megaliths. The King's and Queen's Chambers of the Great Pyramid, Giza, is of imported granite, which ionises the air; at the apex of many pyramids was a block of polished black granite or iron, called the Benben. These design features may have produced

increased ion levels and so improved crop yields (Burke and Halberg 2005). The huge granite blocks which comprise the Kings chamber of the Great Pyramid were transported some 600 miles north from Aswan. The Egyptians distinguished between limestone, symbolic of the mundane world, and granite, which to them was symbolic of spirit (Devereux 1992). Egyptians called granite 'maat' – *stone of spirit*. The passage grave of Newgrange, Ireland and the amazing monuments around Carnac, Brittany, are mainly of granite.

Ionisation of the atmosphere, and 'earth lights', have been recorded on high granite outcrops (Devereux 1990). Records of light phenomena at granite monuments are numerous, such as at Chun Quiot, Cornwall. Concerning Dartmoor, peculiar light phenomena have been seen, such as at Hexworthy and Drizzlecombe (Devereux 1990). Many more may have gone unreported (see Chapter 17).

Granite is a radioactive rock, if only low levels. Radon meters are installed in Cornish houses to detect the accumulation of this harmful gas given off by granite. The King's Chamber of the Great Pyramid also has high radon levels. The *Dragon Project* found that stone circles containing granite megaliths have exceptionally high levels of gamma radiation. The granitic Cornish fogous, for example, have been found to contain high levels of radiation. It has been suggested that low 'homeopathic' levels of radiation may have healing qualities (Devereux 1989). At Machu Picchu, a Peruvian shaman, Don Eduardo Caleron, gets his students to place their foreheads and spines against specific sacred stones to make a psychic connection. These 'power rocks' are also of granite (Devereux 1992).

On Cox Tor, a hill not composed of granite, I found pieces of red granite on the cairns **(top image, p. 93)**. This must have been imported, underlying the magical properties of granite. Is this another example of transferring 'pieces of place'? (Devereux 2001). Red granite has been selected for many ancient sites and can be found in the locations of some of Britain's 'heart centres', such as at Croft Hill, the centre of England (Biltcliffe and Hoare 2017).

Everything on Dartmoor boils back to granite. I believe that the rocks of the tors, with their overhangs, caverns and rock basins, were perceived as interfaces between this world and the spirit world of the Dreamtime and the ancestors. Perhaps long ago, as psychoactive substances kicked in, the simulacra became animated; these were then no longer just images of spirits, but ***were the spirits***.

Granite soundscapes

One means of opening the door between the worlds is through the properties of sacred sound. Drumming, chanting, singing and the use of wind instruments may have been used in conjunction with the ingestion of hallucinogens. The aim was to achieve 'out-of-body' experiences, as is the case with indigenous cultures today. The experiencing and co-creation of sound is one that has largely been ignored in former research of prehistoric cultures. Archaeology has been deaf to acoustics until very recently. But phenomenologist champion Prof Chris Tilley has argued that we must experience the landscape and rock outcrops with ALL our senses. In an article in *Archaeology Today* (2001), archaeologist Aaron Watson considered that, '... many Neolithic monuments possess unusual acoustic properties that give sound strange, otherworldly aspects. We cannot be sure that acoustic properties were exploited thousands of years ago, but it seems highly likely that they were'. My work inside West Kennet Long Barrow, Wiltshire, has highlighted acoustic hotspots (Knight 2011), and Steve Marshall has ascertained the optimum frequencies of the chambers (Marshall 2016). At Dwarfe Stane, a rock-cut tomb in Scotland, voices were used to achieve a certain resonance and found that the massive blocking stone, and the air itself, seemed to 'shake vigorously'. It was commented that, '... one person can induce many tons of stones to appear to come alive' (Watson & Keating 1999). Some believe that 'journeying' to a drum beat can improve the immune system (Williams 2010).

A research venture, The *Landscape and Perception Project,* coordinated by Paul Devereux, has done more acoustic work on sacred sites. As part of this work, Devereux has demonstrated the acoustic properties of the Bluestones at their outcrop in the Preseli Mountains. When struck by a small 'hammer stone', some rocks issue a clang, like a bell. At Carnac, Brittany, a number of horizontal slabs of granite issued bell-like notes when struck, some of which showed signs of wear. The fallen obelisk at Carnac is also of granite and can be struck to produce sound. 'As the notion that unusual sounds were associated with spirits, the idea of the spirit world existing behind rock faces seems to have been fairly universal' (Devereux 2001). Examples of thin rocks being 'lithostones' or 'ringing rocks' (even 'xylophones') have been recorded in North America, Russia, Africa and Thailand, some dating from the Neolithic (Devereux 2001). Some African cultures say that spirits are released when certain natural rocks are struck. Ken Hedges has identified a 'ringing rock' in Riverside County, California, which is one of a collection of granite boulders 1m across in which a group of hollows or 'cupules' has been worn into its surface, probably by human effort. The rock chimes when hit with a small stone, with a range of tones depending where it is struck. The rock is notable because it is balanced on a giant boulder, with space beneath it, similar to the logan stones of Dartmoor (Hedges 1990).

Another 'ringing rock' is Bell Rock, Orange County, USA, which weighs 7 tons and has more depressions on its surface. There is a historical reference that, '... around this granite boulder native Indians gathered in ancient times' (Hedges 1990). Another record speaks of the Yokuts Indians producing bell-like sounds when they struck, 'thin ledges of rock that extended from the ground'. A 'ringing rock' in North Dakota is known as Writing Rock, and is associated with burial mounds and local rock art. The location is special in terms of its acoustic properties and when struck the stone emits sounds that can be heard for some distance across the valley (Devereux 2001). The stone is composed of white granite!

In ancient China, resonant rocks were known as *bayinshi.* In ancient India, stone instruments were developed into a sophisticated musical technology; at Deccan, stone outcrops covered in petroglyphs give out sounds like a gong or bell when struck (Devereux 2010).

St Govan's Chapel, Dyfed, is a tiny chapel wedged into the living rock in a steep-sided crevice. Jumbled rocks and curious stacked rock formations are close by and there is a healing well. There is a legend that the church bell was stolen by pirates, but that it was retrieved by the locals and hidden beneath a rock, which is supposed to ring with the sound of the bell when struck! (Walker 1987). Is this a memory of ringing rocks at the locality, at an ancient site that was later Christianised?

Sites where echoes can be experienced have also been held as sacred to indigenous people, and are sometimes rock art localities (Devereux 2001); '... an echo is a communication between the shaman and the landscape' (Devereux 2010). I have myself experienced how echoes are produced when one speaks or chants into some of the deep cavities in the Avebury megaliths, and in some tor rock shelters.

The wind can also play tricks around outcrops. Ninaistakis is the sacred mountain of the Blackfoot People, and was used for vision-questing because it 'sings'. Carn Kenidjack, Cornwall, is also known as 'Hooting Carn', on account of the noise the wind makes as it is funneled through the rocks. This distinctive set of rocks has a number of legends attached to it and was culturally significant in prehistoric times; a high

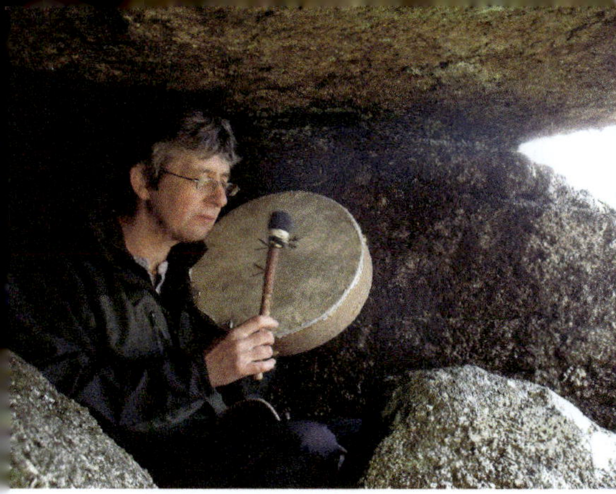

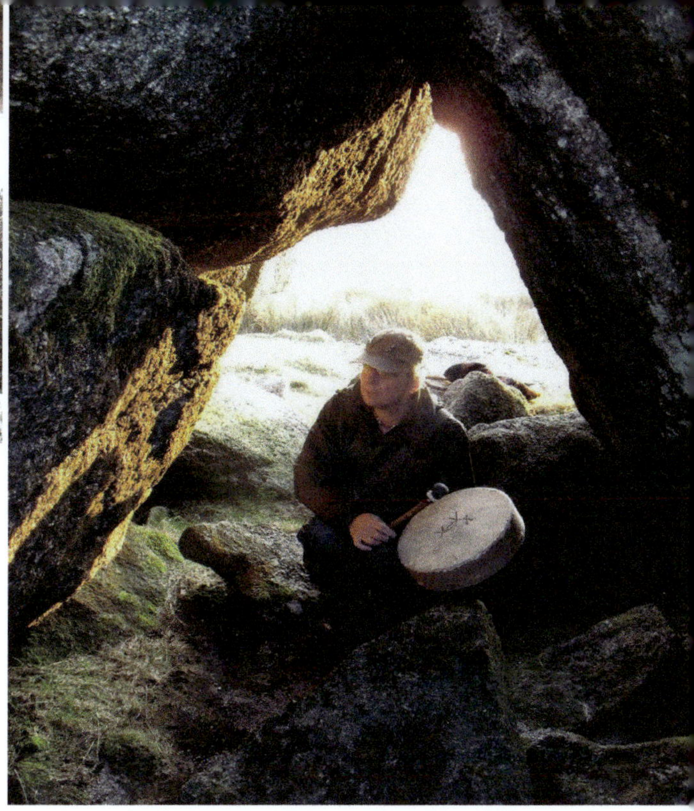

concentration of burial sites can be found in the vicinity. Peculiar sounds are caused by the wind blowing around rock stacks, and through natural cracks and crevices on its summit, much like the tors of Dartmoor (Devereux 2001). Whooping Rock on Easdon Hill (728623) is a logan or rocking stone, so named from the peculiar sounds it used to make when it was moved by strong winds. There are records of these sounds being heard three miles away in stormy weather. Pupers Hill (which includes Pupers Rock - 673674) is said to be a corruption of 'pipers'. Folklore says that two rock piles are musicians turned to stone for making music on the Sabbath. This could be a corruption of memories of peculiar acoustic properties of the rocks, and of people regarding these effects as meaningful.

Dartmoor soundscapes

I believe that prehistoric shamans took advantage of the acoustic qualities of the tors of Dartmoor. It would have been exceptional if they had not! I can personally vouch for the peculiar sound qualities of these high places, whether due to natural or manmade processes. The human voice singing across the landscape, or the gentle beating of a drum, are tools to contact that which is normally beyond reach.

And it is not just drums that can produce sound. Bull roarers are ancient instruments made from a piece of wood, bone or rock attached to a long string, and which are whirled around to produce a low humming sound. They were made famous by the Australian Aborigines. Steve Marshall has used them to great effect at West Kennet Long Barrow; 'Almost every culture in the world has independently invented the bull roarer; it is so ubiquitous that it would be surprising if it was **not** used in Neolithic Britain' (Marshall 2016). Perhaps these were used on Dartmoor back in prehistory; I can imagine the night time silence of the moor being broken by the hum of a bull roarer, swung around by a solitary shaman standing on a granite stack.

On windy days I have heard the wind produce strange sounds as it whistles around outcrops, or when it has blown through voids formed by the collapse of overhangs. In some indigenous cultures it is believed that peculiar sounds are the spirits speaking to people through the rock surfaces. The sound of a waterfall, or even the trickle of water, can be enough to inspire the imagination, or trigger otherworldly experiences.

I have personally experienced the deep and moving resonances whilst positioning myself in some of the narrow crevices, cavities and overhangs of the Dartmoor granitic tor outcrops. Often my voice seems deeper and richer, especially in confined spaces or when I am pressed up against a rock face – the rocks and I both vibrate in unison when I hit the right pitch. Over Tor, near Merrivale is such a place (557753). Here a cavern has been formed by a large collapsed slab of granite. Beneath, the sound is amplified and very resonant **(images p. 79)**. Going off from this overhang are even more confined spaces, where one is forced to curl up in a womb-like space, with legs in a foetal position. Chanting and drumming here is very powerful.

Similar acoustic resonances were achieved inside the 'dolmen' on Hawk's Tor **(images p. 112-4)** and at Showery Tor, Cornwall **(left),** which also affords a granite overhang with acoustic properties. Perhaps this is one of the effects sought in the granitic chambers at Newgrange, the Great Pyramid, and other Neolithic sites. Special sound effects have been experienced at *natural* places for millennia.

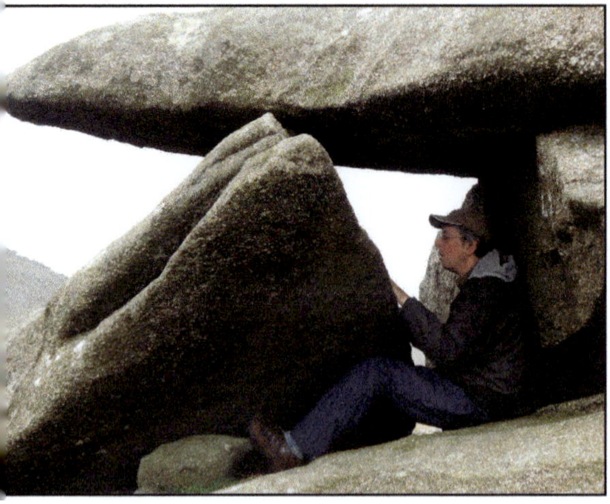

Echoes can also be produced if the human voice is directed towards an appropriate rock formation, such as under an overhanging ledge. It is also interesting that in 2010, Neil Mortimer and Mark Pilkington experienced echoes at the Grey Wethers stone circles, which is composed of granite megaliths (Mortimer & Pilkington 2011).

I think more work remains to be done on striking thin slivers or overhangs of granite, to see if they resonate sound, like elsewhere. I have not yet found one that sounds like the Preseli 'bells', but when I have struck some rocks with another piece of granite, I have experienced echoes and loud 'thuds', which were also dramatic.

Sometimes it has been the *lack of sound* that has been powerful for me. I was once on Pew Tor (west of the Merrivale Stone Row), in a total white-out; the mist had descended, consuming my world. I wrote the following: 'Immersing my body in the mist is as a rare occasion. Visual distractions are removed. All sounds muffled, even my own footsteps. There is no birdsong, or even the whisper of the wind. Yet I am not alone'. It was an environment that was conducive to conversing with 'something', be it only myself. My senses were heightening and sharpened – I was metaphorically and literally standing 'on the edge'. Sometimes we only appreciate the sanctity of sound through the sanctity of silence. I was told the following by the spirit of the place: *'It is important to bring other people to this place. To spread the word. To experience all that I am, and all that you are. Let the land open your mind and heart to what is really going on, not what you have been taught by those with closed minds'.*

Tors as landscape foci

The term *ritual landscapes* is used for extended areas of monuments, Avebury, Stonehenge and the Boyne Valley being excellent examples. But, in terms of the wealth and spread of prehistoric monuments, is not the whole of Dartmoor a ritual landscape? Dartmoor's wealth of archaeology over virtually the entire moor provides what really is an incredible connection to our distant ancestors. On Exmoor it is the valleys and the coombes that tell you where you are, whereas on Dartmoor, and

Bodmin Moor for that matter, it is the tors that orientate, providing points of reference. So it was in ancient times. We should not consider ancient monuments and tors in isolation, for the prehistoric shaman would not have embraced the concept of unconnected landscape features. Everything interacts with everything else in the shaman's universe, and by extension sacred sites are also interconnected. A profound interrelationship was present between a ritual monument and its surrounding landscape, a symbiosis that must have been particularly potent regarding the tors; 'Whether enclosed or not, it would seem that the tors had long been significant places within the landscape' (Davies 2010).

The tors were landscape markers, and possibly named, as far back as the Mesolithic. No two tors are alike, and with practice they would have been readily identified, as myths and names were birthed. When they named an outcrop, or a feature on it, there was probably a myth related to it or, sooner or later, would have had. The myth is then perpetuated by a physical presence on the landscape; the natural and the mythological are inseparable. Speaking of the granite tors of Bodmin in the Mesolithic, Chris Tilley concluded, 'The tors were, in effect, non-domesticated 'megaliths', or stone monuments, sculptured by the elements and imbued with cultural significance in the Mesolithic imagination' (Tilley 2010).

Back in the 19th century, a certain Mr A Lewis undertook a detailed survey of the stone circles of Bodmin Moor, and came to the conclusion that, '... each of these circles was placed on the exact spot that it occupies, because this spot was in a certain direction from the hills I have mentioned' (Lewis 1895-8).

In SW Wales, Prof Chris Tilley noted how it was the hills and rock outcrops that were the dominant focal points on the land, not the monuments (Tilley 1994). He also pointed out the high places and outcrops determine where to expect to find the manmade sacred sites. He notes how Carn Ingli, a prominent outcrop, is visible from several dolmens, whereas the monuments themselves are not intervisible from each other. Tilley also suggests that dolmens were not burial sites at all, but rather symbolic references and meeting points on paths of movement, drawing attention to landscape features of local clan mythology (Tilley 1994). He noted how some Neolithic sites were located below prominent tors, and also that most Bodmin stone circles were within sight of at least four tors, with sometimes seven. In nearly all Bodmin Moor stone circles the closest tors to the circles were to the north, in eleven of thirteen cases. In many traditions, north is the direction of earth, gestation, dreaming and the ancestors. The positioning of circles takes account of a few metres, enabling extra tors to be visible (Tilley 2010). I have found this to be evident on Dartmoor, as I will highlight later. The cultural importance of tors is also confirmed by the location of settlements, which often take the numbers of tors visible into consideration. For instance, there are twenty settlements visible from Gutter Tor, and fourteen from Hen Tor (Klemen 2015). The erection of longstones may have also referenced places that were culturally important, such as the tors; this was found to be the case in the relationship between menhirs and granite outcrops in Brittany (Tilley 2014).

Haytor Rocks is an excellent example of a landscape focus. This massive exposure of granite rises above the moor east of Widecombe-in-the-Moor. It is said that on clear days the tor is visible from up to 40 miles away. It is a popular tourist and walking destination, and its sheer faces challenge rock-climbers. Much of the tor is of red granite, which is found at some of the 'heart centres' of Britain (Biltcliffe and Hoare 2017). Several simulacra can be found on the two main outcrops, and I have already described a triangular stone at the tor **(image p. 62)**. On my many walks across the moor I noticed how Haytor's characteristic double, twinned, summit was visible from certain monuments, and that these were sometimes several miles away. This is

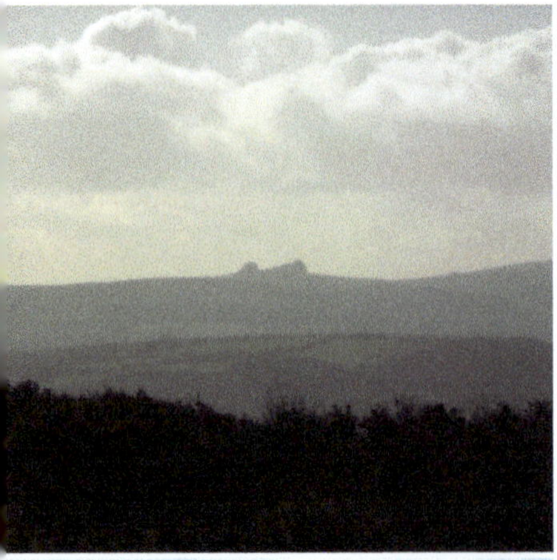

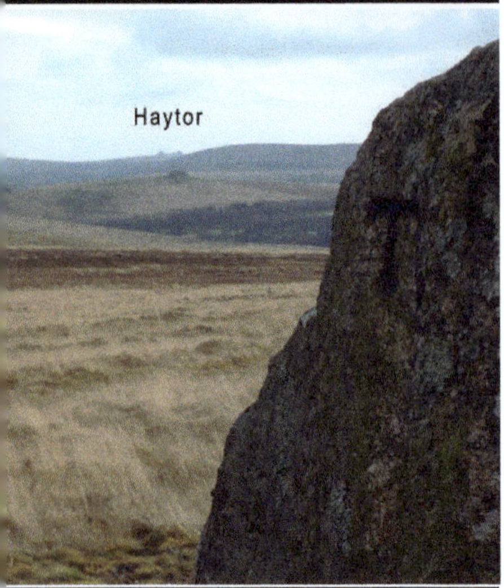

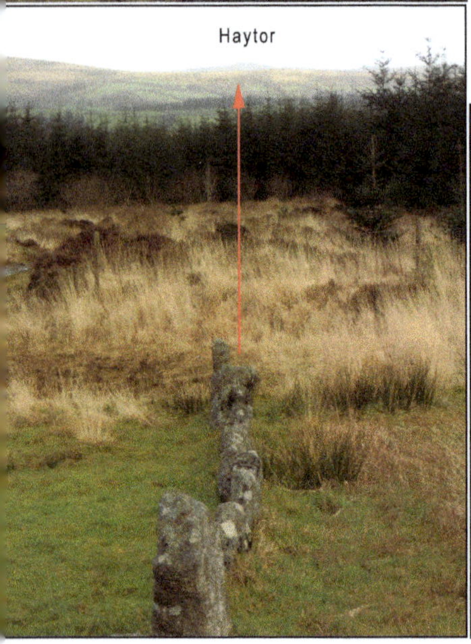

interesting, considering that at 457m the tor is nowhere near the moor's highest peak; plus it nestles near the SE corner of Dartmoor, not in a central location. Haytor shows few signs that its twinned summits were encultured. Prof Chris Tilley suggests, '... the most significant hills in the landscape were *too* spiritually powerful to have any monuments located on their summits in the Bronze Age' (Tilley 2010).

I have already described how twin-peaked hills are sacred around the world (p. 24-5). Haytor's distinctive twin peaks are locally visually dominant. However, it was only when I started walking to monuments around the moor that I realised that several were positioned to take account of the intervisibility of Haytor. Sometimes this visibility was only possible from the monuments themselves, not from nearby. I will list some here.

The first is the view **(top)** of Haytor from the stone circle on Mardon Down (767872), NE of Moretonhampstead. The tor is not visible until one approaches the stone circle, from where it straddles the skyline. Although other tors are visible, it is the double summit of Haytor that draws the eye. As I left the circle and walked north towards Giant's Grave, I noted that the tor disappeared from view.

Next is the view of Haytor from the White Moor Stone (634895), over 11 miles distant. From here **(left)** the tor is only visible due to a dip in the intervening skyline! Haytor is also the focus of the short row of stones leading from the cist on Lakehead Hill (644776), which clearly align with it **(lower left)**. The last example is from the cairn at the summit of Hameldown Tor (703806). Haytor becomes visible **(lower right)** as one approaches the cairn from the Grimspound settlement.

Other good places from which to see Haytor's double

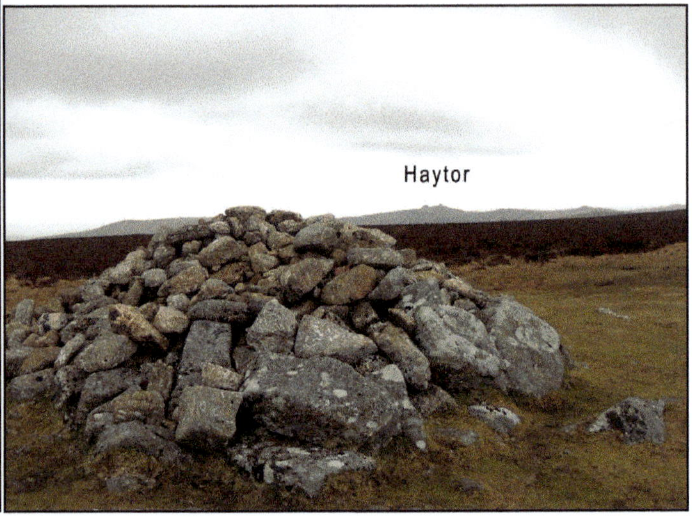

peaks as a skyline feature is from Figgie Daniel, Easdon Hill, and the triple stone row below Cosdon Beacon (at the north end of the moor), the latter of which I illustrate **(image p. 145).** Haytor is also visible from several tors that have rock basins. These include Bellever Tor, Cobblestone Tor, Kestor, Bag Tor, Rippon Tor and Gidleigh Tor. Although these are natural, the shamans regarded such places to be particularly potent - a combination of the sacred twin peaks and water-bearing granite. To complement Haytor, I have noted how Sharpitor and Leather Tor appear as a twinned hill, due to line-of-sight, when viewed from Yellowmead **(images p. 188 & 189)**.
These examples serve to illustrate how landscape features miles distant were of relevance to our ancestors. Speaking of the Butterdon ridge complex of monuments, Peter Klemen remarks that, 'This whole area, compared to the NE and NW areas of southern Dartmoor, is noticeably lacking in any major tors. However, they still form important focal areas for the surrounding archaeology' (Klemen 2015). As I have walked along ridges and through valleys, different tors have come into view and then ceased to be visible. The landscape is constantly changing and, as Klemen and Tilley observed, it is the tors, not the monuments, that are often the visual foci, drawing to them our eyes, our feet, and our minds. Perhaps each Dartmoor tor, as with hills and outcrops around the world, was endowed with a different mythology; as the landscape was walked, so too the myths of Dartmoor's prehistoric people unfolded before them. The tors embodied and personified the Dreamtime.
I shall return to the concept of tors as landscape foci when I look at the locations of more monuments in detail later. I shall also return to the tors because of their rock basins, propped stones, and logan stones. Chapter 12 will look at the relationship between some stone rows and tors, and in Chapter 13 I will demonstrate how tors are integral elements of the sacred landscape around Merrivale.

The case for clitter

'The clutter of clitter is like the litter in my mind'. (P Knight, Dartmoor notes)

Clitter is an evocative Cornish term to describe boulder and stone spreads found down slope of tors and granite hills of SW England, although the term has now been applied to similar deposits in other areas of the world. It is now assumed that clitter formed following the large-scale frost-shattering and the subsequent weathering and downhill movement of material during periglaciation. From a cultural perspective, in terms of human interaction, the clitter has lain where it is now since at least the Mesolithic, with little or no natural movement (Bender et al 2007).
These boulders are strewn around Dartmoor, the greatest concentrations of which are around or below the tor outcrops. But we need to look at clitter in terms of it having potency unto itself, as being meaningful in ancient times: 'Since the first human use and encounter with the granite uplands of Cornwall, we can plausibly infer that the tors had enormous cultural significance as landmarks, orientation points, places invested with stories, myth and meaning... but what of clitter? Clitter does not carry the same kind of contemporary cultural baggage as the tors' (Bender et al 1999). Little work has been done on the cultural modification of clitter spreads. Which rocks are human-placed and which are in situ? 'Archaeologists have paid little attention to clitter because it was regarded as natural rather than cultural, seeing it as nothing more than a source of building stone in prehistory' (Tilley 1995). However, some clitter may have been regarded as sacred even if left in situ, whilst others were 'stood up' when seen as significant. Clitter expressing unusual shapes were incorporated into hut circles, whilst several settlements were built where no effort was made to remove 'unused' clitter

from between the dwellings. As I have approached many tors the clutter of the clitter spreads has presented marked obstructions to my progress, metaphors for the obstacles in our lives. After the steady rhythmic meditative walking of open moorland, the clitter presents different experiences: the clitter and outcrops now require the sinuous weaving through and over obstacles, jumping or stepping up and then down, zigzagging like a serpent around boulders. I now need to concentrate on every step. I am slowed down. As a result I start to see simulacra, phallic and triangular stones, many lying prone, others 'uprighted'.

Through regular engagement with these natural unmoved stones, prehistoric people may have been emotionally attached to them. Some archaeologists concur: 'When one first starts to look hard at clitter the eyes hurt, the stones begin to swirl like looking at an Escher print. A pattern is no sooner seen than it is lost, as the stones appear to be an ever changing kaleidoscope of forms. Such effects would be ideal in inducing trance-like states, important in shamanistic experiences and the capacity to mediate between worlds' (Bender et al 1999).

Work by archaeologists at Leskernick, a prehistoric hilltop settlement in Cornwall, revealed the spiritual and cultural importance of clitter, in that these granite stones were held to be special. Some stones were clearly more important than others, although it is not always possible to tell which ones were which! Profs Bender, Hamilton and Tilley summarise thus: 'We have a hunch or feeling that they [clitter] were important because of their size, shape and location along pathways... It is born out of our own practice and engagement with the stones leading to a growing awareness of their surfaces, angles, layouts, shapes, textures... Perhaps this contemporary experience of the stones meshes with the way the stones were experienced in the Bronze Age (Bender et al 1999). And they later conclude that, ...we have good reason to think that the clitter, rather than being left untouched as 'natural' forms, has been culturally transformed' (Bender et al 2007).

The inhabitants of Leskernick enhanced the significance of clitter boulders where they lived, by incorporating them into their dwellings; by joining up enclosure walls to areas of clitter and rock outcrops; by encasing boulders with uprights and surrounding them with small stones at their bases; and by clearing away stones from around important rocks (Bender et al 1999 & 2007). I have found the same to be the case on Dartmoor at several places. In fact there are close similarities between the use of clitter on Bodmin and Dartmoor. This is hardly surprising, as the edges of the two moors are only about 10 miles apart, and both are pre-dominantly granite.

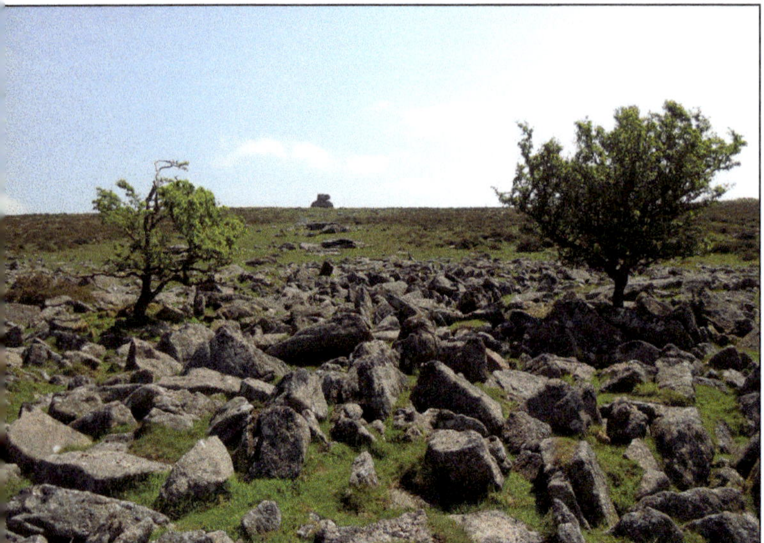

Here is a typical clitter field, dominated by Hangershell Rock on the skyline **(left)**. A hut circle nestles in the clitter field, and two hawthorns rise tenaciously from earth and rock.

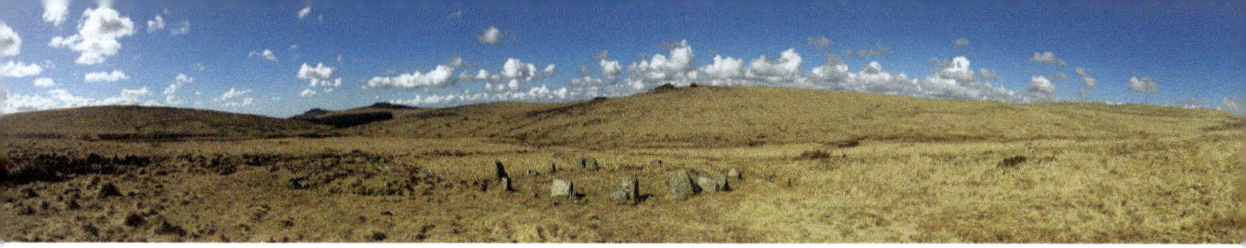

8. Enculturing of the Tors

'Man does not have the only memory. The stones remember.' (Hopi)

Enculturing is a term used by archaeologists to describe natural places, such as the tors of Dartmoor for instance, that have been embellished or enhanced with monuments, rock art or votive offerings. Modern thought is that people enhanced natural sites to 'stake a claim' on a location or landscape, or sought to improve or modify the qualities already present, or to honour deity, spirit of place or the ancestors. Perhaps this was in part to secure their future, as they associated themselves with *permanent* landscape features: 'Prehistoric people could have imitated these impressive and durable features of the landscape in their own constructions, in which case they may have sought to give their monuments an impression of age and permanence' (Bradley 2000).

Several archaeological investigations on the moors of SW England have concentrated on the enculturing of the landscape. However, the problem apparent in these studies has been the frequent inability to distinguish between culturally affected features and those resulting purely from geological processes, such as weathering. Is a pile of rocks at the foot of a vertical rock face the remains of a denuded cairn or merely scree, or the product of erosion?

The enculturing of high places by enhancement has parallels across the world, such as at Delphi and the Minoan peak sanctuaries. The Minoans regarded imposing natural places as sacred long before the erection of any temples. The peak sanctuary at Jouktas, Greece, was constructed around a natural rock fissure, which is where offerings at an altar were excavated (Bradley 2000). At Filitosa, Corsica, a megalithic site was constructed on a rocky spur. At the western end stands the Monument Ouest, a great 6m high outcrop of rock around which has been constructed a series of chambers, the stones of which are still piled up against the natural rock (Service and Bradbury 1993).

Although little work has been done on Dartmoor dealing specifically with enculturing, examples elsewhere in the UK have been studied. The Neolithic settlement at Rinyo, Orkney, was built up against a stone outcrop on the landward side of Faraclett Head. Because water would flow down the face when it rained, a complex system of drains was built to channel the water away from the houses. This could all have been alleviated if the houses had been built just a few metres away from the foot of the cliff face (Garnham 2004). Clearly it was important to connect with the living rock, to be in direct contact with it, even though it required more effort to do so.

At Kynance Gate, Cornwall, a prominent natural outcrop had been the focus of Neolithic offerings, and later became the focus of a Bronze Age settlement: 'It was as if people wanted their entire existence to revolve around this outcrop – a portal, perhaps, to the Otherworld' (Williams 2010). Evidence from Roche Rock, Cornwall, suggests

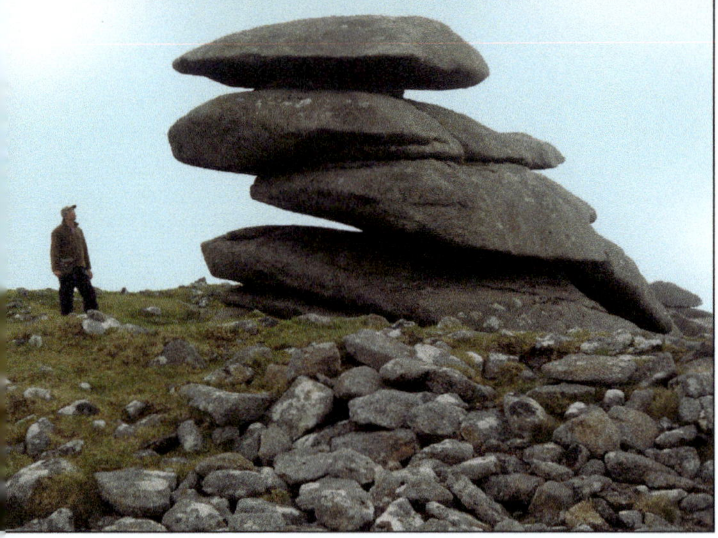

that commemorative offerings were made at some tors (Davies 2010). I recently visited the impressive Showery Tor simulacrum on Bodmin Moor **(left)**. All around the granite stack are the remains of what was once a huge cairn (seen in the foreground). At Carn Brae, Cornwall, the innermost enclosure surrounds a huge granite outcrop, leaving little room for monuments. The stone walls of the enclosures run from one outcrop to another. The enclosure has *monumentalised* some rock outcrops that resemble megaliths and megalithic tombs, incorporating these natural yet curious features into the walls. On Dartmoor there is similar evidence at White Tor and Dewerstone (see below). The Carn Brae settlement gathered around a huge granite simulacrum known as the Carn Brae Giant (Devereux 2013). Prof Chris Tilley adds that, '…on Bodmin Moor there can be no doubt that Neolithic people embellished several natural rocky outcrops, probably because of the strange appearance of the landforms' (Tilley 1996). The Dartmoor tors were encultured in this way. The tors were seen as ancestral monuments, erected by the ancestors or the beings of creation myths. To add to these places was to align oneself with the spirit world.

It is not just large tor outcrops that were encultured. At Leskernick, also in Cornwall, the Bronze Age settlement was subject to excavation: 'Ten metres to the south of this house [a hut circle] is a large natural rock pile. It looks just like a small tor, has uprights placed around it, a cleared area in front of it, and may have an associated offering platform. We suggest that this is an important shrine within the settlement area and the occupants of house 3 were probably closely associated with its guardianship. The people of Leskernick had created, within their settlement, a tiny replica of the great tors' (Bender et al 1999). I have found that people were also attracted to small outcrops on Dartmoor, as I shall soon demonstrate.

Enhancement of Dartmoor tors – Neolithic

'For the people of an old culture, all their mutually owned territory holds numinous life and spirit' (Snyder 1990).

If certain tors were already important places in the Mesolithic, then it can be assumed that there was journeying to them from the lowlands on a regular basis. By later monumentalising these routes, with tombs and megaliths, the people were referring back to previous journeys to the highlands. It has been suggested that some of the moor's stone rows may be Neolithic in origin, a subject I shall return to later. With the Neolithic impulse to erect stone monuments, people were also referencing the spiritual Dreamtime myths of the high tors (Davies 2010).

The Neolithic of Dartmoor is generally approached with reference to its long barrows and chambered tombs. These include Spinster's Rock and Corringdon Ball **(images p. 14)**, Gidleigh and Cuckoo Ball. This is a meagre number considering the extent of Dartmoor. They occupy relatively lower ground, suggesting that they are associated with settlements in the lowlands. However, there are rock formations, such as propped stones and the natural 'dolmen', as at Hawks Tor, which look artificial. It is not beyond the realms of plausibility that the people of the earlier Neolithic might have thought these fantastical natural features as constructions created long ago by the Dreamtime creators of the world. Indeed, some of the rock outcrops of the tors have a visual similarity to Early Neolithic dolmens. On my recent trip to Rough Tor, Bodmin, it was noted how two deep, roofed gullies resemble the passages of Neolithic chambered tombs **(right)**. Two of these gullies are up to 15m long, are acoustically resonant, and align to Condolden Barrow on the skyline. I have found similar examples on Dartmoor. Were natural formations like this used for ritual, and the inspiration to build passage graves?

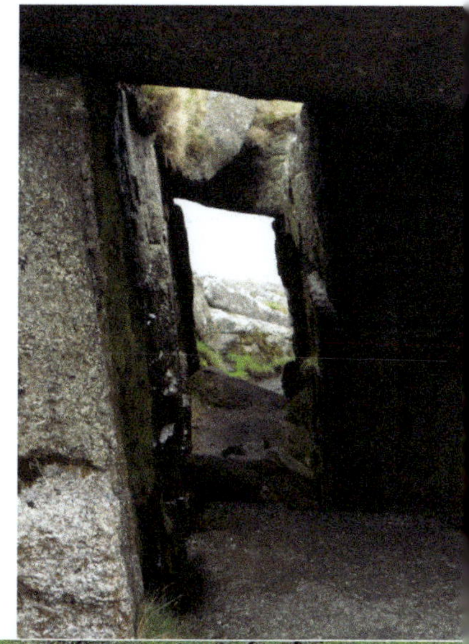

Despite the paucity of Neolithic monuments on Dartmoor, there are impressive enclosures on White Tor (or Whittor) and Dewerstone. These are larger than their Bodmin equivalents, and afford views of Cornwall. They are considered to be seasonal gathering places, rather than settlements, due to the scarcity of domestic finds (Newman 2011); were they the gorsedds of their day? They crown tors that stand on obvious routes up to the high moors. Marking the visible edge of the granite when following the rivers upstream, they were on the boundary between the lowlands and high moor (Davies 2010). Both sites continued to be visited in the Bronze Age, with the building of cairns, and local reaves focus on White Tor.

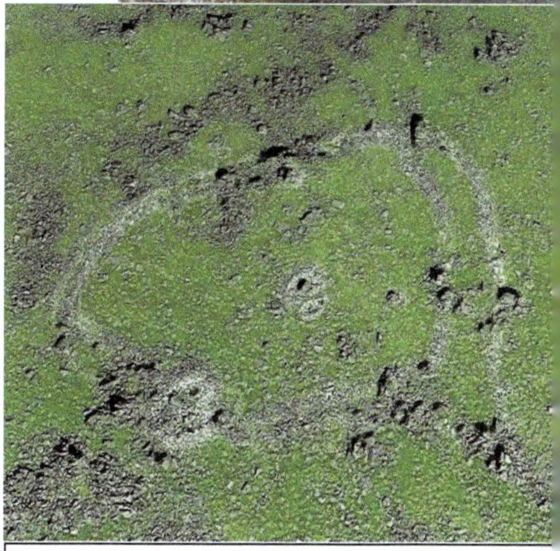

White Tor (c. 543786) rises north of Merrivale, east of Peter Tavy. Several springs arise from its base and feed the River Tavy and Colly Brook. The hill is not of granite, but a dark metamorphic rock, the kind found in many of the river beds lower downstream around the moor. I visited the tor when winter was bearing its teeth on a cold and wet day in February 2016. The brooding presence of the tor towered above as I ascended via one of the Bronze Age reaves. On arrival at the summit, it was clear that rock outcrops were the focus of the, now degraded, encircling Neolithic walls **(image p. 14)**. In this Google Earth image **(centre)**, these lines of rubble can be seen connecting the rock outcrops (the latter revealed by their shadows): 'Closely spaced parallel rubble walls define the edge of the plateau, forming a circuit, and take advantage of several prominent rock outcrops, which have been incorporated' (Newman 2011). Two enormous cairns were built on top of the ramparts, incorporating both outcrop and Neolithic rubble **(right)**. There is no evidence that these walls were defensive in purpose, or that this was a settlement.

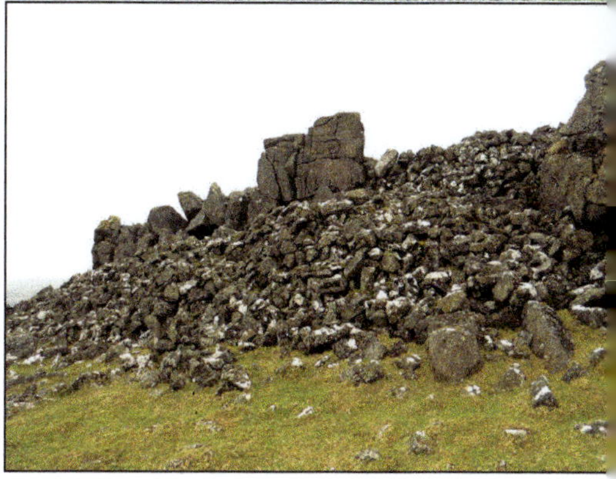

No attempt was made to clear the clitter from inside the enclosure. Clearly these were ceremonial, ritual places of great symbolic relevance; up until this time there were no enclosed spaces on the open moor, so this was culturally groundbreaking.

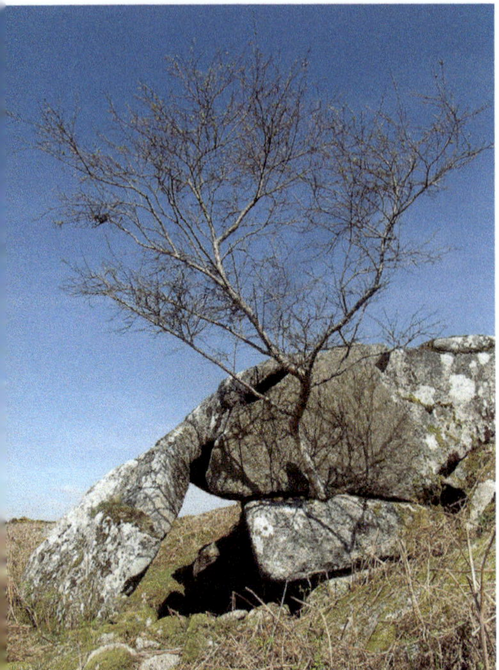

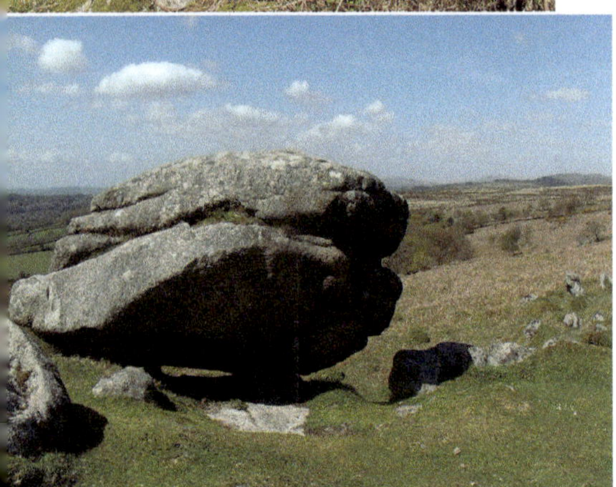

Dewerstone, NE of Plymouth (c. 538640), is an inspiring Neolithic site, constructed directly above a precipitous valley at the convergence of the River Plym and the Meavy. This site affords commanding views; from this lofty spur there are vistas of Cornwall, South Devon and the Plym Estuary. This site mirrors the Carreg Siglo rocking stone, Wales, a site of bardic congresses, which stands at the convergence of the Taf and the Rhondda (Cope 1998). At Dewerstone, double stone walls enclose the neck of a spur with an inner rectangular enclosure that houses a hut circle. There is an internal clitter spread and, as at White Tor, I found that the walls focus on, and incorporate, rocky outcrops. The walls change direction at two of these crags. On my visit to the site on a sunny day in May 2016 I traced the low remnants of the surviving wall rubble, and in doing so some previously unrecorded features of significance were revealed.

At the NW corner, where an outcrop signals a change in the direction of the Neolithic walls, a west-facing simulacrum is evident **(left)**, displaying a stern-looking eye. From its thin mouth protrudes a Silver Birch, much like a country yokel with a stalk of hay sticking out of the corner of his mouth! And against the nose of the simulacrum was propped a granite slab, positioned as to create a cavity beneath. Whether this neat fit was by human design, or was regarded as being created by ancestral means, it may once have been of spiritual significance. Were the Neolithic people focusing their walls on these features?

Further along the walls, on the west side, another rock outcrop can be found, this time within a small copse of trees. To my amazement, a megalith, for it *is* a standing stone, is stood on top of the outcrop. On the west surface of this stone is a rock basin! This is a classic example of the enculturing of a natural outcrop with a standing stone which itself had been selected because it displayed a sacred rock basin **(image p. 135)**. It is not known if the stone was erected in the Neolithic, or was a later Bronze Age addition.

More was to come at Dewerstone. At the south end of the site, near the largest and highest outcrop, stands a huge, 2m high logan stone **(above, lower image)**, pivoted on a small base, just where the inner enclosure meets the summit; the walls were aligned with this boulder (they can be seen to the right). An intriguing, small manmade hollow sits on its top surface. And the summit itself has the appearance of an area where meetings of elders took place, or around which the community gathered to do business. Horizontal laminated surfaces invite one to sit and gaze back over the whole site, and to the distant tors and sea beyond.

Although I could find no special features at the outcrop in the NE corner of the site, it was from there that I could most readily hear the sounds of the river rushing by below – heard and yet unseen. Dewerstone speaks of ceremony rather than occupation, and is one of the finest examples of a Neolithic enclosure in England.

Enhancement of Dartmoor tors – Bronze Age

'Cairns acted as cultural markers in a spiritual passage to the roof of the world.'
(Bender et al 2007)

It was during the Bronze Age that Man left his most notable evidence of his presence on Dartmoor. As well as the iconic stone rows, megaliths and stone circles, this period is significant for the large scale enculturing of tors, in the form of cairns: 'This was no longer a landscape through which one could move without being constantly reminded of its symbolic potency' (Tilley 2010). Unlike the tumuli or round barrows of chalk regions, such as in Dorset and Wiltshire, on Dartmoor the soils are thin and the bedrock much harder, resulting in cairns being the chief means of burial.

On Orkney, it has been noted how chambered cairns are sited to overlook, as well as being seen from, particular areas (Garnham 2004), and that their entrances look out across the land which had been farmed by the interred. Building a cairn not only encultures a tor but also lays claim to the land around it, and its resources; the dead remain relevant to the living. Did these tor cairns literally draw up the latent power of the rock beneath, which is ultimately the foundation of all life on the land. Like the rock outcrops around which they were often piled, the cairns spoke of eternity in terms of people's survival, of their right to be there. Prof Trevor Garnham: 'It looks as if the burial cairns were less tombs than some kind of house for the dead, containing, controlling and storing the particular form of spirit energy or force associated with the bones' (Garnham 2004).

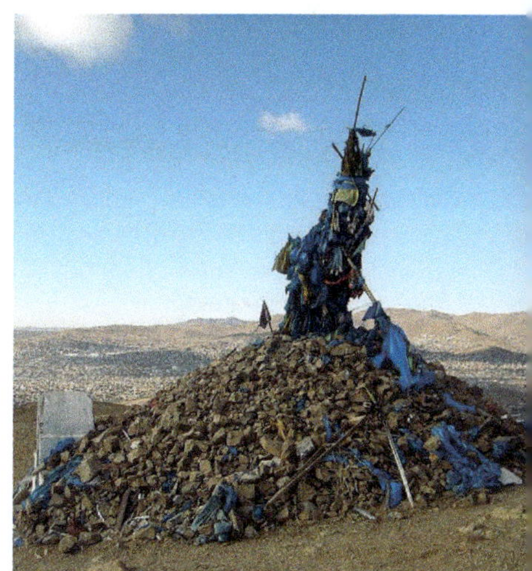

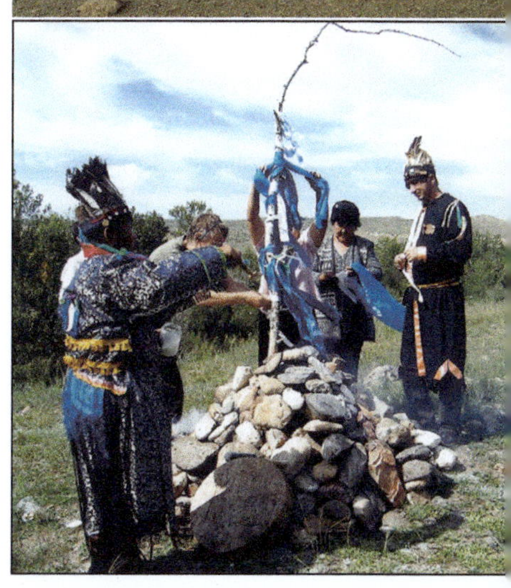

The songlines of the Australian Aborigines are sometimes marked by cairns. The African Bushmen and the Hottentots erect cairns of stone at sacred sites. The Mongolian shamans of today perpetuate an ancient tradition of building cairns, called *oovos*, for the worship of high places and the sky spirits **(right)**. There are hundreds across the country and they are decorated with blue fabric. People gather at these sites today for spiritual purposes, including the offering of votive objects **(right)**. Back in prehistory, were the cairns of Dartmoor similarly embellished with votive offerings and symbols of power?

There is a class of cairns known as *'prestige cairns'*, those with a diameter of more than 20m. These tend to be located at highly visible places and are in locations that are usually away from any settlement, and yet are intervisible from them and other nearby monuments. Concerning the larger cairns of Bodmin, Prof Tilley concluded that burial does not seem to have been their primary function, but were, '... an element of a more extensive series of ceremonial rites' (Tilley 2010). At some burials, white quartz was left as offerings, perhaps as metaphors for the 'bones' of the deceased and of the land itself. These were laid to rest with the dead, confirming their close relationship to land, even in death.

That cairns can be constructed to surround particular tors or rock outcrops was noted by Grinsell (1978) and Turner (1990), as well as recently on Bodmin Moor (Bender et al 2007). These are generally known as 'tor cairns' .The Bronze Age enhancement of tors can hardly be described as subtle. People displayed an 'in your face' claim to the land, by associating themselves with the spirit of place; it was, after all, *their* ancestors that were interred on the tors. However, evidence of burial is often lacking, and excavations of twenty five cairns opened up on Bodmin since 1939 show only 48% were ever used for funerary purposes, evidenced from cists, urns or skeletal fragments that have survived the acidic soils (Tilly 2010).

The relatively small amount of stone required in building Bronze Age cairns (and stone circles), compared to the massive stone monuments of Neolithic, could be explained by people making more intimate and subtle references to landscape, at natural, ancestral places, such as tors, enhancing what was already there. After all, tors had always been ancestral reference points - the time had now come to enculture them. Concerning Leskernick, on Bodmin Moor, 'Nearly every one of the encircling hills has a large cairn or cairns on their summit. In some cases the cairns encircle, build upon, or incorporate rock stacks and tors. In other cases, the cairns break the smooth contours of the hills to create, in effect, artificial tors' (Bender et al 1999 & 2007). On Bodmin Moor there are at least twenty one such tor cairns, where natural rocky outcrops are the foci, some of which are completely encircled by cairn rubble. Others completely envelope large boulders, known as grounders, rendering them invisible. My research shows that this practice was equally prevalent on Dartmoor.

Over time, the cairns may have become the primal permanent landscape focal points, replacing the role previously held by the tor outcrops themselves, '...a cultural triumph over the sleeping powers of the rocks' (Tilley 2010). Bronze Age Man was now feeling he was in control of all he surveyed.

In many ancient cultures, ancestral sites were often gathering places for specific ceremony, ritual and perhaps celebratory feasting, and yet were avoided by people at other times. This is similar to how churches usually only have services on Sunday. Prof Chris Tilley has argued that access to tors, which were sacred places in every sense of the word, became more and more restricted during the Bronze Age. These were controlled by elites who maintained their power through their deeper, mystical knowledge of the landscape (Tilley 1996). In Aboriginal Dreamtime landscapes there are places where unauthorized access is forbidden, such as at certain rock art sites, which are visited only by elders. Giant Rock, a huge boulder in the Joshua Tree area of California, is held to be sacred by Native Americans, so sacred in fact that only the chief is allowed to go near it. Everyone else has to wait nearly a mile away while the Chief communed with the spirits of the *'Rock People'*, who had prophesied that, '... the Mother would split open and a new era would be revealed'.

I believe the encultured tors of Dartmoor were such places, deemed to be high, even dangerous, places where ancestral spirits dwelt in their cairns. An embargo of movement regarding certain Dartmoor tors would further add to their mystique. This exclusion defined boundaries between the realms of Spirit, where, '... intelligent nature can behave with all its wild unpredictability' (Kane 1998), and the land over which Man at least had some control. The boundaries of these two worlds are liminal portals, places of exchange, conduits between people and spirit. Embargos of the tors also acted as a means to prevent 'contamination' between worlds, as these places were seen as energetically permeable. Only totem animals and spirits, and of course the shaman (using knowledge, skill and ritual) were capable of passing from one to the other. Many myths warn against excessive curiosity, and how this can lead to dire consequences. Mythologising the tors with layers of power and warnings ensured that the curious and unprotected were kept at bay. I have argued that this was also true of chambered tombs, where only shamans and initiates would enter the inner sanctum of the ancestors (Knight 2011).

In a study of Drizzlecombe and Butterdon Hill, Peter Klemen notes that in both areas tor cairns are clearly the visible focal points on all the highest summits. They are markers, a series of intervisible locales across the moor. A distant rounded, featureless hill, that may not have attracted one's attention or have meaning, becomes culturally important by the placement of a large cairn (Klemen 2015).

Tilly found fifteen cairns on Bodmin Moor where rocky outcrops or boulders were the focus of the cairn builders, such as at Rough Tor, Brown Willy and Tolborough Tor, as well as the Watch Croft barrow, West Penwith. The cairn at Watch Croft was built around the only local rock basin **(drawing, p. 125)**. At Carn Downs, near Men-an-Tol, one of the stacks has five rock basins on its upper surface, and around this was built a cairn. Tilley concluded, 'There is a clear relationship between siting of the cairns in relation to 'chambers', rock stacks, fissures and solution basins' (Tilley 2010). I shall look in detail at the sanctity of rock basins later.

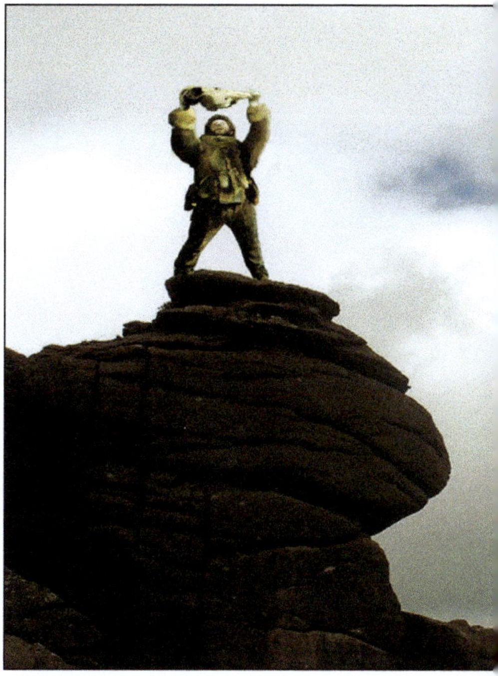

Moses, Jesus, and many saints, went to deserted high places to contact their higher power. During the Bronze Age, the shamans spent time alone on the cairns of the forbidden tors. On their return they may have been greeted by waiting clan members, who, as the wise one spoke, hung on their every word. Perhaps the shaman held aloft a bull's skull, which he had used for divination **(right)**. Today, we are removed from contact with our ancestors, whereas on Dartmoor they were all around, their cairns clearly visible, to be approached by shamans through drumming, ritual and trance dance: 'The earth and its living soul is the source of the shaman's power, not the hallucinogenic drug that lifts the veil... it is the dancing ground, not the drug, which facilitates the visions of other worlds' (Trwoga 2006).

Dartmoor tor cairns

'The tor cairns acted as ceremonial foci' (Bender et al 2007).

On Dartmoor, I sought out tor cairns that had already been recorded. I also explored the moor for any unrecognised examples that might have been out there. I believe that more examples of cairns built around outcrops and boulders await discovery, at unexcavated or undamaged cairns, where potential outcrops are completely hidden. Also, it is possible that recent restorations of tor cairns may have reburied rock outcrops. It is important that records are kept of any cairn/outcrop juxtaposition when this work is undertaken.

I have already described the Neolithic enculturing of White Tor **(images p. 14 & 87)**. I also examined Bronze Age cairns on the tor **(below)**, which were constructed to enclose natural rocks: 'Two of the outcrops have cairns built around them... and a cairn has been constructed around a boulder' Newman (2011). The summit has no large drops or steep rock faces, just several very broken up outcrops, reminding me of the Preseli bluestones outcrop. The rock is not granite, but a dark metamorphic rock, and the tor is also a focus for Bronze Age reaves. From the summit plateau, I could see the flagstaff on Roos tor, plus its flat-topped logan stone; Great Mis Tor, Great Staple Tor and Cox Tor are all prominent to the south. The cairns on Cox Tor are clearly visible, and Brentor is also discernible to the NW.

The White Tor cairns are piled up around three natural boulders and outcrops – just like Prof Chris Tilley found at Showery Tor and Rough Tor on Bodmin (Tilley 2010). I found one cairn to be built around a huge, split, triangulate boulder, and close by, near the flagstaff, the rubble of a second cairn has been built around another large boulder, this time accompanied by an adjacent flat, altar-like stone. Both can be seen in the

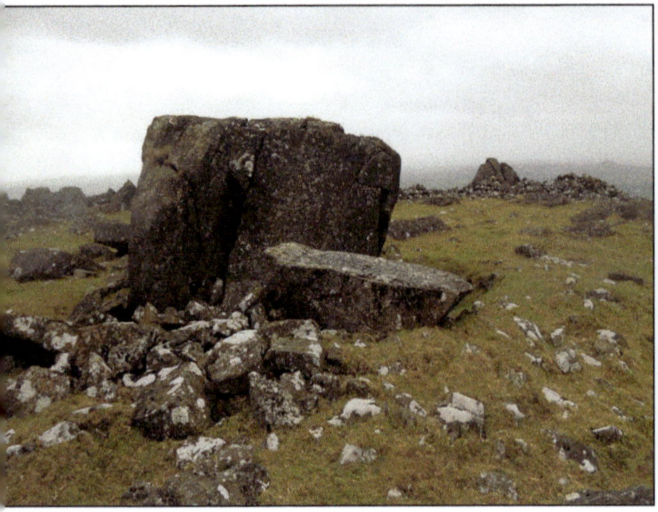

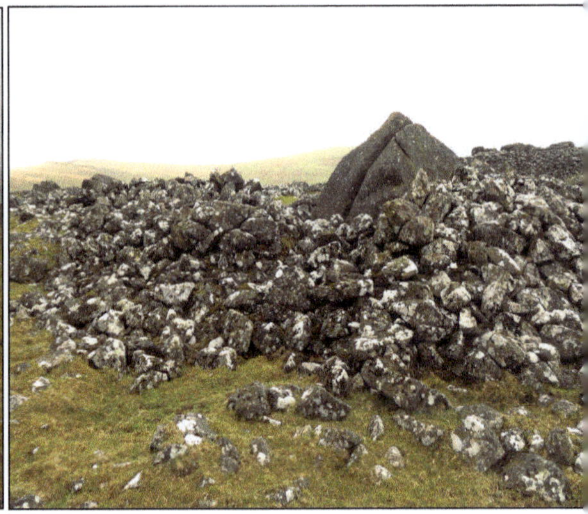

image here **(above left)**. Another denuded cairn **(above right)** had likewise been constructed around a large, fractured grounder, accompanied by a triangular standing stone on the south side, similar to that on Easdon Hill **(image p. 61)**. The Bronze Age people of Dartmoor were honouring the natural rock, paying homage to it, probably because they believed the rocks themselves were imbued with spirit, the life-force of the land. They were aligning themselves to these forces.

What was evident on my visit to White Tor is that the cairn rubble is often covered with growths of white lichen, which is evident in the two images above. Presumably this was the case in the Bronze Age. When the cairns were constructed, did they outwardly face the sides of the stones that were coated with lichen, thus rendering the cairn highly reflective? This was also observed on Cox Tor (see below). Although the name of the tor may have derived from *whit,* meaning *holy,* it may equally have derived from the gleaming white, lichen-encrusted cairns and rocks.

Also, no attempt seems to have been made to remove the rock debris from within the White Tor enclosure: 'Any activity that took place here must have been inhibited by the lack of clearance' (Newman 2011). This would suggest that the site was still ceremonial rather than occupational, and that clitter was culturally important.

Cox Tor, near Tavistock (c. 531762), is another magnificent hill that offers distant views to White Tor, Bodmin, Brent Tor, Stanton Hill, Vixen Tor, Great Staple Tor, Great Mis Tor, and to a sliver of shimmering sea to the south. Merrivale is hidden by the ridge of the Staple tors. With lofty 360° views, I have felt like an eagle surveying its territory. The rocks around the summit trig point have huge growths of pure white lichen on them, as at White Tor, like a dusting of snow. The rocks are fragmented and sometimes point angularly upwards. A hollowed out cairn lies desecrated next to the 442m trig point. This is the Cox Tor Ring Cairn Circle. It is 21m diameter and is built up around natural craggy outcrops, which also exhibit three rock basins, up to 1m across. Sadly, the cairn was modified for the 1887 jubilee celebrations (Turner 1990). On the north side of the outcrop is a good place to see the remains of the cairn material piled up against the rock face **(centre)**. As at White Tor, much of the cairn rubble is enveloped with white lichen. Was this used for effect when the cairn was built, placing lichen-covered surfaces on the outside? This would have been very reflective, just the chalk was at Silbury Hill and West Kennet Long Barrow (Knight 2011, Marshall 2016). Blocks of *imported* red granite **(right)** and white quartz also comprise the cairn – more white! Prof Tilley found quartz in the Bodmin cairns.

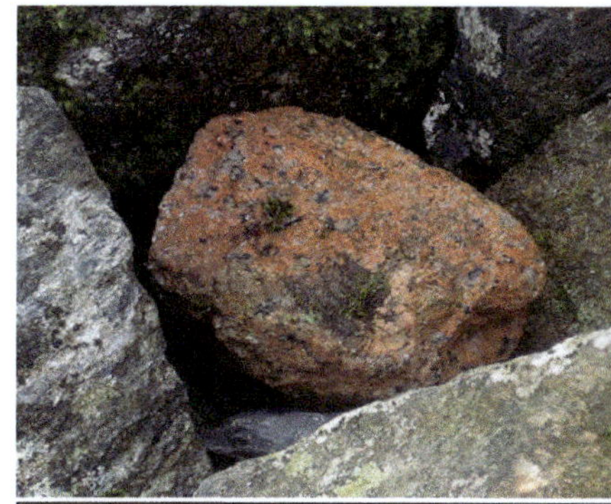

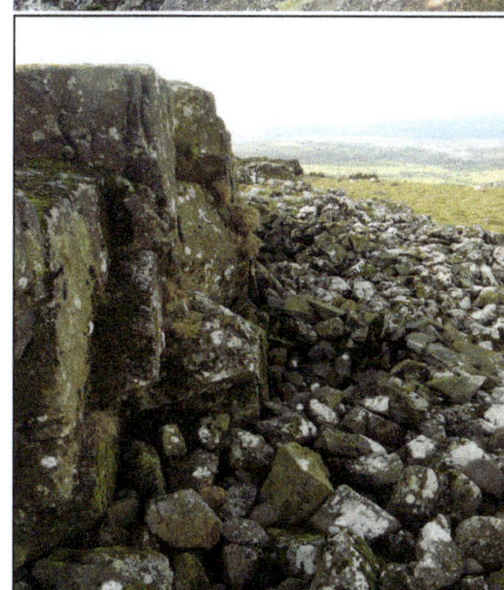

Walking north across the flat ridge at Cox Tor, another cairn is encountered; this is visible as a white, glistening mound from the trig point outcrops. White quartz and red granite of blocks were again found in the cairn material; red granite, as at White Tor, was imported from elsewhere as it is not natural to this hill. Is this another example of people transferring 'pieces of place' around the landscape? This cairn has a slight depression in centre, and appears at first to be free of outcrop. However, bedrock is visible on the north side, onto which the cairn has been piled **(below right)**. From here, the eye is drawn in the direction of good views to the valley in the north, and Brent Tor beyond.

A third cairn is close by to the north, although this is smaller and much degraded. But this too has also been built on small rock outcrop, which has been revealed at its centre due to material having been removed. An 'entrance' aligns with Brent Tor in the distance **(image p. 34)**. I also observed that Roos Tor and Great Mis Tor are aligned from these cairns; did this influence their location?

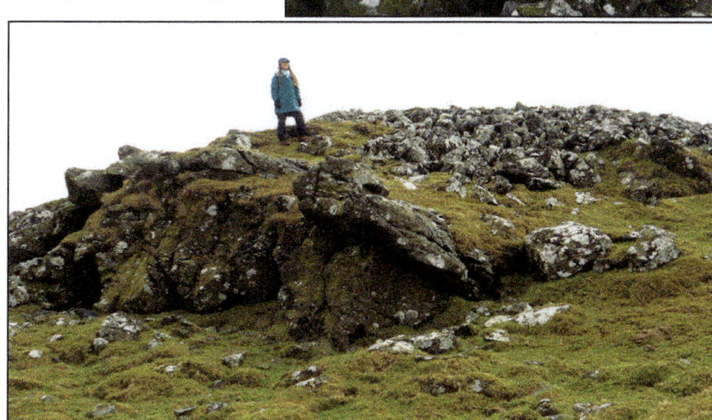

Looking to Cox Tor from elsewhere, the cairns are often skyline features. Just as on Bodmin Moor, these cairns are clustering around sacred tor outcrops to *enculture* them.

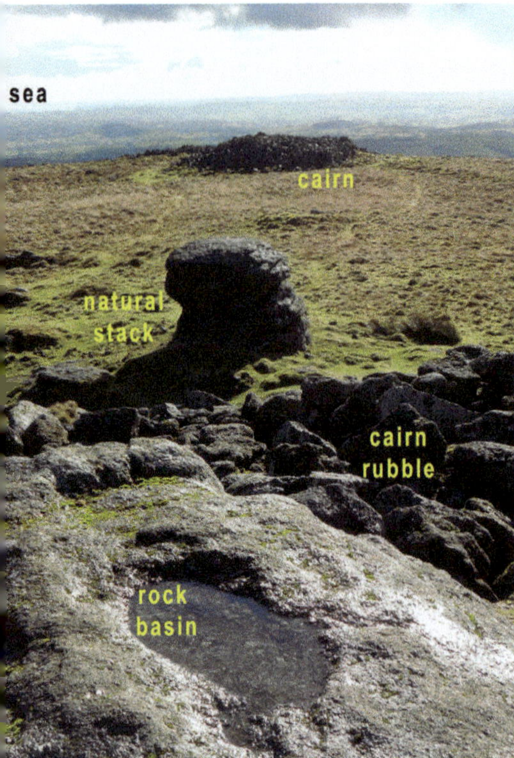

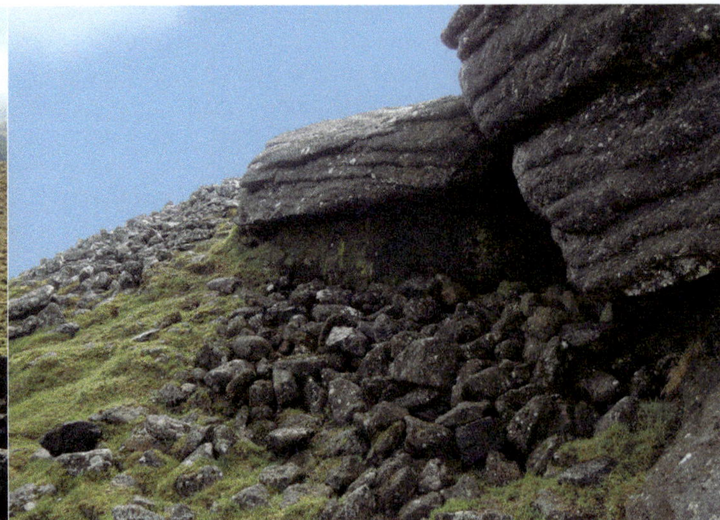

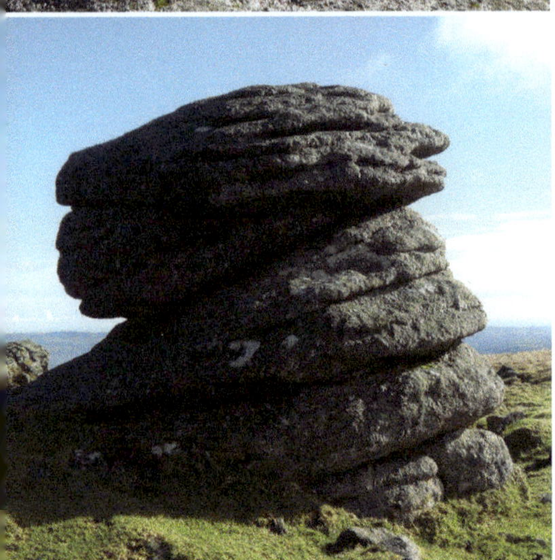

I have already described two of my visits to Rippon Tor (c. 746755) in the winter of 2016, one under clear skies, the other during a rainy whiteout. Both visits elevated my soul when I reached the summit, from the point of view of its wonders - a tor cairn, a significant granite stack, logan stones, and a rock basin!

At the summit of Rippon Tor is a trig point mounted on an outcrop. With excellent 360º views, I felt my spirit soar, as if I were an eagle looking down on the landscape below. A large expanse of sea is visible to the south, including the Plym estuary, and from here the top of Haytor, which draws one's attention, coincides with the distant skyline; to the west is a flatter, gently-undulating landscape.

As one approaches the summit the rubble of a cairn becomes evident **(top right)**. This represents the remains of what must have been another substantial embellishment of the tor. It has been recorded as, 'A cairn built around the tor. Diameter 25m, height 4m, internal diameter 4.5m. In the centre is a boulder 3m wide, 2m thick, 2.5m high' (Turner 1990). It is officially the Rippon Tor Stone Ring Cairn, and adheres stubbornly to the sides of the granite outcrop.

To my delight I found two rock basins on the top surface, filled with water, and which were involved in an alignment with a nearby solitary rock stack and cairns to the SW **(top left)**. This natural stack stands in isolation, a pillar of granite around 2.5m high. It is clearly the 'stand-out' feature of the tor, and may once have been regarded as a sacred 'monument' of the ancestors. It has two anthropomorphic simulacra, one on either side of the stack, like Janus heads looking in opposite directions across the land **(above, bottom image).**

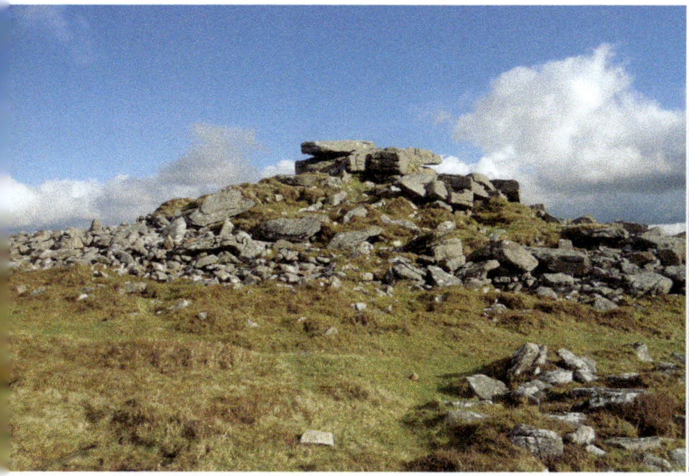 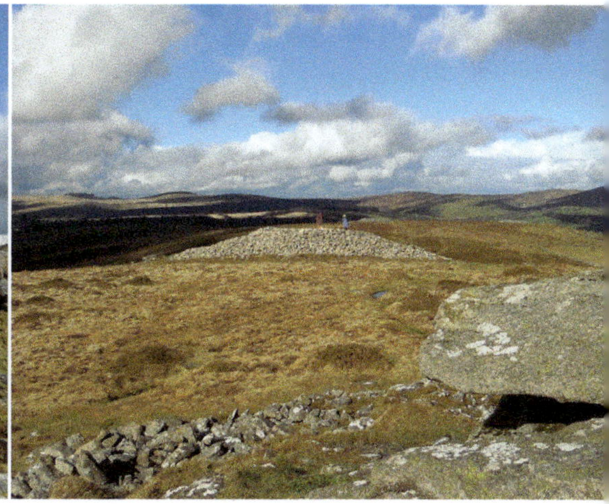

At Corndon Down, NE of Dartmeet (c. 686743), there is another enculturing tor cairn, at the main summit outcrop, which stands at a lofty 434m. This is a rounded hill, and the ascent is a gentle one. Here there is another N-S ridge, with valleys incised into the land on two sides. Several tors are visible to the south and east, including the prominent Sharp Tor, less than a mile south. The summit stack on Corndon Down is surrounded by the cairn rubble, which abuts up against the 5m high outcrop **(above left)**. This outcrop has three grooves/channels running approximately N-S on two of its surfaces. On this summit, Bronze Age shamans were again seeking to capture and control the power of the granite rock. There also appears to be cairn material around a nearby small stack to the south of the main outcrop. North along the ridge, occupying a small rise, sits another cairn (686747), a large, prominent feature seen from the main summit **(above right)**. On the NE side, natural rocks protrude from its base. On the cairn itself, a depression in the centre exposes two small horizontal rocks, which may be bedrock. Sharp Tor is not visible from this cairn, hidden by the summit; the focus of attention has now moved north to more distant tors, and the location of this cairn ensures it can be seen from a nearby settlement.

Just west of Corndon Down looms Yar Tor (c.678740), another ridge outcrop that rises to 416m. Between the two tors a stone row marches across the valley floor. Yar Tor means 'Hart or Stag Tor', and several small outcrops, up to 3m high, occupy the southern summit, but no notable stacks. There is an undulating skyline to the north, and a deep winding valley below to the west. The cairns on Corndon Down are visible on the eastern skyline. On the summit of Yar Tor another pillaged cairn **(right)** grows almost organically from the bedrock - Man and Nature conjoined. In modern times, the cairn known locally as 'Maze Cairn', has been built up in the form of walled enclosure, accessed via a spiralling entrance. The eye is drawn south to Sharp Tor and the glint of the sea, and the stone row is visible to the east in the valley below. Natural overhangs just south of the summit provide shelter, just as they did long ago **(right)**.

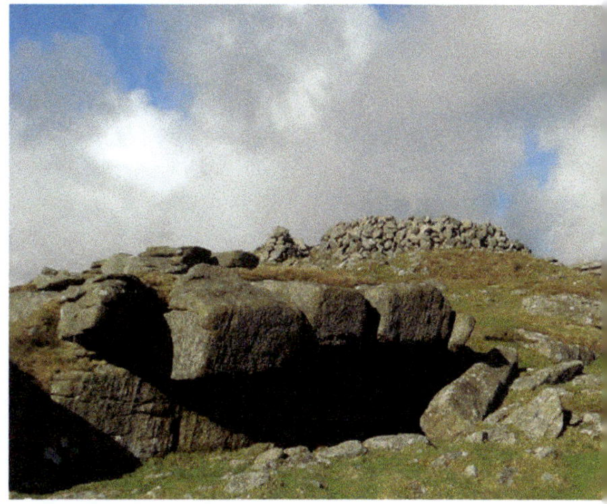

Near the southern extremity of Dartmoor is Ugborough Beacon (667592), which dominates the small town of South Brent, NE of Ivybridge. It consists of a N-S granite ridge, with cairns at the southern end, whilst the highest point (378m) is at the northern point, known as Beacon Rocks. On this northern area stands a wonderful cairn (shown as 'Tumulus' on OS maps), west of the largest outcrop. There are seven stone rows, ten settlements and nine cairns visible from Ugborough Beacon, confirming its cultural importance (Klemen 2015). When approaching from Western Beacon or Butterdon Hill, three cairns stand out on the skyline.

West of the main outcrop of the Beacon, a large tor cairn, 15m diameter, was constructed to incorporate a substantial area of a small exposed outcrop **(below left)**.

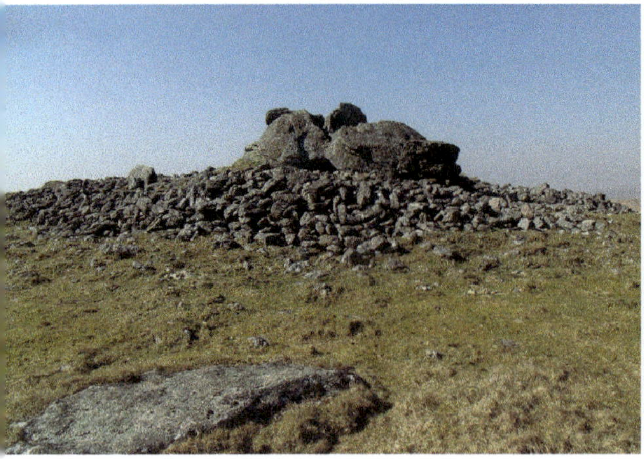

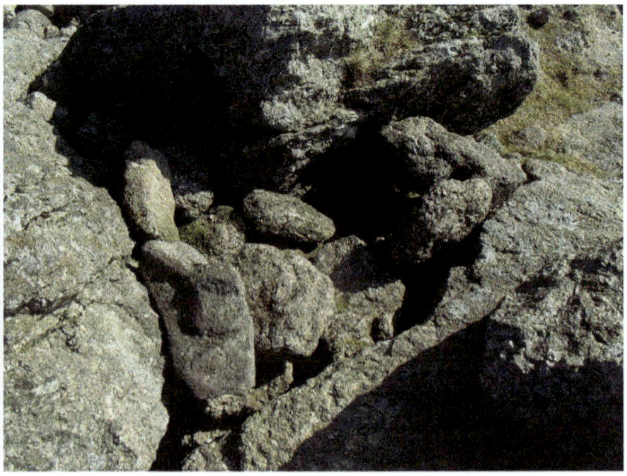

The outcrop is totally surrounded on all sides by the debris, the 'tumulus' of maps (667592). The outcrop is 2.5m high, and on inspection I found cairn rubble in the crevices between the highest boulders – suggesting that cairn material may once have completely concealed the rocks **(above right)**. A split and collapsed logan stone crowns the outcrop **(image p. 106)**, and a small cavern has been formed under it as a result. Was this sacred stone and the tomb-like space the focus of burial? This is one of the most compelling examples of the enculturing of a natural outcrop on Dartmoor. On top of nearby Beacon Rocks there are four rock basins to be inspected **(image p. 134)**. The views from this granite outcrop are breathtaking. From here there are fine 360° views, back to other cairns on this ridge, to those on the hills to the west (on Butterdon Hill and Western Beacon), and across open moor to the north. I could see a cairn that marks the southern end of the stone row that crosses the saddle and goes to Piles Hill. Processions along the row would have been visible from here.

This has been a small selection of tor encirclements I have visited. Many more exist across the moor, notable ones being on Yes Tor, Rook Tor and Branscombe's Loaf. Mention should also be made of the 'Inner Pupers Stone Ring Cairn Circle' (675674). Turner described the rock outcrop here as being encompassed by a cairn 13m diameter. The platform is now only half a metre high, although some natural outcrop protrudes through the remains of cairn rubble. Nearby, at the Outer Pupers (672673), there is a, 'stone ring circle which encloses a flat-topped granite outcrop... 17m diameter' (Turner 1990). Also, I have already shown the view of Haytor from a cairn next to the summit outcrop on Hameldown Tor **(image p. 82)**.

The dates of most cairns seem to fall between 2200 and 1700 BC. We may never know all tors do not have cairns enclosing bedrock, or why some boulders were not covered, but it is clear that symbolically important locales on the landscape were being accentuated. The foci of these sites was the granite outcrops. It is possible that cairns accumulated over generations, just as people add to cairns today as they pass. Perhaps people were leaving tokens of themselves thousands of years ago. Whenever I leave these high places some of myself is indeed left behind. It was these large boulders or outcrops, which the cairns were built around, that held the spiritual significance to people of the Bronze Age. They enhanced natural features to bring them into their culture - into their hearts and minds. And they were meant to be seen from below, from where people dwelt. Referring to Bodmin Moor, Chris Tilley considers that the enculturing of such powerful ancestral places may have been an exertion of power and control, enclosing the knowledge associated with them and limiting other peoples' access to it (Tilley 1995, 1996). Such a scenario may well have been the case on Dartmoor.

Substitution

'The imprint of a sole is fleeting, that of our soul is immortal'.
(Philip Wells, Gatekeeper Conference, 2016)

Prof Chris Tilley advocated a classification of phenomenological criteria, to be used when describing sacred sites (see p. 41-2). *Substitution* was the erection of a sacred site, such as a cairn, on a hill that otherwise has little or no natural rock outcrops. People were creating artificial 'tor outcrops' no less, and 'false cresting' hill summits, pulling the eye to an otherwise barren hill. Symbolically, these can also represent the belly or breasts of the Goddess. If some were intended for burial (and many were not), perhaps the intent was to inter a deceased in a symbolic womb, for their rebirth into the spirit realms. It was their soul, after all, that was immortal.

Dozens of Dartmoor's hills which show little or no rock outcrops, and have a rounded, gentler profiles, have been enhanced with cairns. Some of these can be visible, despite their relative small size, from miles away. I have been amazed from how far I can see the profile of these restored cairns **(right)** on Cosdon Beacon (636915), despite it being one of the northernmost hills of Dartmoor. At a lofty 550m above sea level, it was on the main cairn here that I held a sheep skull aloft and howled across a rain-soaked, overcast moor, and also left a votive offering **(images p. 22 and 48)**. I have since recognised these cairns, often as tiny bumps on the skyline, from many places across the moor, such as Hameldown Tor, Little Hound Tor, Mardon Down, Water Hill, Scorhill, Kestor, Watern Tor, the Shovel Down Stone Row, and several other places; many people looking towards these bumps on the skyline would not necessarily know what they were looking at.

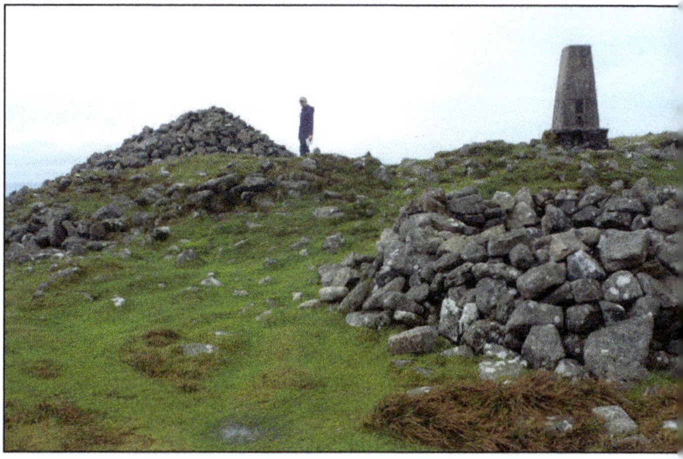

Water Hill is another good example of the embellishment of a round, outcrop-free hill with a cairn. This modest hill (672813) rises behind the Warren House Inn, just north of the B3212. To the S and SW the skyline is gently undulating, and the sea shimmers in the sunlight. The cairns on Cosdon Beacon are visible, as well as the Somerset levels to the NE; Kestor makes an appearance to the north, as the land here drops away in

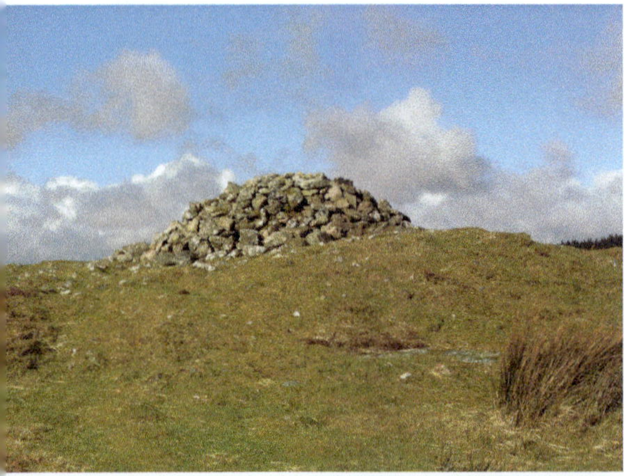

every direction. From being a hill that was otherwise unremarkable, the construction of this single cairn **(left)** made Water Hill a cultural focus. The ancestors were now watching over them, and could be accessed. Most cairns on Bodmin did not receive burial (Tilley 2010). Of the ones that did receive bodies, I wonder if these prestige burials were those of shamans. Clearly only an elite member of society would be given such an elevated position after their death, to oversee the living: 'The shaman would continue to serve their community as they had in life' (Trwoga 2006).

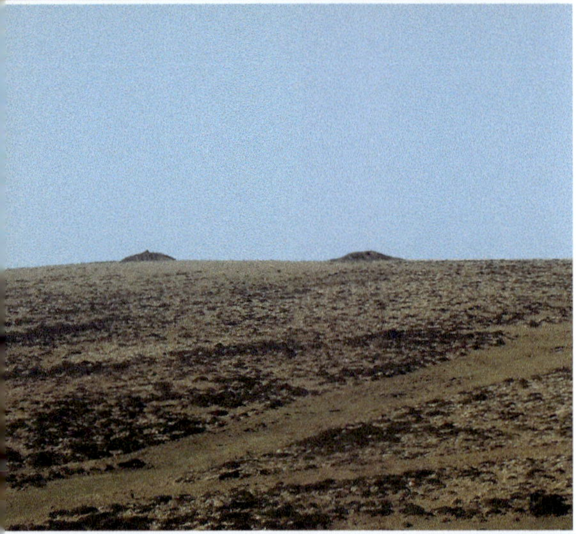

When viewed from the east or west, the great undulating ridge that is formed by the (outcrop deficient) heights of Western Beacon, Butterdon Hill, Piles Hill and Sharp Tor, is peppered with strategically placed cairns, often located in relation to local stone rows. These cairns **(left)** are on Butterdon Hill, and are being viewed from the tumulus on Ugborough Beacon. The next image is a close up of one of the Butterdon Hill cairns, and the triangular stone erected in front of it **(below)**. The walk along the ridge from Western Beacon to Piles Hill follows boundary stones and stone rows for much of its course, as several cairns come into and go out of visibility on distant, rounded hills, of which most are examples of *substitution*.

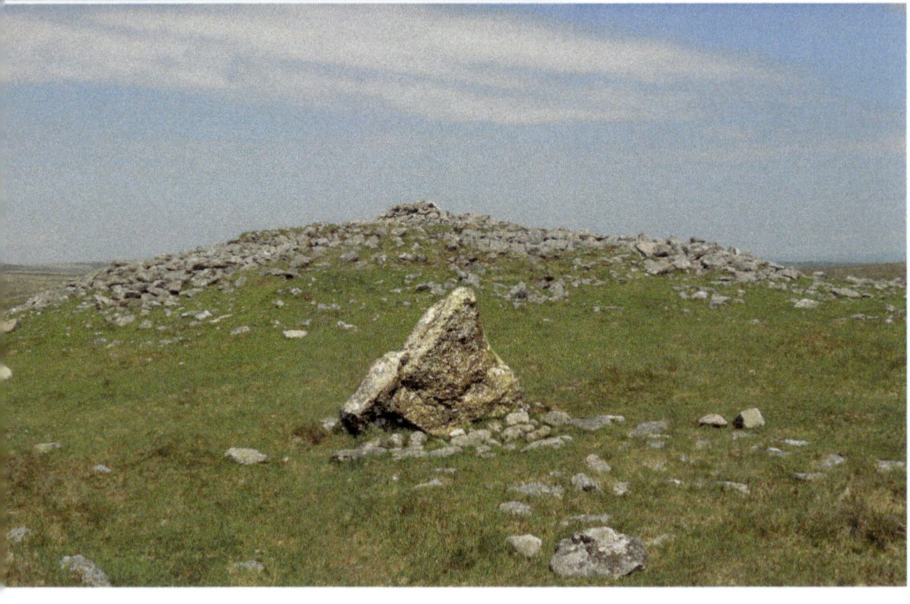

'Stones are the pages of this hill's book.'
(Jan Farquharson in Bender et al 2007)

At the southern end of this ridge, Western Beacon rises to 334m and affords magnificent views of the moor to the north and the sea to the south. But there is no natural bedrock to be seen, save for a quarry at the southern tip. Clustered around the summit are several large cairns, some restored, and some containing red granite, and all of which imbue the summit with 'false outcrops' and 'false crests'. This hill, otherwise devoid of features, is encultured on a grand scale, with cairns that are visible from miles away; they also mark a lunar alignment **(image p. 198)**. Three of the cairns **(right)** align with Ugborough Beacon, with its rocky outcrops and collection of cairns **(images p. 96)**, seen here on the skyline.

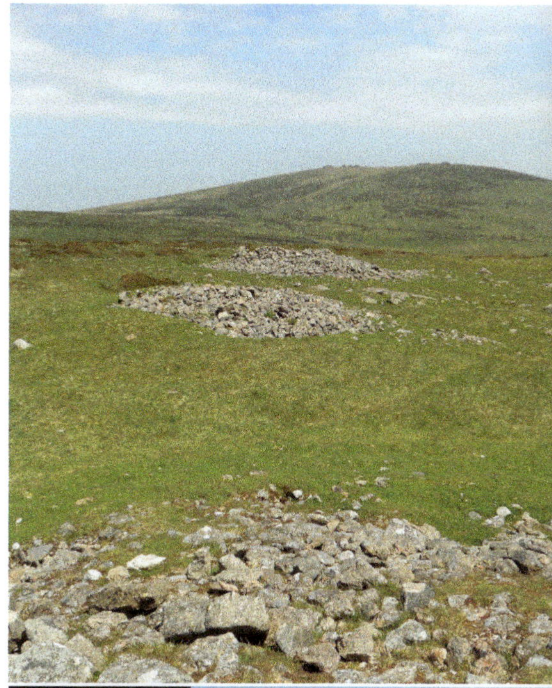

Long range visibility is also apparent regarding several other hilltop cairns, such as those on Cox Tor, Rippon Tor, Piles Hill, Hameldown Tor, Corndon Hill, Eylesbarrow, and Stall Moor. Another good example is King's Barrow on King Tor (709814), which is a very prominent summit feature on a very rounded hill with few other features. There seems to have been a desire to position tor cairns in relation to other tors. These cairns were meant to be seen from afar, and often from other summit cairns; perhaps it was felt that the ancestors needed to communicate with each other. Seeing their ancestors up on the hills may also have brought people comfort, as well as staking a claim on their patch of moor.

Hangershell Rock (654593) is a small granite outcrop **(image p. 84)**, adjacent to the Butterdon Hill stone row. Simulacra grace the 6m high outcrop, yet my lasting memory is of the high number of tor and hill-top cairns that were visible on the skyline from the top of the tor. Cairns on Piles Hill, Butterdon Hill, Ugborough and others were all visible. This view shows two of the cairns on Butterdon Hill, as seen from Hangershell Rock **(right)**; a total of five cairns are visible from this outcrop, as well as four prehistoric settlements. Three megaliths formerly stood to the east of the tor (Klemen 2015).

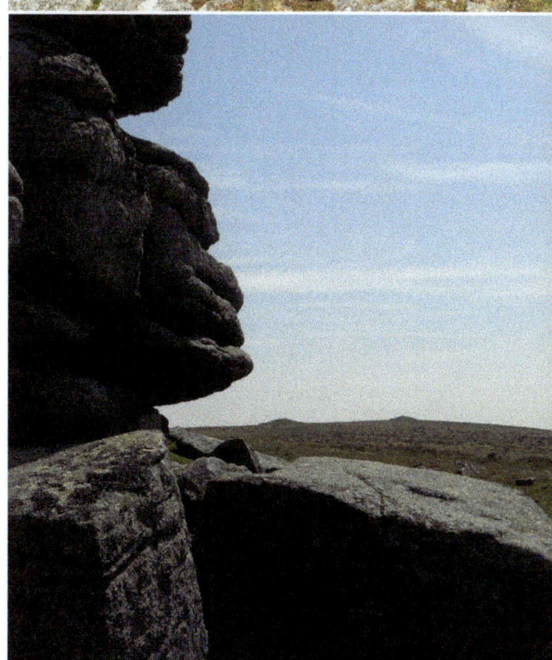

Into this mix we must also place several cairn circles, which were also situated on lofty locales, some of which may have had nothing to do with burial of the dead. Regarding Dartmoor: 'At least twelve ring cairns are on or near tor outcrops, suggesting that the latter were special, and tell us something about the way in which meaning as assigned to features in the natural landscape' (Gerrard 1997). These are amongst the 'prestige' cairns, located where they could be seen from miles around. Nearly all are located on hilltops, deliberately sited as eye-catching features, perhaps following the tradition of the Neolithic long barrows (Newman 2011). There is a debate, of course, as to whether a good many sites are cairn circles or stone circles, as many lack any inner mound or cist. This example here **(below)** *is* a cairn circle, at the north end of Mardon Down (767877), NE of Moretonhampstead. The remnants of an inner chamber and mound survive, surrounded by a circle of ten stones and an outer circle of low kerb stones. From here the land falls away to the north, with views also to the west to east. Cosdon Beacon and Sharp Tor are visible, and Exmoor in the distance. On a visit to Mardon Down on a crisp winter day, I sat on one of the stones, turning my face from a chilly east wind. The poem that came to me at that moment is repeated on the image below. Minutes later a shower came over, followed by a fantastic rainbow, which reached the ground at each end. It was a moment when I felt truly blessed to have been there, having walked in the footsteps of my ancestors.

I have been advocating for many years how we should not regard prehistoric monuments as secular and lying on the landscape in isolation. They must, I believe, be taken as an inter-related network on a landscape they all share, which was the mindset of the people who built them. These places 'hold the space' and encapsulate the very resonance of the landscape. They are anchored and approachable, permanent and reassuring. People were moving around the landscape from place to place, from tor cairn to tor cairn, along stone rows etc. In fact it may have been this very movement across the land that was integral to their attachment to it, and of their learning. The tor cairns were a key element of this connection with the land and their ancestors. In

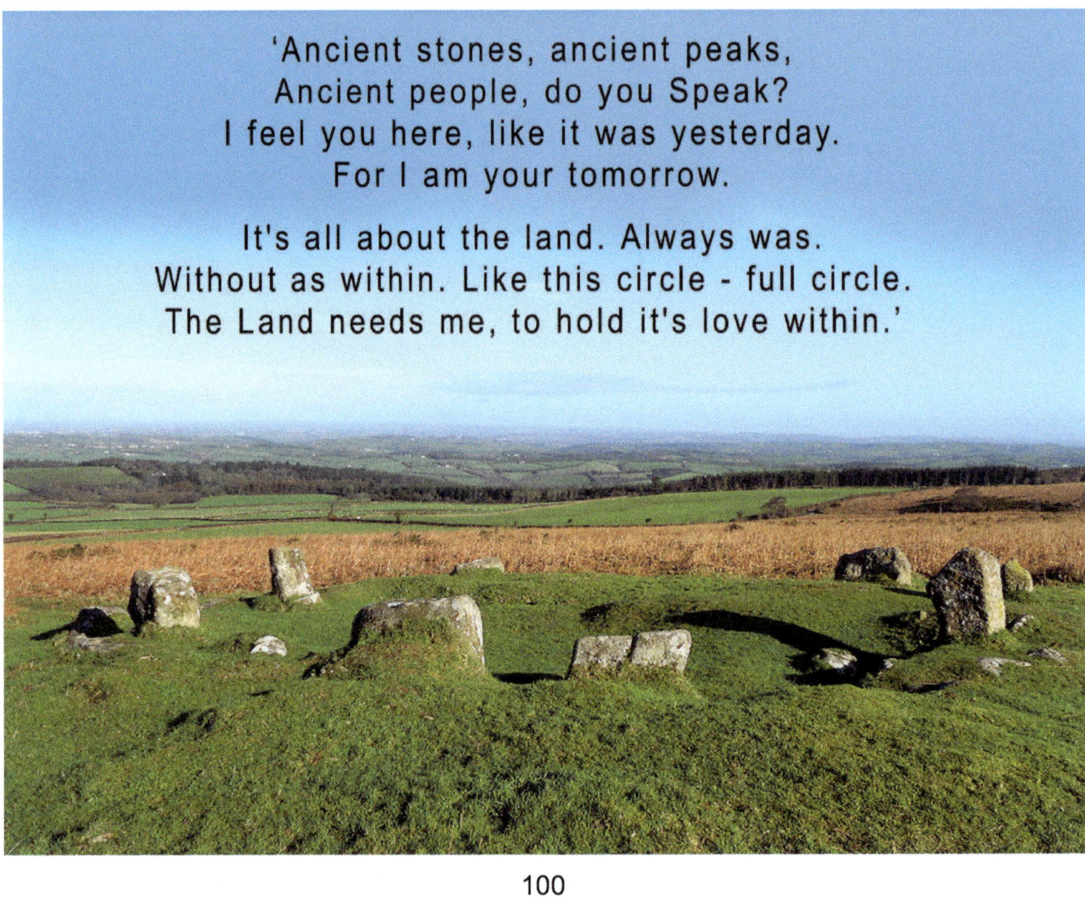

depositing a stone on a cairn, people were leaving part of themselves there, in the company of their ancestors.

Later I shall delve more into the visibility of hilltop cairns as seen *from* monuments, such as stone circles and stone rows in particular. I shall also refer back to enculturing of tors in relation to settlements. Another aspect of experiencing cairns is through their earth energies, which were dowsed and readily felt at virtually every cairn that was studied in this project. I shall look into this further in Chapter 17.

I have spoken much about the lost sanctity of tors, how we no longer regard them as spiritually relevant. A remnant of the former respect for such places can be found at Crockern Tor (616757). This tor **(images below)** was 'encultured', in effect, for the local Stannary Parliament, making it the historical omphalos of Dartmoor. It was the most central point accessible by the old trackways. As a site equidistant from the four stannary towns, it balanced competing claims for pre-eminence. Some say it is named after Old Crockern, a 'guardian spirit of the moor': Folklorist Bob Trubshaw relates: 'In former times Crockern Tor was personified as a grim old man riding a skeleton horse. The sound of the bones rattling on the rocks could be heard on stormy nights. Local people evocatively recognise the gurt old spirit of the moors, Old Crockern himself, grey as granite, and his eyebrows hanging over his glimmering eyes like sedge, and his eyes as deep as peat water pools. The ghostly Wish Hounds, a version of the better-known spectral Gabriel Hounds, are said to emanate from Wistman's Wood, which is less than a mile away' (Trubshaw, 'At the Edge' website). I wonder if Old Crockern is a corruption of Cernunnos or Odin, leaders of this Otherwordly *wild hunt*? These, in turn, are Iron Age equivalents of prehistoric ancestral spirits and Otherworldly beings seen to inhabit the moor, who were later demonised by the Church. There are several simulacra on Crockern Tor, one magnificent example of which is shown here **(below right),** with its long face and pinned back ear. I wonder if it once was the overseer of prehistoric ceremonies and gorsedd-like gatherings.

'Your ancestors are never far away, and places such as this are sacred liminal spaces, where worlds merge' (Knight 2007).

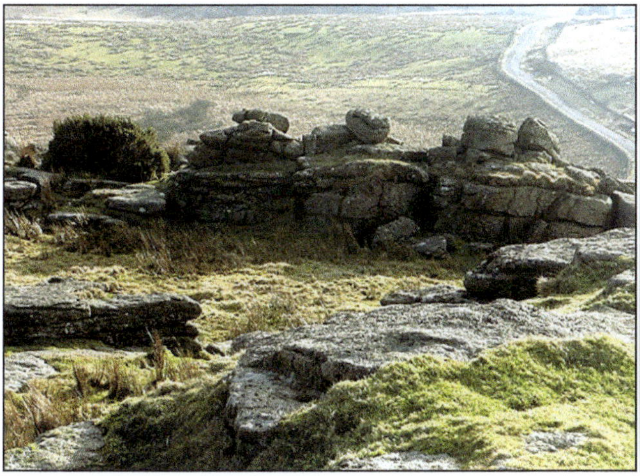

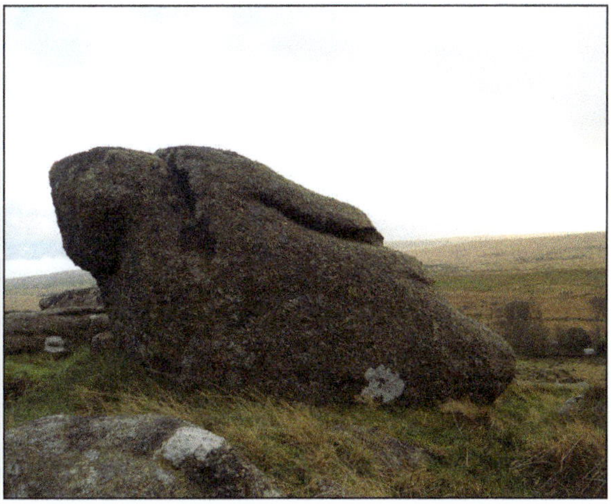

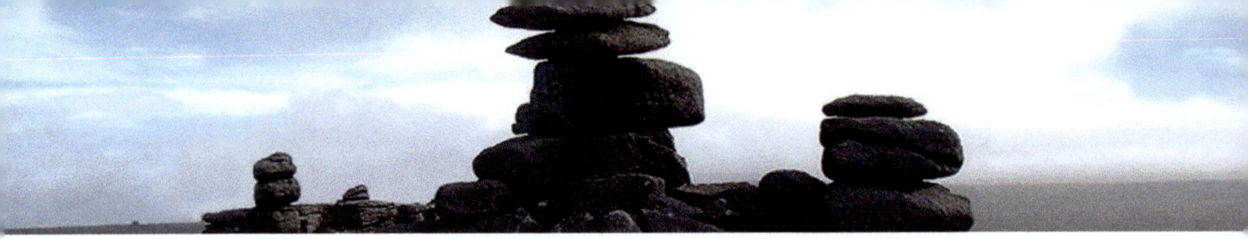

9. Balanced Rocks

'We will, we will rock you.' (Queen)

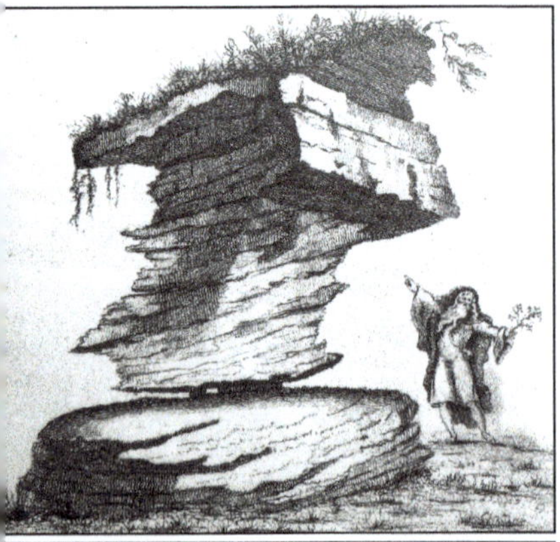

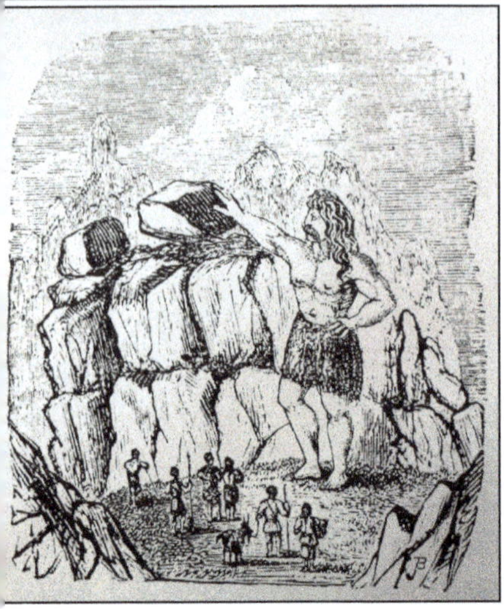

Ancient rock and roll

One of the attractions of Dartmoor, and one which certainly possesses a 'wow factor', is the scattering of amazing balanced rocks, sometimes called logan stones, that can be found precariously positioned on many of its tors. These curious granite formations seem to defy gravity, in much the same way as the balancing artistry of Andrew Goldsworthy, perched as if they are preparing for an impending collapse. They inspire our imagination and test our nerve when we dare to stand on them. Sometimes the smallest pressure can achieve a movement of a large boulder or outcrop. At one time it was thought that these remarkable shapes must have been carved and erected by human means. Amongst antiquarians, the Druids **(left)** were the favoured protagonists, although a race of giants was also suggested, due to the sheer scale and weight of the rocks **(left).** Shown here are two 18th century antiquarian drawings.

We now know that these wondrous rock sentinels are the result of geomorphological erosion processes. The rocks became loosened from the parent bedrock through weathering along joints in the granite. Eventually they may be attached to just a small stem of rock, or may detach, pivoting on a small area of underlying rock. Logan stones are also known as 'plinths' by geologists. Today, the term logan is often applied to any stone that is precariously balanced, even if it has lost its rocking attributes, if it indeed ever had any. They may be totally composed of the immediate geology or, in the case of erratics, may have been dumped by glacial action. Examination of Dartmoor's logan stones shows they are the result of the weathering of rock stacks. However, in the case of propped stones (large stones that are balanced on multiple grounders), there is a case to be heard that the components may not be the result of the weathering at all.

Although logan stones are natural, that does not mean they were not held in wonder, and even had spiritual significance, to our ancestors. Considering the reverence and folklore that has been attached to these balanced stones across the world, it would be highly exceptional if the examples on Dartmoor had not been not similarly revered in

prehistory. You may recall that our ancestors, as with tribal cultures today, may have believed that the amazing tor outcrops, with their simulacra and logan stones, were built by the ancestors or Creation gods. These were the 'temples' of their day: 'Natural sites often acted as sacred places for our ancestors' (McDonald 2011). In Cornwall, logan stones have an alternative name, that of 'Judgement Stones', from their association with the Druids (Miller and Broadhurst 2000). The famous Cheesewring, on Bodmin Moor, has Druidic associations.
The name *logan* means *'little hollow'* according to some. It comes from the Scottish Gaelic - there was once a Logan Clan. It may have derived from Loeg or Lugh, the Celtic sun god. Others believe that the word derived from *'log'*, which in an English dialect means *'to rock'*. In fact, in some parts of the UK, rocking stones are called logging stones. The word 'log' might also be connected with the Danish word 'logre', which means to 'wag a tail'. Some have suggested that the word comes from a Cornish expression for the movement that someone makes when inebriated – that the rocks roll like a drunkard!

The reverence of balanced rocks

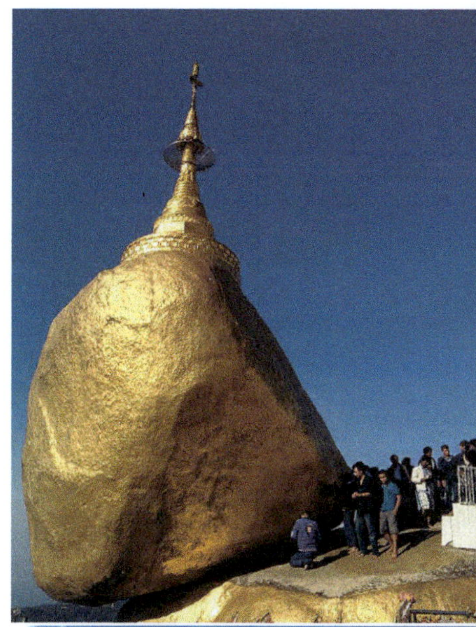

'These peculiar rocks were raised by the Druids.'
(Dr William Borlase, 18th c.)

Around the world, precariously balanced rocks have been endowed with spiritual significance, many of them possessing ancient folklore and legends. I have already made reference to the Devil's Marbles of the Australian outback **(image p. 25)**, which are sacred to the Aborigines.
The Golden Rock (Kyaik-htiyo or Kyaiktiyo), is perched atop a cliff near Yangon, Burma, and is one of the most sacred sites in the country **(right)**. It is about 7.6m in height and has a maximum diameter of around 7m. According to legend, the Golden Rock is precariously suspended on a strand of the Buddha's hair. The rock seems to flout gravity, as it appears to be perpetually on the verge of sliding off the hill. It is covered with gold leaf pasted on by devotees and at the top is a small pagoda. A glimpse of the 'gravity defying' Golden Rock is said to be enough to convert a person to Buddhism.

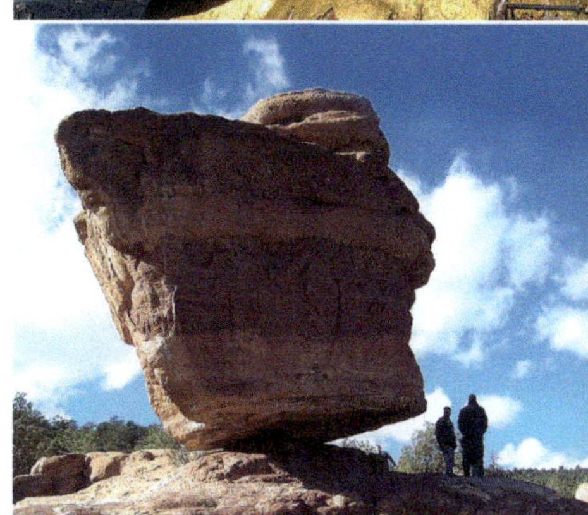

The *Garden of the Gods*, Colorado Springs, USA, is home to incredible red sandstone formations that display several balanced rocks, some of huge proportions. Archaeological evidence shows that prehistoric people visited the area from c. 1330 BC. At around 250 BC, Native American people camped in the park, using natural shelters and overhangs. It is thought that it was these peculiar rock formations, including the balanced rocks, which drew the Indian nations into the area. The example here **(right)** is called, quite simply, *Balanced Rock*.

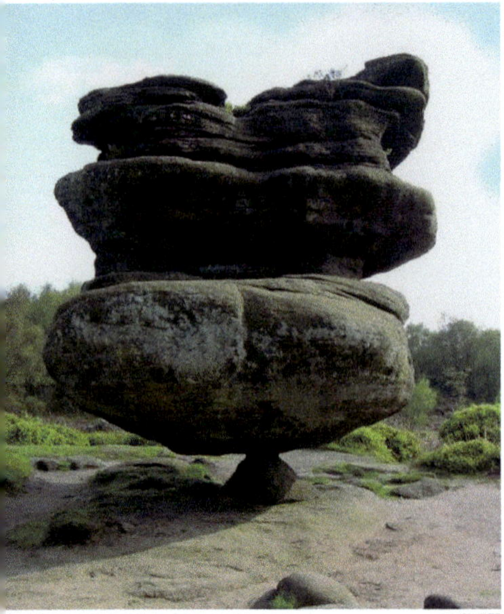

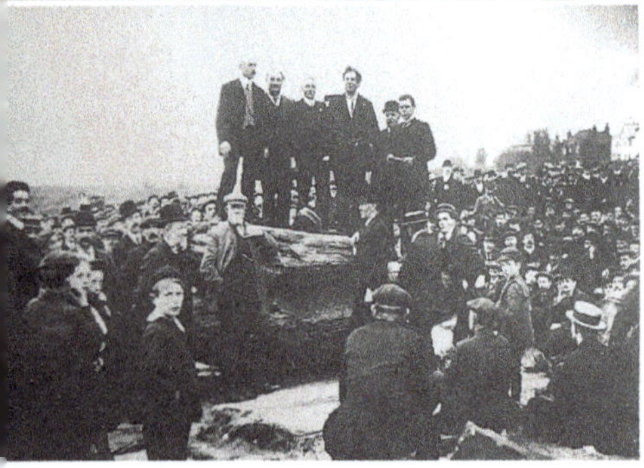

Brimham Rocks are a remarkable outcropping of rocks near Harrogate, North Yorkshire. Several simulacra and balanced rocks make it a popular tourist destination. Occultists Blavatsky and Olaus Magnus saw the rocks as the sites of ancient oracles and divination rites, evidence of a lost civilisation. The amazing Oracle Rock, or Druid's Idol, is shown here **(left)**. It is amazing that this 200 ton, 4.5m high, top-heavy monolith is perched on a mere 30cm wide pyramidal sliver of rock, the result of 18,000 years continuous erosion. Other local simulacra are called the Sphinx, Watchdog, Turtle, Camel and the Dancing Bear.

A logan stone discovered on South Uist, Herbrides, marks the point of midwinter sunrise when viewed from the Barp Barrow (Michell 1989). On the Great Orme, at Llandudno, the Maen Sigl stone was formerly a rocking, logan stone from which St Tudno preached. This hints that the stone was already revered by locals, and was turned into an open-air pulpit by the saint (Walker 1987). The Buckstone, or Frog Stone, at Staunton near Monmouth, was supposedly a Druidic altar and also has witch-related folklore. It could formerly be rocked on its small pivot. Nearby is a rock called the Sacrificial Stone (Walker 1987). The Pontypridd Rocking Stone has long been the scene of ceremony and oratory by the Welsh Druids and Nationalists. Political meetings were held there as late as 1910, as shown in this image **(left)**. The men in the centre are standing on the stone to address the rally. Also in Wales, the Carreg Siglo rocking stone, which stands at the convergence of the rivers Taf and Rhondda, is the site of bardic congresses (Cope 1998). Recent work has shown how rocking stones in the Pennines and Cumbria were enhanced with manmade stone settings (Shepherd 2014). These examples are but remnants of how culturally important rocking stones once were.

Another well-known example is the Logan Rock of Treen, in Cornwall. This huge stone weighs 80-90 tons, and is one of the best known rocking stones. In William Mason's dramatic poem 'Caractacus', the character Modred addresses Vellinus and Elidurus, and proclaims the following, referring to magic, giants and the rock having special properties:

'Thither, youths,
Turn your astonish'd eyes; behold yon huge
And unhewn sphere of living adamant,
Which, poised by magic, rests its central weight
On yonder pointed rock: firm as it seems,
Such is the strange and virtuous property,
It moves obsequious to the gentlest touch
Of him whose breast is pure; but to a traitor,
Tho' ev'n a giant's prowess nerv'd his arm,
It stands as fixt as Snowdon'.

Also in Cornwall, the amazing balanced rocks of Showery Tor **(images p. 80 and 86)** inspire the heart and spirit; the presence of acoustic properties and rock basins would have added to the tor's mystique in times long gone. Nearby, Rough tor is also graced by a summit logan stack, also topped by rock basins, and where another logan stone invited my attention **(lower right image, p. 3).** It was as if the giants and gods of old had balanced the rock, in a state of eternal equilibrium, and were looking down with amusement at my reaction.

A gigantic outcrop called the Agglestone, at Studland in Dorset, could formerly be coaxed into rocking (Knight 1996, 1998). This is all the more incredible when one considers that it's estimated weight is about 400 tons! Also known as the Devil's Anvil, the rock has Druid folklore; the name comes from the Anglo-Saxon *'Helig',* meaning *'holy'*, and *'Aggle'*, old Dorset dialect meaning *'to wobble'*. Sadly, due to erosion, the rock has collapsed and no longer pivots. Nearby is a small outcrop known locally as the Puckstone (Knight 1998).

Dartmoor balancing acts

'Balanced in a moment of perfection' (Lyrics by Carolyn Hillyer).

Archaeologists had already suggested that granite logan stones and propped stones at Brown Willy, the highest point on Bodmin Moor, may have had significance to prehistoric people (Bender et al 2007); one of the stones with rock basins on its surface rocks as one walks across it. Prof Chris Tilley has noted logan stones in Penwith, Cornwall, that appear to have been culturally significant (Tilley 2010).

You may recall that in 1862, the President of the Archaeological Association regarded Dartmoor as, "... a natural Druid Temple – one great mass of logan stones and rock idols". Even this learned fellow recognised that these peculiar weathered outcrops held a certain mystical quality, and that this may have been the case long ago. Amongst the towering granite wonders of the tors, surely the balanced 'logan' stones would have been held as particularly meaningful. Even today, walkers and cyclists may stop and marvel at how several tons of granite could possibly be perched on the smallest pivot, refusing to slide off despite the severest of angles. It can also be disconcerting as the earth suddenly moves below you if you accidentally walk across one! It is hard to find any large tor that does not have balanced rocks to some degree, several of which I will show here. I can see how our ancestors would have regarded them as being the handiwork of the ancestors or gods – no human could possibly achieve such feats of equilibrium.

Several *'logan stones'* are shown on the 125,000 'Explorer' map produced by the Ordnance Survey. Some have been named and imbued with folklore. There is a logan at Rugglestone Rock, to the east of Widecombe-in-the-Moor (723764), which is shown on maps, and gave its name to the Rugglestone Inn. The Nutcrackers at Sharpitor, in Lustleigh Cleave, was once a mighty logan stone that has now collapsed **(images p. 43 & 44)**. *Nut Crackers* on Rippon Tor (743753), was once a popular walking destination for Victorian gentry, such was its famed balancing act **(right)**; a rock some 4m long, weighing 14 tons, could still be rocked prior to 1895 and was used

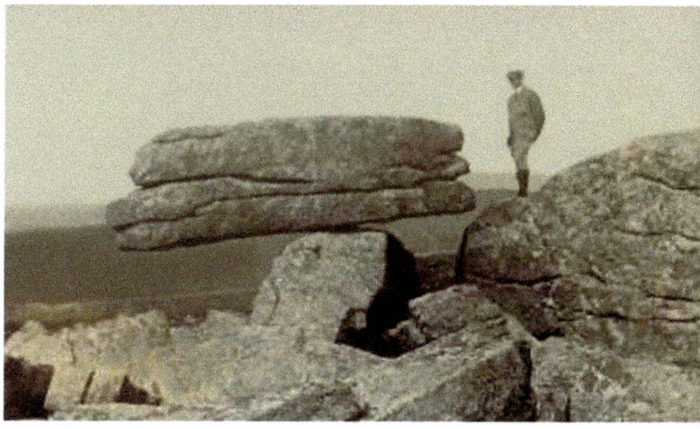

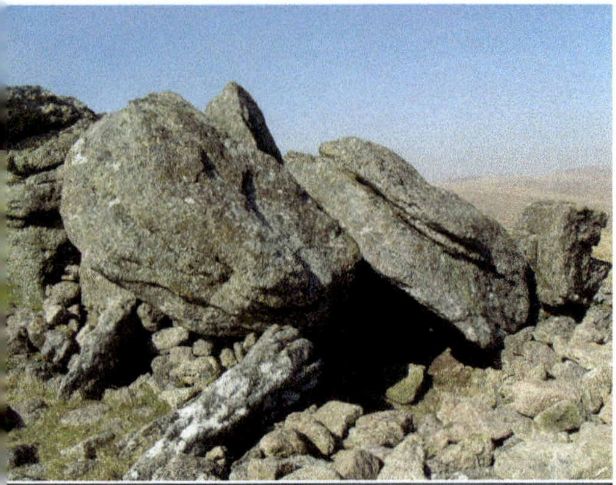

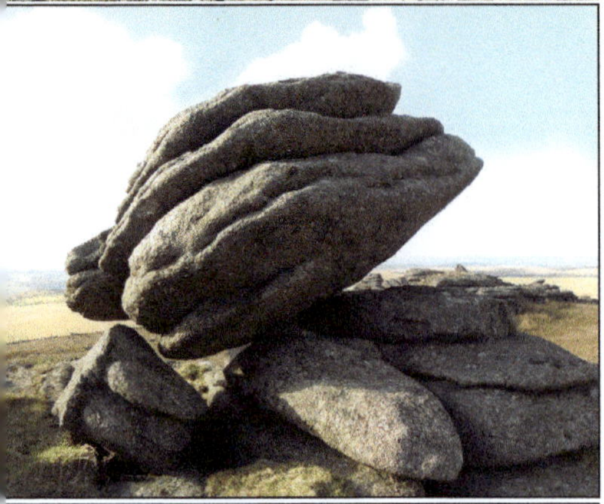

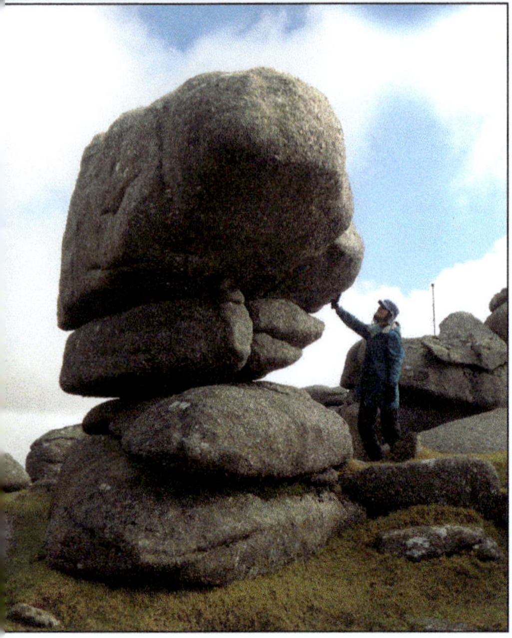

by locals to crack nuts! Local folklore from the 19th century records that the stone was consulted by locals for solving difficult problems; it was an oracle stone! This may, of course, only hark back to the early antiquarian belief that logan stones were connected with the Druids, but we should not rule out older oracular use. The Iron Age priestly class *were* in Southern Britain, and may have regarded such stones with reverence.

I have already shown the relevance of the large balanced stone at Dewerstone **(image p. 88)**, which forms the focus of manmade structures. At Hound Tor, another balanced rock resembles a pixie head **(image p. 57)**. Enculturing of balanced stones is demonstrated by the cairn constructed around a collapsed/split logan at Ugborough Beacon **(top & p. 96)**. A rockable logan on Thornworthy Tor has now slipped. The rocking attributes of the Hanging Stone at Hangerstone Hill (617862) have been restored by the Army.

A fine example of the 'seemingly impossible' is on show near the summit of Great Mis Tor (563768), NE of Merrivale. This massive rock, weighing several tons, seems to defy gravity as it teeters on the brink **(left)**, as if hesitating before it launches itself down the tor. The rock is just a few metres from the Mistor Pan, a great rock basin **(images p. 130)** and the two features may have given this tor added significance and potency.

Whooping Rock, on Easdon Tor, SW of Moretonhamptead (728623), has rocking stone folklore, and is so named from the peculiar sounds it used to make when moved by the wind. There are records of the sounds being heard three miles away in stormy weather, and one can see how our ancestors may have regarded these effects as being of supernatural origin.

Amongst its colossi of granite stacks, Great Staple Tor exhibits many fine logan stones, often perched atop of lofty stack **(image p. 69)**. Nearby is another fine example of a precariously balanced stack (shown as 'logan stone' on OS maps) at the summit of Roos Tor (543766), just west of the flagstaff **(left)**. This top-heavy stack has a rock basin on its upper surface, and is just metres from a propped stone and other rock basins (I shall return to this important locality in Chapter 13). How can such features not have held people in awe and wonderment thousands of years ago? This rock is very difficult to scale, and I believe that most people would have not tried. But I can envisage the shaman, standing on the top, magically producing water from the hidden basin, holding it aloft as his clan

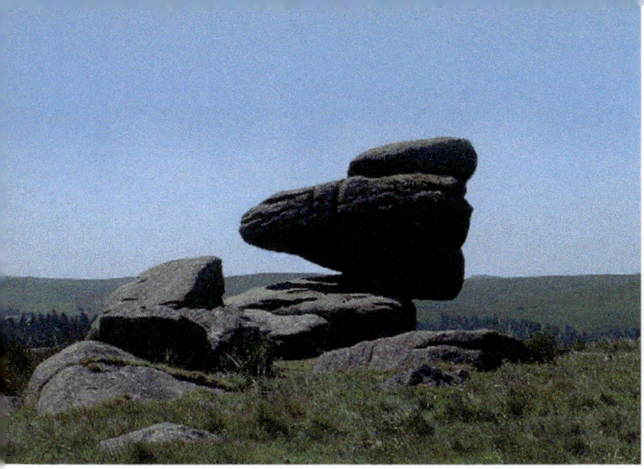
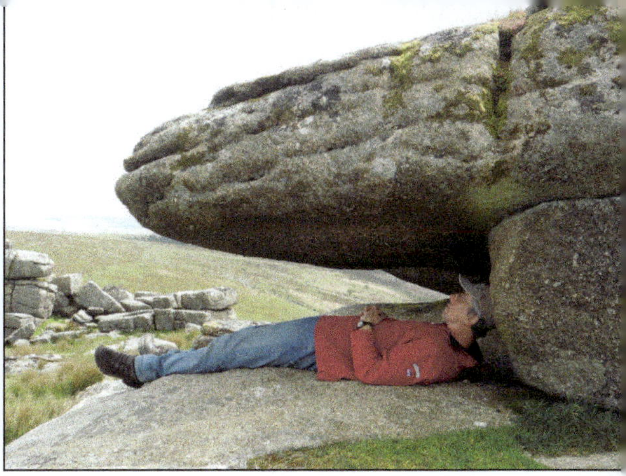

members looked on in amazement. Is it any wonder that these rocks would have been regarded as having magical powers?

One of the most impressive logan stones of Dartmoor, in my opinion, is that topping the north stack of Black Tor, SW of Princetown (574718). This balanced rock **(above left)** gifts us a large overhang under which one can lie **(above right)**, above which is a striking simulacrum **(top image p. 58)**. This head, along with another on the south outcrop **(lower right image, p. 58)**, gazes south in the direction of the stone row in the valley. I led a group to this logan stone in 2016 for the Megalithomania Conference, and demonstrated how people can lie beneath the overhang. Several of the attendees did likewise. I said to those assembled that, as I lay there, beneath tons of granite, I knew that thousands of years ago someone had also lain there.

I found this fabulous whale-like logan next to 'Irishman's Wall' on Belstone Tor **(below)**; nearby is a propped stone, which I discuss later **(image p. 114)**.

One feature of many logan stones is that they may often have a rock basin, sometimes containing water, on their upper surfaces. Work on Bodmin has suggested these features had cultural significance in prehistory. So I shall return to this aspect in Chapter 11.

Dartmoor never stands still. Erosion and time will ensure that logan stones will inevitably collapse, to be replaced by new ones. Several thousand years down the line, I can envisage Bowerman's Nose and the simulacrum at Easdon Tor **(images p. 56)** acquiring rocking attributes, and may likewise inspire wonder and awe, just as similar examples did thousands of years ago.

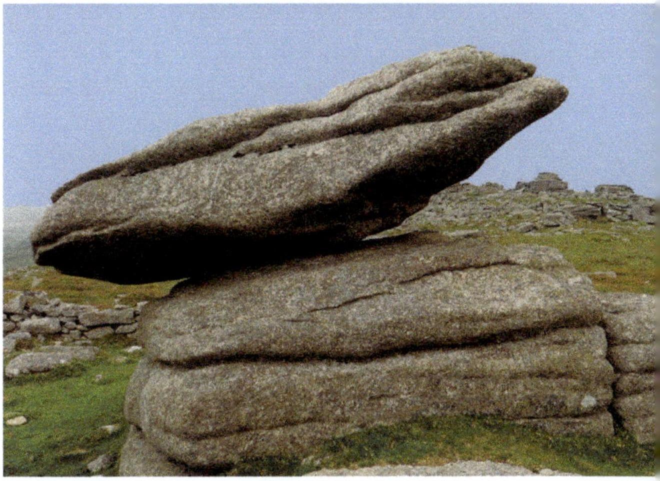

The wonder of balanced stones continues today; some of Andy Goldsworthy's art installations comprise of stacked stones which similarly display gravity-defying feats. On a recent visit to Hadrian's Wall, I helped construct a balanced column of several river cobbles and pebbles. To create such an acrobatic ballet was satisfying and connecting. I left part of myself on the banks of the river that day.

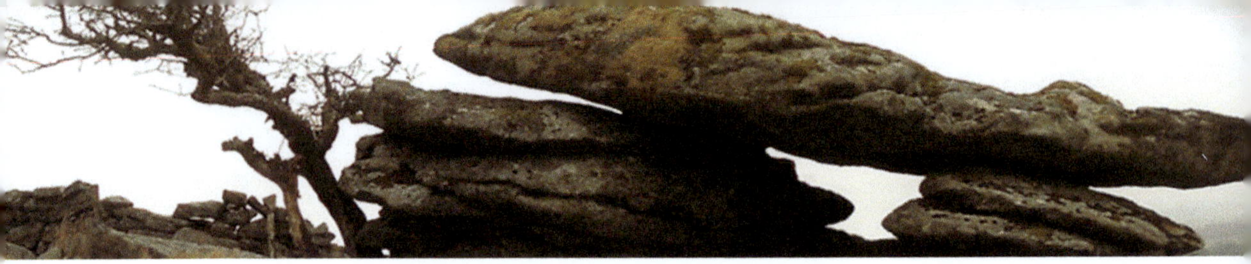

10. Propped Stones

'Thou wilt make me an altar of stone, thou shalt not build it of hewn stone; For if thou lift thy tool upon it, thou hast polluted it.' (Exodus 20:25)

Erratics or prehistoric engineering?

Ramblers walking through Scotland, Wales, the Lake District and Northern England may come across huge boulders and rocks which appear not to be of the local landscape, and many of which are perched on a much smaller pedestal, sometimes of a different geology. These are usually glacial erratics, dumped by glaciers during one of our Ice Ages. In other areas, however, propped rocks (rocks which are held off the earth by the support of smaller 'grounders') are found where there is little or no evidence of transportation by glacial action. And in the case of the granite propped stones of SW England, including Dartmoor, many seem to have been deliberately placed in position by human effort. It is only recently that archaeologists have began to embrace the concept that not all huge boulders supported by grounders are the natural result of glaciation or erosion, naturally coming to rest in their current position. The problem is often how to discern between natural erratic and a structure resulting from human intervention. Perhaps the observations of erratics and other balanced rocks gave prehistoric people the idea of erecting their own.

It is fortunate for my research on Dartmoor that some work on propped stones has been carried out on Bodmin Moor, which is local to Dartmoor, and is chiefly comprised of the same geology, i.e. granite. Before we look into comparing the two moors concerning propped stones and their cultural significance, let us take a look at precedents that have been regarded as sacred places in their own right.

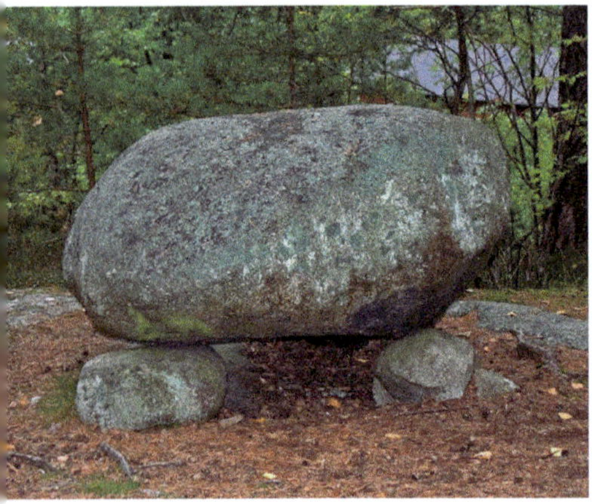

Sacred propped stones

In Sweden, a specific type of Iron Age grave is known as *uppalla sten*, consisting of a rock resting on smaller supports. They are always part of burial grounds. This example **(left)** stands near Stockholm. In Native American folklore, propped stones serve as benchmarks for sacred 'spirit paths'. Good examples are Tripod Rock, New Jersey, and the Lynn Dolmen, Massachusetts. Tripod Rock, in the Pyramid Mountain Natural Historical Area, is generally thought to be an erratic or 'perched boulder'. This famous multi-ton, Pre-Cambrian rock is balanced on three small supports

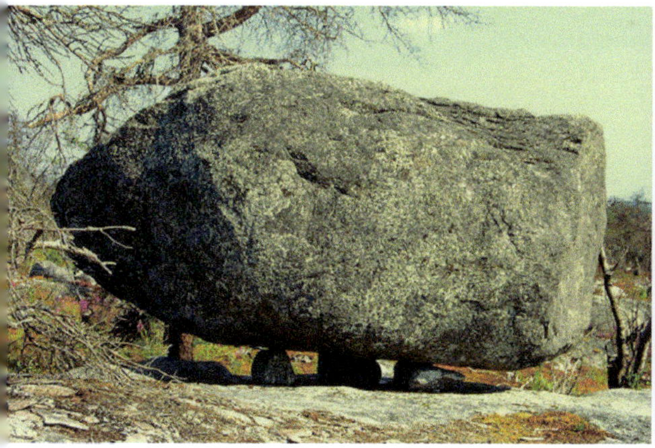

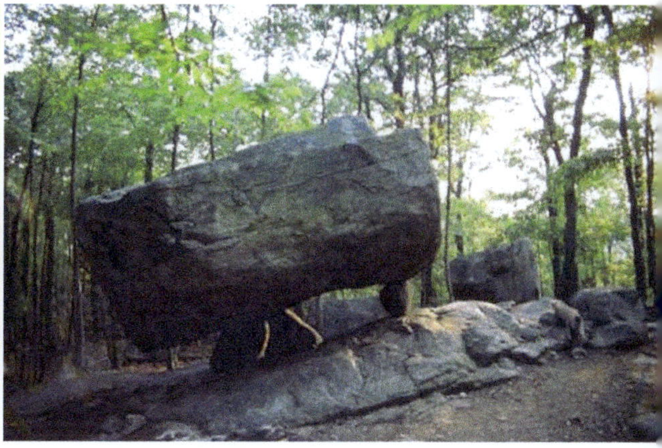

(above right). Roughly 6 metres long, 3 metres wide, and 2.5 metres high, its weight has been estimated as c.127 tons. The stones, however, show no signs of glacial rounding, or tumbling, as would be expected. There is a peculiar triangular crest running the length of its top. The entire point of contact between the main boulder and its support stones form a 3-4-5 triangle, and local tradition says it was put in position by the medicine of Native Americans. It starts to get even more interesting with the fact that about 12 metres NW of Tripod Rock are three boulders that, with it, form another triangle, and two of which are partially balanced on smaller stones. The apex rock is about 3 metres away to the northeast. During the early 1980s, the site was surveyed and it was noted that from the site a large boulder located at the top of the ridge marked the summer solstice sunset. Within a year of the survey a home was constructed on that site and the rock was displaced by earth-moving machinery. Today the sun sets against the far ridge near the edge of a residence and is only partially visible. Some other propped stones in New England, USA, have also been found to be astronomically aligned, which statistically is highly unlikely if they are natural. Elsewhere in the Americas, propped stones are associated with prehistoric cultures; Balanced Rock, in New York State, consists of a huge capstone supported by blocks of white quartz: it has been found to be located over a magnetic anomaly (Burke and Halberg 2005). A huge propped stone at Vottovaara Mountain, Canada, is sacred to indigenous cultures **(above left)**.

Here in the UK, recent work has led to more propped stones being regarded as archaeology rather than having settled through natural processes. At Alcomden Rocks in West Yorkshire, a propped stone occurs very close to a rock surface full of rock basins. David Shepherd has looked at propped stones in Yorkshire, Cumbria, Cornwall, Wales and Ireland, and suggests these stones had cultural significance, even if though they may be 'natural' (Shepherd 2013 & 2014).

At Hendraburnick, Cornwall, a feature called a 'quoit', which was previously thought to have been natural, has been identified as manmade, and is also emblazoned with cup marks. Here, a long block of epidiorite stone is supported by slate bedrock; the geology of the large stone is not to be found on the hill. Excavations by the Cornish Archaeological Society in 2013 yielded arrowheads, mace heads and flint implements, most dated between Late Neolithic to Bronze Age. Freya Lawson-Jones (York University) regards it as, '... a 4000 yr old altar, if you will'. Another granitic Cornish example can be seen at Carn Brae, where, 'A natural rock formation, resembling a megalithic tomb, was built into the wall of the Neolithic enclosure' (Bradley 2000).

Capping the hill above the prehistoric settlement at Leskernick, also in Cornwall, is a dramatic flat-topped, 2.8m long, propped stone, known as 'The Quoit', discovered in

1995. It was built to mimic the natural balanced stones down the slope, and was erected in such a way that at midsummer, the setting sun shines through the peep-hole space beneath (Hamilton et al 2000, and Bender et al 2007). This propped stone is considered to be older than the Bronze Age settlement, and probably Neolithic; a date of 3687 BC best fitted the astronomical alignment. The 'quoit' is also sighted on the skyline from a nearby stone circle: 'The austere tabular stones at the top of the hill, like the tors on other hill tops, were particularly powerful – they were perhaps the source stones…' (Bender et al 2007). Also on Bodmin, on Carburrow Tor, a 4m long propped feature called the Cannon Stone has a, '… megalithic-like chamber underneath… with two step-like features at the top end through which one can squeeze' (Bender et al 2007). A nearby cairn only becomes visible as one passes through this space. A propped stone at the entrance to Carn Lês Boel is supported by small stones that raise it slightly off the ground. It has a partner stone, now half-buried on its side, and together may have served as a gateway to a ritual space.

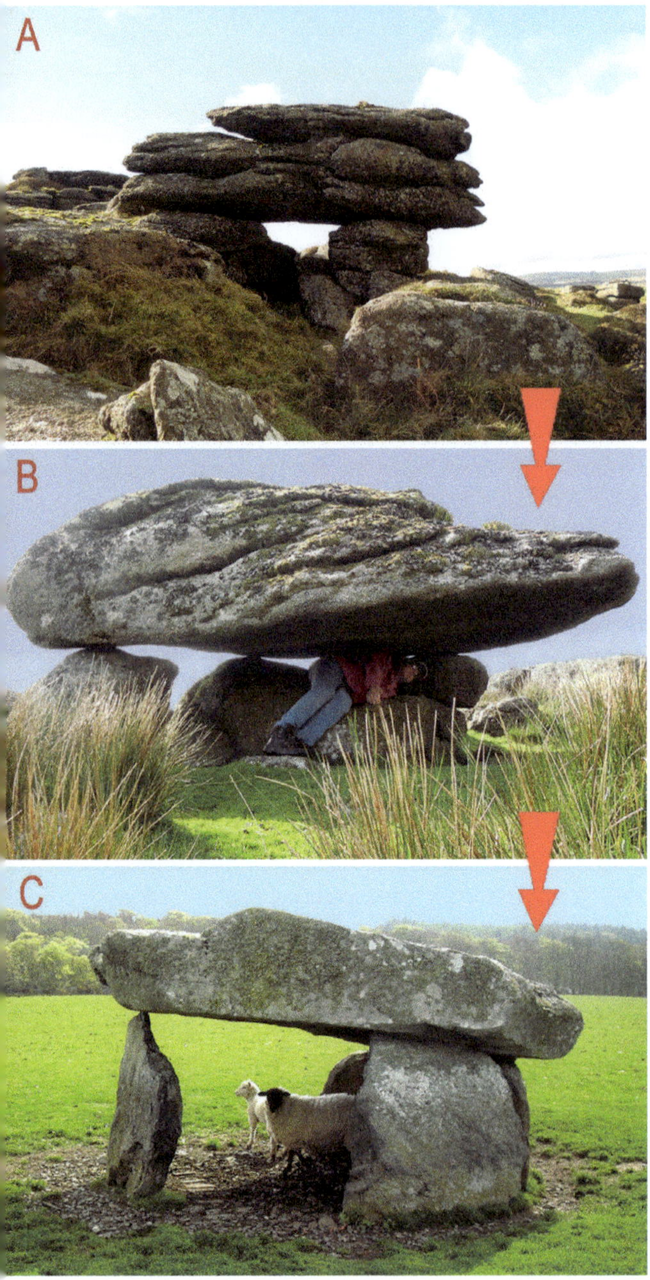

Several tor enclosures, such as Helman Tor on Bodmin, contain propped stones. It has been commented how these large boulders may have been manipulated to point in a certain direction, and, 'One might even speculate that the propped-stones at some enclosures may have been propped up to create special places for bodies to lie in' (Davies 2010). Richard Bradley suggests that dolmens may have been built to resemble tors (Bradley 1998).

On Brown Willy, a relevantly positioned propped stone marks the point where Rough Tor, to the north, disappears from view when walking north along the ridge (Bender et al 2007), or, conversely, comes into view when walking south.

Dartmoor's propped stones

Julian Cope considers that, 'In Cornwall, the natural rocking stones known as logan stones inspired that area's dolmen obsession, with high-flying capstones perched upon fine granite uprights' (Cope 1998). I think the logans in turn inspired the propped stones, which were developed further into the more complex Neolithic dolmens, or cromlechs. This can equally be applied to Dartmoor. Although some propped stones may be natural and fortuitous, I will present evidence that several on Dartmoor (as on Bodmin) *were* in fact erected by people to be *monuments*, or at the very least were natural features that were *modified* to some extent. Glacial erratics tend to have been tumbled and generally have rounded edges – Dartmoor's examples do not! ***They are local.*** In SW England, regarding propped stones, '... there is no geomorphological process that creates that' (Bender et al 2007). So if we embrace the premise that propped stones *are* monuments, we can enquire as to whether they were either balanced boulders about to fall and were supported to stop their demise, thus monumentalising them, or whether they were raised from scratch, with no prior 'history'.

The word dolmen literally means *'stone table'.* French archaeologist Roger Joussaume: 'The French word dolmen is a corruption of British origin, a misreading of the Cornish word *tôlven,* which was not an artificial construction at all, but a boulder left naturally perched on humps of rock' (Joussaume 1998). *Tôlven* should not be confused with *tolmen,* the Cornish for *'holed stone',* although there may have been some cross-fertilisation, for some dolmens, such as Trethevy Quoit, have perforated capstones that may have been rock basins. The term 'stone table' is certainly applicable to propped stones.

This process/development from propped stone to dolmen is demonstrated here **(images opposite)**. Image **A** is a natural feature at the north end of Yar Tor, which is also imbued with a simulacrum. It shows how weathering has formed a 'tunnel' or void.

Image **B** is a truly stunning example of a propped stone which I have no doubt was erected by human means. It had already been suspected as being a monument: 'A possible propped stone at Lower Hartor Tor, demonstrating how it is positioned on the grounders and showing its similarity in appearance with a megalithic chambered tomb' (Klemen 2015). It stands on the south side of the small tor (604675), which outcrops NE of the Drizzlecombe stone rows. It is well worth the walk to its isolated landscape setting, as I would class this as a monument in every sense of the word. A huge 'capstone' over 3m long is balanced on four grounders; another view is shown here, looking from the SW **(right)**. Close by, the face of a simulacrum on the north side of the tor looks towards the midsummer sunset; here, a logan stone offers an overhang under which one can sit. On the surface of the highest stack sits a 30cm diameter rock basin, and a 2m overhang enables one to nestle underneath. The propped stone overlooks the convergence of two river valleys and there is a cairn and a Bronze Age settlement to the SW. I believe that the occupants associated themselves with this structure; they encultured this small but important tor outcrop. From here, outcrops of Higher Hartor Tor on the skyline mark the direction of the midsummer sunset.

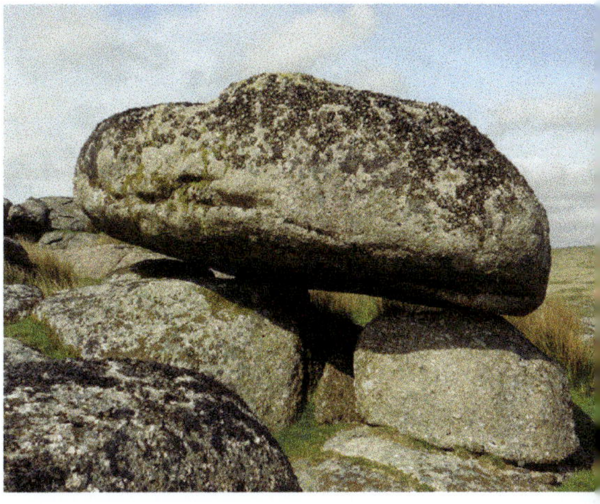

Finally, image **C (opposite)** shows a typical Neolithic dolmen, this example standing on Anglesey. One can see how this pays homage to the previous two structures. I believe these natural features inspired dolmens, just as natural features have been the inspiration for architecture around the planet. We now know that many dolmens where not erected to contain burials, and may never have been covered by an earthen mound or cairn. They have always been freestanding, open to the elements, accessible by the living – like the granite propped stones they so closely resemble. Many chambered tombs and passage graves do incorporate huge boulders in their construction, 'pieces of place' that were moved across the landscape, to bring the spirits of the landscape into these monuments.

I shall now look in more detail at some excellent examples of propped stones on the moor that I think are archaeologically relevant.

Hawks Tor

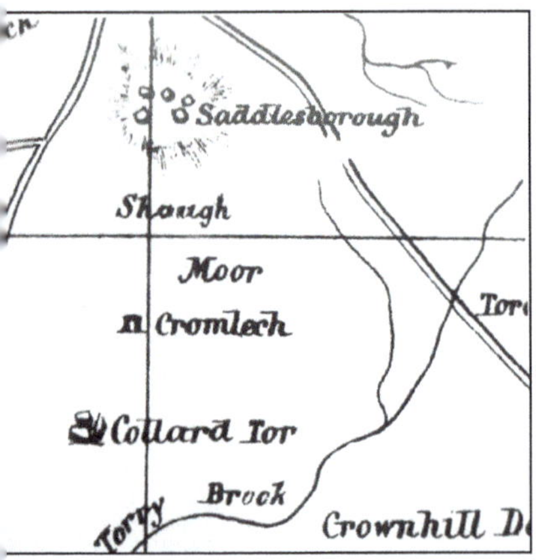

If the structure and landscape setting of the Lower Hartor Tor propped stone was stunning, the one on Hawks Tor (or Hawk's Tor) is exceptional. This small tor (553625) sits at the SW extremity of the moor, on Shaugh Moor, close to the huge china clay works. It has long been suspected that a propped stone here **(centre and bottom)** came to be in its present position through *prehistoric* human effort, and not some natural process or modern action by quarrymen. S Rowe (1848) thought it to be a cromlech, as is shown on this early map **(left)**, where it is shown as 'Cromlech'. RH Worth, however, considered it to be a natural grouping of rocks and outcrop (Worth 1971). On the Dartmoor Trust Archive website a 1940 photo shows it as a 'Dolmen'. A photo dated 1956 is accompanied by this text: 'A small tor, where joints in the granite have formed an aperture resembling a chamber. The roof has been artificially raised on one side on a boulder possibly to make a shelter.' The question is – when was it raised? The Prehistoric Monuments Record of Dartmoor describes the site as a, 'Possible chambered tomb'. In his excellent guide to the moor's ancient sites, William Lethbridge lists the site as 'Hawk's Tor, Dolmen?' in the index. Although he considers the rocks to be undoubtedly from the tor outcrop, he adds, '… I don't think it can be dismissed lightly to suggest the tor was utilised as a dolmen, a cromlech, for this is what it was once thought to be…' (Lethbridge 2015). William, I am inclined to agree. When approaching the site from the north **(centre image)** it resembles a dolmen on the skyline; this may have been the desired effect.

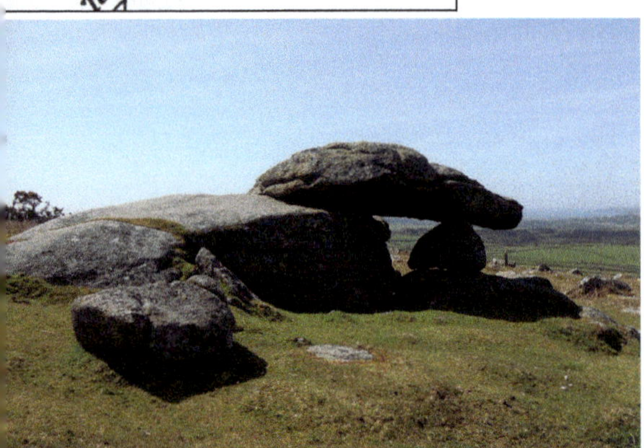

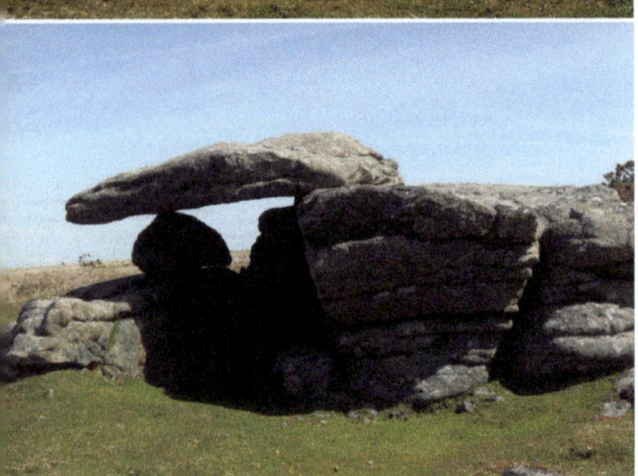

A huge 'capstone', 5.5m long and 3m wide protrudes from the top of the outcrop, supported by a 1m wide boulder **(left)**; it only makes contact with underlying rock at four small points. Quarrymen had tried, but failed, to chisel a slice off the capstone, evidenced by eleven chiselled indents. This slab forms a

cavity below some 3m long and 2m wide, formed by outcrop on three sides, and an entrance which opens to the SW, with fine views to the sea. From the top of the capstone, Sheeps Tor, Sharpitor, Brentor/Brent Tor, Bodmin Moor, and even Cox Tor and Great Staple tor in central Dartmoor, are visible.
The height of the roof of this rock shelter is around 2m high, just high enough for me to stand fully upright. It has been noted previously that the capstone was once part of the outcrop but it was rotated when it was moved, evidenced by the change in the grain of the rock. This is confirmed by a white vein of quartz that runs through the outcrop. The vein on the capstone is now 85° to its natural run through the outcrop, shown here by red arrows **(right)**. It is interesting that archaeologists at Leskernick noted how, at a propped stone known as the Monkey Stone, the joints of the supported block and those beneath did not match the upper block; it had been, '... moved approximately 85° in an anticlockwise direction' (Bender et al 2007). What I think is relevant at Hawks Tor is that the vein here continues below the supporting stone, but does not pass through it. The stone is not a freak of weathering – it has been placed there from somewhere else.

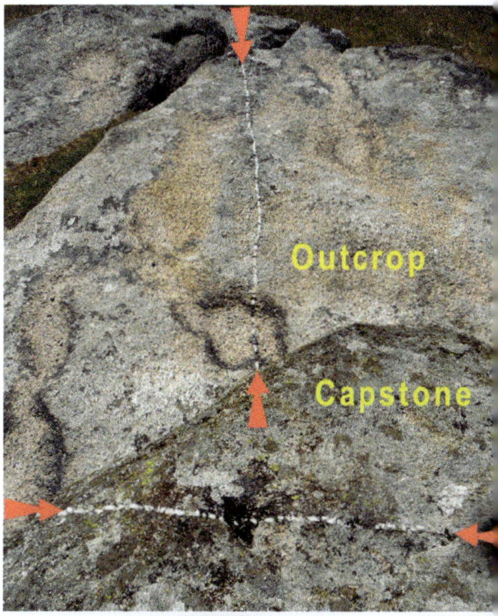

It may also be possible that there was the collapse of a natural overhanging slab, covering a cavity that was already regarded as a sanctuary. A support was installed by levering up the capstone to create, in effect, a dolmen. This 'capstone' also has a 1m diameter rock basin, which has been dry on my visits but looks watertight. The 'newly-exposed' rock surface, now visible due to the rotation of the capstone, has several shallow depressions, which resemble immature rock basins. The rock looks 'fresher' than the top of the capstone. Cracks in the rock and around the basins are home to tiny red sedums.

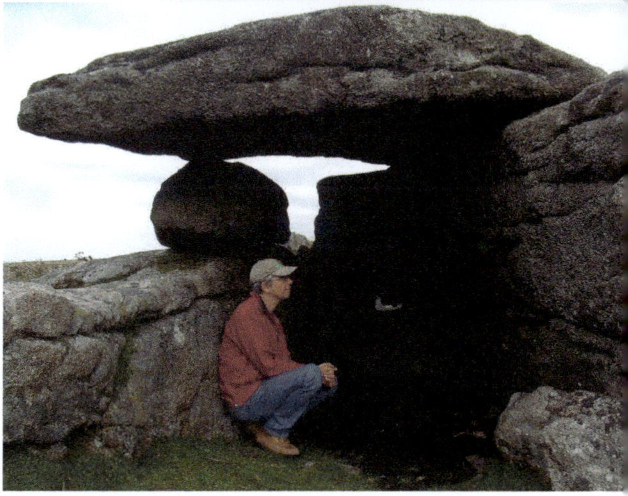

Dowsing showed an energy node in the cavern, and a current that flowed out through the entrance. I had found a sheep's jaw on my way to the site, and left it as an offering on the ledge inside **(right)**. I then tuned into the spirit of the place and a poem was gifted to me **(top image, next page)**. Chanting revealed a resonance that seemed to respond best to a low toning. I recommend visiting this sacred place, which is usually frequented by ponies, sheep, and perhaps the occasional hawk. Spending time at such places is nurturing for the soul.
Belstone Tor, at the opposite end of the moor SE of Okehampton, is a rocky ridge with three prominent summits. The outcrops are dominant from the Nine Stones cairn circle **(images p. 190 & 207)**. In May 2016 I was following the energies of the St Michael Line (details later), which flow from the Nine Stones up to the heights of Belstone Tor. With some delight, I found a propped stone perched on top of one of the

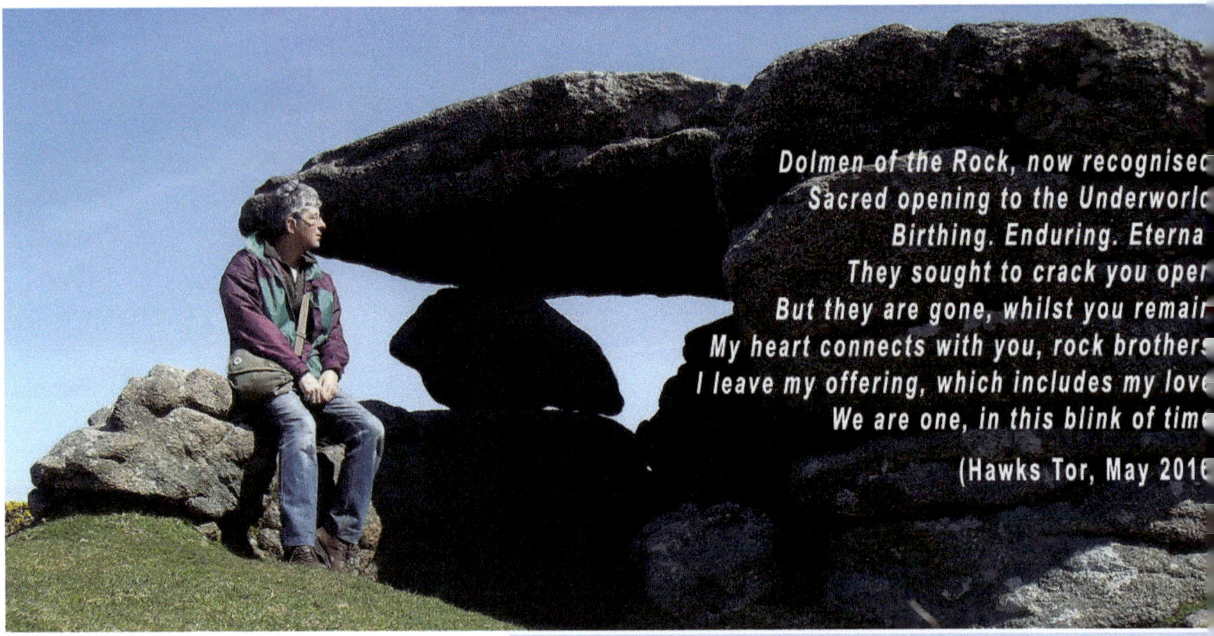

highest stacks at the southern end of the tor (613918). It is 2m long **(right)**, and is prominent on the skyline, affording 360° views as the ground falls away in every direction. Any ritual activities on the nearby level area below the rock would have been overseen by this distinctive and impressive feat of tor enculturing.

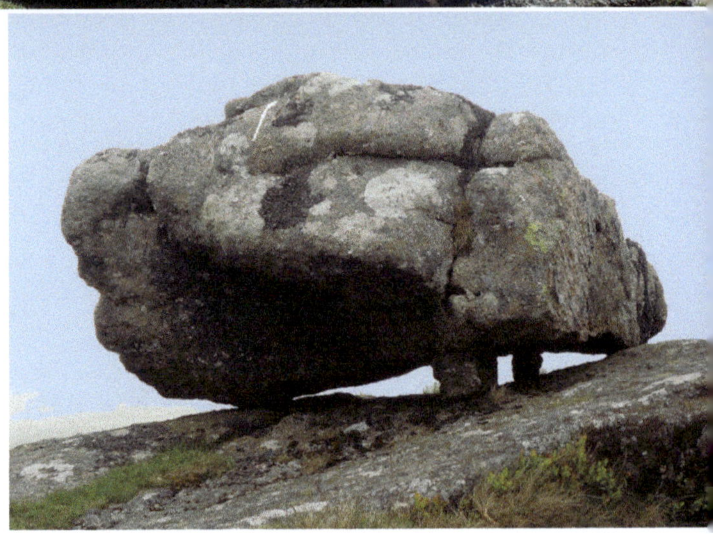

Bag Tor is a small outcrop of granite (762758) under the shadow of Haytor, its mighty neighbour. The setting of the rocks overlooks the valley of the River Sig. I was drawn to this small tor as it was recorded as being home to a rock basin. But as I approached the outcrop from the east it became apparent that next to a fallen logan stone, and the rock basin stone, stood a propped stone **(opposite page, top images).** The 2m+ long slab has clearly slipped or been pulled from the outcrop, upon which the one end still rests. The stone has separated from the outcrop below, and beyond the bedrock it rests on two small, angular stones. A simulacrum face at the lower end seems to survey the valley, as if it is about to launch itself off the tor; it seems unsure whether or not to let go and dive into the landscape below - one day it may pluck up the courage.

As I sat within the rock basin adjacent to the propped stone, under the shade of a guardian holly tree **(image p. 3)**, I tuned in to the spirit of place and, with chilled fingers, wrote the words of my poem, shown later in the rock basin chapter **(image p. 134)**. I could feel the presence of my prehistoric ancestors there, as if it were yesterday.

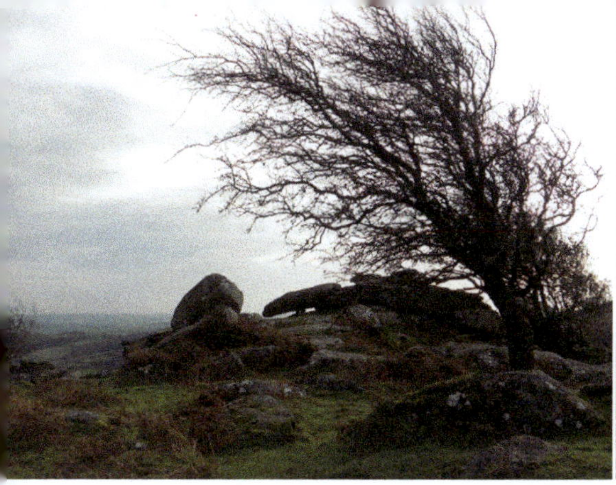

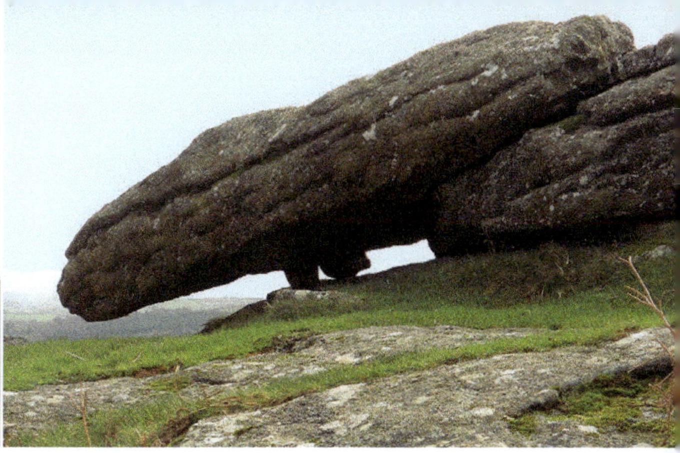

Above: Bag Tor Propped Stone

The Healing Stone, at Batworthy, west of Chagford, is another special stone setting. The stone sits on a small islet midst a stream (662864), nestling by a wall, NE of Batworthy Corner. It was brought to my attention by local resident Jim Hamer during a weekend workshop I was leading in June 2016. It is also known as Cow Bridge, and as the group arrived several cows were indeed in attendance. A local farmer's wife had told Jim how her husband used to sit on the stone to cure his rheumatism, and that other locals found it 'comforting' to sit here when ill. The stone is about 2m long by 1m wide. Jim also confirmed that the Mary current of the St Michael Line flows through the stone. I immediately noticed that the top stone was supported by several smaller ones, **(right)** producing a void beneath – it is a propped stone! Several of our group, unprompted, immediately sat on the slab, such is its enchanting draw **(below right)**.

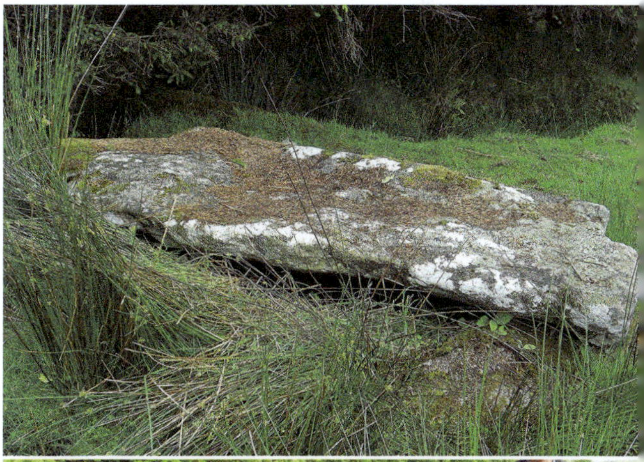

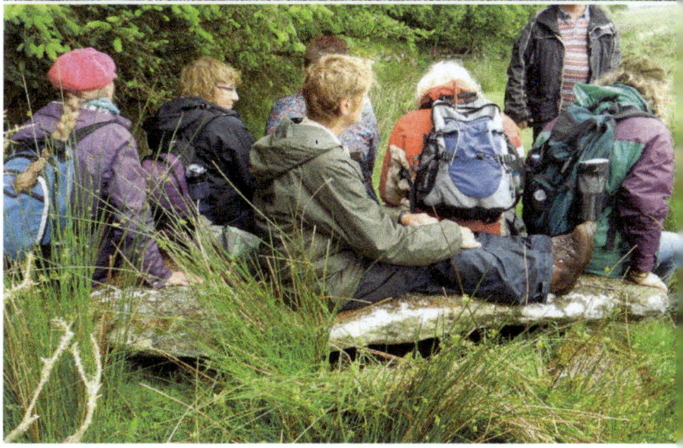

Roos Tor is a fascinating outcrop of granite north of Merrivale. I shall return to the tor in detail later, when I include its many wonders in the Merrivale Shamanic Landscape (Chapter 13). For now I would like to outline a fine propped/logan stone at its summit **(F in images p. 168 & 169)**. To the west of the flagstaff sits a 'capstone' over 2m long, which is supported, as if by magic, by what was originally one stone, which has now cracked into fragments. Close by, another stone lies in a small gully, 2m to the south; this can be rocked and may have once supported the overhang of the capstone. The propped stone overhang is deep enough for a claustrophobic effect to be experienced by anyone lying beneath, as several tons of granite appears to push down onto you. The granite is suspended just inches above the face of anyone lying

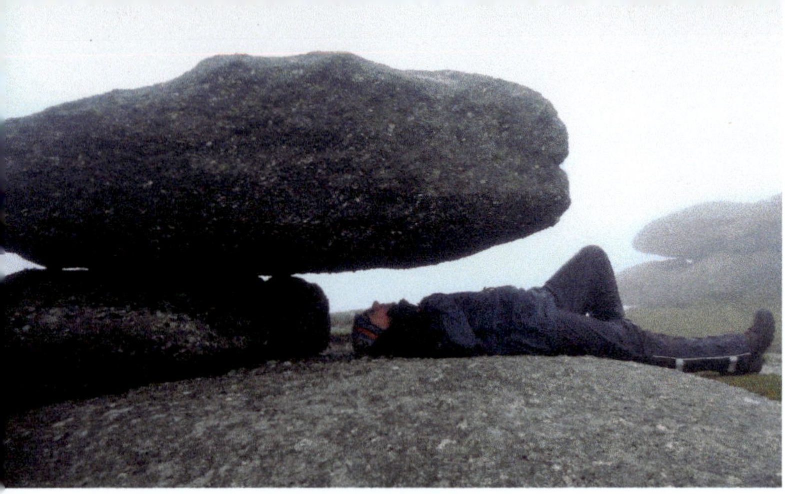

supine beneath **(left)**. And on the occasions when I have lain beneath **(image p. 73)**, I have momentarily wondered if this was to be the day on which the rock finally chose to topple over! Did the facilitating shaman induce similar fears to a prehistoric initiate below by standing on top and rocking it! Even if not manmade, surely this remarkable rock would have inspired people to use it, and perhaps copy it.

Another boulder next to the largest rock basin on the Roos Tor outcrop sits as if an attempt was made to prop it up following a collapse, evidenced by small rocks that have been wedged in beneath a huge slab of granite; this also occurs on Over Tor, where small rocks lie beneath a larger slab.

Hucken Tor is small outcrop of granite to the south of the Merrivale stone rows, and as such I will include it in the Merrivale Shamanic Landscape. The words 'rock basin' are shown on OS maps here, and this is what originally brought me here **(image p. 161)**; a great set of which can be found on stacks built into old walls (552741). One of these stacks is a logan stone, balanced at a precarious angle. But my attention was soon drawn to a huge propped stone nearby, just down slope to the north. The stone is kept company by a guardian hawthorn, which clings adamantly to the living rock **(left and bottom image)**. The capstone is 4m long, up to 2.5m wide, and 0.5m thick. The suspension of the huge slab creates a 0.6m void beneath, enabling one to crawl from one side to the other. Looking through the propped stone void, Pew Tor is framed, so that sunsets from mid-winter through to the spring equinox would be visible to anyone inside. The capstone's long axis points to an azimuth of 300°, to Vixen Tor in the valley below. From here, the fine simulacrum **(images p. 163)** is in profile. The plateau below plays host to a stone circle, the Longstone, and stone rows. To the north, mighty tors reach up to the heavens.

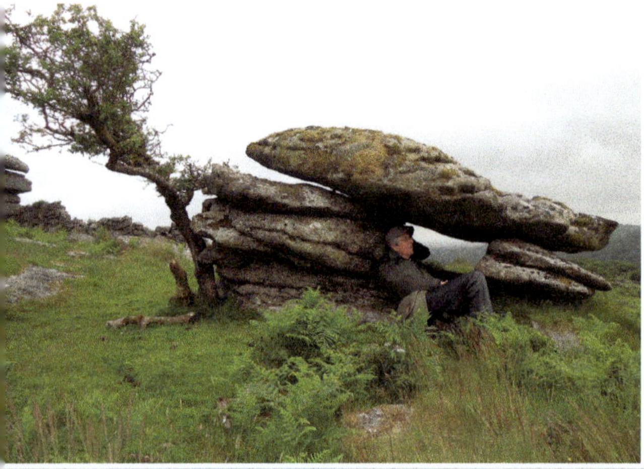

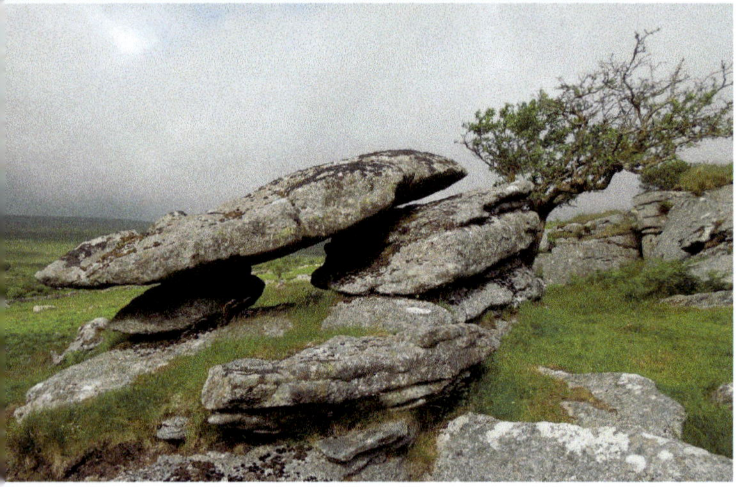

The last example I shall show here **(right)** is that at Black Tor, to the SW of Okehampton. It is located midway between the two northern stacks of this isolated outcrop (567585). The views across the valley of West Okement River to Corn Ridge beyond are stunning. An ancient oak forest occupies the valley floor below. I had been 'tipped off' to this site by a photo I had seen online. A 1.5 mile trek from Meldon Reservoir was worth it. I found the 'propped stone' and soon realised that it is probably natural. A slab of granite overhangs by 2m, and is held up by an elongated rock beneath. A void beneath, about 1m high, was large enough to receive me. I chanted and found that the acoustics of the void were profound, my voice sounding deeper, resulting in a slight echo. Although probably not manmade or modified, I still think that our distant ancestors may have sat in such places for rituals and rites of passage. And, as I have said, such places may have inspired people to purposefully prop up stones. There is another point to this story too; if I had not walked across the moor to check out this stone setting, I would not have found the huge 'bison' or 'auroch boulder' **(image p. 37)**. Perhaps that was the whole point of my journey to Black Tor that day.

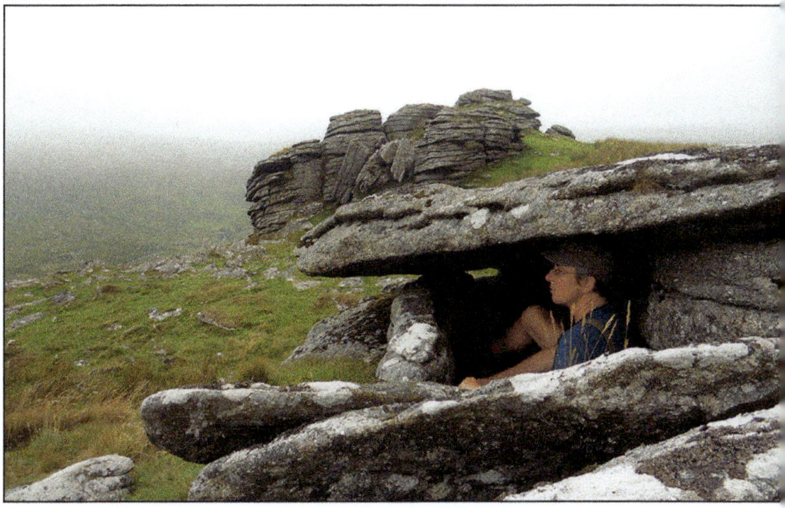

Having spent time at many propped stones across the moor and elsewhere, I constantly feel that these places cry out for recognition, to be seen as having been culturally relevant to our ancestors. They are places where we can sit, be still, to listen and be receptive, to lay bare, not conceal. We weave narratives into the land, from the warp and weft of our experiences, and those of today are as valid as were those of people thousands of years ago. Places like propped stones are where we can open our minds to epiphany, to receiving the wisdom inherent in the landscape. Recognition that pieces of landscape can be regarded as monuments, whether originally erected or simply perceived and utilised, means that I have radically changed the way I connect with a landscape. Landscape features can be artefacts, whether people enhanced them or not (Bradley 2000). When do geographical features, such as a simulacra, cease being 'natural' and become monuments? To the Dartmoor shaman, such a distinction was blurred. All monuments are constructed of 'pieces of place', and as such were sacred even before they were raised or enhanced. People drew from the power of Nature and from features seen as having been created by ancestral beings; they sought to replicate these works of the gods - deity was thus always close at hand.

'The Propped Stone of Leskernick mimics the natural propped stones found on the slopes below many of the tors of the moor.'
(Bender et al 2007.)

11. Rock Basins – Cauldrons of Life

'Of all the key elements in former sacred geographies, water was perhaps the most ubiquitous.'
(Devereux 2013)

Less than 3% of Earth's water is freshwater, and of this 30% is under our feet as groundwater. Water is always on the move – a moving target we are constantly trying to pin down. The very nature of water as a prerequisite for survival was one of the factors that led to it being regarded, universally, as sacred. Most of the world's religions and early civilisations believed in the healing and ritually purifying attributes of water, and as such is an integral element of many ancient myths (Knight 2015); the majority of Aboriginal 'songlines' include water holes. Water is associated with intuition and psychic powers and the subconscious, and the daily ebb and flow of tides links water to the moon. Rivers are symbolic of the human lifespan, from their source (birth) to where they meet the sea (death). There is a transient, spiritual and ethereal quality to water that pulls on our emotions; from the dramatic plunges of great waterfalls, to the anastomosis of gently flowing, mature rivers; from sacred wells and springs to mysterious deep pools and lakes; from the delicate morning dew drops gracing spiders webs to the deep and dark subterranean flows of cave systems.

Many of the great prehistoric monuments of the world are intimately associated with water courses, such as Newgrange, Stonehenge, Egyptian temples, and the Great Serpent Mound in Ohio, USA (Knight 2015): 'Neolithic sites seem to have been located next to watercourses, particularly at points of transition' (Vicki Cummings, *in* Scarre 2002). The Nazca Lines of Peru intersect or change direction at former riverbeds, where precious water emerged onto the Pampas (Devereux 2010b). Plynlimon mountain is the 'Heart Centre of Wales' (Biltcliffe and Hoare 2017). It has five peaks, and the Wye and Severn are born on the mountain. Interestingly, it is shown as 'Plym' on old maps, suggesting an origin to the naming of the River Plym on Dartmoor; its source is also high on the moor.

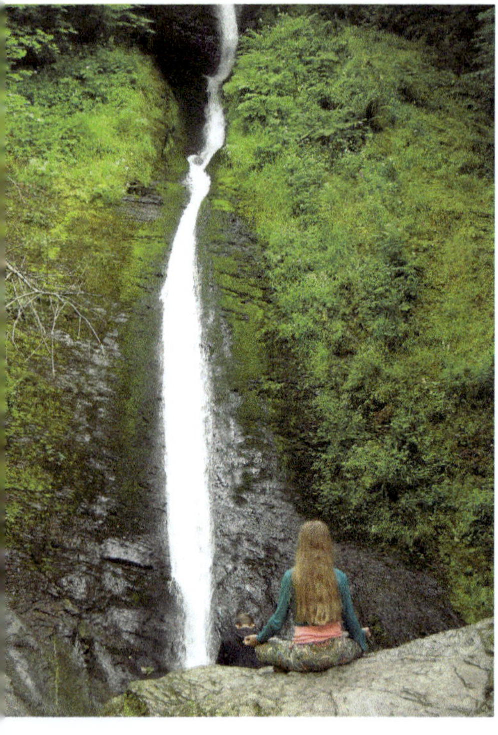

Negative ions have a positive and healthy effect on humans, and these manifest where water is in motion, such as at streams, waterfalls, and seashores. Even next to a raging waterfall one feels peace and a sense of balance **(left)** as here at the

White Lady, Lydford. Water places are conducive to entering altered states and many holy springs and wells around the world are associated with sacred dream sleep. Sacred riparian ceremonies have taken place alongside holy rivers for thousands of years, a tradition perpetuated in the Bible by Jesus and John the Baptist.

Water is often heard even when it cannot be seen, possessing an acoustic depth and dimensionality of presence as it travels through places, linking them. Rain can be heard and felt if one's eyes are closed; the cacophony of a waterfall may be heard a long way off, and yet may only come into view at close range. What did such invisible roars once mean to people?

Rock basins

During my many trips to Dartmoor, I began to notice depressions full of water in the bedrock on some of the tors. Initially, I thought nothing of these in terms of them having possessed spiritual attributes back in prehistory. But then it gradually dawned on me that these striking water features embedded into otherwise barren rock may have been regarded as special. A little research proved my hunch correct.

It is generally believed that natural rock basins were formed by the repeated freezing of water in surface irregularities of granite, where the expanding ice and frosts gradually prises out the individual crystals, particularly the softer feldspars. These start as small irregularities in the rock but over thousands of years become larger and deeper as the granite matrix dissolves, leaving glistening deposits of quartz at the bottom. Both mechanical and chemical weathering can give rise to these smooth, bowl-like depressions, also known as solution basins. Lichen may also be an agent in weathering, as their hyphae penetrate and weaken the rock. Rock basins generally occur on the flat surfaces of the highest stacks of granite, and come as something of a revelation when one reaches the summit, to be greeted by a small pool of water, previously unseen from below. Buzzards and other birds can sometimes give the game away, as they visit the basins during dry spells.

William Borlase noted rock basins in 1754, and carried out the first systematic record of them. He thought them to have been carved out of the living rock by Druids, as he also considered to be the origin of the teetering logan stones, which are often capped by a basin: 'The purest of all water is that which comes from the Heavens, in snow, rain or dew; and of this the Ancients were not ignorant' (Borlase 1754). The leaders who held 'the wisdom and knowledge' would disappear from view from the clan members waiting below, only to return with a pitcher of 'holy' water. He envisaged water being collected from the lips and channels that issue from many basins, and that objects such as mistletoe and oak leaves may have been dipped in the waters of the basins to bless or purify them. He even suggested that the basins would be used for scrying or hydromancy, depending on what was observed in or on the waters. This ancient form of divination was recorded in ancient Persia. Shown here **(right)** is one of Borlases' sketches of the rock basins on the summit stack at Carn Brae, Cornwall.

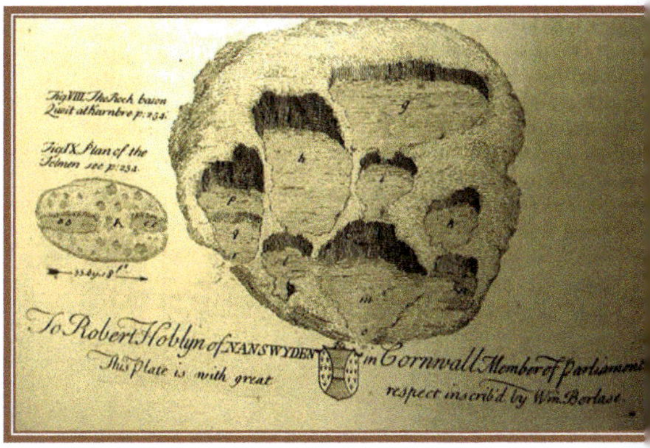

His theories concerning the spiritual uses of rock basins fell out of favour with archaeologists, chiefly because it was discovered that the prehistoric monuments of Britain did not owe their origins to the Iron Age

Druids at all. The concept that natural features in landscape, such as rock basins, could be invested with spiritual and cultural relevance was also many decades in the future. Rock basins became forgotten, only to be mentioned every now and again in local guidebooks and by folklorists.

All this was to change, however, when anthropologists and explorers started travelling the world, bringing back with them records of how aboriginal cultures held rock basins in high regard, even as sacred places. Let us have a look at some of these.

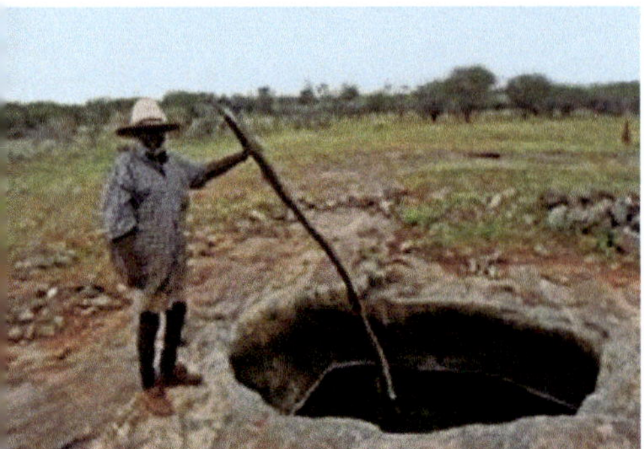

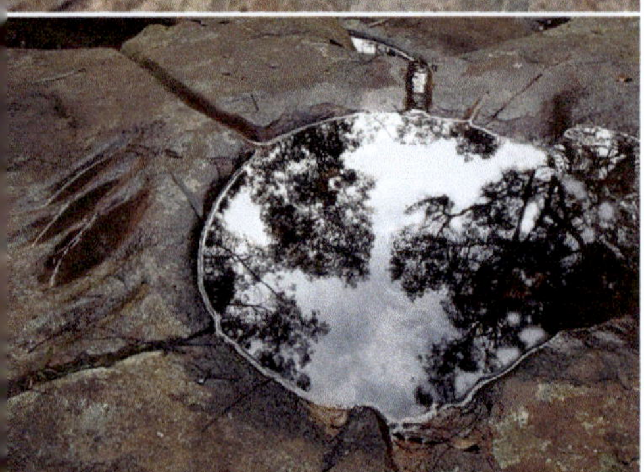

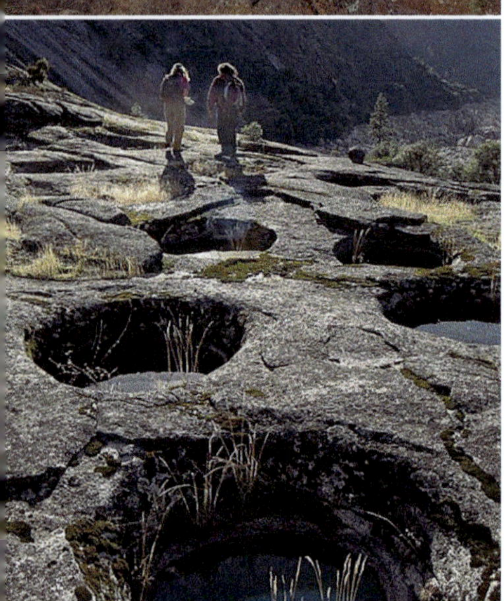

Global reverence of rock basins

Rock basins occur around the world where granite is weathering, but they can occur in other rocks. On top of Uluru, Australia, the Aborigines have woven three rock basins into their mythology, seeing them as where Ungata, the leader of the Kunia people, bled to death. A water-filled rock basin at Ilpili, near Alice Springs, is a metre across and yet, although only a few cms deep, it stays full even through droughts. The local Aborigines sing ancient Dreamtime songs into the night nearby and make black tea with water from the waterhole (Snyder 1990). Another site recorded in the Alice Springs area comprised a 9m blade of rock standing balanced on end which stood next to a small waterhole. It was a teaching or 'dreaming' spot (Snyder 1990). As already mentioned, Aboriginal songlines are often connected by rock basins **(top)**. Water soakage is important in Aboriginal mythology, and most sources of water are associated with Dreaming stories. Well-defined grooves are shown here **(left)** in the sandstone beds of Camp Fire Creek, near Sydney. The grooves were formed by Aboriginal people sharpening axes.

The Western Arnhem Land Aborigines believe that rock is male and water female, and that where the two meet are places of great power. At Canoelands, Maroota, ancient Aborigine rock paintings and engravings are etched into rock close to a cascade of four rock pools. Multiple small pools occur next to rock art in the Terrey Hills (Stanbury and Clegg 1990). One rock basin on King Rock, Western Australia, holds up to 7 million litres of water! Some basins are large enough to have well formed overhanging side walls. Elsewhere, Afghan camel herders clear out the debris from rock basins so they can collect more rainwater.

Early American Indians, including the Miwok people, lived for thousands of years as hunter-gatherers in the Sierra Nevada region. Carved rock basins **(left)** have been found associated with their ancient settlements, arrowheads and small stone tools. The basins average more than 1m in diameter and some are nearly 1m deep. To create them, Miwok tribe members built fires on the *granite* surface, heating the rock until it fractured. They then crumbled and pounded the fractures with stone tools and removed the debris, inch by inch, until the basins were formed (Moore and Gillett 1993). The Indians were mimicking natural rock basins in the area. It has been suggested that the water held in these basins was used for ritual initiation. Perhaps they were also used for grinding corn, which would combine the practical and the spiritual; in grain rituals, these basins would imbue the fertility of the grains they are grinding up. Similar cylindrical depressions can be found on the top surface of a granite outcrop in Texas, known as Enchanted Rock.

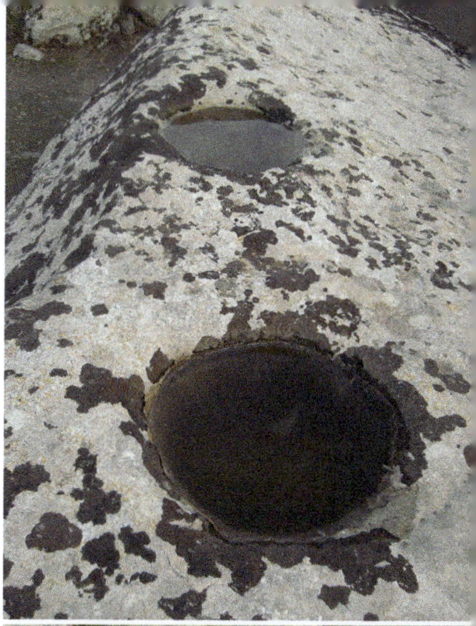

For many years I have partaken in pilgrimages to ancient sacred sites, and on recent re-examination of my photographs I have identified rock basins at several places. On my visits to the Neolithic sites of Malta I captured some rock basins that seem to have been incorporated into the temple complexes, as if the sites themselves were built around them. On my 2007 trip to Hagar Qim, next to the main temple entrance, I photographed a prone stone with two water-filled rock basins on top surface **(top)**. Even then they made an impression on me, and I noted others scattered around the temple. At Kordin III temple, one stone had been hollowed out, and subdivided into seven divisions – the number of human chakras **(right)**. Were people laid down in these waters for ritual submersion?

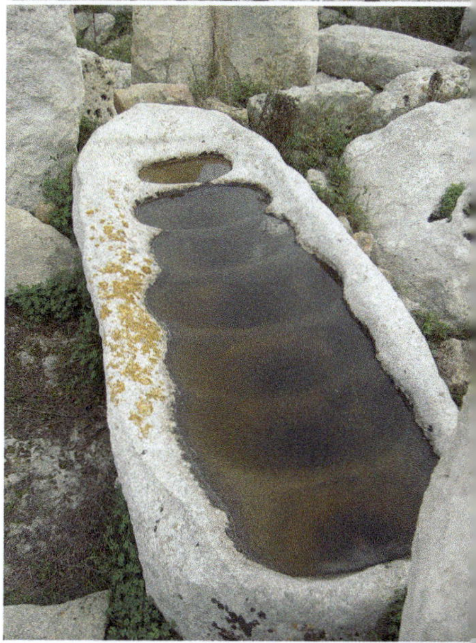

I visited Di Li Muri on Sardinia in 2007. It is now obvious that a natural rock at the very heart of the prehistoric stone setting displays what I now recognise as ancient, eroded rock basins. The rock is clearly the focus for the site, and even has an 'altar' niche carved on one side, seen on the right side of rock here. This also forms the gaping mouth of a zoomorphic simulacrum **(right)**.

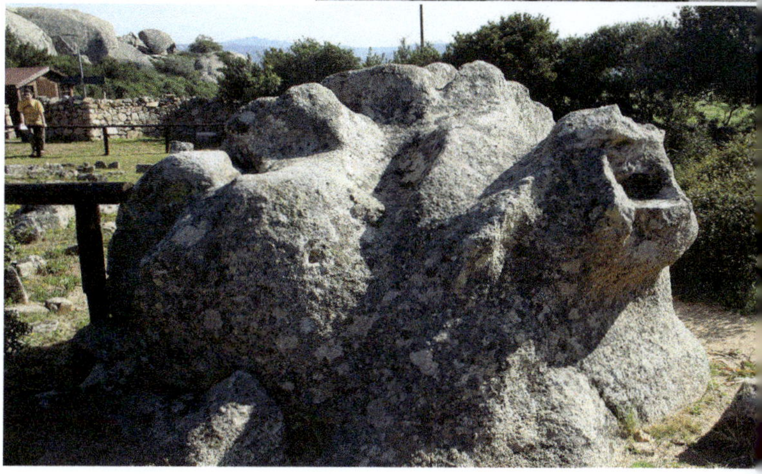

The menhir at St Uzek, Brittany, has been Christianised by the mounting of a cross on the top. But there is also a rock basin on one side, showing that the megalith may have been sacred even before it was stood up. Some of the megaliths at Avebury look as if the depressions on what was once their upper surfaces when they lay on the earth, may have been receptacles for 'holy' rainwater.

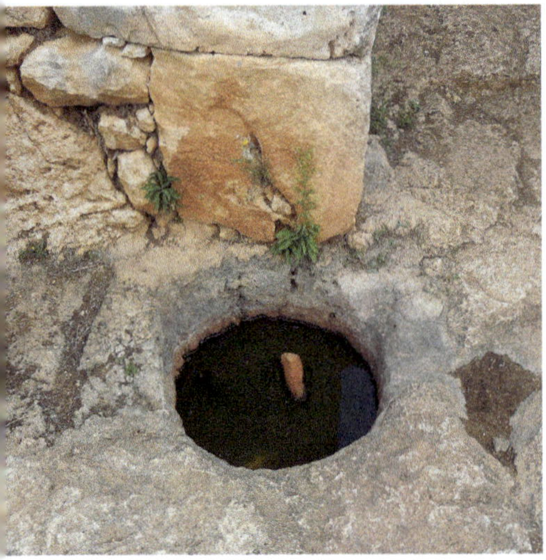

In 2013, I noted holed stones and rock basins around the site of Talati de Dalt on Menorca, and yet more natural basins can be seen midst the temple at Torretrencada. I also found another rock basin that is clearly manmade at Torralba d'en Salort. The whole temple complex of Torre D'en Galmes seems to have been set onto a rock outcrop perforated by numerous rock basins **(left)**, and more artificial ones have been added. The main entrance has an altar-like block of stone with an enhanced, elongated rock basin.

In recent years, Prof Chris Tilley has championed the cultural relevance of rock basins, chiefly in Cornwall. But he also cites a rock surface of Cambrian age near Simrishamn, Sweden, where there is a display of Bronze Age rock art, surrounding a central 3m diameter basin-like depression, the latter of which lacks any rock art (Tilley 2004). Tilley also noted that in the Huat Leon region of Brittany, many of the heavily weathered granite outcrops, which rise to up to 10m out of an otherwise flat landscape, were pitted with rock basins and channels. What is more, most of the menhirs were erected between tens of metres, and no more than 2km, from these outcrops. There was intervisibility between these outcrops and the menhirs in the vicinity, which was mostly lacking between the menhirs themselves. Some of these outcrops also bore cup marks. He suggests that each menhir was associated with a particular outcrop, from which its stone derived, and that ceremonial ways ran between the outcrops and the menhirs. He also cites the Men-Marz menhir, at Brignogan, which is indented with 15cm deep solution basins and interconnecting channels. This was the upper surface of the stone when it lay on the earth; this suggests that it was chosen because it already had significance when it was *'natural'* (Tilley 2004). This is complemented by the dolmen at Cruz Moquen, Brittany, the granite capstone of which is undulating with pronounced hollows. It is said that at full moon, woman would raise their skirts on front of the dolmen in the hope of becoming pregnant (Burl 1985).

Sacred rock basins of the British Isles

Although few have previously thought the rock basins of Dartmoor were once revered, elsewhere around the British Isles both folklore and recent research would suggest otherwise.

In Ireland, near Glengarrif, Co. Cork, rock basins on boulders are known as bullauns or bulláns (=*bowl*), and across Ireland are subject to local reverence. Some traditions speak of water that is drunk from basins cures warts and rheumatism, and even cures barren women of their infertility (Hadingham 1974). Water from a rock basin set into a low mound next to Louch Drumgay, County Fermanagh, cured sore eyes. Other basins near churches have been used as baptismal fonts. Legend says that the head of St Aid, the 6th century Bishop of Killaire, hit at stone at his birth, leaving a hole in it, which collected rainwater which cured all ailments. Bullauns are also found in Sweden, Lithuania and France.

In 1896 Thomas Westropp wrote, 'Basin Stones occur not infrequently at or near dolmens, e.g. at Kiltanon and Newgrove near Tulla, and at Ballyganner and Cappaghkennedy on the borders of the Burren, at the last of which five appear in one slab'. In the Life of St. Mochulleus, written in 1141, a basin 'like a large *hydria*' was found in a polished block of stone when the saint was levelling the site of his church on Tulla Hill. A large block with two basins is amongst the remains at the place of inauguration of the local kings at Magh Adhair Tulla, Co. Clare; at Magh Adhair, within the enclosure to the north of the mound, is a bulláun (basin) stone made of a purple conglomerate **(right)**, brought to this spot from elsewhere. Some have suggested that the bulláun played a role in inauguration rituals; '... the man who would be king washed himself with the sacred water of its basin, using as a symbolic soap, a red stone fixed in the rock' (Westropp 1896). One large bulláun stone at Temple Feaghna, Co Kerry, lies next to the old graveyard, and has eight basins on top. This block is associated with St Feaghna and was involved in Good Friday pilgrimages (Hadingham 1974). These are probably all remnants of pre-Christian reverence for rock basins. This last example is from Co Cork **(right)**.

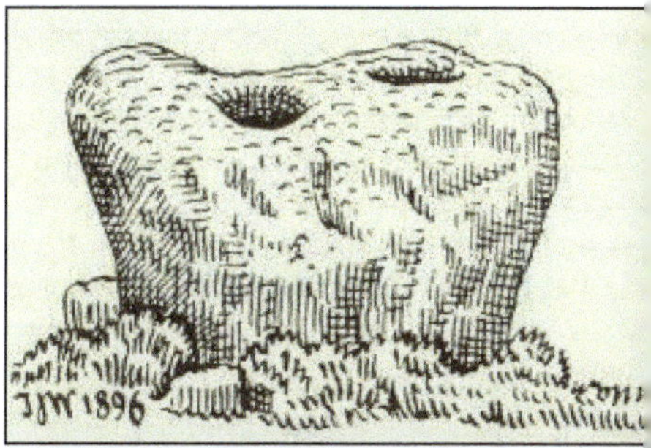

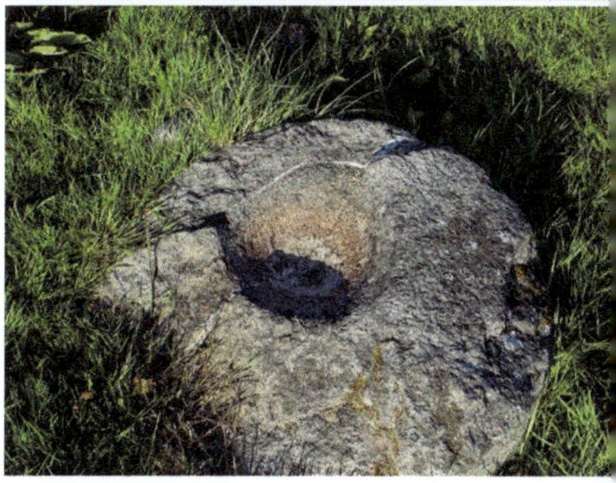

Bullán rocks are particularly fascinating as they are usually associated with some particular local story. Some Irish basins were 'cursing stones', from where a curse could be sent to someone if their name was uttered whilst a stone was turned in the basin. Later, in Scotland and Ireland, these were turned into prayer stones, whereby one could rotate the stone whilst praying for others. These usually relate to how the stone was created or else the stone forms an essential prop (usually magical) to some other event. Such stones are also known as Bride or Biddy stones. It is said that when quartz rocks are ground in the depressions this can affect one's psychic abilities (Biltcliffe and Hoare 2017). In 2012, a cursing stone was found on Canna, Scotland, which has been dated c. 800AD. Another of similar age has been found on the Shiant Isles.

In Scotland, rock basins at Stob an t'Sluichd, in the Cairngorms, are deep enough to receive a person up to their waist. It has been observed that on windy days the action of the wind can reach down into the water and produce a swirling action. It's as if the gods themselves are stirring the water with their fingers! In Lilloch Burn and Glen near Neilston, in East Renfrewshire, witches are associated with numerous potholes that have worn into each other, giving rise to fantastic shapes.

On a ridge called Creag a Chree ('*rock of the trembling/rocking or cattle'*) near Arperfeelie, Yorkshire, are the remains of several ancient hut circles, one of which has a rock basin stone within. Tradition has it that in the early 1800's a local farmer took this basin stone to his house, but as night fell his family was greatly disturbed by strange noises, which became louder, until on the third night the noises were disturbing the whole valley; a thunderous voice was then heard ordering the farmer to return the stone. The farmer returned the stone and peace returned to the area. This stone was regarded as beneficial in terms of infertility, as local folklore contests: '... childless women bathe in its cloud drawn waters immediately before sunrise.' Elsewhere, in the upland regions of the North Yorkshire Moors and Northumberland are many open landscape 'rock basins' stones and cylindrical depressions on rocky outcrops, some formed naturally, others modified, and some entirely manmade (Smith and Walker, 2011). Rock basins across Northern England are often accompanied by cup and ring marks, many of which are very weathered (Smith and Walker 2011). The link between rock basins and simulacra is displayed on the North Yorkshire Moor in a large boulder called the Beast Stone; a rock basin lies within the 'head' of the beast (Smith and Walker 2011). That some of the smaller rock basins may be manmade was hinted at by the discovery of a large flat stone *inside* a basin which had been ground smooth on its underside as a result of creating the basin (Smith and Walker 2008). At Gayles Moor, Co. Durham, two cup marks with multiple rings sit on opposite sides of a rock basin, the three features forming an alignment on the surface of a large rock (Beckensall 1999). At Lordenshaws, Northumberland, rock basins and long channels are adjacent to cup and ring marks.

One rock basin inside the Iron Age fort at Old Berwick (Northumberland) has Druidic folklore and is called the 'Bloody Trough', from its association with sacrifice. Either side of the Drake Stone (another large Northumberland outcrop) are two large rock basins. The location has Druidic associations and 19th century healing folklore. In Lancashire, several rocks displaying rock basins have been named, such as the Buttock Stone, Saucer Stones, and the Bride Stones. There are more Northern examples.

Ley lines champion Alfred Watkins mused as to whether rock basins are connected with ancient ley systems. He noted that a ley involving the Longstone, Forest of Dean, stands within metres of a natural rock with a basin on its surface, with a notch in the side of it. He did not regard this as natural. He suggested that the basin may have received oil, which was burnt for beacon purposes (Watkins 1925). On the Belinus Line (Britain's longest alignment) stands Etching Hill, on Cannock Chase, Staffs. At the centre of the summit is a hollow (like a rock basin), once part of a Bronze Age burial cist. A node of yin and yang energy, belonging to the alignment, can be dowsed here (Biltcliffe and Hoare 2012).

Cornish rock basins

The theories I will soon expound, namely that Dartmoor's rock basins had spiritual/cultural relevance to prehistoric people, have been given validity, in my opinion, by the work done in recent decades by forward-thinking archaeologists, some of whom I have already mentioned (Bender et al 2007 and Tilley 2010). They have suggested that at various Cornish sites, particularly on Bodmin, the location of several monuments and settlements were determined, to various degrees, by the location of granite stacks and boulders incorporating rock basins, which they often call by their geological term, solution basins. What is important is the geographical proximity of the two moors, the virtually identical prehistoric living practices and monuments, and that the tors of both moors are predominantly granite, from the same batholith in fact **(image p. 8)**.

Prof Chris Tilley has produced a good survey of rock basins in West Penwith, citing well over 100 examples. He is insightful in his observation that, 'The tors, and the solution basins, would have been variously regarded as the petrified shapes of ancestral beings, or as the result of the actions of the ancestors who sculpted the rocks and created the chambers in them... and who carved out the solution basins' (Tilley 2010). Back in 1754, William Borlase had suggested that the purity of the water in the basins had been important. Concerning the granite outcrops of Bodmin Moor, Tilley concurs: 'The incorporation of solution basins may be all about connecting the purity of rain water, with death rites involving a requirement for purification... places where water collects, falling from the heavens and filling the solution basins of the high tors, were of great significance...' (Tilley 2010). Let's look at some of Cornwall's rock basins.

Watch Croft Barrow is a cairn to the north of the famous holed stone at Men-an-Tol. Based on the 1872 excavations, it seems that the cairn **(right)** incorporated a grounder boulder of granite which had a solution basin on its upper surface (shown here as the dark circle towards the right end of rock A). It looks as if the cairn was built around a rock stack and that the rock basin may not have been covered – it was meant to be exposed and utilised! Other solution basins occur on outcrops close by the cairn (Tilley 2010). The cairn overlooks Men-an-Tol, which is thought to be significant, as the holed stone here is now regarded as a solution basin that weathered all the way through and was uprighted **(right)**. Holed stones due to this process are rare, as rock basins usually weather through the sides before a hole can be eroded straight through. Another fine example occurs in situ on Zennor Hill, which looks like it has reached a phase just preceding that, when it can be detached from the rock and erected as a megalith. These large in situ perforated rocks must be of great antiquity, and may have had significance back in prehistory (Tilley 2010). The Tolmen stone and Tolvan Stone, at Gweek, may be other examples of how rock basins morphed into megaliths.

The Giant's Stone or Rock, north of Zennor, is 5.5m long and 1m thick and has three deep rock basins on its upper surface. At Zennor Hill, wind worn rocky outcrops yield basins that accompany cairn material; the example shown here demonstrates how the Men-an-Tol holed stone may have looked prior to its removal from the parent outcrop **(right)**. The spectacular rock basins at Bosworlas Rocks (NW of the Boscawen-un stone circle) were referred to as *The Giant's Chair* by Borlase in a 1769 book on Penwith's stone sites. This view shows the telltale signs of a well-eroded rock basin as seen from below the granite stack, betrayed by the deep niche sculpted in the rock **(bottom image)**.

Tilley noted that most Neolithic and Bronze Age enclosures occur on hills, and that are in close proximity to tors possessing solution basins. Indeed, some of the most important prehistoric ceremonial sites of Cornwall, notably Rough Tor, Carn Brae and Helman Tor, have very high numbers of rock basins. At Trencrom, an Iron Age hill fort was previously a single-walled Neolithic enclosure. There is a well at the location which may have been constructed for the former inhabitants. Cairns and hut circles can be seen in the level area enclosed by the stone and earth banks: 'On the largest of these cairns are some rock-basins, known as the Giant's Chair, the Giant's Cradle, and the Giant's Spoon' (Tilley 2010). In similar vein, the Neolithic settlement site of Carn Brea was literally built around outcrops and boulders incorporating

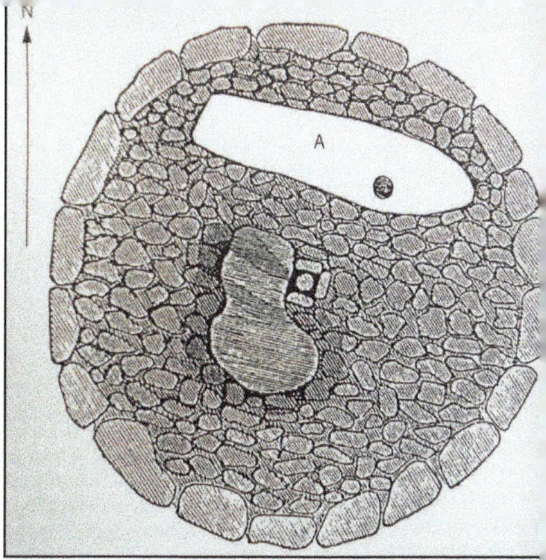

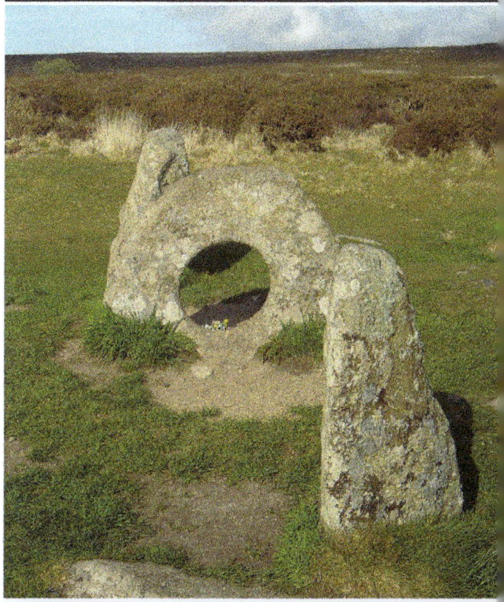

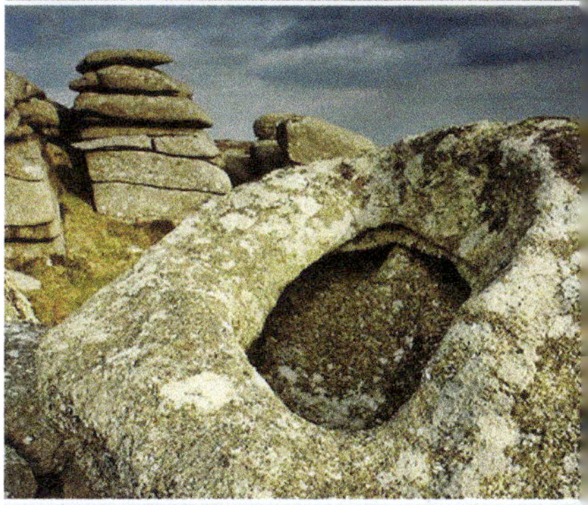

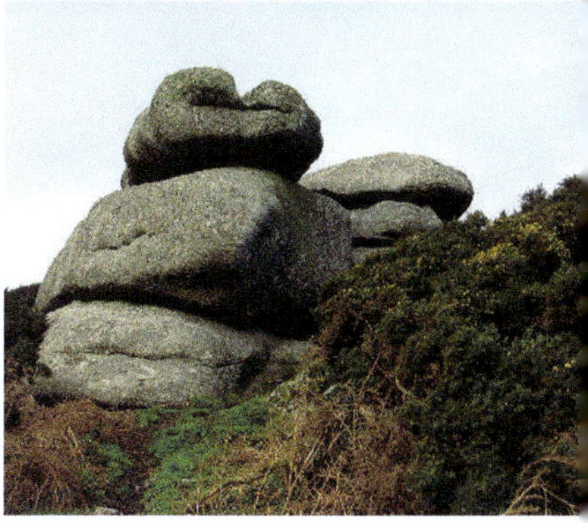

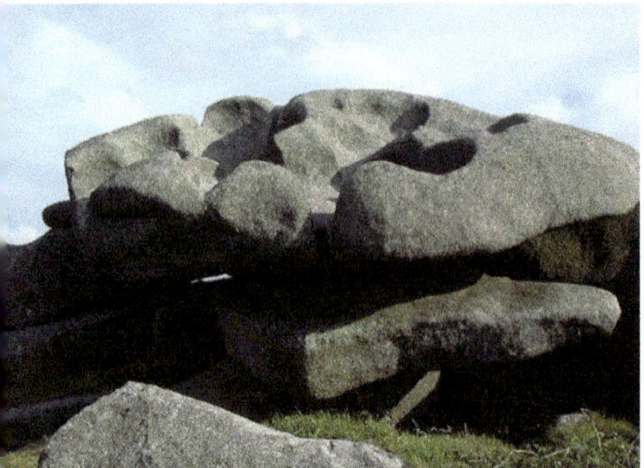

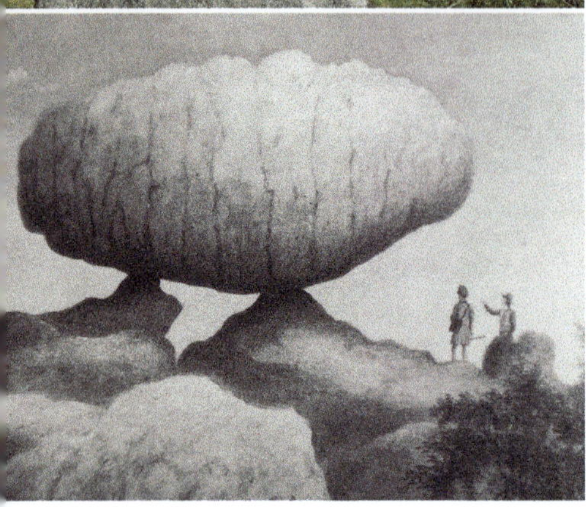

deeply eroded rock basins. The central summit stack is a leaning block of granite with basins, known as the Cup and Saucer **(left)**. It was the spiritual focus of the settlement, literally overseeing all those who dwelt in its shadow.

At Chapel Carn Brae (a different site in Penwith), a former rock basin stone (now eroded through) has been uprighted vertically against the granite outcrop, such was its cultural importance **(image p. 132)**; this compares to some Dartmoor examples (see below). The hill is an important site, showing evidence of late Neolithic and early Bronze Age activity. The Tolmen, at Constantine, was a truly massive rock that has been estimated as having weighed around 700 tons **(left)**. It was a logan stone, and is recorded as, '... being an egg-like stone, placed on two natural rocks... pits and channels carved into its upper surface which were thought to be the work of the Druids' (Michell 1982). These are referring to a system of rock basins, which are seen as the undulating upper surface in this 18th century illustration. This amazing edifice was disgracefully destroyed by quarrymen in 1869.

Further to this, at Creeg Tol (meaning *holed stone*), there is a large natural boulder displaying several rock basins, not far from the Boscawen-un stone circle. Known locally as the Giant's Footprints, the basins still hold water. And on the Isle of Tintagel, a depression in the natural rock at the summit is known as King Arthur's Footprint, and a series of 18 circular depressions on a rock ledge nearby are called King Arthur's Cups and Saucers. Some of these periodically hold water (Broadhurst 1992).

Hamish Miller and Paul Broadhurst have speculated whether rock basins on Giant's Rock, Zennor, were used for scrying when full of water (Broadhurst and Miller 2000). Broadhurst later discusses rock basins further: 'Some of them seem to be deliberately joined by channels chiselled into the rock so that the waters may flow from one to another... it is impossible to look at them, brimming with water from the heavens, without thinking that certain of these 'basins' have been deliberately widened and hollowed out' (Broadhurst 1997). He romantically calls them 'rock-chalices' and notes how, at the Cheesewring, '... a large basin flashes with sunlight as the pure water brims over the stone'. He suggests that the Druids may have utilised these basins, calling them 'Druid's fonts', and that these waters were particularly sought as it was undefiled. Broadhurst has identified several rock basins in the boulders around the sacred outcrop of Roche Rock, on the St Michael Line (Broadhurst 1997).

Work by archaeologists (Bradley et al 2007 and Tilley 2010) on Bodmin Moor (not far to the west) inspired me to visit the area, to check out what may have been relevant to Dartmoor. Regarding the Rough Tor, Brown Willy, Catshole, and Kilmar group of tors - '... the Neolithic activity has not necessarily been focused on the most elevated hills, but upon the ones with the most rock basins... the presence of the solution basins at Catshole has most probably influenced the location of the cairn' (Smith and Walker 2011). On my visit to Showery Tor **(images p. 80 & 86)** I could see from below that the highest surface was pitted with rock basins. This site is thought to be one of the major prehistoric foci in the area. On the highest stack of nearby Rough Tor, considered by Chris Tilley to be the pre-eminent sacred tor on the moor (Tilley 2010), several huge granite outcrops are honeycombed with rock basins. Many held water on my visit, and some had channels from which water would flow when the level is high enough. But the highest stack of all, at the SW end of the granite tor, was home to a spectacular and deeply eroded rock basin **(below, left)**. This was large enough and deep enough to be used as a seat. This rock overlooks the rest of the ridge, and I believe that someone of authority (the chief or shaman) may have sat in the depression thousands of years ago. Here you can see me seated in the rock basin, like a king on a throne! I could survey the whole landscape from this lofty chair; a place where the spirit can soar, like the buzzards that flew overhead. I show, for comparison, an old photograph of the Stone Mare of Locronon, in Brittany **(below, right)**. Local women would visit the

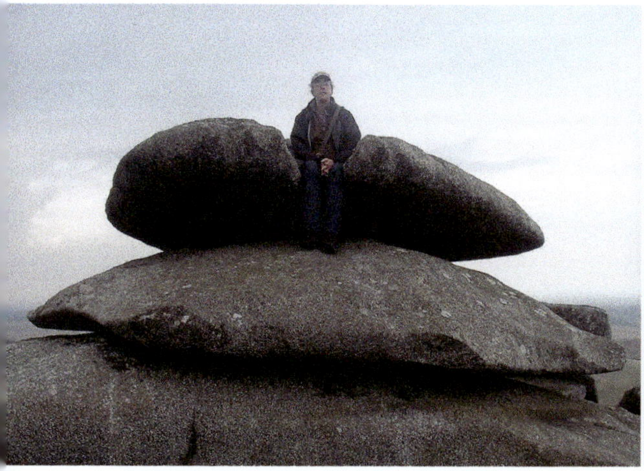

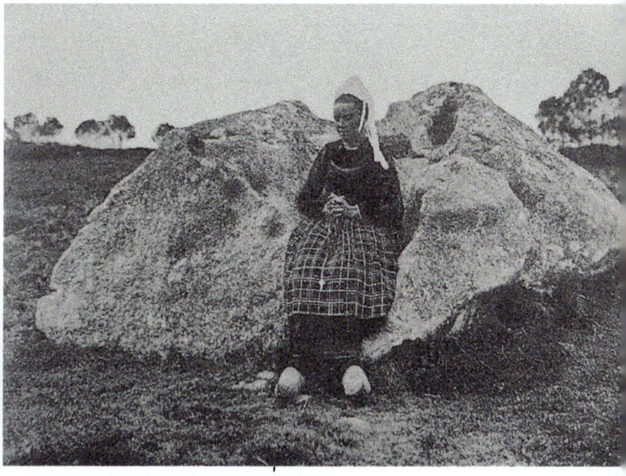

granite boulder, which is covered in large rock basins. It was said that barren women would come here to procure fertility. The stone sits next to a church and was probably the sacred site that the Church replaced. It makes me wonder if such attributes were once given to such rocks in Bodmin, Dartmoor and elsewhere. Folklore speaks of babies being passed through the holed stones of Men-an-Tol and the Tolven Stone (Cornwall), demonstrating the connection people once had between holed stones and children, childbirth and fertility. Most rock basins would hold newborns.

Close by, the towering mass of Rough Tor was encultured with the piling up of cairn material against the living rock, and a local long cairn in the vicinity is near to outcrops with rock basins; Chris Tilley considers that, '... the proximity of the long cairn to this stone seems likely to have been significant' (Tilley 2010). Rock basins are on some of the tabular rocks at Brown Willy, Bodmin, one of which gently rocks when stood upon (Bender et al 2007).

The last basin stone I want to detail before we plunge headlong into Dartmoor's examples is that of the rock stack known as King Arthur's Bed, at the west end of Trewortha Tor on Bodmin (named on OS maps at 241757). On the highest outcrop, on a precariously balanced stack, is a series of rock basins that weathering has conjoined to enable a person to lie within its 1.5m wide depression (see also Smith & Walker 2001). There is a recess to receive a person's head and shoulders. Even though there was rainwater at one end, a primal urge was to lie in this sunken space **(top left, next page)**, which felt nurturing, womb-like, and truly ancient. It was felt that shamanic dream sleep may have taken place at this lofty isolated place; people were living life on the edge, at this liminal meeting place of two very different worlds. Nearby are two

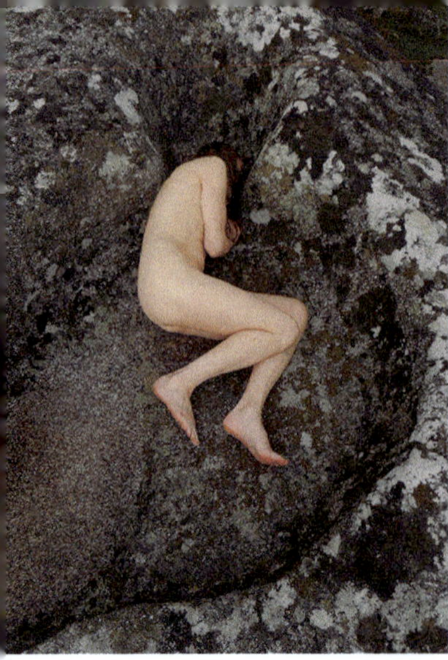

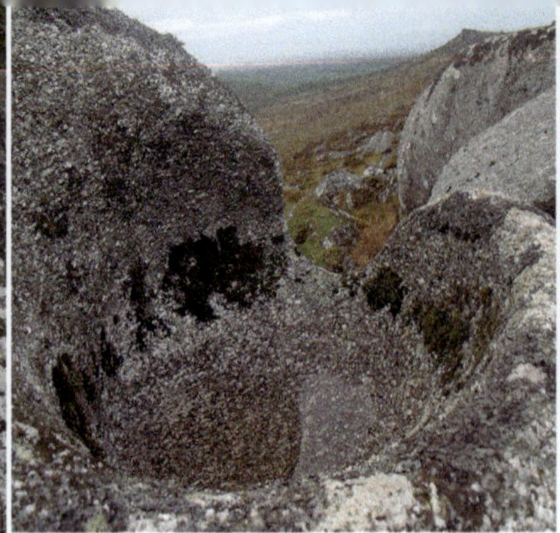

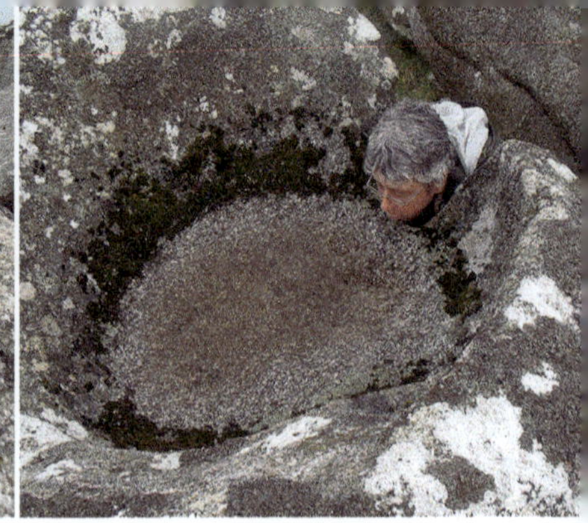

more rock basins, which have pronounced deeply-cut openings **(above centre)**, large enough in which to place one's head to directly partake of the water **(above right)**. This indentation is on the same side as a gully, in which I could stand to access the water; this sacred notch is well-defined and clearly manmade. I wondered who else had taken the sacred waters here thousands of years ago?

Dartmoor rock basins

Although the OS Dartmoor 'Explorer' map is marked with several 'rock basins', it soon became apparent to me that those marked are but a small percentage of what is really out there **(see map p. 139)**. It is one thing to seek out those designated by the Ordnance Survey, which in itself can be both challenging and rewarding, but to 'stumble upon' examples not on any maps is nothing short of revelatory. One stands on top of a solid stack of granite and yet at one's feet is an almost perfectly round sculpted depression full of water. The emotional mix of wonderment and mystery wells up from within, along with the feeling that, '... this means something'. Work at Brittany, Cornwall and elsewhere in recent decades has advocated that these crucibles of water were equally awe-inspiring to our prehistoric ancestors, as they are to indigenous cultures today. Rock basins hold the purest of waters, gifted from the skies; here granite and water meet in a kind of alchemy, the granite being the 'holy chalice', receiving the holy water. The water from the heavens was seen as the purest water obtainable, undefiled, before it had chance to touch the ground – like the Druids did with mistletoe. I have experienced the sense of sanctity as the waters of rock basins are drank. Perhaps people also left votive offerings in rock basins in gratitude. Some solution basins are on rocking or logan stones; were these rocked to mix up a concoction held within basin waters? Perhaps vessels collected the rainwater as it poured out of the basins via manmade notches and channels. Channels or grooves lead water from many basins, at times for it to cascade into a lower basin; some grooves have been proven to be artificial. Some basins have undercut lips, suggesting erosion through the action of swirling water. Other basins have vertical sides, suggesting the erosion is slower and long-term.

The entire landscape is an ancestral creation, so perhaps, as with indigenous cultures today, the simulacra, logan stones and rock basins may have been regarded as the petrified remains ancestral beings, or that these incredible forms had been carved by them. In many other ancient cultures, high places are where gods/ancestors entered the world of Man, and from which they often departed it. Perhaps the rock basins were such portals, as well as places of animal sacrifice, or used as ritual fire pits. The world axis, or axis mundi, connects the shamanic worlds of sky, earth and underworld, which can be traversed via this axis. This generally passes through an opening, or doorway, a liminal conduit through which the soul of the shaman can pass during ecstatic trance. Were these one of the functions of rock basins?

The art of scrying is an ancient practice whereby the sun or moon is reflected in water and the patterns of the reflection, as well as surface ripples, are interpreted. Was this another ancient use for rock basins? Although the term oracle can be used for a person, it was often associated with a place where prophecy and oracular visions took place. These were often at remarkable geological formations, with unusual acoustic properties, or where faulting caused vapours or light phenomena to surface. These phenomena were often woven into the mythology of cultures; Men-an-Tol has oracular folklore attached to it – it is a holed stone which was formerly a rock basin. Holed stones are seen as 'spirit holes' around the world - were the holed stones and rock basins similarly viewed in SW England? Rock basin waters were clearly quenching the soul, not just the body.

Perhaps rites and ceremonies might have included water that apparently came out of solid rock. People may have gathered below in the natural amphitheatre of a tor. A shaman above them, standing upon the rock (which may have been taboo to anyone else) would recite an invocation, and then lower their hands to the solid granite and scoop up water, as if by magic, from the rocks, a gift from sprit of place, from the ancestors. To those assembled, who could not see the rock surface, it would appear that the water was being drawn out of the rock itself (Davies 2010). I have performed a similar 'rite' during my recent group tours of Dartmoor, as I produced, as if by magic, a cup of water from the top stack at Over Tor **(right)**; there were exclamations of 'wow' and so forth from surprised attendees! Was this 'wow-factor' achieved on these tors thousands of years ago?

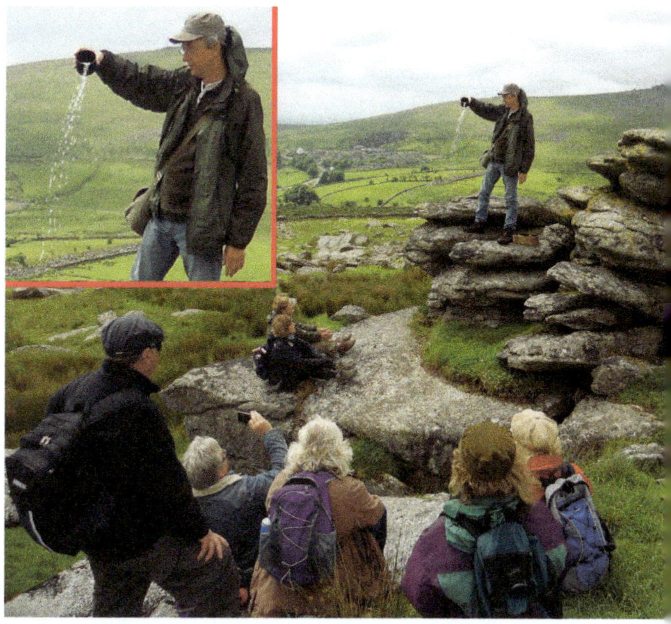

Graham Robb has unearthed the following concerning a French tradition: 'In the Aeduan capital of Bibracte, the Celts filled a pink-granite basin with a liquid that served a ritual purpose. The basin was astronomically aligned, reflecting the upper world both visually and mathematically, while its elliptical concavity suggested a birth passage and a connection to the lower world. Mead is a product of both worlds: it comes from the bees of the air and the wheat that taps the nutrients of the earth. Cauldrons and tankards filled with mead were buried with tribal chiefs... Perhaps, then, this was the sacred beverage that filled the basin at Bibracte' (Robb 2013). Is it possible that Dartmoor's rock basins were similarly filled with ritual libations for consumption at special times?

Another possible use for basins is for the burning of hallucinogenic, psychoactive plants, which we know were being consumed in prehistoric Britain (Knight 2011, Devereux 1997). Perhaps the carved stone basins found within Neolithic sites like Newgrange and Knowth (Ireland) and Le Hogue Bie (Jersey) were also for libation and/or water-immersion ceremonies.

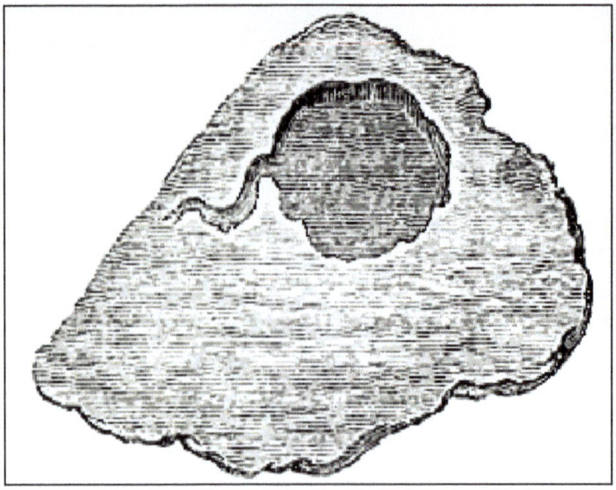 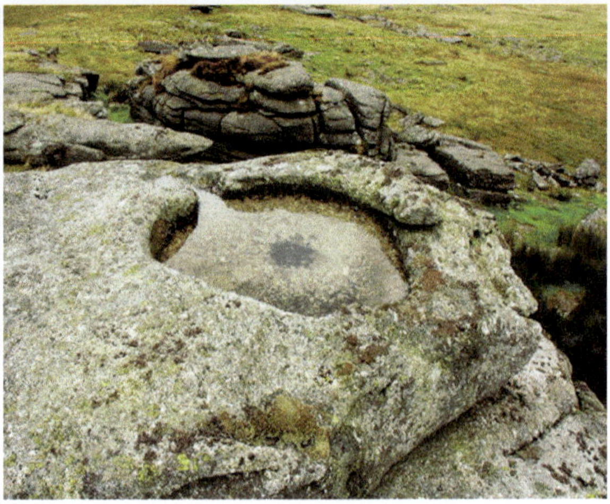

One of Dartmoor's rock basins does suggest that it was once a sacred place. The rock basin on Great Mis Tor (NE of Merrivale) is often said to be the finest example on the moor. It sits on the highest stack of the eastern outcrop of the tor (562769), at around 528m above sea level, just north of the summit flagstaff. Interest in the basin is recorded in 1291, 1609, and during the 19th and 20th centuries; a drawing made in 1830 is shown here **(above left)**. One can see a sinuous channel leading from the basin, and such features have been suspected as being manmade. This basin is frequently found to contain water **(above right)**. It is interesting that the basin is also known as the Devil's Frying Pan. Places associated with Satan are often the result of Church 'spin' to demonise Pagan holy places. The tor also has Druidic folklore. Some researchers have suggested that the evolution of rock basins can be measured in thousands of years, rather than hundreds, so most of the moor's large basins will have been around in prehistory; they were probably regarded as sacred even then. It is interesting that this basin overlooks a precariously balanced logan stone, just metres to the south **(centre image, p. 106)**. Standing on this summit is like communing with the gods, with spectacular views of White Tor, the logan stone stack on Roos Tor, Cox Tor, and also a thin slice of sea to the SW. I shall return to Great Mis Tor in Chapter 13, as it is an element of the *Merrivale Shamanic Landscape*.

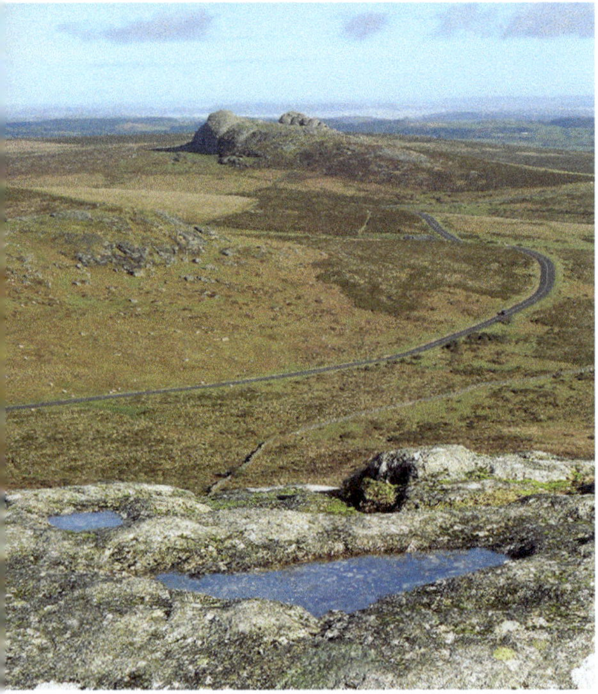

Rippon Tor is fine granite outcrop, just SW of Haytor (747756), which rises to a height of 473m at the trig point. I have described how my experiences of the tor was radically different under varying weather conditions (see p. 40). It was an absolute delight that two rock basins **(left)** were revealed to me, embedded in the summit stack, as they are not shown on maps. More than this, the tor summit outcrop had been encultured by an encirclement of cairn material **(top right image, p. 94)** – which had in effect also encircled the rock basins. I have also shown an alignment between cairns, a notable simulacrum and these rock basins **(image p. 94)**. Standing on the summit, with an eagle eye's view, it is the rock basins that seem to hold centre stage – this is where to stand. Haytor, with its double-summit horns or breasts of the Goddess, is prominent to the NE, with Saddle Tor in the middle distance **(bottom image opposite)**. I drank the waters of the basins, and both my thirst and my very soul were quenched. I dowsed a spiral of energy coming up out of one basin; master dowser Guy Underwood found rock basins to be foci for earth energies (Underwood 1972).

Kestor Rock is a granite outcrop to the west of Chagford, thought to have been named after the Kestral. It is one of my favourite tors, even though it is smaller than many. Its elevation of 437m affords views north to Exmoor, and to the west the high tors in the army ranges project into the skyline. Across the ridge of Shovel Down, half a mile west, marches the famous stone rows. Despite OS maps showing 'rock basin' (singular), I have counted a total of nine basins on the tor - four on the north stack, three on the central area, and two more on the southern edge of the outcrop. The largest basin **(right)**, at over 2m across, is actually visible on Google Earth, as a dark water-filled dot on the grey granite. Some of these basins are very ancient and eroded, no longer capable of containing water, but others still do; of the ones that can, a winter visit is recommended, or after rainfall. When the shallower basins hold water they show up the large crystals of feldspar and quartz **(top)**. The water in these basins can be surprisingly warm, energised by the sun.

It is said of the largest and best known basin here has not been seen to be empty of water since it was cleared of peat in 1856, but one local informant, Jim Hamer, told me that he has seen it empty. The depression is around 2m wide; in 1856 the depth was measured as, '... 31ins [78cm] and half way down the basin a diameter of 50ins [127cm]'. Prior to this date farmers filled the basin with peat and even fenced it off to stop sheep falling in. Folklore also tells of how an angry farmer told his adulterous wife to empty the basin, but that she could use nothing more than a sieve. On my winter visits in 2015/6, the basin was almost full **(image, back cover)**; by June 2016 the water level had dropped to about 45cm from the rim. When I did some shamanic drumming next to the main basin **(second image)** I felt the energy was circulating out of the water anti-clockwise, and was being drawn up into my body. The feeling was

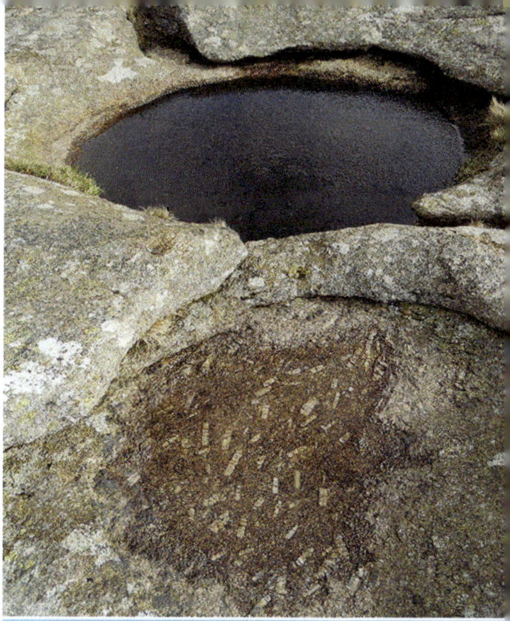

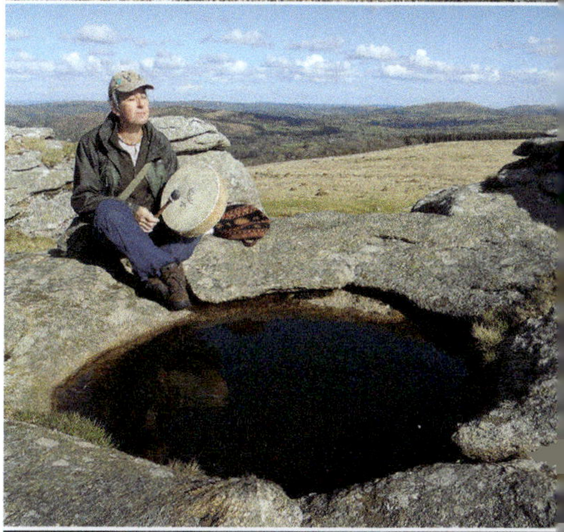

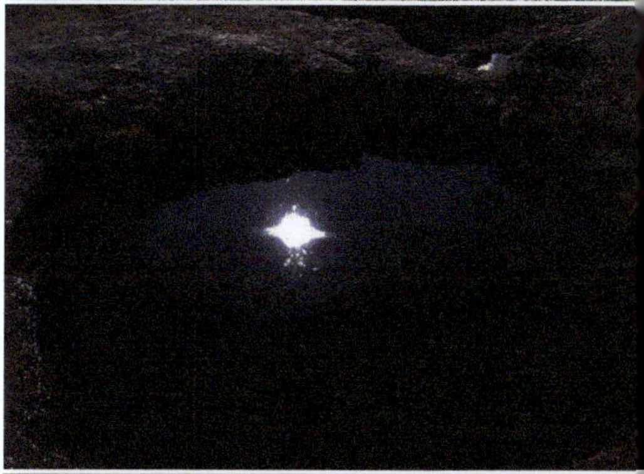

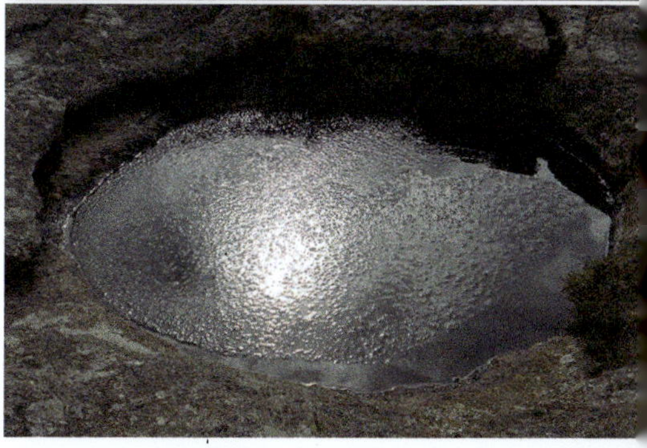

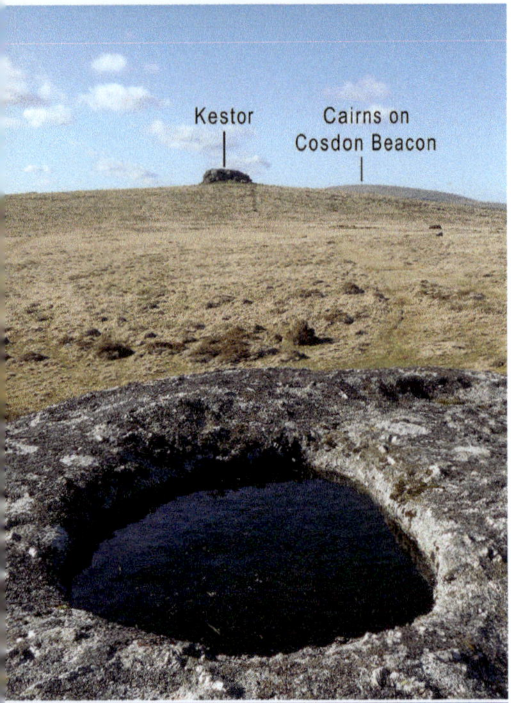

ecstatic, and moved me around as I sat on the naked granite. I believe this large basin was used for scrying, as signs and portents were sought in the reflection of the moon or the sun. The moon may also have been seen to potentise the waters **(third image, previous page)**; the lunar light pulls you in to another realm – the light at the end of a watery tunnel. When the sun reflects on the surface of the basin, it engenders a hypnotic effect. On another occasion, I arrived to find a thin layer of ice covering the surface **(bottom image, previous page)**; to plunge my fingers through this icy veneer was like breaking into another world. As I have said previously, same landscape, but not. By visiting rock basins under different conditions, times of the year, or times of the day or night, then diverse experiences will be gifted to you.

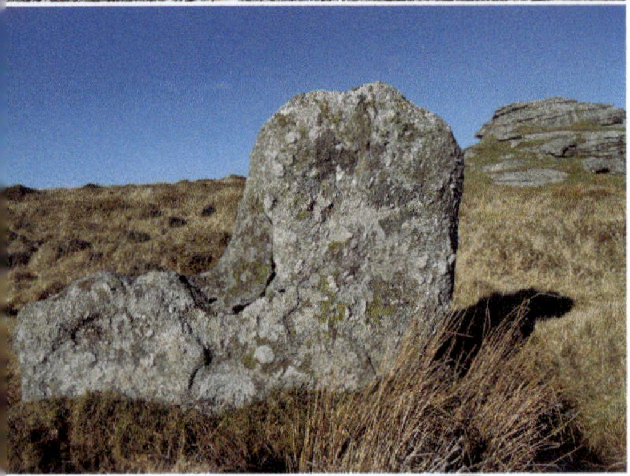

Middle Tor rises not far south of Kestor (669858), a small outcrop with unusually white granite with huge megacrysts, which also holds big open secrets. I have already shown the huge simulacrum, like a surfacing dragon, on its north side **(bottom left image, p. 58)**. On my visit in February 2016, I had already perceived the simulacra and lay beneath the overhang it forms. I was then drawn to stand on the summit where, to my amazement, was a water-filled rock basin – directly above the head of the dragon! I broke the thin ice that was on the surface and put some drops of water on my third eye: 'Blessings and thank you'. I stood on the summit, on the dragon's head, and howled towards Kestor to the north, which sits on the skyline **(top)**; due to a dip in the slope at Kestor, the cairns on Cosdon Beacon are visible.

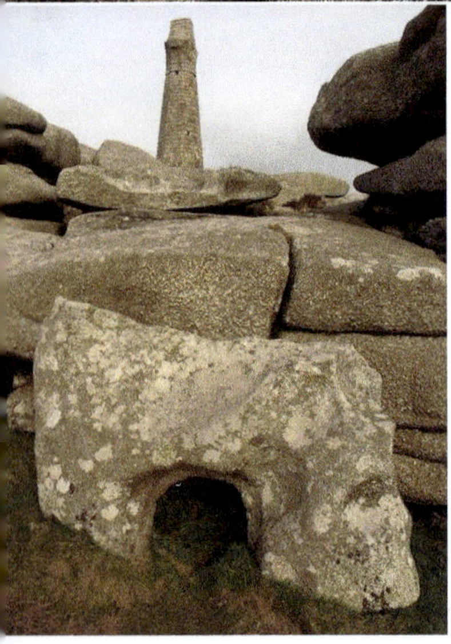

But there was more to be revealed at Middle Tor. In March 2016, as I walked west from the tor towards the longstone (660856), I saw a standing stone **(centre)**, about 75m from the outcrop. A thin slab of granite had clearly been stood up vertically; it stands 1.2m high, nearly 2m long and yet only 30cm thick. A huge 'bite' was missing on the top edge, and it was clear that long ago this had been a rock basin. I have found this reverence for former rock basins elsewhere, such as at Over Tor **(images p. 175)** and Dewerstone **(image p. 135)**. Prof Chris Tilley regarded uprighted rock basins as culturally relevant when he came across them at Chapel Carn Brae and Carn Brae in Cornwall (Tilley 2010). Of the Chapel Carn Brae example Tilley comments, '... this rock must have been dislodged from the top of the rock outcrop and set up as a shrine below'. The same could be said of the Carn Brae example, shown here - the upended stone in the foreground displays the arc of a basin **(left)**. I believe we

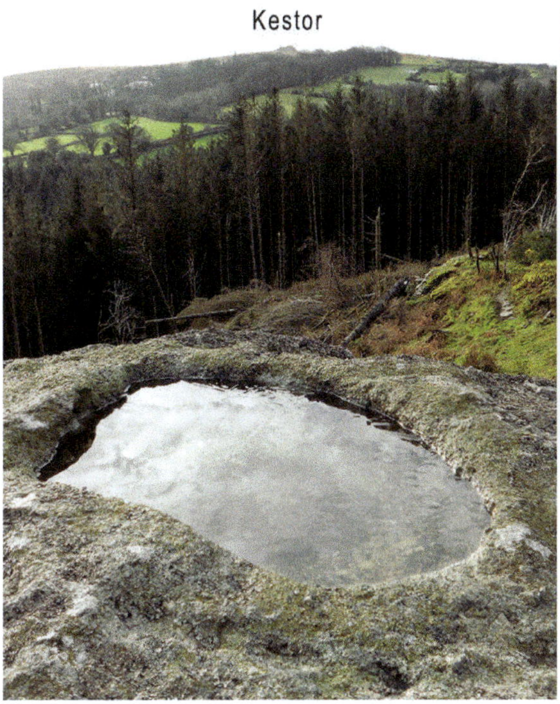

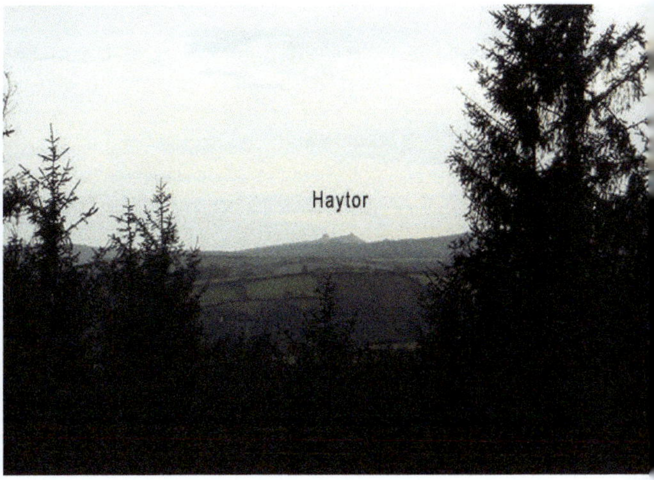

now have Dartmoor examples. These demonstrate how, even when they could no longer hold water, the eroded basin stones were revered sufficiently to become monuments.
Another tor with rock basins in the vicinity of Kestor is Gidleigh Tor (671878), which sits midst a plantation overlooking the North Teign River. I have shown a view of the tor earlier, demonstrating how tors may have appeared in the Mesolithic **(top image, p. 12)**. On a visit to the tor in January 2016, I unexpectedly found two rock basins on the highest stacks; subsequently I have found that one even shows up on Google earth! A thin crust of ice covered part of largest rock basin, which was approx 80cm x 50cm **(above left)**. A gully separates the two basins, both of which contained water on my visit, and this gully enabled me to lean over to take the waters.
From this important vantage point on Gidleigh Tor, I could see the cairns on Cosdon Hill; Kestor Rocks is prominent to the SW. To my surprise, the holy double-summit of Haytor was once again visible on skyline to the south **(above right)**. The intervisibility between these rock basins and other sacred places must have made this relatively small tor greatly significant. As with monuments, the geographical context of rock basin sites may have been more important than we have previously thought.
As I stood on Gidleigh Tor, with chilled face and hands, the following words came in, as if the rocks themselves were coaxing me to write:

I gaze into a pool of eternity
I am drawn into your mystery,
I see the sky below me, in waters still
My world has turned upside down in winter chill,

But what is up and what is down
If I fall in, will I even drown?
My head spins as I am pulled asunder
Into a land of dreams and wonder

I shall return when the moon does shine
Into this Otherworld of my mind.

Another outcrop with rock basins is Bag Tor (763757), which sits under the shadow of its mighty neighbour, Haytor. I passed attendant guardian hawthorns, greeting them. I approached the rocks, from where I enjoyed fabulous views to the sea to the south. It is guarded by a tenacious holly tree and nearby is a propped stone **(image p. 115)**. The tallest stack has several basins on its surface. On the west side of the outcrop, water can drain out through a hole from the deepest basin. I sat inside this basin, crouched up, almost foetal-like in the cold wind. It seemed nurturing to sit there, as if I had been invited. More inspiration came in as I spent time inside the sacred depression **(below)**; although, to be honest, depression was far from my mind.

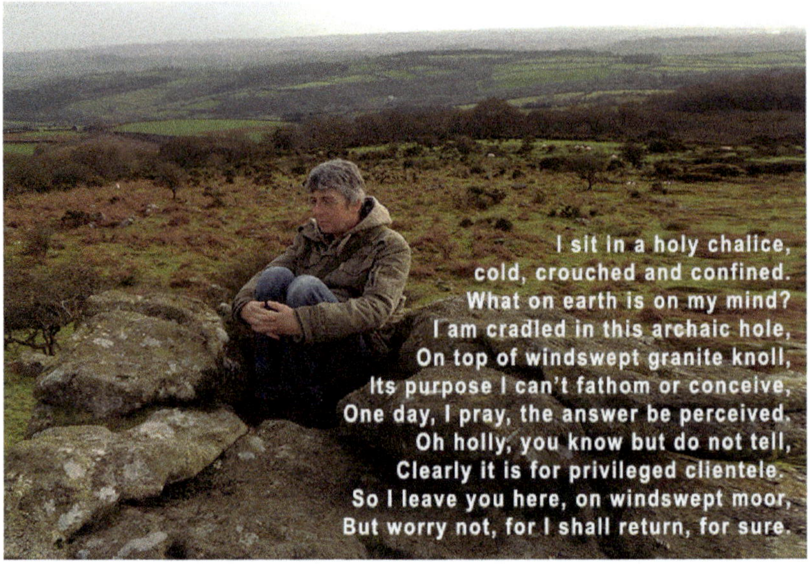

The next basins I would like to share are on Beacon Rocks, on Ugborough Beacon (668592), between Ivybridge and South Brent. This magnificent hill rises majestically north of the A38. The views from Ugborough Beacon are spectacular; it is a fine vantage point from which to view ceremonies processing along the stone rows along Butterdon Hill to the west, and of the cairns on the ridge. The hill was encultured with three cairns/tumuli, one of which is wrapped around a natural outcrop **(images p. 96)**.

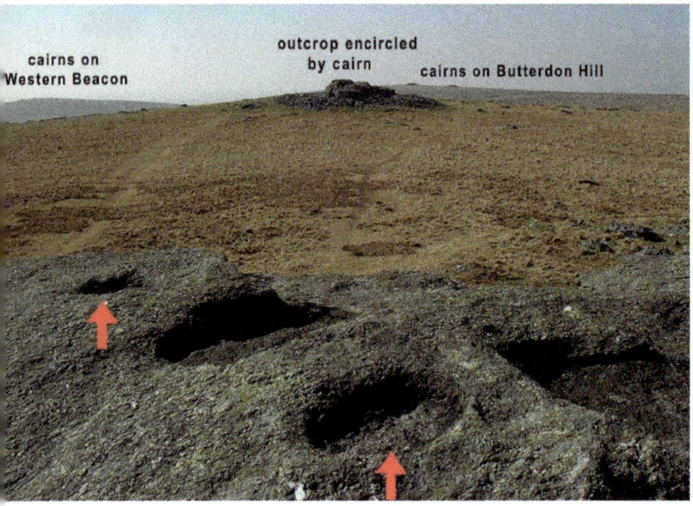

Close by, the eastern outcrop here is known as Beacon Rocks, a small outcrop up to 3.5m high. When I ascended the rocks I found four rock basins at the northern end. Two are old, up to 1m wide, their sides now too worn now to hold much water. But my attention was drawn to two other smaller ones close by, which look *freshly chiselled out – they are manmade!* These have diameters of 30cm – 45cm, and unlike the smooth features of the ancient basins, these have rough edges **(left)** and sharp crystals perturbed from them; shown here with red arrows. They also contain sprinklings of loose quartz grains at their base. I have come across similar elsewhere, and I am convinced that attempts were made in prehistory to replace defunct basins with new ones. It has been said, that the theory that some rock basins are manmade, does not hold water (excuse the pun). Yet some of the basin stones at Barnsdale, North Yorkshire Moors, seem to have been enhanced by additional cutting, and on the Cheddar Stone (on the same moors) there is faint 'chiselling' at the base of the basin outlet: 'If people saw the rock itself as a membrane between worlds, then by scraping away a little of its surface, perhaps they thought that they might make contact with this alien realm' (Williams 2010). Perhaps people were creating new portals. Bender and Tilley et al, working at Leskernick, concluded that prehistoric people may have thought that the basins *were* carved by their ancestors, so to create new rock basins was seen as an alignment with those forces. I think the whole issue of manmade rock basins needs to be reassessed.

I return now to the Neolithic encampment at Dewerstone, which I described earlier **(images p. 88)**. I have demonstrated how a logan stone and a simulacrum were foci in defining walls and boundaries. On the west side of the enclosure walls, a rock outcrop within a small copse of trees has been used as a focus for the wall. To my amazement, a 1.5m tall megalith has been erected on top of the outcrop, on the outward surface of which was a rock basin! Here I show it in profile, so the concave depression is seen to good effect **(right)**. This is a classic example of the enculturing of a natural outcrop with a standing stone which itself was selected because it holds a sacred rock basin. It is not known if this stone was erected in the Neolithic, or was a later Bronze Age addition. It is yet another example of how there are 'open secrets' all around us, if we have eyes with which to see them.

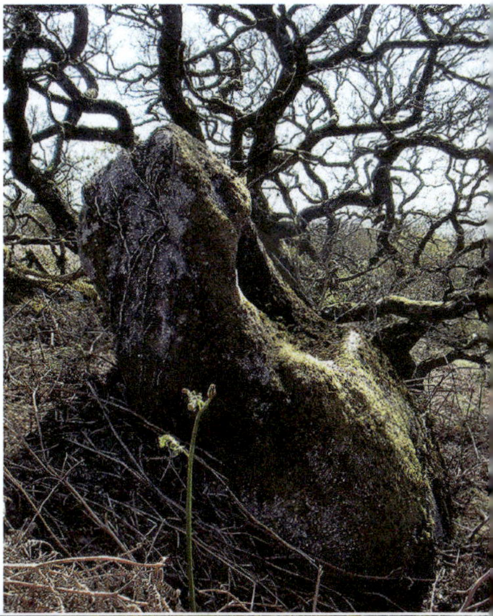

The Tolmen Stone

'Like a Japanese Zen painting, it is the space that is crucial, not the solid form that surrounds it, as are the silences between drumbeats.' (Knight 2007)

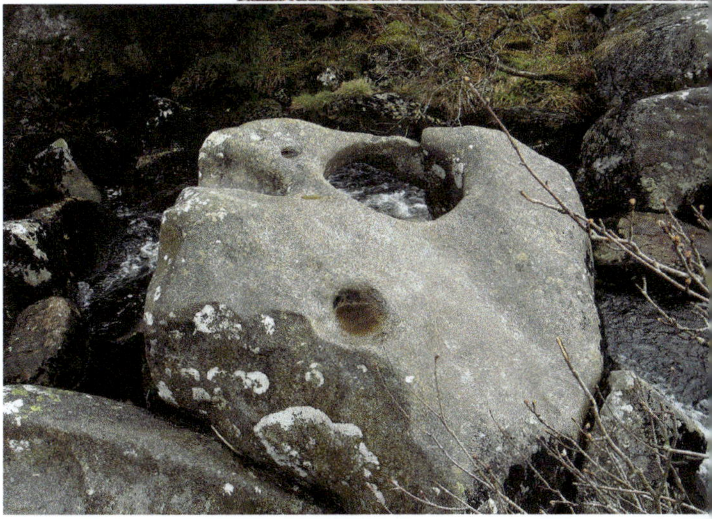

The last rock basin I shall illustrate in this chapter is that of the Tolmen Stone **(right)**, a huge granite boulder that sits in the North Teign River (655871), due south of the Scorhill Stone Circle. It is on the opposite side of the river from where the western edge of the Batworthy plantation descends to the river. The name comes from Celtic *tol,* meaning *hole,* and *maen*, *stone.* Although not marked on OS maps, it is one of the wonders of Dartmoor, in my opinion. This massive boulder is taller than a man and is notable for a rare rock basin that has weathered all the way through the rock. It manifests on the upper surface as a metre wide portal. One can pass down through the shaft onto a thin ledge at river level. At times of extreme wet weather, it has been know for the stone to be completely consumed by the raging torrents of the North Teign (pers. comm. Jim Hamer). Close by, on the top surface, another large basin has broken out at its side, whilst there are smaller ones close by.

Folklore says the Druids are associated with the Tolmen Stone, and that people are cured of rheumatism and arthritis if they pass through the orifice. Another legend says that if you plunge through the hole into the river you will glimpse the future, and be gifted with 'second sight'. Other folklore says that unfaithful wives would have to wash in Cranmere Pool, run three times around Scorhill Stone Circle and then pass through the Tolmen Stone. This may be a memory of Druidic 'lustration', which was a cleansing ritual. It is this opening, the water-born breach, that possesses the power to heal.

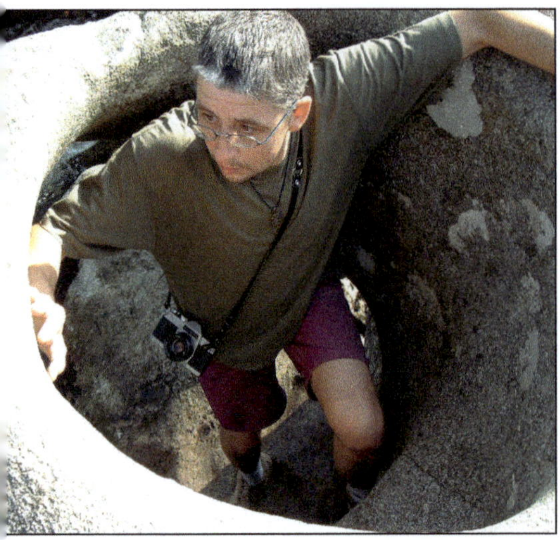

I have passed through this magical aperture many times, as have attendees of my weekend workshops and day walks. It is a yoni, a rite of passage re-birthing channel, through which people once plunged into the purifying waters below. The hole is a vulva through which we may pass naked, leaving behind all the illusions of ego. It is a place of rites of passage, as every birth is, where people may be coaxed down into, or emerge up through, this sacred portal **(left)**. In my novel, *Thirteen Moons – Conversations with the Goddess,* the hero drops naked through the hole, plunging into the waters below as a purification ceremony, to demonstrate his resolve and announce his intent to the spirit of place.

Dowsers say that negative ions are produced at fast-flowing water, and that these can enhance one's health. The roar of the fast waters here adds to the energy, atmosphere and mystique – it is like the roar of a dragon. If the hole is connected with oracles, then the Tolmen stone can be seen as its all-seeing eye. The river here is strewn with more boulders, over which the fast waters cascade. These can be seen as obstacles in our way, and yet as water takes the line of least resistance, so could we. After all, the softest of elements eventually erodes the hardest rocks.

Further down the Teign, east of Leigh Bridge, there is the Puckie Stone, another large boulder which has a rock basin some 1m across and several cm deep. Unfortunately, I do not have the space to list all the rock basins that are out there for the reader to encounter. However, I shall discuss the rock basins at Vixen Tor, Pew Tor, Little Mis Tor, Hucken Tor and Roos Tor in the chapter on the Merrivale Shamanic Landscape. It is there that I will also describe another rock basin stone that has been metamorphosed into a megalith. Although there are many rock basins strewn across the moor, I can recommend the following localities, which offer water for the pilgrim during wet spells, and uplifting scenery all the year round: Lower Hartor Tor (604674), Cox Tor (531762), Gutter Tor (578668), Hawk's Tor (554626), Black Tor (573718), Mel Tor (693724), Combestone Tor (671718), Littaford Tor (616769), Bel Tor (697729), Figgie Daniel (735823) on Easdon Hill **(image p. 56)**, Little Bee Tor (616772) as well

as Honeybag Tor (728788). As I have said, this list is not exhaustive, and you may find others not marked on any map, as I have done. Good hunting!
The sources of rivers on Dartmoor occur in the regions of the most intense collection of tors. These tors stand above the spring lines, yet I have been on tors and seen mini waterfalls and rivulets flowing off rock outcrops, which are then absorbed by the soil or flow away down the hillside. The rivers really do have their origins here. It is as if the ancestors, simulacra, the spirits of place, are gifting, or at least blessing, the moor's rivers. The spirits of the tors and high areas are literally 'reaching up' to the clouds and 'pulling' down the water. Any water flowing or dripping off such high outcrops, or captured in rock basins, could be seen as 'holy water'. At the Preseli Mountains, the source of the Stonehenge Bluestones, former springheads were dammed, by crude walls of rock, '... as if the Stone Age people wished to collect the water pure and unsullied from within the earth' (Devereux 2010). I would urge the reader to commune with water in all its forms. The waters of rock basins become alive and animated as ripples glisten and dance in the breeze. Rock basins are bizarrely compelling, and seem to call out for an acknowledgement of their ancient cultural relevance. Their healing water is given unconditionally to those who seek.

Dartmoor rock art – a link to water?

Dartmoor has some rare examples of rock art, and when I visited some during the winter months I have found them to be pools of rainwater. As receptacles, it occurred to me that they too may have been symbolically linked to water.
Water seems to have had a symbolic, as well as practical, association with the rock basins and the cup and ring marks of Northern England. Perhaps the observation of a raindrop falling onto the water and creating ripples gave birth to the concentric circles found carved in the vicinity of rock basins in the North (Smith and Walker 2011). The ripples are literally frozen in time.
On rock outcrops and boulders of Europe Atlantic seaboard area, 90% of prehistoric motifs are circular (Trwoga 2006). The cup and ring marks or concentric circles frequently have a straight line or groove coming from the heart of the design and cutting through the circles – similar to how the rock basins of Dartmoor have channels coming from them! It is interesting that the majority of British cup and ring marks are not on megaliths at passage graves, but are on open landscape outcrops. Many British and European rock art is accompanied by rock basins (Beckensall 1999).

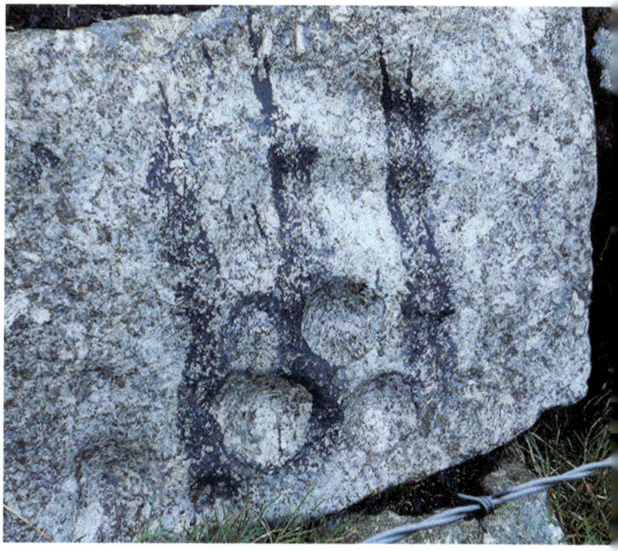

Documented examples of prehistoric rock art on Dartmoor include the following:
On the west side of a track at Holmingbeam, east of Princetown (595753) there is a granite boulder built into a wall, on which are incised 12-14 cup marks **(right)**. At Brisworthy (559651), there are cup marks on a granite boulder built into a trackside wall (Beckensall 1999). Finally, at Lower Dunstone (716758), south of Widecombe-in-the-Moor, there are 13 shallow cups on a large granite boulder

called the Dunstone **(below left)**. The rock resembles a seal or walrus, and may also be a propped stone, as space can be seen below the huge boulder. The rock stands close to the Dunstone Cross, seen here towards the right **(below right)**, restored to its original position next to the Dunstone in 1980. A granite boulder/outcrop lies in between them, and I consider this site to have once been the omphalos or ritual centre of the local area. From here, tors and cairns rise on the skyline to the east. Dowsing has proved an energy flow between here and a new 'dolmen' in a nearby garden.

It is generally accepted that these three examples were natural rocks once lying flat on the earth, like most of their counterparts in Northern England and elsewhere. These small depressions would have filled with water – sacred symbolism conjoined with the divine gift from the skies.

A map showing the Dartmoor basins mentioned in this chapter is on the next page. It should be noted that several of these localities possess multiple rock basins. Grid references can be found in the preceding text.

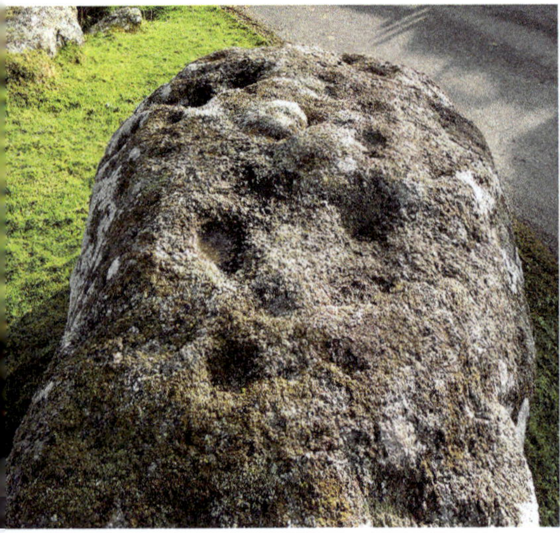

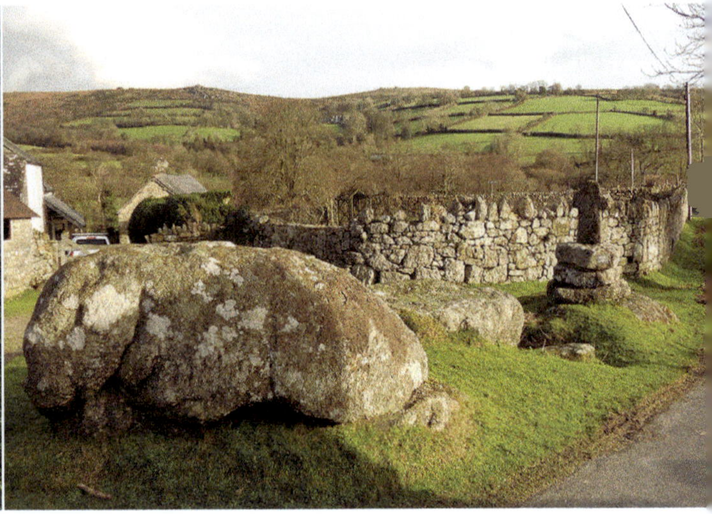

The Dunstone, with cup marks, and nearby cross (right)

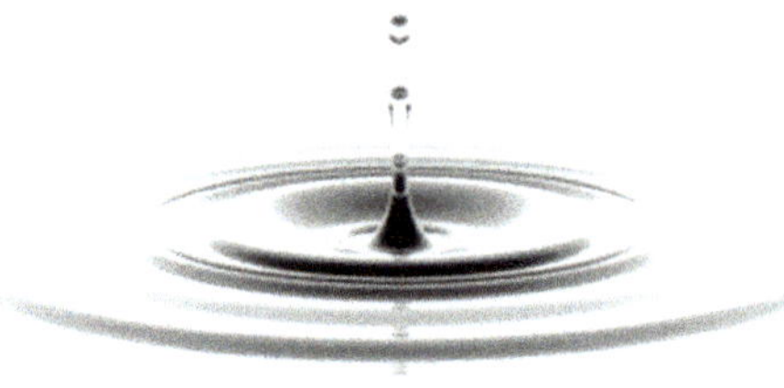

'Water is the mirror that has the ability
to show us what we cannot see.'
(Masaru Emoto)

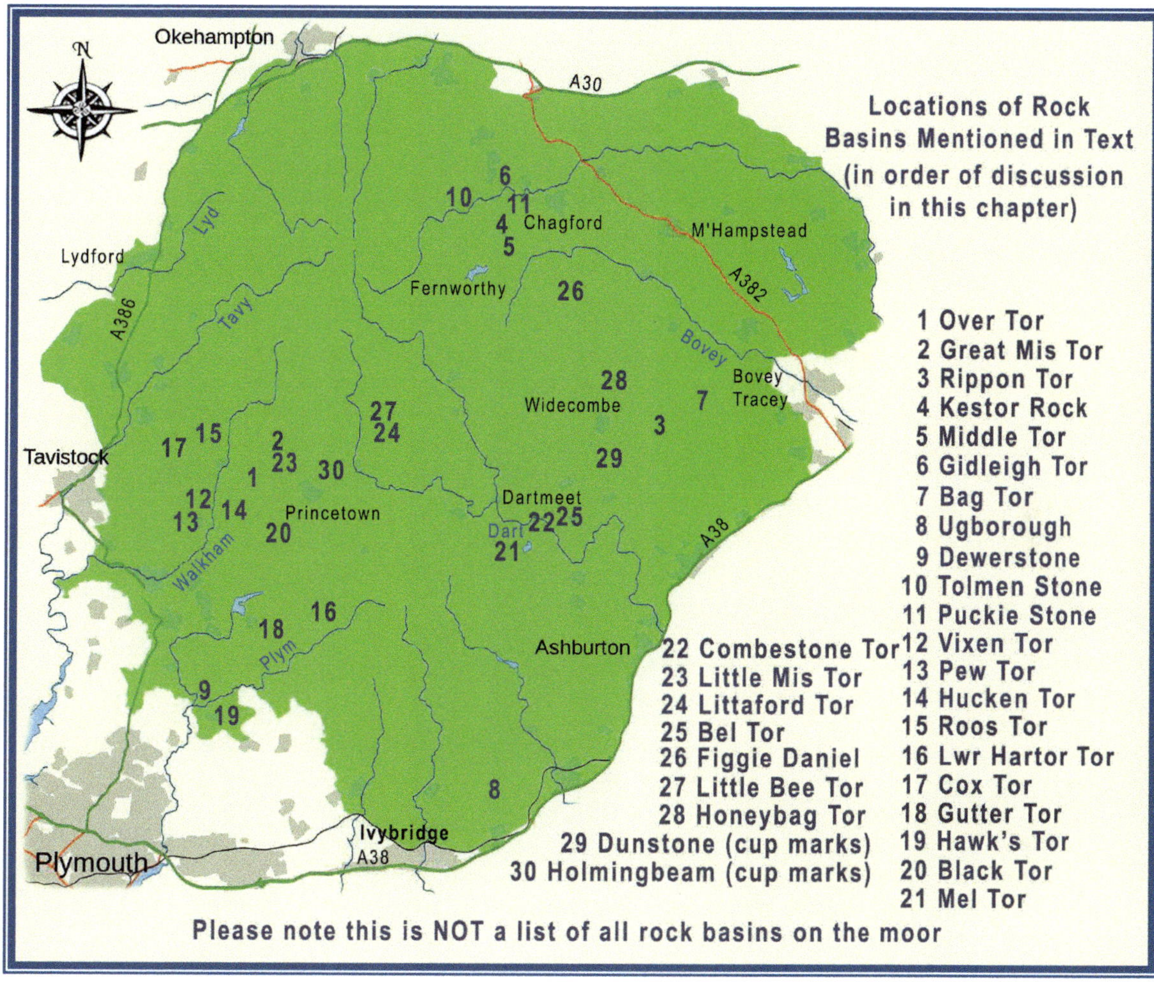
Locations of Rock Basins Mentioned in Text (in order of discussion in this chapter)
1 Over Tor
2 Great Mis Tor
3 Rippon Tor
4 Kestor Rock
5 Middle Tor
6 Gidleigh Tor
7 Bag Tor
8 Ugborough
9 Dewerstone
10 Tolmen Stone
11 Puckie Stone
12 Vixen Tor
13 Pew Tor
14 Hucken Tor
15 Roos Tor
16 Lwr Hartor Tor
17 Cox Tor
18 Gutter Tor
19 Hawk's Tor
20 Black Tor
21 Mel Tor
22 Combestone Tor
23 Little Mis Tor
24 Littaford Tor
25 Bel Tor
26 Figgie Daniel
27 Little Bee Tor
28 Honeybag Tor
29 Dunstone (cup marks)
30 Holmingbeam (cup marks)
Please note this is NOT a list of all rock basins on the moor
N
Okehampton
A30
Chagford
M'Hampstead
A382
Lydford
Lyd
Tavy
A386
Fernworthy
Bovey
Bovey Tracey
Widecombe
Tavistock
Princetown
Dartmeet
Dart
Walkham
A38
Plym
Ashburton
Ivybridge
A38
Plymouth

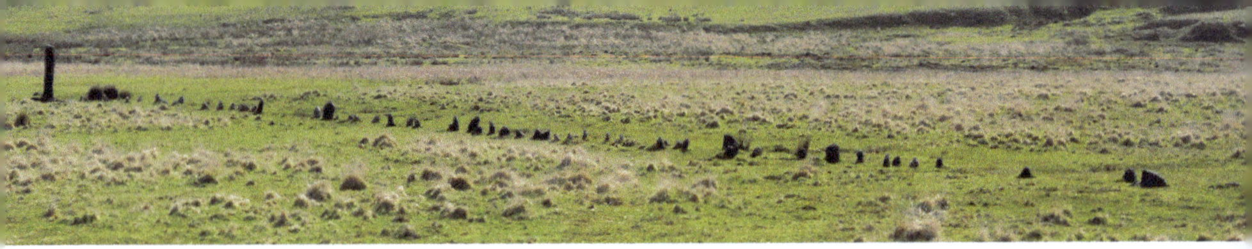

12. Stone Rows and their Landscape Setting

'It is important to recognise that monuments cannot be considered in isolation.' (Bradley 2000).

Stone rows are some of the most enigmatic prehistoric monuments found around the world; over 1000 examples are known in Britain. From Brittany to Avebury, from Scotland to Ireland, and across Cornwall back to Dartmoor, have I walked these mysterious megalithic configurations. Even now I have not got to the bottom of all of the levels of significance they had to our distant ancestors. Nor has anyone else if they are honest. Many are single rows of stones, whilst others are double, forming avenues. There are also examples of triple rows. They often sinuously snake across the land, like at Avebury **(right)**. Other complexes subtly change direction or add additional rows, such as Carnac, Brittany **(lower image)**. Some have been found to feature astronomical alignments (see Chapter 16), whilst dowsers see them as channelling earth energies (Chapter 17). Stone alignments may, on occasions, incorporate stone circles, as at Callanish.

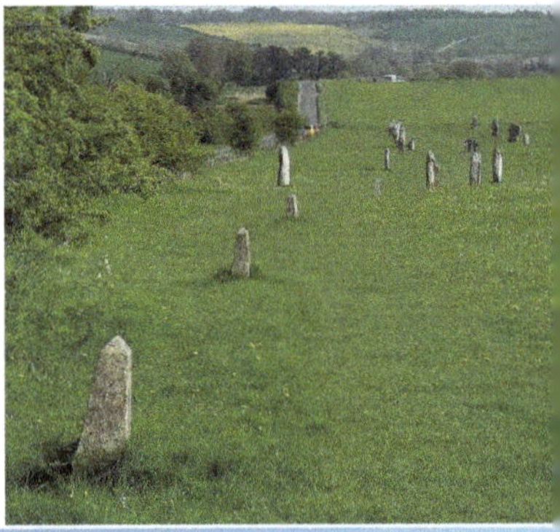

Like most megalithic sites I have studied, I think there is not one definitive answer as to their purpose; they were multifunctional, multipurpose, and operated on many levels, from the practical to the shamanic. My aim here is to demonstrate my theories about Dartmoor's rows and avenues, primarily from a phenomenological point of view. I will demonstrate how they were positioned on the landscape with intricate care, *as an experiential element of it.*

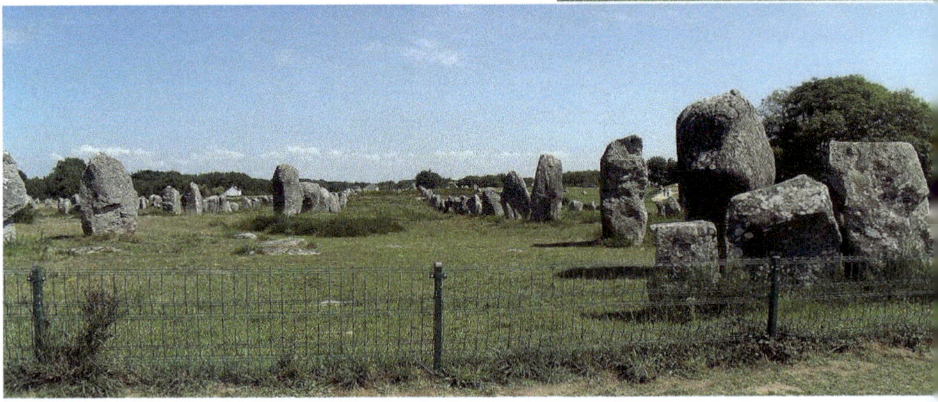

Bodmin and elsewhere

Once again, I shall glean from the findings of excellent archaeological research that has come out of Bodmin Moor in recent years (especially those of Sue Hamilton, Barbara Bender and Chris Tilley). These undoubtedly throw light on the stone rows of Dartmoor. It had been generally accepted by academia that stone rows were all erected in the Bronze Age. New research suggests that at least some of the stone rows of Bodmin Moor were under construction towards the end of the Neolithic, i.e. the early 3rd millennium BC. This is in keeping with rows at Avebury and Brittany, which are considered to be Neolithic. On the moors, they were probably used by people visiting the area seasonally, mainly during the summer months (Bender et al 1999). The modest size of stone row components has been commented on: '... they were not primarily erected to be seen at a distance... the stone row acted as a processional way through the landscape' (Bender et al 2007). That there is a spiritual/cultural element to rows has been advocated: 'These were stones by which to learn, by which to remember, by which to orient, and by which to think' (Bender et al 2007).
At Leskernick, Bodmin, it was noted that, 'As one walks along the stone row, which is 317m long, the tip of Rough Tor comes into view as the walker approaches the terminal area. Although the stone row is made up of small knee-high stones, excavation has demonstrated that the terminal consisted of three dramatic stones of up to 2m high, which are positioned to maximize the view of Rough Tor'. In other words, *the location and the orientation of the row takes account of landscape features.* This is confirmed elsewhere. For instance, on the Isle of Jura, in Scotland, geophysical surveying techniques have revealed that one standing stone formerly had a stone row leading up to it that was aligned with the Paps of Jura: '... the eye is led directly to the domed summits of the Paps' (Devereux 2013).
There is frequently an association between stone rows and cairns; at the Leskernick settlement complex, this has been noted, asking the question as to where the mundane ends and the spiritual begins: 'What was the 'role' of these monuments, and their associated rituals, in the routine experiences of everyday life?' (Bender et al 1999). We will later ask the same question about Merrivale.
The shapes of the stones selected for stone rows also seem to have been a factor on Bodmin (Bender et al 1999). Likewise, the setting of triangular and flat-topped stones on Dartmoor at the termini of stone rows, is a recurrent theme (Burl 1993). Triangular stones have been thought to represent the female/yin principle (Meaden 1991). Megaliths that become anthropomorphised carry with them the essence and presence of the dead, as 'petrified ancestors' (Klemen 2015) as at Avebury and West Kennet Long Barrow (Knight 2011), bringing the monuments to life. Stone rows are frequently accompanied by burial cairns, to the extent that some cairns are incorporated within the rows themselves; these monuments evolved, to the extent that some stone rows were built at sites of pre-existent cairns.
After the rows were erected, additional cairns were sometimes added at a later date. Sites may continue to evolve over long periods of time: 'Where stone rows seem to be the focus for a group of cairns, it may be assumed that a succession of later cairns was placed there because of the pre-existence or association of the older monuments in the group, suggesting very strongly that these places fulfilled sacred, funerary and ceremonial roles over many generations' (Newman 2011). It is usually difficult to ascertain which came first; sometimes the cairns are set within the rows, at other times at row termini, or alongside. Stone rows provided a conduit between the living (stone rows are about movement) and the dead (cists and cairns), 'spirit ways' along which the departed souls moved. Many indigenous cultures still believe that spirits travel in

straight lines (Devereux 1993). Other researchers have made the link between the straight nature of stone rows and ley lines, landscape alignments that are still viewed as an heretical concept by academia.
Prof Chris Tilley considers the Bodmin stone rows to be all about conscious passage across the landscape: 'Stone rows seem to be a metaphor for movement, transition and change (Tilley 2010). Cairns and other rows come into view and then pass away from view as one traverses the land; 'Together the rows and cairns are representative of different areas where different memories or practices were related' (Klemen 2015). I have often felt as if I am being directed and choreographed across the landscape, directed along the rows of stones. But where from? And where to?

Dartmoor stone rows

I am not going to describe all the stone rows of Dartmoor, as this would be a near-impossible task. New rows are being unearthed almost annually, and more entombed examples are no doubt awaiting discovery. In any case, good guides to the best sites are already out there (Gerrard 1997, Walker 2005, Lethbridge 2015). Rather, I will present a selection of stone rows I have experienced, with the object of demonstrating certain concepts and 'ways of seeing' that can be applied to other stone rows - how to walk in the footsteps of our ancestors. See the map on p. 157 for locations.
These alignments of stones are one of the enigmas of Dartmoor, and can consist of single, double or triple rows. Dartmoor has the largest assemblage of stone rows in the UK, with around 80 examples, a total which may well grow as more emerge from the peat and heather. Some have associated folklore, such as at Stall Moor **(below left)**, where the circle of 26 stones are known as the Dancers and Kiss-in-the-ring. They are said to be girls who all kissed a young countryman on the Sabbath, and were turned to stone – the stone row are those who had pursued the man.
In general, stone rows and circles occupy flatter areas, sloping ground with clitter fields, near to where settlements and small cairns were often sited, whilst the ridges and tors were where large cairns were built, sometimes inside hilltop enclosures. They are often located within amphitheatre-like topography, within a bowl, surrounded by higher terrain. Many are situated on gently-sloping saddles between high ground.
One is invited, it seems to me, to be focused on the immediate area. This is particularly the case with several of the rows that pass through clitter fields, such as at Butterbrook. No attempt was made to clear the clitter out of the way (Klemen 2015), suggesting that the 'impeding' stones were an integral part of the stone row experience. The terminal stones on Dartmoor are often triangular, tapered at the top, such as at Merrivale and Drizzlecombe.

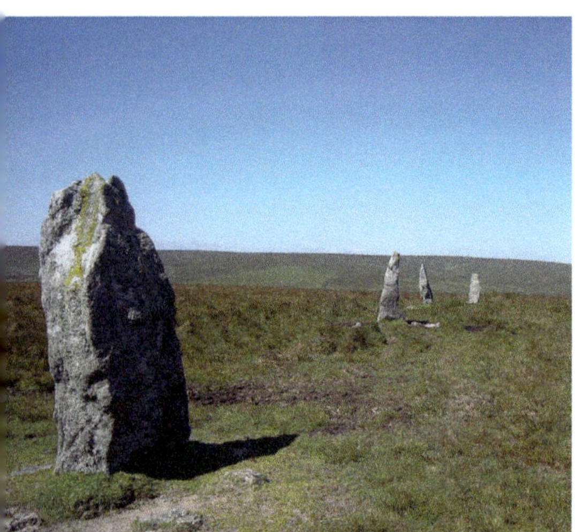

Dartmoor's stone rows are generally thought to be Bronze Age, due to their associations with cairns of that age. However, one isolated newly discovered row at Cut Hill (599827), revealed datable finds from around 3700–3500 BC, suggesting that some rows may be Early Neolithic in origin (Gerrard 1997, Newman 2011); Chris Tilley has suggested similar for some of the Bodmin Moor rows. The Cut Hill row is unusually high at around 600m above sea level, whereas it has been demonstrated that most of

Dartmoor's stone rows lie close to the 300m contour, which may represent the upper limit of cultivation in the Bronze Age (Gerrard 1997). This seems to be the case with eight documented rows on Bodmin Moor, seven of which are located between the 250m and 300m contours. The longest row is that from Green Hill to Stall Moor, which marches across the moor north to south for more than 3.4km (over 2 miles), terminating in a great cairn circle. All the examples with a length of over 500m are singular rows. Cairns are sometimes situated so as to be on the skyline when walking a long stone row, as I will soon demonstrate.

With few exceptions, the stone rows of Dartmoor start from a cairn or cist. Of the eighty alignments, 59% have a terminal cairn (Butler 1997). In nearly half of the rows a cairn lies at the upslope end. Rows are usually associated with gradients of less than 10% - fairly level, gently sloping ground. The rows seem to shepherd us to the cairns, as well as focusing the mind in the here and now. Are these rows a physical realisation of the soul's journey, whereby people created symbolic routes to direct the souls of both the living and the dead?

There does not seem to be a prevalent direction for stone row alignment, although some do align with astronomical events, such as solstices. I shall deal with this subject again in Chapter 16. Although astronomical alignments have been suggested (Lockyer 1906, Walker 1995) this does not mean that the majority of stone rows were aligned with key astronomical events in mind, as many do not seem to have been. Some regard stone rows to have no astronomical significance at all (Gerrard 1997), but I think that we should not debunk all celestial links. Some astronomical associations have recently been advocated at Scorhill, Drizzlecombe and Hingston (Walker 1995), and I shall return to these soon, along with others I have perceived. What I *have* found is that the *location* of stone rows enables astronomical alignments, such as solstices, ***using the tors as the markers***, just like the outliers at some stone circles. So, even though a stone row may not have any astronomically relevant azimuths, there may be significance in the *direction* of intervisible landscape features. However, in my experience, the most common alignments are not celestial, but rather with water sources, a subject which I shall return to soon.

Stone rows were often respected by those who later built stone walls in their vicinity: 'In some places the reave builders respected stone rows and avoided crossing them' (Newman 2011). At Hurston Ridge and Holne Moor, reaves run parallel with stone rows; the latter is a triple stone row south of Combestone Tor (675710), and other examples occur on the moor. At Yar Tor, however, two reaves cross the stone rows with seemingly little respect. At the Hook Lake double stone rows (641653), the component stones connect two Bronze Age enclosures, and comprise part of the walls of the south enclosure. Rows do not appear to form boundaries, but were cultural clan anchors – monuments of belonging.

I think the key element of rows is that movement across the landscape is suddenly directed and fixed. And not just for the living. Stone rows represented pathways for the departed ancestors to move along, and were part of a way of bringing the dead 'back to life', so they could be contacted. Rows facilitated spirits to come back out into the physical landscape, from within the cairns where the dead resided. By walking the rows, the living and the dead would commune. In this respect, movement in both directions is important. For the living to move/walk towards a cairn is the process by which they come to meet *specific* dead. Walking the stone row away from the cairns may have been part of the process through which the dead are coaxed back to the world of the living. I felt as if the ancestors were walking side by side with me, communicating as I walked several rows and avenues. This could be described as quite literally 'walking your talk', as movement seems to be a key part in the process.

My most memorable moments on the moor have been whilst I have been in motion across it. As one passes the terminal points, which are generally well defined, one exits liminal space, and returns to the realm of the physical, of the living and of the open moor, with freedom of movement and unrestricted space.

Intervisibility

I have already shown how the stone row at Challacombe Down affords a fine view of the Grimspound Bronze Age settlement **(image p. 17)**. Most stone rows cannot be seen until one is relatively close to them, generally well within half a mile. Clearly, it was more important as to what was seen *from* them. Tors and other features may come and go as one walks a long stone row; in a landscape that at first appears static, it is in motion as I move around it. It seems possible that the tors were conveyed with added significance because they were the sources of the material for the stone rows and circles and, conversely, the power of the stones came from them having been derived from the tors. I shall also deal below with what seems to be the association between water and stone rows, be it proximity or visibility.

The presence and intervisibility of cairns along the stone rows is primal, as they almost pull the pilgrim along to the next. It is as if the ancestors themselves were compelling you to join them. At Corrington Ball, a stone row (665612), with accompanying cairns, looks across a small river valley to where cairns and the long barrow stand on the far side. An unassuming stone row can be found at Yar Tor (c.681740), and yet, as I entered the stone avenue/rows (walking north), Sharp Tor, which had been prominent to the south, was no longer visible. My focus of vision and movement was down slope and northwards. However, having walked southwards back up the row, Sharp Tor rose from the land as I exited the row, a spot marked by cairns; the row is aligned with the tor. Also, it is from this location that a thin slice of sea became visible to the south! Also noticeable from the row were cairns to the west on Yar Tor, and more on Corndon Down to the east. It seems that location is everything.

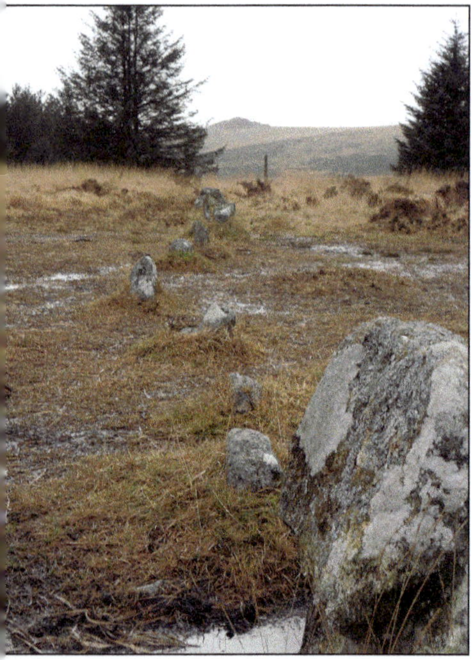

I have already demonstrated how a short stone row and cist on Lakehead Hill (644776) is aligned with the horned summits of Haytor **(lower left image, p. 82)**. This is clearly intentional. This stone row once extended westwards, and the remains of it appear 100m from the cist. On my visit I saw how it aligns with the granite crags of Longaford Tor **(left)**. The row is sinuous, but the tor is its focus. Originally this end of the row would have afforded a 360° vista, including Bellever Tor, dominant to the south. Sometimes the intervisibility between stone rows and other stone rows, distant cairns and settlements is taken to extremes, such is the intricate placement on the landscape of the observation point and that which is being observed. For instance, from the two Corrington Ball stone rows, five other stone rows, plus eight settlements and six cairns are visible (Klemen 2015). I have stood at these rows and seen cairns straddling the skyline of Piles Hill and Butterdon Hill to the west. From the Glasscombe Corner stone row (661607), no less than nine Bronze Age settlements, plus three other stone rows and four cairns, are visible (Klemen

2015). Although most stone rows could not be seen from these settlements, chanting and drumming would have been audible, and ritual fires observed. The emphasis seems to have been to see places of the living and cairns *from* the stone rows, not the other way round.

Other examples can be found of rows aligning with tors. For instance, the Challacombe row (690807) aligns with Birch Tor, whilst the Higher White Tor row (618783) aligns with the tor.

An impressive 135m triple stone row can be found at the eastern foot of Cosdon Hill, near the northern extremity of the moor **(right, and p. 157).** This site can be waterlogged in winter months, and is located close to the source of the waters of Cheriton Combe. The three rows are aligned with a cairn north of the summit (637917), even though they are not intervisible. From the rows, views are magnificent and very distant from azimuths 15° to 180°, from almost north to due south. As with Merrivale, the rows sit on a plateau. The west section, which ends in a cist, heads off at 90° (equinox sunrise), but then changes direction and heads more northerly. My head felt dizzy when I rested against one of the 'blocking stones'. Perhaps we should call them 'portal stones', marking the meeting place of living with the dead. I really sensed the liminality of the space here.

The blocking stones are aligned to the SW, so I suspected a midwinter alignment. But when I stood behind them I saw they were aligned **(right)** with a very distant Haytor! I have shown elsewhere how this sacred hill was the focus of attention **(images p. 82)**. Also, as I walked south across a sodden moor, I looked back and saw how the rows exquisitely mirrored the hill line beyond **(below)**. I have seen a similar effect with the Merrivale stone rows when viewed from the nearby settlement **(image p.181)**.

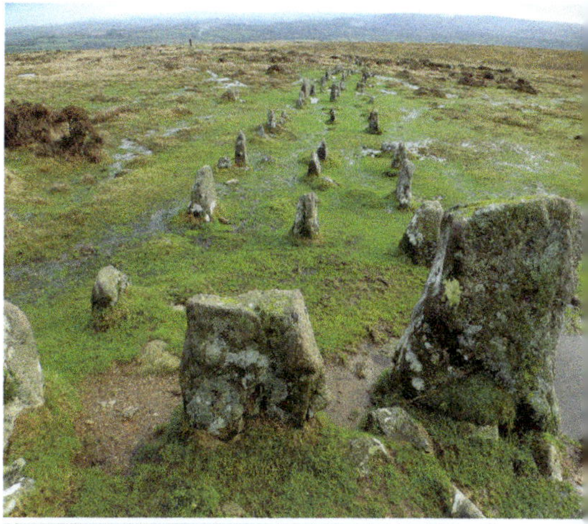

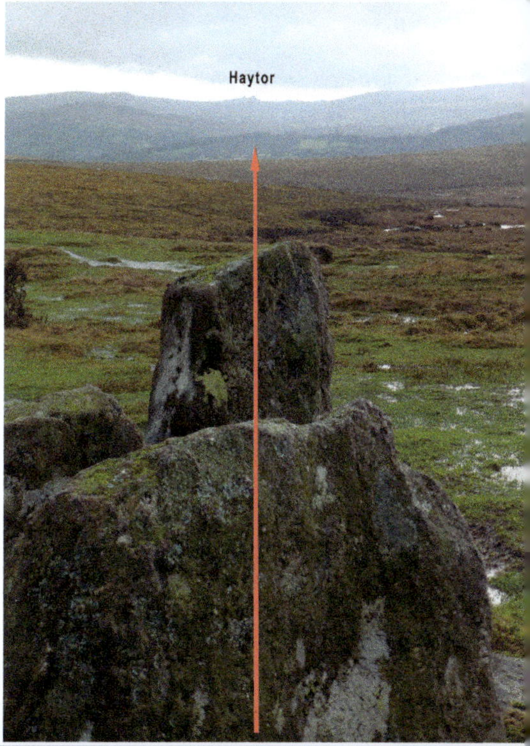

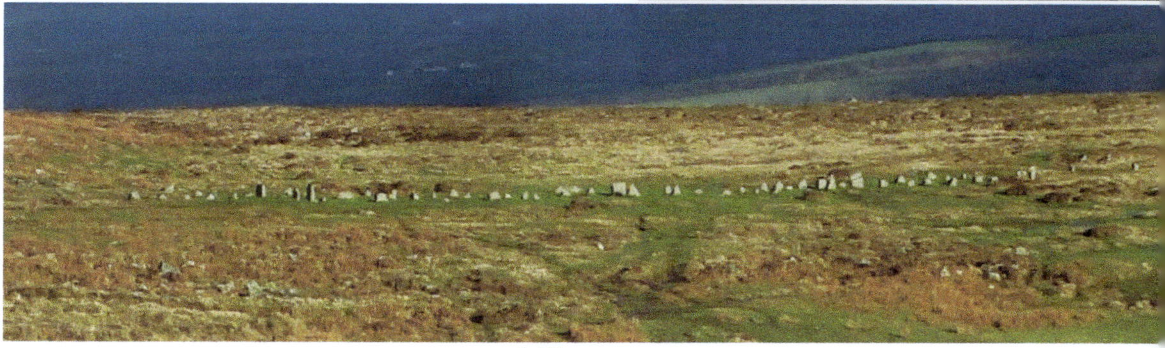

Stone rows and water

That the megaliths of Newgrange, Avebury and Stonehenge all have tangible connections with nearby rivers has been well documented by archaeologists (Burl 1979, Parker Pearson 2012). On Dartmoor, however, there is a more subtle, almost imperceptible, relationship between many of the moor's stone rows and water. This was brought home me on my many visits to rows over the winter half of the year, when the moor was frequently sodden; summer walkers and cyclists will have no idea how much rainwater is held on the land after prolonged rainfall. Stone rows that march across dry and parched land in summer, become waterlogged and engulfed by squelchy ground and deep pools in winter. It must be acknowledged that this would have been the case when the stones were erected, and therefore part of the stone row experience. Water is purifying and a gift from the gods or ancestors, as we saw with rock basins. There is also the challenge of physically getting to, from, and along stone rows during wetter conditions; this feels more shamanic in intent, making a spiritual connection with the life-giving waters of the land.

Jeremy Butler saw a connection between rivers and stone rows: 'There is a detectable riverine association, since half the total [of stone rows] are within 200 to 300m of a riverbank, sixteen of them near the springs of minor tributaries' (Butler 1997). Recent work (Mortimer 2013, and on the Heritage Journal website) has also advocated that stone rows have a connection with water, either through their close proximity to rivers, or else through an intervisibility with the sea. At the Hook Lake double stone rows (641653), the site is upslope from the stream of that name, where it converges with another brook. From the top of the rows, a thin shimmer of sea is visible on the skyline, whereas it had not been from the lower end. At Hart Tor (576716), the sea comes into view as one proceeds westwards along the row, yet is not visible from the eastern end. From the Shaugh Moor stone row, a thin sliver of sea is visible (and a stream flows by one end of the row). At the Brent Fore Hill stone row (668613), as one walks east along the row, the sea comes into view on the skyline. As they are often at the opposite direction to the cairns of the rows, do these chinks of sea represent life? I also suggest that, during shamanic trance journeys, the sensation is often one of travel, or of plunging downwards, as if in a tunnel. There is often light at the end, often as one reaches ancestral worlds. Is this symbolically replicated with stone rows, the light at end of the tunnel being the glistening waters of rivers and the sea?

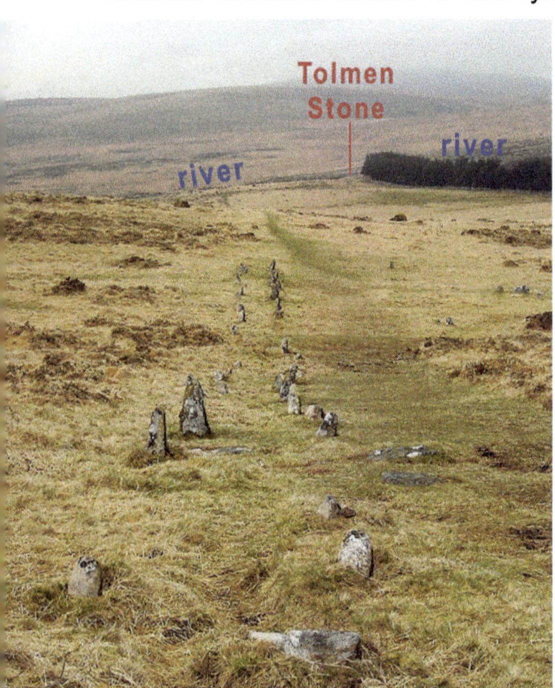

Neil Mortimer observed that two stone rows near Sharpitor aligned with the somewhat distant confluence of the Tamar and the Tavy rivers. He also found that the 3.2km stone row at Stall Down (c. 632623) affords extensive views of the Devon and Cornwall coastlines. The row may have once extended to a cairn further south, just upslope from two springs. Not far north, the Upper Erme Stone row runs for 3.7km across open moorland, and is the moor's longest row, originally comprising up to 2000 megaliths (Mortimer 2013). Mortimer noted how this row actually crosses the River Erme, as well as one of its tributaries, Red Lake. To this I can add that the southern section of the stone row noticeably changes direction so as to align with the convergence of the Erme and the Bledge Brook. As I have said already, only from the cairns at the south end of the Yar Tor stone row does the sea become visible. It was also clear to me that it is significant that two streams pass between the Corrington Ball long barrow and the stone row west of it. Further to these, Conies Down stone row (586790) aligns with the springhead of Conies Down Water; the stone row below Great Trowlesworthy Tor crosses a stream (576638); and a stone row below Penn Beacon (595633) passes three springheads, which produce an almost impassable barrier in winter months.

The stone row at Shovel Down (660858) heads north and down slope towards the North Teign River **(image opposite)**. One of the Bronze Age reaves here runs from the stone row down to the river. As I walk down any of the stone avenues (there are three at the northern end) I can feel the river (which is unseen) drawing me down towards it; in it sits the Tolmen Stone – as if awaiting my return.

Let us look at a number of other stone rows where, at each place, a veritable ballet ensues between stone rows, tors and water.

Drizzlecombe

The Drizzlecombe complex of stone rows and cairns (c. 593670) is one of the prehistoric wonders of Dartmoor. Three stone rows, plus cists, cairns and Bronze Age settlements are sited in close proximity to the River Plym, to the east of Burrator Reservoir. The landscape setting is stunning, as various tors give a backdrop to this compelling collection of monuments **(map below)**. As with many other sites, the complex is just upslope from a river confluence, that of the Plym and the Drizzle

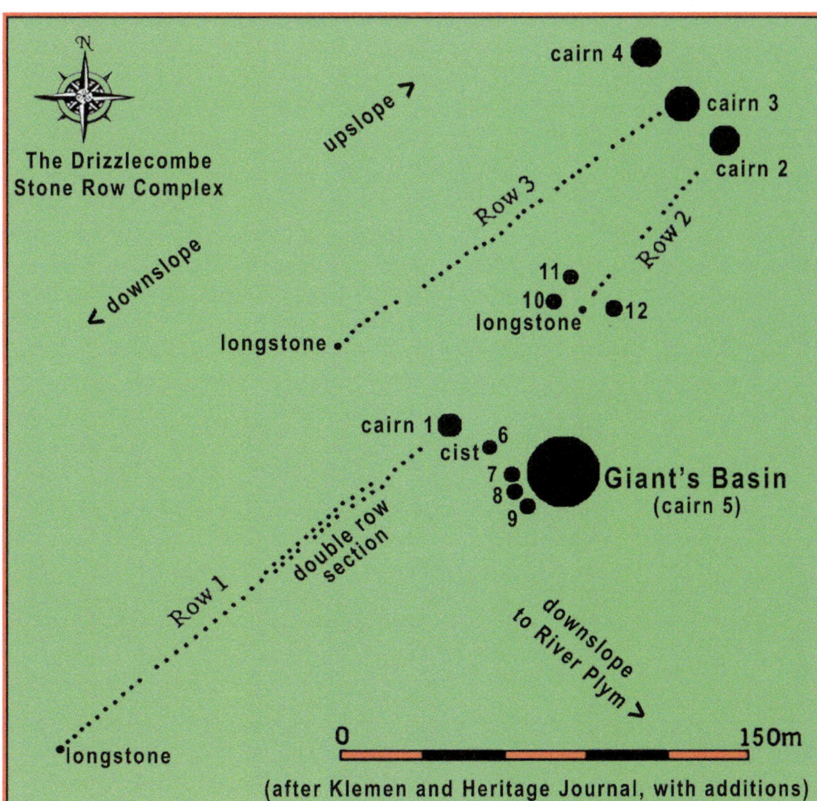

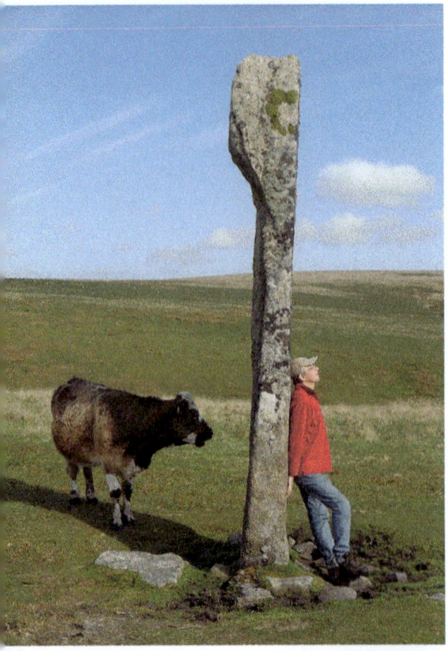

Combe stream; it is a landscape setting naturally graced with sanctity. As with elsewhere, I am not so much going to describe the archaeology in detail, but rather my experiences and observations from a phenomenological perspective.

All three of Drizzlecombe's long granite rows have cairns at the upslope end, and tall longstones at the down slope termini. The rows echo the course of the River Plym to the south, and views are afforded up the river valley towards its source on Crane Hill. Drizzlecombe is enclosed in a bowl-like amphitheatre, as is Merrivale. Settlements were established just beyond cairns 2, 3 and 4 **(see map)**, and more lie to the east, south and west. As has been said, stone rows seem to be a metaphor for movement, transition and change (Tilley 2010), and this megalithic complex was right at the heart of the daily lives of the clan. Each row is approximately NE–SW, hinting at solstice alignments, although Eastern Tor seems to be the focus of row 3. Row 1 is about 160m long, terminating in a 2.5m high triangular longstone, tapering at the top; its long axis is aligned with the row. Part of this row is double, forming an avenue **(left)**. Row 2 is about 90m long, with a 4.2m megalith at its terminus, the largest megalith still standing on Dartmoor. It was re-erected in 1893 when the original socket hole was located, and was measured at 5.5m when lying on the ground. A distinct feature of the stone is the face or bulb at the top, on the east side **(top)**. Row 3 is about 150m in length, terminating with another longstone, over 3m tall (Thomas 1976). The sheer size of the longstones suggests they were brought in from outside the immediate landscape setting (Klemen 2015).

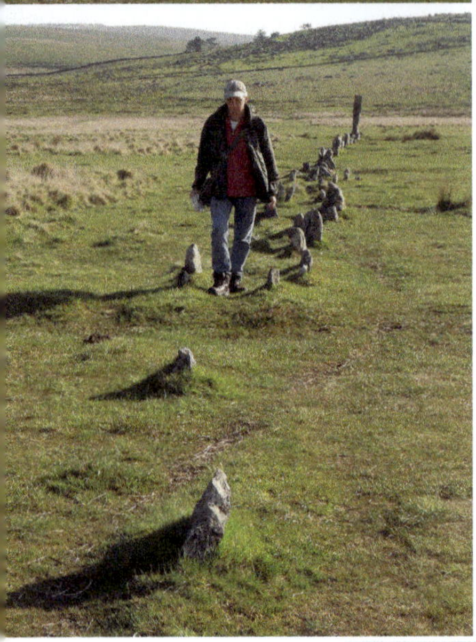

Movement around the complex reveals some interesting revelations. As one walks up and down the rows **(left)**, the small size of the stones becomes apparent, with the exception of the terminal longstones. One has to bend over or crouch down to touch them. One can easily place one's legs astride them. Clearly the size of the stones was not of prime importance here. I felt I was being led across the landscape along prescribed routes, from river to cairn, from cairn to longstone, and on to the settlement, and back again. If Tilley is correct that stone rows are about movement, this is apparent at the longer rows like Drizzlecombe. It is also about the contrast between the visuals and freedom of the vast open landscape, and the physical confines of a row. It required discipline to surrender myself to the rows.

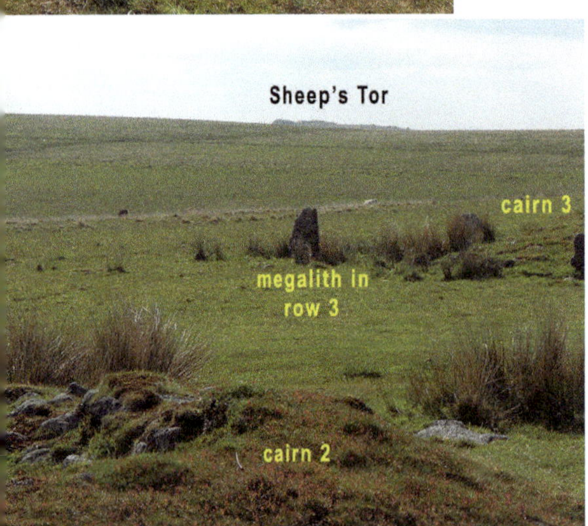

Features in the landscape come and go as one walks down from the high ground at the NE end of the site. From cairns 2, 3 and 4, the top of Sheep's Tor is seen. The tor is aligned with a taller stone in row 3, when viewed from seen from cairn 2 **(bottom image, opposite)**. But on walking down row 2, I noted how the tor gradually recedes into the skyline, until it has gone from view completely at the Longstone. From cairns 2 – 4, the sea is visible as a thin shimmering line to the SW, and remains in sight down slope, even as far as the longstone of row 2. But as one leaves the stone and approaches cairn 1, the sea drops from view, hidden by higher intervening ground.

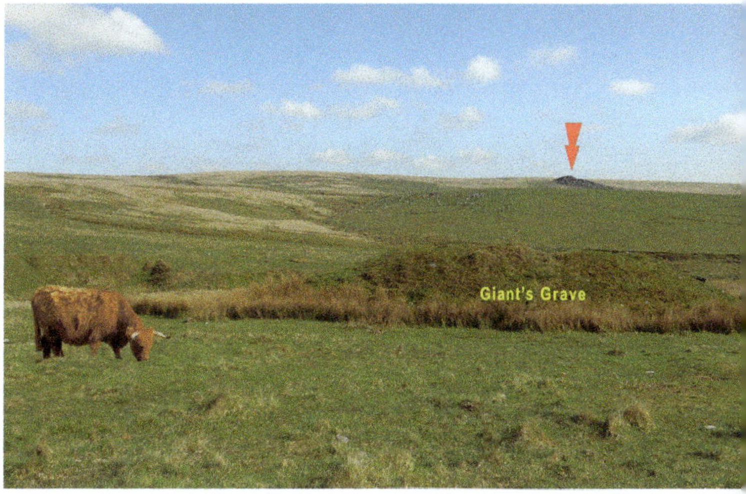

On arriving in the vicinity of the 'bulb' megalith and the huge Giant's Grave (cairn 5), I scanned the skyline again and noted that Hen Tor had now broken the skyline **(above)**, which it had not done previously, even though it had been visible (red arrow in image). Hen Tor was encultured with hut circles and walls. From cairn 5, an alignment involving cairns 5, 6 (a cist), cairn 1 and the longstone at the end of row 3 was apparent, in the direction of azimuth 308°. The skyline in this direction is above the observer, and I believe this alignment marks the first contact of the sun with the horizon at midsummer solstice in the Neolithic. Did the view of Hen Tor and the direction of the summer solstice determine the position of these monuments? It has also been noted that as one ascends row 1, from a point just before the row becomes double, Giant's Basin or Grave begins to obscure the view up the Plym valley, and by the time one is halfway along the double section, the mound blocks all views up the valley. From where the double row ends, one can again see up the valley (Klemen 2015).

Standing where row 3 meets cairn 3, I could see that one of the stones that comprised the cairn circle also seemed to be doubling as a 'blocking stone' for the stone row. The stone was set with the long axis at 90° to the row. From here is an exquisite alignment of this stone, the longstone of row 2 and Great Trowlesworthy Tor, which just rises above the skyline **(right)**. This alignment is specific to just a few metres.

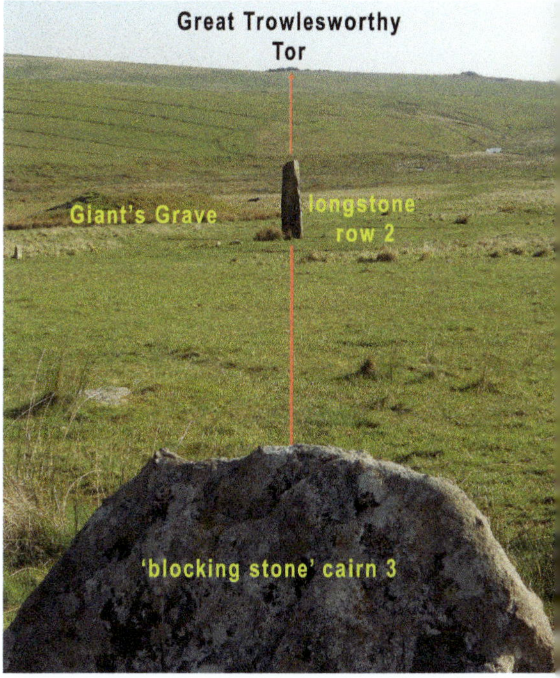

But it is not all about looking to distant horizons. The 'bulb' or head protruding from the longstone of row 2 **(top image, opposite)** is only appreciated when standing at right angles to it, which is why I believe cairns 10 and 12 are positioned where they are! They are located where these stone features can best be appreciated: 'The 'bulb' brings a very distinct dimension to the stone and gives it an almost anthropomorphic look and breaks the 'formal' look of the stone from the west' (Klemen 2015). The stone is also very phallic in appearance from these cairns. The longstone is also notable for the mica crystals that give it a distinct appearance, which is different from the longstone at the end of row 3, which is notable for its tourmaline and large white feldspars.

To sum up, the Drizzlecombe stone rows are specifically nested within a landscape 'bowl'. Views to the west, south and east are somewhat restricted, preventing any experiences apart from the immediate landscape; to the north only Sheep's Tor pops up from the middle distance hill line. Experience seems to be '... focused 'in' and 'onto' this area' (Klemen 2015). Once one arrives at the hilltop settlements which encircle the complex, there are 360° vistas, with views of Great Mis Tor, the Staple Tors, Sheep's Tor, Gutter Tor, with the sea and Bodmin Moor in the distance. I did conclude that Gutter Tor was important to the builders of the rows, as this tor stays visible from everywhere within the complex. I believe it to be relevant that there are several rock basins on the tor. When approaching Drizzlecombe from the east, over Giant's Hill, it is Gutter Tor and Sheep's Tor that are prominent on the skyline. In fact, Gutter Tor is the focus of reave systems, and a hut circle **(image p. 195)** was erected on the summit.

I shall return to Drizzlecombe later, when I look at the archaeoastronomy and earth energies of this amazing prehistoric complex.

Hingston Hill Stone Row and Cairn Circle

The stone row at Hingston Hill (sometimes referred to as Down Tor row) is one of the most evocative of the moor's stone rows **(below)**. It has been described as, '... the most magnificent of all the prehistoric monuments on Dartmoor' (Lethbridge 2015), a sentiment which I can endorse. It is situated in isolated open moorland (c.588694), not far north of Drizzlecombe, and is a hidden gem, visited only by those pilgrims who take

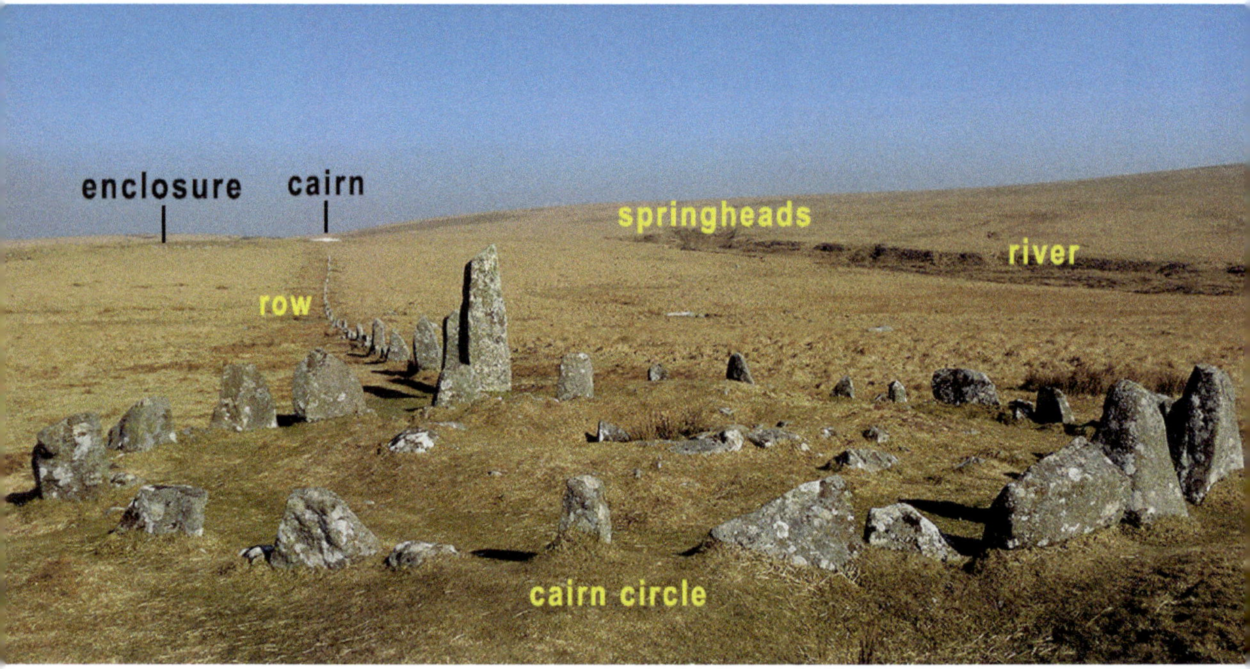

the mile long uphill trek from the nearest parking (568693). Like many other stone rows, it marches across gently sloping terrain, in this case for 350m from NE-SW. The row of 161 stones terminates in three megaliths which are 1.6m, 2m and 2.8m tall respectively as one approaches the SW terminus **(right)**. At this end there is a 12m diameter cairn circle comprising 25 stones. At the NE end stands a 1.5m high triangular 'blocking stone', and beyond that a large cairn which is aligned with the row. The row is clearly not straight, and veers to the north in the centre section. Restoration of the stones was carried out in 1894.

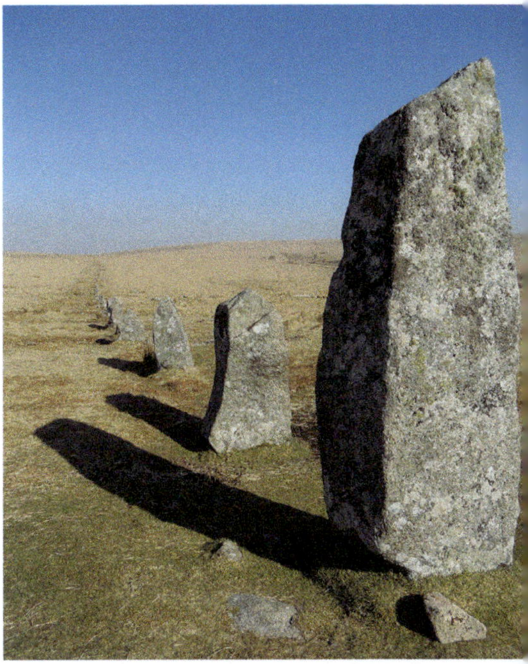

I visited the stones on a cold but sunny day in March 2016, and approaching from the south was in awe; what a landscape setting – 'big country'! From the site, Combeshead Tor is dominant to the SW, although the rest of the landscape is undulating, with distant skylines. The cairn circle is a delight, and I felt the energies of the place. The tall megalith next to the circle gave out a message: "I am strength, standing the test of time, through the eons'. From this point the tops of Great Staple Tor, Great Mis Tor and Roos Tor were just visible – just! Was this an intentional effect? Walking to a small cairn to the NW of here the landscape opens up, with views of Sharpitor, Leather Tor, Down Tor, Great Staple Tor, and better views of Roos and Great Mis Tor.

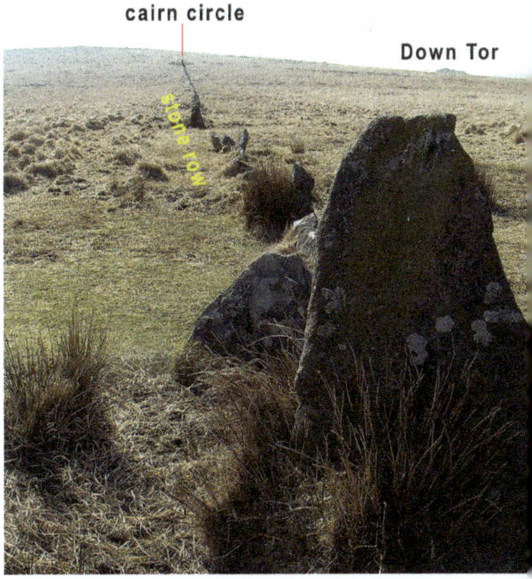

Walking the row, it was clear that it rides a saddle, as the land gently drops away either side. The centre of the row also dips noticeably before rising again at each end. By mid-row the land gradient ensured that Roos Tor, Great Staple Tor and Great Mis Tor had gone from view. These all come back into visibility from the NE end of the row, by the triangular blocking stone. From this stone the top of Down Tor has also subtly risen above the skyline **(right)**.

It was not until I reached the cairn beyond the row (592694) that Sheeps Tor came into view; it just peeks up over Hingston Hill, above the row and cairn circle at the SW end. This tor was not visible from the row, and suggests that this cairn was located here (further east away from the row) because it afforded the view of this tor. Some stones were found lying on the ground that indicate the row may have once continued up to this cairn. It has been said that a thin wedge of sea is visible (between Great Trowlesworthy Tor and Gutter Tor) from this end of the alignment (Heritage Journal website), but I could not confirm this on my visit. The cairns on Eylesbarrow are certainly visible on the skyline to SE. From these cairns, I looked down like an eagle on the whole ceremonial landscape.

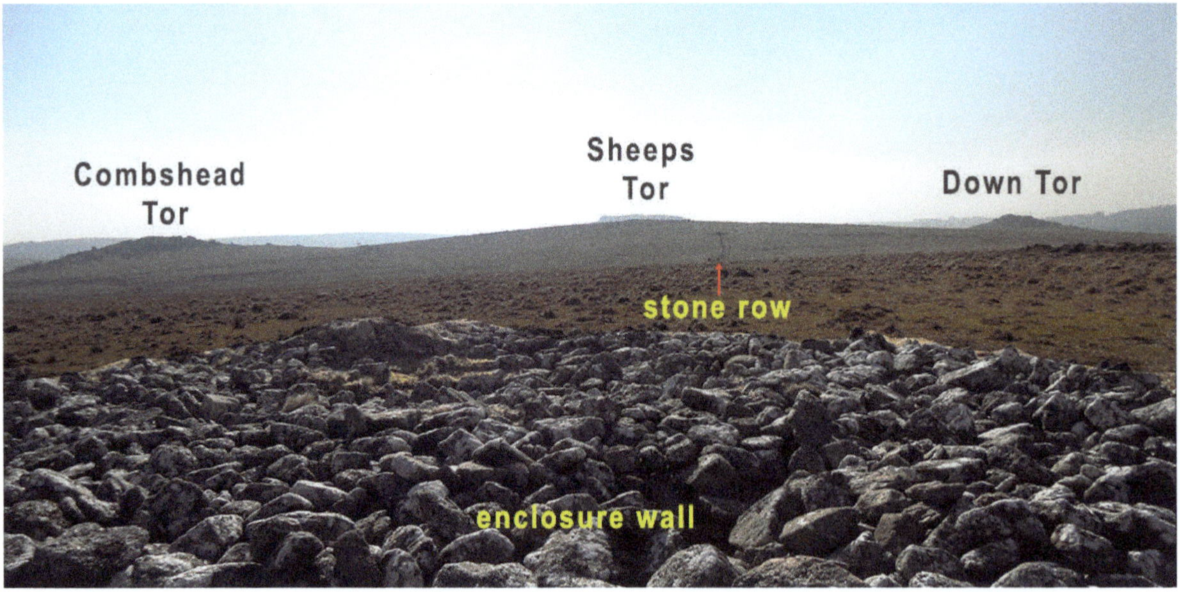

It was from an enclosure (591694), next to this eastern cairn, where the views are perhaps the best - 360° in fact. From the centre of the enclosure the stone row aligns with Sheeps Tor, which has now appeared over Hingston Hill. The row marches up the slope towards it, changing its direction to do so. The stone row in the ceremonial landscape is now beautifully framed by Combshead Tor and Down Tor **(above)**, which now punctuate the skyline. What a backdrop our ancestors forged for themselves!

To the south of the row is a spring line **(image p. 150)**, which feels like a sanctuary, with high banks and multiple springheads (592692). The entire length of the stone row is visible from the top of the river banks. This mirrors the stone row/river association at Drizzlecombe, which also has the river to the south. Examination of OS maps further reveals that the Hingston complex is surrounded by springs and streams, which also give rise to extremely boggy conditions during winter. In fact the row itself is sometimes waterlogged, which, even in dry spells, is evidenced by reeds.

Jack Walker has undertaken notable work on the astronomical alignments of Hingston Hill, which I shall return to. I shall deal with the energies dowsed here in Chapter 17.

Hart Tor/Black Tor Stone Rows

Two smaller stone rows with cairn circles can be found in a beautiful river valley setting (576717), just SE of Black Tor, SW of Princetown. The rows are easily accessible from the car park on the B3212, although they are shielded from the sights and sounds of the traffic by Black Tor; its granite outcrops dominate the view to the north. These are further examples of stone rows descending a moderate slope in the direction of a river, one of which ends within metres of it. More than this, the southern row is aligned with the convergence of the River Meavy and Hart Tor Brook. Unfortunately a tinner's gully has cut through both rows.

One of the rows is a double configuration, an avenue along which to walk. The poorly preserved south row is singular. Both rows end with cairns at the upslope end, the north one being enclosed by a well-preserved cairn circle. Coming down from Black Tor I could see the rows nestling in the landscape, as if the stones were walking down to the river to drink **(top image, next page)**. I had to ford the river to access the rows,

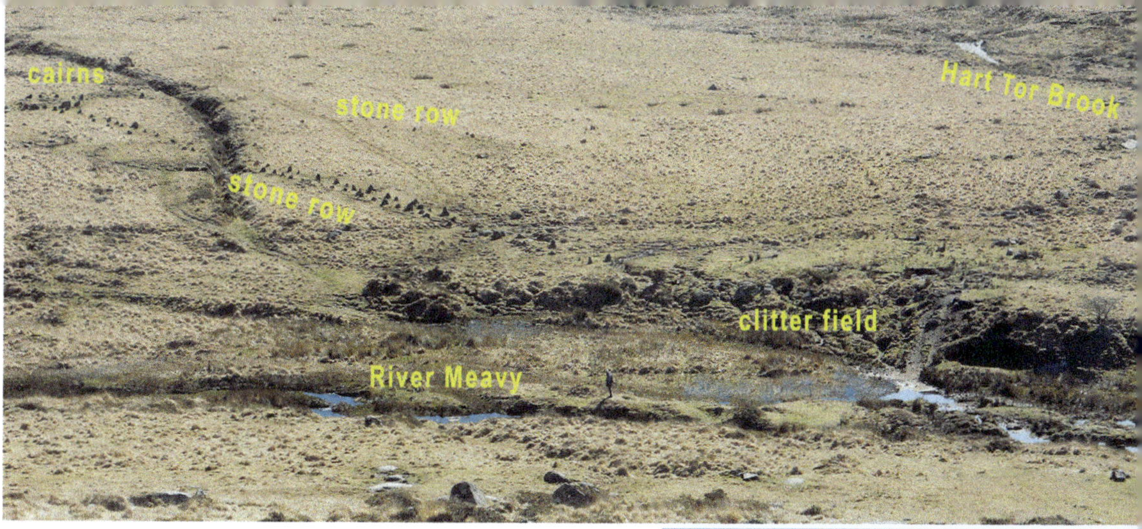

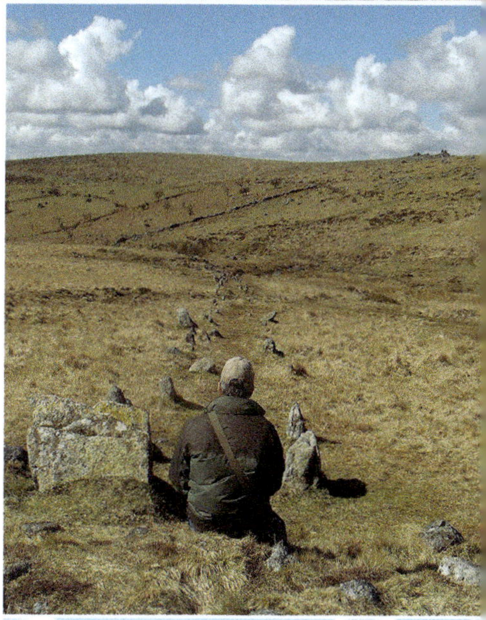

which is tricky due to marshy ground either side in winter. The sunken area marks the convergence of the streams, and has the feeling of a sanctuary about it, like that near the Hingston row. On the other side of the river are large clitter and river boulders, which blend seamlessly with the start of the main stone row. Walking up the double row there is no focus in the distance. But walking down slope one is drawn towards the river; several tors are also visible in this direction. Black Tor is high on the right, its huge simulacrum **(lower right image, p. 58)** overseeing the ceremonies that may have been held here. Sharpitor and Leather Tor rise to the left, and due south a cairn graces Raddick Hill.

At the top, a fine cairn circle terminates the row, with another cairn close by to the SE, from which the shorter row heads off down to the river. From the cairns, I could see an ancient settlement to the west. One of the cairn circle stones is very triangular whilst another seems to be doubling as the 'blocking stone' for the stone row. I settled down next to it, looking back down the row **(centre)**. The cairn seems to represent death, whereas the river, at the other end of row, is symbolic of life. Sitting here the energy rose up into my throat and I got a sensation as if someone was choking me, which continued until I started to walk back down the row. I realised afterwards that I had not asked permission to go on to the cairn!

Another phenomenon that may have determined the end of the row is that from here Leeden Tor now appears above the skyline, top right in this image **(centre)**. Also evident to me was that these two cairns, at the end of the stone rows, were aligned to the cairn on the skyline on Raddick Hill **(right)**. It's all about seeing with new eyes.

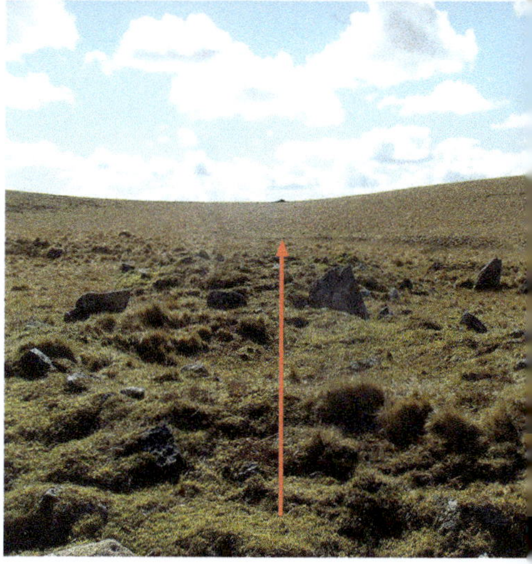

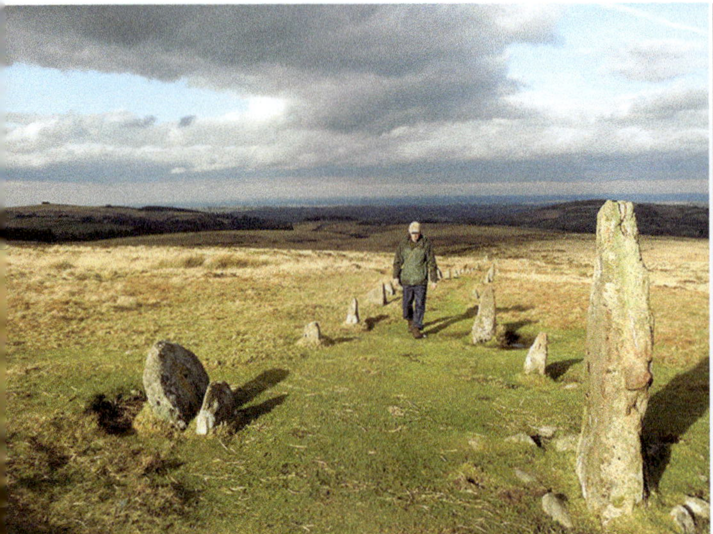

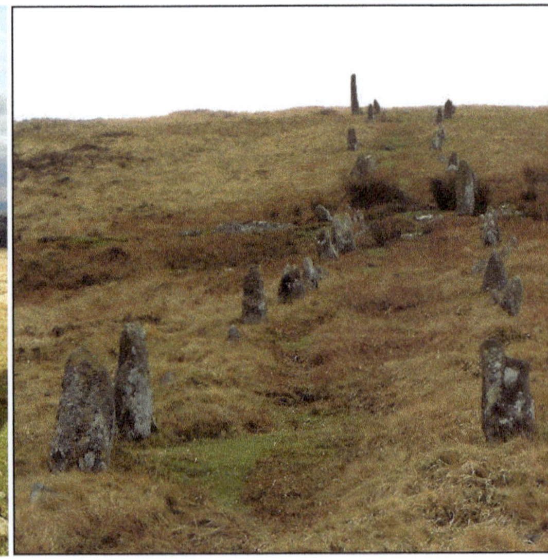

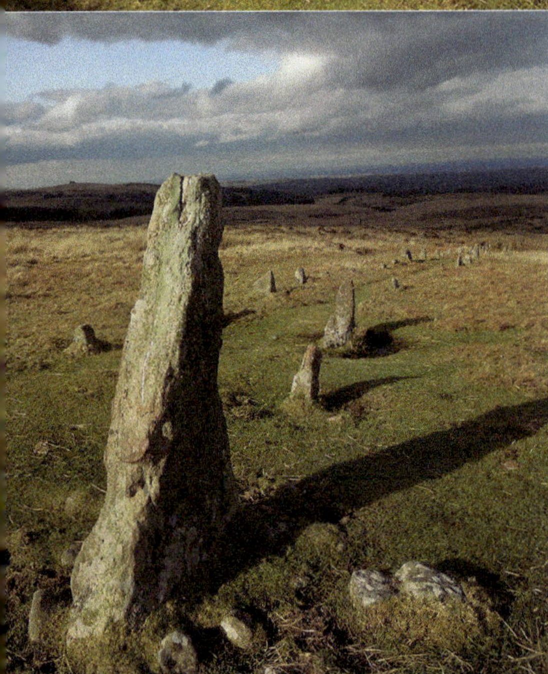

I shall return to this site later, as it was found to be very active with dowsable energies. I have led walks to these rows as part of my own programme of weekend shamanic workshops, as well as for the Megalithomania Conference. Attendees agree that this place is both powerful and beautiful. The 'spirit of place' dwells here. Again, there is an alchemical fusion of granite, water and Man.

Hurston Ridge

The next row I shall highlight is a double row on Hurston Ridge (673825). This row has commanding views of Kestor and Middle Tor, which break the skyline to the left side of image **(top left)**; Meldon Hill and Exmoor are visible to the north. The row marches across a N-S ridge, and the tallest stone (nearly 2m tall) is at the southern end **(left)**; it appears phallic from one direction and triangular from another. I also noted the numerous blocks of quartz lying around. The rows occupy a high triangular area bounded by the sources of Lowton Brook and Metherall Brook, and the valley of the North Walla Brook to the east - water again! The stone rows are very boggy in winter, with reeds and ponds, and small rivulets flow cross their path.

Walking the rows northwards I felt I was being directed down slope to both the North and South Teign rivers. The north end of row is all about the view north, with extensive views from NW to NE. However, when I turned around and looked back south, the tall megalith, plus a couple of other stones, now projected into the skyline **(top right)**; this effect can only be achieved from this terminal. The phallus rises erect from of the sodden landscape; or has it been thrust *into* the land, penetrating it with its fertilising power?

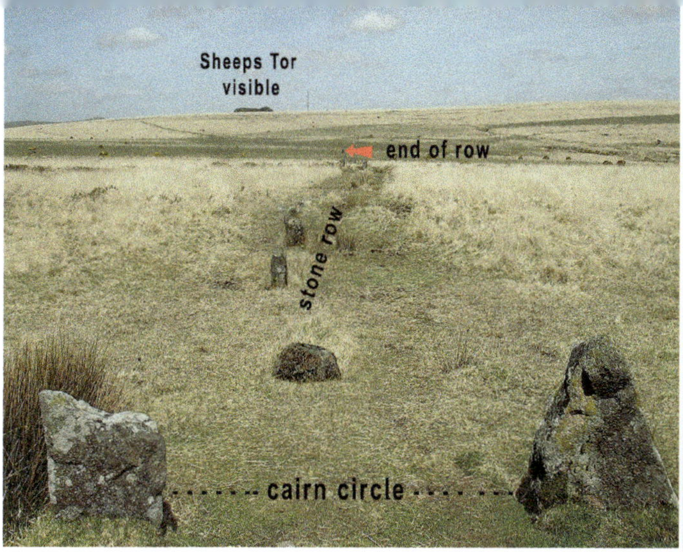

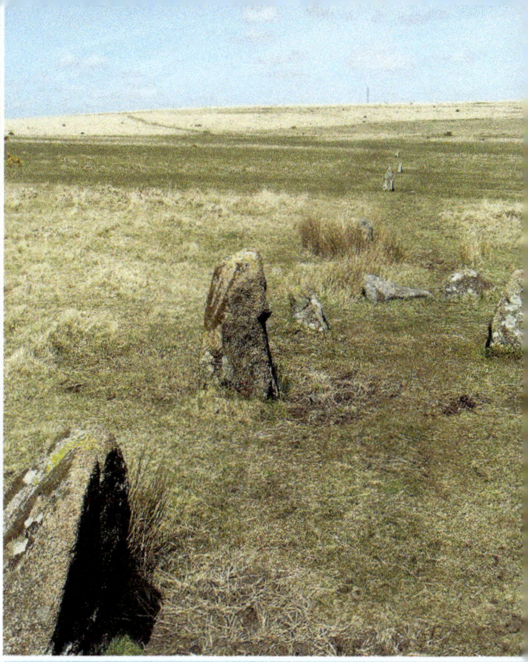

Brisworthy Stone Row

This row (c. 563658) is set midst fabulous terrain, tucked away near the SW corner of the moor, north of the Brisworthy stone circle. A fine cairn circle stands at the south end of the row, a triangular stone marking where the circle meets the row. The row is over 500m long, and bends noticeably north (left) as it proceeds in a northerly direction, as if turning towards Sheeps Tor, the top of which rises out of the skyline to the north **(above left)**. From the cairn circle the sea is also visible to the SSW. Some stones in the circle are of distinctive a red granite, as are some of the stones comprising the rows. The stone row also seems to be double in places, although many stones are missing; some stones are over 1m high, but most are much smaller.

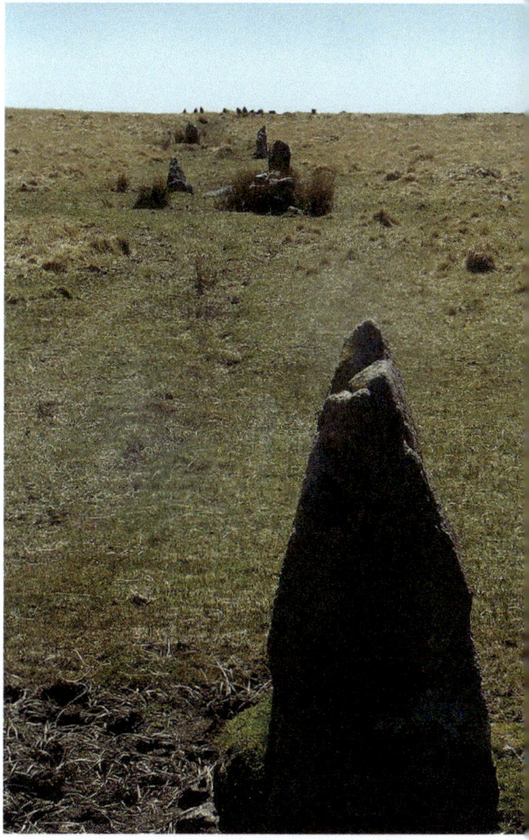

In May 2016, as I walked north and down slope from the cairn circle, I noted reeds and small pools, suggesting that this area must be boggy and waterlogged in winter. From the centre of the row, I noted that Sheeps Tor had gone below the skyline **(above right)**. At this point the row is double and a square, blocky stone, like an altar, sits on the earth. Is this stone here because it marks where Sheeps Tor disappears from view going north, or comes into view walking south?

Where the stones peter out at the north end a line of reeds can be followed, filling the gaps, and I noted that animal dung also followed this line. More reeds followed - the low ground just to the east of row is called Legis Mire. Further on the reed line splits into two lines, one of which goes to a 1m prone stone 100m further on. Are the lines of reeds marking the earth energies following the former route of the row?

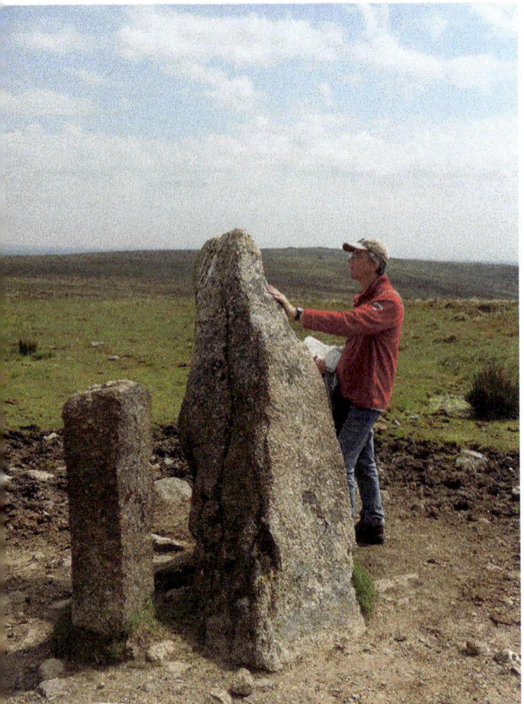

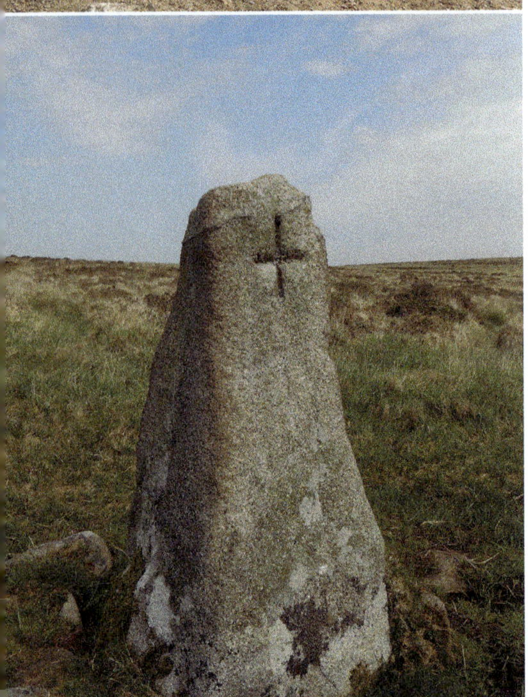

From this north terminal point I turned around to see that the cairn circle was now standing plumb on the skyline! **(bottom image, previous page)**. I felt as if my movement was again being choreographed across the landscape; I was being led out onto the open moorland in one direction, and by walking back south along the row I was once again being drawn to a cairn circle – to the place of the ancestors.

In May 2016, I walked the long stone rows of Butterdon Hill and Piles Hill. One of the largest longstones (653607) is the restored terminal **(left)** of a row that runs for over a mile. I found astronomical alignments with nearby cairns when viewed from this stone. Not far south long the row stands Hobajons Cross, a stone that has been Christianised with an inscribed cross **(lower image)**. Other longstones here are also used as boundary stones. However, what impressed me the most was how various hilltop 'prestige' cairns appeared and then passed from view as I followed the row (see p. 91 & 96).

The recurring themes concerning stone rows seem to be their association with water, cairns, and the way that tors come into and go out of view as perspectives change. Movement is the key to unravelling and experiencing stone rows. We need to see them as places of memory and cultural attachment, as liminal linking places, where knowledge was learnt, taught, passed on by walking, as well as talking whilst walking: 'They are pathways of knowledge' (Klemen 2015). People were active in social and spiritual engagement, but not just with each other, but rather in the context of their environment. These rows reflected their knowing of their past and present and, who knows, perhaps even what was to unfold in their future. Some megaliths of the rows became anthropomorphised, carrying with them the very essence of the dead. When we walk a stone row today we are still walking in the footprints of our ancestors.

Next, I shall look in detail at arguably Dartmoor's finest stone rows, those at Merrivale. But, more than this, I will argue that the whole landscape around these rows was part of an extended ceremonial/shamanic landscape.

'The body becomes the primary tool in which you gather in knowledge and experiences... the body is central, but not a frozen static one, one on the move and active.' (Klemen 2015).

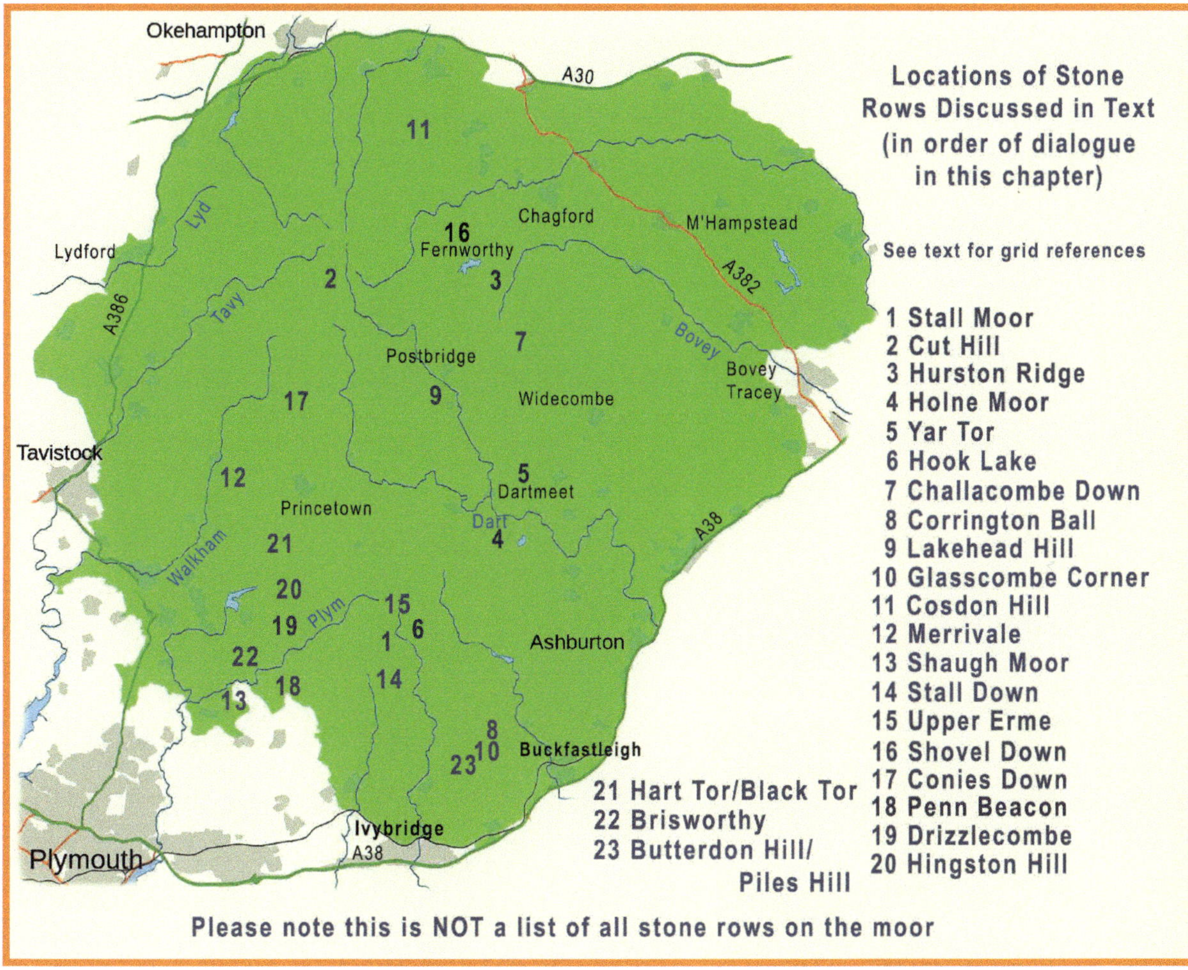
Locations of Stone Rows Discussed in Text (in order of dialogue in this chapter)
See text for grid references
1 Stall Moor
2 Cut Hill
3 Hurston Ridge
4 Holne Moor
5 Yar Tor
6 Hook Lake
7 Challacombe Down
8 Corrington Ball
9 Lakehead Hill
10 Glasscombe Corner
11 Cosdon Hill
12 Merrivale
13 Shaugh Moor
14 Stall Down
15 Upper Erme
16 Shovel Down
17 Conies Down
18 Penn Beacon
19 Drizzlecombe
20 Hingston Hill
21 Hart Tor/Black Tor
22 Brisworthy
23 Butterdon Hill/ Piles Hill
Okehampton
A30
Chagford
M'Hampstead
Lydford
Lyd
Fernworthy
A382
A386
Tavy
Postbridge
Bovey
Bovey Tracey
Widecombe
Tavistock
Princetown
Dartmeet
Dart
A38
Walkham
Plym
Ashburton
Buckfastleigh
Ivybridge
A38
Plymouth
Please note this is NOT a list of all stone rows on the moor

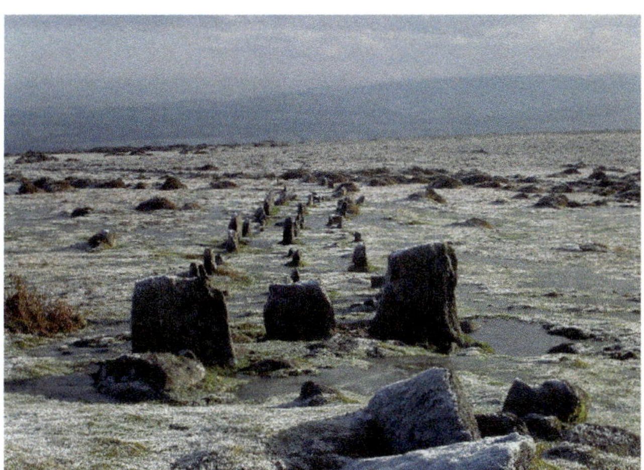

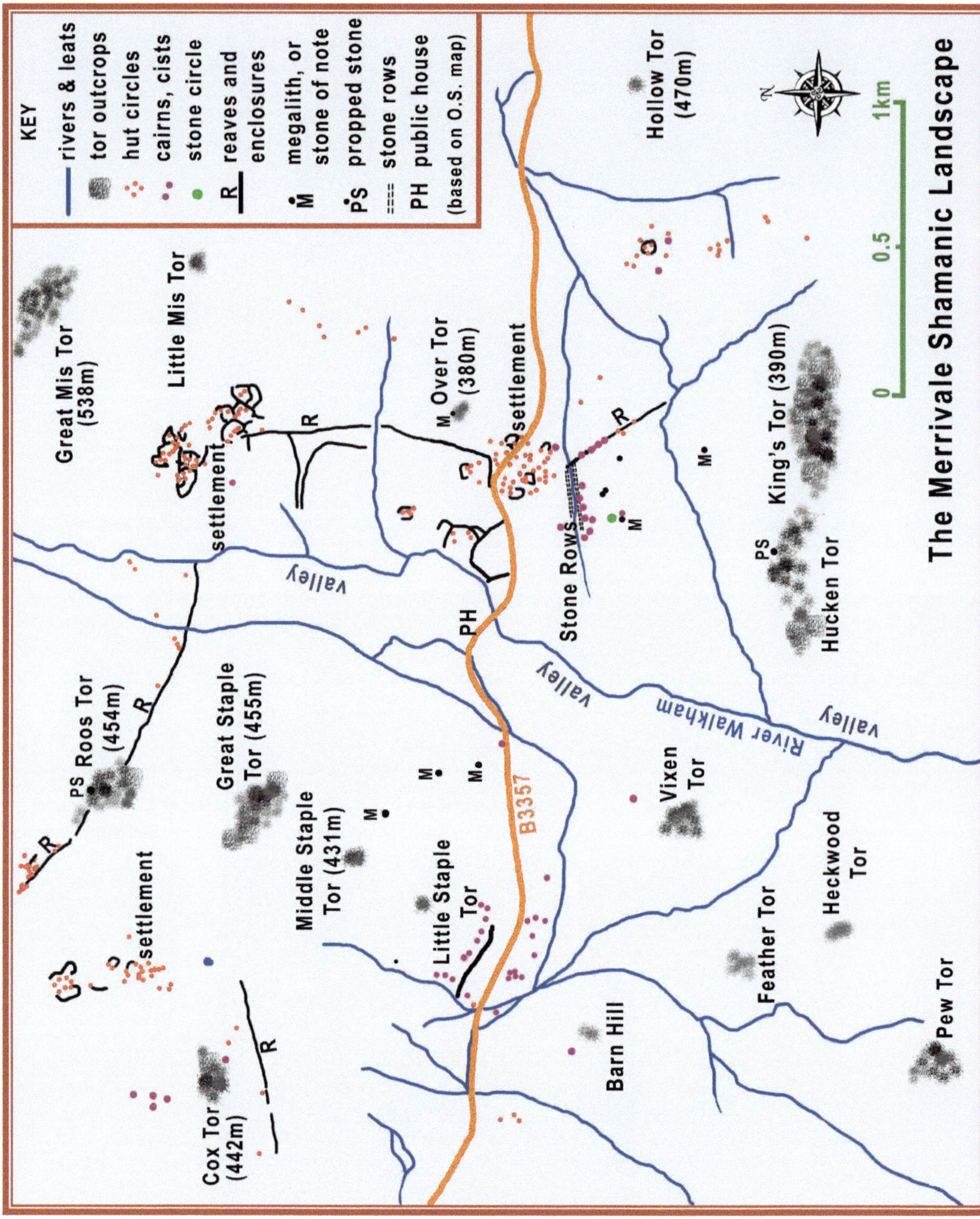

The Merrivale Shamanic Landscape

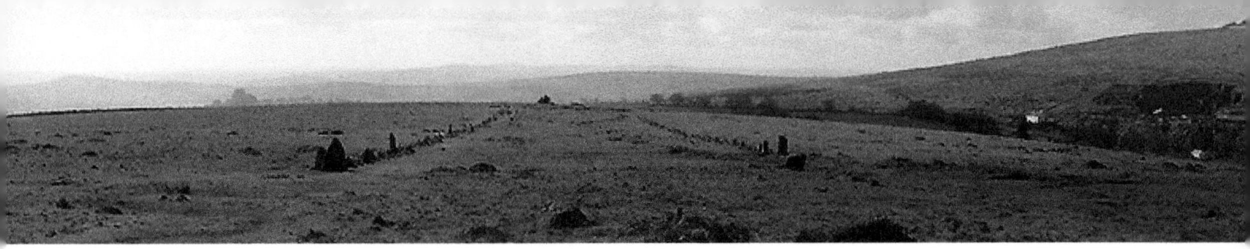

13. The Merrivale Shamanic Landscape

'In the past, people lived within territories that conformed to natural criteria.'
(Bender et al, 1999).

Situated just metres south of the B3357, and served by two car parks and a pub, the Merrivale stone rows are probably the most visited prehistoric monuments on Dartmoor. The setting is stunning, with tors and high hills on all sides, and distant views to the sea and Bodmin Moor. Thousands of people walk the two double rows every year, and many also marvel at the longstone, the stone circle and the cists nearby. Many come to tune in to the energies which move pendulum and dowsing rod alike. Others lean against stones and meditate, whilst many come with camera in hand to witness sunsets. I have been here more times than I can remember, but it is only in recent years that I have come to realise how the Merrivale stone rows and other monuments are located with reverence to the surrounding high places, which hem in the site on most sides. The crucible landscape held within the tors holds settlements, cairns, cists, stone rows, and megaliths. Sitting around the 340m mark, the stone rows are dwarfed by the tors, several of which rise to 400m and 500m above sea level. Like at Drizzlecombe, a natural bowl-like amphitheatre has been utilised; it is a 'ritualised landscape', such as those in other high areas, such as Stanton Moor in the Peak District, Kilmarton, Bodmin Moor, and the Preseli area of Pembrokeshire. Often I have walked through this landscape and been in awe of it, as my spirit soared; walking as a means of revelation.

This prehistoric complex straddles a whale-backed ridge, sitting on a plateau which slopes gently downwards to the River Walkham **(map opposite)**. The ridge also drops away to the north and south – the location of the ancient rows was chosen with great forethought. And watching over Merrivale are towering tors, their rock outcrops appearing in silhouette, like rock giants gazing from on high **(image p. 35)**. It is as if the ancestors or spirits themselves are holding court, overseeing all that transpires below. This has been commented on before: '[Merrivale is] ...encircled by the granite crowned tors that ring the area like abstract gargoyles' (Trwoga 2006). Prof Chris Tilley spoke of the natural bowl in the landscape in which Leskernick's monuments sit as, '... the omphalos of the saucer', with higher tors and hills forming the rim. I believe that Merrivale's monuments are located within such a natural amphitheatre.

Some of the water courses shown on the map are natural, whilst others are 'modern' leats, connected with mining and quarrying. But water is never far away on this landscape, especially in the winter months, when the streams are in full flow, the rock basins full, and the ground often waterlogged. The eternal and ancient dance between water and granite is the ever-recurring theme on Dartmoor.

Don't forget that these high tors may have been taboo to ordinary folk (Tilley 2010). The shamans alone may have had access during most of the year. There was mystique here, and at its centre was the belief that the granite rocks were endowed with spirits. By bringing granite blocks down to the plateau to build their homes and monuments, Bronze Age people were transporting sacred 'pieces of place', blurring the lines between the living and the dead, between the everyday and the profound.
Other researchers have recorded astronomical alignments at Merrivale, and special mention should be made of the work of Jack Walker (Walker 2005) and John Edwin Wood (Wood 1978). I will briefly mention some astronomy in this chapter but, as it is more an exploration of the landscape, and of moving around the various elements therein, I shall leave most of the astronomy of Merrivale, including my own observations, until Chapter 16. In similar vein, most of the earth energies and dowsing experiences will be dealt with in Chapter 17.
I now would like to take the reader on a landscape sojourn, clockwise, around the tors that overlook the stone row complex, gradually coming down into the monuments themselves that nestle on the plateau. This journey will be blessed with stunning scenery, amazing simulacra, propped stones, thirst-quenching rock basins and more. Much has been made in recent years about Orkney, the Boyne Valley, Avebury and Stonehenge in terms of landscape settings; Merrivale rivals the best.

King's Tor

This mighty edifice of granite (557738) rises to about 400m, and is the nearest high tor to the stone rows, rising less than 1km to the south. It is a sad testimony that the hill has been severely decimated by quarrying, and it is often difficult to tell what is natural clitter and what has been extracted and left strewn about the slopes. I always feel sadness here, knowing that my experience is radically different from that of my prehistoric forebears. And yet there are several overhangs and ledges on which to perch, and some steep vertical faces near the summit which also exhibit small simulacra. Several large gullies can be walked through, and there are boulders often precariously balanced and jumbled up. On the highest outcrop I found a 60cm diameter and 3cm deep rock basin, which did not contain water on my visit.
From the upper slopes of the tor the view north over Merrivale is awe-inspiring. Four tors grace the skyline to the NW **(below)**, and one can just make out the stone rows, reaves, the Longstone and the stone circle. Note how the rows appear to mirror the

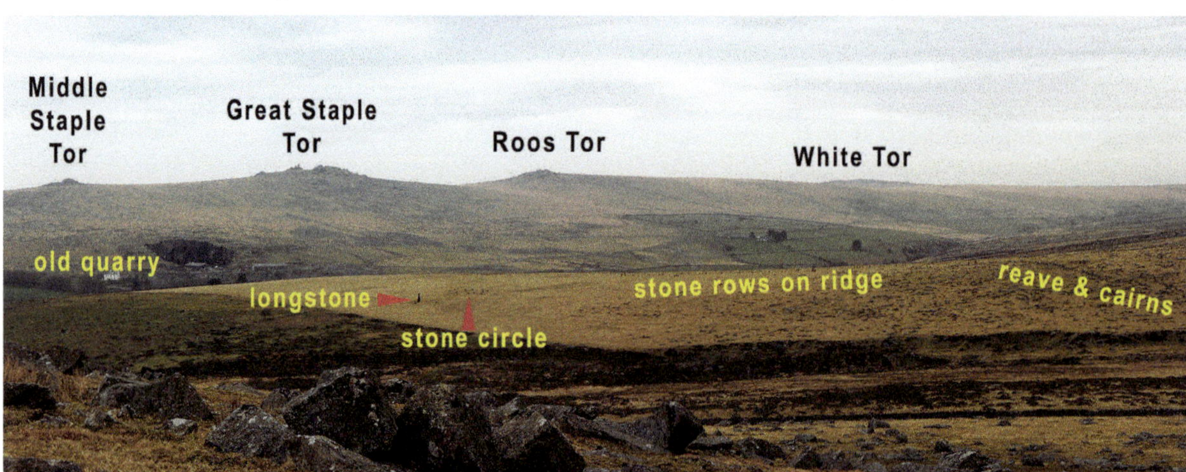

line of the ridge, like the triple row at Cosdon Hill **(images p. 145 & 157)**. From up here the amphitheatre-like bowl of the landscape is appreciated.
At the western end of King's Tor, as the ground begins to slope down to a clitter field, the most amazing simulacrum is passed, in the form of a 2m long dragon's head! I paused for a while, and it seemed to me that the dragon **(right)** was pleased that it had been perceived. No wonder our ancestors, as do indigenous cultures today, believed that the land was inhabited by mythical beings. This earth dragon faces west towards the setting sun; it was also pointing the way to the next place of interest – Hucken Tor.

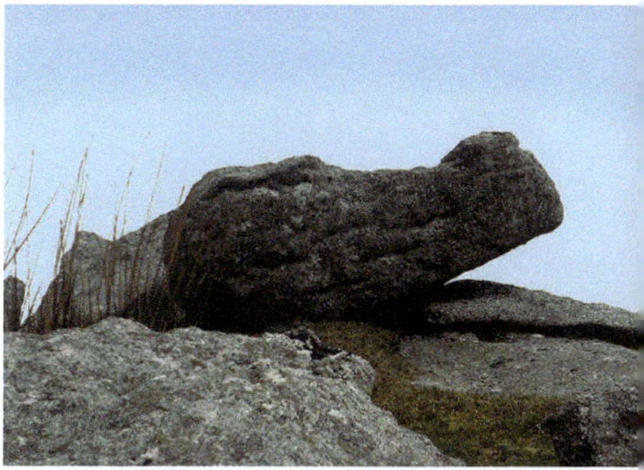

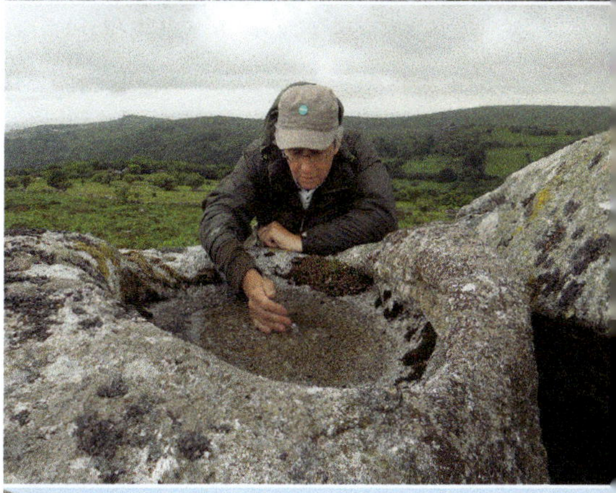

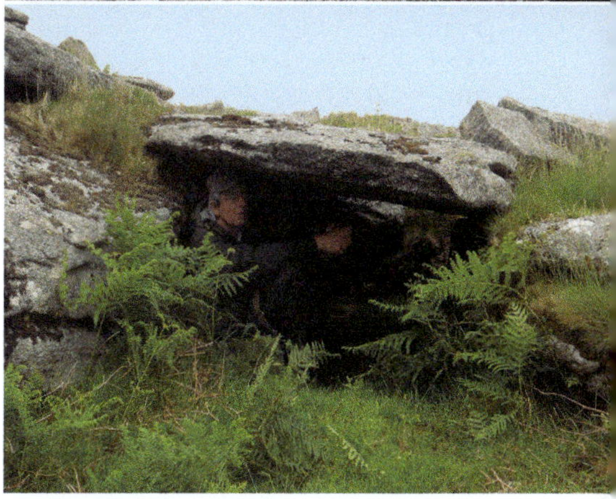

Hucken Tor

This collection of small granite outcrops rises down slope from the western end of King's Tor. The stone circle and longstone appear aligned with the tor's highest outcrop. The stone rows are discernible, and the wonderful simulacrum head of Vixen Tor is now well seen, in profile. Some stacks form the focus of a N-S stone wall which passes up the hill and through them (552740). Climbing to the top of the southern stack I was rewarded with a rock basin, almost 1m in diameter, some 20cm deep, with lots of white quartz lining its base. It was June and yet the basin still contained water. I dipped my hands in the water and drank **(centre)**. I wondered who else had been doing similar here thousands of years ago. This simple act of taking the waters linked me to them. Next to this is a slab of granite which slopes precariously north, as if it could slide off at any moment! This has six smaller, eroded, basins, some of which have spouts, including one that looks rough and manmade. The basins show up as grooves when viewed from below the outcrop. The Merrivale stone circle and Longstone appear aligned with these basin-bearing rocks. People were aligning themselves with natural ancestral places. Just north of this stack is the amazing propped stone described earlier **(images p. 116)**. But there was more to be revealed at this little-visited tor. Just east of the rock basins is a rock shelter, formed by the suspension of a slim block of granite between two outcrops **(bottom image, above)**. This 'capstone' appears to have slid, or been coaxed, from the adjacent outcrop. At over 1m high it resembles a dolmen, although its age cannot be ascertained. If it is ancient, I believe our prehistoric ancestors would have used it. I sat inside, pondering the sacred landscape spread out below me, knowing that it was a mindscape, born of *my* beliefs and experiences.

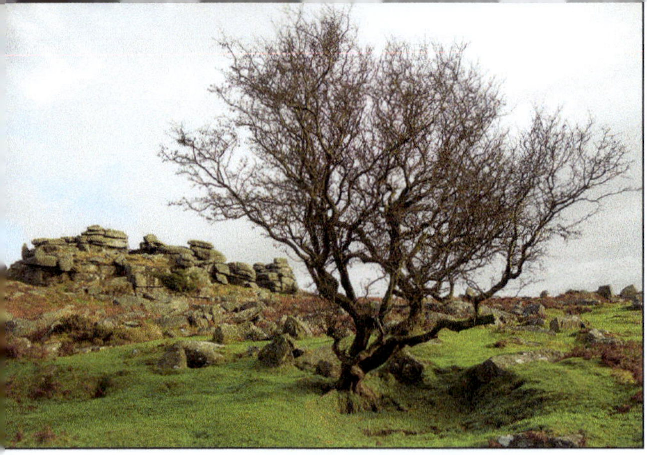

Pew Tor

This modest tor rises at the SW extremity of the Merrivale environs. It climbs to around 320m on the west side of the valley of the River Walkham. From the tor summit, it is difficult to make out the stone row due to the distance, but in the Bronze Age, fires and smoke from the settlement would have been evident. On approaching from the road to the west, a guardian hawthorn **(above)** tenaciously clings to the rock-strewn earth. The tor is known locally as the residence of the Piskie King, and it is said that his palace lies here, deep underground. On some nights the wee folk can be heard, although the entrance to their domain has never been found.

I have visited this tor on sunny days and white outs. On one murky day, the mist had descended, consuming my world. I wrote the following: 'I immerse my body in the breath of the dragon. Held by it. Enveloped by it – willingly. My visual distractions have been taken away from me, all sounds becoming muffled, even my footsteps. No birdsong, or even the whisper of the wind'. Yet for me, the fog was not an environment of fear and trepidation, but that of a liminal space of self-realisation. My senses were heightening and sharpened – I was metaphorically and literally, 'standing on the edge'.

I also wrote this midst the same white-out: 'The top feels alive, the granite lives! Weird shapes and limbs project skywards, some melancholic; the place resembles a graveyard of dragon bones'. Two simulacra appeared as the mist lifted. The first bore an open mouth, poised to speak to me from across the ages **(top image p. 75)** seemingly welcoming me in to this liminal world; it said, 'Well done to have perceived me - your mind is opening'. The other also had a wry smile, with a black eye **(below left)**. A ledge below the head allowed me to sit and shelter.

On the top of the summit stack are eroded and conjoined rock basins **(below right)**, which were recorded back in 1829. The view from these ancient receptacles is uplifting, as on this visit. Early antiquarians thought this to be a place of the Druids, and it was called the 'Seat of Judgement', the 'Druid's Chair', and 'Piskie's Pond'. I have shown how eroded rock basins can be used as seats **(images p. 127 & p. 134)**. When seen from the Merrivale stone row, Pew Tor is aligned with the midwinter solstice sunset, and my observations of this event will be discussed later.

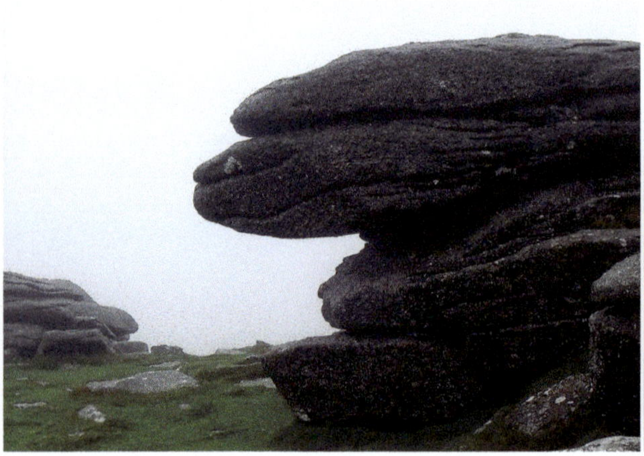

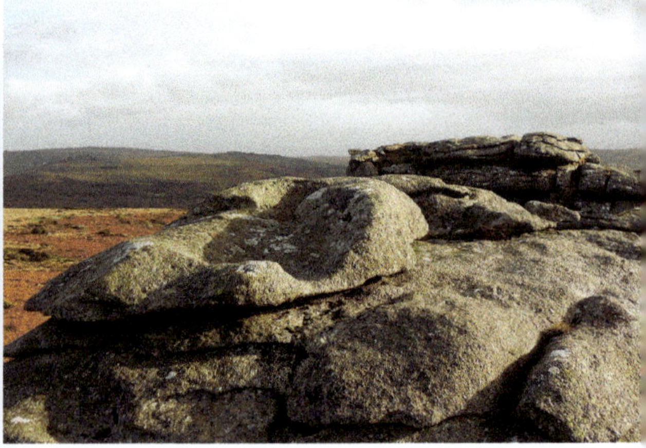

Vixen Tor

Vixen Tor is somewhat unusual in that is it is a dip, not far above the River Walkham. This relative lack of prominence is more than made up for by the presence of one of the most impressive and largest of Dartmoor's simulacra **(top)**. Some early guide books do describe the tor as looking like a sphinx! A jumble of rock surrounds vertical granite walls, and nearby is a standing stone **(image p. 63)** and a burial cist. The huge rock giant surveys the plateau with a knowing, sideways glare, and faces directly towards where the standing stone and cist are located, suggesting that this feature was a factor in place selection. Just north of the tor, a small stack of granite (incorporated into fencing) is capped by a rock basin. The basin contained water during my winter visit, and a groove serves as an outlet or collection point from which to receive water **(lower image)**. From the basin, the simulacrum is seen in profile, looking left, at the top of the image.

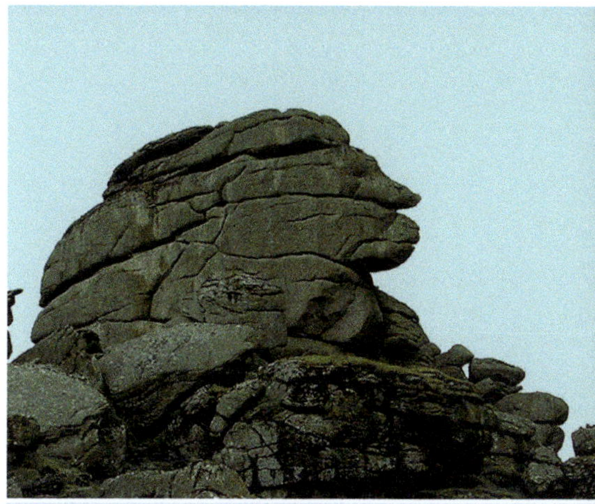

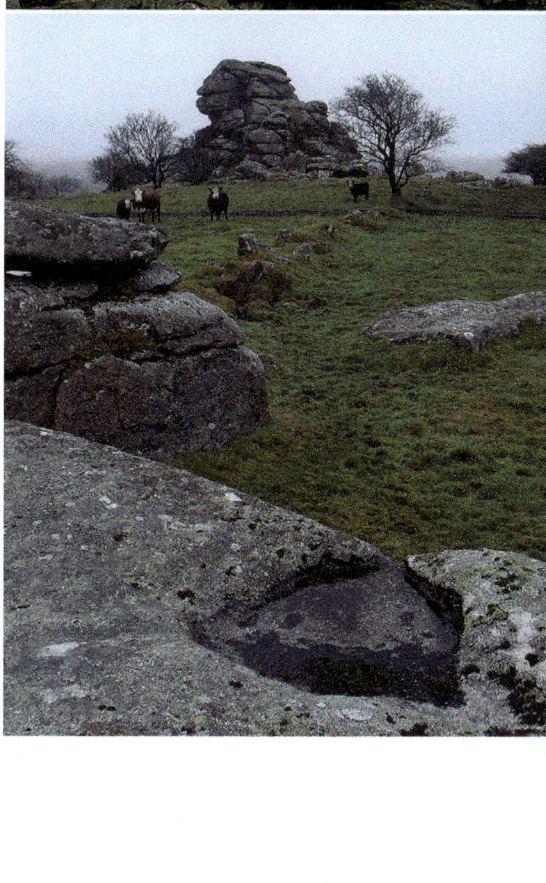

The name of the tor may have derived from its association with the fox, but local folklore tells the tale of *Vixiana the Witch*. She was supposed to dwell in a cave located deep in the granite bowels of the tor. She stood six feet tall, with a hooked nose and deep sunken eyes - a 'truly frightening sight'. At sunrise and sunset she would stand on the rocks, watching and waiting for lone travellers. She would then summon up a thick mist, engulfing the traveller, at which point she would call out, falsely directing them to safety. They became trapped in a bog, and on hearing their screams, Vixiana would summon the mist to clear so as to watch their final struggles. This gruesome tale is actually typical of many around Britain, thought to mark a former sacred site, often associated with a Pagan wise woman, to be later subjected to negative propaganda.

I have been to Vixen Tor in sunshine and fog, and my most memorable visits have been under the latter conditions. On one occasion I was walking above the level the cloud base. As I left the car I called out, 'I am here. I am here!', announcing my arrival to the land, and offering my blessings and intent. A crow/raven answered my invocation from a nearby tree. I walked across a squelchy land, a lunar landscape of granite boulders: '... the clitter is like the litter of my head'. Passing sodden ponies, I crossed into the tor field via the granite outcrop with the rock basin hewn on top **(right)**. I approached the huge simulacra and looked up at the massive gnarled head that towered over me: 'Hello old friend'. I sat beneath the overhanging chin of the rock giant,

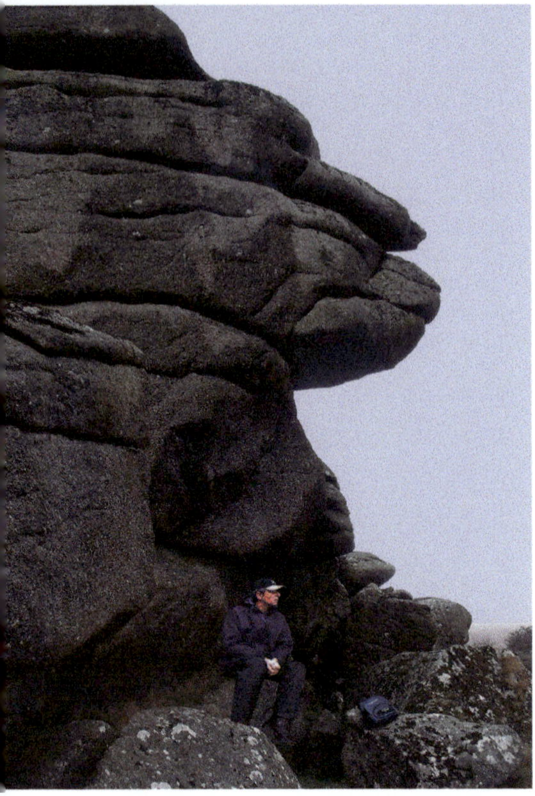

sheltered on the leeside from the rain and wind **(left)**. My gaze mirrored that of my granite brother. A sense of great peace descended. I asked, 'What is it I need to know? The answer came almost instantly: 'The wisdom you seek is within you. You have done all this before'. Then a crow/raven croaked from somewhere close by. I was left almost breathless: 'An open heart is the key!' More crows/ravens squawked in the distance, as if to say, 'You got it brother'. Feral urges rose within as I stood on naked granite, like a wolf surveying his territory, my back arching as I sent my wolf 'howl!' out across the shrouded landscape. When it was time to leave, I turned to thank the spirit of place and said my farewells. Some part of me remains there.

The sun sets over Vixen Tor around Imbolc when viewed from the east end of the north stone row at Merrivale. From the blocking stones at the west end of the south row it is 243° azimuth to Vixen Tor. I believe that in the Bronze Age, people watched the sun gradually move from setting over Pew Tor to its setting over Vixen Tor (around mid February), signifying that spring had arrived. I shall return to the astronomy in more detail later.

Continuing around the landscape in a clockwise direction, Heckwood Tor, Feather Tor and Barn Hill are three fairly inconspicuous hills, with some small outcrops. Barn Hill marks equinox sunsets from the stone rows. Beyond it, the land begins to rise and finds Little Staple Tor at around the 380m contour. This outcrop is slightly elevated above the stone row, which can be seen on the ridge below. This small tor gives us a sampler of the mighty granite tors to the north - a stunning backdrop to the Merrivale complex.

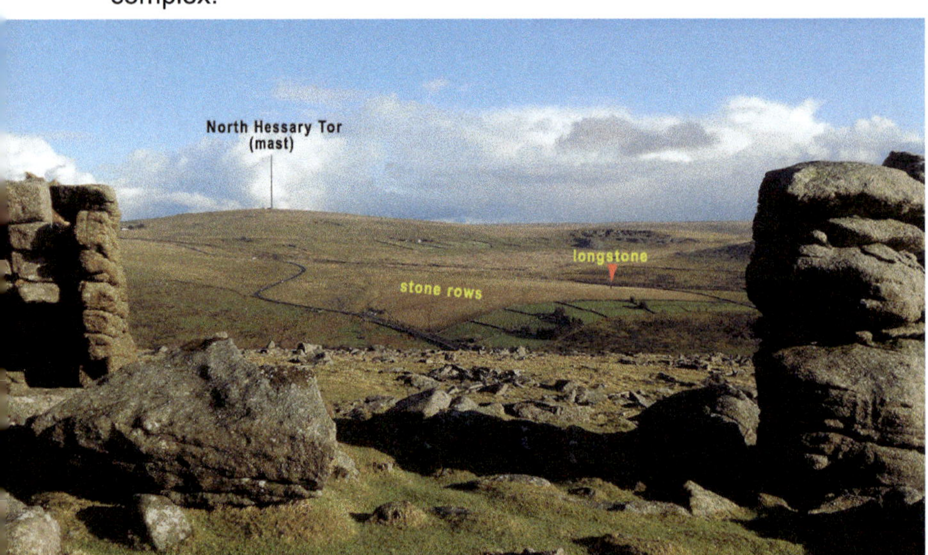

View across Merrivale from Middle Staple Tor.

'The human mind is geared to try to see patterns in apparent randomness' (Paul Devereux 2010).

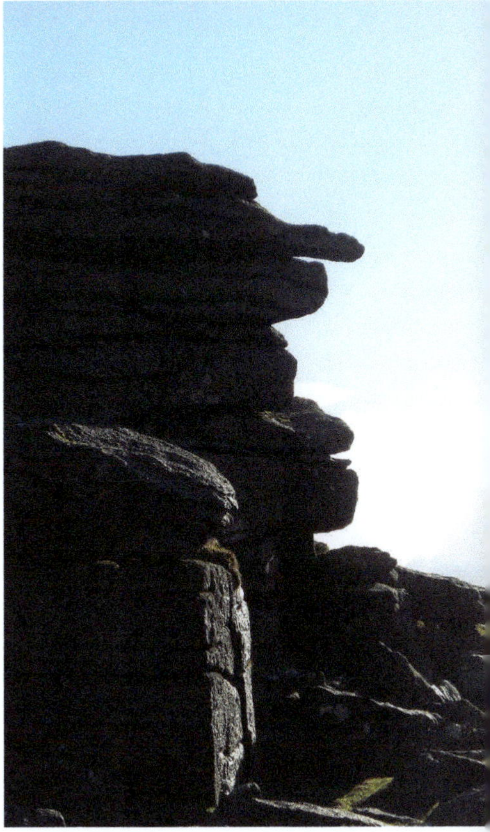

Middle Staple Tor

This fine granite outcrop rises to 431m above sea level. At only 1.5km from the stone rows, it affords fine views of the plateau; the larger stones of the row and the longstone can be made out under good conditions. A gap between two outcrops allows a 'window' view down to Merrivale **(bottom image, opposite)**. There are also fine views of Vixen Tor below to the south, and Great Staple Tor to the north. The glistening shimmer of the sea and the estuary at the Tamar Bridge are also well seen. To the west rises Cox Tor, and some of its cairns grace the skyline. On the northwest side of the main outcrop of Middle Staple Tor are two fine profiled simulacra; the top one sports an extremely long, thin nose **(right)**, whilst the face below seems to be sticking out its tongue! Other faces are in evidence, and these 'spirits of the granite' would not have gone unnoticed by our distant ancestors; the rock giants gazed eternally across a mythologised landscape.
Middle Staple Tor is also intricately involved in an alignment with three megaliths and a cairn down at the Merrivale complex (Wood 1978). I shall return to this and other alignments later **(images p. 201 & 202)**.

Great Staple Tor

This tor is one of the most magnificent of Dartmoor's outcrops. Rising to a height of 455m, its huge granite pinnacles seem to defy gravity, as if the giants of old have stacked them up. Logan stones perform balancing feats, and simulacra seem to be around every corner. The rocks play tricks with your mind – as eyes and minds long closed are opened. I have already shown some of these colossal edifices **(images p. 3, 35, 47 & 69)**. The landscape is lunar-like, with huge boulders, gullies and angled slabs everywhere. I am often reduced to standing still to take it all in, or rotating my body so as to let the rocks dance around me. Rock basins can also be found on some of the stacks, although many of these are too steep for me to scale.
The tor offers superb views across the Merrivale landscape, as well as south to the sea. Bodmin can be perceived on distant west skylines, whilst Brent Tor rises like a volcano to the NW. There is a fine view of Merrivale, which nestles in the landscape over 100m below; individual stones cannot be made out, but they are there none the less. Smoke from fires during the day, and flames during night time rituals, would have been readily observed from up here. Perhaps even the sound of distant drums and bull roarers would have reached up here, breaking the silence of the tor.
My visits to Great Staple Tor have produced radically different experiences – one landscape, but rather many. From bright sunshine to fog and rain, they all offered magic and wonder, which was gratefully received and acknowledged. Whether I am solitary or leading group tours, this tor always delivers.

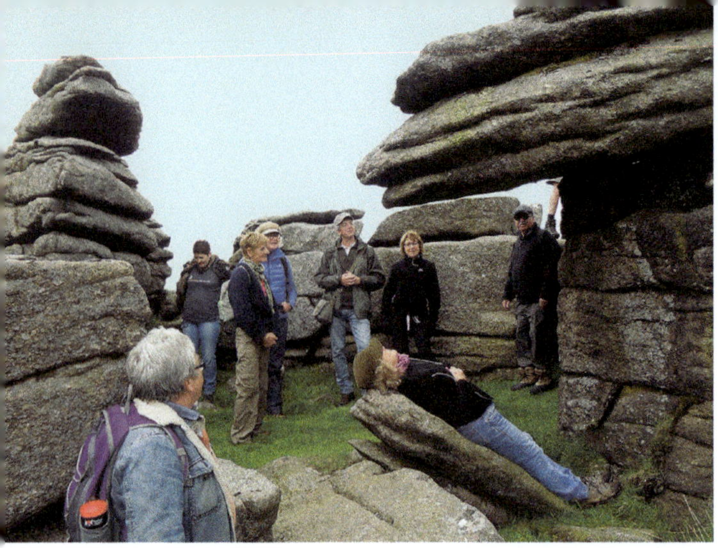

On the eastern side of Great Staple Tor, there is a 4m long 'tunnel' in the granite, which can be entered and experienced. It also offers shelter from the rain. I could not help thinking that this would have been sought by those doing lengthy vision quests here thousands of years ago.
Also on the east side, just below the summit, is a precariously balanced rock with a simulacrum at one end, with dark eyebrows and mouth **(left).** Directly below is an angled stone which can be leant against. On a recent tour I led, many of the dozen attendees felt the urge to recline beneath the huge overhang. During wet weather, water drips from the tip of the simulacrum onto the face of anyone lying on the inclined stone. These waters, straight out of the 'mouth' of the rock giant, may have been regarded as sacred. Close by are the two guardian simulacra, which I have already shown **(top of front cover, & banner top of p. 50)**. The three simulacra and the inclined stone make this a sanctuary, and those present on my tour felt the 'power of place'. We were in a holy place, and one that owed nothing to any modification of the natural features.
On the north face of the NW outcrop of the tor is a wonderful simulacrum which I have named 'Toothless Crone' **(below left)**. She is open-mouthed, as if to call out a 'hackle cackle!' across the moor! I could see why our ancestors believed the Goddess is in the land. The rays of the sun illuminated her in a cascade of rainbows. Just beyond this there is another rock basin on the summit of a stack at the very NW tip of the tor; beyond it is a balanced stone. The view from here is extensive, to the cairns on Cox Tor and over to Brent Tor and beyond **(below right)**.

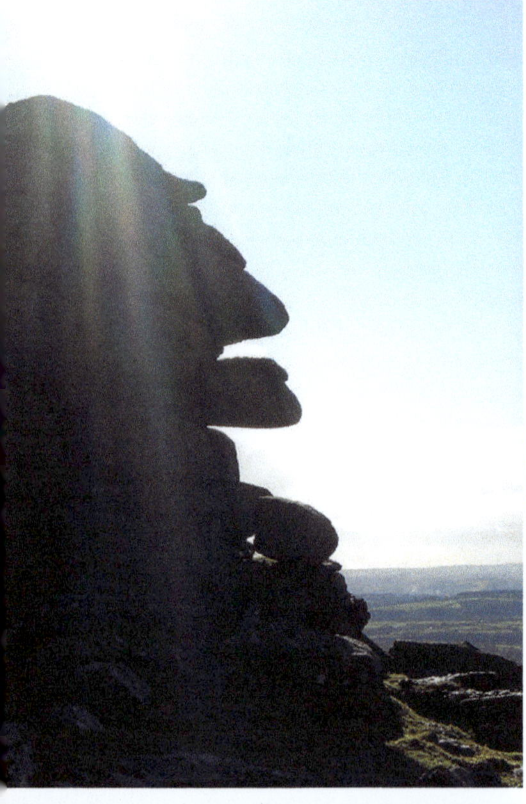

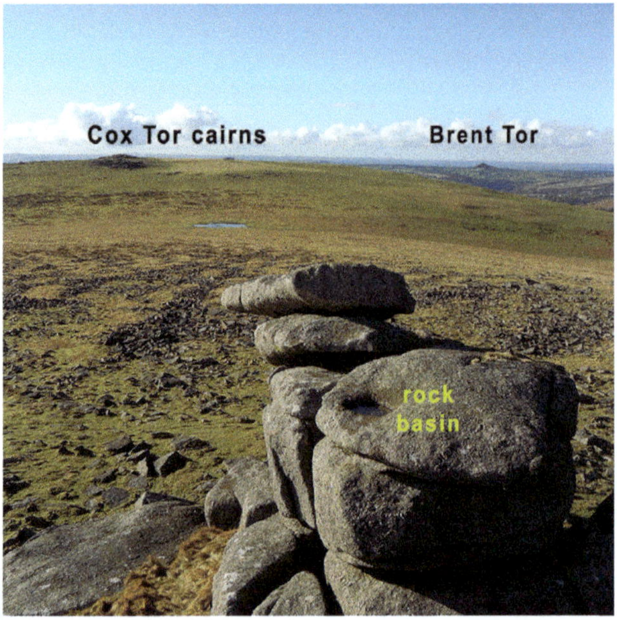

Roos Tor

This granite tor rises to 454m just north of Great Staple Tor, and 2km north of the Merrivale stone rows. It can be identified by the flagstaff on its summit, from which a red flag is frequently unfurled, warning when the army land to the north is out-of-bounds. Each tor on the moor is unique, and the difference between these two is marked. Roos Tor lacks the vertical piles that characterize Great Staple Tor, but its spread of granite clitter and lower outcrops is almost as extensive. From the first time I visited Roos Tor I knew it was a special place, and had been so in prehistory. Here, on this one tor, all the elements that I had seen across Dartmoor seemed to come together in one place; rock basins, rock shelters, a propped stone, simulacra, overhangs, caverns and ledges, have all made this a place I never tire of experiencing. And with each visit, more is revealed to me. The distant 360° vistas are uplifting, and the moor to the north opens up for the first time on our journey here.

The name may derive from the Anglo-Saxon word *Hruse,* which simply, and appropriately, means *'rock or hill'*. In 1826, Eliza Bray wrote of her visit to Roos Tor and here is a brief synopsis of her record:

"*We met an aged shepherd, who was collecting his flock, and informed us the hill we were ascending was Roosetor. This name may possibly be derived from Rhôs or Rôo, signifying, in Welsh or Cornish, a healthy mountain... The south side of the tor has a grand and picturesque appearance. Two immense piles of rocks are of so pendent a form as to threaten every instant to fall upon the beholder... On another pile, which was fifteen high, we found two basins - one two feet by one and a half; the other one foot in diameter... Another pile, though much lower, we ascended with the greatest difficulty. On the top of it were a few imperfect basins. But a mass of rocks, near the latter, afforded us a very curious specimen of the works of the Druids. On the uppermost stone of the mass we discovered a basin, in depth a foot and a quarter, with smaller ones surrounding it, and little channels communicating with others in a serpentine direction'.*

She records rock basins and balanced logan stones, features shown on this early OS map **(below)**. She associates features with the Druids, but I believe that this tor was once a sacred place for local people centuries before the Druids; it has all the elements needed for shamanic ceremonies and vision quests; it is a stone's throw from several settlements, whose occupants may have climbed these hallowed outcrops. The Great Western Reave, the Bronze Age boundary work that marches across the moor for over 10km (Gerrard 1997), runs up the slopes of the tor, clearly using it as a focus, as at White Tor, Sharpitor and elsewhere. From here the reave runs down to the Merrivale complex, passing by the eastern end of the stone rows. The early map considered the reave to be an 'Ancient Trackway'.

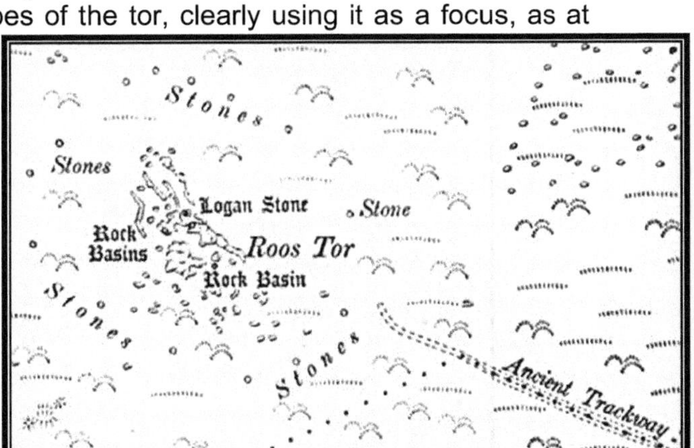

As with other places, I have visited Roos Tor in hail, sunshine and rain. Each a different and unique experience. Whether with friends, groups, or by myself, I always find it to be a place where I can explore my outer and inner landscapes. I will now share some of my findings, with

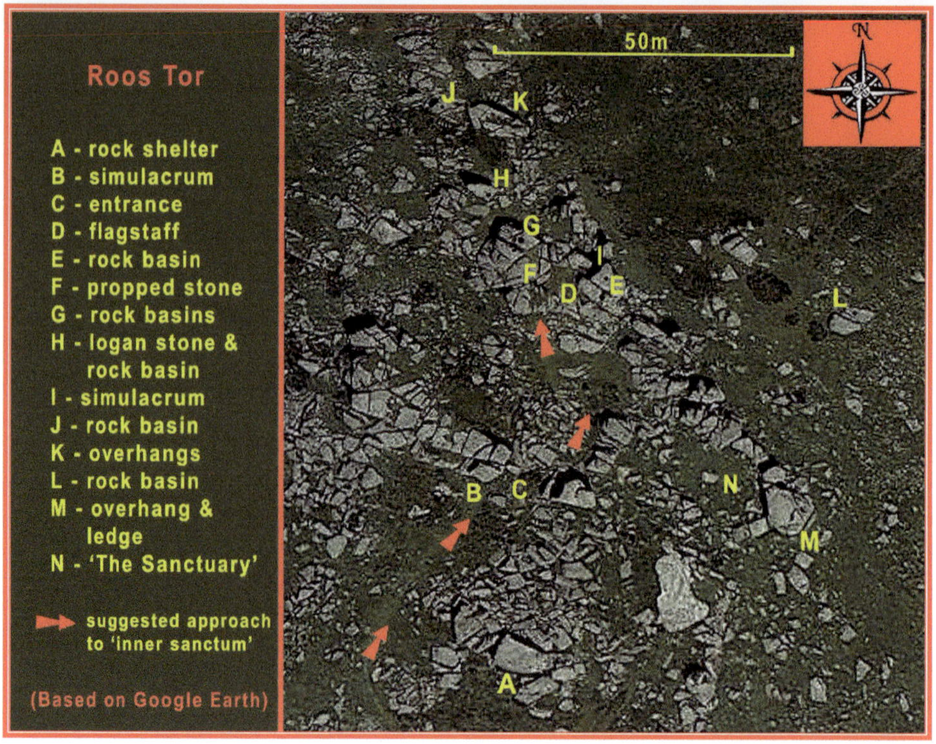

the aid of a fine Google Earth photo **(above)**, onto which I have added letters so I can guide the reader around the tor. The red arrows mark what I feel is a ceremonial route that may have been used in ancient times; I have often felt as if I was being manoeuvred to follow this particular way up to the inner sanctum. This concept of 'funnelling' was observed by archaeologists on Brown Willy, Bodmin Moor, where it was felt they were, 'moving in procession' and that there was a, 'correct path of movement' along the ridge, passing cairns, propped stones and rock basins (Bender et al 2007). Today there is a well-trodden path that brings many up to the tor summit (from the south side), and my arrows (see map) mirror this. As I have followed this yellow brick road, I have stepped into a place that seems like a time capsule, frozen in granite. It is a place to unleash the spirit.

First stop **(A)** is a south-facing rock shelter, a 2m void beneath a massive granite boulder some 5m across and 3m high, full of large crystals, and which overhangs at

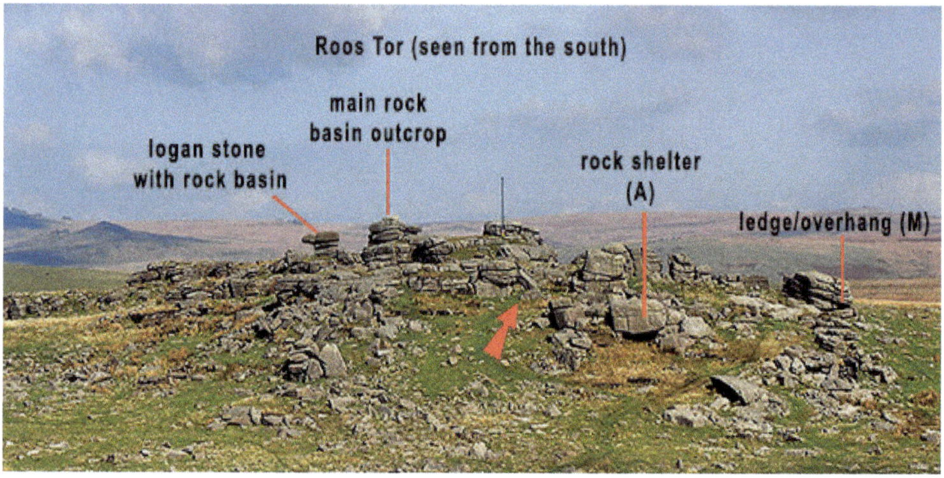

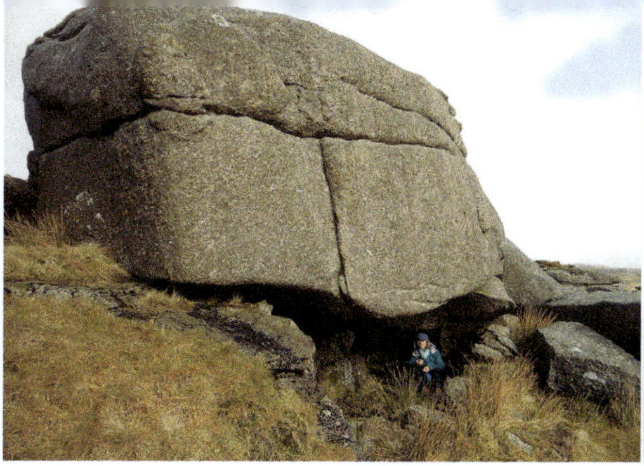
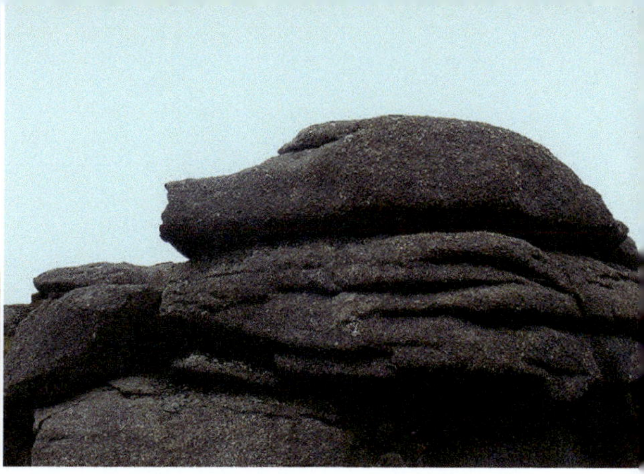

quite an angle **(top left)**. Although this is a natural sanctuary, a dry stone wall, now mainly collapsed, used to shield those within. Reeds and puddles occupy some of the floor space, whilst there are also stones large enough to perch on. On one occasion I sheltered here with Sue Wallace during a sudden hail storm; inside was still and calm - a sanctuary. The view from within is to Great Staple Tor, the stones and stacks of which rise out of the skyline to the south. From in front of the shelter I could see Merrivale, and just make out a couple of the larger megaliths. Although I generally felt nurtured, at times I have felt moments of uncertainty as I see that the huge boulder rests at an acute angle on the bedrock below. Will today be the day it slides off?

The footpath that has been forged to the summit follows the red arrows of my images. Standing guard, high on a granite outcrop, is a beautiful simulacrum (B), in the form of an elongated head with slanted eye and pursed lips, facing westwards **(top right)**. Is this guardian rock giant asleep? The simulacrum and the rocky outcrop opposite frame the entrance (C), as we are gently guided upwards into the inner sanctum of Roos Tor; it has the feel of entering a temple.

Through the gap we are led to the left to the summit, where the flagstaff (D) is planted. From here there is a large expanse of sea visible to the S and SE, which glistens when the sun is in the south. The enclosure of settlements can be seen in the valley this side of Cox Tor, and Brent Tor rises to the NW **(below)**. Behind the flag pole is a flat surface of rock on which two rock basins can be found (E), and from where this image was taken **(below)**. The propped stone (F) has been shown before **(image p. 116)**,

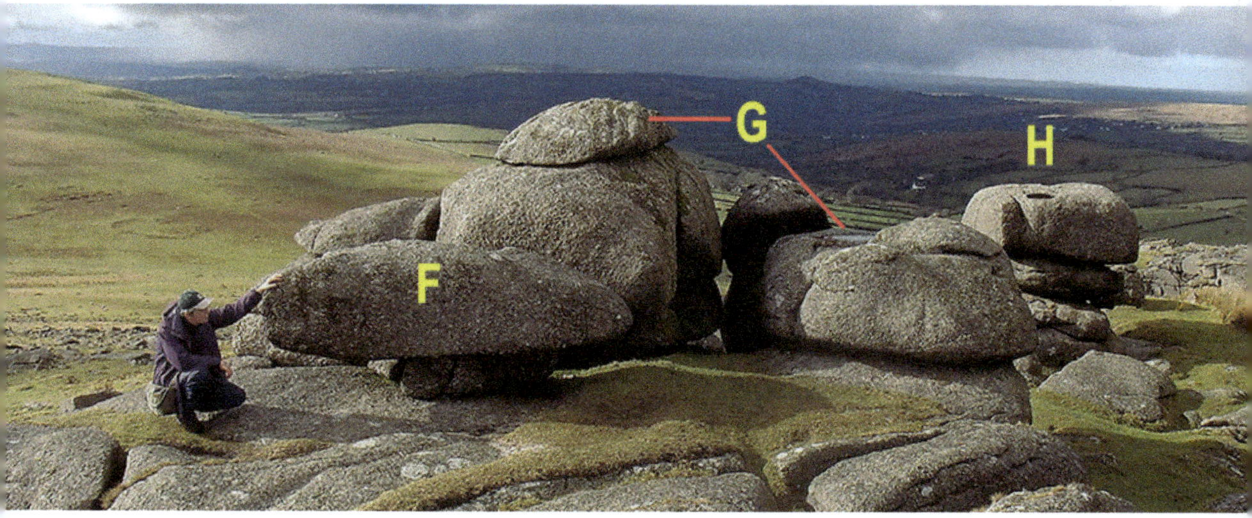

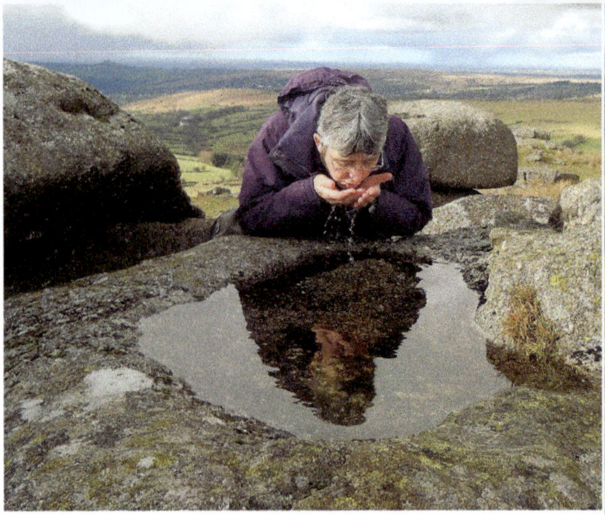

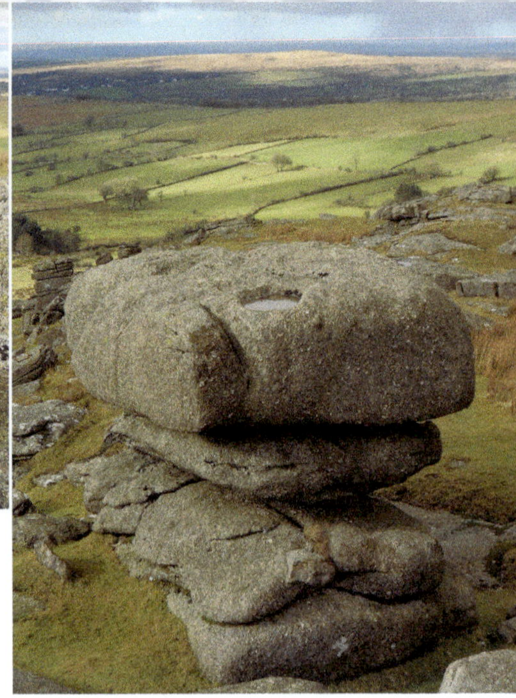

and I have found that to lie beneath this boulder, which pivots on a cracked stone, is a surreal experience **(image p. 73)**. The jagged edges of quartz crystals hang just inches above one's face and can sometimes induce a feeling of claustrophobia. Just 2m to the south of the propped stone is a small boulder sitting in a gully. It is not earth-fast and can be rocked. I wonder if this once supported the overhanging end of the 'capstone'.

Just around the corner is the fine, 1m diameter rock basin (G) that is the jewel in the crown of Roos Tor. Channels are cut into the granite to drain the waters away. It has contained water on all my visits, and I have drunk from these sacred waters with gratitude in my heart **(above left)**. A small gully enables access to the waters. Overlooking this basin, on the adjacent stack, are two more, deeply eroded basins, resembling seats. These holy waters, gifted from the sky and the granite, were probably regarded as magically potent thousands of years ago, as shamans collected the life-giving elixir for spiritual purposes.

From here there is a fine view of the rock basin on the top surface of the balancing logan stone stack beyond (H).This top-heavy stack **(above right)** is 4m high and the top half is considerably wider than the lower **(bottom image p. 106)**. Reaching the waters of this basin is via a more precarious ascent. The landscape setting of this place is breathtaking, as a 'big sky' meets distant skylines. From the main rock basin (G) to this Logan stone is an azimuth 310° - midsummer sunset!

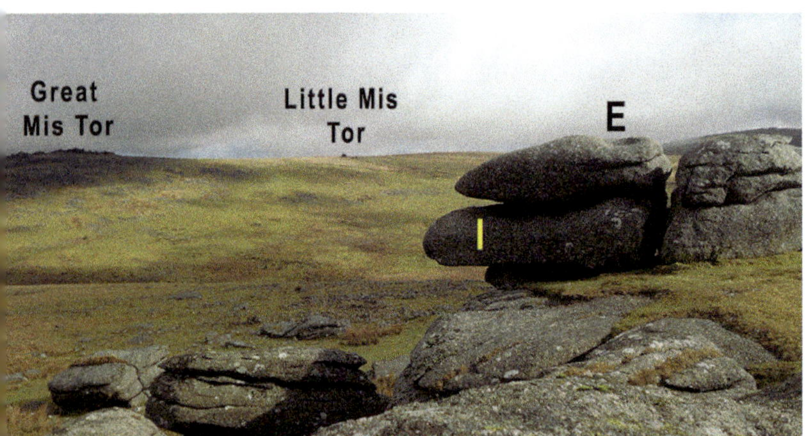

Looking back towards the flagstaff there a fabulous simulacra (I on Google Earth image), which I have coined *Big Nose!* **(left)**. This giant gazes north, towards the Neolithic enclosures on White Tor. It is worth considering that this simulacrum was here when Neolithic people visited; if anything, any weathering has 'softened' its features since those times. Note that the rock basin which we visited earlier (E) is on top of the head. This mirrors simulacra/rock basin/propped stone links elsewhere, such as at Lower Hartor Tor and Hucken Tor. In this image, Great Mis Tor and Little Mis Tor adorn the skyline.

Walking past the simulacrum, down to lower ground, bearing left one can skirt along the foot of the outcrop of the main basin stone. Note how small boulders are trapped beneath the main slab of granite. Have these been pushed into this void to stop the rock above collapsing further? Standing at the foot of the logan stone stack (H) one can appreciate its balancing act **(image p. 106)**. Beyond this, to the NW, there is another rock basin on a low outcrop (J). From here follow the steep rock faces around the north side of the tor, which offer some overhangs and crevices (K). About 25m east of the flagstaff is a low granite outcrop, on top of which is another rock basin (L).

Follow the granite rock face as it turns south and, where it peters out there is the next site of interest (M). Here a fine projecting overhang is accompanied by an elevated ledge, and one can get into the 60cm gap beneath **(right)**. I feel that thousands of years ago this had been a place of initiation; to lie supine with the granite just inches from one's face is a bizarre experience. This is a place to spend some time, held and nurtured by the strength of granite. From here Great Staple Tor and the Merrivale plateau comes back into view. Beneath and low down to the right of the ledge, a narrow void can be carefully entered, which comes out on the other side of the outcrop. This low 4m long cavern is not for the faint-hearted; one is completely held within the womb of the Earth Mother. One a recent tour, one of the attendees, Jim, crawled through, remarking how it was both a claustrophobic and re-birthing experience.

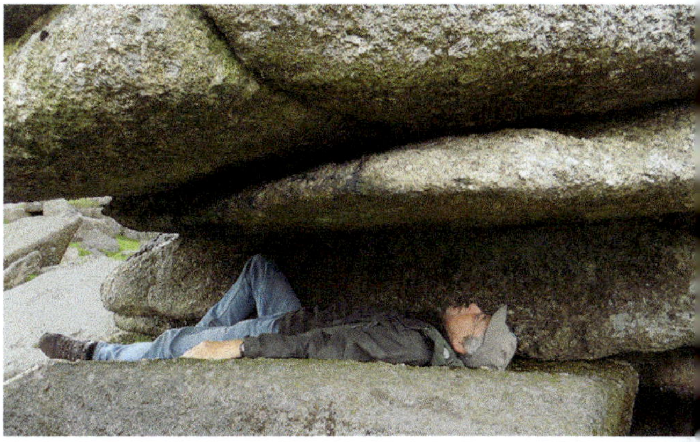

From here, walk upwards and north briefly, where a clear, grassy arena will be found, (SE of the flagstaff). This sanctuary (N) hosts a low altar-like slab of granite at its centre. Several seams and lenses of red granite are seen around the tor outcrops, and lots of red granite rocks litter the ground. Here, there is a large lens in situ at the east end of the sanctuary, the redness of which shows up well when wet, or wetted. This area may have been a focus for ceremonies in ancient times. During one of my weekend tours, we sat here to share our experiences after a quiet meditative time, where attendees had spent time on their own. Two women present felt they had to sit astride rocks to 'tune in'; one felt like the wind was music. Another lady, 'felt my goddess dancing happily around the tor', whilst another was drawn to kiss, 'to snog' a rock surface: 'It felt sensuous and sexual' she commented. Someone else sheltered beneath a low overhang, which 'felt like a womb'. A male attendee witnessed three guardians standing next to him, an experience so lucid that it reduced him to tears. He was told to focus on, and visit, Brent Tor, which was visible in the distance. All those present agreed that Roos Tor was a sacred sanctuary, a temple no less.

Moving on around the landscape in a clockwise direction, one can follow the Great Western Reave down into the valley **(top image p. 17)**, where the low stone walls of hut circles survive. After crossing the River Walkham, a Bronze Age settlement is passed. Looming on the skyline is Great Mis Tor, which pulls one ever upward and onward, through increasingly challenging clitter fields; on my visits, the tor seemed to know I was approaching.

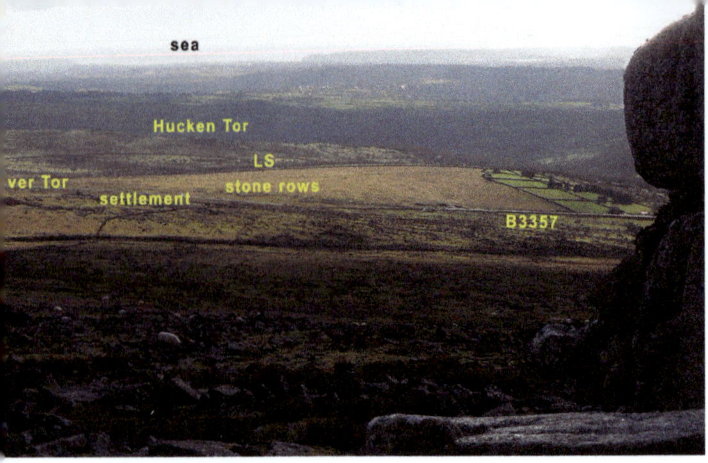

"Great Mistor near the centre stands,
Looming above the dreary lands;
Here heathery wastes, and there the mires,
Surround for miles the rocky spires;
O'er hill and dale and wavy plain
The eye will seek for bounds in vain."
(Rev. E. W. L. Davies – 1863)

Great Mis Tor.

Several large granite outcrops with high rock walls, simulacra and sheltering overhangs, conspire to make Great Mis Tor an impressive place to visit. This tor is big time, no shrinking violet. From the northernmost outcrops the land drops away, and there is a good view of White Tor, and the stone circle and hut circles on the other side of the Walkham. Down in the valley, to the north of the tor, a stream called Dead Lake Well feeds the River Walkham, and is said to be the haunt of piskies. These wee folk imbued the waters with positive attributes; should a group of people come to drink, the first person to partake of the waters would marry by the end of that year (Crossing 1997). From Great Mis Tor, on clear days, I can make out the logan stone stack on Roos Tor and, surprisingly, the large pond between Roos and Cox Tor, due to a dip in the ridge. To the south **(above)**, the Merrivale stone row and the Longstone (LS above) can be perceived – just – and there is also a thin sliver of glistening sea beyond. The sense of elevation is exhilarating; I feel my inner hawk come on, and want to ride the thermals over the land. At almost 540m above sea level, I believe it to be the highest point from which the Merrivale stone row complex can be seen.

The Mis Tor Pan, or Devil's Frying Pan, is a large rock basin **(images p. 130)** on the highest outcrop of the tor **(below).** The name of the tor may have derived from Misor, a Roman and Phoenician sun god. Was the sun's dazzling reflection in the waters of the rock basin connected with sun worship? (Others think the name may have come from 'mist', in which its peaks are often obscured). The rock basin was first recorded in 1608 and has, inevitably, been connected with the Druids; the depression has a spout/outflow, which has been regarded as manmade. In 1867, a parish boundary was established through the centre of the tor, using the rock basin as a mark.

Near the north end I found a small stack with a rock pool below, level with the ground, set upon granite platform **(right image, p 49)**. I have drunk of its crystal clear waters and given thanks and blessings. One is compelled, drawn even, to the highest rock outcrop, where the flagstaff stands. Near to it is the gravity-defying balanced stone that looks as if it will topple at any moment **(centre image, p. 106)**. Our ancestors must have thought that only the gods could perform such feats. This boulder is perched just metres from the rock basin, just north of the flagstaff. On the south side of the main outcrop, at the base of the steep rock face below the flagstaff, is a cavern. This is very enclosed, inviting the pilgrim to sit inside, enjoying the view south to Merrivale.

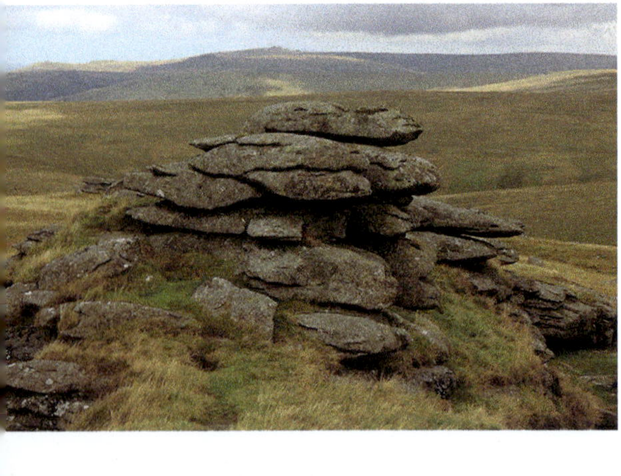

During winter months, the ground on Great Mis Tor is surprisingly boggy, with reeds and ponds aplenty. On one visit I tuned in and asked, 'What is the story with this tor?' It came back to me that it is all about water: the rock basin, the boggy ground and pools, the valleys/river below, views of sea in two directions, as well as the estuary. Many of these granite outcrops are dripping water after wet weather. And below, the River Walkham is birthing, growing as it snakes away to the sea. This is a metaphor for our lives, from birth to maturity. This was a surprising revelation considering the height of the tor. But, as I have said previously, Dartmoor is all about granite and water.

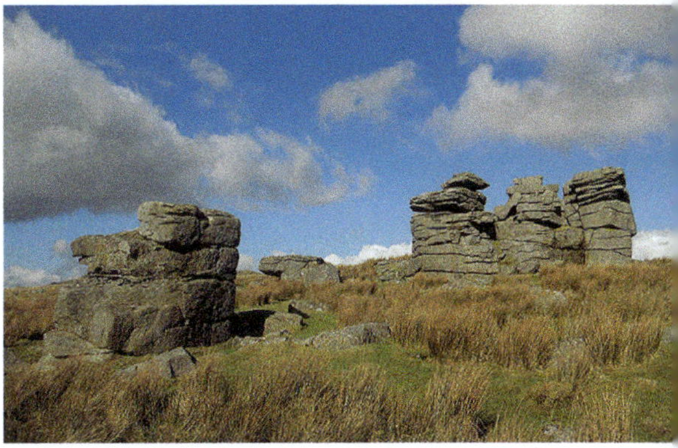

Little Mis Tor

This small tor **(right)** is the smaller cousin of Great Mis Tor, its mighty neighbour. It stands about 500m to the south as a cluster of relatively small outcrops, on the 480m contour line. It is only 1.5km from the stone rows, which are visible. Despite its small size, its position on a ridge ensures it is visible from quite some distance away, such as from Cox Tor, Pew Tor and beyond. I had found previously that visiting tors of smaller stature can still nevertheless be rewarding. Little Mis Tor did not disappoint. Views to the west and south are stunning, as one looks across the Merrivale landscape to the sea and the Tamar Bridge. Brent Tor has appeared to the NW due to a dip in the skyline to the north of Roos Tor. Cox Tor is visible on the other side of a saddle between Great Staple Tor and Roos Tor, with Bodmin Moor beyond **(below right)**. White Tor also shows itself to the north.

The main outcrop has a 2m overhang on the east side, with an amazing crone-like anthropomorphic face **(below left)**, with eye and protruding tongue! I knew she was pleased with my acknowledgment of her. A ledge beneath her chin provides shelter and a place to ponder life. Access to the top of the outcrop is best achieved from the east side, and I was delighted to find two rock basins, both holding water, at the NW end of the stacks. I drank from one, offering grateful thanks. Ripples on the water did a dance before my eyes **(below right)**.

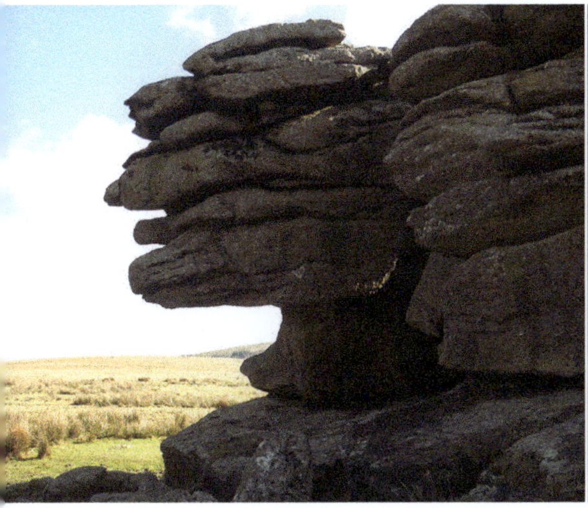

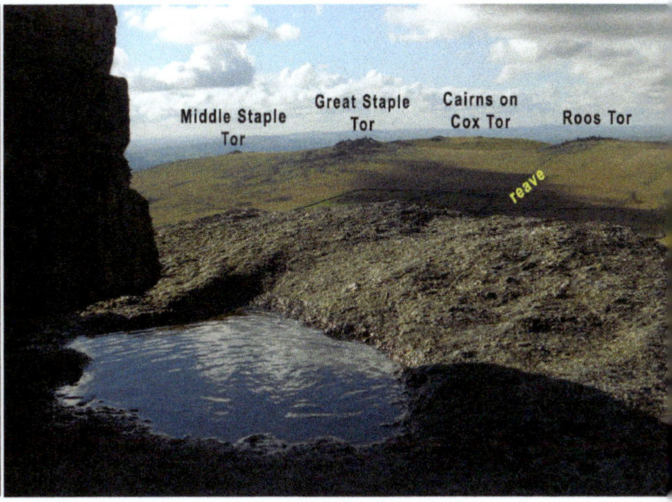

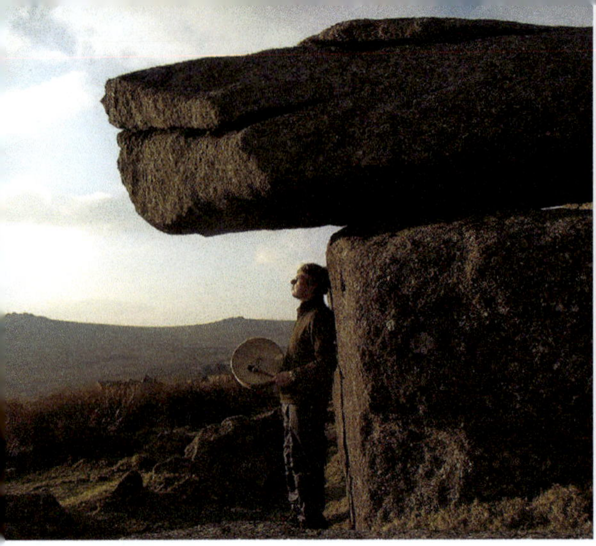

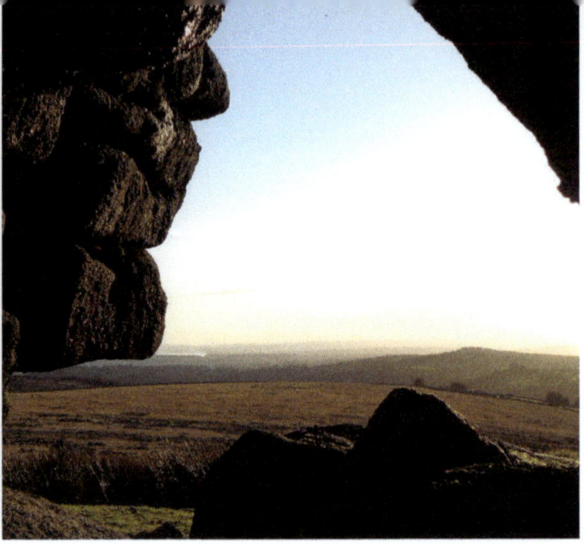

Over Tor

This small, unassuming tor (557753) is not even named on OS maps, and on the latest edition of the OL28 Explorer map is only shown as a very small outcrop, just above the English Heritage emblem. The tor is named by archaeologist Sandy Gerrard (Gerrard 1997, fig. 75), and is the closest outcrop to the stone rows. I was instinctively drawn to this outcrop whilst studying the Bronze Age settlement that straddles the B3357 **(map p. 158)**. Yet within this small granite locale is an uprighted simulacra with rock basins on one side, a rock basin that holds water, a cavern with acoustic properties, a short stone alignment, and more! This outcrop really epitomises the Dreamtime, of seeing with 'new eyes'.

Approaching the tor from the south (from the settlement and road) one negotiates a clitter field, which slows ones progress; I was brought into the here-and-now, made to focus on the immediate space around me. Low overhangs and small caverns on Over Tor invite inspection, some displaying unusual red and green crystal deposits, whilst others can be acoustically resonant. One overhanging balanced rock resembles a hound's head sporting a cheeky grin **(above left)**. Immediately in front of where I am standing is an alignment of small rocks, which I believe is manmade.

But it is the 2m high cavern formed by the slippage of a large granite slab that draws me in. I found this to be acoustically resonant **(images p. 79)**, as have other people with whom I have shared this enclosed space. Drumming and chanting inside on recent group tours produced powerfully-felt effects, which we called *Over-tures*! The most resonant places seem to be at the fissures and cracks. The chanting of deep Ohms seems to reflect back from the naked granite, and my drum 'overtones' to a slow, heartbeat rhythm. My voice becomes full and deepens when I stand up at the triangular apex of the cavern **(left)**.

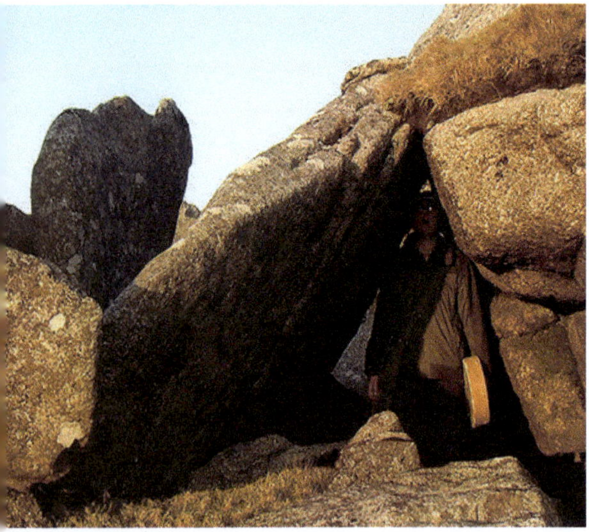

The setting sun shines into this recess during the winter half of the year, and the Merrivale complex of stone rows and settlement hut circles are easily seen below on the plateau; Pew Tor, Vixen Tor and the sea lie beyond **(above right)**. Can you see the rock spirit that gazed with me over this sacred landscape?

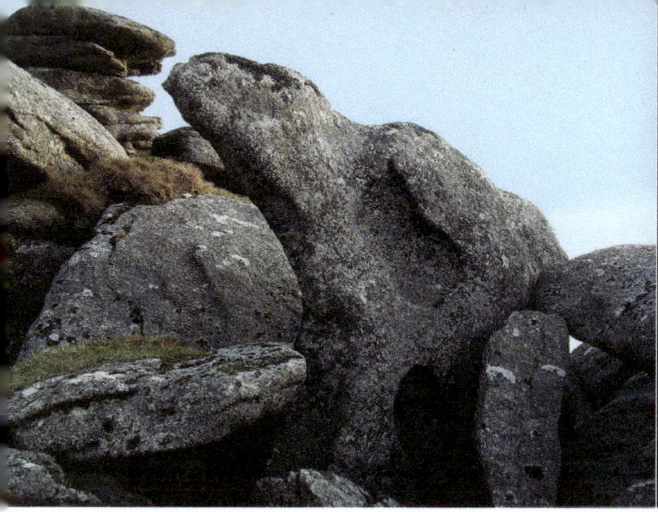

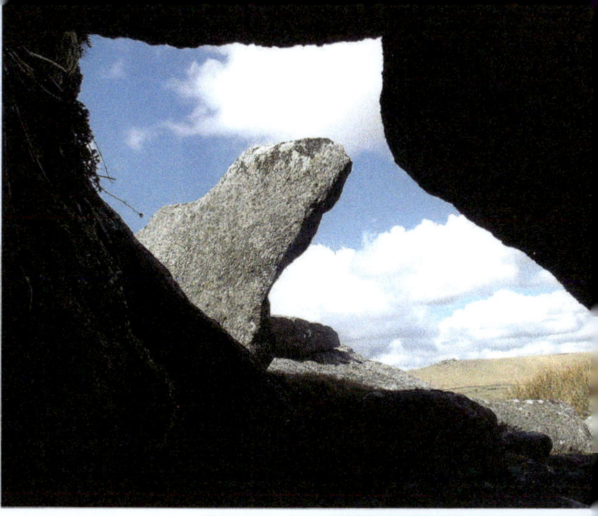

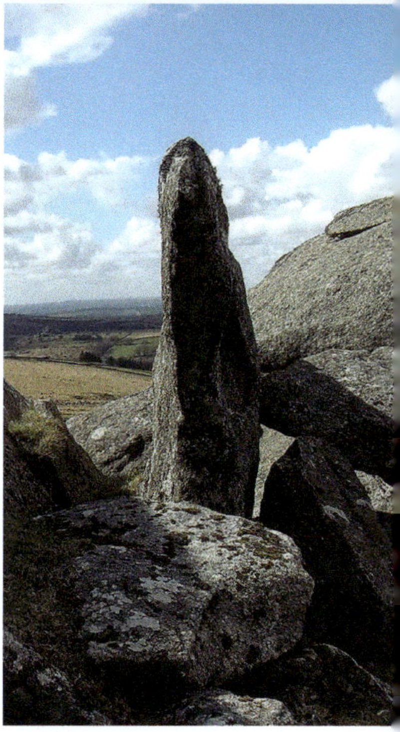

Exiting through the rear of the cavern, one encounters one of the most notable simulacra on Dartmoor, and one that man has had a hand in. A thin slab of granite, 2m high, has been uprighted and tightly wedged into the vertical **(right)**, and the whole rock forms a simulacra that has been variously described as a bear, an eagle or dragon **(above left)**. What is amazing is that two worn rock basins adorn the north side, which must have been the old top surface when the slab was horizontal on the outcrop. The top, eroded basin, forms the 'neck' of the creature. There are other recorded examples of the reverence and enculturing of slabs displaying former rock basins (Tilley 2010); I discuss this further on p. 125-7. I have found two more Dartmoor examples, on Middle Tor **(image p. 132)** and at the Neolithic site at Dewerstone **(image p. 135)**. This creature rises vertically from the jumble of granite like an eagle, its wings folded behind. It looks to the sky as if about to take to the air. From inside a small recess at the rear of the 'cavern', the bear/eagle looks in, towering over the observer **(above right)**. Everyone on recent group tours saw the relevance of this simulacrum, several before I had even introduced it. Similar forms across the world have been regarded as significant **(images p. 51 and 52).** In some cultures, the bear is believed to be the ancestor of humans (Gunn 2010). I can imagine shamans and initiates gathering around this holy rock thousands of years ago, the 'bear' becoming animated due to the flickering of torch flames, with the help perhaps of psychoactive plants (see next page for details of a night visit). An Aborigine sacred site in the Alice Springs area comprised a 9m thin blade of rock standing balanced on end. It stood next to a small waterhole, which was known as a teaching or 'dreaming' spot (Snyder 1990). This thin slab at Over Tor is also visible from the west side of the tor **(bottom image, opposite)**, and from quite a distance down slope.

Moving around to the south side of the summit, a 30cm diameter rock basin, which often contains water, can be found on one of the higher ledges. It is very roughly cut and irregular, as if manmade; I have suspected as much elsewhere, as at Ugborough Beacon **(image p. 134)**. You may recall how, at Over Tor, I enthralled one group, who could not see the rock basin from below, by producing water from solid rock, as if by

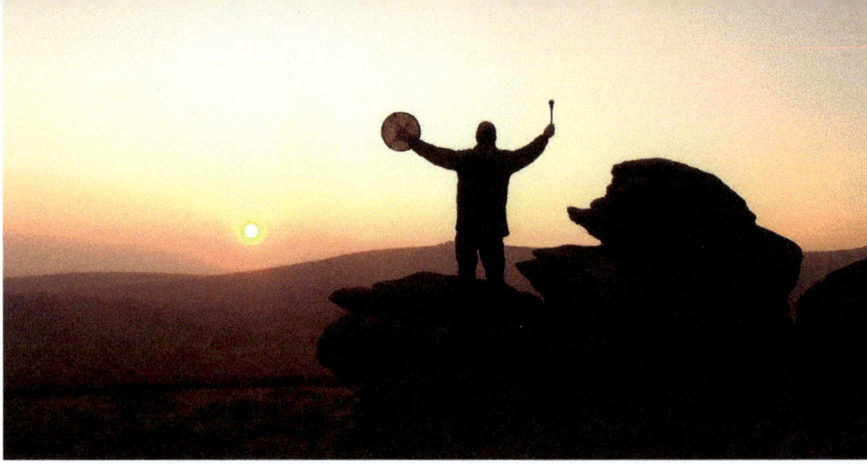

magic **(image p. 129)**; there were exclamations of 'wow' and so forth from attendees below! Was this 'wow-factor' pulled off by shamans to gatherings long ago?
Over Tor is a fabulous vantage point from which to see the Merrivale complex below and, at one time, the round houses of the Bronze Age community. The smells and sounds from the settlement would have been experienced by anyone up on Over Tor, and yet the shaman, elder or initiate, was separate from his kin, divorced from the world of the living to reside with the rock 'bear', and ancestral spirits. Any time of the year, the outcrop is a good place to witness sunsets, as I have done. I have drummed the sun down, and howled my wolf howl across the land; and chanted, 'Peace and Love to the land' **(above)**. It was after doing this at one sunset that I looked down and was first shown the rock basin! It was as if I had been gifted it. To my right you can see an open-mouthed simulacrum, announcing that nightfall is imminent.
On a recent full moon visit to Over Tor, I was moved by its atmosphere and majesty. The moon did not show due to cloud, but as my eyes adjusted to the dark, I found that, even without the light of the Silver Lady, I could see the texture of the lichen and crystals on the rocks. The granite simulacra loomed up out of the darkness, and the silence and sense of peace was palpable. The bear/eagle simulacrum was stark, standing upright in the night. Sue Wallace and I tuned in to the spirit of this rock, and were told, *'strength, be strong, be true to your heart. Speak from the heart. Look to the skies like I, not down in despair'*. I had indeed suspected this was an oracle site. I flashed my torch, moving it around, and the shadow cast behind the rock danced; the creature became animated, seemingly of its own accord. Any fires lit here in ancient times would have produced a similar effect. Sue tuned in whilst astride the back of the beast, and was inspired to write some prose **(image p. 214).** This simulacrum has also been found to have astronomical alignments **(image p. 201)**.

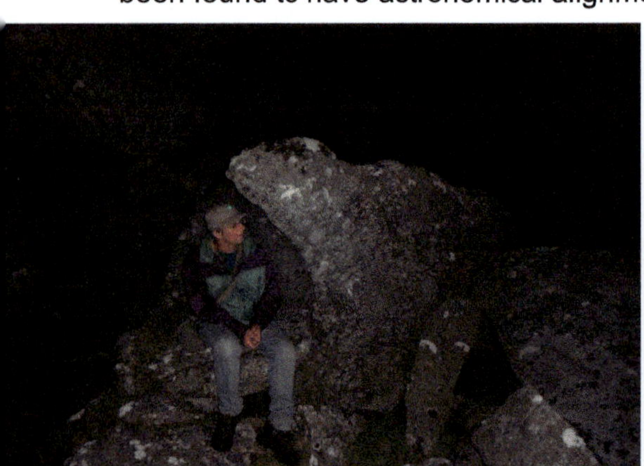

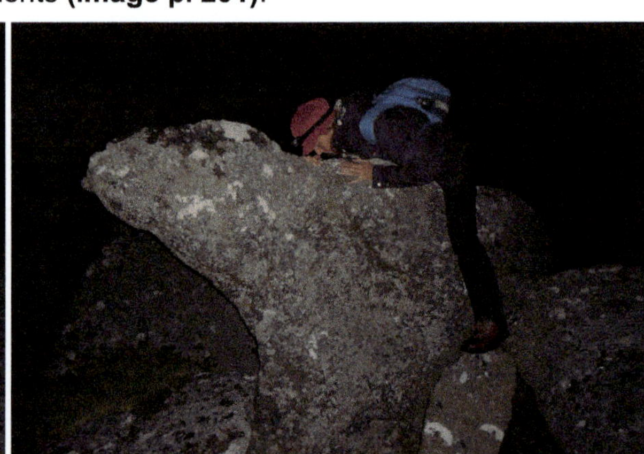

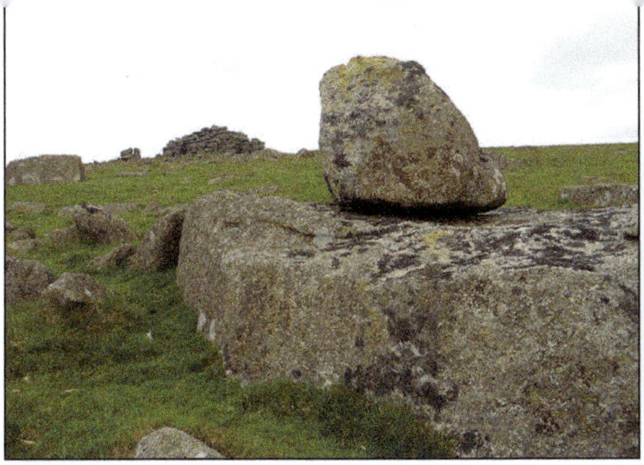

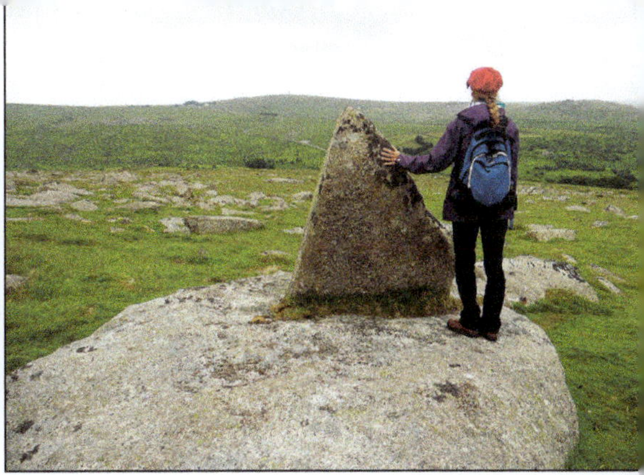

Middle
Staple Tor stone settings

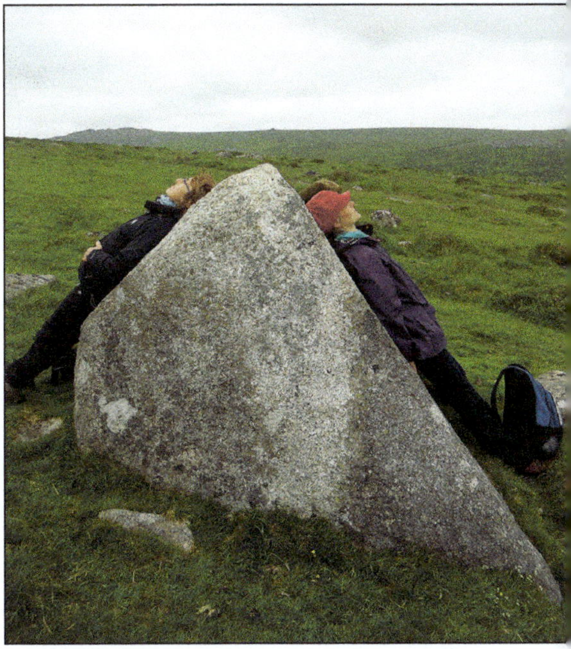

During a tour I led in June 2016, the group was returning from Middle Staple Tor, heading to where we had parked at the B3357 milestone (545751). Descending the steep slopes to the south of the bridle path, we came across three unusual stone settings amongst a clitter spread. The northernmost (542754) was a 1m high stone, set up on a large, earth-fast clitter boulder; it was within sight of Middle Staple Tor, which was on the skyline **(above)**. The group found it to spin a pendulum that was held over it. The next interesting setting was further down the slope, but just within sight of the previous (543753). A 1.5m tall triangular stone is again set on a large slab/outcrop of clitter **(top right)**. Both these remind me of a similar stone setting above Grimspound **(top image p. 63)**, and they each afford good views of Over Tor and the stone rows at Merrivale.
The third site of interest was a further 150m down slope (544752), just above a water course. This took the form of a pyramidal rock **(bottom image)**, with flat faces up to 2m high. The granite was unusually white, gleaming with feldspar and quartz. Some of the group reclined against the rock and felt the energies passing through it.
It is not clear when the first two were set in place; the last one does seem to be natural clitter, if unusual. Examples of such settings on Bodmin Moor have been regarded by archaeologists as culturally significant to our ancestors, whether natural or modified (Bender et al 2007). I have already discussed how unusual rocks are held as sacred shrines across the world (Chapters 6-8). All three settings stand out on the landscape and are either on, or close to, the alignment from Merrivale to Middle Staple Tor **(map next page).**

Merrivale

At last, we come down from the lofty heights of the surrounding tors, and walk Merrivale's immediate landscape. Like Stonehenge, Avebury, and many other major prehistoric sites, Merrivale is a whole complex of sites of different ages and varying designs, which would have lent themselves for diverse purposes. The famous stone

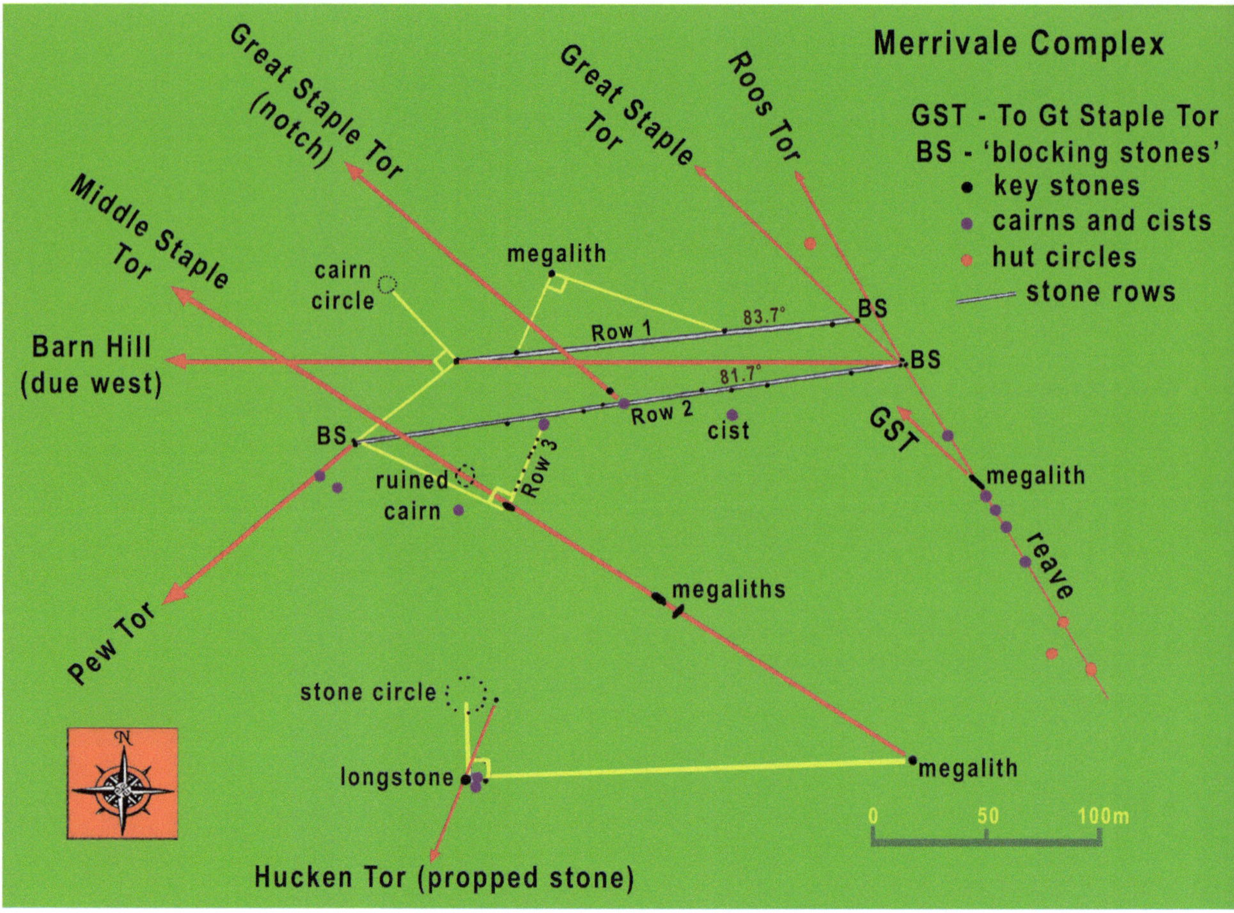

rows are world famous, but stand alongside cairns, cists, standing stones and a stone circle **(above)**. A Bronze Age reave passes by one end of the rows, and people were living in close proximity in a settlement; the living and the dead co-existed.

There has been some notable work carried out regarding the astronomy of the complex in recent years (Walker 2005 & Wood 1978), and I shall return to this aspect in Chapter 16. In Chapter 17, I shall also deal with the powerful earth energies that are dowsed here. For now, after a brief introduction to the complex, I shall concentrate on the main premise of this book, that monuments were located with exquisite care on the landscape that they might align with prominent natural features.

Merrivale is unique on the moor in that it has two stones rows that are double for their entire length – two stone avenues running almost parallel. There is a smaller third row too, which is much shorter. The complex nestles on a gently sloping ridge at around the 340-350m contour lines. As with Drizzlecombe, the rows lie in a natural landscape bowl. Both rows have larger terminal stones, some of which have been termed 'blocking stones' **(BS in map above)**. There are cairns nearby, plus one cist that is actually set into a row; this row/cairn association is consistent at many stone rows. A cairn is recorded at the east end of Row 1 (Dartmoor National Park Authority 2004). The Great Western Reave passes the stone rows on the east side, and some cairns are embedded within it.

Paul Devereux has long discussed the possibility that the Stonehenge Cursus and stone rows like Merrivale may be associated with spirit flights of the dead (Devereux

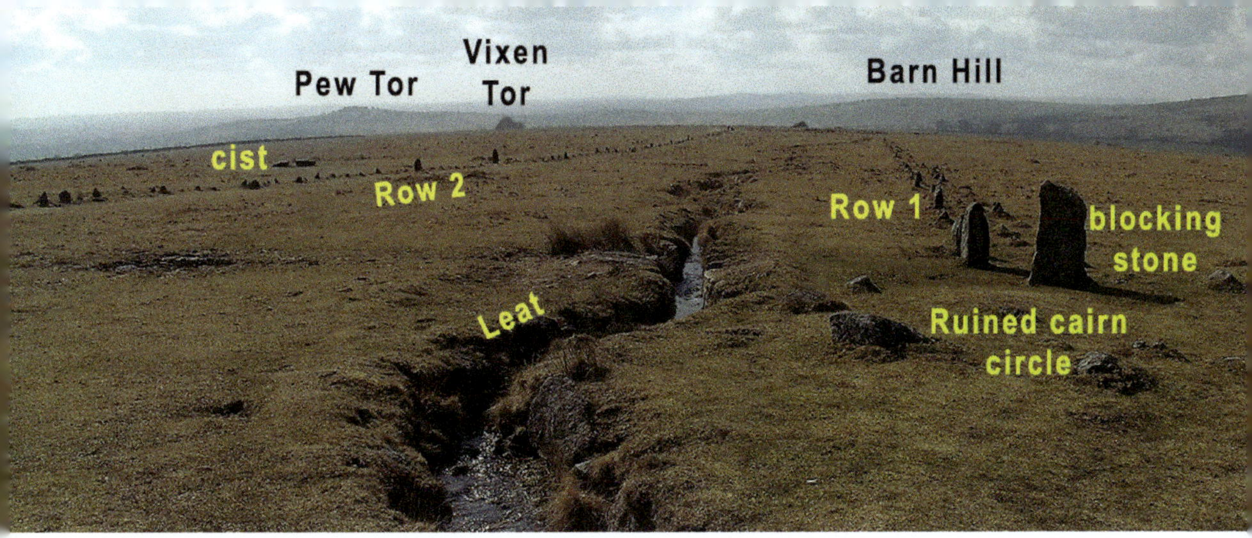

2010). It may be relevant that the 81-83° azimuths of Merrivale's rows are identical to the azimuth of the Stonehenge Cursus!

Like many other sacred sites, Merrivale has a yielded finds that suggest a long range of dates, namely from around 2,500 to 600 BC. I have already discussed the possibility that at least some of Dartmoor's stone rows may date to the Neolithic.

Stone Row 1, the northernmost, is a double row some 182m long. It is thought to have 186 stones (Wood 1978) and its azimuth is 83.7°, not quite east-west. The tallest stones are over 1m tall at the east end, and only three other stones approach this height (marked on map). The remnants of a cairn circle lie at the east end **(above).**

Stone Row 2 is the southern one, and is also a double row, some 263.7m long (Wood 1978). Its azimuth is 81.7° and has 266 stones. The usual numbers of stones visible in these two rows is usually less than the numbers given here, as peat and soil has obscured some that are smaller or have fallen. Again, the larger stones are at each end, although seven large ones can be seen down the rows, which contrast with the small size of the stones generally. Stone Row 3 begins with a cairn and heads off at an azimuth of 203°, ending in a small 'blocking stone'. This row is only 42.3m in length and has 41 stones, most of which are now buried in the earth; 17 small stones are generally visible. Another row has been suggested next to the Longstone (see map), where there is an alignment of three small stones.

Merrivale's stone circle is formed by 11 stones, all less than 1m tall, which form a circle almost 19m in diameter, the smallest on the moor (Lethbridge 2015). From here the equinox sun sets into Barn Hill (see Chapter 16). Just south of this stands the Longstone, a 3m tall ithyphallic megalith. It may have had a twin, for another slender longstone lies prone to the SE. An eroded cairn lies between them. On a recent tour I led for Megalithomania, dowser Shaun Kirwen noticed how several stones in the Merrivale rows had their long axis aligned with the Longstone.

The water that flows between Rows 1 and 2 **(above)** is a leat, built in the 1880s. And don't be fooled also by a number of pillar-shaped granite stones inscribed T/A that stand to the east of the reave. These are modern waymarkers of a route between Tavistock and Ashburton.

Some right-angled triangles are produced in the design of the complex, which must have been integral to the original design, and later development. Four examples are shown here (in yellow on the map), based on the work of Dr John Edwin Wood (Wood 1978). Prof Alexander Thom (1967), and Robin Heath with John Michell (2004) have provided proof that our ancient ancestors had a deep knowledge of geometry and surveying techniques. They plied their ancient craft at Merrivale for sure.

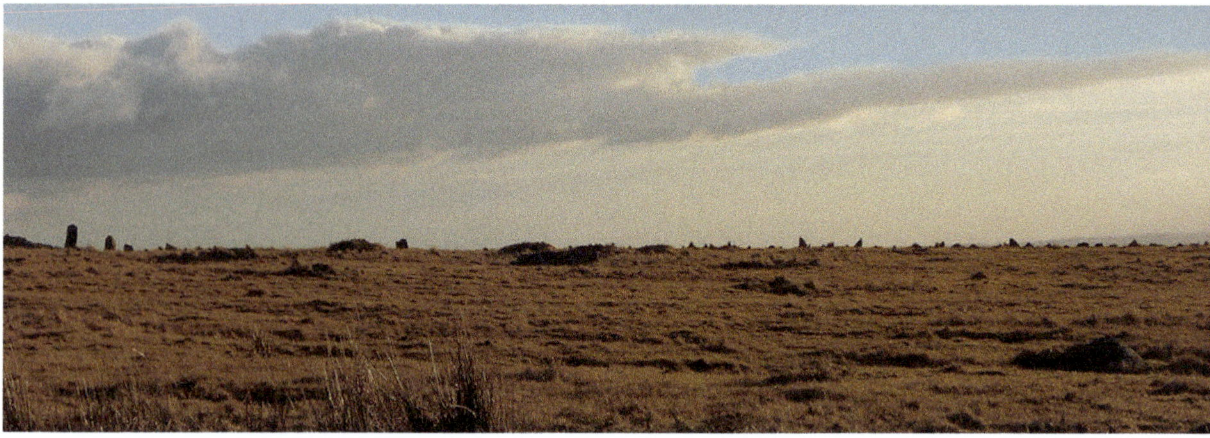

A large settlement of 35 round houses **(map p. 158)** lies north of the rows, and straddles the B3357, extending towards Over Tor: At Merrivale, '... there is an integration of tombs and ritual space... the dead are still the focus of ritual experience in the Early Bronze Age' (Trwoga 2006). The places of the dead are near to where the living dwell; perhaps the stone rows are the liminal spaces where two worlds meet. Walking up from the dip in which several huts circles are located, I saw that the rows appear on the skyline from the huts nearest to them **(above & image p. 196)**. It is as if the ancestors themselves are standing on the ridge, watching over the living below.

Walking the stone rows is a sacred act, where we are, quite literally, walking in the footsteps of our distant ancestors. Movement is controlled along prescribed routes, with cairns as foci; the cairns at the ends of Rows 1 and 3, and the one halfway along Row 2, have been dated around the same time as the rows (Dartmoor National Park Authority 2004), whilst the others around the complex appear younger. In Row 1 we are being led upslope to the cairn at the east end. In Row 2 we are led from either end to a stone cist in the centre of the row. Row 3 also has a cairn at one end. At the lower end of all three rows there are no cairns, suggesting that perhaps we are being led down to the River Walkham – symbolic of life. This is evident elsewhere, such as at Shovel Down and the Hart Tor rows. When walking towards the river at Merrivale, we also look towards more water - the sea.

I never tire of walking these rows, and pausing to sit against the blocking stones. Come snow or rain, come sunshine or fog, these stone rows always hold their mystique, keeping their secrets. I have been here for several sunsets, to watch the solar orb march along the skyline as the year progresses. And as I am standing here watching the sun god set, I know that thousands of years ago someone was doing likewise, from where I am standing. Those moments link my heart to those who have long fallen on sleep – I am joined to them; the concept of time, that I am told separates them and I, just melts away. I can see why people once believed, right here on Dartmoor, that the ancestors were always close at hand.

Landscape alignments of Merrivale.

I had recorded alignments with landscape features for my previous books on Dorset, West Kennet Long Barrow and the Cerne Giant (Knight 1996, 2011, 2013). With these in mind, I returned to Merrivale with 'new eyes', with those of the phenomenologist (Tilley et al), and of the prehistoric shaman. And I had questions. Why is the Merrivale complex here and not somewhere else? Do the tors have anything to do with where individual monuments are located? And can I connect with this ancient landscape in a deeper way, as my ancestors once had?

The Great Western Reave is the Bronze Age boundary work that marches across the moor for 10km. As it approaches the rows from the SE, 5 small cairns lie on top or next to it. Walking north along the reave it is apparent that a long section of the reave, and the cairns set into it, are aligned with Roos Tor, which straddles the distant skyline. In this image **(below left)** a tripod stands on one of the small cairns, with Roos Tor behind. Roos Tor was the focus of the reave-builders.

Standing on the same reave, stands a megalith, the long axis of which has been angled so as to align with Great Staple Tor **(centre)**. I have placed the tripod on a different cairn here, that is also on this alignment. Such 'open secrets' are for all to behold with those 'new eyes'. Some of the taller megaliths of the two main stone rows

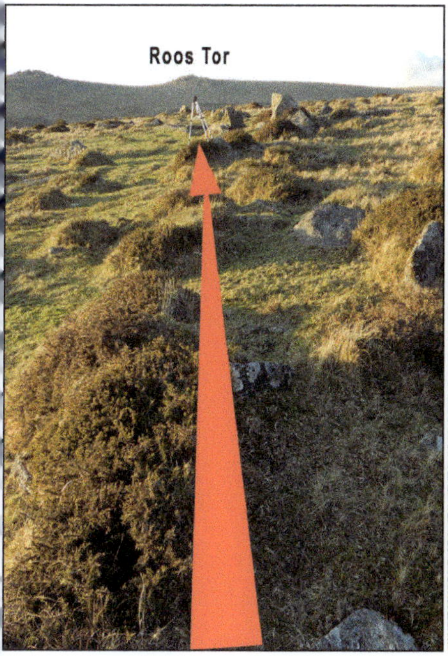

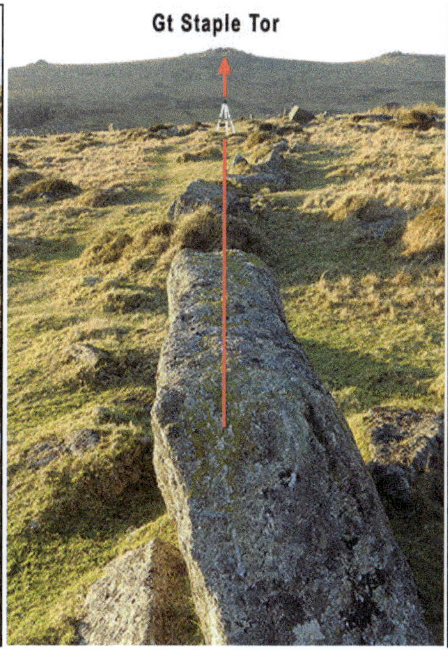

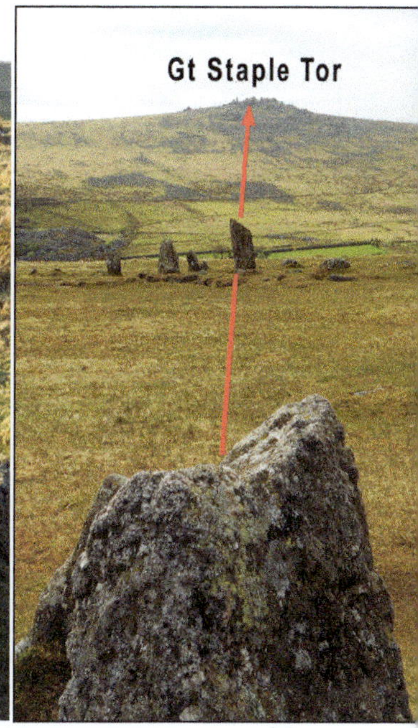

also align to point to distant tors. One example here shows how the tall stone at the east end of Row 1 aligns with the second stone in from the east end of Row 2, so as to align with Great Staple Tor **(right)**. Three other tall stones in the two rows form an alignment with Great Staple Tor. For example, from the cist set into Row 2, one will see a small outlier close by to the NW. This forms an alignment to a notch to the left of the summit of Great Staple Tor **(map p. 178)**. This is an astronomical alignment, which I shall return to in Chapter 16.

It has also been noted (Wood 1978, Walker 2005) how the west end of Row 1 aligns exactly east-west with the east terminal stones of Row 2. This may have been one of the factors in determining the azimuths that the stone rows were set.

Another impressive alignment involves 5 features: a megalith to the east of the Longstone, two more that sit NE of the Longstone, a stone at the end of Row 3, and a nearby ruined cairn. All these monuments form an alignment with Middle Staple Tor. This was first recorded by John Edwin Wood (Wood 1978). The image here **(next page, top left)** is from the 'megaliths' near the centre of the map, looking to Middle Staple Tor. From here, the stone rows ride the ridge top, mirroring the view from the settlement on the other side, shown on p. 179.

From the eastern edge of the stone circle, the Longstone aligns with the summit of Hucken Tor **(next page, lower left)**. Moreover, the outlier just east of the stone circle and the Longstone, aligns with the propped stone and the stack on Hucken Tor on which sit the rock basins **(shown on map, p. 178)**. Once again, our ancestors have left us subtle signs of their deep connection with their landscape.

The last alignment I want to illustrate for now is one involving a large, 2m long boulder to the south of the complex, just north of King's Tor. It sits not far north from the tall stile that scales an east-west wall (approx. 556743). The rock **(below right)** is unusual, a simulacra that is smooth, rounded, and resembles a sleeping bear or buffalo. I had been drawn to it from afar but it only when I stood at the rock did I see that it was perfectly aligned with the Longstone and Great Staple Tor. Whether the rock was moved here, or else its location was 'fortuitous', we may never know, but the alignment exists and would have been noted by our ancestors.

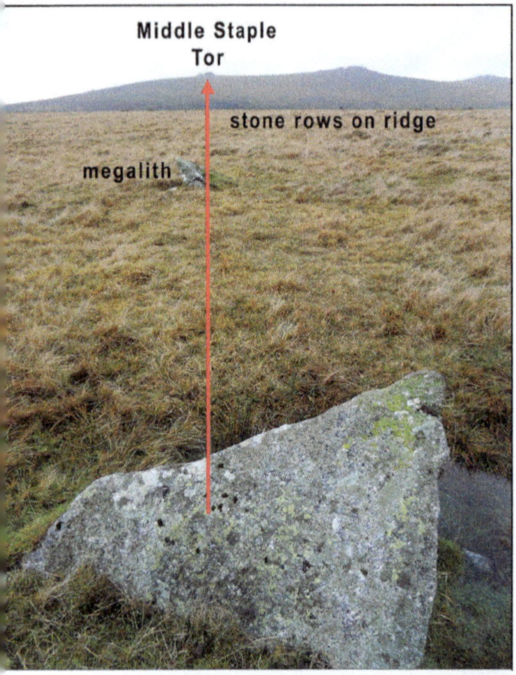

I shall return to the wondrous landscape of Merrivale in Chapters 16 and 17, when I look at astronomy and dowsing. I hope this chapter has shown how Man and landscape were in synthesis, and how people erected monuments with exquisitely on the land, in balletic harmony with it.

People were born, lived their lives, and died here. And whilst all this was playing out, the ancestors looked on, from the cairns and the tors **(top next page)**; but, more than this, they watched over people from the megaliths of the stone rows. In the prehistoric mind, the ancestors were omnipresent, and Merrivale epitomises this symbiosis between the living and the dead.

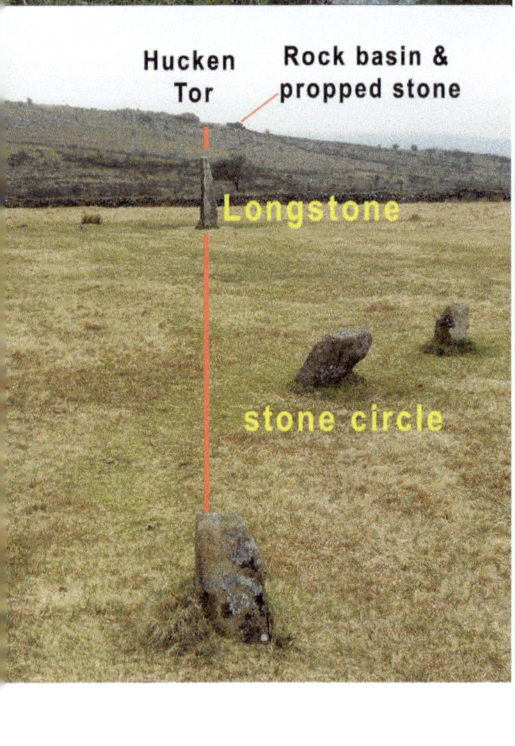

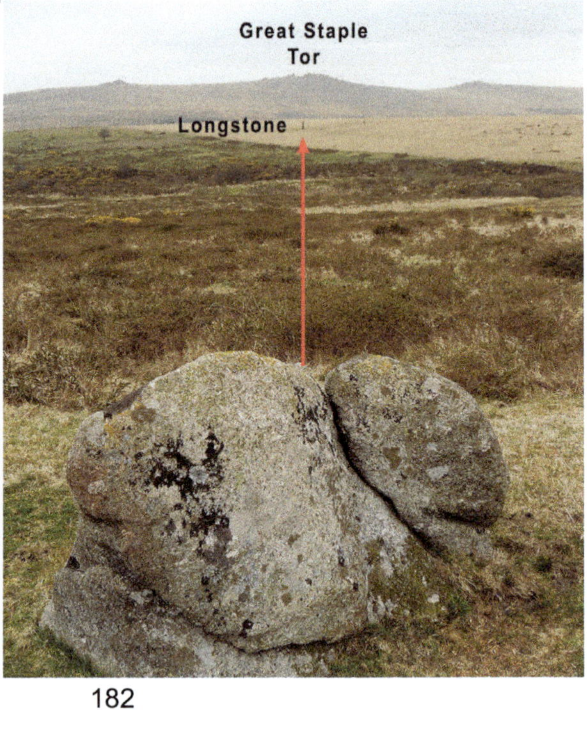

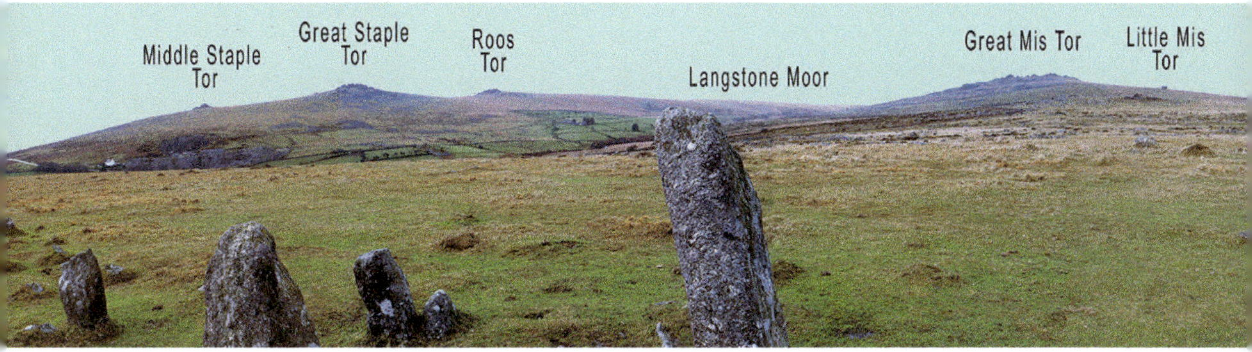

Looking north from the eastern end of Row 1.

'The staggering array of ritual monuments associated with Merrivale indicates the strategic and spiritual importance of this area to those people who lived within its influence'
(Dr Sandy Gerrard, 1997.)

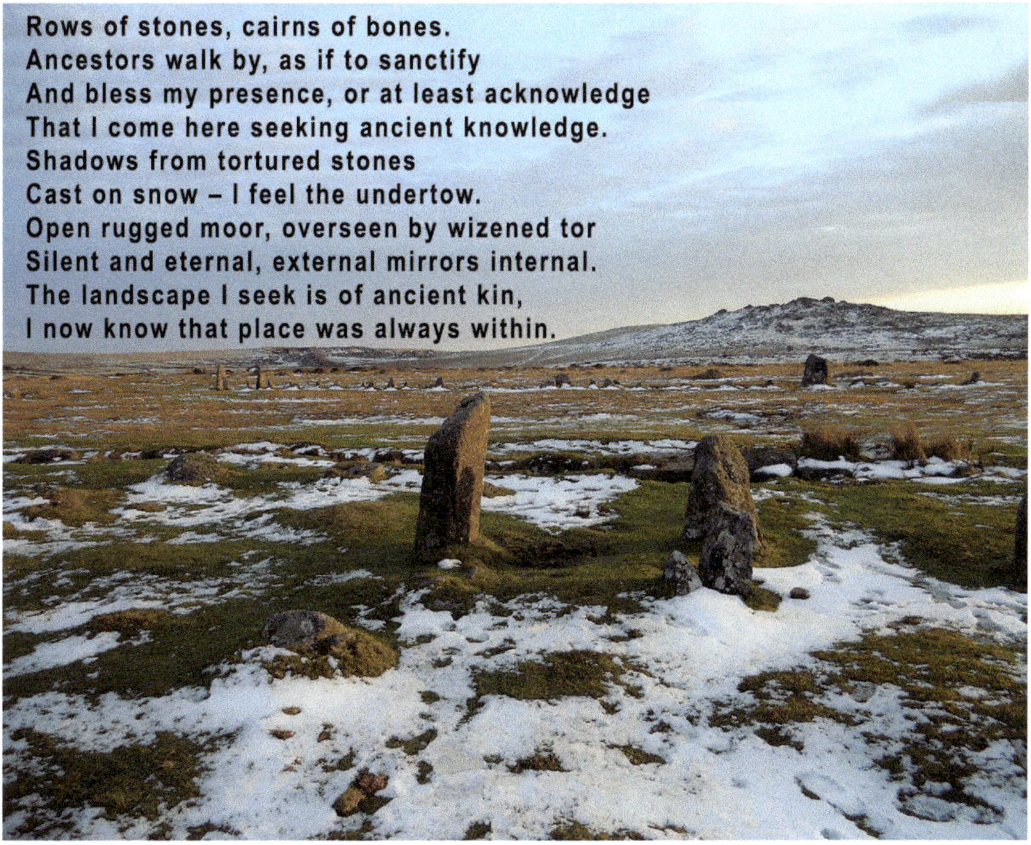

'Merrivale Snow Poem'. January 2016. P Knight.

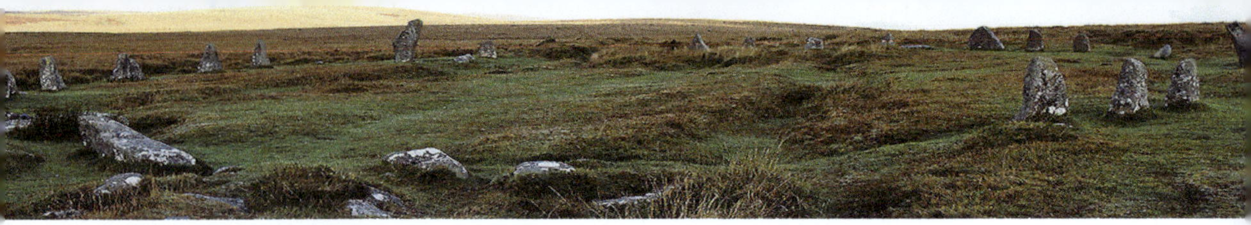

14. Circular Stone Settings and Their Landscapes

'The ancient temple sanctuaries are usually located in powerfully numinous places in the landscape. This numinous quality evokes for me a sense of the gods as potent elemental forces' (Nanson 2011).

The circle is one of the basic building templates of the Universe, a symbol of harmony and balance around a dimensionless point. The Greeks considered it a perfect shape, possessing neither a beginning nor end (Knight 2015). In many cultures and spiritualities, to step into a circle is to enter a sacred space, possessing a deeper significance to that outside. A circular stone setting (the circle) and a stone row (the line) are such contrasting geometric forms, suggesting that their functions were of a different nature. The circle suggests encirclement and movement within, continuity, cycles of time; whereas rows invite movement to somewhere else, directing us out across a greater landscape - they link places.

Some of the greatest prehistoric sites in the world involve circular stone settings. Stonehenge, Avebury, Newgrange, Castlerigg, the Ring of Brodgar, even Classical Greek and Roman temples, were designed to circular, or near-circular, templates. Previous research has suggested that landscape setting was an important element in stone circle location. This is sometimes in relation to astronomical alignments, where the sun or moon may rise or set over geographical features.

In this chapter I have included recognised stone circles, cairn circle and ring settings. There seems to be grey areas between these three categories. Some so-called 'cairn circles' lack internal burial, like official 'stone circles'. However, at Brisworthy stone circle (see below), a low rubble bank surrounds 75% of the circle, which may indicate it is in fact a ring cairn (Gerrard 1997). At the Merrivale and Langstone Moor stone circles, there is evidence that a second circle of stones may have stood outside the first. At Yellowmead and Shovel Down there are four concentric circles: 'Care should be taken in unequivocally identifying these structures and it is possible that the stones were originally covered by a cairn which has since been removed' (Gerrard 1997). So I am not going to split archaeological hairs about whether this or that circle is a true stone circle or the remains of a burial site. My brief is still primarily to demonstrate the importance of landscape settings to circle settings, regardless of their purpose.

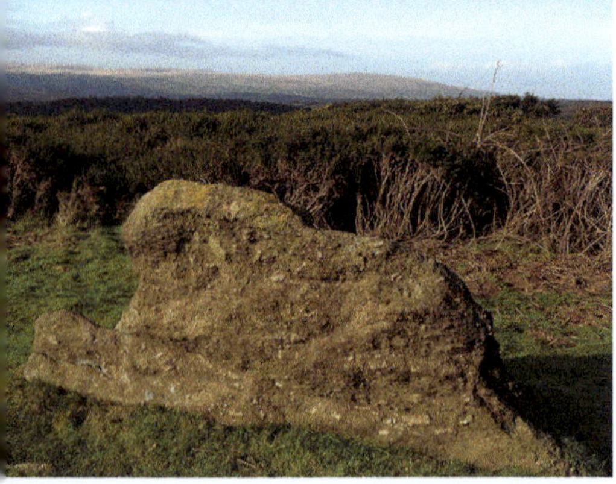

A layer of charcoal was found at five of Dartmoor's stone circles, showing that fire played a part in the ceremonies. The shape of megaliths was also important, and there are those bearing simulacra; the 'running hare' shown here **(left)** is one of the

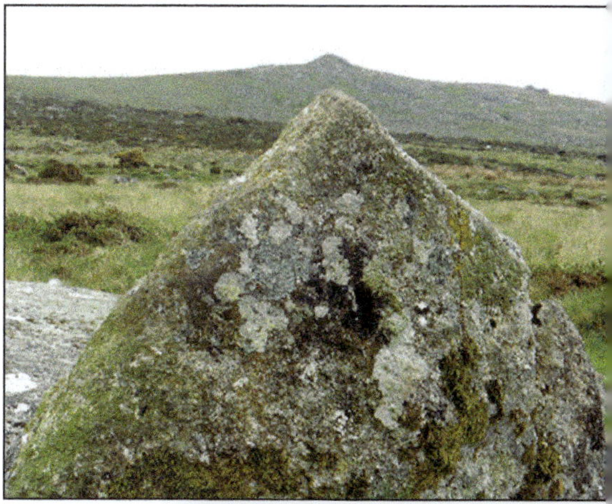

megaliths at the Mardon Down stone circle. I have already demonstrated the importance of phallic and triangular stones in prehistory.
Sometimes the shapes of megaliths can mirror or mimic distant skylines, as has been found elsewhere, such as at Castlerigg. I have found some on Dartmoor. In this example **(right)**, see how the tip of this triangular stone at the 'Nine Stones' cairn circle at Belstone (612928) duplicates the summit of Belstone Tor. Helen Woodley found another 'mimic' at the Grey Wethers double stone circles (639832), where the shape of one stone matches the form of Bellever Tor on the skyline (Devereux 1991).

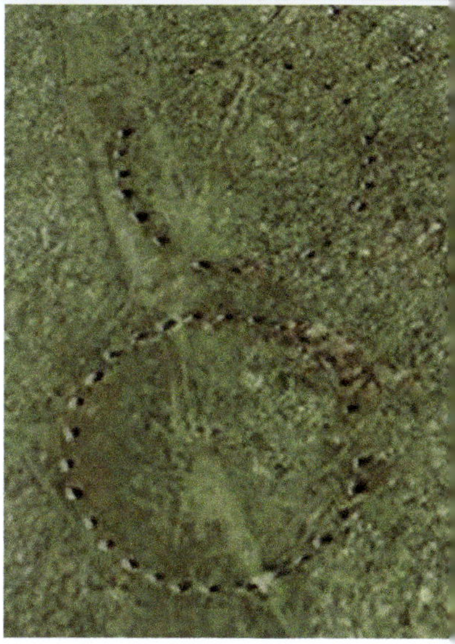

Stone circles started to be constructed towards the end of the Neolithic, i.e. the early 3rd millennium BC, and were used by people visiting the area on a seasonal basis, probably during the summer months (Bender et al 1999). Stone Circles total 18 in number on Dartmoor (Gerrard 1997), nearly all of which sit over 300m (1000ft) above sea level. Stone circles can be singular, or in pairs, such as the Grey Wethers, which stand on a gentle slope; they show up well on this Google Earth image **(right)**. Each Dartmoor circle is unique, varying in diameter from 19m diameter at Merrivale to 38m at Mardon Down. No attempt seems to have been made to create a perfectly round circle, even though this is relatively easy to do with a post and a long stretch of rope. Alexander Thom's book proved that many circles were laid out to complicated geometrical theorem. The gaps between the stones suggest that they were designed to look outward from within, out across the landscape (Bradley 1998). Prof Chris Tilley found that on Bodmin Moor very few cairns are located in the immediate vicinity of stone circles (Tilley 2010), and this is a general rule of thumb on Dartmoor.
Some circles have folklore attached to them, such as being people turned to stone due to some indiscretion. The Stall Moor circle has 26 stones, known as the Dancers and Kiss-in-the-ring. The stones are said to be girls who all kissed a young countryman on the Sabbath, and were turned to stone. Unfaithful wives had to visit Scorhill **(banner p. 184)** and the Grey Wethers as part of their penitence (St Leger-Gordon, 2001).

Landscape settings

I have already described and illustrated some circular stone settings, namely Mardon Down **(image p. 100)**, Hingston Hill **(image p. 150),** Lakehead Hill **(image p. 62),** and Langstone Moor **(image p. 47)**. These are all in locations that enable views of significant landscape features.
As I have stated, Chris Tilley (2010) found that most of Bodmin moor's stone circles were within sight of at least four tors, with up to seven being visible. Sometimes the positioning of circles takes account of a few metres, to enable extra tors to be visible. The visibility of Rough Tor seems to have been important when viewed from the two stone circles near Leskernick, (Bender et al 2007). The North Circle at Leskernick has

a large earth-fast boulder at its centre, showing that these natural rocks were of great significance (Bender et al 2007). The summit of Rough Tor is visible from the southern stone circle, but disappears from view at precisely the point where one enters the northern stone circle (Bender et al 1999). All Bodmin stone circles are located within 2km, or considerably less, from a prominent tor, and in nearly every in case, 11 out of 13 in fact, the shortest view (i.e. the closest skyline) is to the north (Tilley 2010).

Stone circles are not isolated, solemn places, but are an element of a dynamic terrain. They express a cultural 'belonging' to the landscape by the people who erected them. In general, flatter plateaus are occupied by stone circles, on sloping ground, often with clitter fields, rather than on hill tops. They can be situated on ridges, as are stone rows, and seem to have been chosen for their extensive vistas. There are exceptions to this hill top rule; for instance, the Mardon Hill stone circle is on a ridge summit, with amazing views across the moor; I think the relevant criteria here is the visibility of Haytor to the south **(top image, p. 82)**.

Prof Tilley noted that *all* of Bodmin's stone circles are located a short distance from streams or substantial boggy areas, and which may have been natural boundaries marking out areas of sacred space (Tilley 2010). On Dartmoor, it has been noted that four of the larger circles are situated in the watersheds between major rivers (Gerrard 1997). The Grey Wethers are upslope from both the East Dart and the North Teign, and the area around the circles is very boggy in winter months. The Sherberton circle (639732) is exquisitely placed between the two major flows of the West Dart and the River Swincombe, as well as a boggy area of springs just to the north.

Tilley recorded that the stone circles of Bodmin Moor usually have one particular tor as its primary visual focus, and in most cases the tor is north of the circle. Looking at it another way, as seen from the tors the circles are aligned with the midday sun. I have found that on Dartmoor this is less obvious, although it does occur. For instance, the White Moor circle is visually dominated by Cosdon Beacon to the north; the Sherberton circle is south of Bellever Tor; Legis Tor is a prominent feature to the north of the Brisworthy circle. The Yellowmead stone setting is dominated by the looming presence of Sheeps Tor, which is NW of the circle. But there are also exceptions. I think the close location to water is the overriding incentive to circle location, and positioning was *ideally* dictated by both the visibility of tors *and* proximity to water. Let's look at a few examples in more detail.

The Scorhill stone circle **(below)** is near the confluence of the Gallaven Brook, Walla Brook, and the North Teign. The areas west of the circle are almost impassable after heavy winter downpours. This fine circle has a selection of triangular and phallic stones, and the views beyond the circle are stunning. To the north rises Cosdon

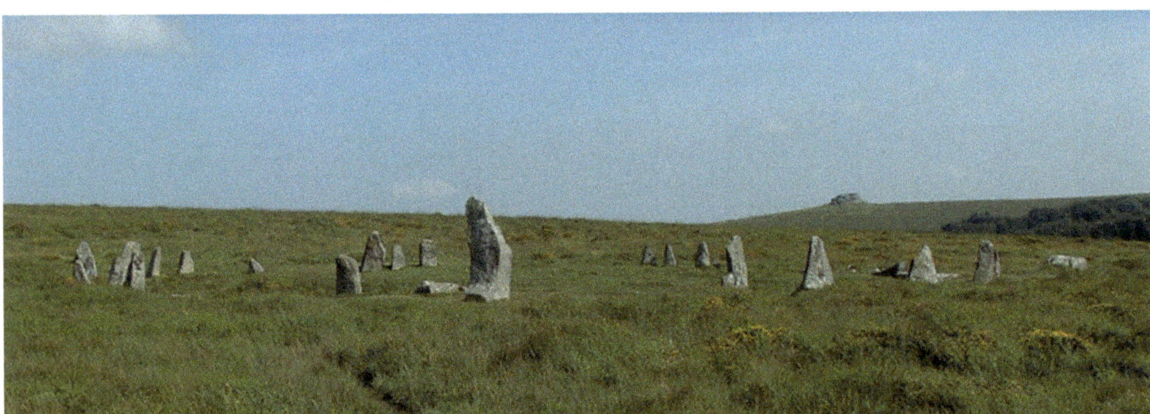

Beacon, capped by cairns, and the characteristic form of Watern Tor **(image p. 68)** is on the western skyline. To the south, the Tolmen Stone sits in the North Teign River. To the SE, Kestor marks the midwinter sunrise **(image p. 200)**.

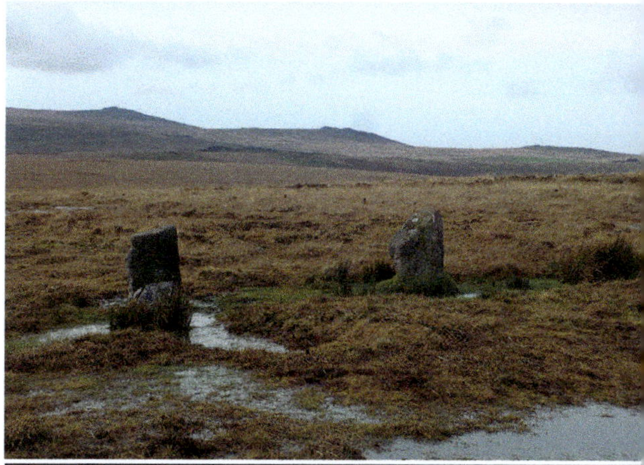

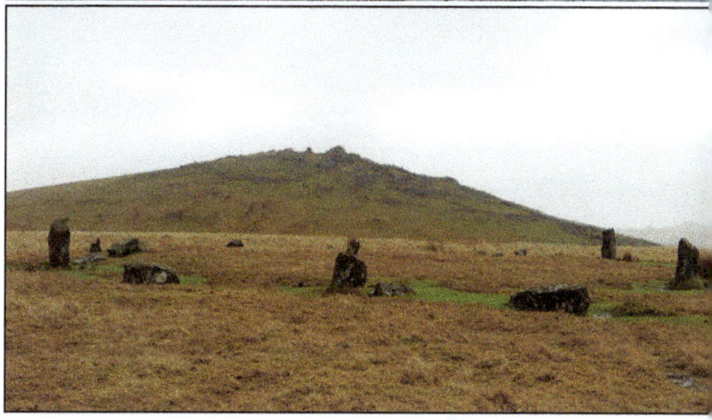

The Little Hound Tor or White Moor stone circle (633896) is quite isolated **(right)**, enclosed by boggy ground during the winter months, as I have found to my cost! Its isolation is part of its magic. The stones stand on flat area in the saddle between Hound Tor and Little Hound Tor, with views from the NW, through the south, right around to NE; it feels like landscape setting is all here. From here at least ten tors are visible; when one walks away from the circle to the north or south, the number of tors visible falls – the circle is placed to view the optimum number of tors. From here, I saw an alignment with Kestor Rocks and Haytor **(centre image, p. 82)**. This is close to the midwinter sunrise.

The Langstone Moor stone circle **(lower image above)** is just north of the River Walkham, east of the head of Colly Brook (557783); the circle stands on a ridge, and the land here, particularly down slope to the west, is very watery during much of the year. The setting is magnificent, and has been compared to that of Castlerigg, in the Lake District (Lethbridge 2015). The views are distant towards the SW, as the eye is drawn to the sea, Great Staple Tor and Roos Tor **(image p. 47)**. But it is the lofty mass of Great Mis Tor that dominates the view, seen here, which rises above the settlements and the River Walkham, out of view below. This tor would have been sacred to the inhabitations of the settlement (c. 558779), who raised cairns just south of the circle. The location of the stone circle ensures a view down the Walkham valley and that the Merrivale plateau is visible, whereas from further north it is not.

The Brisworthy stone circle **(below)** stands near the SW edge of the moor. It sits on a gentle incline, which slopes south to both the Legis Lake Brook and the juvenile waters

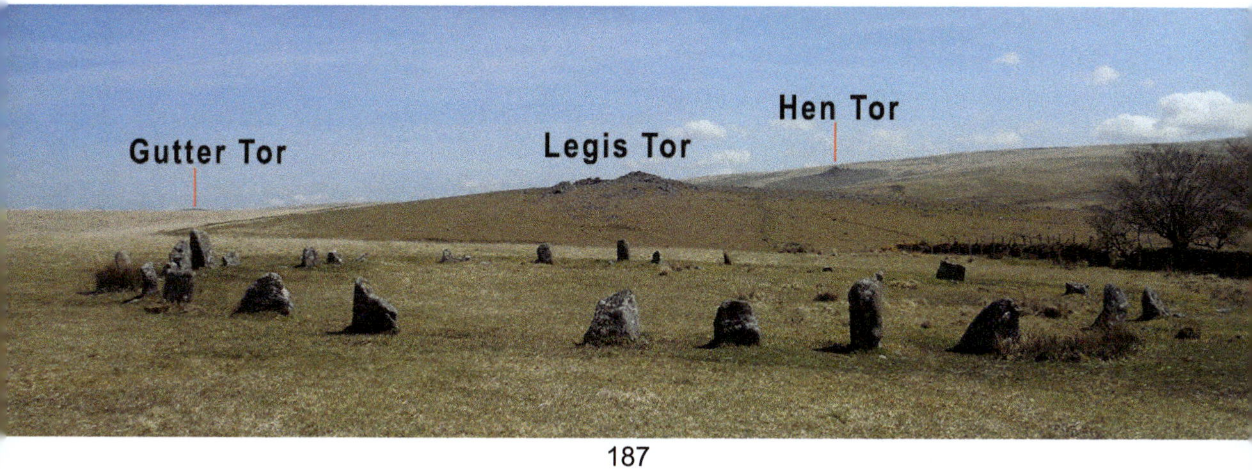

of the River Plym. It is another stone circle set in a stunning landscape. One's eye is focused east to Legis Tor and Hen Tor (which has a substantial clitter spread), whilst Great Trowlesworthy Tor rises to the SE. There may have been views of the sea to the south before the china clay works spoil heaps were created. From here the very top of Gutter Tor very subtly breaks the skyline, which would not have gone unnoticed by the circle's designers. The positioning of the circle also enables an intricate interplay between the circle, the tors and the heavens; from here the equinox sun rises in between Legis Tor and Hen Tor, and the midwinter sun rises over Great Trowlesworthy Tor. Man, the landscape and the cosmos in harmony. I dowsed earth energies here, which I shall return to later **(image p. 208)**.

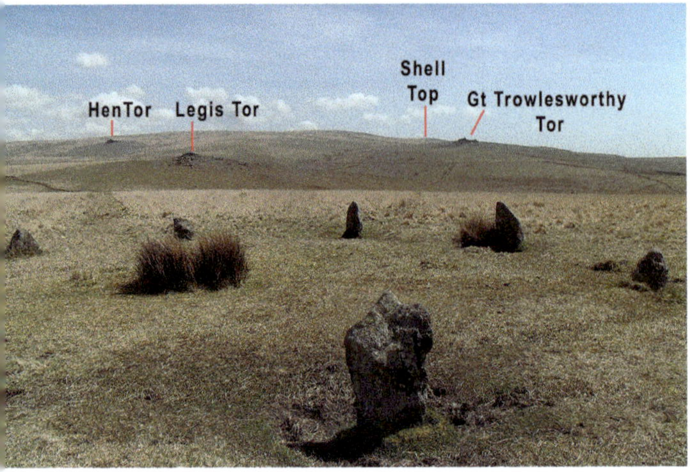

To the north of the circle marches the Brisworthy stone row, with the cairn circle (563658) at the south end **(images p. 155)**. The 'big sky' expanse of the moor from here is breathtaking. Of interest here is the view SE from the cairn circle **(left).** In the short distance that separates the stone circle and the cairn circle (about 450m), the relative positions of Legis Tor and Hen Tor have reversed. Compare this view to that of the previous page; from the stone circle, Legis Tor was on the left of Hen Tor, and now it is on the right. I had noted similar in the White Tor area **(images p. 47),** where Roos Tor and Great Staple Tor appeared to change places. It is a constant wonder to me how landscape features change over such short distances, a phenomena that would have been observed by our ancestors. From the cairn circle, the midwinter sun rises over the cairn on Shell Top, before 'hanging' over Great Trowlesworthy Tor.

Yellowmead Stone Setting

Yellowmead stands SE of Sheeps Tor (575677), and is one of the jewels in Dartmoor's crown. Again, its stones stand on gently sloping ground **(below)**, with springs and rivulets in close attendance. It is classed as a 'multiple stone ring', with an outer

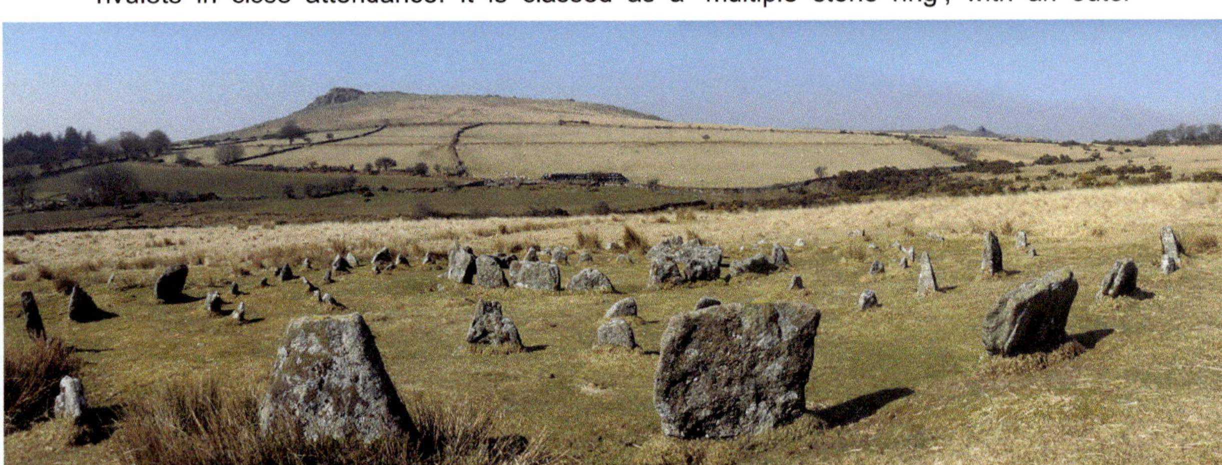

diameter of almost 20m, and there is no evidence that a cairn ever covered it. The site has been restored, consisting today of 99 stones forming a 4-fold concentric setting, with the remains of stone rows joining the circle on the west side. Although the site has been restored, it is clearly seen that the spacing of the stones is not uniform, plus the fact that the circles are irregular **(below right)**. Presuming that the original socket holes were used in the restoration, this irregularity could be down to the circle builders following the flows of earth energies. And perhaps people were walking each circle, gradually making their way into the sacred centre. The bulge in the SE corner of the outer circle is in the direction of the midwinter sunrise.

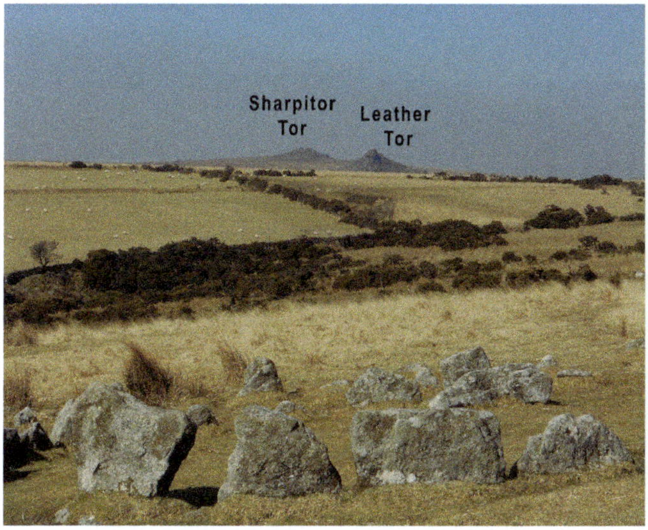

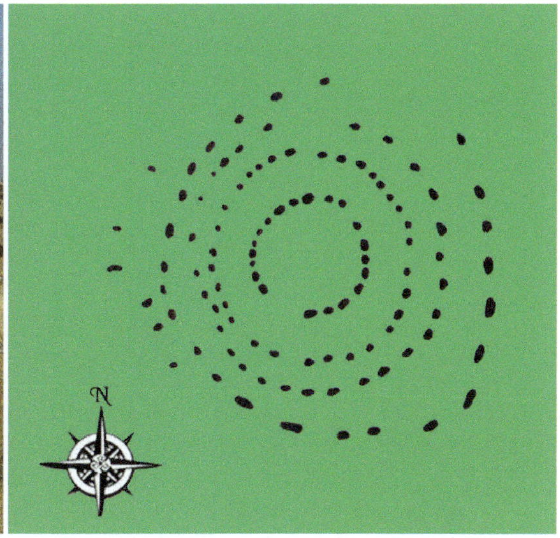

But it is the landscape setting that truly 'sells' Yellowmead. Sheeps Tor is a dominant feature on the NW skyline **(image p. 188)**, and into it sets the midsummer sun. Gutter Tor, with its settlements, rock basins and cairns, is prominent to the south and there are distant views to Down Tor in the east. And yet there is something more subtle going on here. The tops of Sharpitor and Leather Tor rise out of the skyline to the north, and perspective has created another example of the horns or breasts of the Earth Goddess **(above left)**. Leather Tor is particularly pointed, resembling a horn. Earth energies were dowsed at Yellowmead, which I shall return to later.

Comparable with Yellowmead is the 'cairn circle' that sits where the two northern stone rows converge on Shovel Down (659861). From here the rows lead the pilgrim down to the North Teign River **(image p. 146)**. A phallic longstone used as a boundary stone lies close by **(image p. 60)**. Antiquarian John Page mapped the cairn circle as a 'triple circle'; Turner (1990) says there are 'four concentric stone rings... 29 visible stones', whilst it has recently been described as a 'fourfold cairn circle' (Lethbridge 2015). Two earthfast boulders are incorporated into the design **(right)**. I have suspected for some time that the small stones comprising this structure originally defined a walk-in spiral, now much damaged. Several attendees of my tours have walked this spiralling path to the centre. This may suggest that the living walked it thousands of years ago. Or perhaps symbolism is involved, the spiral leading the dead into or out of the sacred centre. Dowsing has confirmed that earth energies spiral into the heart of the cairn.

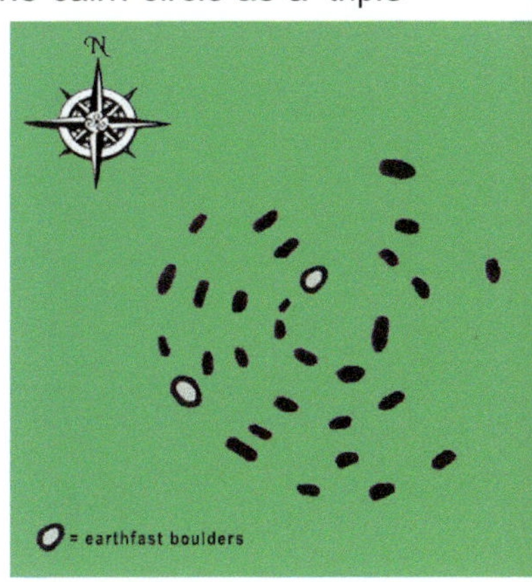

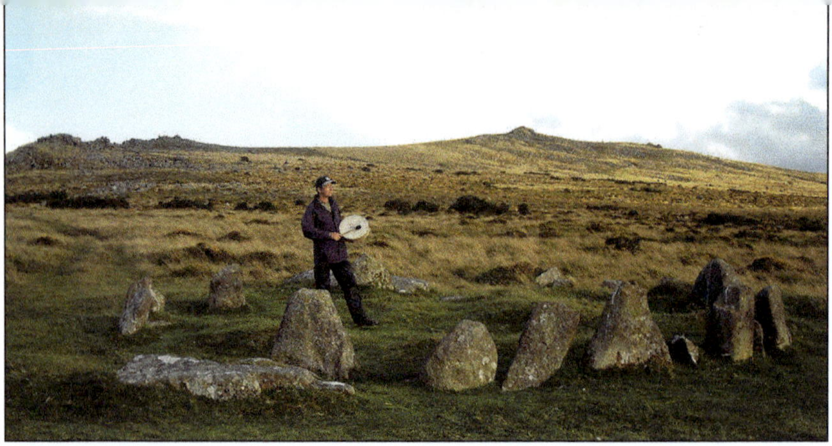

Going around in circles

I have already told the story of how I was inspired to put pen to paper at the Mardon Hill cairn circle **(image p. 100),** by the views to the north, as well as having felt the presence of the ancestors. The circle seems to represent the eternal cycles of the universe, of life, of the cycles of our own lives. As well as possessing sacred space, circular stone settings also possess sacred times, occasions when they seem to come to life. This can be a sunrise or sunset, moonrise or moonset, a solstice or, indeed, as when the rainbow was manifest before my eyes at Mardon Hill. Some of my most memorable times have been when I visited circles to observe a significant event, some of which I will highlight later in the chapter on astronomy. But we can also be co-creators of sacred time and sacred space at circles. Our presence and activities can be a reciprocal exchange of energies between us and any place; I have visited the Nine Stones cairn circle at Belstone Tor several times. The setting of the circle is wondrous: it nestles below the tor **(above)** and yet offers extensive views of distant tors to the S and SW. I have drummed in the circle and felt the bond between the ancestors and myself – the drumbeat crossed over eons that separate us. Dowsing at the circle is also a powerful experience **(images p. 207);** a place is never static, never empty, rather always dynamic and changing.

This is true when one considers the changeable weather and seasons on Dartmoor. I had visited the Soussons Common cairn circle and cist (676788) previously, but on January 16, 2016, I was on the moor after snowfall. The land was enchanted and I happened to pass this circle and decided to stop. The snow was crisp on the ground, crunching beneath my boots **(below)**. Some people had beaten me to it earlier that morning, their footprints perforating the snow; it was as if the ancestors themselves had been there prior to my arrival. The modern plantation encroached on three sides, and yet a view opened up to the south with distant views of a snow-dusted landscape, with Bellever Tor on the skyline. It made me appreciate the efforts of Bronze Age people, who dwelt on the moor through snow covered winter months. Of all my visits to this circle, this one will live the longest in my memory. The circles of life and death are indeed eternal.

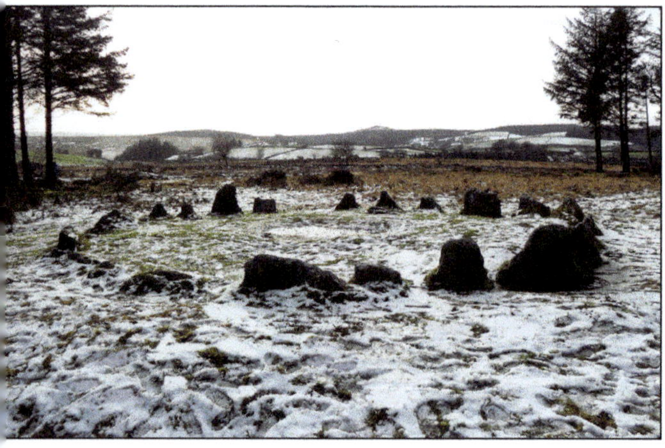

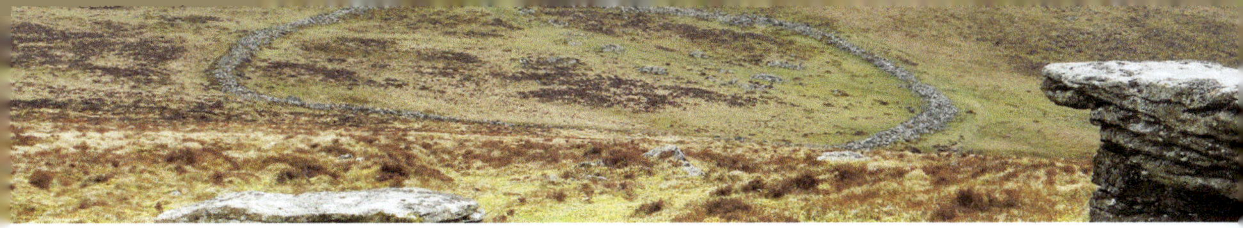

15. Settlements – Design and Landscape Settings

'House walls did much more than simply contain people and animals; they touched and contained ancestral forces ...'
(Bender et al 2007)

When we stand inside the dry stone walling of a Bronze Age hut circle (the remains of a round house), it is impossible to really grasp that people much like you and I lived, worked and died here. The stones do not hold the laughter of children, the smells of cooking, or the tales told around hearth and camp fire. It is also difficult to grasp the concept that symbolism, perceived ancestral presence, and landscape connectedness, determined the location, design and use of prehistoric houses and settlements. It is only in recent years that these dwelling places have been approached with new eyes, seeing them as part of the sacred landscape: '... the domestic was as ritualised, as symbolic, as any lonely cairn or stone row' (Bender et al 2007). Today we separate the routine from the profound. This arises from the compartmentalising of our lives, making clear distinctions between the 'everyday' and 'religious' or 'ritual', and that never the twain shall meet. It was not always so: 'Dividing the sacred from the profane is a modern construct that had no bearing in the past... everyday life was ritual and ritual was everyday life' (Williams 2010). The routines of everyday life, the feast days, and the ceremonial, once blended seamlessly into each other.
There are in excess of 5000 examples of hut circles on Dartmoor (Gerrard 1997), showing a variety of sizes, designs and construction techniques. The stone walls of these prehistoric houses, which were once covered by timber and furze roofs, can resemble stone circles. The internal diameters vary between 3m and 14m. They can often be defined by a single entrance, with upright door jams still in situ, and the majority of these open up to the SE, possibly avoiding the strong westerly winds, as well as capturing the morning sun. Perhaps entrance orientations also had something to do symbolically with the midwinter solstice sunrise. Many hut circles occur in groups, or settlements, which are often enclosed by a stone wall or enclosure; some lack clear entrances, suggesting they doubled up as animal corrals. The number of Bronze Age remains on Dartmoor illustrates how it was a central and important *occupied* landscape during this period (Klemen 2015).

Clues from Bodmin Moor and elsewhere

Once again, I shall use the recent work by archaeologists on Bodmin Moor to see if it can throw light on Dartmoor's Bronze Age settlements.
Several settlements on Bodmin are situated on the west side of hills, and not on the generally more sheltered eastern sides, and some are on highly exposed areas. Some

other factor determined location selection, one of which may have been the intervisibility of tors (Bender et al 2007). At the Bronze Age settlement of Leskernick, the round houses were embedded in clitter fields, and little attempt was made to clear the area to make life easier. Profs Bender, Hamilton and Tilley conclude that, '... the people of Leskernick regarded the stones as ancient sentient beings...', and that the rocks had, '... a protective function guarding the population of the hill from potential sources of evil and danger'. The rocks lying on the land were respected: '.... the stones, their sizes and shapes, textures and form were appropriated and symbolically empowered by those who lived there...' (Bender et al 2007). They also concluded that not all hut circles were dwelling houses, just as not all buildings in a modern town are for habitation. One hut is called the 'Shaman's House', and is orientated to Rough Tor (Bender et al 2007). It was found that many hut circles at Leskernick had 'backstones' at the opposite side of the house from the entrance, which were often pyramidal or of large dimensions. Midst some of the huts they found small rock piles, miniature stacks which, '... mimic the tors' (Bender et al 1999).

The Neolithic settlement at Barnhouse, on Orkney, includes some structures that are described as 'ritual buildings', where habitation was not the primary intent (Garnham 2004). Structure 8, for instance, had an entrance which looked out at a megalith called the Watch Stone. At Skara Brae, Orkney, the dead were buried beneath the living, under the bed!. The similarity in design of houses and chambered tombs on Orkney has been noted, suggesting a symbolic function in the design of settlements such as Skara Brae. Cairn-like structures within and between houses at Leskernick show transition from being homes of the living to houses of the dead (Bender et al 2007).

Perhaps burial of the dead in the ground mirrored the birth of a plant from a seed, which had also been interred in the earth. People were relating to natural processes of planting and growth, in their case rebirth of the ancestors. The deceased were 'planted' into the earth, that seemed to, '... embody nature's rhythms of eternal return' (Garnham 2004); plants regenerate themselves by means of their own death. It was hoped that the spirit/presence of the ancestors would continue to dwell in the same places as the living.

At Leskernick, a river, clitter field, cairn, an outcrop, a propped stone, and a 'Shaman's House' are linked by, '... an almost magical wall' (Bender et al 2007). A seemingly mundane structure like a boundary or enclosure wall connects both spiritual monuments and natural features. It has been suggested that the stone row and circles at Leskernick predate the settlements, which suggests that the living wanted to be associated with the places of the ancestors.

Later in the Bronze Age there may also have been a move from rituals being carried out at stone rows, to rituals being carried out within round houses, and in settlement fields in the form of 'shrines' constructed around selected large outcrops (Bender et al 1999). Archaeologists reached an understanding that the inhabited slopes of Leskernick Hill were full of large rocks serving as shrines. Just as the houses had interior shrines (the backstones), the fields and enclosures also contained them. It was concluded that several hut circles were not just for habitation. The Kogi of Columbia, for instance, have a structure called the *'Nuhue,* the *World House'*, a ceremonial building symbolising the rhythms of the cosmos (Garnham 2004).

'For the people who lived both on and off the moors,
the stones were the ancestors or ancestral beings,
or the work of the ancestral beings.'
(Bender et al 2007)

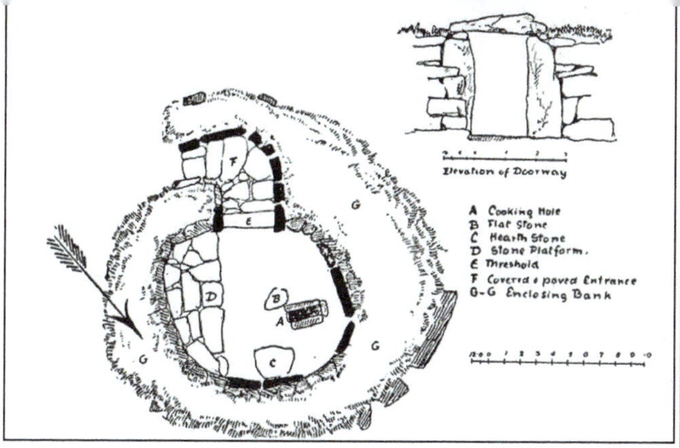

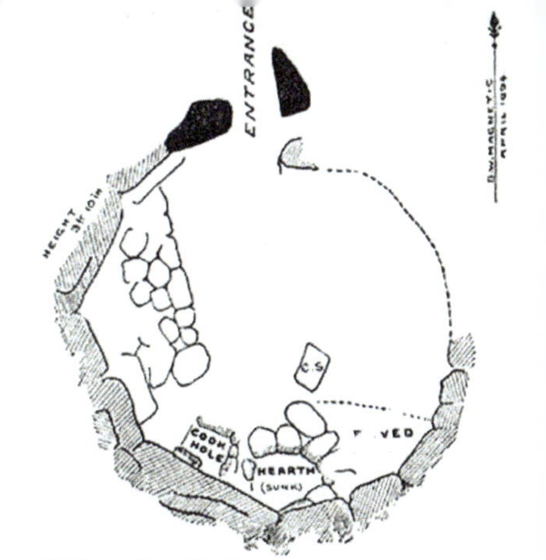

CIRCLE Nº VII

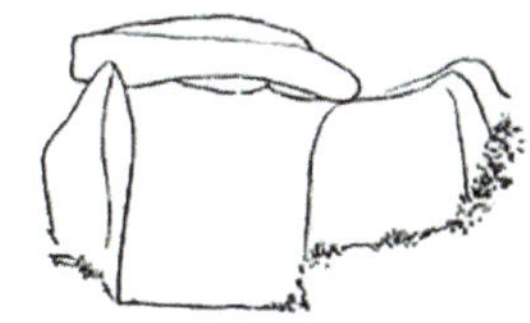

ELEVATION OF ENTRANCE

Dartmoor settlements

At least 488 prehistoric settlements with enclosures have been recorded on Dartmoor (Gerrard 1997). Both Bodmin and Dartmoor became more populated with a rapid expansion from around 1600 BC, when the grasslands were of better quality than today (Bender et al 2007). Bronze Age settlements are often associated with reaves, stone boundary walls which can cross the moor for miles. This is the earliest sign that the land was being divided up due to land 'ownership'. The dividing up of the land by means of reaves was often accomplished by using the tors and skyline cairns as foci. A Bronze Age person growing up at Grimspound **(below right)** would have developed an intimate knowledge of the local topography and inherent myths, as well as a partial familiarity of the broader landscape of the moor, perhaps even down to the sea; people were on the move in the Bronze Age, due to trade, visiting relatives, pilgrimage and inter-clan 'unions': 'No man is an island – nor settlement either. One way or another, there was a criss-crossing of pathways and of movement over the moor' (Bender et al 2007).

Settlements and small round house clusters are sometimes enclosed in walls, thought to hold or exclude livestock, as well as to define extended family units. At some sites the 'finest' hut circle lies outside the surrounding wall and has been interpreted as the 'Headman's Dwelling' (Butler 1997). But surely, the chief or high status person would be at the heart of his or her community. My interpretation is that these external houses were those of the shaman, wise-woman, or equivalent. In aboriginal cultures the shaman or 'medicine man' often lives somewhat removed from his settlement.

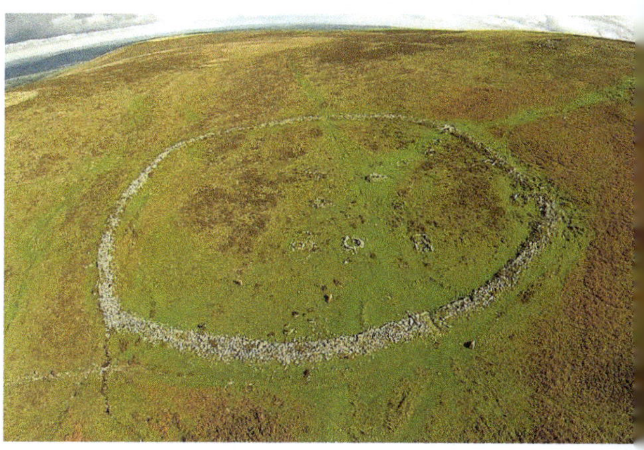

Round houses usually survive as a circular or oval area enclosed by a stone or earth wall. In a study of 1500 hut circles, 85% are of a simple round plan, 2.5% had a porch, 10.5% were conjoined with another, and 1.7% had a forecourt (Gerrard 1997). Many are paved internally with stones or slabs, have hearths, and a 'dias' - a raised area thought to be for sleeping. Some huts have recesses in the walls – stone age cupboards. The plans of two huts at Grimspound are shown here **(above)**. Some have benches or tables, whilst others show evidence of a central

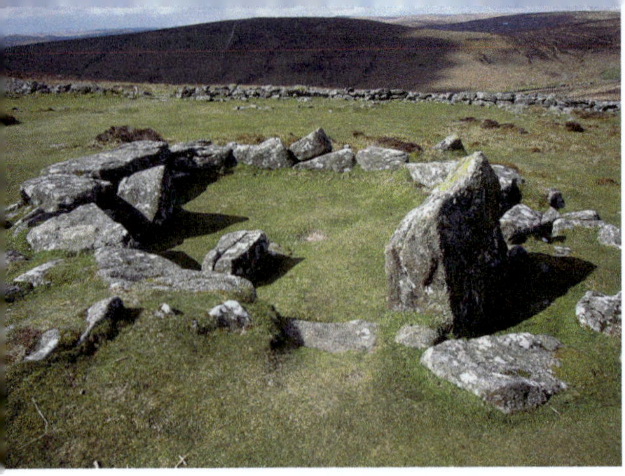

wooden pole, which presumably supported the roof. Grimspound **(left)** has 24 hut circles, all double rings of stone walling up to 1.7m high, with rubble infill. In 1797 the site was called, 'One of the principle temples of the Druids'.
On Dartmoor, the orientation of the entrances is at times haphazard, whilst others seem orientated so as to face away from the prevailing winds. However, this is not always the case, as evidenced by huts at White Tor, Cosdon Hill and Roos Tor, where house doorways can face adverse aspects. At Grimspound, the entrances all face downhill, which would have let in the westerly winds.

Hut circles and stone

On my visits to Bronze Age settlements on Dartmoor, I have noted how often phallic and triangular stones are present in the hut circles. Was this for purely practical purposes, or was selection due to perceived symbolic shapes? I then discovered that triangular and phallic stones were uprighted into houses of the Leskernick settlement. Recent work there by archaeologists has suggested that the shapes of rocks used in round house wall construction may have been a factor in selection: 'We regard shape as a key element in the choice and arrangement of stones on the hill [Leskernick], whether it is a stone incorporated into a structure such as a house or compound wall...' (Bender et al 1999, 2007). A dwelling can be imbued with symbolism, representing the cosmos of the inhabitant's world (Bender et al 1999). I have also found some examples on Dartmoor of large 'backstones', like those seen at Leskernick.
Some hut circles incorporate earth-fast boulders, called grounders. Were these a means by which people attached themselves to the land, to ensure their own permanency, just as tor outcrops were encultured with cairns?
It has been noted how modern stone workers seem to have avoided certain settlements, ignoring the plentiful supply of stone scattered around. Perhaps such places were left alone due to superstition, which spoke of them being the abode of pixies, goblins and spriggans (Bender et al 2007).

Settlements, monuments and landscape

The availability of water is the dominant criteria for the location of most settlements and smaller farmsteads. The largest accumulations of habitation are in the environs of rivers, which is the same the world over. Water is essential for life on Earth, and humans are equally dependant on its life-sustaining properties. But there is also a close association between settlements, tors and spiritual monuments, which can be seen to have 'fine-tuned' the location of dwellings.
Stone rows and their cairns are often found close to settlements, for example at Drizzlecombe, Hurston Ridge, Shovel Down, Merrivale, and Hingston Hill. A hut circle at Assycombe is located near the west end of a stone row (660826). Around the Shavercombe Tor enclosures, there are cairns in between hut circles. The Hook Lake double stone row (c. 641652) is flanked by hut circles, and the southern end of the row is included in an enclosure wall. The north end of this settlement is close to the Stall Moor stone row. South of Combestone Tor, triple stone rows (675710) run parallel with

a reave that connects hut circles beyond both ends. Other stone rows have *solitary* hut circles near them, often located in isolated places, away from rivers. Are these shaman's houses, the dwellings and ritual places of those officiating at the rows? Good examples are on Stall Down (632623) and Shaugh Moor (553633).

At Drizzlecombe, one of the best views of the landscape 'bowl' in which the stone rows stand is from the settlements upslope, (north east) of the complex. The site is flanked by the Drizzle Combe and Plym rivers, and yet is removed from them on a relatively well-drained hill. The stone rows converge on these settlements. The view from the enclosure walls is shown here, with the Drizzlecombe stone rows below **(right).** Great Trowlesworthy Tor, Eastern Tor, Hen Tor and Gutter Tor are also in attendance when viewed from this fine vantage point.

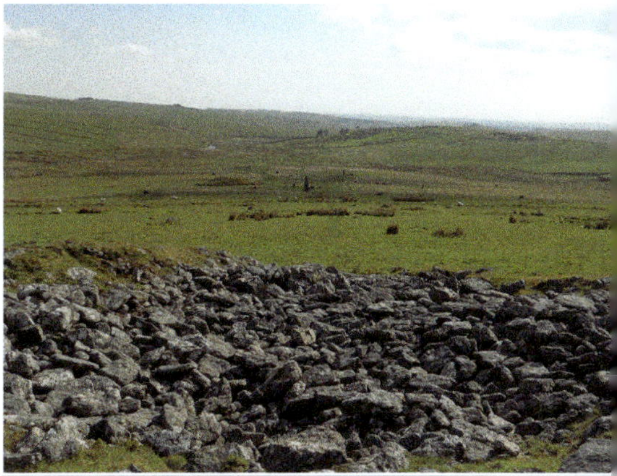

Standing midst the Whittenknowles Rocks settlement, on the ridge west of Drizzlecombe (585671), there is clitter everywhere, to the extent that it is difficult to differentiate between clitter and the 38 hut circles. From the top of the settlement there are extensive 360° views, which include Great Mis Tor, Great Staple Tor, Sheeps Tor, Gutter Tor, the sea, and Bodmin Moor in the distance, and the stone rows marching across the land below.

I find it equally fascinating that hut circles, indeed whole settlements, can be found high up on the tors, well above the rivers. This enculturing of tors is well demonstrated at Gutter Tor, where a settlement was established to the SW of the main outcrop. My interest was raised by an isolated hut circle and enclosure built on the NE side of the outcrop **(right)**. Rock basins on the summit of Gutter Tor may have confirmed the sanctity of this place to our ancestors. From here, the Drizzlecombe complex is stretched out before one's eyes to the east. Is this isolated hut another example of a shaman's house or ritual building?

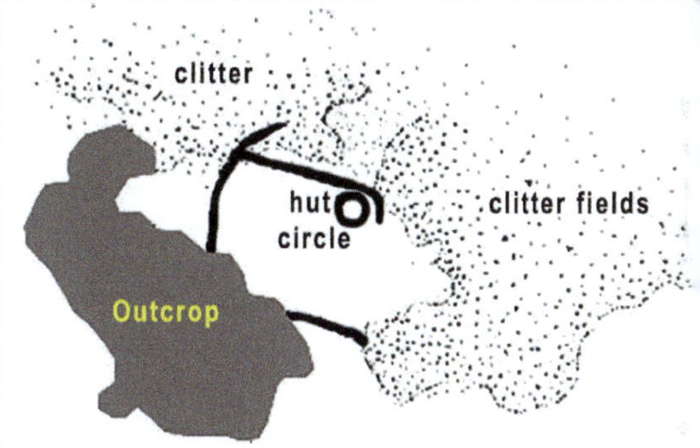

Gutter Tor enclosure and hut circle
(after Klemen 2015)

Gutter Tor is visible from twenty Bronze Age settlements (Klemen 2015), which is remarkable when one considers that, at 350m, it is not a particularly high tor. There are a number of tors that can viewed from multiple settlements, such as Sheeps Tor (visible from 15 settlements), Hen Tor (14), and Legis Tor (11).

Hen Tor (or Hentor) is a small but notable outcrop east of the River Plym (593653), which attracts our attention from the Drizzlecombe stone rows and from Brisworthy **(images p. 187 and 188).** Here two enclosures were constructed within the clitter spread. One enclosure forms an arc around the outside of the NW edge of an extensive clitter spread, and inside this the ground was still not cleared of stones (Klemen 2015). Many of the hut circle entrances look out over the Drizzlecombe complex. The hut circles and walls are often accompanied by exposed clitter and rock outcrops, which form one side of the enclosures. Again, it is often difficult to distinguish between 'natural' and 'cultural' rocks. The point is, the builders of the settlement did not make a distinction; the 'profound' and the 'mundane' were one and the same. The

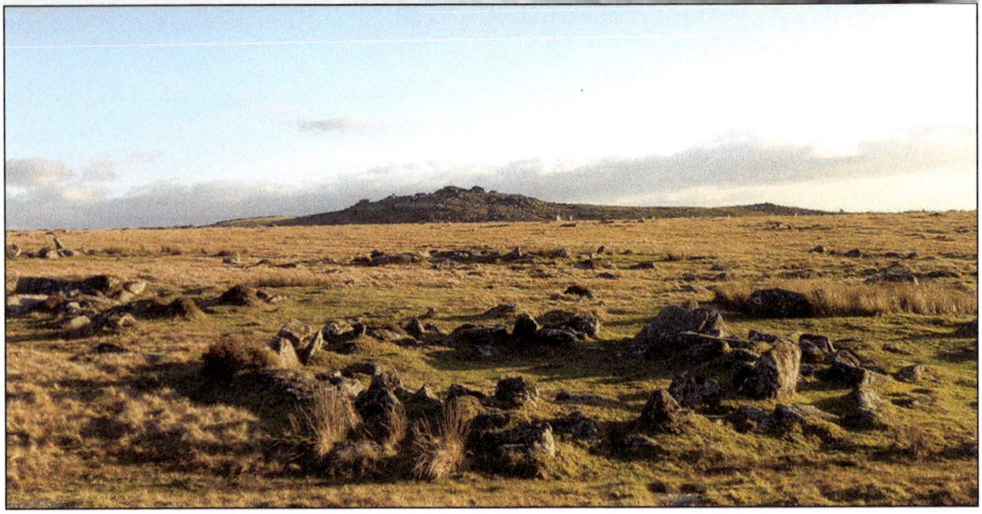

rocks of the clitter spreads were not simply selected at random as a resource for construction, but were deliberately selected, and even culturally transformed (Bender et al 2007). Exposed stone was seen as the bones of the moor's body, and as such anchored the people to the landscape.

Merrivale has been covered extensively earlier, in Chapter 13. It is perhaps Dartmoor's most accessible and best preserved Bronze Age settlement and is visited by thousands of people every year, or be it as a consequence by those primarily visiting the famous stone rows. Sauntering around the settlement is a powerful experience, and one gets the clear sensation that the ancestors, who lived and died here, are still watching over us. Perhaps they have left some essence of themselves behind. As I walk through the entrance into a hut circle, I can imagine being greeted by the inhabitants thousands of years ago. The stone rows can be seen straddling the ridge nearby, with King Tor **(above)** and Pew Tor (**below)** beyond. I often wonder which hut was that of the shaman of the settlement. Was it one of the huts nearest the rows, slightly removed from the heart of the community? Was he or she the bridge, the conduit who helped people through that liminal zone between the living and the ancestors, the latter of whom were never far away in this mindscape?

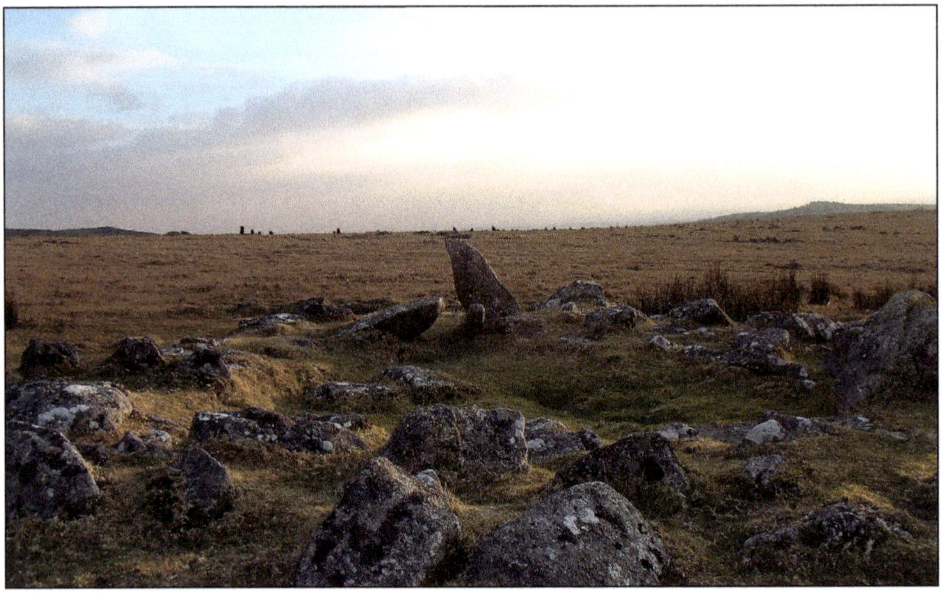

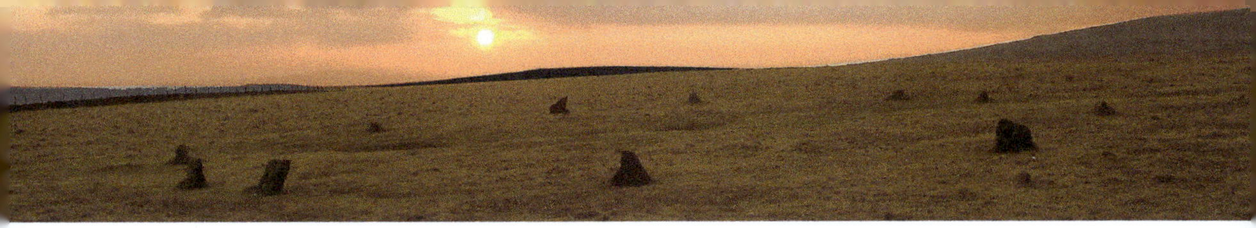

16. Sun, Moon and Stars – Prehistoric Astronomers

'Twinkle twinkle little star,
How I wonder what you are'.
(Trad.)

Ancient star-gazers were looking up at the skies long before Man arrived on Dartmoor. Neanderthal Man was arranging burials to align east-west; Mesopotamian, Greek, Egyptian, Chinese and Babylonian cultures all recorded the observations of the movements of the sun, moon and stars. British archaeology, until recently, was slow on the uptake regarding Neolithic astronomical alignments in Britain. This is somewhat strange, considering the famous Stonehenge mid-summer sunrise alignment has been acknowledged and accepted by academia for many decades. Many considered Stonehenge to be unique, a 'quirky' exception.

But the writing had been on the wall for some time. In 1720, John Toland noted how Callanish was astronomically aligned to the sun, confirmed in 1808 by Thomas Headrick. When Alexander Thom (1967) accurately surveyed hundreds of British prehistoric sites and found precise alignments with the sun, moon and the stars he received a cold and cynical academic reception. So too with Gerald Hawkins' initial work on the alignments of Stonehenge (Hawkins 1963). Recent work by Martin Brennan in Ireland (Brennan 1994), and by Nicholas Mann and Philippa Glasson on Glastonbury and Avebury (Mann & Glasson 2007, Mann 2011), has convincingly argued the case for astronomical alignments involving Neolithic sites. It has been discovered that 80% of the Neolithic houses on Orkney are orientated so their entrances are on a NW – SE axis, midsummer sunset and midwinter sunrise. My work on the megalithic sites of Dorset revealed astronomical alignments (Knight 1996). Similarly, my research on West Kennet Long Barrow (Knight 2011) and the Cerne Abbas Giant (Knight 2013) revealed more astronomical configurations. Archaeologists are finally recognising that, '… orientation is as important as architecture and artefacts to anyone examining the ritual centres of prehistory' (Burl 1983).

Dartmoor skies

The main work to date that has explored, in some detail, the astronomical alignments of Dartmoor's prehistoric sites is *'Dartmoor Sun'* by Jack Walker (Walker 2005). In this wonderfully well-illustrated book, Walker convincingly advocates, through good research and direct observation, alignments for both Merrivale and the Hingston stone rows and cairn circle. At Drizzlecombe, Walker also observed that the tall terminal longstone of Row 1 casts a shadow directly down the row of small stones at midwinter,

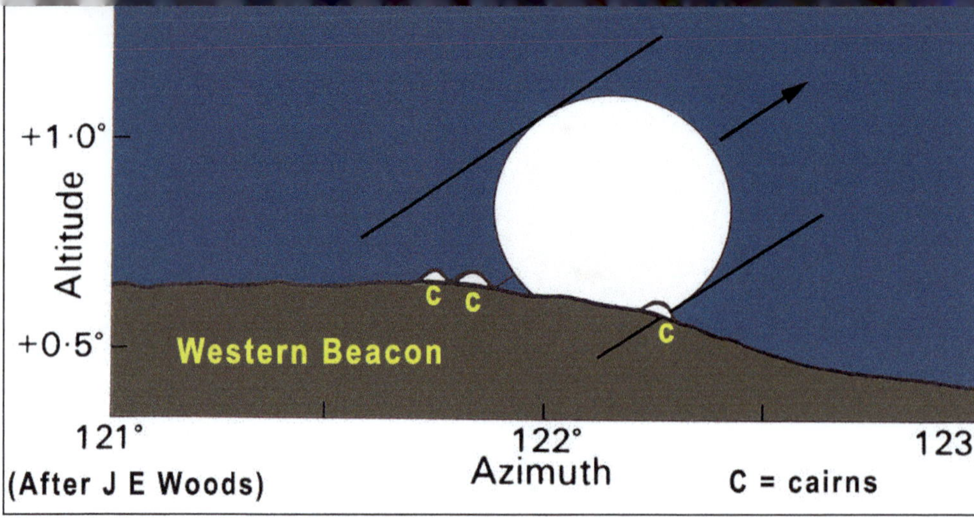

just a few minutes prior to sunset. He also noticed that all three longstones took it in turn to cast shadows down their own row! This is an excellent set of observations by Jack and shows how people were using light and shadows for calendrical purposes; perhaps the shadows cast down the rows also had symbolic significance. I will dip into Jack's work later on.

John Edwin Wood, in *Sun, Moon and Standing Stones',* also looked at astronomical alignments of Merrivale, particularly in relation to skyline features. He also describes lunar alignments at a former stone circle at Cholwichtown, destroyed in 1964 by china clay works; he calculated that every 18½ years, when viewed from this circle, the moon, at the southern lunar standstill, would rise out of three cairns on the summit of Western Beacon (654576), 6.5km distant **(above)**. Wood also describes two lunar alignments involving a circle setting at Lower Piles (646602). These involve the moon setting into a natural notch at Rame head, and a major northern standstill involving Penn Beacon, 5km to the NW (Wood 1978).

However, it is worth reflecting on the fact that way back in 1872, G W Ormerod wrote a paper on how he considered the area around the Neolithic dolmen known Spinster's Rock (701908) to be an astronomical observatory. He noted a series of concentric circles and avenues of stones west of the dolmen, one avenue of which aligned with it. His map **(below)**, also includes stones observed by two other gentlemen antiquarians. A Mr Polwhele saw the stones in 1793, describing the complex as, '... a sacred way, and two rows of pillars and several columnar circles'. Depending on the accuracy of the map, solstice alignments may also be inferred. The stones were later removed for building purposes. These early antiquarians believed it to be a Druid observatory; the local village is Drewsteignton, which means, *'Druid's Town on the Teign'.*

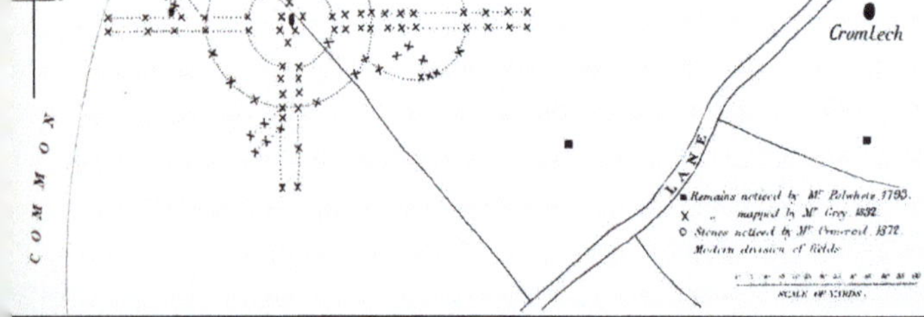

On my many pilgrimages across Dartmoor, I have invariably had my compass with me. But this is not just to assist me should I get lost, but also to help me ascertain the azimuths of landscape features and monuments regarding possible astronomical alignments. I would like to share some with you here. Some are created by locating monuments in relation to certain tors, so the sun or moon rises or sets over them at certain times of the year or lunar cycle. I have also surmised that some of the natural holes, gullies and crevices I have encountered on tor outcrops may have been ritually used when the light of the sun or moon entered them. This is ongoing research, save to say that a rock tunnel on Rough Tor, Bodmin, lets in moonlight at major standstills.

From the propped stone on Lower Hartor Tor **(images p. 110 & 111)**, the midsummer sun sets over Higher Hartor Tor, which is on the skyline. Another propped stone is involved in a midsummer sunset alignment at Leskernick, on Bodmin (Bender et al 2007).

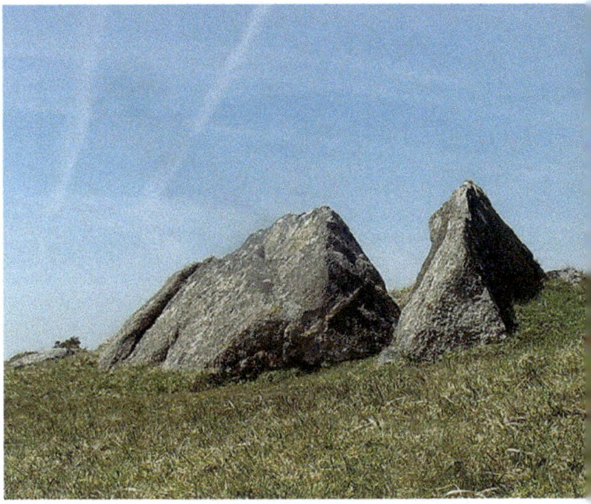

From the Brisworthy stone circle **(image p. 187)**, the equinox sun rises (due east) on the skyline in the space between Legis Tor and Hen Tor. Furthermore, when I was standing at the circle, I noticed some boulders on the skyline to the NW **(right)**. The azimuth (290°) is that of the midsummer sunset, allowance having been made for the altitude of the skyline (10°). John Michell has demonstrated how natural rocks can mark astronomical alignments, such as a hill-crest boulder on South Uist, which marks the midwinter solstice sunrise from a nearby barrow (Michell 1989). Jack Walker noted alignments marked by natural rocks at Hingston Hill. I think there may well be many more astronomically aligned 'natural' stones awaiting discovery across the moor.

From the re-erected longstone on Piles Hill **(top image p. 156)**, one gets a fine view of the outcrops and cairns on Ugborough Beacon. From this longstone, the moon at major standstill rises over the Beacon; at no other time can it do this as viewed from this longstone. Did this determine the location of this particularly tall stone? Furthermore, as seen from the summit of Western Beacon, the midsummer sun hangs over Beacon Rocks on Ugborough Beacon shortly after rising. This point is marked by the tor cairn (tumulus on map). Cairns on Western Beacon align with this event **(top image p. 99)**.

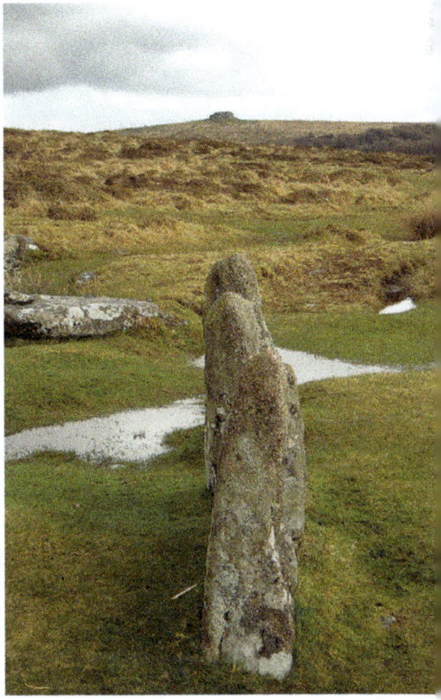

The Hawk's Tor propped stone **(images p. 112-4)** opens up to the SW, enabling midwinter sunsets to be observable.

Scorhill is one of the most popular of Dartmoor's stone circles **(image p. 186)**. In that image Kestor Rocks can be seen on the skyline towards the right. The outcrop is at an azimuth of 137-138° from the circle, which, allowing for an altitude of approximately 4°, means the midwinter sunrise should rise over the outcrop. On previous visits I had noted how three stones of the circle aligned to the tor, which I thought was significant **(right)**. This tor is a sacred site, with several rock basins on its summit. Was this one of the reasons Scorhill was located here, so the midwinter sun could rise over Kestor? I have had two tries at confirming this alignment and the best I have managed is this image **(top left, next page)**, taken on December 20th, 2015. The sun has already risen and is clearly to the right of the tor. I would welcome observations of the midwinter sunrise for

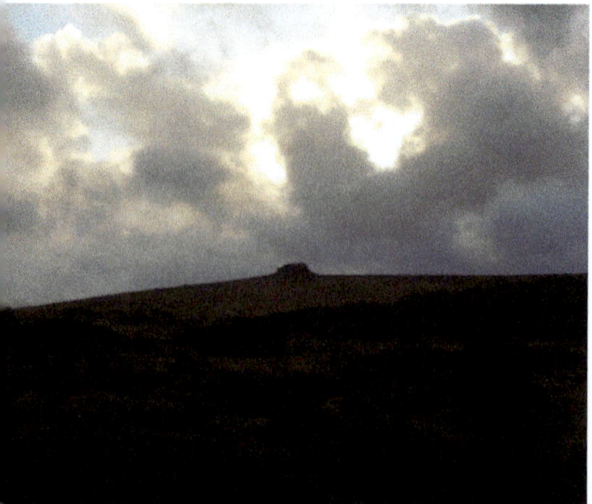

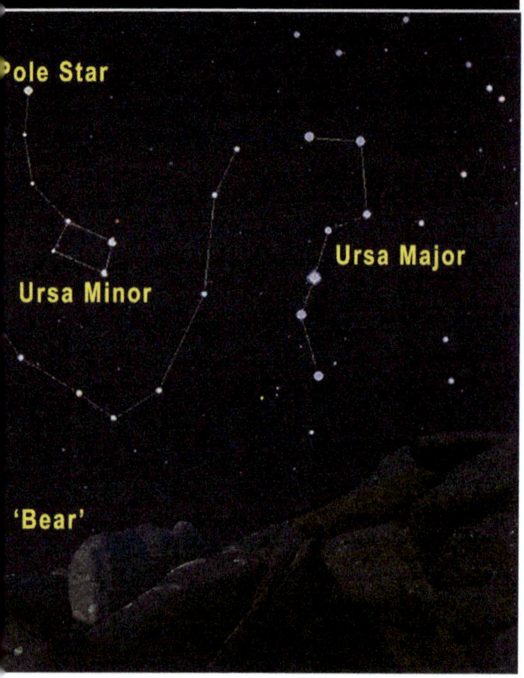

future editions. This complements a study by J Barnatt showing evidence for 13 solar alignments between six stone circles and six prominent tors on Bodmin. Brown Willy, for instance, marks equinox and midsummer alignments depending from which circle it is viewed. From the Stannon stone circle the May Day sun rises through a cleft on Rough Tor (Barnatt 1982).

The azimuth from the Black Tor logan stone and simulacrum **(top images p. 107)** to Leeden Tor is 270°**,** or due west. This is the sunset at equinox; I suspect people may have once taken note of such an alignment, even if it is 'natural'. Also at Black Tor, I noticed how Brent Tor is visible due to a dip in the intervening skyline: at 310° azimuth this is close to the midsummer sunset.

You may recall the 'bear' simulacrum at Over Tor **(images p. 175-6)**. I have been up to the tor during the night, but not under clear skies. After one visit, Sue Wallace asked me if the simulacrum was facing the constellation of Ursa Major, or the Great Bear (the bear is her totem animal). I followed this lead. The bear on the tor is facing NE, and is looking slightly up to the heavens. And, sure enough, for much of the winter months, the stars of Great Bear (or the Plough) are in that direction, coming into alignment with the bear's head earlier each night **(left)**. The Little Bear, (Ursa Minor), would be visible to the north all through the year. The scene here is around 10pm, January 23, 1500 BC.

The rock bear also faces the midsummer sunrise, looking up to the higher skyline over which the sun rises at that time. I believe that it is possible that our distant ancestors, with their profound knowledge of the heavens and their grasp on mythology and symbolism, may have made this connection. The landscape, the stars, and Man in harmony.

Hingston Hill

In *'Dartmoor Sun'*, Jack Walker records his observations of the midsummer sunrise at Hingston Hill circle and stone row **(images p. 150-2)**. As the sun rose at midsummer the shadows of the three largest stones (where the stone row meets the cairn circle) would be cast on the next one – each was a gnomon. The shadow of the large standing stone nearest to the cairn was cast into the centre of it. Furthermore, as the sun continued to rise, part of the stone row was aligned with it, and each smaller stone cast their own shadows in such a way that they just reached the next stone at ground level. The spacing between them is immaculate! He also demonstrated that later, as midsummer morning proceeded, more alignments took place using shadows. Similar shadow effects have been found for the Heelstone at Stonehenge and with the former

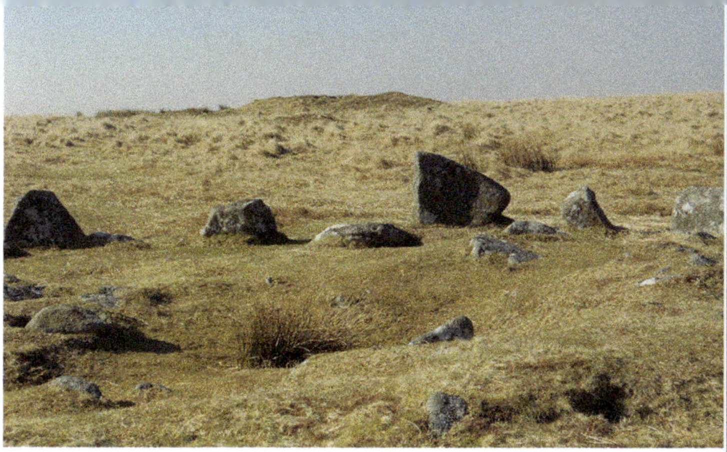

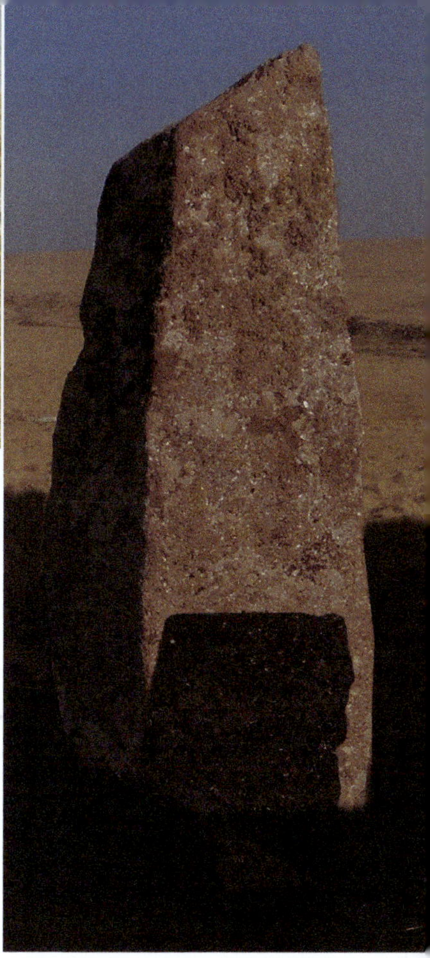

Obelisk at Avebury. Later on in the day at Hingston, a nearby cairn is positioned in such a place that it marks the midsummer sunset when viewed from the cairn circle; this cairn is an obvious feature on the skyline when viewed from the circle **(above)**.

Midwinter sunset is marked by one of the cairn circle stones acting as a gnomon, casting a shadow on the tallest stone of the stone row **(right)**. This midwinter sun sets into a small tor on Hingston Hill, when viewed from the main terminal megalith. Hingston Hill is an amazing place at which to demonstrate how our ancestors were in tune with not just the landscape, but also the movements of the sun.

Merrivale and the skies

In Chapter 13, I described the wondrous landscape around the Merrivale prehistoric complex, and how monuments were positioned to be in sync with the landscape **(map p. 178)**. As elsewhere, the people here were also looking to the skies, and accurately building their sites to reflect their knowledge of celestial events.

Alexander Thom (1967) noted that the Longstone at Merrivale is almost exactly due south from the stone circle, making it a good midday meridian marker; when the longstone's shadow points to the centre of the circle then the sun is due south. John Edwin Wood did the first accurate surveying and sacred geometry of the Merrivale monument (Wood 1978), in which he noted alignments to tors. In terms of my studies, I was delighted that he insightfully calculated that, in the Late Neolithic and Early Bronze

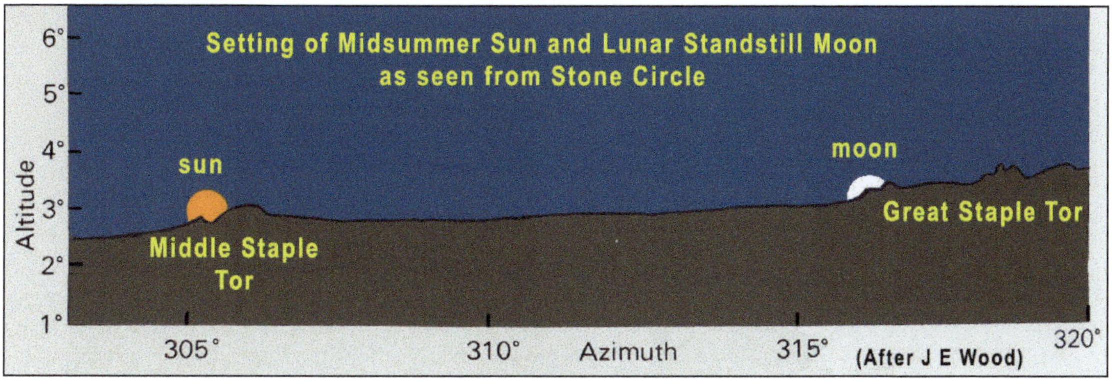

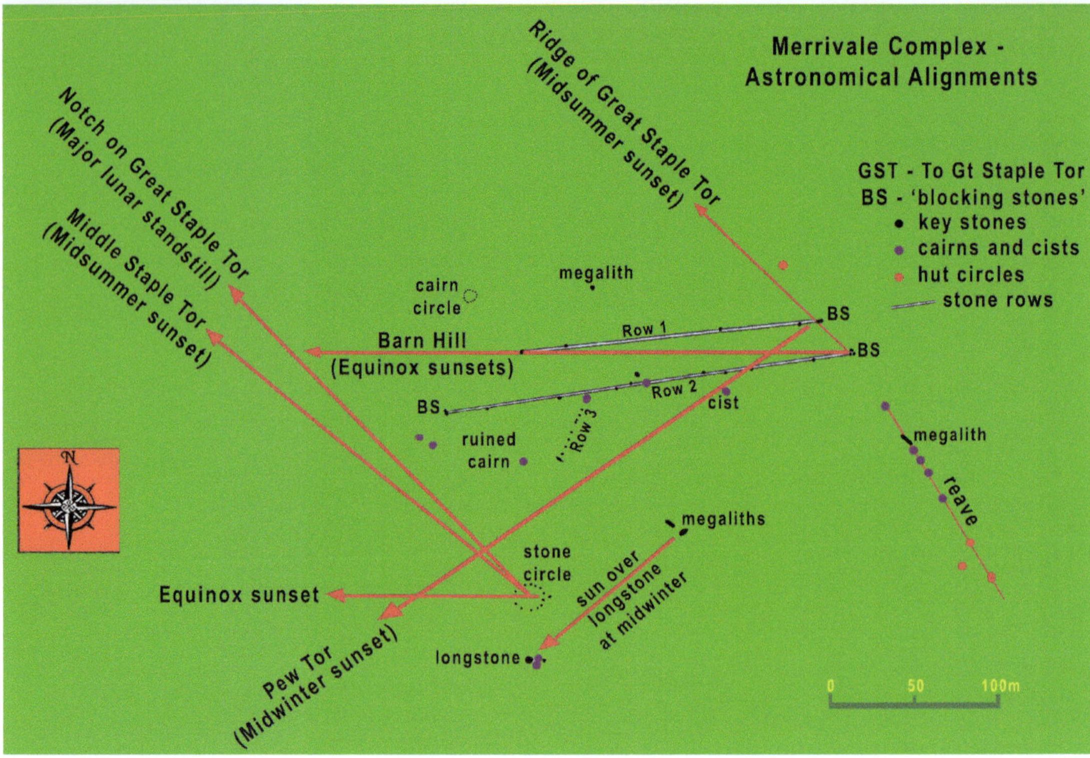

Age, Middle Staple Tor marked the midsummer solstice when viewed from the stone circle **(bottom image, previous page)**, and that moonset at the major lunar standstill (the most northerly the moon can rise and set every 18.61 years), was exquisitely marked by a notch in a small outcrop on the south part of Great Staple Tor (seen to the left of image on p. 35). Our ancestors even made allowances for the height of the skyline when positioning the stone circle.

The map above shows most of the astronomical alignments worked out by Jack Walker, John Wood and myself. It can be compared to the similar map on p. 178. Some tor alignments remain, whilst others are added involving monuments. From the onset, I must stress that the images do not do justice to the profound experiences. To stand in the places of ancestors as the sun goes down and the moon rises is awe inspiring. For as I watch these events unfold, I know that someone else was watching the same scenes unfold long ago. This time is liminal, as the day passes into night, light to dark, distant views submitting to the all-consuming darkness of night.

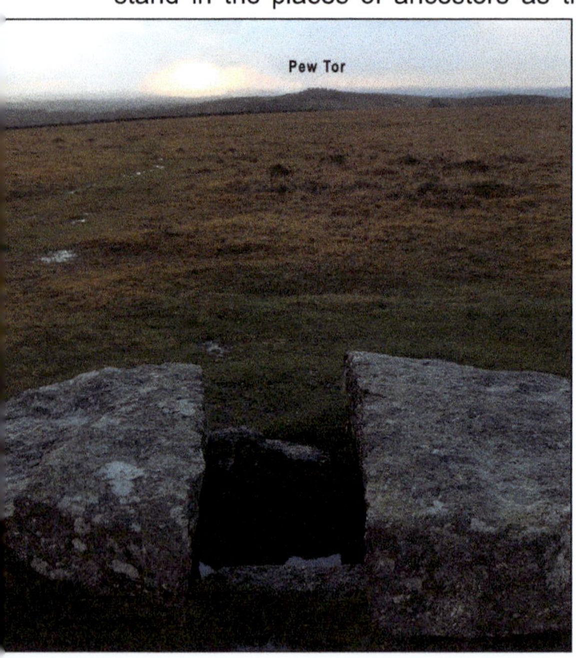

At midwinter, the sun sets into the southern slopes of Pew Tor, which is aligned with the east end of Row 1 and the cist **(map above)**. I captured this event myself on December 20, 2015; this is the view from the cist **(left)**. Jack Walker also noted how one of the megaliths NE of the Longstone is the place to stand to get the midwinter sun hovering over the Longstone prior to its setting. I took my shots of the sun over the Longstone a few weeks later in January. The sun was already moving north along the skyline, now setting into the summit stacks of Pew Tor. This phallic stone was casting long shadows which I measured to around 50m. This moment will remain with me forever; there was a dusting of snow underfoot, as the sun god seemingly paused, balanced on the tip of the Longstone **(right)**. An alchemical fusion of sunlight and granite.

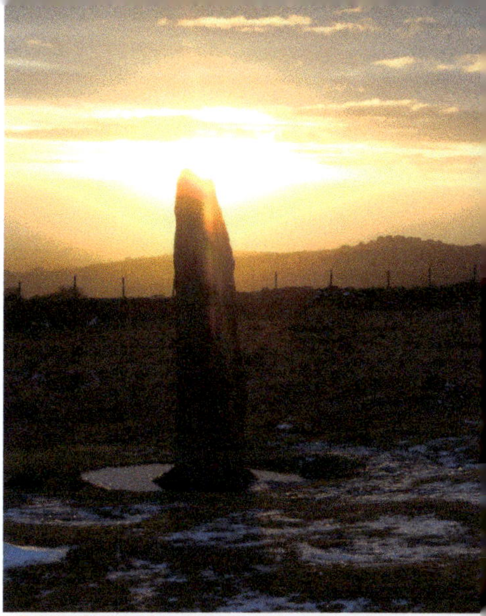

Jack Walker also insightfully observed that, around midwinter, shadows were cast on to the blocking stones at the east end of both Row 1 and 2, by the next stone in the row, which acted as gnomons. This effect was seen at Hingston Hill. I was fortunate to capture the Merrivale phenomena myself **(centre)**. I found that the effect continues for a while, for I saw the shadows on the blocking stones in mid-January. By equinox, it is a different set of stones that are now casting shadows on to the blocking stones. The whole arrangement works as a calendar.

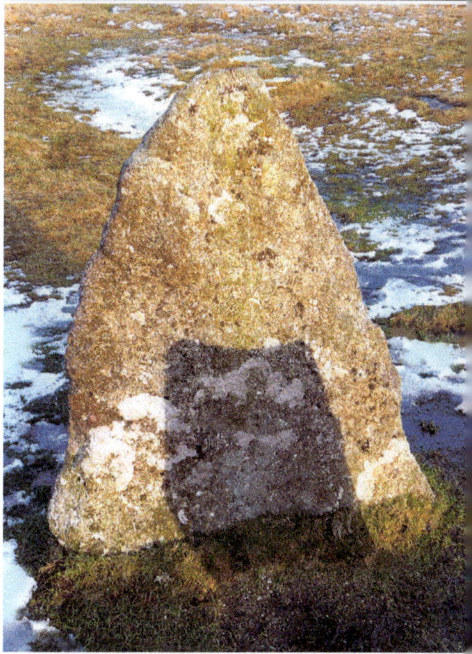

Around Imbolc, the early February fire festival, the sun sets in the vicinity Vixen Tor. On occasions, the huge simulacrum seemed to be announcing the sunset – overseeing it. It will be seen that a line drawn from the west end of Row 1 and the east end of Row 2 exactly aligns with the equinox sunsets, in March and September each year. I took the next image on March 17, 2016, from the west end of Row 1, to show how the rows are not equinox aligned in themselves, and how the sun at this time sets into Barn Hill **(bottom right image)**.

It was at equinox that I also recorded the sun setting in line with the stone circle and the small outlier just east of it **(below left)**. From here the sun still sets into Barn Hill, but to the left of the summit. The stone that is the foresight for the alignment (shaped like a moon-gazing hare, below the sun) has a long axis that points to the blocking stones at the west end of Row 2. From this stone circle the top of Vixen Tor exactly

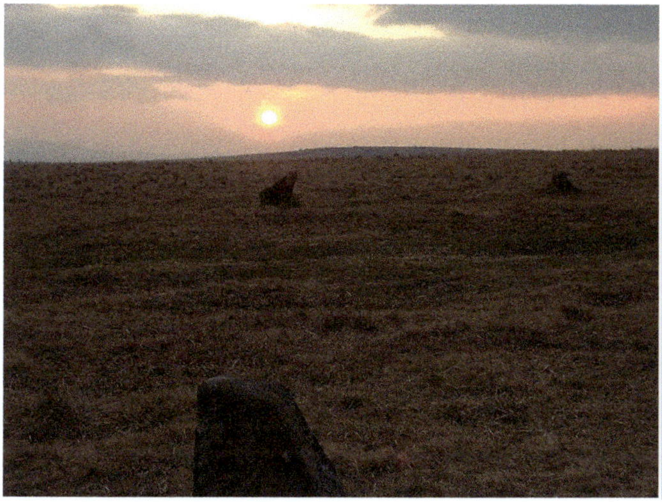

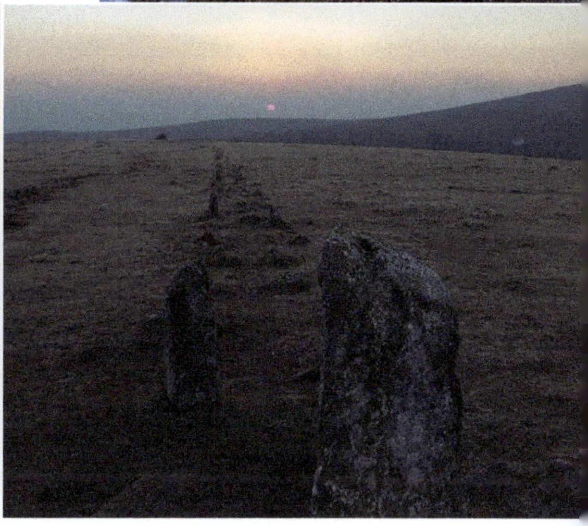

coincides with a dip/saddle north of Pew Tor, and appears to rise out of the valley as one walks west from the circle.

At around the midsummer solstice, the sun sets into the skyline ridge just to the left of the main stacks of Great Staple Tor (see Walker 2005 – recommended!). The triangular blocking stone of row 2 and the first two stones of Row 1 align with this event. Shadows from the blocking stones of Row 1 reach across the ground like fingers, pointing to the triangular blocking stone. But, once again, things change over very short distances. Observing the midsummer sunset from the stone circle back in prehistory, the sun set into Middle Staple Tor **(see lower image p. 201, and map p. 202)**. The setting point now is only slightly different to what our ancestors observed back in the Bronze Age.

What is evident is that Merrivale is to do with marking *sunsets,* rather than sunrises, although that is not to say that these were not honoured.

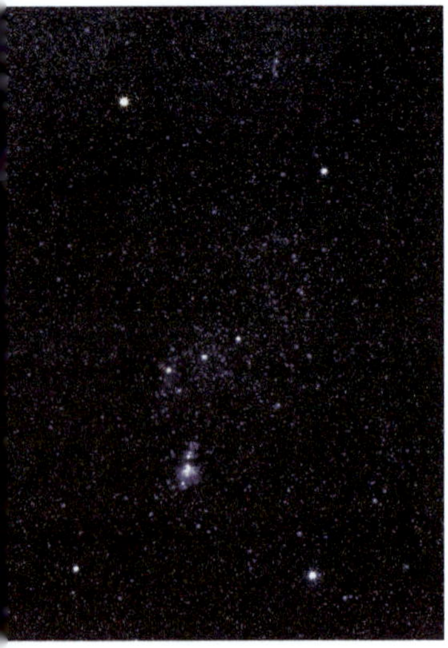

Orion

As for the azimuths of the two stone rows themselves, I think they may be in alignment with where Orion **(left)** was setting c.2500-2000 BC. Before that, in the Early Neolithic, most of the 'Hunter' configuration was setting to the south, but by the Bronze Age the constellation was setting further north, and more stars were aligning with the stone rows. This large constellation would have set into Pew Tor and over Vixen Tor at this time. It is the brightest constellation in the sky, and dominates winter skies, and I have shown elsewhere that Orion was involved in myths and alignments across the ancient world (Knight 2011, 2013). Orion's Belt is said to be mirrored on Earth by the layout of Thornborough Henges and the Giza pyramids. At around this time, Taurus the Bull was also hanging over the western horizon prior to it setting into Barn Hill.

Experiencing

Although it is to be applauded that our prehistoric ancestors worked out the movements of sun, moon and stars, it must be remembered that they did so by sitting out on the landscape, for years on end. But not just observing, but also experiencing. The breathtaking beauty of a red sunrise, or the spellbinding sight of the moon as it rises over a tor, must have moved them, as it does us today. I urge readers to experience these liminal moments between day and night and, indeed, to walk the moor under darkness. A kindred spirit, Jim Hamer, who lives on the moor, has told me how he annually watches the sunrise at the midsummer solstice from the top of Kestor Rocks. He tells me that quite a few people gather there now, and that it is a powerful and moving event to witness. This image was taken by him on one such gathering; the light of the sky is reflected waters of the rock basins **(left)**. At moments like this one can feel the heavens, the Earth and ourselves aligned by some force much greater than the sum of its parts.

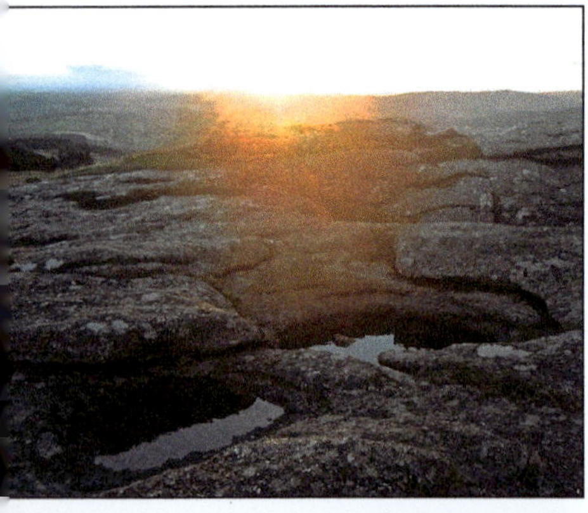

'Hello darkness, my old friend,
I've come to talk with you again'
(Simon and Garfunkel)

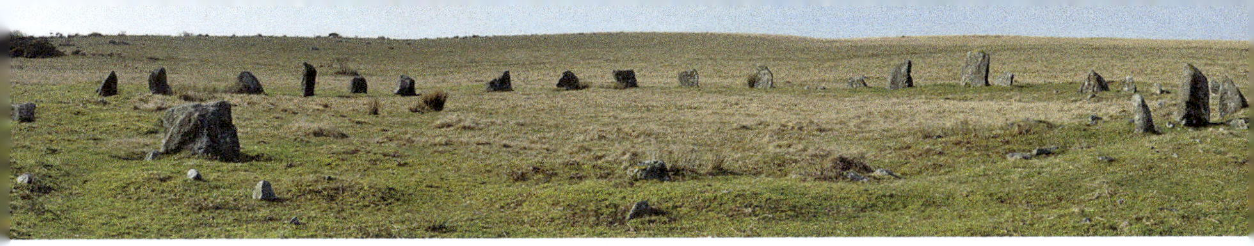

17. Earth Energies - the Pulse of the Land

'The mysterious earth-currents which thrill the clay in our bodies'
(Rudyard Kipling, *Kim.*)

Aboriginal cultures believe that there is a life-force, a spirit, which permeates the land. This is often personified as a dragon or serpent, myths of which go back thousands of years. Detecting these forces through dowsing is an ancient science, where the object of the exercise has often been to locate underground water. Today, this ancient practice has undergone a renaissance, and one of the areas where it has flourished is the dowsing at ancient sites. Dowsers have even been invited to archaeological excavations, where their efforts can save much time and money, and reveal that which is normally unseen and may have even been missed. Today, farmers still employ dowsers, or water diviners, to locate a new water supply.

I have been a dowser for over 20 years and can confirm the value of dowsing as a tool for unravelling our heritage. People who develop sensitivities to earth energies can delve into new levels of knowledge at sacred sites, as they tap into the very forces that our ancestors interacted with thousands of years ago. I have included dowsing in this book because the general premise has been to *experience* the landscape holistically, using every sensory experience at our disposal. Dowsing with rods or pendulums, or by simply 'tuning in' to a place, has been, for me, a vital element of connecting with Dartmoor. Shamans who once walked the moor had greater sensitivities than we do today; they lived and breathed the moor, developing a level of connectedness that can only be found today in aboriginal cultures. Dowsing can help bridge the gap.

Dowsing Dartmoor

'Developing a relationship with these places of power is the goal.'
(James Endredy 2002)

Way back in 1937, Scottish mystic and antiquarian J Foster Forbes suggested, in a BBC radio interview, that the quartz-rich rocks comprising stone circles were designed to attract the Earth's electrical and magnetic currents, which were then accumulated in nearby tors on Dartmoor (*in* Michell 1989). Master dowser Guy Underwood came to Dartmoor and wrote of his findings (Underwood 1972). He mapped the energies at Spinster's Rock at Drewsteignton **(images p. 14 and 198)**. He found the dolmen to be located above a blind spring or energy node, as well as be the focus for six concentric circles of dowsable energy. This is in common with the findings of dowsers across the world, who have likewise found dolmens to be energy foci.

Underwood also suggests that natural features, such as rock basins, balanced stones, and notable boulders, are part of the landscape energy matrix, of which our ancestors would have been well aware. He also found that the gullies present at most tors are channels for, '... the passage of geodetic lines', considering that tor summits are foci for energies. I have dowsed this effect at gullies on Roos Tor, as well as powerful energies coming out of the rock shelter on that tor **(image p. 169)**; the band of energy was the width of the huge boulder above the shelter, and its energy flowed away with the rainwater rivulets.

Perhaps this is what lies behind heightened sensitivities and strange sensations that so many people on my tours comment on. Is this the ethereal element behind the beliefs of ancient people that high places were the abode of gods and ancestral spirits? And did people think that strange lights seen at such places were otherworldy beings? Triboluminescence is a phenomena in which light is generated when chemical bonds of minerals in a rock are scratched or rubbed together; light can be emitted from fractured crystals when under stress through friction, such as along fault lines. The Native American Ute of Colorado made rattles filled with quartz crystals. These emitted light when rattled (visible in night ceremonies). Aborigines see quartz tools as being particularly potent (Tilley 1994). Could the synthesis of earth lights, radiation, magnetism, and the presence of quartz, all have contributed to the ancient mystique of the granite tors of Dartmoor. Paul Devereux has produced a good summary of the study of these *'earth lights'* (Devereux 1990). He cites many examples of strange light phenomena near to fault lines, granite outcrops, localities sacred to the local indigenous, and places that have fairy folklore. Lights reported near Ashburton in 1898, were described as 'of a phosphorescent nature... auroral displays'. In 1915, strange lights were reported in the vicinity of the old tin mine at Hexworthy, east of Princetown, which roused the interest of the military. Light phenomena were also reported around Drizzlecombe in 1981 (Devereux 1990): 'Earth lights phenomena haunt specific terrains: faulted geology, mountain peaks and ridges, bodies of water and areas of mineral deposits' (Devereux 1989). Dartmoor ticks all these boxes!

Underwood found that Dartmoor's rock basins mark 'geodetic nodes' and that the energy exits the basins via the channels that are often present. At Rippon Tor and Kestor Rocks I dowsed spirals of energy coming up from the basins.

Underwood saw the balanced, or logan, stones as being as important as standing stones and considered they may have been, '... deliberately sited with reference to the geodetic pattern'. It is interesting that work on balanced rocks and propped stones in the USA has shown that huge propped stones supported by blocks of white quartz stones are positioned over magnetic anomalies (Burke and Halberg 2005).

Guy Underwood also comments on huge sloping boulders, called *rostra,* he found below Vixen Tor; he found them to mark blind springs. Turning to monuments, he dowsed that stone rows often marked important looping energy flows. He cites a, 'good but short example' at Cowsic Bridge, near Two Bridges. He comments on rows that consist of 'wavy lines', and cites Merrivale as being two rows where the energies vary with the lunar cycle. I have noted the sinuous aspect of several stone rows on Dartmoor, and dowsing has confirmed the serpentine nature of their energy flows. Are we picking up what mythologies speak of in terms of mythical serpents?

If Dartmoor has a claim to fame in the dowsing world it is probably because the St Michael Line traverses the northern stretches of the moor. This famous alignment runs across England from Cornwall to East Anglia. The seminal work on the line is, '*The Sun and the Serpent*' (Miller and Broadhurst 1989), which traces its course of almost 400 miles. Two dowsable flows of energy were found to follow the axis of the alignment, like the twin serpents of a caduceus (Knight 2015). The Mary current flows through churches dedicated to St Mary or other female saints, as well as through springs and wells; the Michael flow generally goes through churches dedicated to male dragon-slaying saints, such as St Michael and St George.

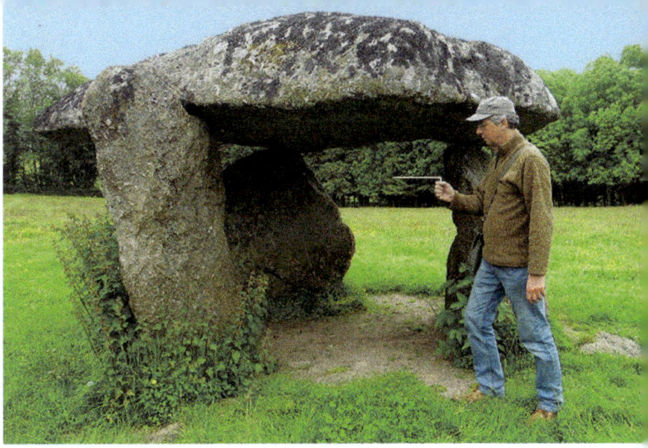

On Dartmoor, the Mary current courses through Brent Tor, Mary Tavy, across the open moor to the churches at Gidleigh and Throwleigh, then on to Spinster's Rock, vacating the area via Castle Drago and Fingle Bridge. The Michael energies go through Brent Tor, Lydford, Yes Tor, the Nine Stones, Belstone Tor and exits the moor heading off towards Hittisleigh. Cosdon Hill marks the actual axis of the St Michael Line. I have dowsed the Mary current at Spinster's Rock on several occasions **(above)**. There is a powerful energy spiral under the capstone. By comparison, I have also dowsed an energy spiral/node at the entrance of the propped stone 'dolmen' on Hawk's Tor **(images p. 112-4)**.

As this study is primarily focused on the relationship between monuments and tors, I decided to check out the results of Miller and Broadhurst concerning the Michael flow between the Nine Stones cairn circle and Belstone Tor **(image p. 185 & 190)**. Carol Stone and I dowsed the Michael energy as it flowed into, through, and out of the cairn circle, where we marked the flow with sticks, coloured red here for clarity **(below left)**. We then followed the current up Belstone Tor, along the ridge **(below right)**, from where it descended and left for the open moor to the east. It was this dowsing that lead

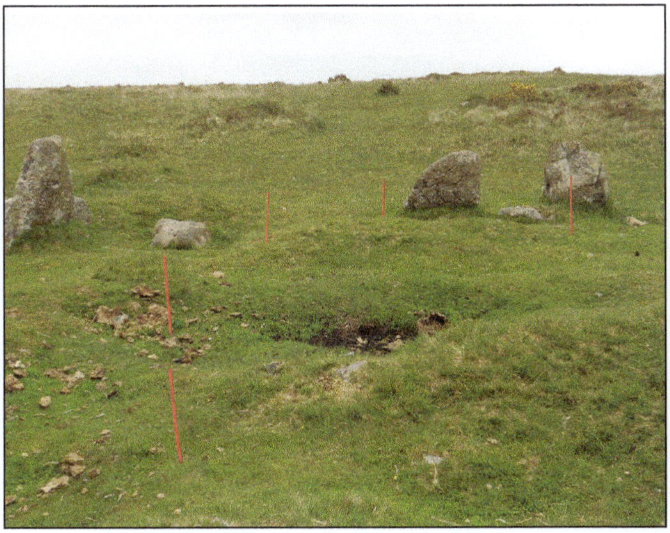

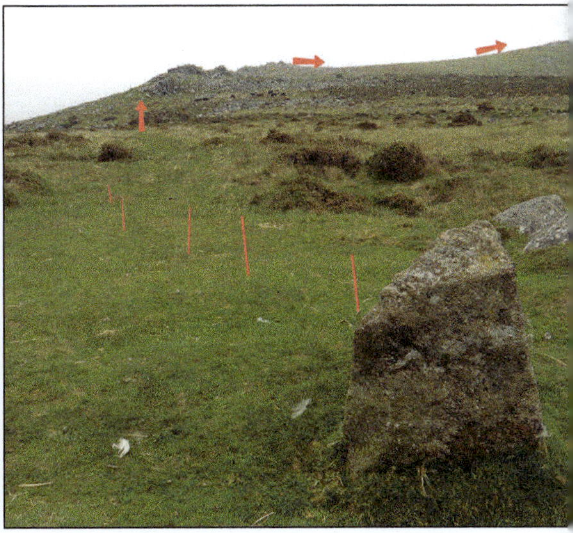

to the discovery of the propped stone on Belstone Tor **(image p. 114)**; I have found that when I walk the moor with an open, enquiring mind, being receptive to what may unfold, then anything can happen, and often far beyond expectations.

It has been stone rows that have attracted the avid attention of dowsers over the years. They have readily felt the flows of energy that are channelled by the stones, and maintain that the serpentine nature of many rows is down to the builders following these energies. Guy Underwood found an association between underground and overground energy flows at stone rows (Underwood 1972). On the Mid Atlantic

Geomancy website, dowser Sig Lonegren speaks of dowsing the Merrivale stone rows: 'There's at least one vein of water flowing underneath each stone in both pairs of rows. I find this at all of the rows on Dartmoor that I've dowsed, They follow different patterns at different rows. Some work like a braided pattern. At the longer pair of stone rows at Merrivale, veins of primary water snake back and forth down the rows'. This seems to confirm the findings of Guy Underwood. Lonegren also found that blind springs were absent in the settlement nearest the rows. However, he did find that the hut circle nearest the rows *did* have energies coming up. His perception was that this hut was that of a female priest/shaman. I had suspected this on my visits.

Carol Stone and I also dowsed the Shovel Down stone rows and the longstone (660857). As we proceeded down the avenue of stones, the varying width of the space between the two rows had the effect of altering the width of our auras. The energies were flowing down slope, as if leading us down to the North Teign River. At the cairn circle (659861), we dowsed energies spiralling into the centre of the eroded mound, channelled by the remaining small stones **(bottom image p. 189)**.

At the Drizzlecombe stone rows, Sue Wallace and I did a detailed mapping of the energies. The energies primarily flowed southwest, down slope, in all rows on the day of our visit **(map p. 147)**. The sinuous nature of the rows was directing the flow across the landscape. Sue dowsed around the huge Giant's Basin, finding that energy was flowing into it from Row 1 and 2; one of these flows came from the longstone at the SW end of Row 2. At this stone I felt a 'happy bubble' consume me. The centre of Giant's Basin was marked by anticlockwise spiralling energy. We also noted that there are lots of reeds around cairns 1, 2 and 3, but none around cairn 4, which is one not at the end of a stone row. To us, it seemed that the reeds were a sign of underground water, associated with the energies we dowsed down the stone rows. All of these cairns had anti-clockwise spirals on them, as at Giant's Basin. It is interesting that I dowsed anticlockwise energy spiralling on cairns at Corndon Down and Water Hill, and that two of the cairns on Cox Tor similarly had anticlockwise spirals. Guy Underwood called these 'left hand spirals', and thought them to be 'primary spirals' marking blind springs. He thought such a place to be, '... the esoteric centre of the Old Religion, as well as being the actual centre of its monument' (Underwood 1972).

I dowsed the Brisworthy Stone Row in May 2016 **(images p. 155)**. Where stones get fewer at the north end, I saw that a line of reeds could be followed, marking blind springs, filling the gaps. Amazingly, there were lines of animal dung marking the denuded row. Dowsers have known for a long time that animals are very sensitive to energy flows, congregating at places that feel good. Energy was flowing down slope, which is what I had found at the Hurston Ridge row.

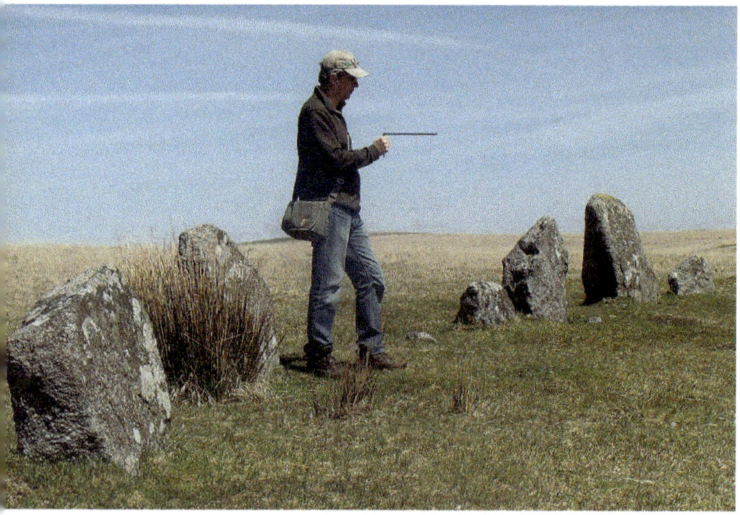

At the nearby Brisworthy stone circle **(image p. 187 & 205)**, the two largest stones on the north side were an energy doorway, into which energy was dowsed coming into the circle, seen here to the right hand side of the image **(left)**. I dowsed that this was coming from the stone row and cairn circle to the north. Energy was also flowing around the stone circle itself, which is often the case.

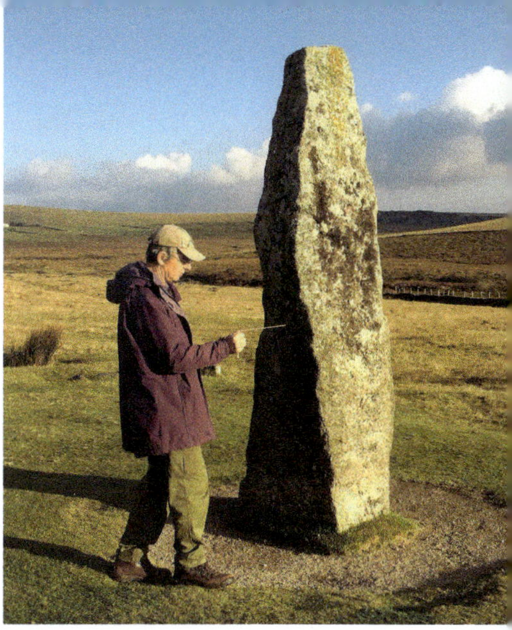

At the Hart Tor stone rows, just east of Black Tor, SW of Princetown **(images p. 153)**, I dowsed that the energies were flowing up one row and back down the other. There were lots of blind springs/nodes around the two cairns at the ends of the rows, and the energies from the rows carried on up the hill beyond. I felt energy was being drawn to the cairns and then directed down the rows to the river. I sat at the end of one row **(centre image p. 153)** and felt as if I was about to be sucked down the rows to the river below – like riding down in a water flume! The energies were palpable.

Sometimes dowsing can detect the 'energy imprint' of that which has gone from the physical. Sue Wallace dowsed that the stone row at Hingston Hill **(images 150-2)** once continued beyond the present NE terminus, and that it may have extended up the slope to the cairn (593694). If this was once the case, and that former stones have been removed, it could explain why there are no large blocking stones or a cairn at this end of the present terminus.

On several occasions I have dowsed around the Merrivale complex with friends, and groups I have led. It really has everything for the novice to try out regarding dowsing - – stone rows, a stone circle, megaliths and more. Walking down the avenues of stones is a powerful experience, partly due to the energies in which one is immersed. Dowsing around the Longstone **(above and map p. 178)** has revealed that it is attracting energy from across the landscape, and that it is 'in conversation' with the stone circle nearby. An energy flow can be detected from the Longstone, through the remains of the cairn nearby, and on to the fallen longstone to the east; a blind spring spiral marks the damaged cairn. On one occasion I sat with my back on the triangular blocking stone at east end of Row 1. Looking down the sinuous rows, I felt as if I was being physically pulled down the avenue – it was like looking down a tunnel. The effect was so powerful that I felt dizzy. I also sensed subtle energy coming towards me eastwards up the avenue of stones, which were plunging into the earth through the blocking stone, and through me! The energies were being grounded, and so was I.

I have found dowsing to be an essential element of my connecting with the landscape, and with my ancestors who walked it. I am always eager to help others experience these mysterious forces, as shown here at Merrivale **(right)**.

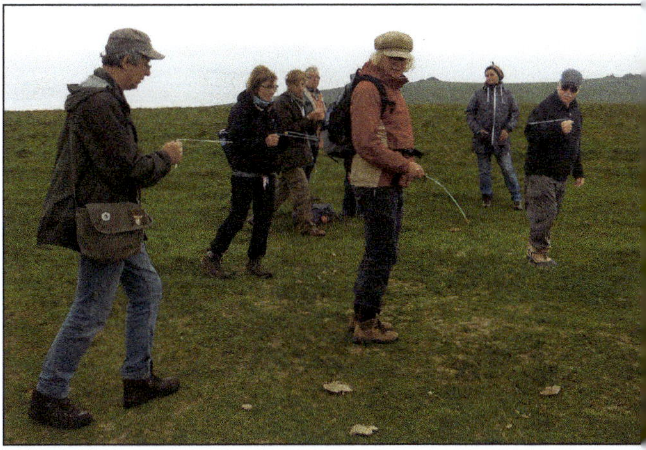

'The dragon shall be in the tumulus, old, rich in treasures.'
(Beowulf)

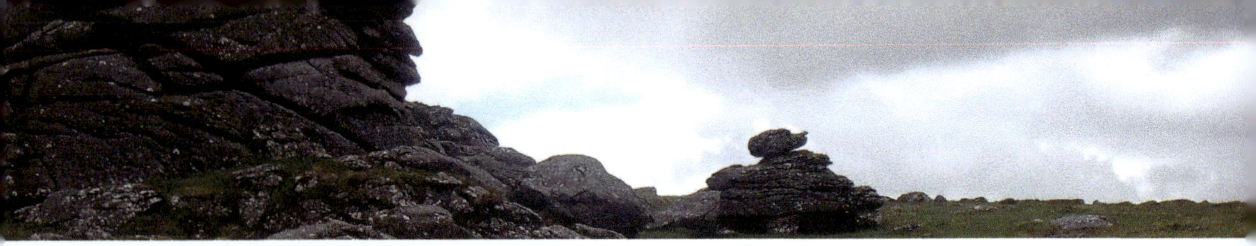

18. Open Hearted Moor

'If Nature is your teacher, your soul will awaken'
(Goethe's *Faust*)

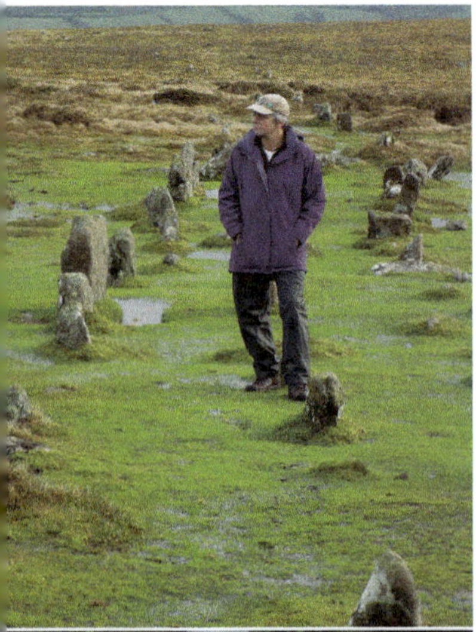

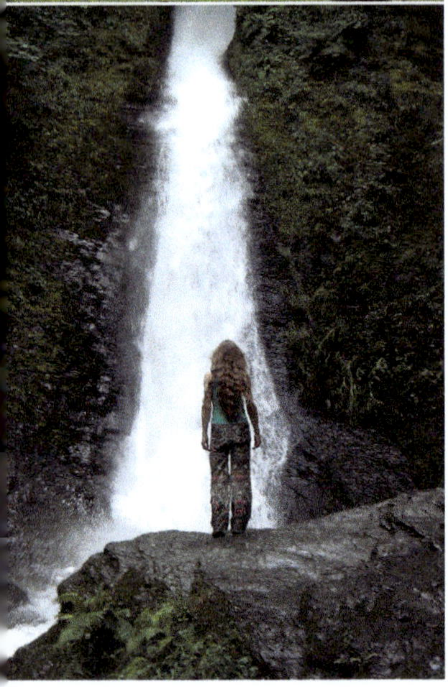

This book has not been so much a guide to the prehistoric wonders of Dartmoor, but rather a new way of seeing, of experiencing, of being. The premise has been that by mindfully communing with the land we can get some inkling of how our ancestors lived there, and of the nature and purpose of their monuments. This is based on the concept of phenomenology, championed by archaeologist Prof Chris Tilley, which, in my mind, is the conduit I had long waited for; it offered me a link between the world of academia and the 'alternative'. It suggests that we shift our enquiries from concentrating on the structure of monuments and sacred sites to how they may have once structured people's perceptions. The same is true of landscapes.

This has been the story of my own personal journey through Dartmoor's ancient landscape. In reality, it has mirrored my own journey of self-discovery. For going without is always a means of going within - sauntering for the soul. For walking can be revelation, the soil for visionary experience. The landscape mirrors our own moods and emotional fluctuations. Nothing is ever constant on the moor, something is always happening, changing: 'Temporality is thus at the heart of a phenomenological study' (Tilley 2010). If it rains suddenly, I do not curse my luck, but open up to different experiences. Some of my most profound moments on the moor have been when I have had rain dripping off the end of my nose, or not being able to see far beyond it! There is often a harsh beauty on the moor. The land can indeed be wild, so how do we respond to this - through fear? Or through a boundless curiosity that can take us beyond where we were, to see the world how it *really* is, and not how we have been taught it is.

The landscape is a metaphor for how we view the world; we can interpret what we experience symbolically, seeing the land as an extension of ourselves, perceiving the land as a physical body - the Great Mother. The moor is all about granite and water; the hard and the soft. Yet the soft can erode away the hardest rock.

Dartmoor landscapes possess endless mindscapes, for that's what the land is, a projection of our mind: '... each state of mind provides us with a view of nature... changing how we see the world actually changes the world for us... our worldview is actually *embodied* within us' (Devereux 1996). We have an open invitation, I believe, to stand on the weathered edge, metaphorically - and sometimes physically. Pushing beyond fears and trepidations has taken me to states of exalted emotions that I thought were impossible merely by walking, sitting, or just being. This is the perhaps the realm of the poet, but it was also the world of the prehistoric shaman, who stood on that ledge thousands of years ago, in mist, rain and fog, howling across the moor. This is the shaman who has inspired and guided me through my own fear barriers, and, when I did break through, it was *always* a profound experience. This is the way of the shaman, who hugged rocks, stood naked on rugged, windswept outcrops, plunged into icy rivers, and spent days in solitary meditation.

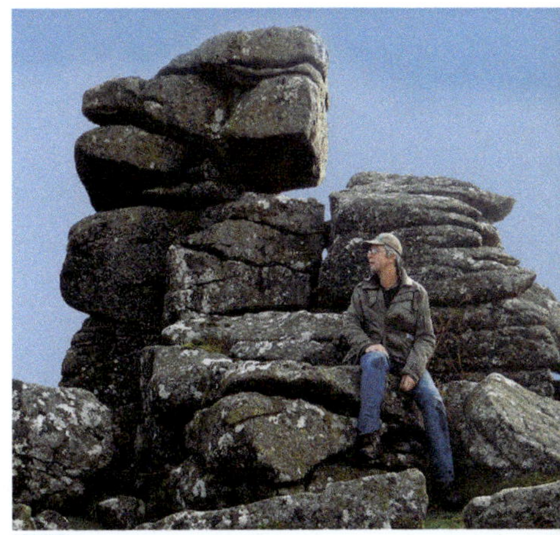

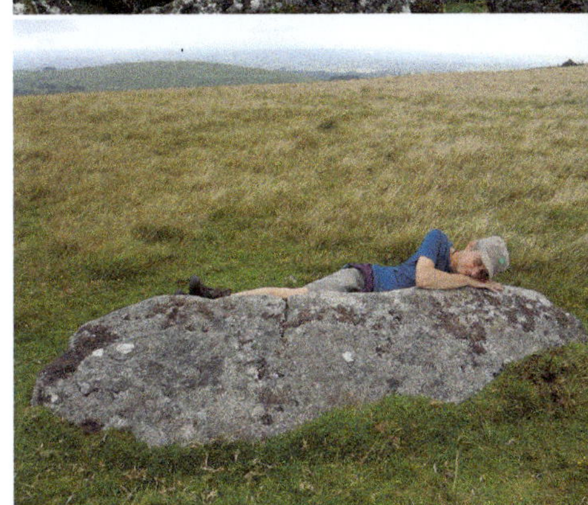

Prof Chris Tilley advocates experiential, cognitive archaeology; if we wish to find out the whys and wherefores of our ancestors' beliefs and activities, there is much we can learn by putting ourselves in their moccasins, standing and sitting where they did, like here at Figgie Daniel **(right)**, walking where they walked, and looking at sunrises and sunsets as they did – with wonder and awe. And as the "bones" of the Dartmoor landscape are essentially the same today as in the Bronze Age, we should be able to have similar physical/sensory interactions as people in the past. Then, as now, it is the experiencing of landscape through all of our senses that holds the key: 'All that the world offers as clues to its own nature is the evidence available to our senses' (Michell 1979). Perhaps to be *consciously aware* of what is being experienced is our point of power.

An open and enquiring mind is key. Ask yourself why people chose to stand where they did; what were they looking at and why? We are coaxed to immerse ourselves fully on a tor, to walk around the rock debris, to view the outcrops from different directions. What does an outcrop look like under the full moon, compared to under the midday sun? Does the tor dispense different narratives depending on which direction I approach it or walk around it – clockwise or anticlockwise? Does a simulacrum's 'expression' change as I move, and what lies in the direction it is looking? Their craggy, wizened eyes stare through the doorways of time, and so can we. I once asked myself what it would be like to lie on the earth with a fallen longstone brother? What would it be like for the stone? Everything is relative – do I touch a stone or does the stone touch me? We enjoyed the hug **(lower image)**.

Water is in our blood, literally. A close connection with water precedes our birth, in our mother's womb, and when the waters break we are born into the world. We never lose that subconscious connection with it. Water on the landscape is often heard even when it cannot be seen, possessing an acoustic depth and dimensionality of presence as it travels through places, linking them. Rain can be felt and heard if one's eyes are

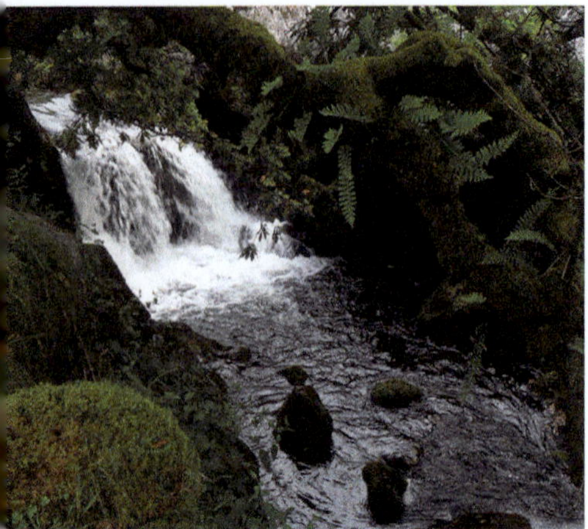

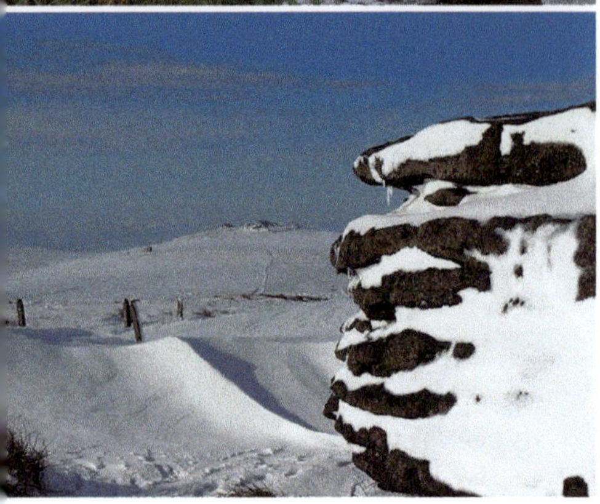

closed. The roar of a waterfall may be heard a long way off, and yet may only come into view at close range. What did this invisible roar mean to people? The White Lady at Lydford is an emotive place **(bottom image p. 210)**. My night visit there was a totally different experience compared to during the day; my other senses took over as my eyesight was impaired by the darkness. The waterfall sang and roared, as its column of light punctuated the darkness. Rivers are other places where we may get the feeling we are being watched, that fairies and pixies could step out at any moment and join you on a moss-covered rock **(left)**: 'Of all the key elements in former sacred geographies, water was perhaps the most ubiquitous' (Devereux 2013).

The range of environments that Dartmoor gifts us is endless. From thunderous waterfalls to lofty tors, from snow-covered 'Christmas card' landscapes **(left)** to jagged granite outcrops. Ancient oak forests lure us into their canopied wonderland, into scenes reminiscent of a set from *Lord of the Rings.* And, as we do all this, we may sense that the ancestors and nature spirits are close at hand.

I make no apologies to those who may feel I swing from archaeology to 'New Age', from hard evidence to myth, from good referencing to dowsing. For I have looked at Dartmoor holistically, not through the eyes of one discipline. I have trawled the internet and academic papers, as well as embodied the landscape directly. This is how it should be, to find out the whole story. And, whether we are overtly 'spiritual' or not, Dartmoor cannot be known without embracing our own facets and foibles, out there on the land. For life is not all airy-fairy; even prehistoric shamans shat in the woods!

I urge you to explore these landscapes in all weathers, at all times of the year, in rain and shine, in groups or on your own, during the day and through starry, moonlit nights. Each experience will be unique, for every Dartmoor landscape you walk is unique, as Nature gives us constant messages. The same landscape can potentially offer you a multitude of different experiences every time you venture across it. These are the mindscapes of the shaman, as we project what is within us out into the world. Tilley was right when he advocated, 'what space is depends on who is experiencing it'. We must learn to walk again, as infants learn to walk, with all our senses, mindfully, in the now, perceiving ourselves as being an element of landscape. The mind is also a landscape of sorts and walking is one way to traverse it. We are being called to totally immerse ourselves in landscapes, and to enter without prejudice or preconception. Connecting with landscape is both reciprocal and symbiotic, for as I walk along I give of myself to the landscape and it gives back. And that it is acceptable not to understand something, for this leads an enquiring mind to realms it may not have previously ventured. As soon as we try to rationalize something, we lose its purity, and potentially cease experiencing it. It is the nature of Man that understanding Nature tends to lead to our overwhelming it.

Sometimes we need to do no more than listen - for that in itself is an act of worship and honouring. When I have tuned in, I have sometimes 'received' poems and other narration. I know not from whence these come, whether from the ancestors, the spirit of place, or whether the site has triggered something within me. Communication through osmosis. The dialogue is often simple, to the point, and I am grateful for that; Nature only does what is necessary, no more, no less. The following dialogue took place when I lay on the capstone of the burial cist at Lakehead Hill **(below)**, within sight of Haytor **(image bottom left p. 82)**:

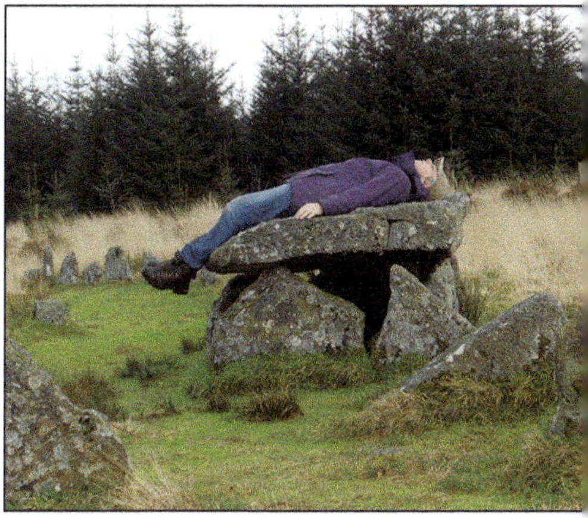

I hear:
I am table and altar
I am the altering table
Come lie on me, do not fear
The dead lay below, whilst the living persevered

I reply:
I am seeing with new eyes, as much as am able,
I will indeed recline on your granite table,
Clearing my mind, of space and time
Ever searching, ever higher I climb.
I know that long ago, others were here,
Clearing their minds of despair and fear.

It is not Keats or Wordsworth. But it is sincere communication. A connecting.
The ancestors are never far away on Dartmoor, and they have left signs across the land. Some are obvious, like stone rows and megaliths. Others less so, such as carved out rock basins, propped stones, and subtle alignments. But they left us much more than this. They left us deeper mysteries to decode; they left us part of themselves. Their presence can still be felt; their wisdom can still be requested, respectfully. This is the way of the shaman. This is the way of those who would seek life's deeper meanings, and those who feel the world is not quite as it once seemed. It is a freeing of the mind. It is also for those who wish to connect with people, long ago, who only took what they needed – no more, no less. Something inside compels us to treat the land as we once did, with respect, with gratitude. To connect with a landscape on a profound, spiritual level is a humbling experience, compelling us to re-evaluate what we class as culturally important today. To regard the land as sacred, as alive, is to go back in time thousands of years, to a time when everyone felt that way. The land is then transformed, becoming redolent with mystique, taking on a perceivable numinous quality. And when one regards the landscape as sacred, by extension one must also regard Planet Earth as sacred. And when one crosses that threshold, we feel compelled to take care of our Earth Mother as best we can. This is the way of the shaman.

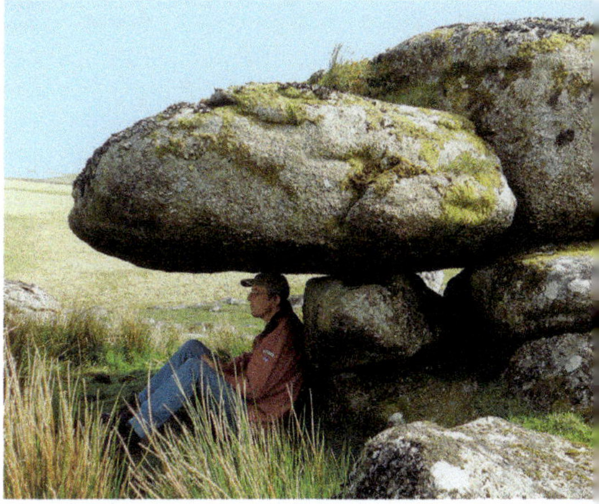

The images of the Earth from space brought back by Apollo astronauts changed things forever. On a collective consciousness level, Mankind realised that our fragile planet, hanging there in the darkness of space, was not merely a resource: 'It was as if life recognised life' (Devereux 1989). The idea that the Earth is alive seems strange to the majority today, but this was the mindset of most people until relatively

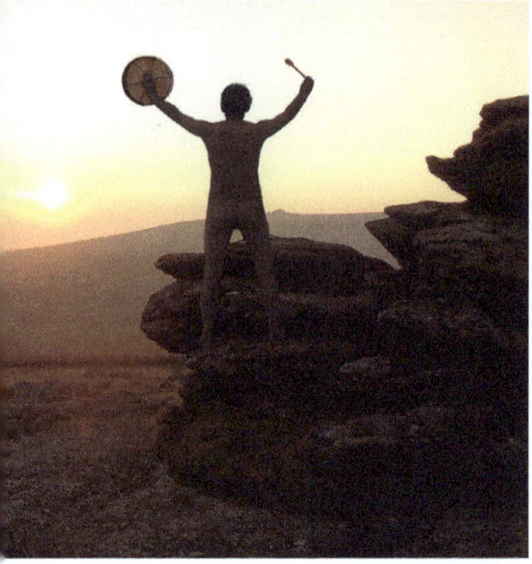

recently in Man's history. As a species we have been suffering from amnesia, a loss of memory of that which once drove our philosophies, religions, art and culture. Truths became hazy myths, landscapes becoming devoid of spiritual dimension. Those images from space, now updated regularly by the ISS, have stirred something within us, inviting us to connect with the Earth once more, to retrieve ancient awareness from the mists of time, in the nick of time. We are being invited to perceive landscapes as interfaces, saturated with cultural and mythic memory which can be accessed, like a library. As I have I said, this can result in a reciprocal and transformative communication between us and landscape; ancient cultures on Dartmoor once possessed this symbiotic relationship.

The more this project progressed, the more potent was the realisation that I was becoming umbilically linked to the land, by a thread of energy and consciousness, which was ever pulling me back to the moor. Even when carrying out day to day activities, the moor would tug at my being, at my heart, drawing me in like a fish on a line. I truly believe I have been given a hallowed gift. My heart has been opened to the beating heart of the Land. My eyes and mind are becoming less filtered, seeing glimpses of clarity at last. My path has changed from straight, predictable and safe, to one of winding blind bends and rocky uneven tracks. It truly is a road less travelled - but it is a yellow brick road. I now know that I walk the same hallowed ground as those who had gone before me thousands of years ago. And it is onto this canvas that I lay down my own story, my 'future myths'. I am not 'home' yet, but I feel I am going in the right direction. In a sense, I guess I always have been.

It is time for all of us to tread gently on the earth, in the footsteps of the ancestors, with joy, an open heart, and with new eyes through which to see. For the spirit of the land has been awaiting our return for far too long.

'The natural world is filled with mysteries that lie hidden within its very fabric.'
(James Endredy 2002)

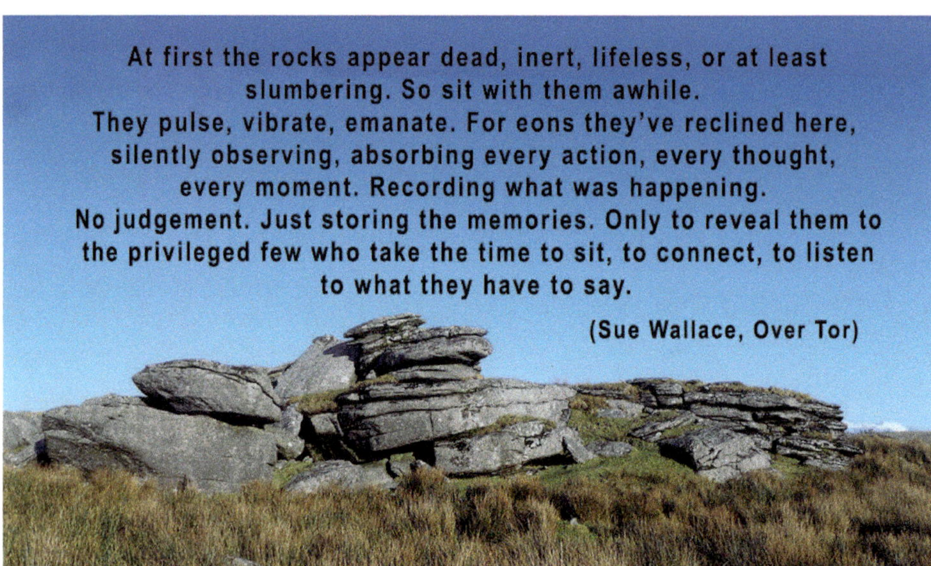

Acknowledgements

I would like to thank the following people, whose images were placed for free use on Wiki Commons: Mike Norton, Hogweard, Herbythyme, Nilfanion, Graham Horn, Jon Constant, J Y Lewis-Williams, Onderwijsgek, Daniel Schwen, Gerard Lovett, Thomas Schoch, Kathy Cox, Herby Talk Thyme, Sheila Russell, Ash, SwedeSwede, Henri Breuil, Patricia, Carl Bloch, Mark Fickett, Derek Harper, Labongo, Guy Wareham, Martin Vorel, M Macheret, EvanS, W Fix, and Del Williams. (Apologies if I missed anyone – let me know!) I also thank Jim Hamer for his image of the Kestor sunrise.

The painting of hunter-gatherers is by Viktor Vasnetsov, the 19th century painter.

The following websites yielded an abundance of information: Legendary Dartmoor, Megalithomania, Modern Antiquarian, Mid Atlantic Geomancy, The Leskernick Project, and The Heritage Journal.

I thank Emma Kidd, Richard Long and Sue Wallace, for their poetry and prose, and Carolyn Hillyer for her magical lyrics.

I am deeply indebted to Sue Wallace and Carol Stone, who walked the moor with me on several occasions, offering valuable insights during and after the trips, as well as taking several of the photos. I also thank the input of attendees of the Megalithomania Conference tours I led in 2012 and 2016, of my Dartmoor workshop in June 2016; their participation, photos and feedback is appreciated. I thank Gary Biltcliffe, Caroline Hoare and Jim Hamer for information. A huge thank you again to Sue Wallace, for her insights, proof-reading, and lots of patience and support.

And, lastly, I would like to express my gratitude to the Ancestors, whose debt I will always be in; thank you for opening my eyes that they may see.

About the Author

Peter Knight is well known for his inspirational PowerPoint presentations, workshops, and field trips on topics relating to sacred sites, ancient wisdom and dowsing. He has been leading tours to sacred sites since 1995 and has spoken at several international conventions in the USA, Malta, and around the UK. This is the author's 11th published book (for other titles see p. 219). Peter has also contributed to several magazines and journals. He has appeared on BBC local radio, and on TV, such as on Channel 4's *Don Roamin"* with Monty Don, and ITV's *Weekend Escapes with Warwick Davis*. Peter is the founder and organiser of the *Convention of Alternative Archaeology and Earth Mysteries*, held annually in Wiltshire, which gives a platform to both new and leading researchers. In 2004, he established Stone Seeker Publishing, and in 2005 launched Stone Seeker Tours, which promotes holistic tours of sacred sites across the UK.

Peter lives near Avebury and his interests include walking, drumming, world music, dowsing, prehistoric art, astronomy, and shamanism. He is a grandfather, a vegetarian, and follows a goddess-orientated spirituality, whilst honouring all spiritualities and religions. His 'mission' is to help people connect with sacred landscapes, to enhance their lives, and promote planetary healing.

Peter is available to give inspiring full-colour presentations about this book to local groups and societies, as well as to lead field trips across sacred landscapes.

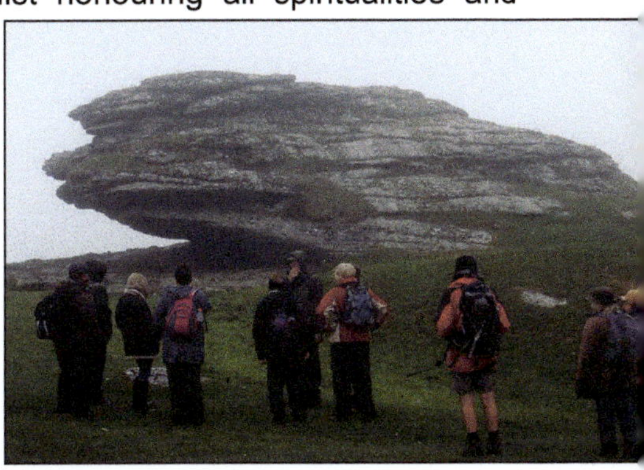

Contact Peter: stoneseeker@waitrose.com

www.stoneseeker.net

References

Barlow, Bernyce (1996), *Sacred Sites of the West.* Llewellyn.
Barnatt, J (1982), *Prehistoric Cornwall: The Ceremonial Monuments.* Turnstone Press.
Beckensall, Stan (1999), *British Prehistoric Rock Art.* Tempus.
Bender, B, Hamilton, S, and Tilley, C (1999), *Stone Worlds, Alternative Narratives, Nested Landscapes.* Leskernick Project: http://www.ucl.ac.uk/leskernick/articles/stone/stone.htm
Bender, B, Hamilton, S, and Tilley, C (2007), *Stone Worlds - Narrative and Reflexivity in Landscape Archaeology.* Left Coast Press.
Bergson, H (1991), *Matter and Memory.* Zone Books.
Biltcliffe, Gary, and Hoare, Caroline (2012), *The Spine of Albion.* Sacred Lands Publishing.
Biltcliffe, Gary, and Hoare, Caroline (2017), *The Centres of the British Isles – and the Cult of the Fire Goddess.* Sacred Lands Publishing.
Bloch, M (1995), *People into Places: Zafimaniry Concepts of Clarity.* In - Hirsch, E, & O'Hanlon, M, (eds.), *The Anthropology of Landscape: Perspectives on Place and Space.* Oxford University Press.
Borlase, William (1754), *Observations on the Antiquities of Cornwall.* David and Charles.
Bradley, Richard (1998), *Ruined buildings, ruined stones: enclosures, tombs and natural places in the Neolithic of South-west England. World Archaeology* 30.1. 13-22.
Bradley, Richard (2000), *An Archaeology of Natural Places.* Routledge.
Brennan, Martin (1994), *The Stones of Time: Calendars, Sundials and Stone Chambers of Ancient Ireland.* Inner Traditions International.
Broadhurst, Paul (1992), *Tintagel and the Arthurian Mythos.* Pendragon Press.
Broadhurst, Paul (1997 ed), *Secret Shrines.* Pendragon Press.
Broadhurst, Paul, and Miller, Hamish (2000), *The Dance of the Dragon.* Pendragon Press.
Burke, John, and Halberg, Kaj (2005), *Seed of Knowledge, Stone of Plenty.* Council Oak Books.
Burl, Aubrey (1979), *Prehistoric Avebury.* Yale.
Burl, Aubrey (1983), *Prehistoric Astronomy and Ritual.* Shire.
Burl, Aubrey (1985), *Megalithic Brittany.* Thames and Hudson.
Burl, Aubrey (2002 ed.), *Prehistoric Avebury.* Yale University Press.
Butler, J (1997), *Dartmoor Atlas of Antiquities: Volume Five, The Second Millennium B.C.* Devon Books.
Cope, Julian (1998), *The Modern Antiquarian.* Thorsons.
Cope, Julian (2004), *The Megalithic European,* Element.
Cowen, James (1989), *The Mysteries of the Dream-Time'.* Prism Press.
Cowen, James (1992), *Aborigine Dreaming.* Thorsons.
Crossing, W (1997), *Folklore and Legends of Dartmoor.* Forest Publications.
Dartmoor National Park Authority (2004), *Merrivale – An Archaeological Landscape.*
Davies, S R (2010), *The Early Neolithic Tor Enclosures of Southwest Britain.* Thesis, University of Birmingham Research Archive.
Devereux, Paul, et al (1989), *Earthmind – Communicating with the Living World of Gaia.* Destiny.
Devereux, Paul (1990), *Earth Lights Revelation.* Blandford.
Devereux, Paul (1991), *Earth Memory.* Quantum.
Devereux, Paul (1992), *Symbolic Landscapes.* Gothic Image.
Devereux, Paul (1993), *Shamanism and the Mystery Lines.* Quantum.
Devereux, Paul (1996), *Re-Visioning the Earth.* Simon and Schuster.
Devereux, Paul (1997), *The Long Trip – A Prehistory of Psychedelia.* Arkana.
Devereux, Paul (1998), *Secrets of Ancient and Sacred Places.* Brockhampton Press ed.
Devereux, Paul (2001), *Stone Age Soundtracks – the Acoustic Archaeology of Ancient Sites.* Vega.
Devereux, Paul (2002), *Living Ancient Wisdom.* Rider.
Devereux, Paul (2010), Pers. Comm. at *Stars and Stones Winter Forum.* Suffolk.
Devereux, Paul (2010b), *Sacred Geography - Deciphering Hidden Codes in the Landscape.* Gaia.
Devereux, Paul (2013), *Dreamscapes: Topography, Mind, and the Power of Simulacra in Ancient and Traditional Societies.* International Journal of Transpersonal Studies, 32 (1).

Endredy, James (2002), *Earthwalks For Body and Spirit.* Bear and Co.
Ferguson, James (1872), *Old Stone Monuments.* The Lost Library.
French, Karen (2012), *The Hidden Geometry of Life.* Watkins.
Garnham, Trevor (2004), *Lines in the Landscape, Circles from the Sky.* Tempus.
Gerrard, Sandy (1997), *Dartmoor.* B T Batsford/English Heritage.
Grinsell, L. V. (1978), Dartmoor Barrows. *Proceedings of the Devon Archaeological Society,* Vol 36, pp. 85-180.
Gunn, Celia M (2010), *Simply Totem Animals.* Sterling.
Gunnell, Y, Jarman, D, et al (2013), *The Granite Tors of Dartmoor, Southwest England.* Quaternary Science Reviews, 612, p. 62-76.
Hadingham, Evan (1974), *Ancient Carvings in Britain.* Garnstone.
Hamilton, Sue, Tilley, Christopher, and Bender, Barbara (2000), *Bronze Age Stone Worlds of Bodmin Moor.* Archaeology International.
Hawkins, Gerald (1963), *Stonehenge Decoded.* Nature, Vol. 200.
Heath, Robin, and Michell, John (2004), *The Measure of Albion.* Bluestone Press.
Hedges, K (1990), *Petroglyphs in Menifee Valley',* in *Rock Art Papers*, 7, (p.75-82).
Jung, Carl (1964), *Man and His Symbols.* Turtleback.
Kane, Sean (1998), *Wisdom of the Mythtellers.* Broadview.
Klemen, Peter (2015), *Dartmoor – A Landscape Study.* Thesis. University College of London.
Knight, Peter (1996), *Ancient Stones of Dorset.* Power Publications.
Knight, Peter (1998), *Sacred Dorset – on the Path of the Dragon.* Capall Bann.
Knight, Peter, and Power, Mike (2000), *Dorset Pilgrimages: A Millennium Handbook.* Power Pub.
Knight, Peter (2007 and 2010), *Thirteen Moons – Conversations with the Goddess.* Stone Seeker.
Knight, Peter (2011), *West Kennet Long Barrow – Landscape, Shamans and the Cosmos.* Stone Seeker.
Knight, Peter (2013), *The Cerne Giant – Landscape, Gods and the Stargate.* Stone Seeker.
Knight, Peter, and Wallace, Sue (2014), *Calne – Gateway to Ancient Wiltshire.* Stone Seeker.
Knight, Peter (2015), *Stolen Images – Pagan Symbolism and Christianity.* Stone Seeker.
Krőnig, Jűrgen (2001), *The Secret Face of Nature.* Gothic Image.
Kumar, Satish (1992), *No Destination.* Resurgence Books.
Lethbridge, William D (2015), *Discover Prehistoric Dartmoor.* Halsgrove.
Lewis, A (1895-8), *Rude Stone Monuments of Bodmin Moor.* Journal of the Royal Institute of Cornwall, 13:107-113.
Mann, Nicholas R, and Glasson, Philippa (2007), *The Star Temple of Avalon.* Temple.
Mann, Nicholas R (2011), *Avebury Cosmos.* O Books.
Marshall, Steve (2016), *Exploring Avebury - The Essential Guide.* History Press.
McDonald, Neil (2011), *The Lake District – A Megalithic Journey.* Megalithic Publishing.
Meaden, Terence (1991). *The Goddess of the Stones.* Souvenir Press.
Meaden, Terence (1999), *The Secrets of the Avebury Stones.* Souvenir Press.
Michell, John (1979), *Simulacra.* Thames and Hudson.
Michell, John (1982), *Megalithomania.* Thames and Hudson.
Michell, John (1989), *A Little History of Astro-Archaeology.* Thames and Hudson.
Michell, John, and Rhone, Christine (1991), *Twelve Tribe Nations.* Thames and Hudson.
Miller, Hamish, and Brailsford, Barry (2006), *In Search of the Southern Serpent.* Penwith Press.
Miller, Hamish, and Broadhurst, Paul (1989), *The Sun and the Serpent.* Pendragon Press.
Moore, Robert, and Gillette, Douglas (1993), *The Magician Within – Accessing the Shaman in the Male Psyche.* Morrow.
Mortimer, Neil, and Pilkington, Mark (2011), *An Archaeoacoustic Observation on Dartmoor.* Time and Mind, Volume 4, Issue 2, July 2011. Bloomsbury.
Mortimer, Neil (2013), *From Moor to Shore – Re-Visioning Dartmoor's Stone Rows.* Time and Mind, Vol. 6, Issue 2. Bloomsbury.
Nanson, Anthony (2011), *Words of Enchantment.* Awen.
Newman, Phil (2011), *The Field Archaeology of Dartmoor.* English Heritage.
Parker Pearson, Michael (1993), *Bronze Age Britain.* English Heritage.
Parker Pearson, Michael (2012), *Stonehenge: Exploring the Greatest Stone Age Mystery.* Simon and Schuster.

Pettit, Paul (1974), *Prehistoric Dartmoor,* David and Charles.
Pitts, Mike (2000), *Hengeworld.* Century.
Robb, Graham (2013), *The Ancient Paths: Discovering the Lost Map of Celtic Europe.* Pan Macmillan.
Rowe, S (1848), *A Perambulation of Dartmoor.* Hamilton.
Russell, Miles (2002), *Monuments of the British Neolithic.* Tempus.
Scarre, C (2002), *Monuments and Landscape in Atlantic Europe.* Routledge.
Scott, George Ryley (1966), *Phallic Worship - a History of Sex and Sexual Rites.* Senate.
Service, Alastair, and Bradbury, Jean (1993), *The Standing Stones of Europe.* Weidenfeld and Nicolson.
Shaw, Alasdair (2012), *Walking Through the Past – Dartmoor.* Archaeoroutes.
Shepherd, David (2013), *Propped Stones: The Modification of Natural Features and the Construction of Place.* Time and Mind, 11/2013. Bloomsbury.
Shepherd, David (2014), *Variations on a Theme: An Account of Some Possible Kerbed Boulders in the South Pennines and Cumbria.* Time and Mind, 2014. Bloomsbury.
Smith, Brian, and Walker, Alan (2008), *Rock Art and Ritual – Interpreting the Prehistoric Landscapes of the North York Moors.* Tempus.
Smith, Brian, and Walker, Alan (2011), *Rock Art and Ritual – Mindscapes of Prehistory.* Amberley.
Smith, V (1966), *Portrait of Dartmoor.* Hale & Company.
Snyder, Gary (1990), *The Practice of the Wild.* North Point Press.
Stanbury, Peter, and Clegg, John (1990), *A Field Guide to Aboriginal Rock Engravings.* Oxford University Press.
St Leger-Gordon, Ruth (2001 ed.), *The Witchcraft and Folklore of Dartmoor.* Peninsula Press.
Thom, Alexander (1967), *Megalithic Sites in Britain.* Oxford.
Thomas, Nicholas (1976), *Guide to Prehistoric England.* Batsford.
Thorley, Anthony, ed. (2012), *Legendary London and the Spirit of Place.* Archive Publishing.
Tilley, Christopher (1994), *A Phenomenology of Landscape: Places, Paths and Monuments.* Berg.
Tilley, Christopher (2004), *The Materiality of Stone.* Berg.
Tilley, Christopher (2007), *The Neolithic Sensory Revolution: Monumentality and the Experience of Landscape.* Proceedings of the British Academy, Vol. 144, p. 329-45.
Tilley, Christopher (2008), *Body and Image – Explorations in Landscape Phenomenology 2,* Left Coast Press.
Tilley, Christopher (2010), *Interpreting Landscapes – Geologies, Topographies, Identities.* Left Coast Press.
Trwoga, Chris (2006), *Shamanism and Sacred Landscapes,* The Speaking Tree.
Turner, J. R. (1990), *Ring Cairns, Stone Circles and Related Monuments on Dartmoor.* In Proceedings of the Devon Archaeological Society, Vol 48, pp. 27-86.
Underwood, Guy (1972), *The Pattern of the Past.* Abacus ed.
Walker, Charles (1987), *The Atlas of Occult Britain.* Hamlyn.
Walker, Jack (2005), *Dartmoor Sun.* Halsgrove.
Walter, Eugene Victor (1988), *Placeways.* University of North Carolina Press.
Watkins, Alfred (1925), *The Old Straight Track.* Methuen (Abacus reprint, 1974).
Watson, Aaron (2001), *Composing Avebury.* World Archaeology, 33:2, p. 296 – 314.
Watson, Aaron & Keating, David (1999), *Architecture and Sound: an Acoustic Analysis of Megalithic Monuments in Prehistoric Britain.* Antiquity, Vol. 73, p. 325-36.
Westropp, Thomas Johnson (1896), *A Folklore Survey of County Clare.* Clasp Press (2000 ed.)
Williams, Mike (2010), *Prehistoric Belief: Shamans, Trance and the Afterlife.* The History Press.
Wood, John Edwin (1978), *Sun, Moon and Standing Stones.* Oxford University Press.
Woodward, A (2001), *British Barrows - A Matter of Life and Death.* Tempus.
Worth, R H (1971), *Worth's Dartmoor.* David and Charles.

Also by Peter Knight

Ancient Stones of Dorset
Published in 1996 by Power Publications. 208 pp. The most comprehensive work on Dorset's megalithic sites. 180 illustrations. Maps of alignments, site plans, and grid references, earth energies, astronomy, newly discovered stones. Recently reprinted.

Sacred Dorset ~ On the Path of the Dragon
Published in 1998 by Capall Bann. 292 pp, 200 illustrations. A thorough work on Dorset's ancient spiritual heritage, including hillforts, wells and springs, hills, alignments, sun and moon, the green man, fairy and giant folklore, dragons, trees, and much more.

Dorset Pilgrimages ~ A Millennium Handbook (with Mike Power)
Published in 2000 by Power Publications. 144 pp (gloss finish), over 100 photographs and line drawings. Day-long pilgrimages across Dorset, visiting churches, stone circles, megaliths, wells, the Cerne Giant, Maiden Castle and more.

***Earth Mysteries ~ An Illustrated Encyclopaedia of Britain* (CD-ROM)**
Published in 2003 by Stone Seeker Publishing. Over 350MB of information – the biggest overview of British earth mysteries ever published. Compatible with Windows Word. Over 250 illustrations. A-Z format, plus resources and fully cross-referenced - like a giant website!

Thirteen Moons ~ Conversations with the Goddess
Published in 2007 (new ed. 2010) by Stone Seeker Publishing. Peter's novel has received rave reviews. The book's hero is contacted by the Earth Spirit on 13 full moons at sacred sites across Europe. The Goddess guides him on how to connect with the Earth Spirit, and divulges what the human experience is all about, how we can live fulfilling lives in harmony with the planet.

The Wessex Astrum – Sacred Geometry in a Mystical Landscape (with Toni Perrott).
Published by Stone Seeker Publishing in 2008. Fully illustrated. The groundbreaking discovery of the huge landscape hexagram, involving Stonehenge, Avebury, Glastonbury, and the St Michael Line; new megaliths, forgotten wells, Knights Templar sites etc.

West Kennet Long Barrow – Landscape, Shamans and the Cosmos
Published by Stone Seeker Publishing in 2011. Fully illustrated. The most thorough guide to this 5,500 year-old Neolithic tomb near Avebury, including Peter's new discoveries. Deals with the landscape, alignments, astronomy, excavations, acoustics, earth energies, shamanism, psychic phenomena and how we can use such places today.

The Cerne Giant – Landscape, Gods and the Stargate
Published by Stone Seeker Publishing in 2013. Fully illustrated. The ultimate guide to the iconic Dorset hill figure. Includes, history, folklore, landscape alignments, and astronomical alignments, including those with Orion and the 'Stargate' of Osiris.

Calne – Gateway to Ancient Wiltshire (with Sue Wallace)
Published by Stone Seeker Publishing in 2014. Illustrated. A guide to sixteen walks (with maps) through the scenery, history and prehistoric sites in and around this Wiltshire town, including local wells and springs, historical curiosities, art installations, churches and much more.

Stolen Images – Pagan Symbolism and Christianity
Published by Stone Seeker Publishing in 2015. This is Peter's acclaimed and superbly illustrated, full colour guide to how Pagan symbols and myths were incorporated in the early Church, for its own agenda. 240 pages of images and surprising insights.

Signed and dedicated copies are available from the author.

www.stoneseeker.net

Aaron's Knock, 60.
acoustics, 21, 22, 77-80, 87, 105, 113, 117, 129, 174.
Agglestone, 53, 105.
Alton Barnes Yew, 50.
ancestors, 13, 17, 19, 20 ,28, 33-35, 39-40, 51, 55, 70, 77, 80, 86, 90, 99, 135, 141, 143-4, 156, 172, 176, 180, 190-1, 195-6, 201.
anthropomorphic rocks (see simulacra).
Apollo/St Michael Axis, 53.
Archaeological background, 10-18.
Ashburton, 7, 71, 157, 206.
Assycombe, 194.
astronomy, 5, 7, 59, 66, 99, 109-111, 116, 129, 143, 145, 149, 150, 152, 156, 160, 162, 164, 170, 176, 179, 184, 187-89, 190, 197-204 (see also moon, sun, stars).
aurochs, 20, 37, 61, 117.
Australian Aborigines, 5, 6, 10, 19, 25, 27-8, 32-4, 45-6, 64-5, 70-1, 79, 89, 90, 103, 118, 120, 175, 205, 206.
Avebury, 19, 23, 30, 53-4, 61, 78, 80, 121, 140-1, 146, 160, 177, 184, 197, 201.
axis mundi, 128

Bag Tor, 83, 114-5, 134, 139.
balanced stones/rocks, 56-7, 65, 67, 73, 79, 88, 94, 96, 102-7, 110-1, 114-6, 119, 126, 128, 130, 135, 165, 167-8, 170-1, 206.
Barn Hill, 158, 164, 178-9, 202-4.
basins (see rock basins).
Batworthy, 15, 115, 135.
'Bear', the (simulacrum), 174-6, 200.
Beardown Man, 16, 60, 72.
Beardown Tors, 12, 72.
Belinus Line, 124.
Bellever Tor, 11, 62, 144, 185, 186, 190.
Belstone Tor, 107, 185, 190, 207.
Bel Tor, 136, 139.
Black-A-Tor Copse, 10.
Black Tor (SW of Princetown), 17, 57-9, 107, 136, 139, 152, 157, 200, 209.
Black Tor (S of Meldon), 36-7, 61, 117.
Bodmin Moor, 10, 13-5, 17, 33, 60-1, 69, 72, 74, 81, 84, 86-7, 90-4, 97-8, 105, 108, 110-1, 113, 124, 126-7, 141-3, 150, 159, 165, 168, 173, 177, 185-6, 191, 193, 195, 199.
Bosworlas Rocks, 125.
Bowerman's Nose, 26, 56,107.
Bran, 65.
Branscombe's Loaf, 96.
Brent Tor/Brentor, 18, 34, 72, 92-3, 113, 165, 169, 171, 173, 200, 207.
Breasts of Aphrodite, 24.
Brimham Rocks, 66-7, 103.
Brisworthy cup marks, 137.
Brisworthy stone circle, 47, 184, 187-8, 195, 199, 208.
Brisworthy stone row, 154-7, 187-8, 195, 208.
Brittany, 53, 59, 77-8, 81, 121-2, 127-8,140.
Bronze Age (by name), 4, 5, 13-8, 20, 25, 33-5, 45, 55-6, 60-2, 69, 82, 84, 86-93, 95, 97, 109-11, 122, 124-6, 135, 141-4, 147, 162, 164, 167, 171, 174, 176, 178-80, 190-3, 195-6, 202-3, 211.
Brown Willy, 91, 110, 126-7, 168, 199.
Brutus, 65.
Bullauns/bulláns, 122-3.
Burrator Reservoir, 147.
Bushmen, 89.
Butterbrook, 142.
Butterdon Hill, 63, 83, 86, 91, 96, 98-9, 134, 144, 156-7.

Cader Idris, 65.
cairn circles, 16, 62, 96, 99-100, 150-6,166, 178-9, 184, 188-90, 197, 200, 202.
cairns, 15-8, 22, 34, 41, 48, 56, 61, 63, 66, 85-7, 89, 90-101, 106, 110, 112, 125-6, 130, 132, 134, 138, 141-3, 146-53, 156, 158, 166, 168, 173, 178-81, 186, 194, 198-202, 208, 209.
Carn Brae, 53, 62, 86, 88, 109, 119, 125, 132-3.
Carn Ingli, 53, 65, 81.
Castle Drago, 207.
Cerne Abbas Giant, 46, 180, 197.
Chagford, 7, 58, 76, 115, 131, 139, 157.
Challacombe Down stone row, 17, 144-5, 157.
Chapel Carn Brae, 126, 132.
Cheesewring, 126.
Cheriton Combe, 145.
circles (see stone circles).
circular stone settings, 184-90.
cists (kists), 17, 62-3, 82, 100, 124, 141, 143-4, 145, 147, 149, 158-9, 163, 178, 180-1, 190, 202, 213.
clapper bridges, 18.
clitter, 11, 12, 15-6, 17, 30, 33, 40-1, 56, 61, 73, 83-4, 87-8, 93, 142, 152, 160-1, 163, 171, 177, 186, 192, 195, 196.
cognitive archaeology, 38, 47, 211.
Combestone Tor, 58, 60, 62, 136, 139, 143, 194.
Combshead Tor, 151, 152.
Corndon Down, 95, 99, 144, 208.
Cornwall (see place names).
Corrington Ball, 14, 86, 144, 147, 157.
Cosdon Beacon/Hill, 22, 41, 48, 63, 97, 100,132-3, 145, 157, 161, 186, 194, 207.
Cox Tor, 34, 41, 77, 92-3, 99, 113, 130, 136, 139, 158, 166, 169, 172-3, 208.
Cranbrook, 18.
Cranmere Pool, 136.
Crockern Tor, 66, 69, 101.
crosses, 9, 121, 138, 156.
Crow Tor, 72.
Cuckoo Ball (burial chamber), 14, 86.
cup marks, 109, 122, 123-4, 137, 139.

Cut Hill stone row, 142-3, 157.

Dartmeet, 7, 58, 62, 139, 157.
Dartmoor National Park, 7, 8, 18.
Dartmoor (geological map) 8.
Dart, River, 7, 9, 139, 186.
Dead Lake Well, 72, 172.
Dean Moor, 17.
Delphi, 64, 85.
Devil, 26, 71-2, 103, 105, 130.
Devil's Frying Pan, 72, 130, 172.
Devil's Tor, 16, 26, 60, 72.
Dewerstone, 13, 15, 86-9, 106, 132, 135, 139, 175.
Dewerstone Rock, 71.
dolmen,14, 76, 80-1, 110-3, 122, 161, 198, 205.
Domnonii, 18.
Dorset, 13, 25, 35, 53, 89, 105, 180, 197.
Down Tor, 151-2.
Dowsing/dowsers, 9, 16, 42, 52-3, 101, 113, 131, 136, 138, 140, 152, 154, 177-9, 188-90, 205-9.
Dragon Project, 76-7.
dragons, 25-6, 40, 55, 65, 136, 161, 175, 209.
Dreamtime, 6, 19, 27-8, 34, 50, 54, 65, 69-71, 77, 83, 86, 90, 120, 174.
Drewsteignton, 71, 198, 205.
Drizzlecombe, 16, 60, 62, 77, 91, 111, 142-3, 147-50, 157, 159, 178, 194-5, 197, 206, 208.
Druid Cross, 71.
Druids, 18, 19, 56, 67, 71, 102-6, 119, 120, 124, 126, 128, 130, 136, 167, 172, 194, 198.
Druid's Chair, 71, 162.
Dunstone, the, 138-9.

earth energies, 16, 42, 49, 66, 89, 101, 113, 124, 131, 136, 138, 140, 150-55, 159, 160, 177-8, 188-9, 205-9.
Earth Mother (Goddess), 25, 44, 59, 166, 171, 189, 210, 213.
earth lights, 77, 129, 206.
Easdon Hill, 61, 72, 79, 83, 92, 136.
Easdon Tor, 42, 56, 106-7.
Eastern Tor, 195.
Egypt, 13, 52, 59, 76-7, 80, 118, 197, 204.
Elephant Dolmen (Sardinia) 52.
equinox, 59, 116, 145, 164, 179, 188, 199, 200, 203.
Erme, River, 9, 146.
Exmoor, 10, 17, 80, 100, 131, 154.
Externstein, 29, 61.
Eylesbarrow, 41, 99, 151.

'false cresting', 41, 42, 97, 99.
Feather Tor, 72, 158, 164.
Fernworthy, 7, 10, 11, 22, 23, 106, 157.
Figgie Daniel, 56, 83, 136, 139, 211.
Fingle Bridge, 207.
folklore, 25, 33, 50-1, 53, 56, 66, 71-2, 79, 101-2, 104-6, 108, 122-4, 127, 129-31, 136, 162, 172, 185, 194, 206.
forests, ancient, 10, 11, 14, 23.
Fox Tor, 72.
Fur Tor, 72.

Gaia (see Earth Mother).
Garden of the Gods, 51, 103.
Genius loci, 28, 42.
geological background, 8-9.
giants, 27, 36, 53, 55, 67, 102, 104-5, 159, 163, 165, 176, 194.
Giant's Grave(Mardon), 72.
Giant's Hill, 72, 150.
Gidleigh, 10, 15, 83, 86, 206.
Gidleigh Tor, 12, 133, 139.
Glasscombe Corner stone row, 144, 157.
Glastonbury, 65, 197.
Golden Rock (Burma), 103.
Goldsworthy, Andy, 9, 45, 102, 107.
granite (introduction to), 7-8.
granite, (radioactivity of), 77.
granite, red, 81, 93, 99, 155, 171.
granite (sanctity of), 76-8.
granite soundscapes, 77-80.
Great Mis Tor, 49, 72, 92-3, 106, 130, 139, 150-1,158, 170-2, 183, 187, 195.
Great Staple Tor, 35, 47, 69, 92, 106, 113, 151, 160, 165-6, 169, 171, 173, 178, 181-3, 187-8, 195, 201-2, 204.
Great Trowlesworthy Tor, 147, 149, 151, 188, 195.
Great Western Reave, 17, 167, 171, 178, 180-1.
Green Hill, 143.
Greeks/Greece, 24-5, 59, 64, 85, 184, 197.
Grey Wethers stone circles, 22, 80, 185-6.
Grim's Grave, 72, 82.
Grimspound, 17, 18, 60, 63, 82, 144, 177, 193-4.
Gundestrup Cauldron, 20.
Gutter Tor, 81, 136, 139, 150-1, 187-9, 195.

Haldon Ridge, 15.
Hamel Down/Hameldown, 18, 60, 63, 72, 82, 96-7, 99.
Hangershell Rock, 84, 99.
Hangerstone Hill, 106.
Hart Tor, 72, 146, 152-3, 157, 180, 209.
Hawk's Tor, 72, 80, 87, 112-4, 136, 139, 199, 207.
Haytor, 12, 37, 40, 56, 62, 81-2, 94, 96, 114, 130-1, 133-4, 144-5, 186-7, 213.
Healing Stone (Batworthy), 115.
Heckwood Tor, 158, 164.
Hell Tor, 72.
Hembury, 18.
Hen Tor, 47, 81, 149, 187-8, 195.
Hexworthy, 77, 206.
Higher Hartor Tor, 111, 171.
Higher White Tor, 145.
High Willhays, 7, 8.
Hingston Hill, 143, 150-2, 157, 194, 197, 199-201, 203, 209.
Hittisleigh, 207.
Hobajons Cross, 156.
holed stones, 125, 127, 129.
Hollow Tor, 158.
Holmingbeam, 137, 139.

Holne Moor, 143, 157.
Honey Bag Tor, 137, 139.
Hook Lake stone rows, 143, 146, 157, 194.
Hookney Tor, 17-8.
Hopi, 85.
Hound Tor, 56-7, 72-3, 106, 187.
Hucken Tor, 116, 136, 139, 158, 161, 171-2, 178, 181-2.
Hunter's Tor, 18.
Hurston Ridge stone row, 60, 143, 154, 157, 194, 208.
hut circles, 15, 17, 61, 83-4, 86, 88, 123, 125, 149, 158, 174, 180, 191-6, 202, 208.

Ice Age, 8, 10, 18, 20, 101, 108.
Imbolc, 164, 203.
Inca, 52, 64.
Iron Age, 18, 71, 106, 119, 124.
Ivybridge, 96, 134, 157.

Kent's Cavern, 10.
Kestor, 12, 18, 58, 63, 72, 83, 97, 131-3, 139, 154, 187, 199, 204, 206.
King's Barrow, 42, 99.
King's Tor (Merrivale), 158, 160-1.
King Tor, 42, 99, 182, 196.
Kogi, 19, 64, 75, 192.
Kumar, Satish, 46.

Lakehead Hill, 62, 82, 144, 157, 185, 213.
Landscape symbolism (see symbolic landscapes & mythologised landscapes).
Langstone Moor, 36, 47, 60, 62, 183, 185, 187.
Leather Tor, 83, 151-2, 189.
leats, 158-9, 179.
Leeden Tor, 68, 153, 200.
Legis Tor, 17, 81, 186-8, 195, 199.
Leskernick (Bodmin), 61, 84, 86, 90, 109, 113, 135, 141, 159, 185, 192, 194, 199.
Ley Lines (re Watkins), 124, 142.
light phenomena, 77, 206.
Liminal/liminality, 11-2, 44, 46, 55, 69, 73, 91, 127, 129, 144-5, 180, 196, 202.
Lithostones, 78.
Littaford Tor, 136, 139.
Little Bee Tor, 136, 139.
Little Hound Tor, 187.
Little Mis Tor, 17, 136, 139, 158, 170, 173, 183.
Little Staple Tor, 158, 164.
Logan stones (see balanced stones/rocks).
Longaford Tor, 144.
long barrows, 14, 86-7.
Long, Richard, 45.
longstones, 16, 47, 60-2, 76, 81, 116, 124, 132, 147-9, 150, 156-7, 159-61, 164, 178-9, 181-2, 184, 189, 197, 199, 201-3, 208-9, 211.
Lower Dunstone, 137-8.
Lower Hartor Tor, 111-2, 139, 199.
Lower Piles, 198.
Lugh, 103.
Lustleigh Cleave, 43-4.
Lydford, 7, 22, 72, 119, 157, 207, 212.

Machu Picchu, 29, 64, 76-7.
magic mushrooms, 22.
Malta, 21, 54, 59, 121, 215.
Maori, 5, 10, 27, 52.
Mardon Down, 82, 97, 100, 185-6, 190.
Mary Tavy, 207.
May Day, 199.
Meavy, River, 88, 152-3, 221.
Meldon Hill, 154.
Mel Tor, 136, 139.
Men-an-Tol, 91, 124-5, 127, 129.
Merrivale, 17, 35, 59, 60, 62, 80, 83, 116,130, 141, 145, 157, 160-2, 164-5, 167, 169, 171-2, 177-84, 187, 194-8, 201-3, 208-9.
Merrivale (astronomy map), 202.
Merrivale Shamanic Landscape, 130, 158-83.
Mesolithic, 4, 10-3, 15, 20, 33, 36, 43, 81, 83, 133.
Middle Staple Tor, 158, 160,164-5, 177-8, 181-3, 201, 204, 211.
Middle Tor, 58, 76, 132, 139, 154, 175.
Midsummer, 59, 66, 109-11, 149, 170, 189, 197, 199, 200-2, 204.
Midwinter, 14, 104, 187, 189, 191, 197, 199, 201-3.
Mistor Pan, 106, 130.
Moon, 19, 25, 36, 38, 54, 61, 72-4, 99, 118, 122, 129, 131-2, 176, 184, 190, 197-9, 201, 202, 204.
Moretonhampstead, 7, 82, 100, 106, 139, 157.
Mushroom Rock, 25.
mythologised landscapes, 6, 10, 23, 26-9, 34, 51, 53, 91, 165, 214.
myths, 6, 7, 11, 14, 24-8, 33-5, 37, 39, 46, 50, 53, 55, 59, 65, 67, 69-71, 81, 83, 86, 91, 118, 120, 129, 200, 206, 214.

Native Americans, 5, 29, 32, 51, 64-5, 68, 71, 78, 90, 103, 108, 120-1, 206.
Natural outcrops as sacred places, 65-7.
Nazca Lines, 118.
Neolithic (by name), 4-5, 10, 12-16, 19-23, 28, 34, 44, 53-55, 57, 59, 61-2, 65, 69-70, 77-81, 85-90, 109, 111, 118, 125-6, 129, 135, 141-2, 149, 170, 179, 192, 197, 202, 204.
Newgrange, 30, 61, 77, 118, 129, 146, 184.
Nine Stones (cairn circle), 113, 184-5, 190, 207.
North Hessary Tor, 62, 164.
North Teign River, 133, 135, 147, 154, 186, 189, 208.
North Walla Brook, 154.
Nutcracker (Lustleigh Cleave), 43-4, 105.
Nutcrackers (Rippon Tor), 105.

Okehampton, 7, 36, 113, 117, 139.
Orion, 204.

Orkney, 28, 85, 89, 160, 192, 197.
Over Tor, 62, 79, 80, 116, 129, 132, 139, 158, 172, 174-6, 200.

Palaeolithic, 10, 59.
Paps of Anu, 24, 25.
Penn Beacon, 147, 157, 198.
perspective (in landscapes), 41, 46-7, 156, 189.
Peter Tavy, 47, 87.
Pew Tor, 71, 75, 80, 116, 136, 139, 158, 162, 164, 173, 178, 196, 202-4.
phallic stones/phallicism, 53, 56, 59-61, 63, 66, 84, 149, 154, 179, 185-6, 189, 194, 203.
Phenomenology, 6, 12, 19, 38-49, 61, 72-3, 97, 180, 210.
Phoenicians, 172.
Pieces of place, 9, 30, 36, 55, 61, 77, 93, 112, 117, 160.
Piles Hill, 96, 98-9, 144, 156-7, 199.
Pixies/Piskies, 57, 72, 106, 162, 172, 194.
Plym, River, 7, 9, 88, 94, 118, 139, 147-8, 157, 188, 195.
Postbridge, 13, 62, 157.
Preseli, 21, 30, 53, 78, 80, 92, 137, 157.
Prestige Cairns, 17, 48, 89, 98-9, 156.
Princetown, 7, 59, 107, 137, 139, 152.
propped stones, 83, 87, 106, 108-17, 158, 160-1, 167-71, 178, 181-2, 192, 199, 206-7, 213.
psychoactive/hallucinogenic plants, 21-3, 55, 75-7, 91, 129, 175.
Puckie Stone, 136, 139.
Pupers Hill, 79, 96.

Quartz, 8, 9, 12, 42, 65, 90, 93, 98, 109, 113, 123, 131, 134-5, 154, 161, 170, 177, 205-6.

Raddick Hill, 17, 153.
Rainbow Serpent, 25, 65.
Raven's Tor, 72.
reaves, 15, 17, 35, 56, 62, 87, 92, 143, 147, 150, 158, 160, 167, 171, 173, 178, 180-1, 202.
Rippon Tor, 40-1, 56, 74, 83, 94, 99, 130-1, 139, 141.
Ritual landscapes, 159.
rivers (as sacred and metaphor), 9, 22, 34, 35, 118-9, 136-7, 146-7, 173, 212.
rivers (see names of).
Roche Rock, 53, 85, 126.
rock art, 24, 27, 78, 90, 109, 120, 122, 137.
rock basins, 4, 9, 12, 22, 28, 33, 40, 42, 56, 58, 61, 67-8, 72-3, 77, 83, 88, 91, 93-4, 96, 105-7, 109, 111, 113-4, 116, 118-139, 146, 150, 159-63, 165-76, 181-2, 189, 195, 199, 206, 213.
Rook Tor, 72, 96.
Roos Tor, 17, 35, 39, 47, 92-3, 106, 115-6, 130, 136, 139, 151, 158, 160, 167-73, 178-81, 183, 194, 206.
Rough Tor, 15, 54, 74, 87, 91-2, 110, 125, 127, 185, 192, 199.
round barrows, 16, 89.
round houses (see hut circles).
Rugglestone Rock, 105.
Rundlestone, 60.

Saami, 29, 52, 66, 70-1.
Saddle Tor, 33, 40, 56-7, 131.
Scorhill stone circle, 60, 97, 135-6, 143, 185-6, 199-200.
scrying, 119, 126, 129.
sea (visibility of), 9, 49, 56, 89, 93-5, 97, 99, 113-4, 130, 134, 144, 146-7, 149-51, 155, 159, 165, 172-3, 180, 187-8, 195.
settlements, 15, 17-8, 35, 61, 69, 81-3, 86-7, 96, 99, 101, 110, 126, 142, 144-5, 148, 150, 158, 171, 174, 178, 180-1, 189, 191-6.
shamans/shamanism, 5, 16, 19-23, 29, 33, 37, 50, 54-5, 64, 66, 68-9, 71, 75-9, 81, 83-4, 89, 91, 98, 106, 116-7, 127-9, 131, 146, 153, 156, 160, 167, 170, 175-6, 180, 193, 195-6, 205, 208, 211-3.
Sharpitor (Lustleigh), 105.
Sharpitor (SW of Princetown), 17, 35, 83, 113, 146, 151, 153, 167, 189.
Sharp Tor (NE of Dartmeet), 95, 100, 144.
Shaugh Moor, 112, 146, 157, 195.
Shaverscombe, 194.
Sheeps Tor, 72, 81, 113, 148-52, 154-5, 186, 188, 195.
Shell Tor, 188.
Sherberton stone circle, 186.
Shovel Down (cairn & rows), 16, 60, 76, 97, 131, 146-7, 157, 184, 189, 194, 208.
Showery Tor (Bodmin), 80, 86, 92, 105, 126.
Shrine Stone, 61.
Siejddes, 52, 70.
Silbury Hill, 93.
simulacra, 9, 12, 15, 24, 28, 33-4, 36-7, 49-63, 66, 68-9, 73-5, 84, 86, 88, 94, 99, 101, 104, 111, 114, 117, 121, 124, 128, 130, 132, 137-8, 149, 152, 161, 163, 165-6, 168-71,174-6, 182, 184, 211.
Solstices (see midsummer and midwinter)
solution basins (see rock basins).
song lines, 6, 27, 46, 89, 118, 120.
soundscapes, 79.
Soussons Down cairn circle, 190.
space (discussion on), 42-44.
Spinster's Rock, 14, 86, 198, 205, 207.
Spirit of place/land, 4, 6, 13, 15, 28, 33, 42, 61, 80, 85, 90, 93, 111, 114, 117, 136, 153, 154, 164, 213.
Spirit ways, 141.
Stall Down, 146, 157, 195.
Stall Moor (row & circle), 99, 142-3, 157, 185.

Stannon stone circle, 199.
Star Carr, 20.
stars, 8, 38, 74, 197, 200, 204.
Sticklepath Fault, 8.
St Michael Line, 53, 72, 115, 206.
stone circles/circular settings, 15-6, 22, 36, 38, 47, 49, 60, 62, 81, 89, 97, 101, 116, 135-6, 143, 154, 158, 160-1, 178-9, 182, 184-90, 199, 202, 204, 209.
Stonehenge, 24, 30, 55, 59, 118, 137, 146, 160, 177-8, 184, 197, 200.
Stone of Destiny, 59.
stone rows, 15-17, 35, 38, 60, 62, 76, 83, 86, 89, 95-6, 98-101, 107, 116, 131, 140-62, 164, 167, 172, 174, 178-82, 188, 194, 196-7, 200, 202-4, 206, 208-9.
Substitution (with cairns), 41-2, 97-99.
Sun, 19, 38, 54, 72, 74, 111, 149, 164, 172, 174, 176, 180, 184, 188-91, 197-204, 211.
Symbolic landscapes, 11, 23-37, 61, 69, 118, 137, 192, 210. (see also mythologised landscapes.)

Tara, 59, 65.
Tavistock, 7, 93, 139, 157, 179.
Tavy, River, 7, 9, 87, 139, 146, 157, 173.
Taw Head, 13.
Taw Marsh, 10.
Taw, River, 9.
Teign, River, 9, 12, 113, 135-6, 147, 154, 186-7, 189, 198, 208.
Temple Tor, 72.
Thom, Alexander, 179, 185, 197, 201.
Thornworthy Tor, 106.
Throwleigh, 207.
Tolmen Stone, 135-6, 139, 146-7, 187.
Top Tor, 62.
tors (as landscape foci), 17, 35, 70, 80-3, 143-5, 151, 187, 192-3, 195.
tors (enculturing of), 13, 14, 15, 17, 24, 41, 69, 85-101, 111, 114, 130, 134, 149, 175, 194-5.
tors (intervisibility of), 11-2, 16-7, 34-5, 56, 82, 95, 99, 116, 143-5, 150, 156, 166, 172-4, 185, 187, 192, 194-5, 199, 201.
tors (mythologies of), 11, 33, 81, 83, 86, 91, 159.
tors (sanctity of), 4, 11, 20, 30, 34, 55, 64-84, 86, 90, 101, 110, 160.
totems, 72.
Touchstone, the, 60.
Tower Hill, 65.
Trewortha Tor (Bodmin), 127-8,
triangular stones, 56, 60-3, 81, 84, 92, 98, 141-2, 148, 151, 153-4, 177, 185-6, 194, 204, 209.
Triboluminescence, 206.
Triple Goddess, 61.
twinned peaks, 24-5, 81, 189.
Two Bridges, 12, 206.

Ugborough Beacon, 41, 94, 96, 98-9, 106, 134, 139, 175, 199.
Uluru, 27, 64, 120.
Upper Erme, 9, 157.
Upton Lovell Shaman, 19.
Ursa Major, 200.

Vixen Tor, 26, 63, 72, 93, 116, 136, 139, 158, 163-5, 179, 203-4, 206.

Walkham, River, 7, 157-9, 162-3, 171-3, 180, 187.
Walking (consciously, as revelation), 5, 6, 36, 39, 41, 44-7, 49, 75, 159, 180, 210, 212.
walking (in the wild), 44-5.
waterfalls, 13, 22, 32-3, 41, 72, 79, 118-9, 137, 212.
Water Hill, 41, 97-8, 208.
water (holy/sacred), 9, 67, 118-9, 121, 126, 128, 136-7, 146, 170.
Watern Oke, 17.
Watern Tor, 68, 97, 187.
Western Beacon, 96, 98-9, 134, 198.
West Kennet Long Barrow, 20-22, 25, 30, 35, 40, 46, 54-5, 61, 77, 79, 93, 141, 180.
West Okement River, 117.
Whitehorse Hill, 16.
White Lady (Lydford), 72, 119, 210, 212.
White Moor Stone, 82.
White Moor stone circle, 187.
White Tor, 13-15, 17, 35, 41-2, 47, 61-2, 72, 86-8, 92-3, 130, 160, 167, 172-3, 188, 194.
Whittenknowles settlement, 195.
Whooping Rock, 79, 106.
Widecombe-in-the-Moor, 57, 81, 105, 137-9, 157.
Wiltshire, 13-4, 19-23, 25, 30, 50, 77, 89, 140-1, 146, 215.
Wish Hounds, 26, 71, 101.
Wistman's Wood, 10, 12, 101.
witches, 56-7, 163.

Yar Tor, 95, 111, 143-4, 147, 157, 186.
Yellowmead, 16, 49, 83, 184, 188-9.
Yes Tor, 96, 207.